THE CASE THAT SHOOK INDIA

The Verdict That Led to the Emergency

PRASHANT BHUSHAN

Foreword by M. Hidayatullah

PENGUIN BOOKS

An imprint of Penguin Random House

PENGUIN BOOKS

USA | Canada | UK | Ireland | Australia
New Zealand | India | South Africa | China | Singapore

Penguin Books is part of the Penguin Random House group of companies
whose addresses can be found at global.penguinrandomhouse.com

Published by Penguin Random House India Pvt. Ltd
4th Floor, Capital Tower 1, MG Road,
Gurugram 122 002, Haryana, India

Penguin
Random House
India

First published by Vikas Publishing House Pvt. Ltd, New Delhi 1978
Published in Viking by Penguin Random House India 2017
Published in Penguin Books 2018

ISBN 9780143442646

Typeset in Dante MT Std by Manipal Digital Systems, Manipal
Printed at Manipal Technologies Limited, India

www.penguin.co.in

MIX
Paper | Supporting
responsible forestry
FSC® C043100

This is a legitimate digitally printed version of the book and therefore might not
have certain extra finishing on the cover.

PENGUIN BOOKS

THE CASE THAT SHOOK INDIA

Prashant Bhushan is an eminent public interest lawyer in the Supreme Court of India, most known for cases such as 2G and Coal Scam. He is also an activist and a founder member of Swaraj Abhiyan—a campaign organization that focuses on various issues such as the environment, human rights, corruption and good governance. He was a prominent member of the group India Against Corruption (IAC) and worked alongside Anna Hazare for the implementation of the Jan Lokpal Bill (Citizen's Anti-corruption Ombudsman Bill).

PRAISE FOR THE BOOK

'An invaluable historical document . . . being re-issued when new questions are being asked about the independence of the judiciary from the PMO'—*Caravan*

'Of general interest [with] contemporary resonances'—*India Today*

Contents

4

VALIDITY OF THE CONSTITUTIONAL AMENDMENT

5

VALIDITY OF THE ELECTION LAW AMENDMENTS

APPENDICES

Foreword

we should worry that the rules so much so that the Supreme Court is not even allowed to decide whether to appeal. This was a thoroughly undesirable feature of the case. Only one case [an [the] Court] was withdrawn from the Supreme Court of the [their] choice. It was not an election case but involved [the] parties in a pending case withdrawn from a [the] court. All the cases [ ] [ ] without animosity by the court and the companions [the one]] [ ] are legitimate. In addition to] [ ] of] [ ] [ ] it is a subject of the High Court

Elections to Parliament and the legislatures of the states are regulated in two ways by law. The first relates to the conduct of the elections by the Election Commission and the second to the personal conduct in it of the candidates. Unlike in other countries, the duty of deciding whether the election was fair and free and if the candidate was guilty of a corrupt practice is entrusted to the High Court and finally to the Supreme Court.

After the election is over, the defeated candidate or a voter can challenge the election of the successful candidate by proving irregularities in the conduct of the election by the authorities and/or by proving corrupt conduct on the part of the candidate. In no other way can the result of the poll be challenged. The courts apply to such cases the standards which they usually apply in trials before them. Such cases are like any other case. The allegations made must be strictly proved. Some judges call these quasi-criminal proceedings. This is not an apt description. They rather resemble the trial of allegations of fraud, subject to this that the benefit of the doubt goes to the successful candidate.

Ordinarily, I have found more perjury in these cases than in others. Political motivation often colours evidence and courts have to be very careful in assessing partisan testimony. This task becomes even more difficult when the actions of the candidate are also partly referable to his official position. Such was the case dealt with here.

The book deals with the election petition filed by Raj Narain to challenge the election of Mrs Gandhi in the 1971 election to Parliament. The author has recorded the day-to-day progress of the case through all stages. He is the son of the counsel for Raj Narain and was presumably present at conferences and in the courts. He has first-hand knowledge of all facts. He has narrated them in a very readable form, describing the proceedings objectively. He has also outlined the many steps by which legislative interference righted what was found wrong at the trial. So much so that the Supreme Court was not even allowed to decide the case in appeal. This was an unusual and undesirable feature of the case. Only one case (McCardie case) was withdrawn from the Supreme Court of the United States. It was not an election case but never afterwards was a pending case withdrawn from the courts. All the events are told without acrimony by the author and the comments that one finds are legitimate.

I have had my share of election trials as a judge of the High Court and the Supreme Court. Twice I unseated ministers and once upheld an election. There is no doubt that Justice Sinha proved equal to the task. He decided every issue adequately and his reactions during arguments were also relevant and proper. Whether one agrees with his conclusions or not, none can accuse him of taking a strained view of facts. It must be remembered that a person in authority can and should always prevent from acting overzealously the officials who go out of their way to act in aid of such a candidate. The higher the position of the candidate and the more the availability of official aid, the more the risk of allegations.

Justice Sinha, in my judgment, has rightly been strict. Although I do not say that I agree with him on every point pro or con, this much I can say, that my approach, by and large, would have been similar. In any event Justice Sinha and Judge Sirica of the Watergate case have much in common just as there is a parallel between Shanti Bhushan and Jaworski in the same case.

I have enjoyed reading the book and have found much that was not in the newspapers and I recommend it to the reader.

Bombay   M. Hidayatullah
1 October 1977   MA (Cantab); LLD,
                                        Bencher Lincoln's Inn and
                                    former Chief Justice of India

Preface to the New Edition

It's been forty years since *The Case That Shook India* was published. The book has been out of print now for more than thirty-five years and during these years many people have asked me for copies of this book, including lawyers, law students and academics. I have been giving out photocopies of the book to several people and then many suggested that I should get it republished. I am aware that this book has inspired a number of students to study and practise law and hope that it continues to do so.

The *Indira Gandhi v. Raj Narain*[1] case was important for several reasons. It was the first time in independent India's history that a Prime Minister's election was set aside. It was also the first time that a constitutional amendment was struck down on the basic structure doctrine that had been propounded a couple of years prior, in the Kesavananda Bharati case (1973). It was also the first time that election laws had been retrospectively amended to validate the annulled election of the Prime Minister. The hearing of the case in the Supreme Court of India took place during the Emergency, when fundamental rights had been suspended, press censorship was enforced and therefore there was no public reporting of the case or its hearings. While it was being heard in the Supreme Court, my notes were probably the only ones available as a record of what really transpired during the hearing. I had taken detailed notes of the hearing including the questions asked by the judges and their responses by the counsels, many of which have been reproduced in the book.

The case also impacted Indian politics in a big way. The elections that ensued after the Emergency saw the wiping out of the Congress and the installation of the first non-Congress government at the Centre. That government however collapsed within two years, due to infighting amongst the leaders of the various parties who had hastily come together to form the Janata Party. This then led to the split of the Janata Party and the formation of the Bharatiya Janata

Party (BJP). This was a landmark development in Indian politics. The BJP contested its first election in 1984, soon after Mrs Gandhi's assassination, when it won only two seats. By the early 1990s, however, the BJP had stirred up the Ram Janmabhoomi campaign, and riding on its back, it won a substantial number of seats, which paved the way for its eventual victory in 1996.[2]

The ascendance of the BJP in the twenty-first century has been one of the most significant events of Indian political history. This can be attributed largely to the vacuum left by the Congress. Modi's rise too can be attributed partly to the anti-corruption movement (Jan Lokpal movement) that took place in the country in the year 2011–12. He used the momentum created by that movement to demolish the Congress with the promise of ending corruption, graft and black money. Arvind Kejriwal also did the same for coming to power in Delhi. Unfortunately, neither of them has appointed a Lokpal yet. In fact, it has been reported that Modi's government has not worked to strengthen the anti-corruption institutions like the Central Bureau of Investigation (CBI), Central Vigilance Commission (CVC), the whistle-blower law and even the Prevention of Corruption Act.[3]

Coming back to the central issue of the *Indira Gandhi v. Raj Narain* case, it is unfortunate that the spectre of dubious electoral funding has not gone away even today, more than forty years after the judgment in the case. Currently the law is that the political parties are allowed to accept cash donations up to 20,000 from each person, which are not required to be reported. Donations above that figure need to be reported to the Election Commission, the details of which can thereafter be obtained by citizens under the Right to Information (RTI) Act 2005. The Association of Democratic Reforms (ADR) has been obtaining such details and has recently discovered that about two-thirds of political parties' funds come from unaccounted sources. Among the national parties, 83 per cent of the total income of the Congress and 65 per cent of the BJP came from unknown sources.[4]

Since parties are not required to keep any accounts of who has donated the money or how much has been received, they simply report that they received a lump sum amount as cash donations from undisclosed donors. This lump sum amount is usually in the multiples of hundreds of crores of rupees. This has led to parties accepting a lot of black money in large amounts from various donors as illustrated in the Birla–Sahara diaries also. On top of this, there is the problem of political parties not coming within the ambit of the RTI Act, though the Central Information Commission (CIC) has ruled that they are 'Public Authorities' within the meaning of the RTI Act, and therefore subject to it.[5] However, all the political parties have flouted this rule, with the result that no citizen can ask political parties about any information that they might have—even about the donors or the expenses. The fact of black money being accepted by political parties in the form of undisclosed cash donations has been a burning issue for some time. In order to show that he was doing something about it, Modi, in the budget of 2017–18, proposed an amendment, which seeks to bring down the limit of allowed cash donations from 20,000 to 2000. This reduction of permissible cash donations would not make any difference to the black money being accepted by political parties and being shown as cash donations, since they are still not required to declare the details. So, whatever is currently declared as cash donations under 20,000 each would now be declared as cash donations of under 2000 each. The total amount would remain the same.

Simultaneously proposed was another amendment to allow donors to give donations to political parties by way of electoral bonds. These bonds can be purchased by anybody from specified banks; they would not carry the name of the holder and can be given to any political party. Thereby the donor, even if he makes a large donation of several crores, would remain anonymous to the Election Commission and even the citizens. This would completely destroy whatever little transparency that exists today with regard to electoral funding. The Finance Act of 2017 brought by the government contains two further changes which will facilitate large amounts of corrupt and anonymous corporate funding to political parties. The earlier cap of a corporation not being allowed to give more than 7.5 per cent of its profits by way of donations to political parties has been removed. The requirement of disclosing the parties to which a corporation has given donations has also been done away with. The net effect of this is that any corporation is allowed to give any amount of donations to a political party/parties anonymously.

On 28 March 2014, the Delhi High Court found the Congress party and the BJP guilty of having accepted several crores of foreign donations from the subsidiaries of a foreign company, which are regarded as foreign sources under the Foreign Contribution

Regulation Act, 2010 (FCRA).[6] However, instead of prosecuting the
functionaries of these parties for violating the FCRA, the government
thereafter brought an amendment to it under which any donations
received from subsidiaries of foreign companies shall no longer count
as foreign sources. The result is that foreign companies can set up
subsidiaries in India and donate any amount of money, even hundreds
of crores, to political parties, without falling foul of the FCRA. This
is an anomalous situation since the Act was introduced to primarily
prevent political parties, politicians, candidates and public servants
from accepting foreign money. Now the situation is that on one hand,
the government is going after small NGOs doing development work
for receiving foreign funds,[7] even after the mandated registration
under the FCRA, but on the other hand, political parties are not only
free to accept any amount of foreign donations but the donors too are
allowed to remain anonymous.

The practice of allowing companies to donate any amount
of money to political parties is pernicious because many of these
companies are involved in contracts with the government or receive
various kinds of favours in return. The existing practice of recognizing
electoral trusts, through which such donations could be made, was
already a device that created one degree of anonymity for the donors,
but now with electoral bonds, there will be complete anonymity and
no limit on the amount of donations that corporations, even foreign
corporations, give to political parties. Political funding remains one of
the major problems of India's democracy. Opaque corporate political
funding has corrupted and polluted India's democracy and allowed
large corporations to control political parties.

It may, however, be mentioned that what the parties report as
donations received (even cash donations) is only the tip of the iceberg.
Most of the donations received are not even reported by political
parties even in terms of petty cash, etc. and most of it is just used in
the black economy.

The role of money power in elections can be traced to a very
fundamental axiom of Indian politics that when people go to cast
their vote, they want to vote for a candidate belonging to a party they
feel has a realistic chance of actually forming the government and not
necessarily their favourite candidate. As a result, many excellent and
meritorious candidates lose out because they are either running as
independents or are affiliated to smaller political parties. For parties

to have a 'winning' perception in the public, they must have great visibility and this visibility is usually purchased by money in the form of advertising, holding large election rallies (which cost a fortune and very often people are brought there by monetary inducement) or in the form of having a large number of paid workers on the ground who are visible.

It is exceedingly rare, though not impossible, for a party with little funds to create such a winning perception. It can only happen if this party has a large number of unpaid volunteers on the ground who give it that kind of visibility or if that party has been instrumental in a large mass-based campaign like the Lokpal campaign that preceded the Delhi election of the Aam Aadmi Party.

This problem of money power playing a major role in elections has led to the phenomenon of, what Anna Hazare calls, 'Money to power and power to money'. In order to break this vicious cycle, several reforms in the nature of elections themselves as well as political funding need to be undertaken. The primary system we need to address is that of 'first past the post', which operates at two levels. First, at the stage of the elections of the candidates themselves—that is, when the candidate who receives the largest number of votes is declared the winner of that constituency. The problem here is that all votes cast for all the other candidates, even if they aggregate for more than 75 per cent in that particular constituency, count for nothing as the candidate who received the highest percentage of the vote cast (25 per cent in this example) becomes the elected candidate. At the second level, first past the post also works in government formation when the party or coalition with more than 50 per cent of the number of seats forms the government and rest of the MPs/MLAs play no role thereafter in the running of the government (apart from hopefully being a constructive Opposition).

This can be broken by replacing first past the post with a proportional representation system. For example, in Switzerland, all the parties are represented in the government in proportion to their number of MPs/MLAs. In proportional representation, parties give a list of candidates and thereafter the voter can casts two votes— one for his favourite party and one for his favourite candidate in those parties. Thus even parties receiving only a few per cent of the votes get at least some representatives elected from their party. Such a system would actually allow the people to cast their vote for the most desirable candidate from their point of view and not only for the candidate who belongs to a party they think has a realistic chance of winning.

The second reform required is that of State funding of elections, which will also give a fair chance to candidates who do not have access to large amounts of money. Under this system, the government would be mandated to refund each candidate, after the elections, the expenses incurred by him/her in proportion to the number of votes received by him/her. Thus candidates without access to much money, if they are popular and if they receive a significant number of votes, would be able to get a large part of their expenses reimbursed by the state.

There have been heartening developments in Indian law in recent years. One of them is that the basic structure doctrine has been further strengthened and several constitutional amendments have been struck down on this doctrine, the latest being the Ninety-ninth Constitutional Amendment which formed the NJAC (National Judicial Appointments Commission).[8] In the *Indira Gandhi v. Raj Narain* case, the amendments in the electoral law that had retrospective operation and legitimized Mrs Gandhi's elections were placed in the Ninth Schedule and for that reason escaped judicial scrutiny. This was a subterfuge on the Constitution. However, now with the I.R. Coelho case of 2007,[9] no law is beyond judicial scrutiny, even if it is placed within the Ninth Schedule.

As the reader will see, the *Indira Gandhi v. Raj Narain* case was undoubtedly a landmark case and a watershed moment in the constitutional, legal and political history of India. This book, I hope, will shed some light on the finer nuances of this case.

April 2017

References

1. AIR 1975 SC 2299.
2. Ian Copland, Ian Mabbett, et al., *A History of State and Religion in India* (Oxon: Routledge, 2012), pp 246–47.
3. Shoaib Daniyal, 'Caged Parrot', Scroll.in, 1 May 2017, https://scroll. in/article/836190/the-daily-fix-the-modi-government-is-using-the-cbi-for-political-gain-just-like-the-congress-did; 'Appointment of KV

Chowdary as CVC the "greatest disaster that will fall on this unfortunate nation" : Ram Jethmalani', LiveLaw.in, 4 June 2015, http://www.livelaw.in/appointment-of-kv-chowdary-as-cvc-the-greatest-disaster-that-will-fall-on-this-unfortunate-nation-ram-jethmalani/'; Archis Mohan, 'Rajya Sabha select committee dilutes anti-graft law', *Business Standard*, 19 December 2016, http://www.business-standard.com/article/economy-policy/rajya-sabha-select-committee-dilutes-anti-graft-law-116121900024_1.html; and Shalini Singh, 'Prevention of Corruption Act: Watered down version will make scamsters look like saints', Firstpost.com, 13 December 2016, http://www.firstpost.com/india/prevention-of-corruption-act-watered-down-version-will-make-scamsters-look-like-saints-3154344.html.

4. *Analysis of Sources of Funding of National and Regional Parties of India—FY 2004–05 to 2014–15*, 24 January 2017, http://adrindia.org/content/analysis-sources-funding-national-and-regional-parties-fy-2004-05-2014-15-0.

5. PTI, 'Political parties come under RTI Act, says Central Information Commission', *India Today*, 3 June 2013, http://indiatoday.intoday.in/story/political-parties-under-the-rti-ambit-cic-india-today/1/278248.html.

6. *Association for Democratic Reforms v. Union of India* (2014) 209 DLT 607.

7. David Dawkins, 'Why does India HATE the help?', *Mail Today*, 2 February 2017, http://www.dailymail.co.uk/indiahome/indianews/article-4182592/Why-does-India-hate-help-Modi-s-war-NGOs.html.

8. *Supreme Court Advocates-on-Record Assn. v. Union of India*, (2016) 5 SCC 1.

9. *I.R.Coelho v. State of Tamil Nadu*, AIR 2007 SC 861.

Acknowledgements

It is difficult for me to imagine how I could have written this book without the help and encouragement of a large number of well-wishers and relatives. I would, however, like to mention my special debt to a few individuals.

I am grateful to my cousins Sumati and Bhagwant Bishnoi who sacrificed much of their vacations for doing the preliminary editing. I also wish to thank my brother-in-law Kenneth Waldron, cousin Ashok Mittal, and family friends R.N. Verma and V.K. Khanna, for giving me valuable suggestions which made substantial improvements in the book.

My thanks are also due to J.P. Goyal, advocate, who secured my entry in the courtroom during the hearings in the Supreme Court and otherwise helped me, and to M.C. Gupta, advocate, who furnished me with much valuable information.

I am profoundly grateful to M. Hidayatullah who spent several hours of his valuable time in going through the manuscript and writing a foreword for the book.

I would like to give a special mention to my industrious colleague, Siddhartha K. Garg, who took the initiative to get the book republished by Penguin Random House and also re-edited the book.

Introduction

The day had hardly begun on 26 June 1975. The streets of Delhi should rightfully have been resting at that time after the previous day's hectic political activities. But this morning they were witnessing a strange kind of activity. Hundreds of police cars were moving silently along the streets in search of their prey. Their prey were no ordinary men. A list of those who were to be nabbed in the midnight operation made up a 'who's who' of those who had asked Mrs Gandhi to quit office. The operation was totally successful. In a coup planned and executed with ruthless military efficiency, Mrs Gandhi that night transformed the country from a working democracy into a dictatorship.

The apparent reasons for this sudden transition are fairly obvious. They perhaps lay in something which took place in a small, inconspicuous courtroom of the Allahabad High Court, just two weeks earlier. On that day, a lone judge, sitting in the High Court, had pronounced a verdict, setting aside the election of the respondent on charges of corrupt practices. This by itself was not unusual. The High Court almost every year set aside elections on charges of corrupt practices. What made the case unusual was the fact that the respondent here was no ordinary person. She was the Prime Minister of the country.

The rumblings set off by the judgment had their culmination in the midnight coup of 26 June. But the story does not end there. With remarkable swiftness, in less than two years, history completed a full circle. The night which began on 26 June 1975 ended on 20 March 1977, with a resounding defeat of Mrs Gandhi and her Congress party, at the polls.

Most people will dispute that it was the 'case' that had brought about this remarkable political revolution. They will say that the 'case' has become the scapegoat for the political revolution which was bound to take place, seeing the political dynamics of the country at that time. Their argument would be that Mrs Gandhi was bound to strike as ruthlessly as she did, whenever her power was threatened. The author entirely agrees with this analysis. But no one will deny that the case at least expedited the process, and made the country go through in a flash what it would normally have gone through in a much longer time. Therein lies the political importance of the case. It was the immediate, though not the real cause of the ensuing revolution.

People will wonder what this history-making case was. What were the charges against Mrs Gandhi? What happened inside the courtrooms? What were the manoeuvrings behind the court? This book is intended to provide the answers to all these questions. It deals with the entire case right from the time the petition was filed in the High Court in April 1971, till it was finally disposed of by the Supreme Court in November 1975. Thus, viewed from a political perspective, this can be regarded as a historical book which focuses on a legal event, which had grave political consequences. However, viewed from a wholly legal perspective, it can be regarded as a case history of one of the most important court battles of our times. There are really two cases involved here. The case in the Supreme Court had become entirely different from the one in the High Court. While in the High Court it was an ordinary election petition, in the Supreme Court, because of the constitutional and election law amendments made to influence the case, it became an entirely constitutional case.

The Supreme Court arguments would be of special interest, as most of them went unreported in the newspapers due to press censorship. The arguments have been presented as the author heard and interpreted them, and therefore the account must necessarily have a bias. The author has tried to avoid bias as much as possible, and whatever bias remains is unavoidable in the circumstances.

Another matter needs to be clarified. As there are no verbatim records of court proceedings, it is impossible to record the exact wordings of the arguments and observations which took place in the court. Therefore, while the account of most of the arguments and observations are given in the first person, they are not necessarily the exact words used by the counsel and judges on those occasions. The first person has been used so that the account remains more lively and interesting, though care has been taken to see that there is no misrepresentation.

1

PRELIMINARY
COURT PROCEEDINGS

1

From Electoral Battle to Court Battle

If any year signifies the beginning of Mrs Indira Gandhi's ascendance to power, it would probably be 1969, when the Congress split took place. Though at that time the faction led by Mrs Gandhi was reduced to a state of minority in the Lok Sabha, she started looking for an early opportunity to consolidate her power. She had to rely on the support of the Communist Party of India—which she did not like—to get Bills passed in the Lok Sabha. However, when the Privy Purses Abolition Bill was stalled by the combined Opposition parties in the Rajya Sabha where they had a majority, Mrs Gandhi was given the opportunity she needed.

On 27 December 1970, the President dissolved the Lok Sabha at the advice of Mrs Gandhi and called for elections in early March. This was one year before the normal scheduled elections which were due in 1972. Although the Opposition parties were somewhat taken by surprise, they recovered quickly and announced they would form an alliance to fight the election against Mrs Gandhi's Congress party. The members of this alliance, which Mrs Gandhi called the 'grand alliance', were all the major non-communist Opposition parties, which included the Congress (Organization), the Jan Sangh, the Swatantra Party and the Samyukt Socialist Party.

On 29 December 1970, Mrs Gandhi held a press conference regarding the elections. At the press conference, someone told her that 'a short while ago in a meeting of the Opposition parties, the Opposition leaders said that Mrs Gandhi was changing her constituency from Rae Bareli to Gurgaon'. To this, she replied emphatically, 'No, I am not.' (Mrs Gandhi had fought and won her first election to the Lok Sabha from Rae Bareli in the 1967 General Elections.)

Meanwhile, the Opposition parties were also choosing their candidates for various constituencies. On 19 January 1971, the Opposition parties which had forged an alliance against Mrs Gandhi's Congress party announced Raj Narain's candidature from Rae Bareli to oppose Mrs Gandhi. He would be their jointly sponsored candidate and even other Opposition parties like the Bhartiya Kranti Dal, which were not members of the alliance, decided not to put up their own candidate from Rae Bareli. The next day, Mrs Gandhi, giving a speech in Coimbatore, lashed out against Raj Narain's candidature from Rae Bareli. She said that 'Mr Narain had been chosen by the Opposition parties to contest from Rae Bareli because he was a well-known Nehru hater and baiter'.

On 25 January, the Election Commission allotted the symbol of a cow and calf to the ruling Congress party of Mrs Gandhi and the symbol of a lady with a charkha to the Congress (Organization) Party led by Morarji Desai.

A few days later, Shanti Bhushan received a telegram from C. Rajagopalachari which expressed his dissatisfaction at the allotment of the cow and calf symbol to the ruling Congress party. He asked Bhushan to challenge this allotment in the court on the ground that it was a religious symbol. Bhushan replied that as the election process had already started with the issue of the Presidential Notification on 27 January, it was not possible to challenge the allotment of the symbol till the elections were over.

The polling dates were 3, 5 and 7 March and the last date for filing nomination papers was 3 February. Meanwhile, on 25 January, Mrs Gandhi's tour programme for Rae Bareli was issued for 1 February. In the tour programme, 11 a.m. was marked out for filing her nomination papers in the District Magistrate's office. In accordance with her tour programme, Mrs Gandhi went to Rae Bareli on 1 February and filed her nomination papers. She appointed Yashpal Kapoor as her election agent. Kapoor was earlier working as officer on special duty in the Prime Minister's Secretariat and he had resigned just a few days before. It is noteworthy that Kapoor, who was Mrs Gandhi's Private Secretary earlier, had resigned at the eve of the 1967 elections and had worked in Mrs Gandhi's election campaign. Immediately after the elections, he had rejoined Mrs Gandhi's Secretariat as officer on special duty.

With the last date for filing nomination papers over, the din for getting party tickets died down and the election campaign of the parties started in a big way. The Opposition parties' slogan was 'Indira *Hatao*' and their main charge against her was that she was responsible for the corruption which had crept into the government in the past two years. Mrs Gandhi who had earlier nationalized the fourteen major banks of the country and had tried to abolish the privy purses of the erstwhile Maharajas was successful in projecting her image as a radical socialist, who was seriously interested in bridging the gap between the rich and the poor as quickly as possible. In reply to the Opposition's slogan of 'Indira Hatao,' she coined her own simple slogan *'Garibi* Hatao'. In every election speech, she said, 'All that the Opposition wants is the removal of Indira, and all that I want is the removal of poverty. Now, it is up to you to decide what you want.' The effectiveness of this rhetoric can only be gauged by the election results.

The polling date for Mrs Gandhi's constituency was 7 March. The day went off uneventfully and counting of votes started on 9 March. Meanwhile on 8 March, before the votes were counted, Raj Narain led a victory procession through the streets of Rae Bareli, thanking the people for their support and for having elected him.

The results started coming in by 10 March and early returns showed that the Congress was heading for a landslide victory, even beyond the most optimistic estimates of the Congress supporters. In her own constituency, Mrs Gandhi routed Raj Narain by more than 1,10,000 votes. Mrs Gandhi polled 1,83,309 votes while Raj Narain could get only 71,499 votes. The only other candidate, Swami Adwaitanand, who had fought as an independent candidate, did not get any significant number of votes.

Raj Narain was a very optimistic man and the victory procession was taken out by him on his firm belief that he would indeed win. The results, however, shook him, and he started believing the stories which were being circulated about the chemical treatment of ballot papers. The results were so surprising that some other Opposition leaders also started believing that the ballot papers might indeed have been treated chemically so that the ink of the actual stamp mark disappeared after some time, and an invisible stamp mark, which had been put on the ballot papers at the time of their printing, appeared on the paper just before counting. If it was true that the marks had been manipulated, then they should have been identically placed on the ballot papers. But the only way in which this could be determined was by examination of the ballot papers, which could only be done by means of an election petition. The fear that such rigging had taken place was perhaps the main reason why Raj Narain decided to file a petition challenging Mrs Gandhi's election. The charges of corrupt practices were at that time regarded as only subsidiary issues. This was the background of the court battle which was destined to create history.

2

The Petition

The Representation of Peoples Act, 1951, specifies that the result of an election announced by a returning officer can only be challenged by an election petition brought before the High Court in whose jurisdiction the election was contested, and that the petition must be filed within forty-five days of the announcement of the result. It was, therefore, some time in mid-April that Raj Narain went to Ramesh Chandra Srivastava, a lawyer of Allahabad known to him, for the handling of the petition. Raj Narain also decided to engage Shanti Bhushan as his senior counsel in this case. Although Raj Narain did not know Bhushan personally, he chose him, as apart from being an active member of the Congress (O), he was regarded as a very competent lawyer who did most political cases without charging any fee. After some junior lawyer had done the initial drafting of the petition, Raj Narain took the draft to Bhushan on 22 April. The initial draft which was brought to Bhushan contained several allegations, and the chief ones were:

1. that the ballot papers had been chemically treated;
2. that Yashpal Kapoor (Mrs Gandhi's election agent) had induced Swami Adwaitanand to stand as a candidate by bribing him to the tune of Rs 50,000;
3. that Mrs Gandhi's agent had distributed quilts, blankets, dhotis, liquor, etc., to induce voters to vote for her;
4. that a large number of voters had been conveyed to and from the polling stations in vehicles provided by Mrs Gandhi's agent;
5. that Mrs Gandhi had incurred expenditure much above the prescribed limit of Rs 35,000;
6. that Mrs Gandhi had procured the help of Yashpal Kapoor for her election while he was still a gazetted officer in the government.

All these, except the first, were made out to be corrupt practices under the election laws (see Appendix 5). If a corrupt practice is proved against a returned candidate, his election is declared void and he is disqualified from holding any public office for six years.

To Bhushan, the petition seemed to be more of a vehicle for propaganda than an election petition. He also did not believe the first allegation, which was the main charge in the petition. So he told Raj Narain that he would only argue the case if it was treated as a serious election petition and not as a propaganda stunt. Moreover, the charge of chemical treatment of ballot papers would have to be deleted from the petition, he said. At that time, Raj Narain, though reluctantly, agreed to the conditions. Bhushan also added three more charges to the petition. These were:

1. that Mrs Gandhi had procured the assistance of a number of gazetted officers and members of the police forces for furthering the prospects of her election by erecting barricades for her visits and constructing rostrums for her speeches;
2. that she had procured the services of members of the armed forces for the furtherance of her election prospects by flying in Air Force planes flown by them;
3. that the symbol of a cow and calf used by Mrs Gandhi was a religious symbol.

At this time, Bhushan was asked about the chances of the success of the petition. 'Negligible' was his reply. Firstly, the case was not strong enough, and secondly, few judges would have the courage to unseat the Prime Minister. 'Nevertheless, we must fight it, on the off chance that it succeeds.'

Next day, Raj Narain came back to Bhushan and told him that he could not sleep the whole night on account of Bhushan deleting the issue about the chemical treatment of ballot papers. Very reluctantly, Bhushan agreed to restore it, though in a different form. Instead of alleging that the ballot papers were chemically treated, the petition now alleged that a large number of ballot papers counted in Mrs Gandhi's favour were not actually cast by the voters and that the markings on these papers were made surreptitiously by some mechanical process. The petition alleged that this would be clear from the fact that the seal marks on these papers were in exactly identical places.

So the final draft of the petition contained the following charges:

1. that Mrs Gandhi had procured the assistance of Yashpal Kapoor for the furtherance of her election prospects while he was still a gazetted officer;

2. that at the instance of Mrs Gandhi, Swami Adwaitanand was bribed to stand as a candidate from Rae Bareli;

3. that Mrs Gandhi procured the assistance of members of the armed forces of the Union for furthering her election prospects by ordering them to fly her to her election meetings in Air Force planes;

4. that she procured the assistance of the District Magistrate and the Superintendent of Police of Rae Bareli and other police officers for erecting barricades and rostrums and making loudspeaker arrangements for her election meetings;

5. that her agent freely distributed liquor, quilts, blankets among the voters of Rae Bareli with the object of inducing them to vote for her;

6. that by using the symbol of a cow and calf she appealed to the religious sentiments of the voters for the purpose of getting votes for herself;

7. that Yashpal Kapoor and other agents of Mrs Gandhi hired a number of vehicles for the free conveyance of voters to and from the polling stations;

8. that Mrs Gandhi and her election agent incurred or authorized expenditure much beyond the prescribed limit of Rs 35,000 for the purpose of the election.

All these, the petition alleged, were corrupt practices under the election laws on the basis of which Mrs Gandhi's election was liable to be declared void. The last allegation in the petition was about tampering with ballot papers.

THE PETITION IS FILED

This petition was presented to the Additional Registrar, Allahabad High Court, on the night of 24 April by Raj Narain along with Ramesh Srivastava. This was, incidentally, also the last date for the filing of the election petition. The petition was listed before Justice W.

Broome. He directed the court to issue notices to the first respondent, Mrs Gandhi, and the second respondent, Swami Adwaitanand.

Mrs Gandhi's Reply

The written statement of Mrs Gandhi was filed on 5 August 1971. In that she denied that Yashpal Kapoor did any election work for her before resigning. She also denied the bribery of Adwaitanand.

It was stated that Mrs Gandhi travelled in Air Force planes on the basis of the standing instructions of the Government of India regarding the travel arrangements for the Prime Minister. The instructions stipulate that the Prime Minister should travel by Air Force planes even when she is not on official duty.

She further denied that the use of Air Force planes by her was a corrupt practice. She said that this facility of Air Force planes for the Prime Minister was like a commercial service created exclusively for her. Further, she denied soliciting the use of the planes; these were provided merely on the basis of her tour programmes.

She also denied that the construction of barricades and rostrums was for furthering her election prospects. These were merely for law and order purposes, she said.

She also denied the allegation of bribery and the conveyance of voters to and from the polling stations.

She further denied that the cow and calf symbol was a religious symbol and that she exceeded the limit on election expenditure.

She dismissed the charge of tampering with ballot papers as fanciful and ridiculous.

The Issues Are Framed

After the written statement was filed, Justice Broome framed the issues for the petition on 19 August 1971. The main issues framed were:

1. Whether Mrs Gandhi procured the services of Yashpal Kapoor for the furtherance of the prospects of her election while he was still a gazetted officer.
2. Whether Yashpal Kapoor had bribed Swami Adwaitanand for the purpose of inducing him to stand as a candidate in the election.

3. Whether at the instance of Mrs Gandhi, members of the armed forces arranged Air Force planes and helicopters for her, flown by members of the armed forces to enable her to address election meetings, and if so, whether this amounted to a corrupt practice under Section 123(7) of the R.P. Act.

4. Whether at the instance of Mrs Gandhi and Yashpal Kapoor, the District Magistrate and Superintendent of Police of Rae Bareli arranged for the erection of barricades and rostrums and loudspeakers for Mrs Gandhi's election meetings, and if so, whether this amounted to a corrupt practice under Section 123(7) of the R.P. Act.

5. Whether quilts, blankets, dhotis and liquor were distributed by agents and workers of Mrs Gandhi in order to induce voters to vote for her.

6. Whether by using the symbol of the cow and calf, Mrs Gandhi was guilty of making an appeal to religious sentiments and committed a corrupt practice under Section 123(3) of the R.P. Act.

7. Whether on the polling date voters were conveyed to the polling stations free of charge in vehicles hired by Yashpal Kapoor or with his consent.

The judge also said that regarding the charge of tempering with ballot papers, he would carry out an investigation of a sample of papers to see whether there was any substance in it.

THE INTERROGATORIES

A few days later, an application was filed on behalf of Narain making a plea to deliver interrogatories to Mrs Gandhi under Order 11 of the Civil Procedure Code. Interrogatories are written questions for which the petitioner can ask the respondent to provide written answers. This was strongly objected to by Mrs Gandhi's counsel on the ground that Order 11 of the CPC which permits interrogatories to be delivered in a civil suit does not apply to an election petition. After hearing arguments of both sides in this matter, Justice Broome granted leave to Raj Narain for delivering interrogatories to Mrs Gandhi.

Mrs Gandhi had engaged S.C. Khare, a senior lawyer of the Allahabad High Court, and a staunch member of the Congress party, to be her senior counsel in this case. Khare, however, was not satisfied by Justice Broome's decision on the interrogatories and he decided to appeal to the Supreme Court.

In the Supreme Court, the case went before Justices Hegde, Khanna and Vaidyalingam. After some arguments were heard by the Bench on this matter, the appeal was withdrawn by Khare on the advice of the Bench.

'Tampering Charge Baseless'

Raj Narain was not happy with Bhushan's attitude towards the charge of tampering with ballot papers. Bhushan was not taking it seriously, while Raj Narain was convinced that the papers had been chemically treated. When Bhushan was in Delhi at that time, Raj Narain took him to a scientist from Bombay who, he said, would convince him that the ballot papers were chemically treated. Bhushan met the scientist at the house of Balraj Madhok, a Jan Sangh leader. The scientist had with him infrared and ultraviolet lamps. He showed Bhushan two identical ballot papers and then projected ultraviolet rays on them. The paper now appeared to have different colours. This, the scientist claimed, proved Raj Narain's charge that some ballot papers were chemically treated. Bhushan, however, was not convinced. He said that these papers were printed in different printing presses, so the texture of the papers might have been different, which could account for difference in colour when observed in ultraviolet light.

Regarding this issue, Justice Broome carried out an investigation of a sample of ballot papers.

On 15 November 1971, he inspected 200 ballot papers cast in favour of Raj Narain and 600 cast in favour of Mrs Gandhi. He found that the seal marks on the ballot papers were in different places and hence there was no reason to believe that they had been tampered with.

'Unreasonable, Vexatious, Oppressive and Irrelevant'

A few days later, a set of thirty-one interrogatories were delivered to Mrs Gandhi by the petitioner. As soon as the interrogatories were delivered, Mrs Gandhi's counsel took objection to these saying that they were 'unreasonable, vexatious, oppressive, unnecessary and irrelevant'.

All the interrogatories related to the issues about Yashpal Kapoor and Swami Adwaitanand. Mrs Gandhi's counsel also pleaded that the particulars set out in the petition did not afford a basis for these issues and hence these issues should be deleted.

COURT DELETES SOME ISSUES

The judge then heard arguments on this matter. Khare contended that since the petition did not specify the date on which Mrs Gandhi became a candidate (as the R.P. Act specified that the corrupt practice must be committed by the 'candidate') nor did it specify the date from which the assistance of Kapoor was procured, corrupt practices on account of Yashpal Kapoor was not made out. Regarding the issue of Swami Adwaitanand's bribery, Khare contended that since the date on which the money was paid was not mentioned, the issue was not made out.

Bhushan, in his arguments, did not press the issue of bribery of Adwaitanand. He, however, contended that since the petition alleged that Kapoor's services had been procured while he was a gazetted officer, and Mrs Gandhi was a candidate, it did make out the charge of corrupt practice.

Justice Broome, however, agreed with Khare and deleted this issue too from the petition.

The petitioner then filed an application for making some amendments to the petition, under Section 86(5) of the R.P. Act, which says, 'the High Court if it deems fit may allow the particulars of any corrupt practice alleged in the petition to be amended or amplified to ensure a fair and effective trial of the petition, but shall not allow any amendment of the petition which will have the effect of introducing particulars of a corrupt practice not previously alleged in the petition.' In the proposed amendment, it was sought to be stated clearly that Mrs Gandhi had been holding herself out as a candidate right from 27 December when the Lok Sabha was dissolved and that Yashpal Kapoor had started doing election work for her right from that time. The allegation that she began holding herself out as a candidate from 27 December was necessary because it is normally held that a person starts attracting charges of corrupt practices only after becoming a candidate. The R.P. Act specifies that a person becomes a candidate when he starts holding himself out as a candidate.

The amendment application was strongly opposed by Khare on the ground that the proposed amendment would have the effect of introducing particulars of a corrupt practice not previously alleged in the petition and hence was not permissible. Justice Broome accepted the argument of Khare and rejected the amendment application on 23 December 1971.

CASE GOES TO THE SUPREME COURT

Raj Narain was not satisfied with Justice Broome's decision and he appealed against the order to the Supreme Court. The special leave petition was heard by a Bench consisting of Justice Hegde, Justice Jagan Mohan Reddy and Justice Mathew.

The judgment in this case was delivered on behalf of the Bench by Justice Hedge, who allowed the appeal. In his judgment, he said:

> But if the petition is read reasonably, as it should be, it is clear that the allegation of the petition is that the services of Yashpal Kapoor were obtained by the respondent when she had already become a candidate and when Shri Yashpal Kapoor was still a gazetted officer. It is true that the ingredients of the corrupt practice alleged is not specifically set out in the petition but from the allegations made it flows as a necessary implication. While a corrupt practice has got to be strictly proved it does not follow that a pleading in an election proceeding should receive a strict construction . . . Moreover, no objection was taken to the issue about Yashpal Kapoor when it was originally framed by the trial judge. Objection was only taken when the petition to set aside the interrogatories was heard. Therefore, it is clear that the respondent was not in the dark about the allegation of this particular corrupt practice.

He therefore ordered that the petitioner be allowed to amend the petition. He also ordered that the issue about Yashpal Kapoor which had been deleted by Justice Broome be restored and recast in the following manner:

> Whether Respondent No. 1 obtained and procured the assistance of Yashpal Kapoor in furtherance of the prospects of her election

while he was still a gazetted officer in the service of Government of
India. If so, from what date?

In his judgment, Justice Hegde found it necessary to mention one other
fact. Justice Broome, when deciding on the amendment application,
had come to the conclusion that Yashpal Kapoor ceased to be in the
employ of the Government of India from 14 January 1971. The facts
were that Yashpal Kapoor appears to have tendered his resignation
on 13 January 1971. The President accepted his resignation on
25 January 1971, but with effect from 14 January 1971. Justice
Hegde said that normally the services of a government servant stood
terminated from the date on which the letter of resignation is accepted
by the appropriate authority. Since in this case it was accepted on
25 January, therefore, it could not be easily concluded that the
resignation was effective from 14 January with retrospective effect. He
ordered that this question be re-examined with reference to Yashpal
Kapoor's conditions of service. Regarding the interrogatories, Justice
Hegde allowed some of them, those which related to the issue of
Yashpal Kapoor.[1]

Meanwhile, Justice Broome had retired in December 1971 and
for a few days the case was with Justice B.N. Lokur. He too, however,
retired a few months later and the case was then taken up by Justice
K.N. Srivastava.

On 27 April 1973, Justice Srivastava framed three additional
issues consequent to the amendment made in the petition. Additional
issue no. 1 was the issue of Yashpal Kapoor which had been recast by
the Supreme Court. Additional issue no. 2 was, 'whether Respondent
No. 1 held herself out as a candidate from any date prior to the 1st
of February 1971 and, if so, from what date'. Additional issue no. 3
was 'whether Yashpal Kapoor continued to be in the service of the
Government of India from and after 14 January 1971 and till which
date'.

---

[1] This judgment was delivered on 15 March 1972. About a year later came
the appointment of Justice A.N. Ray as the Chief Justice of India and the
supersession of the three judges—Justices Shelat, Hegde and Grover. It might
be of interest to know that in an interview with Kuldip Nayar on the eve of
the supersession, Justice Hegde is reported to have said that he was superseded
because of this judgment which he had delivered in Mrs Gandhi's case.

THE STATE PRIVILEGE

Oral examination of the petitioner's witnesses started from 10 September 1973.

One of the witnesses summoned by the petitioner was S.S. Saxena, Under Secretary in the Confidential Department, Uttar Pradesh (UP), who was directed to produce certain documents before the court. He appeared on behalf of the Chief Secretary on 10 September 1973 with the documents, but he objected to produce: (1) The 'Blue Book' entitled *Rules and Instructions for the Protection of the Prime Minister When on Tour or Travel*, (2) Correspondence exchanged between the Government of India and the government of UP in regard to the police arrangements for the meetings of the Prime Minister, and (3) Correspondence exchanged between the chief minister of UP and the Prime Minister in regard to the police arrangements for the meetings of the latter.

The objection was made on the ground of a State privilege, claimed under Section 123 of the Evidence Act. Bhushan objected to the claim of privilege and Justice Srivastava heard arguments on this issue for three days. He argued that the privilege could not be claimed as no affidavit, stating that the documents related to matters of State and that their release would injure public interest, was filed by the minister or the head of the department. This, he argued, was mandatory under Section 123 of the Evidence Act for a claim of privilege to be sustained. He further argued that since portions of the Blue Book had been published, it was not an unpublished official record relating to affairs of the State and hence no privilege could be claimed in that respect.

Khare, on behalf of the respondent, and Kackar, on behalf of the State, argued strongly for the claim of privilege to be upheld. They argued that although no affidavit was filed by the minister or the head of the department, the affidavit filed on 20 September 1973 by R.K. Kaul, Home Secretary, served the same purpose.

Justice Srivastava, however, rejected the claim of privilege and allowed the production of the three sets of documents. At this stage, Khare told him that he would be appealing against this order to the Supreme Court, so he was granted two days' time to produce a stay order from the Supreme Court.

A Special Leave Petition against this order was admitted in the Supreme Court in April 1974 and the production of those documents was stayed. Thereafter, a joint application was filed by both parties for the adjournment of the case, till the Supreme Court finally disposed of the claim of privilege. The case was thus adjourned.

While the case was in the Supreme Court, pending disposal of the appeal, Justice Srivastava also retired, and the case was taken up after the summer vacation by Justice Jag Mohan Lal Sinha. It might be noted here that this case had already been going on for more than three years and recording of the oral evidence had barely started. This was because of neglect by both parties; possibly, they never expected anything to come of it. However, as soon as Justice Sinha took it up, he gave it top priority. Although the Supreme Court was yet to dispose of the appeal on the privilege matter, Justice Sinha told the petitioner to start producing evidence on other issues which were unconnected with the privilege matter or else give them up. If not for Justice Sinha, the case might have dragged on in the High Court for years.

Between August 1974 and January 1975, the entire oral evidence of the petitioner was recorded.

CHAWLA'S CASE

Meanwhile on 3 October 1974, a Supreme Court Bench composed of Justices Bhagwati and Sarkaria gave an important decision on the law of election expenses, in what has come to be known as Amar Nath Chawla's case. The decision in this case was to have far-reaching consequences. Justice Bhagwati, delivering the judgment on behalf of the Bench, comprehensively analysed and interpreted the law as it stood on election expenses. He laid down that the expenditure incurred by any person with the consent or acquiescence of a candidate, or any expenditure of which a candidate takes advantage, or fails to disavow, shall be treated as expenditure impliedly authorized by the candidate within the meaning of the section and has to be included in his return of election expenses. As the facts in Mrs Gandhi's case were that most of the election expenditure was incurred by the Congress party on her behalf, with the express or implied authorization of her election agent, the decision in this case was bound to influence the decision in Mrs Gandhi's case on the expenses issue.

Raj Narain's counsels were very happy with this decision and they felt that now they had a very strong case on the expenses issue. Their joy was, however, short-lived as only a few days later, an Ordinance[2] was promulgated by the government which amended the law on election expenses retrospectively. This was clearly an attempt to nullify the law laid down in Chawla's case. The amendment added an explanation to Section 77 of the R.P. Act which deals with election expenses. It was now provided that any expenditure incurred or authorized by a political party, friends or supporters of the candidate, or any other person (except the candidate or his election agent) shall not be deemed to be and shall never be deemed to have been expenditure in connection with the candidate's election. This amendment was given retrospective effect so as to apply to all cases which were pending before the courts.

It was greeted by howls of protest in Parliament and elsewhere. The timing of the amendment was such that it fooled no one. Almost every one interpreted it as an attempt to interfere with the decision in Mrs Gandhi's case. It was formally enacted into law by the Congress-controlled Parliament on 21 December 1974.

THE SUPREME COURT HEARS THE PRIVILEGE ISSUE

The appeal on the privilege matter came up for hearing in the Supreme Court in January 1975, before a five-member Constitution Bench composed of Chief Justice Ray and Justices Mathew, Untwalia, Sarkaria and Alagiriswamy. It was argued on behalf of the State by the Attorney-General, Niren De, and on behalf of the petitioner by Bhushan. There were two issues involved here:

1. Whether privilege could be claimed even if no affidavit was filed at the time of the presentation of documents by the minister or head of the department concerned.
2. Was such privilege absolute and whether the court could examine the document to see whether they related to matters of State so that their disclosure would injure public interest.

De submitted that the court could not reject the claim of privilege merely on the basis of some technical irregularity, as public interest

---

[2] An Ordinance is a law which can be passed by the executive when Parliament is not in session. It has to be ratified by Parliament within six months or it lapses. The text of the amendment appears in the Appendix.

would be seriously injured by the disclosure of the documents. When he was asked by the Bench as to how the court would know whether the documents really related to matters of State and that their disclosure would injure public interest, De replied that the executive was the best judge of whether certain documents related to matters of State or not. He cited cases from England to show that certain classes of documents, such as Cabinet papers and minutes of Cabinet meetings were privileged per se. Even the court could not look into those to determine whether their disclosure would injure public interest.

The claim of the Attorney-General was strongly contested by Bhushan, who argued that the State could not be the sole judge to decide whether the disclosure of certain documents would injure public interest as the State was a prejudiced party in this matter. To support his claim, he cited the decision of the US Supreme Court in the then recently decided case concerning President Nixon's presidential tapes. In that case, too, the US Supreme Court had rejected the claim of privilege of Nixon with regard to his tapes and had allowed the trial judge to hear the tapes to decide whether they should be brought on record or not. As Nixon's case had not been reported till then, a typed copy of the judgment had been hurriedly procured by Raj Narain's counsel from the US. Bhushan, therefore, submitted that it would be open to the court to inspect any documents regarding which privilege could be accepted or rejected by the judgment on the merits of each document.

The judgment in this case was delivered by Chief Justice Ray on behalf of the Bench. Justice Mathew gave a separate, though concurring judgment. The Bench allowed the appeal of the State, on the ground that the privilege was not lost merely because of the technical lacuna that an affidavit of the minister or the head of the department had not been filed at the first instance. They directed that the High Court should call for an affidavit of the minister or the head of department. If on the basis of the affidavit the court was satisfied that the documents belonged to a class, the disclosure of which would injure public interest, then the privilege should be upheld. However, if the court was not so satisfied by the affidavit, it could look into the documents itself to determine whether they belonged to the privileged class.

3

The PM in Court

Recording of the oral evidence on behalf of the respondent started on 12 February 1975. P.N. Haksar, then Deputy Chairman of the Planning Commission, was the first witness to be examined by Khare. He had come to give evidence on the issue of Yashpal Kapoor's resignation. In his examination, he deposed that Kapoor had submitted his letter of resignation on 13 January 1971 and he had accepted the resignation orally at that very time. Thus a new twist was given to the issue of Yashpal Kapoor's resignation. In his cross-examination, Haksar deposed that he had assumed charge of the office of Deputy Chairman of the Planning Commission of India on 4 January 1975 on a verbal order of the Prime Minister. He was asked by the cross-examining counsel, Bhushan, as to whether government servants could be appointed by orders given orally. Haksar replied that as far as he was aware, temporary government servants could be appointed orally and that a formal order in writing could follow later. In reply to another question, he said that he was not aware of any rule under which it was permissible to make appointments by word of mouth, but claimed that it was known that every appointing authority could appoint a person and terminate his services orally. As in 1971, Haksar was the Secretary-in-Charge of the Prime Minister's Secretariat, Bhushan asked him whether he was aware of any rule authorizing the Secretary-in-Charge of making appointments to the post of officer on special duty (the post which Kapoor held). Haksar replied that he was not aware of any rule, but he believed that a Secretary in the Government of India had very wide powers and that he could make appointments of persons to such a post.

The key witness of the respondent was clearly Yashpal Kapoor. His testimony would be of vital importance to the issues about his resignation, the assistance which he provided to Mrs Gandhi during the elections, and also to the issue of election expenses, and the way he fared in his cross-examination would be of crucial importance to the final decision. Kapoor was produced in court on 18 February 1975. His examination and cross-examination lasted for about eight hours and went on till the end of the next day. Perhaps it was his being key witness that made Kapoor don what could be seen as an air of swaggering arrogance. He paced back and forth in the witness stand with his hands in his pocket. The smile on his face could be perceived as one of condescending power. He probably thought the proceedings to be of minor importance—for him at least.[1] Kapoor certainly did not fare well in his cross-examination. For, in his anxiety to conceal certain things, he made several blunders.

The fact that Kapoor had not put up a good show was clearly perceived even by Mrs Gandhi's lawyers. This was, perhaps, one of the main reasons why it was decided that Mrs Gandhi should herself come to give evidence. For only a few days later, on 26 February, a request was made by Khare to Justice Sinha, that a Commission be set up for the recording of her evidence in Delhi, and that the Commission should have the power to disallow questions which it considered irrelevant for the case. Justice Sinha, however, refused this request mainly on the ground that the Commission could not be given the power to disallow questions at its discretion. It was then decided that Mrs Gandhi herself should come to the Allahabad High Court to be a witness in the case. It is a common misconception that Mrs Gandhi was summoned to adduce evidence before the court. The fact is that Mrs Gandhi had decided to appear as a witness of her own will and on the advice of her lawyers. Whether this advice was sound or not is still a matter of debate. In this context it is of interest that a few days before his death, Pandit Kanhaya Lal Mishra, the former Advocate-General of UP,[2] told Bhushan that when he heard that Mrs Gandhi was coming to the witness stand, he had written a letter to her strongly

---

[1] A detailed summary of the main substance of his evidence appears in Appendix I.

[2] Pt Kanhaya Lal Mishra could have been Mrs Gandhi's senior counsel in this case had it not been for his frail health. In fact he had argued some parts of the case during hearings about preliminary matters.

advising her, in the best interest of her case, not to appear in court. Needless to say, his advice had been ignored.

The dates fixed by the court for the recording of Mrs Gandhi's evidence were 18, 19 and 20 March.

Meanwhile, there was hectic activity among the lawyers on both sides. Mrs Gandhi's lawyers were busy preparing the questions that they would ask her in order to get on record whatever they thought was useful to them.

The activity was even more intense on the petitioner's side. Raj Narain, along with a number of other workers who had worked for him during the Rae Bareli election, went every day to Bhushan's house for lengthy discussions. R.C. Srivastava and the other assisting lawyers, M.C. Gupta and T.C. Porwar, would also be present. Meanwhile, word had been sent to the Congress (O) office at Jantar Mantar in New Delhi to try to unearth any documents which could be used in the court to shake the credibility of Mrs Gandhi. (Jantar Mantar had been the central office of the undivided Congress party before the split in 1969. After the legal division of property took place, Jantar Mantar was given to the Congress (O). It housed a vast pile of old documents, letters and other material.)

The people at Jantar Mantar sent a fair amount of documents and papers for Bhushan's examination. Although a number of them were very interesting and revealed curious things about Mrs Gandhi, Bhushan found only one paper that could be used in the court. It was a letter written by the Lieutenant-Governor of Himachal Pradesh, the Raja of Bhadri, to Mrs Gandhi, who was then the Congress president.

In the letter, the Lieutenant-Governor informed Mrs Gandhi that the Congress candidate had been successful in the Lok Sabha by-election held in Himachal Pradesh. He said that he had thus passed the toughest test that Mrs Gandhi had put him through. This was a devastating letter, as it implied that Mrs Gandhi had asked the Lieutenant-Governor who is supposed to be a neutral observer to help the Congress candidate in the election.

Mrs Gandhi arrived in Allahabad on 17 February. Until then the case had received very little publicity. Although the local newspapers were covering the significant events in the case (like the cross-examination of P.N. Haksar and Yashpal Kapoor), no one gave much importance to the case itself. They regarded it as a futile election petition filed by a poor loser, just to harass the Prime Minister. But with the cross-examination of Mrs Gandhi, the case exploded into the limelight. It was a big event in itself. Never before had a Prime Minister of the country gone to a court to testify. The former President, V.V. Giri, had however once testified before the Supreme Court in his election petition.

There were massive security arrangements outside the court that day. All the gates were manned by policemen and entry inside the court premises was restricted to lawyers and litigants accompanied by lawyers. Apart from these, only a few news reporters, *pairokars* (special attorneys who are acquainted with the facts of the case and who can help counsel in some aspects of the case), and pass holders were permitted inside the court premises. Entry inside Court No. 24, where the cross-examination took place, was severely restricted (Justice Sinha's courtroom was Court No. 5, but Court No. 24 was chosen for the cross-examination because it was at one end of the court, and the restriction of entry around it would not hamper the working of other courts).

People had started pouring into the courtroom from as early as 9 a.m. that day. The security staff had installed a metal detector in the passage leading to Court No. 24 where the evidence was to be recorded.

Just before the proceedings in the court were about to begin, a drama took place outside the court. A man carrying a plastic briefcase was apprehended by the security staff at the metal detector. His briefcase allegedly contained a loaded countrymade pistol. His name was Govind Misra and he was the editor of a two-page newspaper *Vijay*, published from Allahabad. The exact circumstances in which he was caught are still not clear, but the version of the security men was that he was carrying the pistol in his briefcase, when the metal detector picked it up. When he was interrogated, he revealed that for the past four months, he had always carried a revolver with him, as he feared violence from some enemies. He did not have a licence for his weapon but had applied for one. He was kept in police custody for a few days and later released as he was found to be harmless.

The Govind Misra affair however caused quite a sensation in Parliament. Accusations were hurled across the floor. Many legislators demanded a high-level probe into the matter and urged that the security arrangements for the Prime Minister be further strengthened.

Meanwhile, Court No. 24 was completely packed by the time the judge arrived. Among those people who were present in the court were high ranking Opposition leaders like Madhu Limaye, Shyam Nandan Mishra, Piloo Mody, Jyotirmoy Bosu and Rabi Ray. They had come all the way from Delhi to witness the cross-examination. They had been cited as pairokars by Raj Narain. Among those present were also Mrs Gandhi's son, Rajiv Gandhi, and his wife, Sonia Gandhi.

Raj Narain himself was also present in the court. Earlier, when he had told Bhushan that he wanted to be present during the cross-examination, Bhushan had objected to it, knowing the volatile temperament of Raj Narain. He, however, reluctantly agreed to Narain being present when he undertook not to utter a word during the proceedings.

The judge arrived two minutes before 10 a.m. Everybody in the courtroom rose when the judge came in. After taking his seat, he announced that the court conventions dictate that no one should rise when a witness comes in. This however did not prevent some people from rising when Mrs Gandhi came in.

Mrs Gandhi took a seat which was specially provided for her. The normal practice is that a witness stands in the witness box. The deviation from convention was made by Justice Sinha after consultation with Bhushan. Her chair was on a raised platform to the right of the judge so that she was on level with the judge. She looked composed and unruffled as she sat down. If she regarded the ordeal before her as something of great significance, she did not give the slightest indication of it. Her appearance was of one who was performing yet another routine task.

Khare was called upon to lead the examination, and he was visibly excited. He was the first person to question the Prime Minister in court. The main issues which could turn on Mrs Gandhi's evidence were (1) whether she held herself out as a candidate prior to 1 February, and (2) whether Yashpal Kapoor actually resigned on 13 January. Khare's questions were mainly focused on these issues.[3] His examination lasted about an hour.

It was now Bhushan's turn. He was inwardly excited, though outwardly calm, when he got up to begin the task before him. It was a big event for him. Apart from the fact that he would be cross-questioning the Prime Minister, with the whole country watching at least through newspapers, he was also fully aware of the far-reaching

---

[3] The highlights of Mrs Gandhi's testimony are given in Appendix 2.

political consequences of the outcome of this case. This cross-examination could be crucial to the outcome of the case.

Most people who are not familiar with courts visualize a cross-examination as something dramatic where the counsel is supposed to give a theatrical display, Perry Mason style. Most cross-examinations are, however, incredibly dull where little happens in the nature of drama.

The cross-examination had not finished when the court rose that day. That evening, all the Opposition leaders who had come from Delhi to witness the cross-examination were invited for tea to Bhushan's house. Opinion there was almost unanimous, that Mrs Gandhi had fared well on the first day of her cross-examination. She had maintained her composure and was convincing in the manner in which she had answered the questions. Piloo Mody did not enjoy the cross-examination. 'Why don't you heckle her? Annoy her a bit!' he told Bhushan. Bhushan smilingly remarked that on the first day, he had only given her the bait and made her feel confident. 'Tomorrow she will walk into the trap,' he said. Little did anyone know that he was indeed serious and was about to spring a surprise.

Pandit Kanhaya Lal Mishra wrote to Mrs Gandhi at the end of the first day's cross-examination, 'I hear that today's cross-examination has gone off very well. I am pleased about that. But that still does not alter my opinion that you should not have appeared for the cross-examination.' His words were indeed prophetic, and later Mrs Gandhi was to regret not having followed his advice.

Bhushan took only ninety minutes to complete his cross-examination the next day. The tables had indeed turned. The additional written statement containing the decision of the All India Congress Committee about her constituency had caught her off guard. Till the previous day she had been maintaining that she had taken a final decision to contest from Rae Bareli only on 1 February. Her additional written statement said that a final decision regarding her constituency was announced by the AICC on 29 January. When confronted with this statement, she said that the statement was drafted in legal language which she had difficulty in understanding. Bhushan did not give her time to recover her composure. Although he had some more questions, he decided to end at this point, not taking the chance of losing his advantage.

The people at large, who were following the cross-examination, did not, however, catch on to Mrs Gandhi's blunder till the arguments stage, when it was fully exploited by Bhushan. But the more astute observers caught on. The report of the second day's cross-examination was headlined in some of the newspapers as: 'Prime Minister did not know of AICC decision about her constituency' and 'PM cannot follow legal language.'

Mrs Gandhi was the last witness of either side to give evidence. The stage was now set for the main battle, the final arguments. The arguments were to start on 21 April. Both sides started preparing for them.

Meanwhile, some of the documents, mainly the controversial Blue Book, were examined by Justice Sinha on 2 April. These were the documents on which privilege had been claimed. The Supreme Court, it will be remembered, had ruled that the judge could examine them and then either uphold or reject the privilege as he thought fit. The judge accepted the claim of privilege in respect of some documents and rejected the claim in respect of others, which were then exhibited and admitted as evidence.

One further development took place before the arguments started. On 16 April, a writ petition was filed in the court by Raj Narain's lawyers, challenging the constitutional validity of the R.P. (Amendment) Act. It was challenged mainly on the ground that it was discriminatory and thus violative of Article 14 in its retrospective effect.

The stage was now set for the arguments. Raj Narain was in jail at this time because of his participation in a civil disobedience movement. This was not a novelty for him as it was his fifty-second trip to jail since Independence. He had spent more than half the post-Independence period in jails. He, however, was brought every day to Bhushan's house in police custody, to allow him to brief his counsel on the case. Being of a religious bent of mind, he gave Bhushan a queer stone to keep in his pocket during the arguments as a good luck charm. Although Bhushan is not superstitious, the stone remained in his pocket during the entire arguments.

2

IN THE HIGH COURT

4

The Petitioner's Opening Arguments

Opening his arguments on behalf of the petitioner, Bhushan said that he would first address the court on the issue of Air Force planes.

THE ISSUE OF THE AIR FORCE PLANE

The issue read as follows: 'Whether at the instance of Respondent No. 1, members of the armed forces of the Union arranged Air Force Planes and Helicopters for her to be flown by members of the armed forces to enable her to address election meetings on 1.2.71 and 25.2.71 and, if so, whether this constituted a corrupt practice under Section 123(7) of the R.P. Act.'

The corrupt practice outlined in Section 123(7) of the Act is the 'obtaining or procuring or abetting or attempting to obtain or procure by a candidate or his agent or by any other person (with the consent of the candidate or his election agent) any assistance (other than giving of votes) for the furtherance of the prospects of that candidate's election from any person in the service of the Government and belonging to any of the following classes, namely, (a) Gazetted Officers, (b) Stipendary Magistrates and Judges, (c) Members of the Armed Forces of the Union, (d) Members of the Police Forces, and (e) Excise Officers.'

Bhushan said that the facts of this issue were undisputed and it was admitted by the respondent that she flew by an Air Force plane from Delhi to Lucknow on 1 February, from where she went to Rae Bareli by car to file her nomination papers. He submitted that in order to prove the charge of corrupt practice on this issue, he would have to establish two facts: (1) That Mrs Gandhi 'obtained' or 'procured' the assistance of Air Force personnel, and (2) that this assistance was availed for furthering her election prospects.

Counsel argued that there was no doubt that Mrs Gandhi obtained or procured the assistance of Air Force personnel by asking them to fly her from Delhi to Lucknow in an Air Force plane. He said, 'the other side contends that Mrs Gandhi did not solicit the supply of the plane and it was supplied to her under the standing instructions which exist for the Air Force, in respect of travel arrangements for the Prime Minister. These rules were amended in 1968, and Mrs Gandhi was party to the amendment. Previously, the rules provided that Air Force planes were to be placed at the Prime Minister's disposal only for official tours, but after the amendment, the planes are to be supplied even for non-official and election purposes. The procedure now is that whenever the tour programme of the Prime Minister is communicated to the Air Force, it is their duty to place an Air Force plane at her disposal.

'So first she had issued instructions that whenever her tour programme is communicated to the Air Force, they must supply her with an Air Force plane and then she issued her tour programme. This clearly amounts to asking for the plane to be supplied to her. Moreover, even if it can be said that the rules existed from before, they cannot obliterate the responsibility of the candidate to abide by the R.P. Act. An administrative order cannot override a statutory provision about corrupt practices. Moreover, no one could force her to board the plane. The very fact that she boarded the plane knowing that it would be flown by members of the Air Force makes her liable for a corrupt practice.'

Moreover, Counsel submitted, *mens rea* (criminal intent) is not essential for a corrupt practice to be proved. 'Take the Supreme Court's decision in Y.S. Parmar's case.[1] The court held that the very fact that the polling agent was a member of the Armed Forces was enough to attract a corrupt practice even though the candidate at that time was ignorant of the fact.'

Counsel then contended that this assistance rendered by the Air Force did further the election prospects of Mrs Gandhi. He argued, 'The other side says that an Air Force plane is provided for the Prime Minister's security. My Lord, there is no limit to the extent of this

[1] AIR 1959, SC 244, *Y.S. Parmar v. Hira Lal Paul.*

argument. Even the rostrum and loudspeaker arrangements are said to be for her security. If this can be done for the Prime Minister, then such things can also be done for every minister, state minister, deputy minister, in fact, for every member of the ruling party. They are also important because they take part in the lawmaking process. If this were done, the election would become grossly unfair, as the ruling party would enjoy tremendous advantages over the other parties. It is because government servants cannot ignore the orders of the ruling party that Section 123(7) expressly prohibits the procuring of their assistance. The holders of high offices are already in an advantageous position by virtue of their offices. Why should they be allowed to derive any further advantage on the pretext of security?'

Counsel further submitted that mobility was a very important part of the electioneering of a candidate, and said how some leaders once demanded that this facility must also be provided to Opposition parties on payment but were refused by the government.

'She cannot escape the charge of corrupt practice here by saying that her flight to Lucknow was not for her election work but for party work. It is true that from Lucknow she flew to other places for party work and also addressed some meetings outside her constituency on her way to Rae Bareli, but the fact remains that her main purpose for stopping at Lucknow was to file her nomination papers at Rae Bareli. No one can deny that the filing of nomination papers is election work, for without filing the nomination papers, a person cannot even contest the election.'

THE ISSUE OF ROSTRUMS AND LOUDSPEAKERS

Bhushan then took up the issue of rostrums and loudspeakers which was framed as follows.

'Whether at the instance of Respondent No. 1 and her election agent, Yashpal Kapoor, the District Magistrate of Rae Bareli, the Superintendent of Police of Rae Bareli and the Home Secretary of UP, arranged for rostrums, loudspeakers and barricading to be set up, and for members of the Police Forces to be posted in connection with her election tour on 1.2.71 and 25.2.71 and, if so, whether this amounts to a corrupt practice under Section 123(7) of the R.P. Act.' Counsel said, 'The District Magistrate and the Superintendent of Police of Rae Bareli have deposed that they did arrange for rostrums, loudspeakers and barricading to be set up in connection with Mrs Gandhi's election tour but they did so in pursuance of the instructions contained in the Blue Book. The question here is whether these arrangements amount to assistance for furtherance of prospects of Mrs Gandhi's election and whether this assistance was procured at the instance of Mrs Gandhi or her election agents. Another question is, can she escape the rigour of Section 123(7) because this assistance was provided because of the Blue Book instructions. Regarding the second question, I submit, that administrative orders cannot by-pass statutory provisions. If it is provided in the statute that certain acts are illegal, they cannot be made legal by any administrative order.'

Counsel then turned to the question of whether this assistance was procured at Mrs Gandhi's instance. Here too, the instructions contained in the Blue Book were amended in February 1969 with Mrs Gandhi's consent. Before November 1969, the arrangements were only to be made for the Prime Minister's official or non-official meetings excluding election meetings. The amendment provided that the arrangements would also have to be made for election meetings.

'BLUE BOOK—THE INDIRECT MEAN'

Bhushan said, 'Even if the assistance was not directly procured, it has been indirectly procured through a circuitous procedure of Blue Book instructions. If this sort of thing is permissible, then the whole government machinery can be used by ministers for their elections. Moreover, even if the arrangements were made without her instructions, she should have refused to use them knowing that they were arranged by gazetted officers of the state government. She could have asked her party to make arrangements for her rostrums.'

Justice Sinha: Suppose she had only asked the people to vote for the Congress in her meetings. Then would it be 'her' election meeting?

Counsel: She was the Congress candidate there. Therefore, a vote for the Congress means a vote for her.

Counsel told the court that it was not that the state government was making these arrangements on its own. He said that, in fact, the state government had protested against the burden which it had to bear. He displayed a letter from the chief minister of UP to the Prime Minister, in which he had said that an expenditure of Rs 35.08 lakh was incurred in less than two months on security arrangements for the Prime Minister's visits. This, the letter said, was an extremely heavy burden for a poor state like UP which got no benefit from these political tours.

Bhushan then came to the question of whether these arrangements furthered the prospects of Mrs Gandhi's election. He argued, 'The other side contends that these arrangements were for the security of the Prime Minister. Security seems to be their magic word for explaining away all the corrupt practices. I can understand that barricading can be said to be for the Prime Minister's security, but I totally fail to understand how rostrums of particular dimensions are necessary to ensure her security. In fact, the higher the rostrum the less secure she is because it is easier to shoot upwards in a crowded public meeting.'

Justice Sinha: Then why is it that the Blue Book says that the rostrum should be of particular dimensions?

Counsel: Because the bigger the rostrum the better is the image of the person projected. All these are image-projecting devices. Moreover, even if by some stretch of imagination, one reaches the conclusion that the rostrum is for security purposes, I submit, is it impossible to conclude that loudspeakers are for security purposes. Whatever do loudspeakers have to do with security?

Counsel argued that if security was the only consideration involved in the instructions about the rostrums and loudspeakers, then there should also have been similar instructions for public meetings of Opposition leaders.

Justice Sinha: This might be because the Prime Minister's election meetings are expected to be the largest.

Counsel: That might be, but it cannot be said that the smallest meeting of the Prime Minister is larger than the largest meeting of a top Opposition leader. After all, security of Opposition leaders is also very important in a democracy.

Khare at this point got up and stated that two truckloads of policemen were provided for the protection of Raj Narain when he went around. Bhushan replied that the police protection was only to deal with law and order. Bhushan showed the court an issue of *Current*, the weekly news magazine, in which it was reported that Bahuguna, then chief minister of UP, had ordered exactly the same arrangements for his public meetings as existed for the Prime Minister. 'All this,' Counsel said, 'was being done to project an image equal to that of the Prime Minister's. There was no question of security involved.'

THE ISSUE OF EXPENSES

Bhushan then turned to the issue of election expenses which was 'whether Respondent No. 1 and her election agent, Mr Yashpal Kapoor incurred or authorized election expenses in excess of the amount prescribed by Section 77 of the R.P. Act.'

Section 77 prescribes a limit of Rs 35,000.

Counsel told the court that since he was submitting that a lot of expenditure incurred by the District Congress Committee (DCC) of Rae Bareli was impliedly authorized by Kapoor, the R.P. (Amendment) Act of 1974 would become relevant. The amendment added an explanation to Section 77 of the Act. The explanation was 'any expenditure incurred or authorized in connection with the election of a candidate by a political party or any other association or body of persons or by an individual (other than the candidate or his election agent) shall not be deemed to be and shall not ever be deemed to have been expenditure in connection with the election incurred or authorized by the candidate or his election agent.' This amendment was given retrospective effect so as to apply to all cases pending before the courts.

Counsel said that before going to the expenses issue he would first challenge the validity of the amendment.

The Supreme Court decided Chawla's case[2] in October 1974. In that case, the interpretation given to Section 77 of the R.P. Act was, 'When a political party sponsoring a candidate incurred expenditure in connection with his election as distinguished from expenditure from general party propaganda and the candidate knowingly takes advantage of it and participates in the activity or fails to disavow the expenditure, or consents to it or acquiesces in it, it would be reasonable to infer, save in exceptional circumstances, that he impliedly authorized a political party to incur such expenditure and he cannot escape the rigour of ceiling by saying that he has not incurred the expenditure but his political party has done so.'

Counsel said that the validity of this amendment would have to be decided in the light of the interpretation given to Section 77 in Chawla's case.

---

[2] AIR 1975, SC 308, *K.L. Gupta v. A.N. Chawla.*

INTERPRETATION OF THE AMENDMENT

Bhushan told the court that he would first advance his interpretation of the amendment, and if the interpretation found favour with the judge, he would have no quarrel with the amendment. He said, 'The amendment lays down that if any expenditure was incurred or authorized by a political party or a friend or supporter of a candidate, (without being incurred or authorized by the candidate or his election agent), then it will not be treated as the candidate's expenses.' The bracketed words 'except the candidate or his election agent' are of crucial importance here. It seems clear that the intention of the Parliament was only to exclude that expenditure which was incurred or authorized by a political party or any other person but which was not authorized by a candidate or his election agent.

Counsel submitted that a correct interpretation of the amendment would only exclude that expenditure which was both incurred and authorized by a third party, without any hand of the candidate. He argued, 'If we accept their interpretation, we would reach the rather absurd conclusion that even if some expenditure was incurred by the candidate himself, it would not have to be included in his return merely because it was authorized by some other person. This makes the provision for a ceiling on election expenses absurd and ridiculous. There would be no difficulty at all in evading the ceiling. All that the candidate would have to do would be to get a letter of authorization from his political party or friend for any expenditure which he wishes to incur in his election, and it would then be excluded from his return. In fact, usually, a candidate does not spend money on his election from his own pocket; it is provided by his political party or friends and supporters. If their interpretation of the amendment is accepted, nobody would ever come within the rigour of the ceiling.'

Counsel read out the following passage from Justice Bhagwati's judgment in Chawla's case: 'A small man's chance is the essence of Indian democracy and that would be stultified if large contributions from rich and affluent groups are not divorced from the electoral process.'

Counsel submitted that this virtual abolition of the ceiling would convert democracy into moneycracy where only moneyed people would have a chance of sitting in Parliament. He argued, 'When such drastic and unpleasant consequences flow from the rejection of my interpretation, then I see no reason why my interpretation should not be accepted. I quote the well-known principle of law that when two interpretations of statutory provisions are possible, the interpretation which harmonized with the other provisions of the statute should be accepted.'

Bhushan told the court that if, however, his interpretation did not find favour with the court, he would challenge the constitutional validity of the amendment. He outlined the four main grounds of his challenge:

1. That it infringed Article 14 of the Constitution by discriminating against the candidate who abided with the law in the election.
2. That it was beyond the power conferred by Article 327 of the Constitution which only conferred power to make prospective laws relating to elections.
3. That it had the effect of destroying democracy which was the basic feature of the Constitution.
4. That it was a colourable piece of legislation designed solely to secure a particular result in a particular case.

Amplifying his first ground of challenge that the amendment infringed Article 14 (Article 14 guarantees the fundamental right of equality), Counsel said that since the amendment was given retrospective effect, it did not provide an equal opportunity to all the candidates. 'If Mr Narain also knew that the law would be that any expenditure could be incurred by his political party or his friends and supporters, he too could have asked his political party to spend a lot of money for him. He did not do so as he was a law-abiding citizen. But Mrs Gandhi did not care about the law. After she has contravened the law, this amendment is passed in her favour. It involves an absurd classification, a classification between law-abiding citizens and citizens who have no respect of the law, in which the advantage is given to the latter. Where is the free and fair election? One candidate works under an injunction which restricts him from spending more than Rs 35,000 and the other spends several lakhs and later the law is amended with retrospective effect to legalize this illegality.'

Justice Sinha: Have there been other retrospective amendments to the R.P. Act?

Counsel: Not a single one, my Lord. How can we contemplate retrospective changes in the rules of contest in any civilized country.

Counsel then cited a case[3] in which the Maharashtra State Electricity Board had issued an advertisement for the post of an engineer. There were certain conditions for the applicants. The person who was finally selected did not fulfil those conditions but the conditions were later relaxed for him. The Bombay High Court held that the selection was void as it discriminated against other persons who could not apply for that post as they did not fulfil the conditions in the same way as the person selected did. The judges in that case observed, 'When such is the case, it is not permissible for the appointing authority to relax or condone any of the conditions to the detriment of equal opportunity being made available to other candidates whose cases for similar condonation or relaxation could not be considered by the selection committee for want of proper advertisement.'

Counsel submitted that in the present case too, the rules had been relaxed with retrospective effect to the detriment of Raj Narain.

Coming to his second ground of challenge, Bhushan submitted that the amendment was also unconstitutional on the ground that it was beyond the powers conferred on the Parliament under Article 327 of the Constitution. Article 327 reads thus:

> Subject to the provisions of this Constitution, Parliament may from time to time by law make provisions with respect to all matters relating to or in connection with elections to either House of Parliament or to the House or either House of the Legislature of the State including the preparation of electoral rolls, delimitations of constituencies and all other matters necessary for securing the due constitution of such House or Houses.

Counsel said that Article 327 had been interpreted by the Supreme Court[4] and their Lordships had observed that before an election machinery could be brought into operation, one of the requisites which had to be attended to was that: 'There should be a set of laws and rules making provisions with respect to all matters or in relation to or in connection with elections . . .'

---

[3] AIR 1968, Bombay, 65, *MSEB Engineers v. MSEB*.
[4] AIR 1952, SC 64, *Ponnuswamy v. Returning Officer, Nammakal*.

Counsel argued that according to this interpretation, Article 327 contemplates that there should already be a pre-existing law determining the conduct of elections before the election is held. He contended, 'Thus their Lordships have held that lawmaking power of Parliament under Article 327 was only prospective. Article 327 does not contemplate any retrospective law relating to elections. Since the amendment is given retrospective effect, I submit that it is void to that extent.'

Coming to his third ground of attack on the amendment, Counsel argued that it was also invalid on the ground that it destroyed democracy which was the basic feature of the Constitution. He said that the Supreme Court in Kesavananda Bharati's case[5] had laid down that there were implied limitations to the Parliament's power of amending the Constitution.

Justice Sinha: Do these limitations also extend to ordinary legislations?

Counsel: The Constitution amending power is a much bigger power than the power of ordinary legislation. If this limitation applies to the Constitution amending power of the Parliament, then it must also apply to the legislative powers of Parliament.

The author here would like to explain that in Kesavananda Bharati's case which was decided in April 1973, the question before the court was whether the Constitution amending power of Parliament was plenary, and if not, what were its limits. The arguments in this case had gone on for four months before a Bench consisting of all the thirteen judges of the Supreme Court. Eleven separate judgments were delivered in this case which rendered the decision fairly ambiguous. Eminent jurists are still in dispute over the details of the majority view. The operative order, however, lays down that although the amending powers of Parliament are wide, they do not extend to damaging or destroying the basic structure or identity of the Constitution. Nine of the thirteen judges had signed the operative order; four judges, Justices Ray, Mathew, Dwivedi and Beg, had refused to sign it. This case also became controversial due to the fact that it led to the supersession of the three seniormost judges who had decided in favour of the majority view.

Quoting from the judgment of the majority, Counsel showed that all of them had agreed that Parliament's power could not extend to damaging or destroying democracy.

---

[5] AIR 1973, SC 1461, *Kesavananda Bharati v. State of Kerala*.

Counsel argued that even if this amendment was not retrospective, it would still have the effect of destroying democracy in the country. He argued that as this amendment virtually abolished the ceiling on election expenses, it completely negated the small man's chance of being elected to Parliament. He said that in a country like India, where most people were uneducated, money played a tremendous part in the election and unless this money influence was divorced from the election process, democracy would be a distant dream.

Arguing on the retrospective aspect of the amendment, Bhushan submitted that if this power was granted to Parliament, then the party in power could perpetually remain there by manipulating the laws retrospectively. He said, 'They could make retrospective laws to validate the invalid elections of members of their party and invalidate the valid elections of members of the Opposition parties. Has anyone ever heard of retrospective laws regarding the conduct of elections? The idea itself is ludicrous.'

Justice Sinha: This amendment cannot invalidate a valid election. All that it can do is to validate an invalid election.

Counsel: My Lord, if they can validate an invalid election, what prevents them from invalidating a valid election? There is no difference in principle between them. The situation is just like a cricket match which is played first and the rules are made later. Not even that, the rules are made by one of the playing teams. If most of the players of that team were bowled and most of the players of the other team were caught, they could retrospectively frame the rule providing that those who have been caught would be out and those who had been bowled would not be out. Thus the team framing the rules could easily ensure the victory of their team.

Counsel then argued that this amendment had been manifestly enacted to save the election of Mrs Gandhi. He said that since it had been enacted with a view to secure a particular result in a particular case, it was a colourable piece of legislation.

Justice Sinha: There are other people who can benefit by this amendment.

Counsel: It has been couched in general terms merely to avoid embarrassment, although it is clearly done with a view to benefit Mrs Gandhi. All the other people who benefit by this amendment would be just subsidiary beneficiaries.

With this, Counsel ended his arguments on the validity of the amendment.

Bhushan then turned to the merits of the issue of expenses. The return of the election expenses filed on behalf of Mrs Gandhi showed that a total expenditure of Rs 12,892.79 had been incurred in her election. The petitioner had alleged that the return did not include lakhs of rupees which were spent on vehicles used by the Congress Committee for Mrs Gandhi's election, rostrums constructed for her by the state government, loudspeakers installed at her meetings, Air Force planes used by her and payments made to election workers.

Taking up the item of construction of rostrums for eleven meetings addressed by Mrs Gandhi on 1 and 25 February, Bhushan showed a letter from the UP Police Headquarters to the UPCC in which it was stated that a total expense of Rs 17,600 was incurred on the rostrums constructed for those public meetings of Mrs Gandhi.

Justice Sinha: The amendment excludes this expenditure.

Counsel: I am submitting that since the expenses were incurred by the state government, even the amendment does not exclude them. Even if my interpretation of the amendment is rejected and the amendment is not struck down, the expenses incurred by the state government would still have to be included if they were authorized by the candidate. The amendment only excludes expenditure by a political party, an association, or any other person. A government is neither a political party nor an association nor any other individual.

Taking up the expense on the Air Force plane, Counsel told the court that the amount actually paid by Mrs Gandhi for her travel in that plane was at the rate of 33p per mile (that was the commercial air fare at that time). He produced a document to show that the chartered rate of these planes was Rs 16 per mile. He said, 'There is no reason why she should pay less than this. At the rate of Rs 16 per mile, her fare from Delhi to Lucknow works out to Rs 5000, which must be added in the return.'

THE TWENTY-THREE VEHICLES

Counsel then turned to the crucial issue of expenses incurred on the twenty-three vehicles used by the DCC of Rae Bareli during the elections. He contended, 'All these vehicles must have been used for the election campaign of Mrs Gandhi and their use was authorized by Yashpal Kapoor. The return of expenses by Mrs Gandhi, however, shows the expenditure on only one jeep which was in the personal use of Mr Kapoor. It is ridiculous that the election campaign of the Prime Minister was carried on with the use of only one jeep. The other side admits that twenty-three jeeps were used by the District Congress Committee in the three constituencies of that district. They, however, say that since they were used by the District Congress Committee, the expenditure on these could not be included in the return.'

Counsel showed the court a letter written by Kapoor to the District Magistrate of Rae Bareli. In that letter, Kapoor had requested the District Magistrate to release these vehicles which had been requisitioned because they were to be used for the election campaign of Mrs Gandhi. The respondent had also filed a letter written by the president, DCC to Kapoor. In the letter, the president had asked Kapoor to write a letter to the District Magistrate requesting the release of the vehicles which were needed for the use of the DCC. During election time, the District Magistrate can requisition, i.e., call for, any vehicle which is registered in that area, for the use of the government, on payment. If a vehicle has been requisitioned, it can only be derequisitioned, i.e., released, on the request of a candidate or his election agent. He has to state that it is being used in his constituency.

'I do not dispute that the vehicles were used by the DCC but this letter of Mr Kapoor to the District Magistrate amounts to the implied authorization for the use of the vehicles in Mrs Gandhi's constituency. Therefore, the expenses on these vehicles must be included.'

Justice Sinha: But how do we know the amount of the expenditure which was incurred on these vehicles?

Counsel: Chawla's case has laid down that if any expenditure is proved to have been evaded (in the return of election expenses), then it is the duty of the court to make a fair and reasonable estimate and add that to the amount shown in the return. It is unfortunate that the two persons who could have thrown much light on the expenditure on these vehicles were not produced in the court by the respondent. They are Mr Gaya Prasad Shukla who was keeping the accounts for Mrs Gandhi and Mr Dal Bahadur Singh, president of the DCC. The testimony of these persons would have been extremely valuable to the court. They were cited as witnesses of the respondent but later withdrawn. I submit that an adverse inference should be drawn against the respondent for this.

Counsel cited Chenna Reddy's case[6] in which the court had drawn an adverse inference against the respondent for the non-production of relevant witnesses. The judges had noted, 'Inference can be drawn against a party who does not call evidence which should be available in support of the party.'

Making an assessment of the expenditure which would have been incurred on these vehicles, Counsel said that the normal period during which they would have been used would be between 1 February (the date on which Yashpal Kapoor was appointed election agent) and 5 March (the last date of the campaign), which came to thirty-three days. He went on, 'At a reasonable rate of Rs 4000 per vehicle, the total expenditure on these twenty-three vehicles works out to more than Rs 92,000. According to the return of Mrs Gandhi, about Rs 1100 had been spent on petrol for one vehicle alone between 1 February and 5 March. Even if petrol expenses on other vehicles are estimated at Rs 1000 each, the cost of petrol alone would be Rs 23,000.'

Justice Sinha: But all these vehicles might not have been used in the Prime Minister's constituency.

Counsel: A reasonable estimate would be that $^5/_7$ of these vehicles were used in Mrs Gandhi's constituency and $^2/_7$ in the other constituencies. This is because Rae Bareli district consists of seven Assembly constituencies. Out of these, five are parts of Mrs Gandhi's parliamentary constituency. Therefore, $^5/_7$ of Rae Bareli district was in Mrs Gandhi's constituency. Even if $^5/_7$ of the total expenditure on the vehicles was apportioned for Mrs Gandhi's constituency, it would be much more than Rs 35,000 and the corrupt practice would be proved.

DCC BANK ACCOUNT

Counsel then produced the bank account of the DCC which was operated by the president of the DCC. According to this account, between 4 March and the end of April, about Rs 1,10,000 had been deposited by cheques mainly from the UP Congress Committee. Out of this, Rs 85,000 had been disbursed to various people by the end of April. Counsel contended that most of this expenditure must have been incurred by the DCC on Mrs Gandhi's election.

---

[6] 40 Election Law Reports, 390, *M. Chenna Reddy v. V.R. Rao.*

Justice Sinha: How do we know where this money went?

Counsel: It is not necessary to show exactly how much money was spent and where it was spent. If it can be shown that the expenditure of the campaign was such that at least Rs 35,000 must have been incurred, then the corrupt practice is proved.

Counsel then turned to the question of whether the money spent by the DCC on Mrs Gandhi's election had been authorized by Kapoor. He stated, 'These are the circumstances. Mr Kapoor was residing in the guest house of the DCC. All the work of the DCC and of Mr Kapoor was being carried on from the same office. The account of Mrs Gandhi's election were being maintained by Gaya Prasad Shukla who was also an active Congress party worker. Moreover, it was Dal Bahadur Singh who got Mr Kapoor appointed as Mrs Gandhi's election agent. All these circumstances, I submit, overwhelmingly establish that this expenditure was incurred with the implied authorization of Mr Kapoor.'

THE ISSUE OF HOLDING OUT

Bhushan then addressed the court on the issue of when Mrs Gandhi became a candidate for the election. The issue was framed as follows: 'Whether Respondent No. 1 held herself out as a candidate from any date prior to 1.2.71 and, if so, from what date.'

This issue was relevant for the case because the R.P. Act defines a candidate as a person who has been or claims to have been duly nominated as a candidate, and in an election, any such person shall be deemed to have been a candidate from the time when, with the election in prospect, he began to hold himself out as a prospective candidate. Since all corrupt practices are defined in terms of a candidate, therefore, the liability of corrupt practices would only be attracted after the person held himself out as a candidate.

Discussing the law on holding out, Counsel told the court that the Supreme Court in a case[7] had laid down what amounted to holding out of a person as a prospective candidate. They have laid down that a person holds himself out when he announces his intention to contest the elections or when by some act he leads people to believe that he would become a candidate in the election.

---

[7] AIR 1955, SC 775, *Khader Sharif v. Munnuswamy*.

Bhushan contended that Mrs Gandhi had clearly held herself out as a candidate on 29 December 1970, just two days after the dissolution of Parliament. This, he said, was clear from Mrs Gandhi's reply to a question asked by a reporter in the press conference on that date. The reporter had said, 'A few hours earlier there was a meeting of the Opposition leaders and they said that the Prime Minister was changing her constituency from Rae Bareli to Gurgaon.' Mrs Gandhi had replied with an emphatic 'No, I am not.' The original tapes of this press conference had been obtained from the All India Radio and the judge had himself heard them. Mrs Gandhi had explained that her statement meant that she would not be contesting from Gurgaon. She said that she did not mean that she would be contesting from Rae Bareli.

Counsel claimed that the context in which the question was asked, would also throw light on what she could have meant. He said, 'This question had been asked in the context that since there was an Opposition government in UP, would Mrs Gandhi again be contesting from Rae Bareli which was in UP. She was rightly annoyed with this question and replied indignantly, "No, I am not." This clearly meant that she intended to stick to her old constituency. If she had meant that she was not changing her constituency to Gurgaon, then her reply would have been, "No, I am not changing my constituency to Gurgaon."'

Counsel cited four newspapers of 30 December 1970. They were the *National Herald*, the *Statesman*, the *Indian Express* and the *Hindustan Times*. They all carried the news of Mrs Gandhi's press conference headlined: 'Prime Minister not to change her constituency' and 'Prime Minister sticks to Rae Bareli', etc.

Bhushan submitted that her reply to the question had given the whole world the impression that she would be contesting the election from Rae Bareli. He read out the depositions of many Opposition leaders who had come to give evidence on behalf of the petitioner. Among them were S. Nijilingappa (former president of the Congress party), Karpoori Thakur (former chief minister of Bihar), Banarasi Das (former minister of UP), L. K. Advani (president of the Jan Sangh). All of them had understood Mrs Gandhi's reply to mean that she would be contesting the election from Rae Bareli. Counsel charged that Mrs Gandhi's explanation was fabricated by her and could not be accepted by the court.

He then referred to a speech delivered by Mrs Gandhi in Coimbatore on 19 January 1971. In her speech, she had referred to the fact that the Opposition parties had chosen Raj Narain as their joint candidate for Rae Bareli to oppose her, and had lashed out against this choice saying that Raj Narain had been chosen because he was a well-known 'Nehru baiter and hater'. Counsel argued that this speech of Mrs Gandhi clearly showed that at that time at least she assumed that the people knew that she would be contesting from Rae Bareli.

Strongly contesting the truth of Mrs Gandhi's statement that she did not take any decision on her constituency before 1 February, Counsel also placed the tour programme of Mrs Gandhi for 1 February before the court. This was for Rae Bareli and was issued on 25 January. On it were handwritten words, 'file nomination papers' at 11 a.m. at the Collectorate. In her deposition, Mrs Gandhi had explained that this was only a provisional tour programme, and she could easily have changed her mind before that date and file her nomination paper from some other place.

Since this tour programme was secret and not a public document, Counsel said that he was not contending that this amounted to a holding out by Mrs Gandhi. 'But I submit that this completely destroys her case that she did not take a final decision about her constituency before 1 February. I submit that one would have to stretch one's credulity too far to believe that even on 25 January she had not decided to fight the election from Rae Bareli. As far as changing her mind goes, she could change her mind even after filing her nomination paper. If this criterion is applied, then the whole concept of holding out will disappear because it is always possible for a candidate to change his mind and withdraw from the contest before the polling date.'

Bhushan now played his trump card on this issue which completely demolished Mrs Gandhi's stand that she took a final decision only on 1 February. He read out a part of her additional written statement made in August 1972 where she had stated, 'A final decision in regard to my constituency was announced by the All India Congress Committee only on 29 January 1971.' When confronted by this statement during the cross-examination, she said, 'The language contained in the additional written statement is legal language which I find difficult to understand.'

'What is legal about that language, my Lord,' Counsel explained. 'It clearly states a plain simple fact that AICC announced a final decision about her constituency on 29 January. This is political language. Can anyone even for a moment believe that the Prime Minister of India is unable to understand this language.' Bhushan became grave, and said, 'I am extremely sorry to say that she has not been truthful to the court on this point, and henceforth, all her statements should be regarded by the court with utmost caution.'

There was a stir in the court. The Prime Minister had been called a liar by a senior lawyer in the crowded court. The judge listened passively and attentively. He did not say a word.

CREDIBILITY OF MRS GANDHI ASSAILED

Counsel argued that in the face of the mass of evidence adduced by the petitioner to support his contention that she held herself out much before 1 February, the only evidence in rebuttal before the court was Mrs Gandhi's statement. Impeaching the credibility of Mrs Gandhi, Counsel placed before the court a letter written to her in 1959 by the Lieutenant-Governor of Himachal Pradesh. Mrs Gandhi at that time was the Congress president. The Governor in his letter informed Mrs Gandhi about the victory of the Congress candidate in a by-election in Himachal Pradesh. He said that he had thus successfully passed 'the toughest test' that Mrs Gandhi had put him to. Counsel submitted that this clearly implied that Mrs Gandhi had asked the Lieutenant-Governor[8] to somehow help the Congress candidate in winning the by-election. Mrs Gandhi's explanation was that 'the test' mentioned in the letter could have been a 'law and order' test. Ridiculing this explanation, Counsel said that one would have to really stretch one's imagination to read any suggestion of a 'law and order' test in that letter. He charged, 'She did not hesitate to procure the assistance of even the Governor of the state for party ends.'

Counsel then referred to another part of Mrs Gandhi's testimony where she had answered some questions about the Maruti car factory. She was asked whether the Air Force had raised any objection to the acquisition of land for Maruti on the ground that it constituted a security risk to the Explosives Depot at Gurgaon. Mrs Gandhi

---

[8] A Governor in India is only the constitutional head of a state government. He does not belong to any party and is supposed to be politically neutral.

had replied that she did not know whether it was the Air Force or Parliamentarians who had raised this objection. Counsel said that it was strange that the Prime Minister, who is immediately concerned with the security of the country, did not know who had raised the objection, particularly when the factory involved belonged to her own son.

Yet Another Lie

Bhushan then made another interesting revelation. He said that some of the secret documents released by the court on 2 April revealed that on 1 February, Mrs Gandhi did not go to the Circuit House at all before filing her nomination papers. Mrs Gandhi had sworn on oath that she had filed her nomination papers only after talking to Congress workers in the Circuit House. The documents revealed that her original tour programme which included going to the Circuit House before filing her nomination papers was changed at the last minute, and she had gone straight to the Collectorate without first going to the Circuit House.

Counsel submitted that in the light of all these untruths, her statement should not be accepted, and it must be held that she held herself out as a candidate from 29 December 1970.

THE ISSUE OF YASHPAL KAPOOR

Bhushan then turned to the issue of Yashpal Kapoor. It was framed as under: 'Whether Respondent No. 1 obtained and procured the assistance of Yashpal Kapoor in furtherance of the prospects of her election while he was still a gazetted officer in the service of the Government of India. If so, from what date.'

Counsel first dealt with Yashpal Kapoor's resignation date. He submitted that the resignation became effective only on 25 January when an order accepting it was passed by the President. The respondent's case was that the resignation was submitted by Kapoor on 13 January and was orally accepted straightaway by P.N. Haksar, the Principal Secretary of the Prime Minister. The recorded facts were that the resignation was officially accepted by an order dated 25 January. The order, however, said that the resignation was to be accepted with retrospective effect from 14 January.

Counsel first contended that it was not at all clear that the resignation was in fact submitted on 13 January. He said, 'Firstly, it is dated 14 January. Why should Mr Kapoor put the date as 14 when he submitted it on the 13th? Mr Kapoor had said that he had post-dated it because of technical difficulties. What sort of technical difficulties can compel him to post-date his letter, I cannot imagine. Mr Haksar also deposed that the resignation was submitted on 13 January. It is, however, strange that Mr Haksar did not make any endorsement on the resignation letter before passing it on to his secretary. Moreover, your Lordship will see that Mr Haksar's testimony is also unreliable. He says that oral appointments and oral resignations take place every day in government offices. He says that he himself was appointed by an oral order of the Prime Minister and does not know yet whether there is any written order at all. I submit that it is monstrous to contemplate that work in government offices can go on in such a fashion.'

Counsel went on, 'Apart from Mr Haksar, Mrs Gandhi also stated that she remembered the dates of Kapoor's resignation. Remembering the exact date of an event which took place four years ago requires a photographic memory, and it is evident that she does not even have a better than average memory, let alone a photographic memory. She does not even remember any event which took place exactly one month back. When such is the case, how can we rely on her memory about an event which took place four years ago? As far as Mr Kapoor's statement is concerned, I will show your Lordship how completely unreliable his word is.'

Bhushan then took up the question of when Kapoor's resignation became effective in law. He stated, 'The other side contends that Mr Haksar accepted Mr Kapoor's resignation orally on 13 January itself. Mr Haksar, however, did not know of any rule authorizing him to accept Mr Kapoor's resignation. He assumed that he was competent to accept it. This is something like *Alice in Wonderland* where each one thinks that he is competent to do things without citing any rule which authorizes him to do them. There is no rule which authorizes one Private Secretary to accept the resignation of another Private Secretary. Mr Haksar was not competent to accept Mr Kapoor's resignation.

'Moreover, even if Mr Haksar was the competent authority to accept the resignation, it was impossible for him to do so orally. Even the Prime Minister cannot accept a resignation without passing a written order.' Counsel further contended that a resignation could not be accepted with retrospective effect. He said, 'In this case, the order accepting the resignation is dated 25 January, but it is given retrospective effect so as to apply from 14 January. This would raise the question of whether Mr Kapoor was a government servant between 14 and 25 January, when his resignation letter was lying on the table and he could still have withdrawn it. I submit that he must be treated as having been a government servant till the time an order was passed accepting his resignation.'

Bhushan then dealt with the question of when Kapoor started working for Mrs Gandhi's election. He divided the issue into two parts: (1) The work done by Kapoor before 14 January, as before that date he was admittedly a government servant, and (2) the work done by Kapoor between 14 January and 25 January.

Dealing with the work done by Kapoor before 14 January, Counsel told the court that there were two instances of Kapoor's working in Mrs Gandhi's election before this date. 'The first instance was when Mr Kapoor accompanied the railway minister, Mr Gulzari Lal Nanda, to Munshiganj, near Rae Bareli on 7 January. Mr Kapoor has admitted that he made a speech at that meeting. He, however, said that he had only paid tributes to the martyrs in his speech and denied having said anything about the election of Mrs Gandhi.'

Counsel produced an issue of a newspaper of January 1971, in which there was a news item to the effect that both Gulzari Lal Nanda and Kapoor had delivered election speeches for Mrs Gandhi at Munshiganj. Counsel argued that it was extremely improbable that Kapoor had gone with Nanda all the way to Munshiganj merely to pay homage to the martyrs, and that they did not utilize the opportunity to deliver election speeches particularly when elections were in the offing.

The only other evidence of Kapoor having worked for Mrs Gandhi before 14 January was the return of election expenses of Mrs Gandhi. In the return, there are two columns for dates. In one column is entered the date on which the expenditure is actually incurred and in the other, the date on which the expenditure was authorized. It was shown in the return that a voters' list had been purchased on 11 January. The date on which this expenditure was authorized was also shown to be 11 January. Since it was authorized by Kapoor, Counsel said that there was no reason why the court should not give full legal effect to the document and hold it as evidence of Kapoor's work for Mrs Gandhi's election before 14 January. Kapoor had explained that the voters' list was purchased by the DCC on 11 January for whosoever the Rae Bareli candidate would be. Kapoor had, therefore, included this item in the return later.

Counsel then dealt with the work done by Kapoor between 14 and 25 January. He produced another news item which appeared in the *Swatantra Bharat* on 22 January. The report said that Kapoor had arrived in Rae Bareli on 14 January with a convoy of seventy jeeps, thus giving a new boost to the election campaign of Mrs Gandhi. The paper also referred to Kapoor as the chief election agent of Mrs Gandhi. Kapoor had denied this report. He had said that when he met Kamlapati Tripathi on 13 January, he was asked to make a general tour of eastern districts of UP, which was how he had reached Rae Bareli (an eastern district of UP) on 14 January. He had no jeeps with him, he had stated.

Ridiculing Kapoor's deposition, Counsel said that it was an extremely strange quirk of fate that Tripathi had asked Kapoor to go to the eastern districts of UP and Kapoor, going like a nomad, chanced to reach Rae Bareli. 'There is no reason at all to believe Mr Kapoor's deposition and disbelieve the report of *Swatantra Bharat*. The reporter of *Swatantra Bharat* must have been a remarkably good astrologer to have reported on 22 January itself that Mr Kapoor was the chief election agent of Mrs Gandhi. This means that he must have been doing election work for Mrs Gandhi much before 22 January so as to give the impression that he was her chief election agent.'

Counsel further revealed that the return of expenses of Mrs Gandhi also showed that Kapoor had paid a salary to the driver of his jeep from 15 January. Kapoor in his deposition had stated that the driver was working for the DCC from 15 January. When asked as to why he had included the salary paid to the driver from 15 January to 1 February in the return of expenses, Kapoor said that he had done so since there was a big margin available. Counsel charged that this also brought out the fact that the expenses shown in the return were cooked up at a later date and did not represent the actual expenses incurred in the election.

The next allegation relating to Kapoor's work was that he addressed several election meetings on the 16, 18 and 19 January along with important Congress leaders. A number of witnesses had deposed before the court that Kapoor had participated in an election meeting addressed by Chandrashekhar (then a member of the Congress Working Committee) on 17 January. They had also deposed that he addressed further meetings on the 18 and 19 of January. These meetings were also addressed by Prof. Sher Singh (minister of communications). Kapoor denied his participation in the meetings. He said that he had left Rae Bareli on 17 January and was not even present there on 18 and 19 January.

Counsel charged that the story about Kapoor leaving Rae Bareli on 17 January, and proceeding to Bara Banki and Sultanpur, was totally fabricated. He said, 'In fact, earlier, the other side had admitted Mr Kapoor's presence in Rae Bareli by suggesting to one of the petitioner's witnesses that Mr Kapoor in his speech on 19 January did not say "Indira Gandhi *ko jitao*" but merely said, "Indira Congress ko jitao". Later, when the Supreme Court judgment came, asking the High Court to reconsider the date of Mr Kapoor's resignation, the stand of the respondent changed. I find it incredible that Mr Kapoor should leave Rae Bareli and go to the remote districts of Bara Banki and Sultanpur just when important persons like Mr Chandrashekhar and Prof. Sher Singh started arriving in Rae Bareli. Mr Kapoor could not even remember where he had spent the nights while at Bara Banki and Sultanpur. I submit that this completely nullifies the credibility of his statement.'

Arguing on the reliability of Kapoor's deposition, Counsel said that there were many things which cast a grave doubt on his integrity. Bhushan charged, 'His entire deposition is a tissue of lies. He says that he went to Rae Bareli in 1969 merely to cast his vote. It is unbelievable that he was so starved to cast his vote that he went all the way from Delhi to Rae Bareli merely for that.'

Analysing Kapoor's answers about the purchase of a house by his wife in the Golf Links area, Counsel submitted that it was extremely interesting that the wife of a person whose life's savings were only Rs 20,000 wanted to purchase a house which costs more than Rs 4 lakh. 'In the financial position in which Mr Kapoor legitimately should have been, his wife could not have even dreamt of buying that house. He, however, stated that his wife had purchased the house by taking loans of slightly more than Rs 1 lakh each from a bank, her mother and a friend. Mr Kapoor professed that he did not even know the conditions on which the loans were obtained, which is fantastic. As for Kapoor's statement that he has seen this house only once, I wonder whether this is because the house evokes the memory of a shady transaction.'

Counsel said that the next question was whether his assistance was 'procured' by Mrs Gandhi. He contended that there was enormous circumstantial evidence to prove that Kapoor worked for her election entirely at her instance.

Counsel added, 'Earlier too, during the 1967 elections, Mr Kapoor had resigned just before the elections to do election work for Mrs Gandhi. A few months after the elections he was reappointed by Mrs Gandhi as an officer on special duty. Mr Kapoor stated that he had resigned both in 1967 and 1971 to join public life. It is amusing that Mr Kapoor's appetite for public life is aroused only during election times, and his public life is confined merely to do election work for Mrs Gandhi. All this about his desire for public life is again a cock and bull story. Mr Kapoor admitted that before and after resigning in January 1971, he had several discussions with Mrs Gandhi. In those circumstances, with the election so close, the discussions must have ranged over the prospects of Mrs Gandhi's election. He must have got instructions from Mrs Gandhi regarding the election campaign. The fact that he was ultimately appointed the election agent of Mrs Gandhi also strongly indicates that she must have sent him to Rae Bareli on 14 January.'

Counsel further said that the return of expenses filed on behalf of Mrs Gandhi showed Kapoor having authorized expenditure for the election right from 11 January onwards. 'Since Mrs Gandhi has also signed the return, therefore, it must be concluded that she authorized him to keep the account right from 11 January. All these circumstances established beyond all reasonable doubt that Mr Kapoor did all this work at Mrs Gandhi's instance.'

THE RELIGIOUS SYMBOL ISSUE

Bhushan lastly argued the symbol issue which was framed as follows: 'Whether by using the symbol of the cow and calf which had been allotted to the party by the Election Commission, Respondent No. 1 was guilty of making an appeal to a religious symbol and committed a corrupt practice as defined in Section 123(3) of R.P. Act.'

Section 123(3) of the R.P. Act provides that 'the use of or appeal to National Symbol, such as, the National Flag, or the National Emblem, for the furtherance of the prospects of the election of that candidate or for prejudicially affecting the election of any candidate,' would be a corrupt practice.

Counsel said that Mrs Gandhi had admittedly used the cow and calf symbol for her election. The only question was whether the symbol of the cow and calf was a religious symbol. He said that he would overwhelmingly establish this beyond any doubt.

Counsel submitted, 'Your Lordship will see that a similar symbol had been asked for by the Akhil Bharatiya Ram Rajya Parishad in the 1952 elections but was refused by the Election Commission on the ground that it was a religious symbol. Further, a report on the First General Elections in India published by the Election Commission says that "no object having any religious or sentimental association, for example, a cow, a temple, a National Flag, a spinning wheel, and the like are found in the list of approved symbols." The Commission specifically mentions the cow as one of the objects having a religious association. The same Commission which had refused to allot the symbol of a cow to the Parishad in 1952 on the ground that it was a religious symbol had now allotted it to the ruling Congress party.'

Counsel went on, 'Just because the symbol has been allotted by the Election Commission, it cannot cease to be a religious symbol. Moreover, your Lordship will see that it has been allotted on the basis of a very suspicious piece of reasoning. The first preference of the Congress party was "a mother with a child in her arms". The "cow and calf" was their second choice. The Election Commission did not allot the first preference though it was a completely harmless symbol, and allotted the second preference which is clearly a religious symbol. Their professed reason was that since the Congress (O) had been allotted their second preference, they were allotting the second preference to the Congress (R) too.'

Counsel argued that just because the symbol had been allotted by the Commission, the party could not abdicate its responsibility. They had themselves asked for the symbol in the first place. So there was no reason why they should not be made to suffer.

Justice Sinha: Suppose the Election Commission allots a religious symbol on its own without the party asking for it.

Counsel: Even then the election would be void. The purpose behind this provision is that if a religious symbol is used by any one, then no matter whose fault it is, the election becomes unfair and it must be set aside. This is similar to the provision in the election law, that if a nomination paper is improperly rejected by the returning officer, the election is declared void even though it is no fault of the returned candidate.

Counsel then cited a judgment of the Supreme Court[9] in which it is observed that the cow in India has been raised to a status of divinity. He cited another recent decision of the Supreme Court in which it was held that the candidate had committed a corrupt practice by proclaiming that a person voting for the Congress would be guilty of *go hatya* (cow slaughter). Placing strong reliance on these cases, Counsel submitted that they alone clinched the issue and proved that the cow was a religious symbol.

He also cited the *Encyclopaedia Britannica* on Hinduism. The *Britannica*, after explaining the concept of worship in Hindu mythology, says that while many animals are worshipped because of their associations with deities, the cow is 'divine in her own right'. Counsel submitted that something which was merely associated with a deity might not be a religious symbol, but the symbol of a deity itself must necessarily be a religious symbol.

Bhushan next analysed the oral evidence which had come in from both sides on this issue. Both sides had examined one pandit each. While the pandit examined by the petitioner maintained that the cow was a deity, the respondent's pandit denied it. Bhushan humorously remarked, 'Your Lordship will have to arbitrate between the two pandits, so you become a super pandit.'

He then read out a few passages from Mahatma Gandhi's book *Go Seva* (Service to the Cow) in which the Mahatma had said that he considers reverence for the cow as one of the fundamental tenets of Hindu religion. Placing strong reliance on this, Counsel contended that if an authority like the Mahatma had said such a thing, there could be no dispute whatsoever about the cow being a religious symbol.

Bhushan ended his arguments on this issue with the plea that in the face of such overwhelming evidence, it was impossible to say that the symbol of the 'cow and calf' was not a religious symbol.

---

[9] AIR 1958, SC 731, *M.H. Qureshi v. State of Bihar.*

There were two other issues framed in the petition, one relating to the bribery of voters and the other relating to the conveyance of voters to the polling stations. Bhushan did not press these issues as the evidence on these was very flimsy. He ended his arguments by thanking the judge for giving him a very patient hearing after arguing continuously for seven and a half days.

These were two other issues raised in the petition: one relating to the burden of proof, and the other relating to the maintenance of accounts in the polling stations. Bhushan did not press these issues as the evidence on these was very flimsy. He ended his arguments by thanking the judges for giving him over a period of nearly three sittings continuously, a total of about two and a half days.

5

The Attorney-General
Defends the Amendment

While Bhushan was arguing, it was announced that the Attorney-General,[1] Niren De, would appear in the High Court to defend the validity of the amendment of the R.P. Act. The validity of laws made by Parliament is often challenged in various High Courts. The court then serves notice to the Union to defend the law. Usually, the Union is represented by the standing counsel, but in this case, the Attorney-General had come in person to argue.

Commencing his arguments on 5 May, the Attorney-General launched a scathing attack on Justice Bhagwati's judgment in Chawla's case. He said, 'The issue in Chawla's case was a simple matter of fact. Yet the learned judges proceeded to lay down the law on election expenses, which they had no business to do. It is quite clear that the learned judges were laying down their philosophy about elections and how in their opinion there could be electoral reforms in the country. It is easy for the judges to say that there should be equality between candidates, but is it practical? How can there be equality between two candidates, one of whom earns only Rs 100 a month and another who earns Rs 50,000 a month. Even if the limit on election expenses was brought down to Rs 100, could a starving man afford to spend even that on an election?

'The fundamental fallacy of the learned judges in Chawla's case was equating democracy with equality. No democracy has perfect equality. Women do not have the right to vote in Switzerland. But can anyone say that it is not a democracy? Money still plays a very important role in the elections in the United States. Can it be said

---

[1] In India, the Attorney-General is the government's chief legal counsel.

that democracy will be destroyed if absolute equality was not ensured among all the candidates?'

The Attorney-General argued that the distinction made in Chawla's case between expenditure on general party propaganda and the expenditure incurred by the party on individual candidates was illusory. 'How can one distinguish between them? During elections, all expenditure of a party is impliedly for individual candidates. Does the dictum of Chawla's case mean that for general party propaganda you cannot even enter the constituency of the candidate?'

Justice Sinha: You can enter the constituency, but must speak about general party policies. Suppose a party sponsoring a candidate incurs all the expenses for a candidate, can it then be said that the candidate need not file any return of election expenses?

Counsel: Yes. No return need be filed.

'The judges in Chawla's case have gone to the extent of saying that the expense on general party propaganda must be limited. If a small man's chance is the essence of the Indian democracy, why not abolish the political party. I wonder whether social, economic and political justice can be achieved by a ceiling on party expenses. That is crying for the moon.'

Counsel further contended that money power did not make any difference to the prospects of a candidate in an election. 'I fought the election for Parliament in 1951 against a Congress candidate. No one can say that I had less money power than him and yet I lost because of Nehru's posters all over my constituency. Kennedy was elected President of the United States despite the vast money power of the Republican Party against him, simply because women liked his face. Where does money power come into this?'

Counsel then proceeded to cite a number of cases on election expenses which were decided before Chawla's case. He argued that the law laid down in Chawla's case was a clear departure from all previous cases, although the judges had disputed this in their judgment. 'I submit that what the Supreme Court says about earlier cases is not relevant. The High Court will have to interpret the earlier decisions of the Supreme Court in their own way.'

The Attorney-General then dealt with the validity of the amendment. He argued that only two things had to be considered to determine its validity: (1) whether it was within the legislative competence of Parliament, and (2) whether it infringed any fundamental rights mentioned in the Constitution.

He submitted that it was open to the legislature to lay down any legislative policy which could not be questioned by the courts. 'Even if the amendment goes against any decision of the Supreme Court, it will have to be accepted by the courts. Changing the law following a judgment of the court is not disrespect to the court. Chawla's case had created considerable doubt as to what the law was, before the judgment was delivered, so the amendment was made to clarify the law as it stood before Chawla's case.'

Counsel then dealt with Bhushan's arguments that the amendment was discriminatory because of its retrospective operation. He contended that before the petitioner could claim the protection of Article 14, he must first set up a case to show that the law had discriminated against him. 'The petitioner has not done so. He has not even pleaded that he has understood the law to be that laid down in Chawla's case when he contested the election. All the arguments of Bhushan in this regard have been in the air. He has contended that there could be no retrospective laws. I find his contention fantastic.'

Bhushan (interjecting): I never contended that the legislature has no authority to enact retrospective laws. All I said was that retrospective laws relating to corrupt practices were not permissible.

De: I thank Bhushan for clarifying his arguments. In any case he has not cited any authority to support his contention. I will cite many authorities to the contrary.

Counsel then cited a case in which the Supreme Court had declared the Cuttack Municipal Elections invalid due to technical reasons. The Governor had retrospectively validated the elections by an ordinance. The Supreme Court had held this ordinance to be valid.

He also referred to the case cited by Bhushan in which the Bombay High Court struck down an appointment of the State Electricity Board on the ground that the Selection Committee had relaxed the qualifications prescribed in the advertisement. 'The point in this case was that the advertisement had prevented others, who would have applied for that post had they known that the advertised qualifications were relaxable, from applying for it. There is no parity between this case and that case. No one had prevented Mr Narain from contesting the elections.'

Counsel strongly rebutted Bhushan's contentions that Article 327 only empowered the Parliament to make prospective laws. 'The power of the legislature includes power to make prospective as well as retrospective laws. If Parliament can make a law prospectively, it can also do retrospectively.' He also contested Bhushan's contention that this amendment was made to protect a single individual and was thus a colourable piece of legislation. 'There is nothing at all in this amendment to suggest that it was done only for Mrs Gandhi's election. It would apply equally to several other cases pending before the courts. However, even assuming that it was done to protect Mrs Gandhi, it does not affect the legislature's powers to pass such a law. The intention of the legislature cannot be questioned.'

Counsel finally made his submissions on Bhushan's contention that the amendment destroyed a basic feature of the Constitution. 'All that Kesavananda Bharati's case lays down is that basic features of the Constitution cannot be destroyed. It does not say that democracy is a basic feature of the Constitution. The basic features of the Constitution regarding elections are adult suffrage and that no person can be deprived of his right to vote on the ground of race, caste, sex or religion. All other laws about elections are made by Parliament, so they can always change these laws. The corrupt practices are defined by Parliament. If they change the definitions, how can one contend that democracy is destroyed? To say that you can have a better form of government is not the same as to say that you have altered the basic form of democracy. Suppose Parliament had not fixed any ceiling on election expenses, could one say that there was no democracy in the country? Can anyone say that there was no democracy in India before the decision in Chawla's case?'

The Attorney-General ended with a vigorous plea that the amendment could not be challenged as being destructive of democracy, or on any other vague ground. His arguments ended on the afternoon of 7 May after two and a half days.

6

The PM's Counsel

When the Attorney-General ended his argument, Khare was not present in court, as he had gone home only a few minutes earlier complaining of a headache. J.N. Tewari, his junior, requested the court that the rejoinder of the petitioner on the validity of the amendment be heard before the respondent's reply. Bhushan was willing to accommodate him but the judge did not agree. He told Tewari that Khare's absence did not matter, and since Tewari was fully acquainted with the case, he could start the arguments.

Tewari: My Lord, I do not have the paper books (records of the evidence) with me at this time.

Bhushan: You can use my paper books.

Tewari grimaced. He had tried his best to get Bhushan to argue first but his attempts had been thwarted. So with the help of the paper books supplied by Bhushan, he began his arguments on the Air Force plane issue.

Meanwhile, an SOS was sent to Khare, who forgot his headache and rushed back to court. Tewari had been on his feet for only twenty minutes when Khare came back and took over from him.

Starting dramatically, he said, 'Your Lordship will notice that this is not a usual election petition at all.'

Justice Sinha: Not at all.

Counsel: This petition has been filed to provide a platform for the leaders of the grand alliance to malign the Prime Minister. It was filed for the same purpose for which Mr Raj Narain was set up as a candidate against the Prime Minister, for mud-slinging. The scheme of propaganda is much the same as that of Goebbels, which was to go on throwing mud so that something might stick. Even the arguments of the petitioner have been directed at throwing as much mud as possible. I am surprised at the irresponsibility with which the petitioner's counsel has argued the case. He has maintained no sense of propriety at all, making wild and unsubstantiated allegations against the Prime Minister.

Counsel charged that all sorts of preposterous, irresponsible and concocted allegations were made in the election petition, most of which were given up during the trial. 'Even though some of the allegations were sworn on personal knowledge by Mr Raj Narain, he did not bring himself to the witness box. The court has only to see the array of witnesses examined by the petitioner to reach the conclusion that the petition is frivolous and filed solely for political reasons. Mr Nijlingappa, the president of Congress (O), had come to give evidence in this case all the way from Mysore. All that he had done was to produce a newspaper. He had no personal knowledge of anything connected with the petition. Similarly, Mr Banarasi Das (a Congress[O] Leader), Mr L.K. Advani (president of the Jan Sangh) and some other leaders had come all the way from Delhi for the same purpose.'

Counsel charged that all these leaders of the grand alliance were produced only from the point of view of publicity; to create an impression that there was some serious issue involved in the election petition. 'Moreover, when the Prime Minister testified before the court, many leaders of the grand alliance, like Mr Jyotirmoy Bosu, Mr Piloo Mody, Mr Rabi Ray and Mr Madhu Limaye, were present as pairokars (special attorneys) of the petitioner in the court. This itself shows the frivolousness of the petition.'

Counsel further said that this was one case where every adjournment had been sought by the petitioner. This was done so that this platform for political propaganda could continue for as long as possible.

Justice Sinha: Proceedings have been adjourned on the joint request of both parties too.

Bhushan (interjecting): In fact it was they who mostly went to the Supreme Court.

Justice Sinha: You also went to the Supreme Court.

Bhushan: Yes, we went once. They went twice and once on such a frivolous issue that it was given up even before the arguments were completed in the Supreme Court.

Khare told the court that most of the issues originally framed in the petition had been given up by the petitioner during the course of the petition. 'Initially, an issue was framed to the effect that Yashpal Kapoor gave a bribe of Rs 50,000 to Swami Adwaitanand. This was given up by the petitioner's counsel on 16 December 1971. Another issue framed was that a large number of quilts, blankets, dhotis and liquor were distributed amongst the voters of the constituency. The only evidence produced on this issue was the oral testimony of one witness named Buddu. The Buddu summoned by the petitioner was the son of Rubai. But the Buddu produced in the court was the son of Babu. This only shows how lightly they have treated such a grave issue. For all practical purposes this allegation of bribery was also given up.

'Another issue that some voters were conveyed to the polling stations in vehicles arranged by Mr Kapoor has also been given up for all practical purposes. Yet another allegation in the petition was that the ballot box had been tampered with. A simple inspection was done by Justice Broome and it was found that this allegation was also absolutely false and baseless. So three-fourths of the petition has already been given up and what remains could not be treated with any seriousness either.'

Counsel further stated, 'The facts of the issues which are left are known to everyone. Nothing was done secretly or clandestinely by the Prime Minister. The fact that she travelled by an Air Force plane on 1 February 1971 is no secret. All the Prime Ministers in the past twenty-five years have done so. The election meetings addressed by Mrs Gandhi were no secret either. The symbol of the cow and calf was allotted by the Election Commission openly. Mr Yashpal Kapoor was publicly appointed election agent from 1 February 1971. Thus whatever was done was done openly.'

Counsel submitted that the arguments raised by the petitioner seemed to suggest that the burden of proof in election petitions was not on the petitioner. He said that the petitioner had tried to show that it was the respondent who had to prove herself innocent of corrupt practices as if allegations based on conjectures were proof of corrupt practices. Khare also charged that a mass of irrelevant evidence had been collected by the petitioner in the hope that something might come out of it. It was an attempt to fish out a floating straw in order to build up a case.

THE VALIDITY OF THE AMENDMENT

Khare first made his submissions on the validity of the election law amendment. He said, 'The petitioner's contention of the amendment being a colourable piece of legislation is absolutely untenable. Firstly, it does not confer any benefit on the Prime Minister in this case. Even if all the expenses incurred by the party for the Prime Minister were added to her return, the maximum limit would still not be reached. Secondly, the Supreme Court has unambiguously stated in many cases that the courts could not examine the motives of Parliament in enacting a particular law. All that the court can do is to inquire whether Parliament was competent to pass such a law.'

He then referred to Bhushan's arguments that the amendment affected a basic feature of the Constitution. He said that this attack could have been sustainable if the validity of a constitutional amendment was at issue. 'However, even assuming that the limitation applies equally to ordinary legislation, I submit that it does not affect the basic structure at all. The basic structure of democracy has to be found from the Constitution itself.'

Counsel said that according to him the provisions laid down in the Constitution itself about elections established the basic features of democracy. None of these, he said, had been affected by the impugned amendment.

He also rebutted the contention that the Amending Act was discriminatory. He said that all the people who had contested the election in 1971 acted on the assumption that party expenses were not to be included in the candidate's return. 'Chawla's case came in 1974 and had altered this position, placing some candidates at a disadvantage. It was because of this that the Parliament had stepped in to clarify the law.'

Counsel contended that even Chawla's case did not apply to the present case because here the expenses were incurred for the security arrangements of the Prime Minister. 'These were like personal expenses. Suppose a minister fell ill during his election campaign and medicines worth Rs 40,000 were imported for his treatment. Could this be treated as his election expenses? Take the case of a lady candidate who gets a facelift at the cost of Rs 20,000 during the elections. This increases her appeal to the voter. But can it be said that this expense has to be included in the return? Further, suppose the candidate buys a new suit costing Rs 10,000 for every day of his campaign, would that be an election expense? In England too, personal expenses are not added to the election expenses.'

'Retrospective Amendments Earlier Too'

Counsel claimed that there had been many other cases of retrospective changes in election law. He cited the Bihar Legislature (Removal of Disqualification) Act, which read: 'Removal of disqualification for membership—a person shall not be and shall be deemed never to have been disqualified for being chosen as for being a member of the Bihar Legislature or the Bihar Legislative Council by reason only of the fact that he holds any of the offices being offices of the profit mentioned in the Schedule.'

He also cited similar acts passed by other state legislatures. He said that even the First, Fourth and Twentieth Amendments to the Constitution were given retrospective effect. 'If the Constitution can be amended with retrospective effect, why not ordinary laws?'

THE ISSUE OF THE AIR FORCE PLANE

Counsel then took up the issue of the Air Force plane. He said that firstly, Mrs Gandhi did not obtain or procure the services of Air Force personnel, and secondly, it did not further the prospects of her election. Elaborating on his point, he said that obtaining or procuring would mean direct action on the part of the candidate, whereas 'Mrs Gandhi was provided an Air Force plane not because she asked for it but because of the standing instructions which were already there for the tours of the Prime Minister. Way back in 1951–52, a high-powered committee recommended this facility for specified VIPs after studying the question carefully. The other side argues that since these instructions were reviewed in 1968 by a committee headed by Mrs Gandhi, therefore, it amounted to her obtaining or procuring the Air Force plane. This argument is fallacious because the 1968 instructions were merely a re-editing of the earlier instructions. Moreover, this was a decision of the government and not of Mrs Gandhi alone. She was a party to that decision not as a candidate but as the Prime Minister of the country. That decision was taken to ensure the safety of the Prime Minister which is the primary duty of each state.'

Counsel argued that the facility of Air Force planes was necessary even for election tours because the Prime Minister continued to function even during the elections. 'The other side has argued that if the rival candidates could not use Air Force planes, then why should the Prime Minister be allowed to use them? Consider, my Lord, what would happen if the Prime Minister was going to her constituency in a bullock cart, and suddenly a neighbouring country declared war on our country? How would anybody contact the Prime Minister in such a situation? It is for these peculiar situations that the Prime Minister is provided this facility. The advantage which accrues to the Prime Minister because of this facility is a compromise in accordance with international practice.'

Counsel pleaded that the court should give a realistic rather than a literal interpretation of the election law. He said that it was difficult to understand the petitioner's grouse in this regard when chartered planes were available on hire to anyone. He gave the examples of Biju Patnaik, the Rajmata of Gwalior and Maharani Gayatri Devi of Jaipur, all of whom used their own planes for electioneering.

Counsel further argued that if any assistance rendered by any government servant to a candidate was a corrupt practice, then if a person travelled in a railway train during the elections, he would also stand disqualified. 'He is procuring the services of the railway driver, the station master, the signal inspector, etc., all of whom are government servants specified within Section 123(7). But this is not a corrupt practice because these are commercial services provided to every person. Similarly, the facility of Air Force planes is also a commercial service created for the Prime Minister. She paid for her flight in the Air Force plane.'

Justice Sinha: Would paying for the services of government servants make any difference? What is prohibited in the R.P. Act is the obtaining and procuring of any assistance.

Counsel: My Lord, this is like a commercial service for the Prime Minister. The special privilege is given to her for security reasons.

Counsel then contended that the Prime Minister's trip from Delhi to Lucknow did not in any way further the prospects of her election. He quoted from the observations made by the judges of the Allahabad High Court where it was held that if a candidate's car broke down on his way to the railway station and he took a lift in the car of a government servant, it would not amount to a corrupt practice.

Relying strongly on this case, Counsel said that the position here was exactly similar. 'The Air Force officers had done nothing more than to carry the Prime Minister from Delhi to Lucknow which was not even in her constituency but only near it.'

He further contended that the dominant purpose of Mrs Gandhi's trip to Lucknow was to address election meetings on her way to Rae Bareli. All these meetings were addressed outside her constituency. 'Moreover, when she landed at Lucknow on 1 February, she was not even a candidate, because her nomination papers were filed subsequently. So how can it be said that the assistance was obtained by her as a candidate.'

THE ISSUE OF ROSTRUMS

Khare next took up the issue of rostrums and loudspeakers. He placed before the court the original Blue Book instructions issued by the Comptroller and Auditor General to various state governments in 1958. The Blue Book gave instructions to the state governments regarding security precautions for the Prime Minister's public meetings. The rationale for the security arrangements is also given. It says:

> It is the desire of all these persons who collect, to have an uninterrupted glimpse of the Prime Minister and to hear him, and it is for the State authorities to see that this desire is fulfilled. Unless order is maintained at the meeting place, there will be terrific uproar and people who have walked 20 to 30 miles will return disappointed and criminals will have a field day. For this purpose, therefore the place of meeting is broken up into two segments by setting up barricades, and proper loudspeaker arrangements are made so that every one can hear the Prime Minister's speech. The Prime Minister has to stand on a prominent and raised platform so that he can be seen by the congregation from every angle, and proper police arrangements are to be made at all approaches to the place of meeting.

Counsel also read out the amendment which was made to these instructions in 1969 to which Mrs Gandhi was a party. This amendment, he said, was merely a re-edition of the earlier instructions. The amendment says:

> It has been noticed that the rostrum arrangements were not always properly made because the hosts are sometimes unable to bear the cost. As the security of the Prime Minister is a concern of the State, all arrangements for putting up rostrums, barricades, etc., at the meeting place including that of an election meeting will have to be made by the State Government concerned.

Counsel submitted that it was quite clear from the initial instructions that all these arrangements were security arrangements for the Prime Minister. He argued that since the amendment merely re-edited these instructions, it would be wrong to say that they were issued at the instance of Mrs Gandhi. The original instructions, he said, were issued by the Comptroller and Auditor General, who was an independent constitutional authority just like a High Court judge.

Counsel then referred to the letter written by T.N. Singh, then chief minister of UP, to the central government which said that the costs on the Prime Minister's visits were an extremely heavy financial burden on the state. Khare said that T.N. Singh only wanted a reallocation of the expenditure. He did not dispute the propriety, necessity or advisability of the security arrangements for the Prime Minister.

Arrangements for Opposition Leaders Too

Counsel also claimed that similar arrangements were also made for all Opposition leaders. He said that only three things were done for the Prime Minister: (1) provision of police officers for law and order, (2) provision of barricades for crowd control, and (3) provision of rostrums for security purposes. What was done for Raj Narain in his meeting? 'Everything except for the damn rostrum.' Counsel showed a number of documents to prove that Raj Narain directly solicited the help of police and other officers of the government. 'Two full truckloads of policemen were provided for Mr Narain. Some distinction in the quantum of arrangements made for the Prime Minister and Mr Narain is only natural because it is assumed that the Prime Minister will draw larger crowds. If the government felt that

there was need for security of Mr Narain too, they would have also
insisted on the construction of rostrums in his meetings.'

Counsel submitted that the allegation of corrupt practice here was
malicious, politically motivated and irresponsible. 'How could Mr Narain
say that what was legal, justified, and democratic for him was illegal,
unjustified and undemocratic when it was done for the Prime Minister?'

Counsel next contended that this assistance was not for the
furtherance of the prospects of her election. 'The first important
component of an election meeting is the audience. The government
officials did not collect the audience for her speeches. The second
important component is the speaker who gives the speech, which
was given by the Prime Minister herself. The third component is the
decorations which were done by the party. The party even paid one-
fourth of the cost of the rostrums. They did not pay the full cost
because the rostrums have to be of specified dimensions for security
considerations.'

Counsel urged that the court should give a realistic interpretation
of the statute rather than a literal one. He said that the Prime Minister
had to submit to these arrangements made by the state governments.
'It is incumbent on the Prime Minister to obey all the security
arrangements made for her. These security arrangements are made
wherever the Prime Minister goes. Security arrangements were made
when she came to give evidence in this court. There were special
arrangements for her inside the court. She was provided with a chair
on a raised platform unlike any other witness. Did it further the
function of giving evidence in this case?'

Justice Sinha: It did. I could hear her better.

R.C. Srivastava (interjecting): We could see her better.

Counsel ended his submissions on this issue with a plea that this
frivolous and malicious charge of corrupt practice be thrown out by
the court.

THE ISSUE OF YASHPAL KAPOOR

Khare then dealt with the issue about the date of resignation of Yashpal
Kapoor. Referring to the nature of office held by Kapoor, he claimed
that the post of officer on special duty was a purely temporary post,
and that no rules governing his service conditions existed. He said that
three points arose about the date of resignation: (1) Can a resignation

be accepted orally? (2) Who was the competent authority to accept the resignation?, and (3) Did Kapoor cease to be a government servant by not working in his office from the afternoon of 14 January.

He contended that in the absence of statutory provision for the resignation of a government servant, the resignation could be accepted orally by the competent authority. He cited a number of cases to establish this proposition. He also read out a passage from an American journal *Corpus Juris Secondum* which says:

> In order to be effective, the resignation must be made with the intention to relinquish office accompanied by the act of relinquishment. In the absence of a constitutional or statutory provision, no particular formalities are required.

Turning to the facts of this case, Counsel submitted that Kapoor tendered his resignation to Haksar on 13 January which was accepted orally by Haksar on the same date. This, he said, was conclusively established by the oral depositions of Haksar, Kapoor and Mrs Gandhi. There was no reason, Counsel said, to doubt the testimony of Haksar on this point, as he was an honourable man who had held important positions and was then the Deputy Chairman of the Planning Commission. 'In fact,' Khare said, 'when Mr Kapoor approached the Prime Minister and told her of his intention to resign, the Prime Minister's consent implied that she herself had accepted the resignation.'

Justice Sinha: She did not accept the resignation but only consented to it.

Counsel: By implication it follows that she accepted it.

Justice Sinha: How can it follow by implication? She only permitted him to see Mr Haksar in this connection. How does she know whether he actually went to Mr Haksar or not? Whether he actually tendered his resignation or not?

Counsel: In the first place, she herself asked him to see Mr Haksar and secondly, the following day, Mr Haksar told her that he had accepted the resignation.

Justice Sinha: That is exactly the point here. Mrs Gandhi had no personal knowledge about the acceptance of the resignation. She was only briefed by Mr Haksar on this point. Do you mean to say that if Mr Kapoor goes to her and expresses his desire to be relieved, it follows that the resignation stands accepted?

Counsel: Yes.

Justice Sinha: But at that moment the resignation does not even exist. Where is the question of it being accepted, even orally?

Counsel said that the fact that Kapoor had worked for Mrs Gandhi in the 1967 election after resigning from his post would show that he knew that he had to resign before doing any election work for Mrs Gandhi. 'There was no reason why he should not have tendered the resignation before starting work for Mrs Gandhi. There is evidence to show that Mr Kapoor did not work in his office after 14 January, as he had only drawn salary up to 13 January. In these circumstances, I submit that the court must accept that the resignation was tendered on 13 January.'

On the question of whether Haksar was competent to accept the resignation, Counsel cited the Transaction of Business Rules, 1961. Rule 11 of this reads as follows:

> *Responsibility of Department's Secretaries*: In the Department, the Secretary shall be the administrative head thereof and shall be responsible for the proper transaction of business and the careful observations of these rules in that Department.

This, he said, left no doubt that Haksar as the Principal Secretary was competent to carry on the entire business of the department which included accepting resignations.

'Moreover, even the notification in the Gazette shows that the President accepted the resignation with effect from 14 January. All these facts cumulatively leave no doubt that Mr Kapoor ceased to be a government servant on 14 January.'

Work Done by Yashpal Kapoor

Taking up the issue of Yashpal Kapoor's work for Mrs Gandhi, Counsel said that he would divide it into two parts: (1) work done before 14 January, and (2) work done between 14 January and 25 January.

Dealing with the work done before 14 January, Counsel stated that the only evidence to substantiate the petitioner's claim that Kapoor spoke about Mrs Gandhi's election in Munshiganj on 7 January was the oral evidence of a few witnesses of the petitioner. Seeking to destroy the credibility of the witnesses, Counsel said that all the witnesses had stated that Gulzari Lal Nanda, in his speech at Munshiganj, had spoken only about Mrs Gandhi's candidature and had not said a word about the martyrs in whose memory the function was organized. 'I do not feel shy to admit that even in a function in the memory of martyrs, Mr Nanda might have spoken about politics, but is it not possible that he did not speak a word about the martyrs, in whose memory the function was organized.' Dealing at length with the oral evidence of the petitioner's witnesses, Counsel claimed that all these witnesses were partisan and could not be relied upon by the court.

Coming to the oral evidence of Kapoor at this point, Counsel said that there was no reason to disbelieve his testimony. Kapoor had deposed that he had merely paid tributes to martyrs in his speech and not said a word about Mrs Gandhi's candidature. Counsel argued, 'On 7 January, the Congress party had not even taken a preliminary decision about the constituencies of candidates. How could Mr Kapoor say that Mrs Gandhi was contesting the election from Rae Bareli at that time? Why should Mr Kapoor have spoken at that meeting? Nobody has said that Mr Kapoor is a great speaker or a great leader. There are some leaders who are great and some who are merely attendants of great leaders.'

Counsel then referred to the other evidence which existed to show that Kapoor had started working in the election even before 14 January. This was the return of election expenses in which it was stated that the purchase of a voters' list had been authorized by Kapoor on 11 January. Kapoor had explained that the list was purchased by the DCC of Rae Bareli for the candidate who was ultimately chosen to contest from Rae Bareli. Since this list was later handed over to Kapoor, he had decided to include the expenditure on this in the return of expenses. Khare said that there was no reason to disbelieve Kapoor on this point as he could not have been in Rae Bareli on 11 January.

Coming to the question of whether Kapoor had done any work between 14 and 25 January, Counsel referred to the newspaper report which said that Kapoor had arrived in Rae Bareli on 14 January with a convoy of seventy jeeps to launch the election campaign of Mrs Gandhi. He contended that since the correspondent of the newspaper who had filed this report was not produced before the court, the value of the report became nil, and the other side could not rely on it.

Another piece of evidence relied on by Bhushan was the fact that Kapoor's driver was paid from 15 January. Kapoor had explained that the driver was engaged by the DCC from 15 January. So when he was provided with the driver and the jeep on 1 February, he had decided to pay him for the period between 15 January and 1 February. Khare claimed that this explanation of Kapoor was extremely logical and reasonable and there was no reason why it should not be accepted by the court.

The next piece of evidence submitted by the petitioner on this issue was the oral deposition of a number of witnesses that Kapoor had delivered election speeches for Mrs Gandhi in the election meetings organized for Chandrashekhar and Prof. Sher Singh on 17, 18 and 19 January. Khare argued that the allegation of Kapoor's participation in Prof. Sher Singh's meeting on 19 January was made by only one witness, who was a worker of the Opposition party.

Counsel then referred to the deposition of another witness of the petitioner who had stated that he attended a meeting of Prof. Sher Singh on 19 January at which Kapoor also spoke. The witness had produced a printed invitation card which was allegedly distributed for that meeting. Counsel found it strange that the witness had preserved this unimportant card for more than three years. He asserted that no such meeting was held, because Prof. Sher Singh, being a minister, would not go to an unscheduled meeting. He urged that the court disbelieve this witness as he too was an Opposition party worker and had worked as a polling and counting agent for the petitioner.

Counsel further contended that even if Kapoor did deliver speeches as contended by the petitioner, he would still have to prove that they were for Mrs Gandhi's benefit. 'The witnesses only say that Mr Kapoor raised the slogan of "Indira Jitao". Just as the slogan "Indira Hatao" did not mean the removal of Mrs Gandhi from her office but the removal of her government, similarly, the slogan "Indira Jitao" merely meant victory for the Congress. This slogan indicates that Mr Kapoor was engaged in general party propaganda and not in furthering the prospects of Mrs Gandhi.'

Not with Mrs Gandhi's Consent

Counsel then dealt with the second part of the issue: 'whether the services of Mr Kapoor were "obtained" or "procured" by Mrs Gandhi'.

He argued that even if Kapoor worked for Mrs Gandhi's election, it was not with her consent. 'Mrs Gandhi had decided to contest from Rae Bareli only on 1 February as I will presently establish. Therefore, the question of her asking Mr Kapoor to do election work for her before that date does not even arise. They want, your Lordship, to infer Mrs Gandhi's consent only through circumstantial evidence. The circumstantial evidence is that Mr Kapoor resigned from her Secretariat on the eve of the 1967 election, and worked in Mrs Gandhi's constituency. He rejoined the Secretariat soon after the elections, and again resigned before the 1971 elections. Does this lead to the inescapable conclusion that Mrs Gandhi must have consented to Mr Kapoor working for her before 1 February?

'Even if Mrs Gandhi reposed the greatest confidence in Mr Kapoor, it was not at all necessary for her to confide in him her decision to contest from Rae Bareli. Confidence is in relation to the work assigned to a person. Your Lordship may have a lot of confidence in your Reader,[1] but that does not mean that he can dictate your judgments. Mrs Gandhi had at least ten Secretaries who were close to her. That, however, did not make any of them her confidante.'

Counsel submitted that even if Kapoor worked for Mrs Gandhi before 1 February, he must have done so on his own. 'He has admitted before your Lordship that he was an ambitious man and was looking for a public office. Is it unnatural for him to go out of his way to help Mrs Gandhi on his own so that he may be suitably rewarded later?'

THE ISSUE OF HOLDING OUT

Khare next took up the issue of Mrs Gandhi's holding out as a candidate. As a preliminary point, he drew the attention of the judge to the fact that this issue was not there in the original petition. It was only included later by the Supreme Court. 'Though I dare not question the wisdom of the Supreme Court, your Lordship may bear in mind that it is an afterthought.'

Khare said that neither of the petitioner's claims of evidence—the press conference and the CPB decision—amounted to holding out.

---

[1] A Reader is a court assistant.

'The Opposition parties' sponsoring a joint candidate to oppose her is not holding out. They can shout at the top of their voice, but unless Mrs Gandhi herself declared categorically that she would be contesting from Rae Bareli, she had not held herself out as a candidate.' Citing a number of cases to support his contention, Counsel submitted that a case of holding out could only be made out if the candidate made a categorical and unambiguous declaration that he would contest the election from a particular constituency.

He further contended that a person could only hold himself out as a candidate after the election was in prospect. 'The election became in prospect only after the presidential notification calling for the elections was issued on 27 January 1971. The other side contends that the election came into prospect on 27 December 1970 as soon as the Lok Sabha was dissolved. If the mere fact that the election would be held presently is enough to make the election "in prospect", then the next election is "in prospect" as soon as one election is over, because people know that another election would take place five years later. If this is correct, then a person holds himself out as a prospective candidate when he goes to his constituency to nurse it.'

Counsel said that even if the election came into prospect with the dissolution of the Lok Sabha, he would establish that Mrs Gandhi did not hold herself out before 1 February. Khare referred to Mrs Gandhi's statement in her press conference on 29 December 1970. The petitioner had produced a number of Opposition leaders who had deposed that they understood her statement to mean that she would contest the election from Rae Bareli. Khare charged that all these political witnesses were summoned merely for political propaganda and their testimony had no relevance to the case. 'What they interpreted her statement to mean does not throw any light on what she really meant, which is what is really relevant in the case of holding out. Mr Nijilingappa had come from Mysore but the newspaper copy which he brought with him belonged to the Moti Mahal Library, Lucknow. So, he did not even have the newspaper with him in Mysore. He is a frustrated man having political animosity against Mr Gandhi.'

Justice Sinha: Has he not tried to show how he understood the news item about Mrs Gandhi's press conference?

Khare: What he understood from the newspaper is not relevant for Mrs Gandhi's holding out. In any case, Mr Nijilingappa is not an expert on the English language. Mrs Gandhi has clarified that she meant that she was not changing her constituency to Gurgaon, and her statement must be accepted.

The next piece of evidence relied upon by the petitioner was Mrs Gandhi's speech in Coimbatore on 19 January, in which she denounced the Opposition parties' decision to jointly sponsor Raj Narain from Rae Bareli. Counsel explained that this speech of Mrs Gandhi did not mean that she would be contesting the election from Rae Bareli. She was merely attacking the Opposition for the reasons for which they had chosen Raj Narain to oppose her.

LT. GOVERNOR ACTED ON HIS OWN

Khare then launched a strong rebuttal of Bhushan's argument that Mrs Gandhi had asked the Lt. Governor to help the Congress candidate in winning the by-election. Khare argued that there was no evidence to prove it. 'Mrs Gandhi was not only the Congress president at that time but also the daughter of the Prime Minister. Therefore, the Lt. Governor must have been naturally anxious to please her. So he must have helped the Congress candidate on his own to oblige Mrs Gandhi.'

YASHPAL KAPOOR'S INTEGRITY

Khare also defended Kapoor's integrity. Bhushan had referred to the purchase of a house by Kapoor's wife as a shady transaction and had alleged that Kapoor had lied to the court on several occasions. Khare said that he was proud of a man like Kapoor who had started on a monthly salary of Rs 99 and had reached such a height that he could afford a house of Rs 4 lakh. 'If there was anything wrong with the transaction, the income-tax authorities would have examined it.'

TOUR PROGRAMME WAS TENTATIVE

Another piece of evidence relied upon by Bhushan was Mrs Gandhi's tour programme for Rae Bareli issued on 25 January, which included the words 'file nomination paper'. Counsel argued that this tour programme was a secret communication between the Prime Minister's Secretariat and the UP government and could not be exploited for a case of holding out. 'A person can only hold out by a public announcement. Suppose a man tells his wife or writes a secret letter to his friend saying that he proposes to file his nomination papers from a particular constituency on a given date, does it amount to holding out? It only means that at a later stage he might become a candidate. Mrs Gandhi's tour programme meant that she was going to Rae Bareli to consult her constituency before taking a final decision. The words "file nomination paper" mentioned in it were only tentative.'

Justice Sinha: One way of looking at it is that the Prime Minister secretly decided about contesting from Rae Bareli. This decision was secretly communicated by her Personal Secretary to the UP government, who in turn secretly communicated it to the District Magistrate, the whole chain being engulfed in secrecy. There was no question of holding out. Looking at it from another angle, a rather natural inference can be drawn that the constituency had been previously consulted and a final decision to contest from Rae Bareli was being made known by the tour programme.

Counsel: This is not the natural inference because she had not yet made up her mind to contest from Rae Bareli and there were several offers to her to contest from various parts of the country.

Justice Sinha: What was the last date of nomination?

Counsel: 3 February.

Justice Sinha: For which period was the Prime Minister's tour programme issued?

Counsel: 1 February to 7 February.

Justice Sinha: Assuming that the mention of filing of nomination papers in the tour programme was only tentative, did the tour programme mention any other similar tentative place from where she could file her nomination papers? If she was thinking of contesting from some other place, a separate tentative tour programme should have been issued, or a mention made in the above programme.

Counsel: This programme related to only eastern India and there was no suggestion of her contesting from any other place here. The alternative places were Rajasthan, etc.

Justice Sinha: Was there any other tour programme for those places?

Counsel: No.

Justice Sinha: That means she must have made up her mind about contesting from Rae Bareli.

Counsel: Gradually the alternatives were being eliminated. She had practically made up her mind but the decision was not final.

Justice Sinha: You mean to say that if even after reaching Rae Bareli on 1 February, she decided to contest from some other place, she could have reached this new place in time without a previously chalked out programme.

Counsel: Yes. A new programme can be chalked out in a few minutes, and the Prime Minister can be flown in a few hours.

Justice Sinha: In that case, even after a categorical statement, you can still say that there was some reservation.

Counsel: No. A final categorical announcement would amount to holding out.

ADDITIONAL WRITTEN STATEMENT DRAFTED BY GOKHALE AND RAY

Khare then came to the most controversial part of this issue, the Prime Minister's additional written statement in which she had stated that a final decision about her constituency was announced by the AICC on 29 January 1971. Bhushan had charged that this gave a lie to Mrs Gandhi's statement that she took a final decision only on 1 February.

Khare, however, argued that there was no incongruity between the additional written statement and Mrs Gandhi's oral deposition. 'The additional written statement merely says that a final decision in regard to her constituency was announced by the AICC on 29 January. This only means that on 29 January, the AICC finally decided to leave the decision about her constituency to the Prime Minister herself.'

Justice Sinha: That means the AICC did not take any decision?

Counsel: No, the AICC decided to leave the decision to Mrs Gandhi.

Justice Sinha: Normally, if the Board says that it has finally decided about the constituency, what does it mean?

Counsel: The Board decides either normally or abnormally about the candidate.

Justice Sinha: Let us first confine ourselves to normally, which means that on 29 January the Board finally announced its decision as to who would be the candidate from Rae Bareli.

Counsel: Your Lordship should not try to read what is not written.

Justice Sinha (angrily): I have to decide the petition. I will read it in the normal manner.

Counsel: The verdict given in favour of the returned candidate by a majority of over one lakh votes cannot be set aside merely on the ground that there are some minor contradictions in the statement.

Justice Sinha: Admitted that there was some slip in the additional written statement, but when the respondent came to the court accompanied by a galaxy of lawyers, she could have made the position clear.

Counsel: I was ill when the additional written statement was drafted and it was drafted by Mr Gokhale (the law minister) and Mr S.S. Ray (chief minister of West Bengal). It is not surprising that a person as busy as the Prime Minister will not be able to exactly remember her written statement filed four years ago. She may not be able to tally her oral evidence with her written statement word by word. But the fact need not be stretched beyond all proportions.

Counsel contended that while evaluating the oral evidence of Mrs Gandhi, the court must remember that the person holding the office of the Prime Minister of this country was unlikely to say anything false.

Justice Sinha: Her evidence will be treated like the evidence of any other person.

Khare argued that the integrity of a person flows from his or her status. He quoted some observations from the judgment of the Supreme Court in V.V. Giri's election case;[2] the court had said that while evaluating the evidence, the integrity, ability and the status of the witness must be kept in view. Khare contended that when the Prime Minister chose the chief ministers of various states and candidates from various constituencies, she must surely have had the choice of her own constituency.

THE ISSUE OF EXPENSES

Turning to the issue of election expenses, Khare contended that since the expenses alleged in the petition were not specific, but merely general allegations on wild conjectures, the court could not estimate or add any expenses to the return filed by the respondent. He cited a number of cases to support his contention. Counsel said that the

---

[2] AIR 1970, SC 2097, *Shri Kirpal Singh and others v. V.V. Giri.*

petitioner had only made wild claims that Rs 2 lakh was spent on barricading, Rs 1.8 lakh on some twenty-three vehicles, etc., but had produced no evidence to prove these expenses.

'Even if we condone the lacuna of non-specific pleadings, it will still be found that most of the expenses alleged were incurred by the state government. Even Chawla's case does not lay down that expenditure incurred by a government for a candidate could be included in the candidate's election expenses. Chawla's case only lays down that expenditure incurred by the party or friends and supporters of the candidate has to be included if authorized by the candidate. A government is neither a party nor a friend and supporter of the candidate. And in this case, the UP government which incurred this expenditure was headed by the Opposition parties, and was thus an enemy of Mrs Gandhi. How could expenditure incurred by an enemy be included in the candidate's election expenses?

'The other expenditure alleged in the petition was incurred by the Congress party. Even Chawla's case does not specify any limit on the money spent by a party for general party propaganda. No evidence has been led to show that the expenditure of the party was for Mrs Gandhi and not on general party propaganda. With such serious defects in the petition, the charge cannot be upheld even if the amendment was neglected.'

Counsel's next submission was that even if expenditure incurred by the government could be included, the expenditure here was for Mrs Gandhi's security. 'This was like expenditure incurred by a candidate on bodyguards. The expenditure on bodyguards who do no election work for a candidate cannot be treated as an election expense. The state government, when it arranged for barricades and rostrums, did not participate directly or indirectly in the electioneering of Mrs Gandhi. It had merely acted as a bodyguard. However, even if expenditure on the rostrums is to be treated as Mrs Gandhi's election expense, it would only be one-fourth of the total expenditure. This is because the Blue Book provides that the rostrums have to be of certain specifications due to security considerations. In fact, the security requirements made it mandatory for Mrs Gandhi to address the meetings from those rostrums. She could not ask her political party to provide them. Left to themselves, the political party could have made a suitable dais with hardly any expense.'

'Propriety of Kapoor's Action Not the Issue'

Coming to the most crucial part of this issue, i.e., expenditure which was allegedly incurred on twenty-three vehicles used by the DCC, Counsel pointed out that the petitioner had agreed that the vehicles were used by the DCC in three constituencies. The petitioner had contended that since these vehicles were released from the District Magistrate by Kapoor, they must be deemed to have been used in Mrs Gandhi's election. Counsel placed before the court a letter written by Dal Bahadur Singh, president, DCC, to Yashpal Kapoor. Singh, in his letter, had asked Kapoor to get the vehicles released since he was unable to locate the candidates of the other two constituencies. This was because during election time, requisitioned vehicles could only be released by a candidate or his election agent by stating that they were being used in his election. 'At present, the question before the court is not the propriety of Mr Kapoor in getting the vehicles released for other candidates, while under the law he was only permitted to get them released for himself. The real question is whether they were actually used in Mrs Gandhi's constituency. In fact, there is no evidence even to show that these vehicles were hired or even used at all by the DCC. They might have been supplied without payment by friends and sympathizers of the Congress. Moreover, there is no evidence to show the amount of expenditure incurred on them. In such circumstances, I submit that the court cannot estimate and add any expenditure on these vehicles to Mrs Gandhi's election expenses.'

Regarding Bhushan's argument that an adverse inference should be drawn against the respondent for the non-production of two relevant witnesses, Dal Bahadur Singh and Daya Prasad Shukla, Khare argued that if they were all that relevant, the petitioner should have summoned them himself. 'Initially, Mr Shukla was cited as a petitioner's witness but later given up. How can an adverse inference be drawn in these circumstances?'

THE RELIGIOUS SYMBOL ISSUE

Khare lastly took up the symbol issue. He argued that the petitioner had missed one vital point on this corrupt practice. 'He has argued on the assumption that the use of a religious symbol alone was enough to set aside the election. But your Lordship will see that the petitioner must also show that the use of that symbol had materially affected the results of the elections.' Counsel was relying on Section 100(c)(2) of the R.P. Act which provides that the election of a returned candidate could be set aside if the High Court was of the opinion that the result of the election had been materially affected by a corrupt practice committed in the interest of the candidate (by an agent other than his election agent). Counsel submitted that the entire arguments of the petitioner were of no avail because of this defect in his pleadings.

He further argued that the symbol had been allotted to the Congress party by the Election Commission, and Mrs Gandhi, being a Congress candidate, had no choice but to use it. 'The decision of the Election Commission allotting the symbol cannot be challenged in an election petition. The only way it could have been challenged was by a direct suit filed at the time the symbol was allotted. He cited Rule 10(5) of the Conduct of Election Rules, 1961. It reads: 'The allotment by the Returning Officer of any symbol to a candidate shall be final except where it is inconsistent with any directions issued by the Election Commission in this behalf.'

Counsel argued that this rule made it clear that the allotment was final except when it was inconsistent with the directions of the Commission. 'The question then arises: "final against whom?" I submit that it is final against everybody. Finality to something is granted in law to avoid litigation. It is the duty of the court to provide a harmonious construction of the law; the construction which would preserve order instead of creating chaos. If this symbol is held to be a religious symbol now, the election of all Congress candidates who had contested the 1971 election would be set aside, causing total chaos.'

Counsel then quoted from the report of the Election Commission on the General Elections of 1971 (Lok Sabha) and 1972 (state assemblies). The Chief Election Commissioner in his report said, 'The cow may be a religious object held in reverence by the Hindus, but it is difficult to accept the view that a cow represents Hindu religion. Hinduism saw God in everything and in that view whatever was used could be regarded as a religious symbol.' Counsel argued that the fact that the Election Commission had refused this symbol to the Ram Rajya Parishad in 1951 did not make it a religious symbol. The Commission at that time had mentioned the cow as one of the objects having religious or sentimental appeal. Counsel argued that all that was sanctified or sacred was not religious.

Counsel went on to quote from a mass of religious texts which he had brought with him. He cited the *Encyclopaedia of Religion and Ethics* by Hastings which lists the religious symbols of Hindus. The cow is not mentioned in it. Counsel also dug out, from a Vedic scripture, the prescription of the sacrifice of a cow as penance for the sin of killing a Brahmin.

Justice Sinha (amidst laughter): Is it also vice-versa?

Dealing with the oral testimony of the pandits summoned by both sides, Counsel charged that the petitioner's pandit, Raghbar Lal Shastri, had not been fair in maintaining that the cow was regarded as a God. Shri Shastri in his depositions had said that according to Hindu shastras (scriptures), namaskar was offered to a cow because it was a God. Counsel drew the attention of the court to a mantra (hymn) of the Vedas to show that the namaskar mentioned in it was not only offered to cows but to human beings and also other animals. Counsel, therefore, contended that it was wrong to interpret the word namaskar to mean worship,

Referring to Shri Shastri's depositions that the cow had been called the mother of Rudra (a God), Counsel said that it was just an allegory. 'Moreover, motherhood does not bestow godliness. Kaushalya was the mother of Rama who was regarded as God, but thereupon Kaushalya did not become a Goddess.' He also referred to the deposition of the respondent's pandit, Pattabhiram Shastri, who had deposed that the cow, although revered by the Hindus, was not regarded as a god.

After summing up his arguments, Khare ended thus: 'In the end, I appeal to your Lordship not for any favour, but for justice according to law for my client. I also appeal to your Lordship to decide the case like a statesman.'

He ended his arguments on 20 May, after arguing continuously for about thirty-four hours over a period of nine days.

7

The Petitioner's Rejoinder

Opening his arguments in his rejoinder, Bhushan first referred generally to the arguments advanced by Khare and the Attorney-General. 'During the last thirteen days, your Lordship has heard at length the Attorney-General and my learned friend, Mr Khare. I must confess that while both of them have drawn heavily for their submissions on their personal experience of fighting elections, I am under a handicap in this respect. I have not fought any election.

'Mr Khare from his experience was able to enlighten your Lordship about heavy expenses on facelifts and make-up amounting to Rs 20,000. He also told your Lordship about the expenses on Scotch whisky, presumably for keeping up the morale of the candidate, and then he mentioned the huge expenditure on several suits so that the candidate could wear a new one at each election meeting.

'The Attorney-General, on the other hand, told your Lordship about his unhappy experience in the general elections of 1951 which he contested as an independent candidate, and in which, despite the use of his money-power which he said was not too little, he lost on account of the attractive posters of Jawaharlal Nehru pasted throughout his constituency. The Attorney-General concluded from his personal experience that money could not play any significant part in the elections. I was, however, wondering as to whether my learned friend would really have used his enormous money-power during the elections. The ceiling on election expenses in 1951 was fairly low, and I am sure that he must have taken good care to keep himself within the prescribed ceiling. In that event, the Congress candidate opposing him could not have suffered any handicap of money-power and with the other advantages available to him as a party candidate, particularly the high image of the Congress in 1951, it is not surprising that the Attorney-General lost.

'Before going into the various points which have been raised by the other side, I would like to refer to certain submissions of a general nature which have been made by them and which appear very startling to me.

'The Attorney-General so strongly commented on the judgment of Justice Bhagwati in Chawla's case that the Delhi newspapers almost gave a full-page headline, "Attorney-General questions the wisdom of the Supreme Court". I would, on my part, like to cite the judgment of Justice Bhagwati as a very learned judgment by a great judge. It was indeed my misfortune that I was not able to appreciate the significance of the Attorney-General's criticism of the Supreme Court judgment which is binding under Article 141 on this court.

'What was more astounding was the manner in which the *de jure* leader of the Indian Bar referred to the judgment of the Supreme Court in Kesavananda Bharati's case. He frankly conceded that the majority in that case had laid down an important principle about inviolability of the basic features of the Constitution, but proceeded to tell your Lordship that he was not attaching any importance to that judgment. He did not tell us why. But if his reasons could be surmised, it appears that he treated this decision in a cavalier manner, because three of the judges who were parties to the majority decision have been superseded by the government in the matter of appointment to the office of the Chief Justice. If I may say so, with respect to my learned friend, his attitude towards this historic judgment of the Supreme Court was unworthy of the high office which he holds.

'So long as the decision of the majority continues to be binding under Article 141, what can possibly be the relevance of the Attorney-General's ceasing to attach importance to that decision. One has heard of judgments being marked AFR, meaning "approved for reporting". Was the Attorney-General trying to evolve a new concept of the Supreme Court judgments being marked "DAG", that is to say, "disapproved by the Attorney-General", in which event the judgment would cease to be binding on the High Court. Fortunately, no such proviso has yet been added to Article 141.

'My learned friend Mr Khare propounded the doctrine that the credibility of the witness is directly related to his status. If that be so, perhaps the evidence of witnesses should be assessed with the aid of the order of official precedence. I submit that the high office which the witness might be holding is quite irrelevant to the assessment of evidence, particularly in a case in which he is a party and has personal stakes. The evidence has to be assessed in the same way as any other witness. On the other hand, it is a matter of common experience that the people of so-called status would sooner resort to false statements as they have much more to lose than a poor man.

'Mr Khare at some stage asked your Lordship to decide the case as a "statesman" although not as a politician. On my part it would be presumptuous to tell your Lordship how to decide the case, because I know that your Lordship will decide it like a judge and only as a judge. Though a rich businessman has the glamour of money and a politician or a statesman has the glamour of office, a judge is the highest of them all. A great judge lives in the hearts and minds of men. He lives in their hearts on account of his moral stature and in their minds on account of his intellectual stature.

'Mr Khare also desired that the consequences of the decision should be taken into consideration as well. May I, in this connection, be permitted to draw attention to the speech of William Wilberforce in the House of Commons in 1789. He said, "Sir, when we think of eternity and of the future consequences of all human conduct, what is there in this life that should make any man contradict the dictates of his conscience, the principles of justice, the laws of religion and of God."

'A country is great when it worships principles and not men. The glory of justice lies in being based upon principles than on any other trivial considerations.'

VALIDITY OF AMENDMENT

Coming to the points raised by the other side in the writ petition, Bhushan said that the whole premise of the respondent's argument was that the amendment only restored the law as it stood declared by the Supreme Court prior to Chawla's case. He contended, 'Even if there was any controversy about the legal position prior to Chawla's case, it was only on the question of whether express authority was necessary or whether implied authority by consent, acquiescence, etc., would have the effect of making a candidate liable for the expenditure. The explanation added by the amendment does not deal with the matter of express or implied authority but says that all expenses incurred by a political party or any other person shall not be deemed to be incurred or authorized by the candidate. If my interpretation is rejected, the explanation even provides that all expenditure incurred by the candidate himself, as long as it was authorized by a third person, would not be treated as a candidate's election expenses. I can say with great confidence that not a single court has ever pronounced this to be the law.'

Counsel cited the last decision of the Supreme Court prior to the 1971 election to rebut the Attorney-General's theory that the candidate in the 1971 election understood the law to be that which is declared by the amendment. In this case, Justice Shah had observed, 'expenditure incurred by a person other than the candidate for election purposes will not be taken into account (unless incurred by such a third person as the candidate's agent) and when any expenditure is incurred by another person with the express or implied consent of the candidate, the person incurring the expenditure becomes an agent of the candidate'. Counsel argued that this case clearly laid down the principles of express or implied authority.

Counsel strongly contested the Attorney-General's contention that money-power did not play any part in the election. He said that this was in direct conflict with the observations of the Supreme Court in Chawla's case. Their Lordships had observed, 'It can hardly be disputed that the way in which the elections are held in our country, money is bound to play an important part in the successful prosecution of an election campaign.'

Counsel then referred to the Attorney-General's contention that the legislature normally had the power to legislate prospectively as well as retrospectively. The Attorney-General had cited a number of cases to support this. Counsel said that the cases cited by the Attorney-General in this connection were useless, as none of them dealt with retrospective legislation which created a situation in which one person was discriminated against. 'This discrimination was bound to occur in retrospective laws about the rules of contest. Consider the case of retrospective legislation by which a requirement to appear in an interview with ties was introduced after the interview had already been held, and entailed the disqualification of the best candidate on this basis. Could this law be said to be non-discriminatory?'

Counsel wondered whether the Parliament, by making retrospective changes in the rules of an election contest, thought that the country was like the world of *Alice in Wonderland* where executions took place first and trials came later. 'If we do not want this country to be the Wonderland of Alice, laws will have to come first and elections later.'

Counsel further said, 'A strange argument has been raised by the Attorney-General, that Mr Narain has neither pleaded nor given evidence to prove that he had not similarly violated the law on election expenses as it originally stood. He has argued that unless it was shown that Mr Narain had not violated the law, there could be no case of discrimination against him. The fallacy in the Attorney-General's arguments is his assumption that the person is required to plead or prove that he has not acted contrary to law. The law always presumes that a man is innocent until proved guilty. Consider the following illustration. If a law was made that only those who had been stealing property or indulging in copying in examinations would be granted licences for establishing industries, would it be necessary for the petitioner who was challenging the law as discriminatory to plead and prove that he had not been stealing property or copying in the examination himself?'

Referring to the other cases of retrospective laws relating to elections cited by Khare, Counsel said that all these related to removal of disqualifications. 'In these cases, the elections of some candidates were held invalid because they held some offices of profit and were thus not qualified to contest the election. The legislature in these cases had retrospectively removed the disqualification of the elected candidates and thus validated their election. The retrospective removal of this disqualification does not discriminate against the opposing candidate. The election was fought under equal laws. Thus, there is no analogy between this and the retrospective change in the laws relating to corrupt practices.'

Coming to the argument that the Amending Act was against the basic features of the Constitution, Counsel said that it was a matter of deep regret that the Attorney-General had said that although the majority in Kesavananda Bharati's case had laid down the principle of inviolability of the basic features of the Constitution, they had not laid down that democracy is a basic feature of the Constitution.

Counsel quoted from the judgments of the seven majority judges in Kesavananda's case to show that all of them had held democracy to be a basic feature of the Constitution. He said, 'It does not even require a reading of the judgment to conclude that democracy is a basic feature. If democracy is not a basic feature, then what is?' Holding a book on the Constitution in his hand, Bhushan said that perhaps the

Attorney-General understood that book only and not the principles enshrined in it, to be the Constitution of India. 'Perhaps he feels that the basic features of our Constitution are the binding and the printing of this book; and not the principles laid down in it.'

THE EXPENSES ISSUE

Submitting his rejoinder on the issue of election expenses, Bhushan referred to Khare's contention that the expenditure on Air Force planes was not an election expenditure as it did not further the election prospects of Mrs Gandhi. Bhushan contended that the Supreme Court had interpreted election expenses to mean any expense having to do with the election and which would not have been incurred in the absence of the election. He cited a Supreme Court case in which the money paid by a candidate to his party as application fee for nomination was treated as an election expense of the candidate, although ultimately the candidate did not get a ticket from that party and he fought as an independent candidate. So the money was actually used by that party against his interest, but was still treated as election expenses.

He also referred to Khare's argument that since the petitioner had not been specific about the expenses incurred, they could not be taken into consideration. Counsel cited a number of Supreme Court cases to show that even if specific expenses were not pleaded, they would still be taken into account if no prejudice was caused to the respondent's case.

He then dealt with Khare's argument regarding the expenditure on the twenty-three vehicles. Khare had argued that the petitioner had not led any evidence to show that these vehicles were used at all. He had argued that they could have been used in other constituencies or only for general party propaganda. Bhushan submitted that the fact that Kapoor obtained the release of those vehicles was evidence enough to hold that they were used for Mrs Gandhi's election. 'A vehicle can only be released by a candidate or his election agent if it is used in his constituency. Once we have shown that the expense on these vehicles has been suppressed by the respondent, the burden shifts on them to show that these vehicles were not used in their constituency. Otherwise, the court must estimate the expenditure which should have been incurred on these vehicles and, at best, apportion it equally among the three constituencies.'

About the expense on rostrums, Khare had contended that since they were for security, no expenditure on them could be treated as an election expense. Bhushan strongly contested this claim. He said, 'The Blue Book says, "It is the desire of all persons who come, to have an uninterrupted glimpse of the Prime Minister and to hear her, and it is duty of the State authority to see that this desire is fulfilled." It is clear from the Blue Book that the rostrums have to be of specific dimensions so that the people can have an uninterrupted glimpse of the Prime Minister. There is no question of security involved here. Moreover, even if security is involved, the fact remains that the expenditure was occasioned by the election, and this, not whether it furthered the prospects of the election, is the material point.'

Counsel further argued, 'A very peculiar argument has been raised by Mr Khare on this issue. He says that Chawla's case lays down that only the expenditure incurred by a political party or friends or supporters of the candidates has to be included. He says that here the rostrums were constructed by the state government and the state government being run by the Opposition party was not a friend or supporter but an enemy of the Prime Minister. Suppose the candidate, with a gun in his hand, tells his enemy to get petrol filled in his car, then can the candidate claim exemption for this expenditure? The case is exactly the same here. The central government at the point of a gun tells the state government to construct the rostrums for the Prime Minister.'

Justice Sinha: Where is the gun?

Counsel: Article 356 of the Constitution is the gun. It is a provision for the failure of constitutional machinery in states. It says, 'If the President on receipt of a report from the Governor of a State or otherwise, is satisfied that a situation has arisen in which the Government of the State cannot be carried on in accordance with the provisions of the Constitution, the President may, by Proclamation, assume to himself all or any of the functions of the Government of the State and all or any of the powers vested in or exercisable by the Governor or any body of authority in the State other than the Legislature of the State.'

Counsel argued that if a state government did not obey the directions of the Blue Book, it could be said that there had been a failure of the constitutional machinery and the state government could be suspended.

Counsel also disputed Khare's contention that the Prime Minister was bound to deliver speeches from the rostrums constructed for her by the state government. 'There are no statutory provisions that the Prime Minister has to submit to her security arrangements. If she had used other rostrums, she would not contravene any law. Who can force any minister, let alone the Prime Minister, to submit to any security arrangements.'

AIR FORCE PLANES

Giving his rejoinder on the issue of the Air Force plane, Bhushan strongly refuted Khare's contention that since the Air Force plane was not used in Rae Bareli, therefore, there could be no corrupt practice on this account. 'The R.P. Act does not say that the corrupt practice has to be committed in the constituency of a candidate. All that it says is that a corrupt practice must be committed by a candidate for the furtherance of his election prospects.

'Another strange argument raised by Mr Khare is that Air Force planes have been used by Prime Ministers right from the beginning. Can a corrupt practice cease to become so merely because it has been committed from time immemorial? An official taking a bribe cannot justify it on the ground that his predecessor also did so. If this corrupt practice has been committed by all our Prime Ministers, it is time that it was stopped and it can only be stopped if it is held to be a corrupt practice.'

Referring to Khare's argument that the facility of Air Force planes was like a commercial service established solely for the Prime Minister, Counsel said that a commercial service should be available to all people. 'One cannot say that it is a commercial service and yet make it available to only one person.'

DO THEY WANT A COMPROMISE

In his rejoinder on the issue of rostrums, Bhushan said, 'It has been contended by the other side that the petitioner is prevented from complaining against the respondent for obtaining assistance from government officers because he also asked for and obtained the same assistance. I wonder whether the other side wants a compromise, that is, if the respondent is disqualified for the corrupt practice, then the petitioner should also suffer the same disqualification.'

Khare was not present in court, so Justice Sinha jokingly asked Khare's junior, Mukerji, whether he was willing to make that compromise.

Mukerji immediately protested: 'Not at all. Khare never made any suggestion of a compromise. He only pointed out the peculiar stand taken by Mr Narain that although he could commit any corrupt practice, Mrs Gandhi could not.'

Referring to Khare's argument that the rostrums were for security purposes and did not in any way further the prospects of Mrs Gandhi's election, Counsel said that another look at the Blue Book would clearly refute this contention. Reading out the relevant passages, he argued that the real purpose of providing a rostrum of specified dimensions was to fulfil the desire of the people to have an uninterrupted glimpse of the Prime Minister and also so that she could be seen from every angle. 'My Lord, look at the specious reasoning given in the Blue Book. It says, "unless order is maintained at the meeting place, there will be a terrific uproar and people who have to come from 20 to 30 miles will return disappointed and criminals will have a field day." I suppose that the criminals forget their business when they hear the sweet voice of the Prime Minister. I submit that the whole purpose of this arrangement was to make these meetings successful. Since the whole purpose of an election meeting is to further the election prospects of the candidate, these arrangements clearly did so.'

Rounding off his submissions on the issue, Bhushan submitted that the decision on this issue would have far-reaching consequences on elections in India. He said that by delivering election speeches from rostrums constructed by the state government, Mrs Gandhi had not only placed her election in jeopardy but also the elections of her party candidates in whose constituencies she had delivered speeches in the Gujarat elections (which were about to be held). This, Counsel explained, was because the candidates in these constituencies must have consented to Mrs Gandhi making use of these arrangements made by officers of the state government. 'Since a candidate's election is liable to be set aside if a corrupt practice is committed with his consent, the election of all Congress candidates whose constituencies Mrs Gandhi visited in the Gujarat elections could be set aside.'

THE ISSUE OF HOLDING OUT

In his rejoinder on the issue of holding out, Bhushan rebutted Khare's contention that the election would be deemed to be in prospect only after the Presidential Notification was issued. 'Your Lordship will notice that the period for nomination starts as soon as a notification has been issued by the President. Since nominations are part of the election, it is clear that the election process begins on the date the Presidential Notification is issued. The election has to be in prospect at least some time before this date.'

Counsel then cited the meaning of the word 'prospect' as given in the *Webster's Dictionary*. It says, 'anticipation, foresight, something that is awaited or expected'. This, he said, made out quite clearly that the election came into prospect when it was in sight. 'When the Houses of Legislatures are dissolved, a fresh House has to be constituted within six months. Thus elections become imminent and are, therefore, in prospect at that time.'

Counsel further submitted that a person held himself out as a candidate when by some act or statement, he led people to believe that he would be contesting the coming election. Khare had contended that only a final decision taken by a candidate and communicated to his constituents would amount to holding out. 'If he is correct, then any person can start a campaign of character assassination of his rival candidates, bribe all the voters in the constituency, use undue influence, etc., till the time he gets himself nominated as a candidate. He cannot be held guilty of a corrupt practice till then. Even after filing his nomination papers, he can still say that his nomination is tentative, and he may possibly withdraw before the last date of withdrawal. Thus the whole concept of a prospective candidate would be abolished.'

Justice Sinha: Suppose a person commits a corrupt practice before he holds himself out as a candidate, can he be held guilty of a corrupt practice?

Counsel: If the corrupt practice is like a bribery, then the act would itself provide definite proof of holding out. If a person is bribing the people in a constituency to vote for him, then he is clearly announcing his intention to contest the election.

Counsel further submitted that in Khader Sharif's case, a person was deemed to hold himself out as a prospective candidate when he applied for a party's ticket. 'The application for a party ticket is certainly not an unconditional declaration by the candidate that he would stand as a candidate.'

At this point, Justice Sinha read out a passage from a 1955 judgment of the Supreme Court. He said that the Supreme Court in that case had ruled that for holding out, a candidate must make an unambiguous declaration of his intention to contest.

Bhushan: When I say that I am likely to contest the election, it is a clear and unambiguous but not a definite or firm declaration.

Coming to the facts of this issue, Counsel argued that Mrs Gandhi's reply to a question in the press conference clearly amounted to a holding out. 'What is really relevant here is what other people, particularly her constituents, understood the statement to mean. From the newspaper reports and the statements of various leaders, it is quite clear that everybody understood her statement to mean that she would contest from Rae Bareli. Whether she had any reservations at that time is not material.'

YASHPAL KAPOOR'S RESIGNATION

On the question of the date of Kapoor's resignation, Bhushan referred to *Corpus Juris Secundum* cited by Khare. In this, it was said that in the absence of a particular mode of resignation provided by any statutory regulation, a resignation could be oral and also implied. Bhushan said that in this case, however, the position was quite different because of Articles 77 and 166 of the Constitution. 'The Constitution itself lays down the specific mode in which the business of the government has to be conducted and, therefore, excludes any other mode. Appointment of government servants and termination of their services are all parts of the executive actions of the government, and have, therefore, to be in writing.'

THE RELIGIOUS SYMBOL ISSUE

Coming to the symbol issue, Bhushan rebutted Khare's argument: that since the petitioner did not object to the symbol at the time when it was allotted, he could not complain now. He said that in Ponnuswamy's case, it has been held by the Supreme Court that once the election process had begun, nobody could go to court to challenge an order of the Election Commission till the election process was over. It could only be challenged by an election petition. 'The symbol of a cow and calf was allotted to the Congress party on 25 January, just two days before the Presidential Notification was issued. In fact as soon as the symbol was allotted, I received a telegram from Mr C.

Rajagopalachari complaining about it, but as the election process had already begun, nothing could be done about it at that time.'

Counsel then turned to Khare's argument that the petitioner had failed to fulfil an important requirement on this issue by not giving evidence to the effect that the election result had been materially affected by the allotment of the symbol. Khare had relied on Section 101(d) of the R.P. Act which reads: 'An election can be declared void if it is found that the result of the election insofar as it concerns the returned candidate has been materially affected by corrupt practices committed in the interest of the returned candidate (by an agent other than the election agent).' Mr Bhushan said that this provision was only to cover instances of corrupt practices committed by agents other than the election agent. 'But if a corrupt practice was committed by the candidate himself, then the election would clearly become void whether or not the result of the election was materially affected. The allegation here is that the symbol has been used by Mrs Gandhi herself.

'Another very peculiar argument raised by Mr Khare was that the symbol in this case has not been used by Mrs Gandhi but by the Election Commission. He said that since there was no evidence to show that Mrs Gandhi ever displayed that symbol, it cannot be said that she had used it. This is totally fallacious. The very fact that the symbol of the "cow and calf" was her election symbol proves that she used it.'

Counsel referred again to the Supreme Court decision which held that a cow in India has been raised to the status of divinity, and to the *Encyclopaedia Britannica* which says that the cow is divine in her own origin. He submitted that these facts alone were enough to establish that the symbol of the respondent was a religious symbol.

Bhushan concluded his rejoinder on 22 May after arguing for three and a half days.

DR DWIVEDI'S ARGUMENTS

The last arguments in the case were advanced by Dr R. S. Dwivedi, who was a Sanskrit scholar assisting Bhushan on the symbol issue.

He quoted extensively from Hindu scriptures to show that the cow had always been regarded as a deity in the Hindu religion. He cited chapter XVIII of the Mahabharata to show that it contained mantras for worship of the cow. As the cow had been treated as an object of worship, it became a deity and a God, he argued.

Justice Sinha: Do we sell our gods?

Counsel: It is prohibited by religion. Religious people do not sell their cows. They may give it to a *gaushala* (cow protection home).

Justice Sinha: Still, people sell cows. Otherwise, how could common people like you and me get cows? Is there any other deity among the Hindus which is treated in the same manner?

Counsel: What about temples?

Justice Sinha: No Hindu has ever desecrated a temple. Let us see the common man's point of view. When we try to find out what a religious symbol is, we must see how a common man thinks. Is this our deity which we sell, starve and treat so shabbily?

Counsel: Still it is respected by everyone.

Justice Sinha: Everything we respect is not treated as a deity.

Counsel then cited a case where an Adivasi candidate had held out the threat of divine displeasure of an Adivasi deity (a cock) if a voter did not vote on the symbol of the cow. This was held to be a corrupt practice.

Justice Sinha: That was a different case. In this case, if the respondent had said that the voters would invite divine displeasure if they did not vote for the cow, then it would have been different. If we accept a cow to be a deity, then every cow is a deity. Every cow is a God and we must touch the feet of every cow and worship it.

Counsel: There are some persons who do that.

Justice Sinha: What is the percentage of such people?

Counsel: It is difficult to specify the exact percentage, but a substantial number of Hindus do so.

Dr Dwivedi said the problem of the cow being a religious symbol could not be analysed logically as religion was not logical. He said that religion begins where logic ends and the scriptures, as they were religious texts, had to be believed even though they were illogical.

Dr Dwivedi ended his arguments on 23 May, which was the last working day in the High Court before it recessed for the summer vacations.

A UNI reporter present there asked the judge when the judgment would be delivered.

Smiling, Justice Sinha said, 'Counsels have quoted many authorities but none on when the judgment will be delivered.' More seriously, however, he said that he would try to deliver the judgment during the vacations in June.

8

The Verdict

With the conclusion of the arguments, the long wait for the judgment began. Both sides were equally hopeful of winning the case. Bhushan believed that he had better than even chances of winning. Khare, on the other hand, ridiculed the idea of the case being decided against his client, the Prime Minister.

Elsewhere, too, there was a lot of speculation on what the judgment would be. A number of bets were made by enthusiasts of the case and it would be fair to assume that on the date of the judgment, a lot of money changed hands. The noticeable fact was the difference in attitude between those who had witnessed the court proceedings and those who had not. Among people who had heard the arguments, odds offered were even. The people who had not heard the arguments, however, were extremely sceptical about the 'boldness' of Justice Sinha. The general opinion outside Allahabad High Court was that the judge would not have enough courage to declare the election void. The fact of the Prime Minister being the respondent over-awed the people, who made their speculations independent of the merits of the case.

Justice Sinha had constantly been taking notes of the arguments. Thus, as soon as the court closed, he was ready to write the judgment. Before beginning to dictate it, he asked his Private Secretary gravely, 'I don't want the judgment to leak out to anyone, not even to your wife. It is a big responsibility. Can you undertake it?' The Secretary had been with the judge for a long time and was a trusted man. He swore not to disclose the judgment even to his own wife.

MANOEUVRINGS BEHIND THE COURT

The judge wanted to write his judgment in peace. But as soon as the court closed, he started receiving daily visits from a Congress MP from Allahabad, which annoyed him immensely. He requested the person not to visit him. When he persisted, the judge had to ask his neighbour, Justice Parekh, to request the MP to stop bothering him. When even this did not succeed, he decided to disappear. He 'disappeared' inside his house, not showing his face even in his own verandah. All visitors calling on him were told that he had gone to Ujjain, where his brother resided. He did not receive any phone calls either. So from 28 May till 7 June, no one was able to meet him, not even his closest friends.

Before he went into seclusion, however, the judge had another distinguished visitor. In the course of their conversation, the distinguished visitor mentioned that he had been to Delhi recently and that he had heard Justice Sinha's name being mentioned in high political circles there, for elevation to the Supreme Court. Justice Sinha was shrewd enough to understand the implications. He said that he was too small a man for that big chair.

The judgment was almost completed by 7 June. Around that date, Justice Sinha got a phone call from Dehradun. It was the Chief Justice of Allahabad calling. Justice Sinha had to talk to him. The Chief Justice said that the Additional Secretary of the Home Ministry, P.P. Nayar, had met him and he wanted the judgment to be postponed till July. This was probably because of Mrs Gandhi's planned visit to Mexico for the International Women's Year Conference. She probably wanted to be in India when the judgment came. Justice Sinha was angry at this request. After telling the Chief Justice that this was not possible, he immediately drove down to the High Court, to order the registrar to inform the parties and the press that the judgment would be delivered on 12 June.

The parties were informed. Bhushan was in Bombay when the news reached him. Commenting on the date chosen by the judge, he said, 'It is a singularly appropriate date for the judgment. I think the judge had chosen this date because of the Gujarat elections. The polling will be over on 11 June; the counting starts on 12 June. So the judgment will come after the polling is completed, and before any result is declared. Whichever way the judgment goes, nobody can now accuse him of influencing the polling or being influenced by the results.' This analysis was penetrating. As I found out later, this was indeed the real reason why Justice Sinha had chosen that date.

Bhushan met Morarji Desai on 11 June, the day he returned from his election tour of Gujarat. Desai asked him what he thought the judgment would be. This was his reply. 'Strictly on merit, the case is almost impregnable. However, because of the high stakes involved, any normal judge would be subconsciously affected, so I would say that the chances are 75 per cent in our favour.'

Khare was in Srinagar on 9 June. His address was not known. A senior police officer of Srinagar was charged with the duty of locating him. He was finally located and summoned to Allahabad. He managed to reach Allahabad in time for the judgment.

Meanwhile, things were warming up in Allahabad. A special task force of the CID was employed to find out the contents of the judgment. They went to the house of Justice Sinha's secretary, Manna Lai, late on the night of 11 June. He was asked to disclose the judgment. He said that he did not know it (which had an element of truth in it, because the crucial parts of the judgment were added at the last moment by Justice Sinha). When he stayed mum even after much coaxing, they left with a veiled threat. 'We will come back in half an hour. You better tell us the judgment then, if you know what is good for you.'

Manna Lai was frightened, and did not waste any time. Packing off his wife to the house of some relatives, he quickly went to seek refuge in Justice Sinha's house. For that night, he was saved. In the morning, he went back to his house to get ready. Just before 8 a.m., a fleet of cars arrived at his house. The CID was back. With them this time were two of Khare's juniors. They again inquired about the judgment and told Manna Lai that Mrs Gandhi herself was on the hotline. He could tell her the judgment personally. He said that he was getting late and left for Justice Sinha's house.

Manna Lai's harassment did not end there. After the judgment, for many days, the CID kept coming to him to find out about Justice Sinha's visitors during June. They also wanted to find out whether the judge's lifestyle had changed lately. It was indeed strange that the CID should ask such questions as Justice Sinha was known to be a judge of unimpeachable integrity. But this is not so strange in the light of Khare's outbursts after the judgment, when in fits of rage he stated on occasions that the CIA had spent a lot of money to procure this judgment. Here one might also wonder whether any attempt was made to pressurize Bhushan to drop the case. There was actually one extremely naïve attempt to lure him away. It was on 7 May, the day the Attorney-General ended his arguments of the validity of the amendment. B.N. Sapru had thrown a dinner party in his honour. Sapru (who became a High Court judge at Allahabad) was the government advocate who was assisting De in this case. He had been Bhushan's class-fellow, so Bhushan was also invited. During the course of the party, the Attorney-General took Bhushan aside and dropped a subtle hint. He told Bhushan that everybody had formed a very high opinion of him when he had argued the privilege issue before the Supreme Court and that a new post like that of an Additional Attorney-General could be created for him. The Attorney-General, however, added that his (Bhushan's) involvement in politics came in the way, and he wanted Bhushan to sever his connections with it. (Bhushan was at that time the Treasurer of the All India Congress [O]). Bhushan responded by saying that he attached more importance to any contribution he could make in the political life of the country. The Attorney-General tried to reason with him saying that he did not believe that any such effective contribution was possible or practical. The talk ended there. It is interesting to note that after the Janata Party victory in 1977, the Attorney-General in a congratulatory letter wrote to Bhushan that he now saw his point and agreed that it was possible for right-thinking people to contribute to politics.

It was finally 12 June. The High Court compound was swarming with policemen. Justice Sinha's courtroom was packed by 9.30 a.m. Bhushan was not present as he was in Bombay and did not judge it necessary to go to Allahabad for the judgment. This was a tactical error as he later realized. It is indeed strange how this small error of judgment cost the country such a great deal. Bhushan's juniors in the case, R.C. Srivastava and M.C. Gupta, were, however, present in the court. On the other hand, Khare was present with his juniors. The excited and restive crowd in the courtroom waited for the judge to arrive.

Justice Sinha was greeted by the glare of flash bulbs as he drove into the court compound at 9.50 a.m. True to his characteristic punctuality, he entered the courtroom exactly at 10 a.m. Everyone got up for the judge, who bowed and sat down. A hush fell in the courtroom. The judge looked at the crowd and started reading out the operative order. (In the High Court, unlike in the Supreme Court, only the operative part of the judgment is read out by the judge.) He began: 'In view of my findings on issue no. 3 and issue no. 1 read with additional issue no. 1, additional issue no. 2 and additional issue no. 3, the petition is allowed and the election of Smt. Indira Nehru Gandhi, Respondent No. 1, to the Lok Sabha is declared void.' The rest of the order was lost in the roar which reverberated in the courtroom. The judge read the rest of the order quickly and left the courtroom. Nobody heard him. The crowd was raising loud cheers of 'Raj Narain Ki Jai', 'Shanti Bhushan Ki Jai'. They had gone berserk with joy. They lifted Ramesh Srivastava and M.C. Gupta on their shoulders and carried them outside the courtroom and down the corridor in a boisterous mood. Never had such a scene been witnessed in the court.

While there were boisterous cheers in the petitioner's camp, there was despondency and gloom among Mrs Gandhi's lawyers. Khare was dumbstruck. It was evident that he never expected this judgment. Someone brought him water. Slowly recovering his wits, he proceeded to draft an application for a stay order.

The application was drafted in 15 minutes and at 10.20 a.m., a junior of S.C. Khare went to Justice Sinha's chamber to present the application. The application listed two grounds for the stay of operation of the order: (1) That Mrs Gandhi was the leader of the Congress party and in that capacity working as the Prime Minister; and (2) That unless a leader of the Congress party is elected and appointed the Prime Minister, the work of the government will come to a standstill and many complications would arise thereupon. It was, therefore, pleaded that in the interest of justice the operation of the order be stayed.

The judge looked at the application and asked Khare's junior to call the lawyers of the other side. It was perhaps because of the stakes involved in the case at that time that the junior counsel did something highly unethical which he might not have done in other circumstances. He said that he had already informed the lawyers of the other side. This, according to R.C. Srivastava, junior counsel for Raj Narain, was an incorrect statement. Raj Narain's lawyers were totally oblivious of the stay application. It was here that Bhushan paid for his absence. Had he been present, he would have been on the lookout for such a move to get a stay order.

The judge, thinking that Narain's lawyers were not interested, then passed an exparte (after hearing only one party) stay order, staying the operation of the judgment unconditionally for twenty days. This was at 10.30 a.m. As soon as Ramesh Srivastava learnt about the stay order, he rushed to the judge's chamber. He asked Justice Sinha why he was not informed of the stay application. The judge told him what Khare's junior had said. Srivastava told the judge that he would be filing an application for the review of the stay order on the ground that it had been procured by professional misconduct by one of Mrs Gandhi's lawyers. Srivastava was told that this review application could only be filed before the vacation judge and not before Justice Sinha. So although the review application was filed before the vacation judge, it was of no avail as it did not come up for hearing for a few days. After that it was given up by Srivastava.

The judgment of Justice Jag Mohan Lal Sinha ran into 258 pages. These are the highlights of the judgment.

ISSUE OF THE AIR FORCE PLANE

The judge first dealt with the issue of Air Force planes. Accepting the petitioner's argument that the plane was obtained at the instance of Mrs Gandhi, he said, 'Since the tour programme is sent from the Secretariat of Respondent No. 1 after her approval is obtained, and since Respondent No. 1 as Prime Minister knew fully well that thereafter it was the duty of the Air Headquarters to place the plane at her disposal, there is no escape from the conclusion that by sending the tour programme to the Air Headquarters, the Respondent No. 1 required an IAF plane being placed at her disposal.'

He rejected the respondent's argument that since the aircraft was provided on the basis of the Pillai Committee Report on travel arrangements for VIPs, therefore the use of that could not be held to be a corrupt practice. The judge observed, 'The aircraft being manned by the armed forces of the Union, the use thereof under such circumstances can fall within the mischief of Section 123(7) of the Act. Neither the interim Pillai Committee Report nor the Office Memorandum referred to by Respondent No. 1 can under such circumstances salvage the position.'

The judge also rejected the respondent's argument that this facility of Air Force planes was like a commercial service established exclusively for the Prime Minister.

He, however, accepted the respondent's argument that the flight from Delhi to Lucknow was part of a general election tour of the

country. He said that since the halt at Lucknow was only an incidental
halt on an extensive tour of the country, it could not be held that
the dominant purpose of her flight was to go to Rae Bareli to file
her nomination paper. It is, therefore, on this ground that the judge
acquitted her of a corrupt practice.

THE ISSUE OF ROSTRUMS

The judge then took up the issue of rostrums. He held that the rostrums
constructed by officers of the state government enabled Mrs Gandhi
to address her meetings from a dominating position. He observed,
'I do not think it was indispensable for the state government for the
maintenance of law and order or security that its officers should have
taken upon themselves to get rostrums constructed for the meetings of
Respondent No. 1 and to make arrangements for the supply of power
for the functioning of the loudspeaker at the meetings. Both these things
could have been left to be arranged by the political party concerned.'

Coming to the question of whether the services of the state
government officers were obtained or procured, the judge observed,
'As already stated earlier the word "obtained" occurring in Section
123(7) only applied to some effort or initiative on the part of the
returned candidate. Since the programme was sent from the office
of Respondent No. 1 with her approval and contained an implied
direction that the state government may, inter alia, arrange for the
construction of rostrums and for loudspeakers for her meetings, the
needed initiative had thereby emanated from her.'

For these reasons, the judge held Mrs Gandhi guilty of a corrupt
practice on this issue.

THE SYMBOL ISSUE

Taking up the issue of the symbol, the judge made it clear that in
deciding whether the symbol was a religious one or not, he would
not take into account the fact that it was refused by the Election
Commission to the Ram Rajya Parishad in 1952 or the fact that it was
allotted to the Congress party in 1971.

The judge said that the oral testimony of the pandits did not
lead to the conclusion that the cow was regarded as a God in Hindu
religion. He also did not accept Bhushan's argument that Mahatma

Gandhi in his book *Go Seva* (service of the cow) said that the cow was regarded as a God in Hindu religion. He observed, 'To my mind that does not mean anything beyond this: that to carry love for the cow is one of the tenets of Hindu religion. That obviously is based on the fact that since a long time the cow has been treated as sacred in Hindu religion. Everything that is sacred does not become God.'

He then referred to the *Encyclopaedia Britannica* where in the chapter on Hinduism it is stated, 'Many animals, plants and natural objects are sacred in varying degrees, the most noteworthy being the cow. The bull is especially sacred because of his connection with God Shiva, but the cow is divine in her own right and is generally revered as the representative of Mother Earth.' The judge commented that the sense conveyed is that while bulls and other animals are held sacred because of their association with some God, the cow is sacred without any such association. This, he says, did not mean that the cow was regarded as God.

The judge then stated his conclusions on this issue. He said, 'whether the cow is a religious symbol should, in fact, be understood in the sense a common man understands it. The common man in our country does not delve deep into the *Vedas*, *Puranas* and *Smritis* in order to know the identity and status of a deity in Hindu mythology. No one can deny that cows, like other cattle, are bought and sold all over the world since time immemorial. It also cannot be denied that cows are treated shabbily by an ordinary man . . . Again if the cow is a deity, the entire race thereof in this universe should be held deities, which is not very much understandable. The rational view, therefore, is that in view of her high utility, the cow is treated with great reverence. It however cannot be equated with God or a deity.'

The judge then committed what was the most serious error in his judgment. He said, 'according to *Corpus Juris Secundum* "symbol" means an object chosen to typify or represent some idea or quality in something else because of a resemblance in one or more of their characteristics or association.' He said that according to this meaning of the word 'symbol', the picture of a cow and calf cannot be held to be a symbol of a cow herself.

With great respect it is submitted that if a picture of a cow is not a symbol of it, then nothing can be a symbol of a cow.

For these reasons the judge held that the symbol of a cow and calf was not a religious symbol.

THE EXPENSES ISSUE

Taking up the issue of expenses, the judge said that we would first consider the petitioner's case assuming that the Amending Act did not exist and accept the law as laid down in Chawla's case. He added that unless the petitioner showed that the expenses of the respondent exceeded Rs 35,000 on the law declared in Chawla's case, there would be no need to go into the validity of the Amending Act.

As regards the expenses on the twenty-three vehicles used by the DCC, the judge observed, 'The petitioner has not established that these vehicles were obtained on hire and not been provided free of change by some friends and supporter of the respondent.'

He did not accept the petitioner's contention that since Kapoor had got those vehicles released, they should be deemed to have been used in Mrs Gandhi's constituency. For these reasons, the judge did not add any expenditure on these vehicles to the respondent's election expenses.

Coming to the expenditure on the construction of rostrums, the judge agreed that on the basis of law declared in Chawla's case, this expenditure could be included in Mrs Gandhi's election expenses. He, therefore, added a sum of Rs 16,000 which was incurred on the rostrums to the election expenses of Mrs Gandhi. He added another sum of Rs 800 for loudspeakers and Rs 1151 for the electricity for the loudspeakers. He did not add the expenses on the Air Force plane on which Mrs Gandhi travelled from Delhi to Lucknow. It was part of a general election tour of the country, and, therefore, did not further her election prospects.

The judge further held that the telephone expenses alleged by the petitioner also could not be added as they were not pleaded in the petition.

Lastly, the judge added an amount of Rs 232.50 as cost of motor transport from Lucknow to Rae Bareli. According to the return of election expenses of Respondent No. 1, an amount of Rs 12,892.97 was incurred over her election expenses. Adding the aforesaid amount of Rs 18,183.50 to this figure, the total comes to Rs 31,076.47, sufficiently below the prescribed limit of Rs 35,000.

For this reason he held her not guilty of corrupt practice on this issue too.

The judge did not find it necessary to go into the validity of the election law amendment as the validity of that would not have affected his findings on this issue.

THE ISSUE OF HOLDING OUT

The judge then dealt with the issue of the date from which Mrs Gandhi held herself out as a candidate. Observing that the tour programme of Mrs Gandhi for 1 February was issued on 25 January with her approval, and that it contained the words 'file nomination papers', the judge said that 'there appears to be no escape from the conclusion that Respondent No. 1 held herself out as a candidate from Rae Bareli at least some time before 25 January 1971'.

Office Not Relevant

On the question of Mrs Gandhi's credibility as a witness, the judge did not agree with Khare's suggestion that while assessing the veracity of the evidence of Mrs Gandhi, the fact of the high office held by her should be taken into account. He observed, 'it should be conceded that when a person appears in court as a witness and his evidence appears to be natural and probable, the status and respectability attached to him is also taken into consideration to lend further assurance to his testimony. The status and respectability of the witness alone cannot however induce the court to accept his testimony, more so when he is himself a party to the proceedings and interested in the result of the case. In such cases, the evidence of that person has to be assessed without in any manner being obsessed by the high office which he may hold.'

MRS GANDHI'S STATEMENTS INCONSISTENT

The judge noted that Mrs Gandhi's stand during her oral deposition that she only decided to contest the election from Rae Bareli on 1 February was inconsistent with her earlier written statement filed in 1972. Mrs Gandhi had explained the inconsistency by saying that her written statement was drafted in legal language which she found difficult to understand. The judge observed, 'the statement made by Mrs Gandhi to explain the inconsistency failed to satisfactorily explain the same.'

Justice Sinha rejected outright the respondent's argument that the final decision of the All-India Congress Committee mentioned in the written statement was to leave the choice of her constituency to Mrs Gandhi herself.

Regarding Mrs Gandhi's press conference of 29 December in which, in reply to the question whether she was changing her constituency from Rae Bareli to Gurgaon, she said, 'No I am not', the judge observed: 'The answer given by Respondent No. 1, to my mind does not mean anything except that she was not changing her constituency and that she would contest the election from Rae Bareli.'

Justice Sinha also did not agree with the respondent's contention that the election was in prospect only after the Presidential Notification calling for the election was issued on 27 January. He held that the election became in prospect on 27 December 1970, with the dissolution of the Lok Sabha.

In view of all this, the judge concluded that Mrs Gandhi had held herself out as a prospective candidate from 29 December 1970.

YASHPAL KAPOOR

On the question of Kapoor's resignation, Justice Sinha found Haksar's claim fantastic that the resignation of a government servant could be accepted by word of mouth alone. He said, 'The appointment of persons in government offices, more so to gazetted posts, as well as termination of their services, is now governed by statutory rules, and the appointing authority has to act under those rules. It is the implied intention of the rules that there should be an order in writing terminating his services.' He also noted that the plea of oral acceptance of resignation was for the first time set up in the additional written statement which was filed a year after the original written statement. He said that it, therefore, was an afterthought. He further said, 'It is true that according to the gazette notification, the resignation of Shri Yashpal Kapoor has been accepted with effect from 14 January 1971. It cannot, however, be ignored that the order accepting the resignation was passed on 25 January 1971. Till that order was passed the status of Yashpal Kapoor continued to remain that of a government servant despite the fact that the order was given retrospective effect so as to be valid from 14 January 1971.'

The judge therefore held that Kapoor's resignation became effective only from 25 January 1971.

Justice Sinha then took up the aspect of Mrs Gandhi's obtaining the assistance of Kapoor for the furtherance of her election prospects before 25 January.

As the preliminary point, Justice Sinha considered the relationship of Kapoor with Mrs Gandhi. He noted that Kapoor had been working in the Prime Minister's Secretariat and therefore in effect with Mrs Gandhi's since 1951. During the 1967 elections, he had resigned from his job in order to work for Mrs Gandhi's election, rejoining the Prime Minister's Secretariat immediately after the elections. In the 1971 elections, too, he was Mrs Gandhi's election agent. All these facts, the judge noted, indicate that Kapoor had become extremely useful and almost indispensable to Mrs Gandhi.

Taking up the question of when Kapoor had started doing election work for Mrs Gandhi, the judge agreed with the petitioner's contention that Kapoor had delivered an election speech in Munshiganj on 7 January.

Regarding the fact that the return of election expenses showed Kapoor having authorized the purchase of the voters' list on 11 January, the judge held that since there was no evidence to prove that Kapoor was in Rae Bareli at that time, he would not hold that against the respondent.

On the period of 14 January to 25 January, the judge, after examining all the evidence available on this, held that Kapoor reached Rae Bareli on 14 January to launch Mrs Gandhi's campaign. He did not believe Kapoor's statement that he had reached Rae Bareli on 14 January on Kamlapati Tripathi's directions to go on a tour of Eastern UP. He found it extremely improbable that of all the places in Eastern UP, Kapoor chose Rae Bareli without having any prior intention of going there. He held that Kapoor had been in Rae Bareli all those days and had participated in election meetings addressed by Shri Chandrashekhar and Prof. Sher Singh.

Kapoor had stated that he had resigned in 1967 and again in 1971 to do public service. Kapoor had also stated that he had an ambition to get into Parliament. 'That being so,' the judge observed, 'it is obvious that Shri Yashpal Kapoor did not resign in 1967 nor in 1971 for the sake of any public service but only to work for Respondent No. 1 in her constituency and thereby obtained her help in the fulfilment of his ambition.'

Commenting on the reliability of Kapoor's deposition, the judge observed that the statement of Kapoor 'is not a statement of a straightforward nature and on several points it is an admixture of half-truths and untruths'.

The judge further held that all the surrounding circumstances made it almost doubtless that Kapoor must have worked for Mrs Gandhi's election at her instance. The circumstances were that Mrs Gandhi reposed great trust in Kapoor, that Kapoor had submitted his letter of resignation on 13 January after consulting Mrs Gandhi, that he again met her between 21 and 26 January.

Because of these findings, Justice Sinha concluded that the respondent had obtained and procured the assistance of Yashpal Kapoor for the furtherance of her election prospects while he was still a gazetted officer and, therefore, held her guilty of a corrupt practice on this issue.

Justice Sinha made this final order.

'In view of my findings on issue no. 1, issue no. 3 and additional issue no. 3, the petition is allowed and the election of Smt. Indira Nehru Gandhi, Respondent No. 1, to the Lok Sabha is declared void.'

The judge accordingly also disqualified her from holding any public office for a period of six years from that date, as provided by the R.P. Act. The election petition was allowed with costs. The writ petition filed for challenging the validity of the election law amendment was, however, dismissed, because the judge held that the petitioner had not been able to lay any foundation on facts to compel an inquiry into its validity.

3

THE REPERCUSSIONS

9

Rumblings after the Judgment

Mrs Gandhi got news of the judgment at 10.10 a.m. She reportedly stayed calm and asked her Secretary to get the details. Meanwhile her main legal advisers, H.R. Gokhale, the Union law minister, and S.S. Ray, the chief minister of West Bengal, rushed to her house as soon as they heard of the judgment. Palkhivala, who happened to be in Delhi, also rushed to Mrs Gandhi's house.

By the time Palkhivala reached her house, Justice Sinha had granted a twenty-day absolute stay. So in the closed-door consultations which Mrs Gandhi had with her legal advisers, she was told that it was not legally imperative for her to resign because of the stay order. They waited for further details of the judgment to come in.

Bhushan was in his hotel suite in Bombay when he first got the news. He was having a conference with some lawyers, when, at 10.15 a.m. he received a phone call from his brother Vijay Kumar from Delhi. He was elated. His hard labour had paid off.

When reporters reached him, Bhushan was asked whether he thought Mrs Gandhi could continue as Prime Minister. He said that legally perhaps she could, but morally he had no doubt that she was under an obligation to resign. 'Apart from holding her guilty of corrupt practices, the judge has also held her guilty of giving false evidence. Consider what would happen if she went to an international conference and the Pakistani delegate got up and said: "Why are you listening to her? Her word has not been believed even in her own court." That would be very embarrassing for the country.'

Raj Narain got news of the judgment at 10.20 a.m. when a friend of his phoned him from Allahabad. He was overjoyed. Sweets were offered to all who came to his house that day. Commenting on the judgment, he said that Justice Sinha had raised the prestige of the judiciary. He asked Mrs Gandhi to resign at once and warned that no power on earth could save her now.

The Opposition as a whole was overjoyed by the news of the judgment. For them it was a godsend opportunity to remove Mrs Gandhi. They were quick to capitalize on it. The reactions of almost all Opposition leaders were similar: high praise for Justice Sinha and a demand for Mrs Gandhi's resignation. They said that a person against whom the court had recorded findings of corrupt practices had no right to remain Prime Minister. The Swatantra Party leader, Piloo Mody, went further. He said that as of 10 a.m. that day, India had ceased to have a lawful Prime Minister. 'Now we have to see how to deal with this imposter,' he added.

THE CONGRESS REACTION

At 6 p.m. that evening, there was a meeting of the Congress parliamentary board. It was attended by the party president, Barooah, Jagjivan Ram, Chavan and about a hundred other Members of Parliament. The notable absentees in the meeting were Mohan Dharia, Chandrashekhar, Krishna Kant and Ram Dhan. Mohan Dharia, who had been dropped from Mrs Gandhi's Cabinet for suggesting a dialogue with Jayaprakash Narayan (JP), was perhaps the only prominent Congress leader who publicly announced that Mrs Gandhi should resign after the judgment. Chandrashekhar, Krishna Kant and Ram Dhan were also known to hold the same view, though they did not announce it.

The parliamentary board meeting turned out to be merely an exercise of expressing confidence in Mrs Gandhi's leadership. All those who spoke in that meeting spoke of Mrs Gandhi's leadership as indispensable for the country and urged her not to quit. Jagjivan Ram's speech, however, struck a slightly different note. He said that the judgment had at least shown that the judiciary in India functioned without fear or favour. Pointedly avoiding the use of the word 'indispensable', Ram, however, stated that whether in or out of office, Mrs Gandhi would continue to lead the nation.

Meanwhile, various Congress stalwarts and chief ministers of states were rushing to Delhi, trying to outdo each other in expressing their allegiance to Mrs Gandhi. Her house was surrounded by people chanting slogans in her praise. Some of them also raised slogans against Justice Sinha.

That evening, Mrs Gandhi addressed the few thousand people who had gathered outside her house. Leaving the resignation issue deliberately vague, she said that she had always served the people in the past and with their support she would continue to do so in the future.

Thus it seems that she had probably not yet made up her mind on whether she ought to resign. The factors which must have been weighing in her decision were obvious. It was clear that a resignation at that time would give the lie to the Opposition charges that she was a dictator, and give a much-needed boost to her slumping popularity ratings. Then, if she was exonerated by the Supreme Court, she could stage a triumphant comeback. But there was the other side of the coin too. If she left now, someone else would replace here. She could be left stranded if that person refused to make way for her even in the event of a favourable Supreme Court judgment. In politics, particularly that of India, power accrues mainly on the basis of the office which one holds. There is no easy comeback in politics—at least in the short term.

Mrs Gandhi to Appeal

By the evening, details of the judgment had come in and had been studied broadly by Mrs Gandhi's legal advisers. Palkhivala thought that there were very good chances of the judgment being reversed by the Supreme Court. So it was decided that an appeal be preferred to the Supreme Court, and Palkhivala was selected to argue the appeal. Most people found it rather surprising that Palkhivala, the famed lawyer who had been a rather vocal critic of Mrs Gandhi, should deem it fit to accept her brief. One might say that a lawyer's is a professional job, and it is his duty to argue the cases of all those who approach him. But this was not an ordinary case; it was a case with immediate and far-reaching political consequences. If Palkhivala was a political opponent of Mrs Gandhi, he was perhaps obliged not to accept the brief in this case. He was supposed to write an article in the *Illustrated Weekly of India* wherein he was to set out his reasons for accepting the brief, but unfortunately no such article appeared, perhaps because the circumstances changed. However, his public image was considerably tarnished by his acceptance of Mrs Gandhi's brief.

PRESS REACTIONS TO THE VERDICT

The next day's papers were full of the judgment: 'Court unseats Indira. Disqualified for 6 years,' screamed the banner headlines. The *Hindustan Times* in their editorial commented, 'While the stay order was absolute, the judicial pronouncement was not politically obliterated although an appeal was pending in the Supreme Court, and it is to this reality rather than the technical legality of the stay to which the country must address itself . . . The proper course in these circumstances would be for the Prime Minister to resign her office pending disposal of the appeal which she legitimately intends to prefer before the Supreme Court. In doing so, she would not only uphold the judicial process but uphold Indian democracy and the value on which it is found.'

The *Statesman*, in an article entitled 'A Time to Resign', commented that after this judgment, Mrs Gandhi would not be able to command the confidence of the party or of the nation. Advising her to resign, they warned, 'By not resigning, she will be guilty of far more than any violation of an electoral law.'

By and large, the press felt that the judgment would undermine her moral authority, and most newspapers urged her to resign. The world press also reacted fast to the High Court judgment. Their main reaction was surprise at the decision. After the supersession of the Supreme Court judges in 1973, the prestige of the Indian judiciary had been considerably devalued in the eyes of the world, and such a 'bold' decision was thus not expected. The western world, however, was pleasantly surprised at the decision, which was in their eyes an indication of a healthy democracy. They waited expectantly for further news.

The day following the judgment, Mrs Gandhi addressed another rally organized outside her house. The crowd was in a boisterous mood. They performed the bhangra for Mrs Gandhi. An effigy of Justice Sinha was also burnt. Mrs Gandhi, in her speech, made her first comment on the judgment. Obviously referring to the issue of rostrums on which the judge had found her guilty of obtaining the assistance of government servants, Mrs Gandhi said that the rostrums had been constructed by officers of the state government. The state government was headed by the Opposition parties at that time, she said.

On 14 June, there was a news item in some newspapers which said that Justice Jagmohan Lal of the Allahabad High Court had died. Although this Justice Jagmohan Lal was an old retired judge, the people, who were ready to believe anything at that time, inferred that Justice Jag Mohan Lal Sinha had been murdered. The speed with which this rumour gained currency reveals the extent of the erosion of Mrs Gandhi's credibility that had taken place since 1971.

As the days progressed, it became routine for Mrs Gandhi to address five to six meetings outside her house each day. She became increasingly hysterical and critical of the Opposition. All her speeches had the same theme. Lashing out at the Opposition, she said that the Opposition was out to destroy the country. 'They have a single-point programme, "Indira Hatao". They are not bothered with "Desh Bachao". One of the Opposition leaders even wears a badge saying "I am a CIA agent".[1] On 16 June, at a public meeting, she made it clear that she did not intend to resign, and that she intended to fight it out with the Opposition.

PRIME MINISTER OR NOT?

Bhushan saw that Mrs Gandhi did not intend to resign. The Congress party, too, instead of choosing a new leader, was rushing to express confidence in her leadership. So he made another move. Addressing some newsmen, he said that moral considerations aside, legally too, Mrs Gandhi was not the Prime Minister.

Explaining, he said, 'At 10 a.m., when the judgment was pronounced, Mrs Gandhi immediately ceased to be a Member of Parliament, and consequently also the Prime Minister. A person can remain a minister for six months without being a Member of Parliament. But in this case, Mrs Gandhi's election has been set aside, so she ceased to be a Member of Parliament with effect from December 1970 when the last Parliament was dissolved. Her six months having expired, she automatically ceased to be the Prime Minister from 10 a.m. on 12 June. The stay order being given at 10.30, could only revive her membership of Parliament. Her Prime Ministership cannot be revived by a stay order given under the Representation of People Act. That is governed by constitutional provisions. That can only be

---

[1] This Opposition leader was Piloo Mody, who once went to Parliament wearing this badge.

revived by a fresh appointment and by taking a fresh oath as provided by the Constitution.'

Siddhartha Shankar Ray was enraged by Bhushan's statement. He said that he did not understand how a lawyer like Bhushan could say such a thing. He pointed out that Section 116B of the R.P. Act, when dealing with the effect of a stay order, says that in the event of a stay order, the High Court order shall be deemed never to have taken effect.

Bhushan commented on Ray's reply in a public meeting organized by the Uptown Jaycees of Bombay. He said that Ray did not understand the difference between statutory and constitutional provisions. 'Suppose the stay order had been obtained twenty days after the judgment. For those twenty days at least, she would not have been the Prime Minister, and a new Prime Minister would have been sworn in. Does Ray mean to say that even if a stay was given after twenty days, she would have automatically become the Prime Minister? What would be the status of the new Prime Minister then? Therefore, it is clear that with a stay order she would not automatically become the Prime Minister.'

'India Is Indira'

The Congress parliamentary party meeting was scheduled for 18 June. Many people expected the Congress party to choose a new leader at the meeting. But their hopes were belied. The meeting turned out to be no more than a repetition of their earlier exercise of firmly expressing supreme confidence in Mrs Gandhi's leadership. At the meeting attended by Mrs Gandhi and more than 300 Congress ministers and legislators, speaker after speaker got up to shower torrents of praise upon Mrs Gandhi. Urging her to continue, they said that her leadership had become indispensable for the country and she had become inseparable from the people. Swaran Singh went to the extent of saying, 'What happens to her happens to India and what happens to India happens to her.' The Congress president, Barooah, improved upon this and coined the slogan, 'India is Indira and Indira is India.'

There were, however, five notable absentees at the parliamentary party meeting. Knowing what the agenda of the meeting was, Chandrashekhar, Krishna Kant, Mohan Dharia, Ram Dhan and Lakshmi Kanthamma had chosen to disassociate themselves from it.

The Congress parliamentary party resolution was greeted by voices of protests from the Opposition party. Jayaprakash Narayan, commenting on the resolution, said that it was yet another instance of unabashed political immorality of the Congress leadership. 'Here is a clear notice given that no matter what the law of the land might be, Mrs Gandhi will remain the Prime Minister as long as she or the Congress party has the say in it.' In response to the resolution, Piloo Mody composed a poem, which went like this:

Humpty Dumpty sat on a throne,
Humpty Dumpty out was thrown.
All the Queen's asses and all the
Queen's yesmen, could not put
Humpty on the throne again.

Bhushan was hoping that the Congress parliamentary party would nominate a successor to Mrs Gandhi. The outcome of the meeting angered him. Commenting on the meeting, he said that the stay was obtained by Mrs Gandhi on the ground that the Congress party would need some time to elect a new leader. The Congress party had met and no new leader was elected. Therefore, the stay was being clearly misused by Mrs Gandhi. He rang up his junior, Ramesh Srivastava, in Allahabad, and asked him to file an application for the vacation of the stay order on the ground that it was being misused. Nothing, however, came of it, as a few days later the matter of the stay came up before the Supreme Court.

The press was sharply critical of the Congress parliamentary party meeting. The *Statesman* said that the meeting 'was a ritual, and like all rituals followed a predictable course. The purpose was to do reverence to Mrs Gandhi and this was done with the slogans, chants, encomiums and verbal extravagance usual to such stage-managed occasions of which there has been a surfeit since the Allahabad judgment.' B.G. Verghese writing in the *Hindustan Times* said, 'The resolution drafted by the party managers carefully obfuscated the real issues confronting the country after the Allahabad judgment to propound what is no less than Fuehrer principle of the indispensability of Mrs Gandhi's leadership as Prime Minister.'

Meanwhile, Mrs Gandhi's legal advisers were busy preparing for her appeal in the Supreme Court and the application for the extension of the twenty-day stay granted by the High Court. Since the Supreme Court was on vacation, the appeal was to be preferred before the vacation judge, Justice Krishna Iyer. The vacation judge normally sits only on

Tuesdays and Fridays. On Friday, 20 June, Mrs Gandhi's advocate-on-record, J.B. Dadachandji, appeared before the vacation judge at 10.30 a.m. and made an oral plea that an early date be fixed for the hearing of Mrs Gandhi's stay application. He also requested the judge to permit an unusual procedure by which he could file the appeal in the Supreme Court on the same day on which the application for the stay was to be heard. Normally, an appeal is formally filed, and then only is the date for the hearing of the stay application fixed. The law is that as soon as the application is filed in the Supreme Court, the stay given by the High Court stands automatically vacated. Dadachanji made this request so that there was no legal hindrance in Mrs Gandhi's continuance as Prime Minister, in the interim period between the time an appeal was filed and the time when an extension of the stay was granted. J.P. Goyal, advocate-on-record for Raj Narain, did not object to this procedure and so the judge allowed it.

Justice Krishna Iyer fixed Monday, 23 June, as the date of hearing of the stay application, observing that Monday would be a virgin day as he had no other work on that day. He told both parties to exchange relevant papers before that date.

THE 'LARGEST EVER' RALLY

As this was going on in the Supreme Court, a massive rally was being addressed by Mrs Gandhi on the Boat Club grounds. Preparations for this rally had been made several days in advance. It is said that Sanjay Gandhi himself was personally in charge of the arrangements of the rally. Special, free trains were run from all over the country to bring in people to attend this meeting. All the buses of Delhi had vanished from the city as they had been sent to neighbouring states to collect people for the meeting. There were elaborate police arrangements and barricading for miles around the Boat Club. Mrs Gandhi claimed this to be the largest ever rally in the history of this country. It is estimated that about five lakh people attended this meeting.

In her speech, Mrs Gandhi launched a scathing attack on the Opposition parties. Explaining why this rally was held, she said, 'It is not to show strength or to seek support for myself, it is being held essentially to demonstrate the will and unity of the people.'

Apart from Mrs Gandhi, the meeting was also addressed by others. It was once again Barooah who stole the show, further substantiating

JP's statement that he was the court jester of the Congress party.[2] Giving vent to his scholarly bent of mind, he recited a poem, specially written by him for this occasion. He chanted:

Indira tere subah ki jai
Indira tere sham ki jai
Indira tere kaam ki jai
Indira tere naam ki jai.

He capped it by shouting the new slogan which he had invented—'Indira is India and India is Indira.'

This rally, as expected, evoked an angry response from the Opposition. They charged that the entire government machinery was being misused by the Congress party to show their muscle. The response of the press was also unfavourable. The London *Economist* in a penetrating comment said that the blatant misuse of the government machinery by Mrs Gandhi for her Boat Club rally was a move 'ironically reminiscent of the very offences for which she was convicted'.

THE OPPOSITION RALLY

The Opposition was not sitting quiet either. Seeing that Mrs Gandhi had no intention of resigning, they were preparing for a countrywide agitation to force her out of office. They organized a massive rally at the Ramlila Grounds on 22 June. Jayaprakash Narayan was also expected to address that meeting, but could not do so as his flight from Patna was cancelled under rather suspicious circumstances. The meeting was nonetheless addressed by most of the top Opposition leaders which included Morarji Desai and Raj Narain. Thousands of people braved the rain and repeatedly cheered them as they spoke. Their strategy was to mobilize public opinion against Mrs Gandhi's continuing in office, so the theme of their speeches was similar. They asked the people to organize themselves and prepare for a non-violent agitation to force Mrs Gandhi out of office. They, however, did not give a final call for the agitation on this day. They were waiting for the outcome of the Supreme Court hearing on Mrs Gandhi's stay application.

[2] Kuldip Nayyar, *The Judgement: Inside Story of the Emergency in India* (Delhi: Vikas Publishing House, 1977), p. 7.

10

The Stay Order

By the evening of 22 June, the relevant papers regarding the appeal and the stay application had been exchanged by both sides. A copy of the appeal and the stay application was also sent to Justice Krishna Iyer, even though the formal appeal was only to be filed the next morning. Mrs Gandhi, in her stay application, had asked for an extension of the absolute and unconditional stay granted by the High Court. This would stay the operation of the High Court order till the appeal was decided by the Supreme Court.

Raj Narain, in his affidavit, had vehemently opposed the extension of the stay to Mrs Gandhi. Alternatively, he had pleaded that if a stay was to be granted at all, it should only be a conditional stay, the sort which is granted normally by the Supreme Court in cases where charges of corrupt practices were upheld against an elected candidate. A conditional stay has the effect of allowing the person to keep alive his membership of Parliament, but deprives him of all other rights as a member, including his right to vote or participate in the proceedings of Parliament.

It was Monday, 23 June, the day that had been fixed for the hearing of Mrs Gandhi's stay petition in the Supreme Court. Justice Krishna Iyer had chosen the Chief Justice's courtroom for the stay hearing. Although it was the largest courtroom in the Supreme Court, it could accommodate only 150 people. Thousands of people wanted to witness the drama that was to determine the future of Mrs Gandhi and of the country. The eyes of the entire country were focused on the Supreme Court that day.

Out of the 150-odd people who got entry into the courtroom that day, there were about 100 lawyers, about thirty visitors and about twenty-five newsmen. Hundreds of people jammed the corridors outside the courtroom in the hope that someone from inside might come out, giving them a chance to go in. There were hundreds of others who could not even get entry inside the court premises as the gates were closed to prevent more people from coming in. The Supreme Court was surrounded by helmeted policemen wearing brickbat guards.

When Bhushan and Palkhivala arrived, they had to push their way to the courtroom because of the fantastic crowds jamming the corridors. They somehow managed to get inside by 11.30 a.m. The judge arrived punctually at 11.30 a.m. and the stage was set for the arguments to begin. Palkhivala, being the applicant's counsel, was called upon to open his arguments.

PALKHIVALA'S ARGUMENTS

As a preliminary issue, Palkhivala requested that the decision on the stay application be given retrospective effect so that the decision would be deemed to have been given from the moment the appeal was filed. This, he said, was to circumvent a technical difficulty which was arising. This was that the stay of the Allahabad High Court would stand vacated as soon as the appeal was filed which had been filed at that very time. So the question would arise as to whether Mrs Gandhi could remain the Prime Minister till the time the judgment on the stay petition was delivered. Justice Iyer turned to Bhushan who said that he had no objection to it.

'Trial Judge Made Manifest Errors'

Opening his arguments, Palkhivala first contended that the trial judge of the Allahabad High Court had made manifest errors in holding Mrs Gandhi guilty of two corrupt practices. He said that on the issue of whether Mrs Gandhi obtained the assistance of government servants by getting rostrums constructed for her, the learned judge had made a manifest error in not observing the distinction between the government and government servants. Counsel went on: 'The Representation of People Act prohibits the procuring or attempting to procure the assistance of a government servant. But if a government, the state government in this case, itself provides some assistance to a candidate, it could not be regarded as a corrupt practice. In the present case, it is clear that the assistance was provided by government servants acting in their official capacity so that in effect it was provided by the state government and not by government servants acting in their private capacity.'

Counsel further argued that for a corrupt practice there must be a conscious attempt to obtain or procure the assistance, whereas here it was part of the routine security drill undertaken for the Prime Minister. 'If the election was set aside on this ground, it would have alarming consequences. Today it might be set aside for the construction of rostrums, but tomorrow it would be set aside for barricading, and then for police arrangements. There can be no elections in these circumstances.'

Counsel further contended that the trial judge had erred in finding that the appellant held herself as a candidate on 29 December. He said that the first art of politics was to confound the opponent, and Mrs Gandhi was no novice to politics. Therefore, there was no reason why she should have declared herself to be a candidate from Rae Bareli till she filed her nomination paper.

Counsel went on to argue at length the issue of the date of Yashpal Kapoor's resignation, and contended that on the facts of the case there was absolutely no doubt that Haksar had orally accepted Kapoor's resignation on 14 January. Further there could be no doubt of Haksar's competence to accept his resignation orally.

At this point the judge asked Palkhivala not to go into the merits of the case as that would take a long time. Justice Iyer said that the matter before him was only the stay application and not the appeal. Palkhivala said that he was only trying to show how weak the case of the petitioner was, and that it was bound to fail in the appeal.

Offences Are Technical

Leaving the merits and going on to the question of why an absolute stay should be granted, Palkhivala submitted that the offences on which the appellant was found guilty were technical in nature and did not involve any moral turpitude. He said that since the appeal would be disposed of expeditiously by the Supreme Court, therefore, in the interest of convenience and justice, the status quo should not be disturbed for these few days. He said that continuity in the politics of the country would be disturbed if Mrs Gandhi was prevented from remaining the Prime Minister. He also claimed that the nation was solidly behind Mrs Gandhi as could be seen from the massive rallies which were held in her support.

Counsel next submitted that there were some precedents in which an absolute stay had been granted by the Supreme Court, even in cases where the candidate was found guilty of corrupt practices.

Justice Iyer: Are you referring to the cases of 1953 and 1954?

Counsel: Yes.

Justice Iyer: But those are vintage cases. At that time the Election Tribunal was the trial court for election petitions. I do not think there has been any case of absolute stay after the High Courts have been constituted as the trial courts.

Counsel: My Lord, such a case has never arisen before. An election petition has never succeeded against a Prime Minister. So we cannot search for a precedent in a case where there can be no precedent. Your Lordship in this case will be laying down a precedent.

Counsel next contended that public and private justice were clearly in Mrs Gandhi's favour for the grant of an absolute stay.

Justice Iyer: I am mystified by the expression 'private justice'. You mean justice as between two citizens?

Counsel: Yes, justice as between the appellant and the respondent. If an absolute stay is not granted to the appellant, it would cause irreparable damage to her political career. It is easy for my learned friend on the other side to say that there could possibly be no damage to her career if she resigns now and resumes office after she is exonerated by the Supreme Court. But there is no easy comeback in politics. On the other hand, an absolute stay would do no harm at all to Raj Narain. It is also in the public interest that an absolute stay be granted. My Lord, it would be very embarrassing for the country to have a Prime Minister whose hands were fettered by a conditional stay.

Palkhivala said that the aim of the respondent was to inflict maximum damage on the appellant and in such a case where considerations of national security and other international considerations were involved, the respondent should not be allowed to succeed in his plea.

Justice Krishna Iyer at this point asked the counsels of both sides to look up the effect of a conditional stay. He wondered whether both the sides were not shadow-boxing on the issue of absolute versus conditional stay. He said that functioning of the Prime Minister in Parliament would not be affected by a conditional stay as this was governed by other rules. He said: 'The only difference between the two types of stay is perhaps that the voting rights in Parliament are affected. Would it cause irreparable injury to public justice if one member is prevented from voting?'

Counsel: It would be extremely embarrassing for the country to have a Prime Minister who is not allowed to vote in Parliament.

Repeating his vehement request for an absolute stay, Palkhivala concluded his opening arguments.

Palkhivala's arguments concluded at 2.30 p.m. At 1 p.m. when it was time for lunch, Justice Iyer had asked the counsel whether they would mind skipping lunch and continuing the arguments. Nobody objected, so it was probably for the first time in the protocol-observing Supreme Court that arguments continued even during the lunch hour.

BHUSHAN'S REPLY

Opening his reply, Bhushan said that he could not understand the argument that the offences on which the appellant was found guilty were technical in nature. He said, 'When the law provides that certain acts are corrupt practices, it is the duty of each candidate to see that he does not commit these acts. Transgressing the law is itself a major offence. Moreover, in this case, no one could say that the offences are technical. The learned High Court judge has found her guilty of being untruthful before the court. That is not a technical offence.'

Going into the merits of the case, Counsel strongly rebutted Palkhivala's contention that the petitioner's case was flimsy and was bound to fail in the appeal. Bhushan said that the petitioner's case was so strong that it was almost impregnable. He said, 'The learned Trial Judge has only found her guilty on two counts and has given her the benefit of doubt on the other five issues. I have full confidence that the Supreme Court will find her guilty on more than two issues.'

Referring to Palkhivala's argument that there was a fine distinction between a government servant and the government, Counsel said that the whole purpose of the law on this was to prevent misuse of government machinery by influential candidates. There would be no purpose, he said, in prohibiting the procuring of assistance from government servants in their private capacity.

At this stage again, Justice Iyer remarked that he would not be going into the merits of the case, so he urged Bhushan to refrain from arguing on the merits. Bhushan said that he was only referring to the merits because Palkhivala had done so and because Palkhivala was relying on his submission that this petition was bound to fail in the Supreme Court.

Answering a question by Justice Iyer, Bhushan made it clear that he was totally opposed to the grant of any stay by the Supreme Court and it was only as an alternative submission that he was arguing for a conditional stay. Counsel said that he was arguing that a stay should not be granted at all because Mrs Gandhi should not be allowed to remain the Prime Minister. 'Political and moral propriety demand that a person who has been placed under a cloud by being found guilty of corrupt practices should not be allowed to remain the Prime Minister. The court, while exercising its discretion, should consider the value of these healthy moral and political conventions.'

Justice Iyer: Moral or political conventions have nothing to do with legal conventions.

Counsel said that till then there had been no precedent of an absolute stay being granted by the Supreme Court when an election had been set aside on corrupt practices. He explained, 'The reason for this practice is that a conditional stay prevents a person from functioning as a Member of Parliament. It merely allows him to attend Parliament to sign the attendance register so that in the event of the reversal of the High Court judgment, he would be able to retain his membership. The court should go by the principle which lies behind the convention of granting a conditional stay. The principle is that the person against whom charges of corrupt practice had been recorded should not be allowed to function in Parliament. This principle applies with greater force to the Prime Minister. The Prime Minister is the leader of the nation and, being so, should be above all suspicion. In this case she can only be prevented from functioning if no stay was granted by the Supreme Court, not even a conditional stay.'

Alternatively, Counsel submitted that if the court did not accept his plea, then he would argue that the appellant be granted only a conditional stay. He said that the only time when absolute stays were granted was prior to 1954 when Election Tribunals were the trial courts. He said that since this power had been delegated to the High Court, there had not been a single case of absolute stay in cases where charges of corrupt practices were upheld against the candidate. He said that the court should not make a departure from the established convention merely because the appellant in this case happened to be the Prime Minister of the country.

Referring to Palkhivala's contention that the present case was unique because the Prime Minister was involved, Counsel said that he could cite any number of instances where ministers and chief ministers had to quit office on their being found guilty of corrupt practices. He cited the example of D.P. Mishra, former chief minister of Madhya Pradesh, and Dr Chenna Reddy, former Union minister, who were both made to resign by Mrs Gandhi herself, because charges of corrupt practices had been established against them. Counsel also cited the recent instance of the West German Chancellor Willy Brandt who had quit office merely because his Secretary was found to be an East German spy, although Mr Brandt had no knowledge of it. He said that the rationale behind this was that the conduct of a person holding a high office must not only be above board, but must also be seen to be above board.

Bhushan said that no country professing democratic ideals could afford a state of affairs where any individual was considered indispensable for the nation. 'The past history of our country shows that whenever there has been a sudden exit of the Prime Minister due to any reason, the work of the government has gone on smoothly and there has been no difficulty in finding a successor to that person. That is exactly the difference between a democracy and a dictatorship. In a dictatorship, the death of a leader plunges the country into a war of succession, but in a democracy, succession is always a smooth affair having no serious repercussions. This is because democracy envisages a government of laws and not of men.'

Justice Iyer: I am unable to understand this expression. I think we are a government of laws and also of men.

Counsel: That is true, but the importance lies not in the individual but in the institutions of the country. If Mrs Gandhi has to go, I am sure that the Congress party can find some capable person to step into her shoes. If they cannot find anyone capable enough, then I must say that such a bankrupt party has no right to rule the country.

Stay Misused

Counsel next contended that the stay obtained by Mrs Gandhi from the High Court had been misused by her and, therefore, this court should not respond to her plea. 'The High Court had given a stay on a particular representation made by the appellant. The representation was that a sudden exit of the Prime Minister would create a void in the country which would bring the work of the government to a standstill. The stay was given because of the plea that some time was required by the Congress party to elect a new leader. But we find that the Congress parliamentary party met on 18 June and all that they did was to express full confidence in Mrs Gandhi's leadership. Was it not incumbent on Mrs Gandhi to ask her party to elect a new leader in her place? It is no argument to say that the party only wanted her and no one else as the leader. I submit that it is impossible for the party to force her to remain the Prime Minister.'

Bhushan's last submission was that the stay order granted now could produce technical and legal complications if the judgment of the High Court was affirmed in the appeal. He referred to Section 107(2) of the R.P. Act, which says:

Where by any order under Section 98, the election of a returned candidate is declared to be void, the acts and proceedings in which that returned candidate has before the date thereof participated as a Member of Parliament or as a Member of the Legislature of a State, shall not be invalidated by reason of that order, nor shall such a candidate be subjected to any liability or penalty on the ground of such participation.

Bhushan argued that it was this section alone which legalized all the acts done in his official capacity during the pendency of a petition by a person whose election had been set aside. Therefore, although the election is deemed to be void from the very beginning, yet the acts done by such a person till the time the High Court judgment is rendered shall be treated to be legal. He further said, 'But this legality is conferred only to things done by the person till the High Court judgment is pronounced. This does not legalize the acts done by the person after the High Court judgment is pronounced. Therefore, if the stay is granted now, and later on the High Court judgment is affirmed by the Supreme Court, then it would raise the question as to whether Mrs Gandhi was legally the Prime Minister between the date of the High Court judgment and the date of the Supreme Court's affirmation of that judgment.'

Bhushan ended his arguments with an impassioned plea that the court should not grant any further stay to Mrs Gandhi.

PALKHIVALA'S REJOINDER

After Bhushan concluded his arguments, Palkhivala briefly replied to them. He rebutted Bhushan's contention that Mrs Gandhi's continuance as the Prime Minister would be embarrassing for the country. He said that this was only Bhushan's personal viewpoint. According to him, it would be embarrassing for the country if a conditional stay and not an absolute stay was granted. He said that it would be embarrassing for the country to have a Prime Minister who was not able to vote in Parliament. 'The institution of Prime Ministership is involved here. A conditional stay will greatly damage this institution.'

'Stay Was Only to Elect a Leader'

In reply to Bhushan's arguments that the appellant had not abided by the representation made in the stay application in the Allahabad High Court, Palkhivala said that the application presented to the trial judge was drafted hurriedly by the counsel present there and therefore was not properly framed. 'Moreover, the application asked for time to elect a leader of the Congress party. The Congress parliamentary party met on 18 June and passed a thunderous resolution affirming support for the appellant and recognizing her as the only leader. The representation does not say that the Congress party will elect a *new* leader.'

Palkhivala ended with a plea that an absolute stay be granted because a conditional stay would have disastrous consequences for the country. The arguments finally ended at 5.05 p.m., which was one hour beyond the normal sitting time of the Supreme Court.

When asked about when the judgment would be delivered, Justice Iyer said that he would deliver his judgment at 3.45 p.m. the next day.

CONDITIONAL STAY

After the arguments ended in the Supreme Court, Bhushan met some Opposition leaders. Ashok Mehta, the president of the Congress (O), asked him what he thought the judgment would be. Bhushan said that he expected it to be a conditional stay. Mehta was pleased. He said that they would throw her out if it was a conditional stay.

The whole country had followed the arguments in the Supreme Court through the newspapers with great interest. Now all awaited the judgment of the Supreme Court. A huge crowd began to gather around the Supreme Court on 24 June as the time of the judgment approached. The judgment was delivered exactly at 3.45 p.m. The judge had granted a conditional stay. He had, however, clarified in his order that there was no legal embargo on Mrs Gandhi continuing as the Prime Minister.

Going on to the actual arguments advanced, Justice Iyer rejected Bhushan's argument that Mrs Gandhi had misused the stay granted by the Allahabad High Court. He accepted Palkhivala's contention that 'since her party so full-bloodedly plumbed in favour of her remaining in office as Prime Minister, she could do nothing else but remain the Prime Minister'.

He also rejected Bhushan's contention that the High Court had found her guilty of being untruthful before the court and agreed with Palkhivala's argument that the offences on which Mrs Gandhi was held guilty were not the 'graver electoral vices'.

Regarding Palkhivala's argument that the High Court's findings were based on flimsy grounds, the judge observed that he could not take the prima facie view that the justice of the case justifies indifference to those findings.

The judge then noted that in such cases it is the usual practice of the court to grant a conditional stay. He further noted that since 1956, when the High Court was made the Election Tribunal, the Supreme Court had always granted only conditional stays.

He then proceeded to analyse the implication of a conditional stay for the Prime Minister. He said:

This appeal, it is plain, relates solely to the Lok Sabha Membership of the appellant and the subject matter of her office qua Prime Minister is not directly before this court in this litigation. Indeed, that office and its functions are regulated carefully by a separate fasciculus of Articles in the Constitution. There is some link between Membership of one of the two Houses of Parliament and Ministership (Art. 75) but once the stay order is made, as has been indicated above, the disqualification regarding appellant's membership of the Lok Sabha remains in force so long as the stay lasts. However, there will be a limitation regarding the appellant's participation in the proceedings of the Lok Sabha in her *capacity as Member thereof*, but, independently of the Membership, a Minister and

a fortiori, the Prime Minister, has the right to address both
Houses of Parliament (without right to vote though) and has
other functions to fulfil. (Arts. 74, 75, 78 and 88 are illustrative.)
In short, the restrictions set out in the usual stay order cannot
and will not detract from the appellant being entitled to exercise
such rights as she has, including addressing Parliament and
drawing salary, *in her capacity as Prime Minister*. There will thus
be no legal embargo on her holding the office of Prime Minister.
However, this legal sequitur of the situation arising from the
stay of the judgment and order of the High Court, including
the suspension of the disqualification under Section 8A, has
nothing to do with extra-legal considerations. Legality is within
the court's province to pronounce upon, but canons of political
propriety and democratic dharma are polemical issues on which
judicial silence is the golden rule.

After summing up, the judge concluded his order by adding that either
party could apply to the Division Bench of the court for a review of
the order if fresh considerations arose, justifying a change in the order.

Reaction to the 'Stay'

The news of the judgment on the stay order was broadcast by the All
India Radio at 4 p.m. It spread like wild fire across the country.

On the political scene, the Congress as well as the Opposition
interpreted the stay as having vindicated their stand. Barooah
triumphantly pointed out that the judge had clearly said that there
was no legal impediment to Mrs Gandhi's continuance as the Prime
Minister. Commenting on the stay, Gokhale said that there was no
resignation issue now. Most of the other Congress leaders also reacted
on the same lines and appealed to the Opposition leaders to end their
satyagraha. Mrs Gandhi, however, made no comment on the stay.

The Opposition, on the other hand, interpreted the conditional
stay as having vindicated their stand. They all demanded Mrs Gandhi's
immediate resignation. 'Has anyone heard of a Prime Minister who
cannot vote in Parliament?' they asked.

M.C. Chagla, the former Chief Justice of Bombay High Court,
commenting on the stay, said, 'Legally she may be entitled to continue
as the Prime Minister, I have no views on it. But on grounds of

political morality and propriety, she should not hold that high office of Prime Minister with a cloud over her head.'

Reacting to the conditional stay, Bhushan said that it had brought into existence a 'crippled' Prime Minister, because she was deprived of the right to vote in Parliament. He said that even Palkhivala had argued before the Supreme Court that a conditional stay would do irreparable damage to her. Bhushan said that it was still possible for Mrs Gandhi to resign gracefully. He pointed out that even in the Supreme Court order, there was a hint that considerations of healthy political conventions might cast an obligation on a person in these circumstances to resign from the office of Prime Minister.

The press reacted to the conditional stay by calling for Mrs Gandhi's resignation. All the four major newspapers in their editorials next day asked Mrs Gandhi to resign.

The National Executive of the Opposition party met that evening at Desai's house to decide their line of action. Jayaprakash Narayan was also present at that meeting. It was decided at that meeting that if she did not resign, a country-wide satyagraha would be launched to protest against her continuance as the Prime Minister.

The Opposition parties were also going ahead with their plans of holding a massive rally at the Ramlila grounds on 25 June. The rally, which was attended by about two lakh people, was to be addressed by Jayaprakash Narayan.

In his speech, Jayaprakash Narayan appealed to the Chief Justice of the Supreme Court A.N. Ray not to be a member of the Bench which heard Mrs Gandhi's appeal. Making it clear that he was not advancing this plea due to any lack of faith in Ray's impartiality, Jayaprakash Narayan said that since Mrs Gandhi appointed Ray the Chief Justice by superseding three judges, even an honest verdict given by him in Mrs Gandhi's favour would not be accepted by the people. Jayaprakash Narayan also appealed to Mrs Gandhi to resign gracefully. He praised the stand taken by the five dissenting MPs who had asked Mrs Gandhi to resign, and expressed surprise at the quietude shown by senior Congress leaders like Jagjivan Ram and Y.B. Chavan. He also deliberately reiterated his appeal to the police and armed forces not to obey illegal orders of the government. He challenged the home minister Brahmananda Reddy to try him in court for high treason for this statement.

Reddy, however, had other plans for JP. Within eight hours of the speech, JP found himself in detention, though without a trial.

11

Law? What Law?

It was just past midnight of 25 June 1975. The city of Delhi was resting after witnessing another day of intense political activity. But this night, the streets of Delhi were witnessing another strange kind of activity. Police cars in hundreds were moving purposively in search of their prey. A plan which had been hatched by Mrs Gandhi to hold on to power was being put into effect. About twenty-eight years ago while the world slept, India had awakened to freedom. This fateful night, free India was sleeping in oblivion as the country was being transformed from a working democracy into a police state.

JP was asleep at the Gandhi Peace Foundation after an exhausting day when the midnight callers came. He was shaken from his sleep and told that the government found his freedom prejudicial to the security of the State and that he was being detained under MISA.[1] Before he was taken away, JP made one last comment. Obviously referring to Mrs Gandhi, he said, 'Vinash kale vipreet buddhi' (in the face of destruction reason deserts).

Meanwhile, other Opposition leaders were also being roused from their sleep to be surprised in the same way. The midnight operation was not confined to Delhi. In a superbly coordinated and executed plan, the police swooped down on almost all the Opposition leaders all over the country. While Morarji Desai, Charan Singh, Raj Narain, Piloo Mody and Ashok Mehta, etc., were 'picked up' in Delhi, L.K. Advani, Atal Behari Vajpayee, Shyam Nandan Mishra, Madhu

---

[1] The Maintenance of Internal Security Act was enacted in 1971, mainly to nab smugglers and foreign exchange racketeers. It gave government power to arrest people without trial for a limited period, if any act prejudicial to the security of the State was apprehended from them.

Dandawate, etc., were picked up in Bangalore. Others were arrested in cities where they happened to be that night.

The next morning Mrs Gandhi came on air to inform the people that the President had declared an Emergency to thwart the Opposition move to imperil the country's security. The news of the Emergency and the arrests stunned the nation but there were no signs of public protest. What had happened was so unexpected that fear of the unknown had gripped the hearts of the people.

There were, however, some isolated signs of protest. At about 10 a.m. the same day, Palkhivala issued a press note saying that he was withdrawing from Mrs Gandhi's case, because he was horrified by the arrests of JP and other Opposition leaders.

THE STING OF THE CENSOR

Meanwhile, the arrests of other Opposition leaders were continuing, and the news of that was coming on the ticker tapes of all the news networks. At 1 p.m. came the order of the Press Censorship and with that the teleprinters stopped. All newspapers and news networks were ordered to have their material examined by the Censor before publication.

However, even under these conditions, some newspapers managed to show their resentment. The Delhi edition of the *Hindustan Times* and the Bombay edition of the *Indian Express* carried blank editorials which perhaps because of their conspicuousness, spoke volumes. The Bombay edition of the *Times of India* managed to insert a small, subtle news item in the obituary column to evade the eyes of the censor. The obituary said, 'Died, D.E.M. OCRACY, mother of Freedom, and daughter of L.I. Berty, on 26 June 1975.'

The international press, however, which was not subject to any censorship, reacted very sharply to the events in India. The *Times*, London, labelled the clamp-down as a coup d'etat by Mrs Gandhi and said that the 'coup seems to have been planned when Mrs Gandhi's own power seems to be threatened and its first objective was to defend that power, whatever measures were necessary'. *The Economist* in an article entitled 'Empress turns Imperious' commented that with the Emergency, Mrs Gandhi had 'broken all the rules which India remarkably has adhered to in 28 years of democracy'.

Commenting on the events in India, *Newsweek* magazine said, 'By her actions, Mrs Gandhi had served harsh notice that if it came to a choice between the rule of law and the rule of Indira Gandhi, the law quite likely would lose.'

However, it was not all criticism for Mrs Gandhi. The Soviet government organ *Izvestia* called Mrs Gandhi's action 'a blow to the rightist plot'.

PLUGGING THE LOOPHOLES

The next day, the President issued an order suspending the right of citizens to move to courts to enforce the fundamental rights given by Articles 14, 19 and 22. Article 14 grants the right of equality. Article 19 grants the rights of speech, movement, trade, etc. Article 21 deals with the rights of life and liberty, while Article 22 provides the right of being communicated the grounds of detention. The rights were suspended under Article 359 of the Constitution which is the main power which accrues to the government during the Emergency. Article 19 was already under automatic suspension because of the Emergency (due to external aggression) already in force since the Bangladesh War of 1971. (Article 358 provides that Article 19 will come under automatic suspension, as soon as a proclamation of Emergency is issued.)

It is interesting to note here that the proclamation of Emergency of 25 June was an exercise in futility. This is because the earlier proclamation (due to external aggression) had not been revoked. Thus from 25 June 1975, there were two Emergencies in operation. The only difference between these was a matter of words. While the first was due to a threat of external aggression, the second was due to a threat of internal disturbances. Thus, no further powers accrued to the government by virtue of the proclamation of 25 June. All that had been done could very well have been done without a second proclamation of Emergency. The proclamation of 25 June seems to have been a part of the shock tactics employed by Mrs Gandhi to overawe and subdue any opposition in one stroke.

THE CASE IS ADJOURNED

The Supreme Court reopened after its vacation on 14 July. Mrs Gandhi's appeal was listed before the Chief Justice's court that day. Appearing on behalf of Narain, Bhushan sought an adjournment of the case for four weeks on the ground that he was busy in the Back

Bay reclamation case in Bombay which was likely to last for another month. Although this was indeed true, the real reason why he sought an adjournment was that he did not want to argue this case in the atmosphere of crippling fear which was prevailing in the country at that time. Bhushan reasoned that the judges would not be unaffected by it. He believed that the fear would decrease after some time when the situation crystallized further. Meanwhile, due to Palkhivala's exit from the case, Mrs Gandhi had decided to engage the Advocate-General of Haryana, Jagannath Kaushal, to argue the case in the Supreme Court. Kaushal vehemently opposed Bhushan's plea for adjournment. He said that the extraordinary nature of the case demanded that it be disposed of as expeditiously as possible. The Chief Justice, however, accepted Bhushan's plea, and the case was adjourned for four weeks.

The Monsoon Session of Parliament was scheduled to begin from 21 July. As some petitions challenging the proclamation of Emergency on the ground that it was malafide were about to be filed in some High Courts, the Union Cabinet met on 20 July and decided to make an amendment in Article 352. In this article, the satisfaction of the President regarding the proclamation of Emergency was sought to be made non-justiciable. This meant that the judiciary could no longer go into the question of whether the President was really satisfied about the need for the Emergency.

In the Monsoon Session of Parliament, the question hour was suspended. Although Parliament is competent to regulate its own procedure, the suspension of the question hour is highly unusual. Now, for the first time since the proclamation of Emergency, Jagjivan Ram came out openly in support of it. Speaking at the debate on it, Ram said, 'The Opposition wanted to subvert democracy. Mrs Gandhi is known for taking the right action at the right time.'

The Opposition MPs who had not been detained spoke out courageously against the Emergency. They exhorted the Congress MPs to stand up against the tyranny of Mrs Gandhi. But their exhortations were of no avail as the fear was too strong. When the Emergency proclamation came up for voting, there was thunderous approval by the Congress MPs. It was approved by the Rajya Sabha on 22 July by a vote of 136 to 33. The Lok Sabha put its stamp of approval the next day by a vote of 336 to 59.

The Opposition saw that their participation in Parliament was unlikely to achieve much as the rubber-stamp Congress majority

was going to steamroll any legislation that Mrs Gandhi thought fit
to introduce. So they decided to boycott the session. They walked
out before the constitutional amendment making the Emergency
non-justiciable was introduced and did not participate during the
remaining session.

Thus the Thirty-eighth Constitution Amendment, making the
Emergency non-justiciable, was passed almost unanimously by both
houses. It got the Presidential assent on 1 August.

The Supreme Court's refusal to expedite the appeal on the plea
of Kaushal had clearly worried Mrs Gandhi. The consequences of an
adverse decision by the Supreme Court could have been disastrous.
According to Bhushan, the only way in which she could have remained
in office in the event of an adverse Supreme Court decision was by
getting her disqualification removed by the Election Commission,
which had the power to do so under the election law; and then getting
the President to nominate her to the Rajya Sabha. She, however,
would have had to resign the moment the Supreme Court announced
its verdict and then there was no reason why the Election Commission
should have accommodated her. It was probably this sombre thought
that prompted the ensuring spate of panicky legislation.

THE BOMBSHELL

On 4 August, the law minister, Gokhale, exploded a bombshell in
Parliament. He introduced an Election Laws (Amendment) Bill
which sought to amend retrospectively all the corrupt practices on
which Mrs Gandhi's election had been challenged. The amendment
not only took care of the issues on which she was convicted by the
Allahabad High Court, but also most of the issues on which she was
exonerated by the court and on which a cross-appeal had been filed
by Raj Narain.

Mrs Gandhi had been convicted on two charges: (1) That she had
procured the assistance of the District Magistrate and Superintendent
of Police by getting rostrums constructed and loudspeakers installed
for her election meetings and (2) That she had procured the assistance
of Yashpal Kapoor while he was still a gazetted officer in the service
of the government. The amendment[2] now provided that 'any

---

[2] See Appendix 7 for text of amendment.

assistance, rendered to any candidate, by a government officer, in the discharge or purported discharge of his official duty, would not be deemed to be assistance for the furtherance of the prospects of that candidate's election'. This took care of the issue of rostrums, and also the issue of Air Force helicopters and planes, which was the subject matter of the cross-appeal.

The amendment also provided that the date of appointment or resignation of a government servant would be taken to be the date mentioned in the official gazette. This took care of the issue of Yashpal Kapoor. An amendment was also made in the definition of a candidate in the Act. It was now provided that a 'candidate' means 'a person, who has been, or claims to have been duly nominated as a candidate in any election'. The result of this amendment was that since Mrs Gandhi had only been nominated as a candidate from 1 February, she could not have committed any corrupt practice before this date. Yashpal Kapoor's resignation in any case became effective on 25 January. So this issue was doubly covered. The amendment also provided that no symbol allotted by the Election Commission to a candidate would be deemed to be a religious symbol, thus taking care of the issue of symbols. The only remaining issue, that of expenses, was already covered by the 1974 amendment which provided that any expenses incurred or authorized by a political party, etc. would not be treated as the candidate's election expenses. This Bill, however, also provided that expenditure incurred by government officers on a candidate's election in the performance of their 'official duties' would not be treated as the candidate's election expense.

The amendment did not stop at this. It also made a change regarding the Election Commission's power of removing the disqualification incurred by a candidate for the commission of a corrupt practice. Instead of the Election Commission, which till then had the power to reduce or remove any such disqualification, the power was now vested with the President. The disqualification now did not flow as a direct consequence of being found guilty by the courts. It was now provided that the case of each person found guilty would be referred to the President who could impose whatever period of disqualification he deemed fit.

Thus all loopholes were plugged. And it was not as if these amendments made in the R.P. Act were part of the general overhauling

of the Act, which could arguably be said to have become outdated.
Even this subtlety could not be granted to Gokhale. The amendments
made were only of those corrupt practices which were in issue in
Mrs Gandhi's case. No one could argue that these amendments
were not being made to influence the decision in Mrs Gandhi's case.
Gokhale, in his speech in Parliament, did not even attempt to do
so. Addressing his colleagues in the Congress, he told them not to
be apologetic about these amendments. He said that this was being
done to protect an institution which was pivotal to the very functioning
of democracy.

As members of the Opposition parties were not present in the
House, the Bill was passed in the Lok Sabha on 5 August by an
overwhelming majority. The next day it was approved by the Rajya
Sabha and received the Presidential assent.

Since this amendment left no loopholes, one should have thought
that this would satisfy Mrs Gandhi. But it appears that she was not
easily satisfied.

'Overkill'

On 7 August, another bombshell was exploded by Gokhale by
introducing a constitutional amendment Bill in Parliament. The
constitutional amendment was slightly more general than the election
laws amendment as it also related to the elections of the President,
Vice President and the Speaker, apart from the election of the Prime
Minister. In the amendment[3] it was provided,

> any dispute, arising out of the election of the President, Vice-
> President, Speaker and the Prime Minister, would only be gone
> into by a forum constituted by a special law made by Parliament.
> Parliament could also make special laws relating to the elections
> of these dignitaries and those laws could not be challenged in
> any court of the country.

These provisions, however, only related to future elections. There was
a special provision for elections which had already taken place, and in

---

[3] The text of the amendment is given in Appendix 8.

which an order had already been pronounced by a court. This section provided,

> no law made by Parliament, before the commencement of the
> Constitution (Thirty-ninth Amendment) Act, 1975, insofar as
> it relates to election petitions, and matters connected therewith,
> shall apply, or shall be deemed ever to have applied to, or in
> relation to the election of any such person, as is referred to
> in Clause (1) (Prime Minister or Speaker), to either House
> of Parliament, and such election shall not be deemed to be
> void, or ever to have become void, on the ground on which
> such election could be declared to be void, or has before such
> commencement been declared to be void under any such law,
> and notwithstanding any order made by any court before such
> commencement declaring such election to be void, such election
> shall continue to be valid in all respects, and any such order or
> any finding on which such order is based shall be and shall be
> deemed always to have been void and of no effect.

The election of Mrs Gandhi which came under this section was thus declared to be valid and the High Court judgment was declared to be void.

Piloting the Bill, Gokhale sought justification for it on the ground that 'since the Prime Minister had not only been elected by a vast majority but is also recognized throughout the length and breadth of the country as the undisputed leader, she should not be subjected to a process of judicial scrutiny where the election could be set aside even on the flimsiest ground'. The only opposition to this amendment came from Mohan Dharia, who said, 'This amendment is a surrender of parliamentary democracy to the coming dictatorship.' Dharia, however, abstained from voting, and the amendment was passed unanimously by the Lok Sabha. The next day, the Congress members in the Rajya Sabha too gave unanimous approval to the amendment. The amendment was ratified by seventeen states[4] on 9 August and received the Presidential assent on the night of 10 August. This incidentally is the record time for the passing of any

---

[4] A constitutional amendment, after being passed by a two-thirds majority of both Houses of Parliament, has to be ratified by half the state legislatures.

constitutional amendment in India. Only three days had elapsed between the introduction of the amendment in Parliament and the Presidential assent.

The Indian press, which was under strict censorship, could hardly carry the details of the amendments and their effect on Mrs Gandhi's case, let alone comment on them. Comment was, however, forthcoming from the international news media. *Newsweek*, in an article titled 'Law? What Law?', painted a ridiculous picture of Mrs Gandhi. The article said, 'What to do if convicted of breaking the law? Simple. Just change the law, retrospectively. That at least was Indira Gandhi's handy solution last week as she had her rubber-stamp Congress Party majority in Parliament retrospectively legalize the electioneering acts for which she had been convicted.' *Newsweek* also ridiculed the Congress legislators, who, it said, 'laughed and shouted and thumped their desks as India slid further towards totalitarian rule'. *Time* called the amendments, 'The harshest step towards authoritarianism since original clamp down', and labelled the constitutional amendment, 'A ludicrous case of overkill'. 9 August was the last date for the sitting of Parliament. Even this day was not to pass without its surprises. Gokhale, on this date, introduced yet another constitutional amendment Bill in the Rajya Sabha. This amendment gave lifelong criminal immunity to the President, Governors and the Prime Minister for all acts done before assumption of office and during their tenure of office. This meant that a person committing the most heinous crime could escape the rigours of the Penal Code by becoming a Governor even for a day. The Constitution did provide a certain immunity to the President and Governors but this was only during their term of office and applied only to acts done in the discharge of their official duties. This constitutional amendment is without parallel in the history of civilized jurisprudence. One had to strain one's credulity to the limit in order to believe it. One could believe such a thing happening in Idi Amin's country but not in India.

The unanimous approval of this amendment by the Rajya Sabha is indeed an index of the fear which dominated the rank and file of the Congress party. The Congress legislators had lost their voices. They had become dummies, who could be used and manipulated by Mrs Gandhi in any way she chose. They would give their stamp of approval to anything which Mrs Gandhi placed before them.

Since Parliament adjourned the same day, this amendment could not be tabled before the Lok Sabha and, therefore, remained an unpassed Bill. It was, subsequently, never brought before the Lok Sabha, perhaps because of the widespread criticism it generated and the political capital which the Opposition made from it.

Bhushan made his comment on this amendment while speaking in a symposium on constitutional amendments a few months later. He said that for his part he could not see how this amendment could benefit the common people in any way, 'Unless, of course, these dignitaries become modern-day Robin Hoods, who will steal money from the rich and distribute it to the poor. In that case, certainly, the criminal immunity given to these people would be justified. But then I must warn you, my friends, to keep your hands in your pockets, whenever any of these people pass your way.'

The Supreme Court was scheduled to assemble to hear Mrs Gandhi's appeal on 11 August. The Chief Justice, A.N. Ray, had announced the constitution of the Bench which would hear this case. They would be the five seniormost judges of the Supreme Court. Apart from the Chief Justice, they were Justices Khanna, Mathew, Beg and Chandrachud. The amendments, though, had thrown the future of the case into serious doubt. When the newspapers announced on the appointed day that the court would be sitting to hear Mrs Gandhi's appeal, people wondered why this was at all necessary. In their eyes, the constitutional amendment had disposed of the case, and the Supreme Court's sitting seemed to be an exercise in futility.

On the evening of 10 August, Raj Narain's lawyers held a conference to decide what was to be done. There were some suggestions that they withdraw from the case in protest. Bhushan, however, could see no purpose being served by this. It was clear that all that could be done now was to attack the validity of the amendments. It appeared that unless the validity of the constitutional amendments was successfully impugned, the Supreme Court could not proceed with the case. Although Bhushan was clear about the grounds on which he would impugn the validity of the amendments, he decided to ask for another adjournment. Since an atmosphere of helplessness had been generated in the country by the introduction of these amendments, he reasoned that the court was extremely unlikely to go beyond a summary disposal of the case in Mrs Gandhi's favour. He had reasoned that a few days would be needed for it to sink in the minds of the people that all was not over with the case and that the amendments could indeed be declared invalid by the Supreme Court. This would raise the hopes of the people which would, in turn, boost the morale of the Supreme Court.

THE AMENDMENTS ARE CHALLENGED

It was 11 August, the date fixed for hearing by the Supreme Court of Mrs Gandhi's appeal. Entry to the Chief Justice's court was restricted to pass-holders. Passes to lawyers could only be issued by the Secretary of the Bar Association and passes to outsiders were issued under the discretionary authority of the deputy registrar. These restrictions were unprecedented. All people going to that court had to pass through a metal detector and a security check. Some Indian newsmen were granted passes. Foreign newsmen, however, were denied passes on the spurious ground that the seats were not enough, although at least half the seats in the visitors' gallery went empty.

The judges entered the court punctually at 10.30 a.m. in the ceremonial order of their seniority—first, the Chief Justice, followed by Justices Khanna, Mathew, Beg and, finally, Justice Chandrachud.

Mrs Gandhi by this time had changed her lawyer yet again. While Kaushal was retained as an assisting counsel, the charge of arguing the appeal was given to Ashok Sen, who had been the law minister in Nehru's Cabinet. It is ironical that Sen had been 'dropped' from the Cabinet by Mrs Gandhi herself when she became the Prime Minister.

As it was Mrs Gandhi's appeal, Sen was first called upon to make his submissions. In the light of the amendments, Sen's submissions were necessarily brief. He submitted that Mrs Gandhi had been convicted by the High Court on extremely technical grounds. Seeking justification for the amendments, Sen said that the case had become an extremely controversial one in which the judiciary had become dangerously embroiled. It was, therefore, to avoid embarrassment to the judiciary, that the Parliament had taken the responsibility on its own shoulders and clarified the issue by amending the Representation of the People Act. Sen read out the relevant portions of the amendments and submitted that it removed the whole basis on which Mrs Gandhi had been found guilty. Sen then also read out the relevant clause of the constitutional amendment which declared the election of the Prime

Minister valid and pleaded that the case be disposed of according to the mandate of the constitutional amendment.

It was now Bhushan's turn to make his submissions. He told the court that he was left with no option but to challenge the constitutional validity of the Thirty-ninth Amendment. Bhushan told the court that in Kesavananda Bharati's case, the thirteen-member Bench had laid down that 'no constitutional amendment could violate the basic features of the Constitution'. He would be relying on the dictum of that case in his attack on the amendments.

Incidentally, these were the last five judges left in the Supreme Court who had been parties to the decision in the fundamental rights case of Kesavananda Bharati. Out of these, only Justice Khanna was a party to the majority decision which laid down that Parliament was incompetent to destroy the basic structure of the Constitution, even by a constitutional amendment. The other four judges had held that the Parliament's amending powers were plenary.

Bhushan then told the court that since a copy of the gazetted amendment had only been made available that very morning, he had not had enough time to study the ramifications of the amendments and thus frame a proper attack on them. He said that he would, therefore, be grateful if the court adjourned the case for two weeks.

The Chief Justice seemed displeased. He said, 'We want to furnish the case as expeditiously as possible. Why don't you start your arguments straightaway?'

Bhushan: If your Lordships insist, I could start my arguments straightaway, but after two weeks I would be in a much better position to assist you. I can, however, at this moment indicate the line of attack which I will take.

Justice Khanna: Are you going to attack the election law amendment too?

Bhushan: Yes.

The Attorney-General at this point interjected to say that the decision in Kesavananda's case was too vague and he would like a review of the case to clarify the matter.[5]

Justice Mathew: But which Bench, according to you, should do it? (Since the Kesavananda case had been decided by thirteen judges, it could be reviewed only by a Bench of at least thirteen judges.)

---

[5] For the review of Kesavananda Bharati's case, see Appendix 3.

The Attorney-General could not give a categorical reply to this.

Bhushan then briefly indicated the line of attack that he would take. He stated that his first ground of attack would be that the amendment went against the principle of Separation of Powers which was a basic feature of the Constitution. 'Since the amendment eliminates judicial review in the case of the election dispute of the Prime Minister, it goes against Article 136 of the Constitution which is the ultimate power of the judiciary.'

The second ground of attack of Bhushan was that the amendment had the effect of destroying democracy which, he said, was also a basic feature of the Constitution. 'It is not a question of one or two elections, but a matter of principle. If the Parliament can remove one election from the court's jurisdiction, it could also remove all. If this was granted to the Parliament, this would certainly have the effect of destroying democracy.'

The third ground on which he would be challenging the amendment, Bhushan said, was that it destroyed equality, which was surely a basic feature of a Republican Constitution. He said, 'Insofar as it places only the election of the Prime Minister beyond judicial review, it discriminates against other people solely on the ground that the person holds a high office.'

The Chief Justice then held consultations with the other judges for a few minutes, and announced that the case would be adjourned for two weeks, i.e., to 25 August. He directed the parties to exchange their written submissions by that date. With this, the court adjourned.

THE IRE OF THE BAR

The Supreme Court Bar was angered at the indignities to which it had been subjected on 11 August. Firstly, they had to get passes to enter the Chief Justice's courtroom, and then they had to go through a stringent personal security check. The Bar Association met some days later and demanded that the Chief Justice withdraw these restrictions. Ashok Sen, Mrs Gandhi's counsel, who was the president of the Association, met the Chief Justice and communicated this demand to him. The Chief Justice said that he would be willing to withdraw the restrictions if he (Ashok Sen) took personal responsibility for the good conduct of the lawyers. Sen was willing, but the lawyers were not. 'We are not children,' they said, 'that someone has to guarantee our safe conduct.'

On 22 August, the Bar Association met again and passed a resolution that no member of the Association should participate in, or witness the proceedings in Mrs Gandhi's case because of the restrictions. The resolution threatened that disciplinary action would be taken against any lawyer violating the resolution.

On 23 August, Raj Narain's lawyers went to Tihar Jail to consult him. They drafted a petition addressed to the Supreme Court which was signed by Raj Narain. The petition referred to the Bar Association resolution, stating that since all of Raj Narain's lawyers were members of the Association, they would not be able to argue before the court. It was, therefore, prayed that either the Chief Justice withdraw the restrictions, or that the court permit Raj Narain himself to argue his own case in person.

This petition was presented to the Deputy Registrar the same afternoon. Although it was Saturday and the court was not sitting, the petition was immediately transmitted to the Chief Justice. The Chief Justice reacted instantly. At 8 p.m., the Chief Justice told the Registrar to announce that all restrictions on entry for the lawyers were withdrawn. Pass requirements would, however, remain for visitors.

The next day being Sunday, the Bar Association could not meet to withdraw their resolution. A meeting was scheduled for 1 p.m. on Monday, 25 August. It was expected that the formality of withdrawing the resolution would be completed in that meeting.

4

VALIDITY OF
THE CONSTITUTIONAL AMENDMENT

12

'It Destroys Democracy'

When the Supreme Court Bench assembled on 25 August at 10.30 a.m., Raj Narain was represented only by J.P. Goyal, while all the lawyers of the other side were present. This was so because the Bar Association's resolution that no lawyer should attend the Chief Justice's court had not yet been withdrawn, as they had not had time to meet after the concession of their demands. Bhushan had, therefore, decided not to go to court and Goyal was to plead for an adjournment, pending the withdrawal of the Bar resolution. He did so when called upon to argue.

The Chief Justice, being in no mood to concede any further demands in this case, said that he would like to proceed with the case immediately. This provoked Goyal to give vent to his anger. He exclaimed loudly: 'How can we proceed? Your Lordship, the Chief Justice, will have to give an explanation as to why all the members of the Bar were searched on 11 August. Even the lady lawyers were not spared. However, Mulla, a counsel of Mrs Gandhi, was not searched. The Chief Justice will have to give an explanation for this discrimination.'

Chief Justice: Behave yourself, Mr Goyal.

Attorney-General: That will be a contempt of court.

Goyal (violently): All right, punish me! Send me to jail. I am ready to face the consequences. But how can we proceed till the Bar Association resolution is withdrawn.

The Chief Justice was subdued. He explained, 'You see it is such a difficult case for us. All of you should help us in our duty.' At this juncture, Ashok Sen informed the court that the Bar Association meeting was scheduled to take place at 1 p.m. He said that he would inform the court of the decision arrived at after lunch and said that it would be convenient if the case was adjourned till then. The Chief Justice consulted his brother judges and agreed to adjourn the case till lunch.

The Bar Association met at 1 p.m., and in view of the concession of their demand, unanimously agreed to withdraw their resolution.

After lunch, at 2 p.m., all the lawyers of both sides trooped into the courtroom. The judges arrived and the stage was finally set for the constitutional battle to begin.

The counsel for the appellant, Sen, was called upon first to make his submissions. Giving a brief history of the case, he told the court that the appellant was found guilty of two corrupt practices by the High Court. He said, 'These two charges were very technical in nature and the legislature in its wisdom retrospectively amended the election law which took care of them. After that, however, the Thirty-ninth Constitutional Amendment was passed by Parliament, which constitutionally disposed of the case. Seeing that the case had raised a lot of unhealthy controversy, the constituent body decided to take the responsibility on its own shoulders to avoid embarrassment to the judiciary.' Sen then read out the provisions of the constitutional amendment and ended with the plea that the appeal be disposed of according to the mandate of the amendment.

BHUSHAN'S OPENING ARGUMENTS

It was Bhushan's turn now. Getting to his feet, he launched a strong attack on Sen's rationale for justifying the constitutional amendment, saying that it was the function of the judiciary to deal with cases, however complicated they may be. 'The constituent body allows the judiciary to handle all sorts of election petitions, but when the Prime Minister's election is set aside, it suddenly feels that this case is too complex for the judiciary.'

Coming to the validity of the Thirty-ninth Amendment, Counsel summarized his three main grounds of attack on the Amendment Act: (1) That it was not an amendment of the Constitution at all. (2) That if it could be called an amendment at all, it destroyed several basic features of the Constitution. (3) That it was passed in an illegal session of Parliament and was hence infructuous.

The mention of the third ground caused a stir in the court as it was indeed an unexpected and sensational argument. In fact, this argument had occurred to Bhushan only a few days earlier. Although not very optimistic about it being accepted, he had decided to include it as one of the grounds of challenge in order to add to the psychological pressure on the judges. Briefly explaining his arguments on the third ground, Bhushan said that since a large number of Members of Parliament were illegally detained, all the proceedings of the Monsoon Session of Parliament became illegal and void. This amendment, since it was passed in that session, was also void, he submitted.

Attorney-General (interjecting): I wonder whether the court can go into the question of the legality of the detentions without a writ of habeas corpus.

Justice Mathew: Can we have a habeas corpus in these circumstances?

Bhushan: I am not asking for the release of the detenus. But the legality of the Session of Parliament will have to be determined.

Chief Justice: We shall have to consider whether we can go into that or not. In any case that question will arise only after your first two points are decided.

Counsel then referred to his second ground of attack, that the amendment destroyed several basic features of the Constitution. He briefly explained what the basic structure theory meant. He said that the doctrine propounded in Kesavananda Bharati's case was that Parliament could not amend the Constitution so as to destroy its identity. Illustrating this, Counsel explained: 'Nowadays we hear a lot about transplants of various organs of the body. Suppose all the organs of a person's body were transplanted and only a leg or a hand remained, could one say that it is still the same person. Suppose every part of my friend, Mr Goyal's body was to be transplanted and only his thumb remained, would his identity remain the same? Could his wife still recognize him?'

Chief Justice (relieving his ire at Mr Goyal): Mr Bhushan, do you want his heart transplanted first or his brain?

Counsel: Everything, my Lord; his heart, his brain, his legs, his hands. Only the thumb remains. (Everyone, particularly the Chief Justice was enjoying himself.) It is not the bulk of the transplanted part which matters. Suppose a person's brain were transplanted. A brain weighs . . .

Chief Justice: 64 ounces.

Counsel: So if these 64 ounces of a person's body were removed, would his identity remain the same?

Amendment Is Exercise of Judicial Power

Bhushan then proceeded to elaborate on his initial submissions. He said that in order to determine the validity of the amendment, it would be necessary to find out exactly what had been done by it. He read out the entire text of the Thirty-ninth Amendment and submitted that it was only clauses 4(4) and 4(5), which were relevant. They read:

> 4(4) No law made by Parliament before the commencement of the Constitution (Thirty-ninth Amendment) Act, 1975, insofar as it relates to election petitions and members connected therewith, shall apply or shall be deemed ever to have applied to or in relation to the election of any such person as is referred to in clause (1) to either House of Parliament and such election shall not be deemed to be void or ever to have become void on any ground on which such election could be declared to be void or has, before the commencement, been declared to be void under any such law and notwithstanding any order made by any court, before such commencement, declaring such election to be void, such election shall continue to be valid in all respects and any such order and any finding on which such order is based shall be and shall be deemed always to have been void and of no effect.
>
> 4(5) Any appeal or cross-appeal against any such order of any court as is referred to in clause (4) pending immediately before the commencement of the Constitution (Thirty-ninth Amendment) Act, 1975, before the Supreme Court shall be disposed of in conformity with the provisions of clause (4).

At this point, Justice Khanna asked Ashok Sen whether he agreed that it was only clauses 4(4) and 4(5) which were relevant in the present case. Sen agreed.

Reading out clause 4(4) very carefully, Bhushan emphasized the words 'and such election . . . of no effect', submitting that this clause clearly declared the election to be valid and the High Court judgment void, and namely an arbitrary exercise of judicial power.

Justice Khanna: Suppose clause (4) had only said, 'No law made by Parliament before the commencement of this Act insofar as it relates to election petitions and matters connected therewith, shall apply or shall be deemed ever to have applied to or in relation to the election of any such person as is referred to in clause (1) to either House of Parliament', and stopped there, would not the election be, ipso facto, valid?

Counsel: No, the High Court judgment would stand, unless it was declared to be void and the election would continue to be void unless it was declared to be valid.

'Judicial Power Not with Parliament'

Bhushan's next contention was that judicial power could not be exercised by Parliament in the guise of a constitutional amendment. 'The power conferred by Article 368 to Parliament is of amending the Constitution. Parliament can only exercise that power which is expressly conferred to it and no other power. The Constitution lays down the organizational structure of government and distributes the sovereign power among the various organs. Thus an amendment of the Constitution would be one which alters the structure of the government or redistributes power among the various organs of government.'

Attorney-General (interjecting): This argument was not raised in Kesavananda Bharati's case and cannot be raised now.

Bhushan: This point had never arisen in any of the previous cases on constitutional amendment, either in Shankari Prasad, Sajjan Singh, Golak Nath or Kesavananda Bharati. It is arising for the first time now because it is the first time that judicial power is being exercised in the guise of a constitutional amendment.

Counsel proceeded to cite some definitions of the Constitution which made it clear that a Constitution dealt with the structure and organization of the government. 'Such being the character of a Constitution, an amendment to it can only redefine the organization of government and the distribution of power therein. Clause 4(4) doing no such thing cannot be said to be an amendment of the Constitution.'

Justice Mathew: Has any constitutional amendment in the United States ever set aside a judicial decision?

Counsel: As far as I am aware, none.

Justice Mathew: Can Parliament amend the Constitution and give to itself judicial powers?

Counsel: It can, but first it must amend the Constitution to make itself a judicial organ. In that case, Parliament would itself become a judicial organ.

Justice Mathew: The British can pass a Bill of Attainder. This is a judicial function. What is the limitation on the plenary constituent power of Parliament to perform a judicial function?

Counsel: The position is different in Britain due to historical and other reasons. There being no written Constitution, the British Parliament is sovereign. But since a written Constitution defines the limits of the powers of the Indian Parliament, it can only exercise its powers within those bounds.

Justice Mathew: Can the constituent power not extend to executive, legislative and judicial powers which are all powers granted by the Constitution?

Counsel: The power of amending the Constitution cannot comprehend an executive or judicial power, since they are powers of a radically different nature. The constituent body being a delegated authority can only exercise the power which has been delegated to it, which is of amending the Constitution.

Counsel then referred to a Ceylon case[1] in which it was held that the power of amending the Constitution was a legislative power. He argued that since the amendment decided merely one particular case, it was the exercise of purely judicial power and the ultra vires Article 368 of the Constitution.

Amendment Destroys the Basic Structure

Moving to his next point, Bhushan argued that even if clause 4(4) could be regarded as an exercise of constituent power, it destroyed several basic features of the Constitution. He read out excerpts from the judgment of the seven majority judges in the Kesavananda Bharati case to establish the proposition that Parliament cannot in exercise of its amending power abrogate or destroy the basic structure or institutional framework of the Constitution. He contended that once this proposition is established, there would be no escape from its compulsion by saying that the concept of basic features was too vague to be understood.

---

[1] [1964] 2 All ER 785, *Bribery Commissioner v. Ranasingha*.

Justice Beg: Mr Bhushan, this concept of basic features does seem very vague and slippery. I feel that all the provisions of the Constitution are equally essential.

Counsel: What in law is not vague or slippery? If everything was cut, dry and crystal clear, we need not have judges or four Lordships' eminence to apply the law. What about the doctrine that the essential powers of legislation cannot be delegated? What are the 'essential' powers of delegation? Is this not an equally vague doctrine? But it has been interpreted and applied by the court ever since our Constitution came into existence. In fact, Justice Mathew, who although did not agree with the basic structure theory, had said in his judgement:

> I am not dismayed by the suggestion that no yardstick is furnished to the court except the trained judicial perception, for finding the core or essence of a right, or essential features of the Constitution . . . Few Constitutional issues can be presented in black and white terms. What are essential features and non-essential features of the Constitution? Where does the core of a right and the periphery begin? These are not matters of icy certainty; but, for that reason, I am not persuaded to hold that they do not exist, or that they are too elusive for judicial perception. Most of the things in life that are worth talking about are matters of degree and the great judges are those who are most capable of discerning which of the gradations make genuine difference.

Counsel went on: 'What is the difficulty in discerning the basic features? Anyone who reads the Constitution can easily see that our Constitution is a thoroughly democratic Constitution where the rule of law is a recognized institution. One can also see that our Constitution is republican, recognizing the sacred principle of equality before law. Thus, it must be held that at least democracy, rule of law, and equality are basic features of our Constitution.'

Counsel then read out those parts of the judgments in the Kesavananda Bharati case where the basic features of the Constitution are indicated. All the judges had given illustrative and not exhaustive lists of the basic features. Most of them had held democracy and equality to be basic.

Bhushan told the court that he was relying on the following as the basic features of the Constitution:

1. Separation of powers between the legislature, executive and judiciary.
2. Democratic character of our polity.
3. Equality before the law and equal protection of the laws.
4. Rule of law and judicial review.
5. Political justice as enshrined in the Preamble of the Constitution.

Before Counsel could start his argument on how several basic features of the Constitution were destroyed by the amendment, Justice Khanna asked a few questions for clarification: (1) Whether election disputes must be settled by the courts of law, and not by any other body? (2) Whether the provision for election petitions is an essential feature of democracy? (3) If the election of the Prime Minister were to be decided by the Chief Justice, Speaker or Vice President, would the democratic set-up be affected?

Replying to the first question, Counsel said that election disputes could be decided by other bodies if overall supervision of the judiciary was retained by Article 136.[2] As regards the question of whether election petitions are necessary in a democracy, Counsel said that they would perhaps not be necessary if the conduct of elections was itself vested in a judicial body which inquired into the complaints during the election process itself. In reply to the third question, Counsel said, 'Why should only the Prime Minister's election be decided by a special forum? Such arbitrary discrimination, without any rationale, is clearly destructive of the sacred concept of equality.'

Justice Mathew: What about elections to the British House of Commons? Who adjudicates the election disputes there?

Niren De: The House itself does it.

Bhushan: The position in Britain may be different due to historical reasons. After gradual evolution, the Parliament there has become supreme. In India, Parliament is not sovereign. Therefore, we cannot compare the situation in Britain to that in India.

---

[2] Article 136 gives the Supreme Court the power to entertain special leave petitions against the decisions of all courts and tribunals.

Judicial Review Eliminated

Bhushan went on to submit that the first basic feature effected by the amendment was judicial review. 'This amendment makes serious inroads into the powers of the judiciary and is thus repugnant to the separation of power envisaged by the Constitution. One of the main functions of the judiciary in our country has been adjudicating election disputes. In our Parliamentary system, the party who wins the election and comes into power immediately gains control of two of the three wings of the government, namely, the executive and the legislative. The postulate of democracy is that the continuance of that party in power should depend on the continued support of the people. This can only be ensured by free and fair periodical elections. For the elections to be free and fair, it is necessary that some third party, which has no axe of its own to grind, be there to preserve the purity of elections. That is why the function of adjudicating election disputes has been entrusted to the judiciary. The Thirty-ninth Amendment, as it takes away the right of the judiciary to adjudicate election disputes relating to the Prime Minister, makes serious inroads into this power of the judiciary. It is not a matter of one election. It is a matter of principle. If the judiciary's power can be taken away for one election, it can very well be taken away for all elections.'

Democracy Destroyed

Proceeding to his next submission, Counsel said, 'Clause (4) arbitrarily declares the election of the Prime Minister valid. If such an arbitrary validation of election is possible, then democracy could well be demolished in the country. There are certain norms which have to be obeyed by all candidates. The logic is that an election procured by unfair means is not a fair election. The amendment declares that the Prime Minister's election shall continue to be valid even though she might have bribed voters, used undue influence, coerced her rival candidate!

'The other side says that the Prime Minister is very important. That is no answer, because there would be no end to important members of the ruling party who play an integral part in the lawmaking process of the country. Using unfair means they would not even have to get a majority of votes. Only the returning officers would have to declare them to be the returned candidates. No further argument is possible.'

Justice Beg: Could it not be that the unusual excitement and public controversy aroused by this case justified the exercise of this power of amendment?

Counsel: What is the unusual public controversy aroused by this case? It is only that some Opposition leaders were saying that Mrs Gandhi should step down as the Prime Minister till she was cleared by the Supreme Court. Moreover, if principles are sacrificed for expedients, then democracy is finished in the country.

Equality Denied

Counsel's next contention was that the amendment which provides that the election of the Prime Minister and Speaker shall be valid, was seriously repugnant to the principle of equality, which was a basic feature of the Constitution.

Justice Mathew: Equality is a concept which does not admit any easy definition. Instances could be cited where equal treatment might result in actual injustice. Indeed, justice and equality are not always compatible.

Counsel: I agree that equality is not an absolutely rigid concept and people could justifiably be treated unequally if they were placed in unequal situations. But there has to be a rational relation of the classification to the object sought to be achieved. I agree that the Prime Minister and the Speaker are not ordinary citizens. But this does not mean that unequal treatment in election matters is also justified for them. Why should their election not be open to challenge as everyone else's is? If they have committed corrupt practices, why should their election not be set aside, in the same way as an ordinary candidate's election is? In fact, being leaders of the country, there should be stricter standards for them, because if the leaders of the country do not set an example of fair play, then who will?

Justice Beg: Can merely an exception to the rule destroy a basic feature?

Counsel: Equality is a concept to which there would be no exception. Either we have equality or we do not. In fact, Justice Jaganmohan Reddy in his judgment in Kesavananda's case has clearly stated, 'Insofar as the abridgement of the right conferred by Article 14 (equality) is concerned, it would be ultra vires for the reason that a mere violation of this right amounts to taking away or damaging the right.'

No Rule of Law

Bhushan's next contention was that the Thirty-ninth Amendment completely destroyed the rule of law and eliminated judicial review, which were both essential features of the Constitution.

Justice Mathew: If Article 136 were repealed, would it lead to the destruction of a basic feature? (Article 136 provides for petitions of special leave to the Supreme Court against the decisions of all Judicial Tribunals.)

Counsel: Yes. Article 136 is the ultimate provision for overall supervision of the Supreme Court over judicial tribunals. Its repeal would certainly destroy the basic feature of judicial review.

Chief Justice: Can the Constitution be amended so as to exclude the jurisdiction of the Supreme Court in some matters?

Bhushan: Yes, it could. If the Supreme Court was over-burdened with work, some less important matters could be taken away from its jurisdiction and vested in some other body.

Justice Mathew: You are arguing that both judicial review and democracy are basic features. Don't you think that there is a certain inconsistency between the two? Parliament represents the will of the people and when the judiciary strikes down a legislation, don't you think that is acting against the will of the people?

Counsel: A Parliament elected by the people on a certain issue might not represent the will of the people on another issue. Since a referendum on every issue is impossible, therefore the people acting through the Constituent Assembly placed certain injunctions on the powers of Parliament. They provided that Parliament could only exercise its powers in a certain manner and created a judiciary to keep the Parliament in check. Therefore, when the judiciary strikes down a legislation, it is really giving effect to the will of the people.

Justice Khanna: You mean that the judiciary, when it strikes down a legislation, is giving effect to the will of the people as represented by the Constituent Assembly?

Counsel: Yes.

Justice Mathew: But Mr Bhushan, don't you think that the judiciary is an undemocratic institution, as some say, an oligarchic institution?

Counsel: All right, my Lord, we can call it an undemocratic institution, which is necessary for the preservation of democracy.

Continuing his submissions, Counsel said that he was frankly horrified at the manner in which the amendment gave a go-by to the rule of law ('no law shall apply to the election of the Prime Minister, and that the election would continue to be valid, no matter how it was procured').

MONSOON SESSION ILLEGAL

Coming to the third leg of his submissions, Bhushan argued that the Monsoon Session of Parliament in which the amendment was passed was illegal and that all business transacted in that session had hence become illegal and void.

He told the court that most of the Opposition leaders, who were Members of Parliament, were under detention without trial when the amendment was passed. They were not even supplied the grounds of their detention, which is a constitutional necessity under Article 22. Hence the detentions had become unconstitutional.

Counsel was asked by the court whether the detention could be declared illegal without a writ habeas corpus. He replied that he was not asking for the release of the detenues, but if he could prove that on the face of it detentions were unconstitutional, the court would have to decide whether or not the Parliament was legal.

Justice Mathew: If a statute was presented to the court duly gazetted, how could the court refuse to accept its validity?

Counsel: How do we know that it is really the Gazette of India and that what it enacts has been validly enacted in a proper session of Parliament?

Counsel quoted from a 1965 judgement of Justice Gajendragadkar.[3] He had observed, 'Article 212(1) seems to make it possible for a citizen to call in question in a proper court of law the validity of any proceeding in the legislative chamber if his case is that such proceeding suffers not from an irregularity of procedure, but from an illegality.' Amplifying his contention, Counsel said that here there was no irregularity of procedure, but illegality.

He went on: 'On 26 June, an emergency was proclaimed by the President on the advice of the government and a large number of Opposition leaders were detained under MISA. None of them were

---

[3] AIR 1965, SC 745, Ref. Powers and Immunities of State Legislature.

supplied the grounds of detention. On 27 June, the President, on the advice of the government, issued an order under Article 359 of the Constitution, suspending the rights of citizens to go to court for the enforcement of their fundamental rights.'

Counsel said that even though Article 22—which makes it mandatory for the government to supply the grounds of detention to a detenu—was suspended by a Presidential Order, the Article still remained in the Constitution. He quoted from the judgment of Justice Mathew in the Kesavananda Bharati case where he had said, 'A law is a law even if it is not enforceable in a court of law.' Thus Counsel argued that although Article 22 was not enforceable, it still remained the law, and the constitutional obligation of the Government for supplying the grounds of detention was not waived by the Presidential Order.

'I agree that if some members of Parliament are legally arrested, then they forfeit their right to attend the Parliament Session. But since here they were not legally arrested, their right remained and their not being given an opportunity to be present in the proceedings of Parliament clearly rendered the proceedings illegal.'

Justice Khanna: How many Members of Parliament have been arrested?

Counsel: I am not absolutely certain of that, but that would not make any difference to the illegality of the session. Even if one Member has been illegally prevented from attending the session, it would render the proceedings illegal.

With this, Bhushan concluded his arguments on the validity of the constitutional amendment, after arguing for about five days.

13

'PM Can Be above the Law'

There was no doubt that Bhushan's argument had a significant effect on the judges. The Mathew-Bhushan confrontation had been described as 'a Tartar meeting a Tartar'. The change in the Judge's attitude during the course of his argument was also visible to Bhushan. Since foreign newsmen were not allowed entry in the court, they came to Bhushan for briefing at the end of each day's arguments. And each day Bhushan was more convinced of the chances of the amendment being struck down.

THE ATTORNEY-GENERAL'S ARGUMENTS

The other side was shaken by the effect of Bhushan's arguments. Since the validity of a constitutional amendment was in question, the Attorney-General, Niren De, and the Solicitor-General, Lal Narain Sinha, were also defending on behalf of the Union government. The Attorney-General having right of precedence was the first to argue in defence of the amendment. In order to destroy the effect of Bhushan's arguments, De started his arguments with great gusto. He began, 'For five days your Lordships have heard Shanti Bhushan impugn the validity of the Thirty-ninth Constitutional Amendment. On a petty peddling issue, a case is being made out that the Thirty-ninth Amendment destroys the basic structure of our Constitution. In fact, deciding election disputes had always been a privilege of the legislature, not only in our country but in almost all democratic countries. Therefore, how can we call Judicial Review of election disputes a feature of the Constitution, let alone a basic feature. Even in the British system where this power has been delegated to the judiciary, the Parliament retains overall supervision and can always interfere when it wants to.'

Continuing, the Attorney-General raised a preliminary objection against Bhushan's argument that constituent power did not embrace judicial power. He said that this argument was not raised in Kesavananda Bharati's case and hence could not be raised then. 'In Kesavananda's case, the scope and limit of constituent power were examined from every angle, and the only conclusion which emerged was that you cannot destroy the basic structure of the Constitution. What is inserted in the Constitution is solely for the constituent body to decide and the court cannot pronounce upon it. The judiciary is also a creature of the Constitution, and being so, it cannot say that it does not like a particular provision of the Constitution. As soon as an Article is incorporated in the Constitution, it becomes part of it and the judiciary being a creature of the Constitution has to give effect to it.'

Justice Khanna: The judiciary has to see whether the Parliament has exercised its power within the limits laid down by the Constitution. The argument of the other side is that constitutional law must also come within the concept of law, and the problem before us is whether a law can relate to an individual case.

Counsel: I submit that it can.

At this point, Justice Mathew quoted from Blackstone's *Commentaries on the Laws of England* in which it was stated,

> Therefore a particular Act of the Legislature to confiscate the goods of Titus or to attaint him of high treason, does not enter into the idea of a municipal law: for the operation of this Act is spent on Titus only and has no relation to the community in general: it is rather a sentence than a law.

De explained that this dealt only with the ordinary lawmaking powers of the government. The constituent power stood on a different plane. It was all-embracing and could enact a law for a particular person too. He proceeded to read out excerpts from the judgments of the various judges in the Kesavananda Bharati case to establish his proposition that the subject matter was not a limitation on the constituent power. He particularly emphasized the portions of Justice Mathew's judgment where he had observed:

> In other words, irrespective of the subject-matter, the moment a provision becomes validity embodied in the Constitution, it

acquires a validity of its own, which is beyond challenge, and the question whether it relates to constitutional law with reference to the subject matter is wholly irrelevant.

These judgments, Counsel contended, hardly left any room for doubt that the subject-matter was not considered a limitation on the amending power. The Parliament in exercise of its amending power could alter the law in any way it liked.

Justice Chandrachud: Clause (4) of the amendment does not alter the law. It just provides that the election shall be valid.

Counsel: The constituent body in its wisdom can always declare an election valid.

Justice Khanna: Could the amendment have been valid, if it had come after the Supreme Court had finally decided on the merits of the case?

Counsel: Yes, it could. If it can be done now, it can also be done after the Supreme Court judgment.

Counsel further submitted that the Constitution contained detailed provisions about elections. He said that part 15 of the Constitution had been held in Ponnuswami's case to be a complete Code on Elections. He argued that Articles 324 to 329 dealt with all the aspects of elections to the legislature and if the constituent body felt that the elections of the Prime Minister and the Speaker were important enough to stand on a different footing, then it has every right to make special provisions about their elections.

Justice Beg: When Article 329(b) gives Parliament the power to make laws for election to legislatures, why could they have not made these special provisions about the Prime Minister by ordinary legislation instead of by a constitutional amendment.

Counsel: If the constituent body thought that the matter was important enough to be taken into their own hands, their wisdom cannot be questioned.

He then proceeded to cite a number of authorities to prove his contention that the Prime Minister and Speaker because of their high offices stood on a different footing from all other people. This being so, the special provisions for the elections would be justified.

'Constituent Power Comprehends All'

De's next contention was that the constituent power was the fountain source of all legislative, executive and judicial powers. For the constituent body, there was no separation of powers. Therefore, while it was correct to say that the legislature could not exercise judicial power, the same could not be said for the constituent body.

Justice Mathew: Mr Bhushan has argued that a case pending in the court cannot be withdrawn and decided by Parliament. You say that all these things can be done by Parliament in exercise of its Constituent power.

Counsel: Yes.

Justice Khanna: Does the legislature in deciding an election dispute not have to hear the parties concerned?

Counsel: Parliament, when it decides an election dispute in its constituent authority, does not act as a judicial forum. It is, therefore, not incumbent on it to follow the procedure of a Judicial Tribunal. It may or may not hear the contending parties. The reason is that some times when political necessities overwhelm all other considerations, they have to act in a non-judicial manner, even against the principles of natural justice. Discretionary powers must be vested somewhere in the matter of elections to deal with political situations.

Justice Mathew: This court is not concerned with political necessities or demands, nor is the court concerned with the propriety of the amendment. The court is only concerned with whether the amending power of Parliament is comprehensive enough to validate an invalid election.

Counsel: The only limitation is of basic features. There is no other limitation.

Judicial Review Not Basic

De's next main submission was that Judicial Review in election matters was not a constitutional compulsion even before the Thirty-ninth Amendment. He said that Article 329(b) of the Constitution clearly empowered the Parliament to lay down the manner in which election disputes would be decided.

Counsel argued that a fair reading of Article 329(b) clearly showed that the intention of the Constitution-makers was to vest the final authority of deciding election disputes in the legislature. Being so, judicial review of election disputes could hardly be called a feature of the Constitution, let alone a basic feature.

Justice Khanna: Is there anything in Article 329(b) which prevents the Parliament from appointing non-judicial bodies as the authority to decide election disputes?

De: Nothing whatsoever. Power given to Parliament under Article 329(b) is plenary and without limitation.

In support of this contention, he cited Ponnuswami's case[1] in which Justice Fazl Ali had said,

> Strictly speaking, it is the sole right of Legislature to examine and determine all matters relating to the election of its own members.

This reading of Article 329(b), Counsel maintained, was in conformity with the provisions regarding election disputes in almost all democracies, where the final authority in regard to election disputes was the legislature itself. He read out the provisions in the Constitutions of several democracies—the USA, Australia, Japan, France—regarding elections.

In support of the proposition that election disputes do not come within the domain of the judiciary without statutory authorization, Counsel also quoted from an American book, *Corpus Juris*.

He also quoted from *American Jurisprudence*, which says:

> At common law there was no right to contest in a court a public election. The theory being that elections belonged to the political propriety of Government beyond the control of judicial power . . .

Referring to the provisions in England, Counsel referred to the overall authority of Parliament.

These provisions, asserted the Attorney-General, clearly showed that the prerogative of deciding election disputes always belonged to

---

[1] [1952]1SCR 218.

the legislature. 'The reason for such a provision is that public interest is involved in election disputes. An election dispute is not merely a dispute between two contending parties. It involves the rights of the whole electorate.'

He further argued, 'The real question to be examined in connection with the violation of election laws is whether violation was deliberate or otherwise. The courts of law are constrained to follow forensic rules, while the legislature is not. This is why this power vests in the legislature. If the legislature felt that a particular violation of the law was not intentional, it would exonerate the person concerned.'

Counsel further contended that there were several Articles in the original Constitution which expressly excluded judicial review from some fields. 'Although Article 136 gave the Supreme Court the power to entertain a petition of special leave against the decision of any court or tribunal of the country, Article 136(2) provides an express limitation on the Supreme Court's power in respect of the armed forces' tribunals.

'There have been several amendments too, which have excluded judicial review and which have been upheld by this court. The Twentieth Amendment by introducing Article 230(a) had directly set aside a court-judgment which had invalidated appointments of certain district judges. Similarly, the judgments in the Kesavananda Bharati case on Article 31B and 31C are also of crucial importance. (Article 31B provides that no law put in the Ninth Schedule shall be questioned on the ground of violation of any fundamental right. Article 31C provides that no law made to implement the Directive Principles could be challenged on the same ground.) The very fact that these Articles were upheld by the Supreme Court makes it impossible for anyone to argue that judicial review is a basic feature of the Constitution.'

Judicial Review Merely Abridged

De next contended that even if judicial review was a basic feature, the Thirty-ninth Amendment merely involved an abridgement of judicial review and not its abrogation. He said, 'Kesavananda's case laid down that you can abridge, but cannot destroy a basic feature.'

Justice Mathew: Once judicial review is removed, what remains of it?

Justice Chandrachud: The majority view in Kesavananda Bharati seems to bar even touching the basic structure.

Justice Mathew: No, you can touch, but you cannot destroy.

Justice Khanna: What has been said in Kesavananda Bharati is that you cannot change the basic structure.

Counsel: What I am submitting is that the amendment only excludes judicial review in respect of one election. Judicial review in other elections remains exactly as it was. And it is not as if it is the first time that an election has been validated. Elections have been validated ever since our Constitution came into being. The Representation of People Act, 1956 validated some six thousand elections. Apart from that, the Punjab Act of 1952, the Mysore Act of 1957, the Uttar Pradesh Act of 1971 and the Rajasthan Act of 1969, all validated elections. The Rajasthan Act of 1969 had validated a single election. This validation had been challenged but was upheld by the Supreme Court. How can the other side argue that the single election cannot be validated?

Counsel also cited instances of England where statutes had validated elections, quoting from Halsbury's *Laws of England*. Justice Mathew asked him to cite any similar instance in the United States. Counsel quoted from a book on the American Constitutional Law by Trasolini and Shapiro, which said,

> Actually, there have been numerous instances in our Constitutional history, when Supreme Court opinions have been overturned or reversed either by the Court itself or in some other manner.

Counsel then pleaded that the amendment be examined from the practical point of view and not on a theoretical or academic basis.

Justice Khanna: Can we uphold this amendment merely because the offences in this case are technical? Can we, because of the facts of an individual case, uphold a constitutional amendment which is so widely worded?

Counsel replied that the amendment only touched one election and it was thus not very wide in its application.

Equality Not Basic

Counsel strongly contested Bhushan's submission that equality was a basic feature of the Constitution. 'After the court has upheld Articles 31B and 31C, it cannot be argued that equality is a basic feature. However, even if equality is a basic feature, we shall see that it has not been violated.'

Justice Mathew: The principle of equality permits unequal treatment to people who are situated differently. Is there anything in this case to justify unequal treatment?

Counsel: Can anyone say that the Prime Minister and the Speaker belong to the same category as an ordinary candidate?

Justice Khanna: Is that relevant for the matter of election?

Counsel: Regarding equality, only the classification is subject to scrutiny and not the object of the classification. The object is left solely to the wisdom of the legislature. They may or may not disclose why they were making a particular classification.

The Attorney-General could not complete his arguments, and he had only gone thus far when the court rose on 4 September. When it assembled on 5 September, the Attorney-General was not present. The Solicitor-General, Sinha, told the court that De had suddenly suffered an attack of high blood pressure, on account of which he would not be able to attend the court for some days. The Chief Justice showed his willingness to adjourn the case, but Sinha said he would argue on behalf of the Union till De recovered.

By now it looked as if the constitutional amendment would be struck down. De's arguments had not cut much ice with the judges. On the final day of his arguments, Justice Khanna had said, 'Mr Attorney-General, I think this constitutional amendment will have to go. However, the election can be upheld on the basis of the election law amendments, subject, of course, to what Bhushan has to say about those.' This was the position when the Solicitor-General began his arguments.

THE SOLICITOR-GENERAL'S ARGUMENTS

Beginning his arguments, Sinha briefly outlined his main contentions. He said that the Constitution permitted exclusion of judicial review for implementing the Directive Principles of State Policy. 'A similar power must necessarily be conceded when such exclusion is needed in the larger interests of the security of the State. The constituent body, legislating for the larger interests of the State, sometimes makes classifications, the validity of which rests on material to which the court had no access and which might be of highly confidential nature, relating to secret forces inside and outside the country. In such cases, the decision has to be a matter of political necessity and cannot be subjected to judicial scrutiny.'

Counsel further submitted that judicial review of election disputes was not a constitutional compulsion. 'Article 329(b) of the Constitution contemplates that the Parliament could vest the power to entertain election petitions in whatever body it wants, even in itself. In such a case, Parliament could resolve the dispute after receiving a report from a Special Committee. Thus, judicial review could be eliminated without an amendment of the Constitution at all.'

Counsel claimed that judicial review could be validly excluded in certain spheres, specially in respect of Article 14 (the right of equality). This, he said, was clear from the fact that in the Kesavananda Bharati case, Articles 31B and 31C had been upheld.

Justice Mathew: Is rule of law part of the basic structure of the Constitution? If so, would not equality before law be also basic?

Counsel: There can be rule of law without strict equality. Moreover, sometimes rule of law can be stretched for the security of the State.

Arguing further, Counsel said that sometimes for political expediencies, the Parliament had to make classifications which though wrong in ordinary times were necessary to meet those expediencies. 'Life is not mere logic always. The interests of the State sometimes transcend the needs of logic.'

Justice Beg: You are in fact saying that there are no limits on the amending power.

Counsel: I am only saying that when Articles 31B and 31C were upheld, one cannot say that exclusion of judicial review regarding equality destroys a basic feature.

Justice Mathew: Kesavananda Bharati's case laid down the principles that the basic features including equality could not be violated. If a case lays down a principle, but goes wrong in its application, the principle alone would be binding and not its application.

Counsel: When their Lordships laid down that judicial review could be excluded in certain fields, they also laid down a principle. Illustrating his arguments, Counsel said that in Mulki Rules case,[2] the said rules were struck down by the Andhra Pradesh High Court. 'This decision wrought havoc in Andhra Pradesh. So the Thirty-second Amendment had to be enacted which overturned the effect of the court judgment.

---

[2] [1970]1SCR115.

Therefore, sometimes political interests have also to be considered in deciding the validity of an enactment.'

Justice Beg: Mr Sinha, your argument that this amendment bars judicial review can be against the interests of your client, as it may prevent her from being cleared on the merits.

Counsel: No, my Lord. This amendment clearly bars the court from going into the merits of the case. Counsel then read out a passage from Justice Khanna's judgment in Kesavananda Bharati's case to reinforce his contention that the constituent power was unlimited. The passage he read out said, 'All provisions of the Constitution are subject to the amendatory process and cannot claim exemption from that process by being described as essential features.'

At this, Justice Khanna interrupted him and asked him to read the whole paragraph before this. The paragraph read:

> So far as the expression 'essential feature' means the basic structure or framework of the Constitution, I have already dealt with the question as to whether the power to amend the Constitution would include within itself the power to change the basic structure or framework of the Constitution. Apart from that, all provisions of the Constitution are subject to the amendatory process and cannot claim exemption from that process by being described essential features.

Justice Khanna told Sinha that after reading only the extract which Mr Sinha had read, it would seem that he (Justice Khanna) had given Parliament an unlimited power of amending the Constitution, but reading the whole paragraph made it clear that he had not. Therefore, he cautioned Sinha not to read his observations out of context.

Counsel then strongly rebutted Bhushan's arguments that constituent power did not include judicial power. He said that the constituent power included the power to readjust the distribution of legislative, judicial and executive power. 'The judicial power in a given matter could be transferred to Parliament which can act by a simple majority. Therefore, there can be no valid objection to Parliament exercising judicial power, where it is acting by a two-thirds majority.'

Justice Mathew: Can the constituent body exercise judicial power without first reallocating the powers?

Counsel: If they can do it in two steps, why can't they do it in one?

Amendment an Exercise of Legislative Power

Sinha further submitted that clause (4) did not involve an exercise of judicial power. It only seemed to do so. He said, 'Similar objectives can be achieved sometimes by legislative as well as judicial processes. Where the principle is laid down antecedently, its application is made by a judicial process. When the legislature creates a principle and also works out the result in an individual case, the process is legislative. To enable it to take decisions, the legislature has full power to collect materials and supplement the information of its members from all sources.

'A court adjudicates validity. The legislature creates validity, even retrospectively. Validation is lawmaking. A validating legislation does not involve a pronouncement on the correctness of a court judgment. It merely alters the legal position by creating a new law. What has been done by clause (4) is that the entire election law including Section 123 (corrupt practices) has been removed retrospectively for the Prime Minister's election. The result is that since no grounds existed for declaring her election void, the election, by that very fact, became valid.'

Justice Mathew: Would retrospective repeal of the law on the basis of which a judgment has been rendered, automatically render the judgment void?

Counsel: In my humble submission, it would.

Justice Mathew: If the High Court decides on the basis of a Supreme Court decision and the Supreme Court later overruled its decision on that point of law, does the High Court judgment automatically fall?

Counsel: No, not then.

Justice Mathew: Apart from repealing the Representation of the People Act for the Prime Minister, was any other law enacted on the basis of which the election might have been validated?

Counsel: No.

Justice Mathew: Then according to you, on what basis was the election validated?

Counsel: Because there were no grounds for declaring the election void.

Justice Khanna: Is there any instance where an election has been declared completely valid and not that a particular ground of invalidity has been removed?

Counsel could not cite any instance of this, but he did cite a Ceylon case[3] where the disqualification of a particular person had been removed by an Order in Council.

Justice Mathew: What about Liyanage's case? In that case, the Privy Council had ruled that legislation which was designed to affect a single person was invalid.

Democracy Not Affected

Sinha next contended that the amendment did not in any way affect democracy or the concept of free and fair elections. 'Just because judicial scrutiny of a single election is removed, how can one say that the concept of free and fair election has disappeared? One cannot maintain that democracy would be destroyed if the Prime Minister's election was excluded from judicial scrutiny. President Ford of the United States did not come into office by an election. But because of that, can anyone maintain that America is no longer a democracy?'

Fundamental Rights Not Basic

Sinha also submitted that fundamental rights were not part of the basic structure of the Constitution. Therefore, the issue whether the amendment destroyed the equality became academic. He said that Justice Khanna had excluded fundamental rights from the basic structure. At this point, Justice Khanna interrupted Sinha and asked him to see his observations on page 685 in the Kesavananda Bharati case, where he had observed,

> The secular character of the State, according to which the State shall not discriminate against any citizen on the ground of religion only, cannot likewise be done away with.

Justice Khanna told the Solicitor-General that here he had unambiguously held Article 15 (a fundamental right) to be basic. How could Counsel then say that he had found none of the fundamental rights basic?

---

[3] 1932 AC 260, *Abeyesereka v. Jayatilake*.

Legality of Session Unquestionable

Sinha then moved to the last leg of his arguments, the validity of the Monsoon Session of Parliament. 'The essence of the grievance is not the illegality of the detentions of the Members of Parliament, but the consequent interference with their right of participation in the proceedings of Parliament. When a Member is excluded from participation in the proceedings of the House, the matter concerns Parliament alone, as the grievance is in regard to proceedings within the walls of Parliament. In regard to the rights to be exercised within the walls of the House, the House itself is the judge.'

In support of this proposition, Counsel quoted from May's *Parliamentary Practice* which says, 'It is the right of each House to be the sole Judge of the lawfulness of its proceedings.'

He also quoted a case[4] of England in which it was observed: 'It seems to follow that the House of Commons has the exclusive power of interpreting the status so far as the regulation of its proceedings within its walls is concerned.' It was also observed, 'where there is no legal remedy, there is no legal wrong'. Relying on this, Counsel submitted that since there was no legal remedy available to the detained Members of Parliament because of the suspension of fundamental rights, therefore it could not be said that their detention was illegal.

Sinha cautioned the judges on the consequences of Bhushan's arguments. He said, 'The detention of Members of Parliament is by a statutory authority. It would be surprising if the statutory authority, by an order which might turn out to be illegal, could prevent the House of Parliament from assembling and functioning. It would mean that if a District Magistrate acting on his own arrested a Member of Parliament, the House would not be able to function.'

He further argued that these arrests have been made possible because of the proclamation of Emergency which was in force. 'When an Emergency is proclaimed, Parliament has power to approve or disapprove it within two months. If Bhushan's argument is accepted, then the Parliament cannot even assemble to withhold the approval of the Emergency and thus terminate the suspension of fundamental rights.'

---

[4] QB 271, *Bradlaugh v. Gossett.*

Sinha further submitted that the detention would not be declared illegal without a formal writ of habeas corpus. He said that the legality of the detentions could not be challenged in this case as a collateral issue. With this, Sinha concluded his arguments.

14

'Amendment Is Like a Firman'

Immediately after Sinha concluded, Ashok Sen began his arguments on behalf of Mrs Gandhi. Giving his interpretation of the amendment, Sen said, 'Clause 4(4) provides that no law made by Parliament before the Thirty-ninth Amendment will apply to *election petitions and matters connected therewith* of the Prime Minister. This has been given retrospective effect. So it is clear that *not* all provisions of the election law have ceased to apply to the Prime Minister's election. The Representation of the People Act has eleven parts. It is only part six which deals with disputes regarding elections. Therefore, it is only part six which has ceased to apply to the election of the Prime Minister. Since part six confers the jurisdiction to the High Court to decide election disputes, therefore, that jurisdiction has been removed with retrospective effect for the Prime Minister's election. This being so, the judgment which was delivered under part six automatically becomes void. Since the judgment becomes void, the election as a consequence becomes valid. No declaration is required for it.'

Justice Mathew: Does it not require adjudication by a court to say that an order passed by a lower court without jurisdiction is void or would that order automatically be deemed to be void?

Counsel: If the court initially lacks jurisdiction then this order would be automatically void. But if a competent court loses its jurisdiction because of improper exercise of jurisdiction, then its order would have to be declared void.

Justice Mathew: What is the difference? In both cases the order is void.

Counsel: Both cases are the same, but in the latter case it has to be determined whether or not the court exercised its jurisdiction properly.

Justice Mathew: Who will declare the order void? The court or the legislature?

Counsel: If the task is left to the court, then the court. But in the present case, the constituent body has itself declared the order void.

Justice Mathew: What is the meaning of a writ of certiorari[1] if an order made without jurisdiction becomes automatically void?

Counsel: A writ of certiorari is issued to quash a void order.

Justice Mathew: If an order is void automatically, where is the need to quash it?

Counsel: In any case, my contention is that the election dispute in this case has been inquired into and resolved by the constituent body itself. After the High Court lost its jurisdiction, the constituent body took it upon itself to decide the validity of the election. After seeing the effect of the amended law regarding corrupt practices, which retrospectively removed the grounds on which the election was declared void, the constituent body finding no infirmity in the election declared it to be valid. As I am submitting that the chapter of corrupt practices still continued to apply to the Prime Minister's election, the constituent body did take into account the norms provided by the corrupt practices chapter in order to decide the validity of the election.

Counsel then contended that the impugned amendment followed the familiar pattern of all validating Acts. In support of his contention, he cited a few cases. The most recent was one in which the Supreme Court upheld the validation of a single election which had been declared invalid. In this case,[2] the election of one Kanta Kathuria was declared invalid because she was not qualified to contest as a candidate. The Parliament had validated the election by retrospectively removing the disqualification.

Subject-matter No Limitation

Dealing with Bhushan's arguments that judicial power could not be exercised by the constituent body, Sen contended that the subject-matter of the Constitution placed no restriction on the amending power. Once a provision was validly embodied in the Constitution,

---

[1] 'Certiorari' is a writ issued by a court to quash the order of a lower court.

[2] (1970) (2) SCR, 835, *Kanta Kathuria v. Manak Chand Surana*.

it became a part of the Constitution. 'If a provision did not destroy a basic structure, it would be valid, no matter what its subject-matter was. In the hands of the constituent body, there is no division between legislative and judicial power. A constituent power is different from legislative power and is a sovereign power.' Counsel quoted some old cases in which the power of the native Indian princes to issue firmans (royal directives) had been upheld. Equating the constituent body to the erstwhile Indian princes, Counsel pleaded that no restriction could be placed on the constituent body's power to exercise judicial authority.

Continuing his arguments, Counsel said, 'Even assuming that the constituent authority could not damage the basic structure of judicial power, this limitation would be available only in regard to those powers which were exclusively granted to the judicial organ under Articles 32, 226 and 136. In India, there is no exclusive repository of judicial power. The whole subject of election has been allocated to the legislature. It is only an accident that Parliament has chosen to entrust the work of deciding election disputes to the High Courts. If, therefore, Parliament withdraws this power from the court, it cannot be regarded as an encroachment of judicial power.'

When asked by the court whether the constituent authority, when deciding the election dispute, had to follow judicial procedure, Counsel replied that it did not. Advancing a new argument, he contended that a particular function became legislative or judicial depending on whether the legislature or the judiciary was exercising that function. 'In this case, since the power to provide for the disposal of election disputes has been vested in Parliament by Article 329(b), it became a legislative function.'

Justice Mathew: You mean even when the courts decide election cases, they are discharging a legislative function.

Counsel: Yes. In India we do not have a clear demarcation between legislative and judicial powers.

Justice Mathew: Don't bother about separation of powers. Once the power to settle a dispute is given to an authority, how is it exercised?

Counsel: If the authority is the legislature, then it uses a legislative procedure.

Counsel argued that this power had been left to the legislature because an election dispute is a political question. It was not a controversy between the contending parties. It concerned the public and the whole constituency.

Justice Khanna: An election contest is a dual proceeding. It is a matter involving the public as well as the contesting candidates.

Counsel, however, maintained that an election dispute was not between the parties. In support of this he cited a few British cases and also a Supreme Court case.[3] In this case, it was held that an election contest does not mean a contest only between the parties, but creates a situation which the whole constituency is entitled to avail of.

Justice Mathew: What about a suit under Section 92 of the Criminal Procedure Code? The public is interested in this too. But does it cease to be a judicial proceeding because of this? The correct position is that an election dispute lies between the contesting candidates although the public is also an interested party.

Right of Equality Remains

Counsel then advanced another novel argument. He said that the amendment merely protected the Prime Minister's election from challenge on the ground of equality. 'If a particular statute is protected from challenge under Article 14, it does not mean that the right of equality itself has been destroyed. The guarantee of Article 14 still remains as a fetter against all executive and legislative acts. It is only that it does not operate on the protected Act. The right of equality as such still remains operative as before and if it is a basic feature, the basic feature still continues.'

Norms of Elections Left to Parliament

Counsel further submitted that the norms of free and fair elections were not prescribed by the Constitution. 'The Constitution only prescribes that there must be elections. Parliament makes all laws regarding elections and also about the determination of election disputes. Post-election scrutiny of election is not a constitutional imperative nor is it a necessary ingredient of free and fair elections. Free and fair elections may be ensured by the various provisions of the R.P. Act under which a candidate may be prosecuted criminally even in the absence of a machinery for contesting the validity of election.'

---

[3] AIR 1958, SC 698, *Mallappa Basappa v. Basavaraj Ayyappa*.

Merely One Election

Counsel's final submission was that the amendments did not affect the structure of republican democracy, assuming that was a basic feature of the Constitution. He said that the validation of one election cannot alter the character of a democracy. 'Parliament and state legislatures will still be elected by direct election under the laws made by the Parliament. This was just one election out of the 500-odd elections to Parliament which took place in 1971.'

This concluded Counsel's arguments in defence of the constitutional amendment.

KAUSHAL'S ARGUMENTS

After Ashok Sen concluded his submissions, J.N. Kaushal, the Advocate-General of Haryana and the assisting counsel of Mrs Gandhi, also made brief submissions in defence of the amendment.

Giving a rationale for the amendment, Kaushal said, 'The constituent body validated its amendment because it found that the High Court judgment was being used for political purposes by some elements of society. The constituent body had previously seen how this provision for election petitions was used merely to trouble the elected candidates. Your Lordships may just look at the statistics. After the 1967 Lok Sabha Elections, fifty-two election petitions were filed. Only seven were allowed in the High Court and the Supreme Court reversed the findings in four of these. So ultimately out of the fifty-two election petitions, only three succeeded. After the 1971 elections, fifty-eight election petitions were filed. Only three have been allowed by the High Court. The judgment in one was set aside by the Supreme Court so that upto now only two have succeeded, while four are still pending.'

Counsel submitted that the constituent body had validated the Prime Minister's election after seeing how petitions were used to harass the elected candidates.

Counsel did not advance any other new argument. He merely repeated some of the arguments already advanced by the Solicitor-General and Sen. This concluded the arguments in defence of the constitutional amendment.

15

Emergency Measure or Tranquillizer?

Immediately after Kaushal ended his arguments, Bhushan began his rejoinder on the constitutional amendment. Analysing the arguments of the four counsels of the other side, he said that each of them had treated clause (4) of the amendment in a unique manner which was very curious and interesting.

He said, 'The Attorney-General has treated it as a sort of homecoming, as if the Parliament was the principal who had delegated its own functions of deciding election disputes to the judiciary and when it found that the judiciary had acted as a reckless agent, it took back the function from it. The Solicitor-General, on the other hand, has treated it as an Emergency measure. He says that when the constituent body found that forces of chaos and anarchy threatened the security of the country, they enacted the amendment to save the country from these dark forces. Sen has, however, treated it as a relief measure for the Supreme Court. He says that Parliament found that the Supreme Court had suddenly got a case which was too complex and difficult for it to handle. Therefore, the Parliament, like a big brother, took the responsibility of deciding the case on its own shoulders to save the judiciary from the embarrassment of having to take on more than it can chew. Lastly, Kaushal has treated it as a medical measure. He says that it is like a tranquillizer or a sleeping pill for the Prime Minister who was being harassed by a petty election petition.'

Their common complaint, he felt, was that the High Court had applied the same judicial yardstick to this case as they were applying to the case of humbler people. Hence clause (4) was necessitated. He referred to clause (4) being compared to these firmans, and to the argument that an election dispute being a political question was not a matter with which the judiciary could interfere.

Bhushan said that before examining the various questions arising out of clause (4), the effect of its implementation had to be discussed. 'On the interpretation of clause (4), there is an important divergence of opinion between the Prime Minister's counsel and the Union's counsel. The Solicitor-General has said that by clause (4), parts 6 and 7 of the R.P. Act both become inapplicable to the Prime Minister's election. While Sen has clearly argued that part 6 became inapplicable, part 7 continued to apply. (Part 6 gives jurisdiction to the High Court for deciding election disputes. Part 7 provides for corrupt practices.) So while Sinha has argued that in declaring the election valid, the constituent body did not apply the standards in the section of corrupt practices, but their own standards of free and fair elections, Sen has argued that the constituent body must have applied the standards furnished by the corrupt practice section of the R.P. Act. But what is the reality? A proper interpretation of clause (4) leaves no room for doubt that the Prime Minister's election has been declared valid just because she was the Prime Minister. It appears that of all the various interpretations awarded to the amendment, Kaushal's interpretation is nearest to the truth. Mr Kaushal has said that clause (4) retrospectively removed the High Court's jurisdiction in regard to the Prime Minister's election. The High Court judgment therefore automatically becomes void. Thus far I agree. But clause (4) declares the election to be valid. This is not a consequence of the removal of the High Court's jurisdiction. The constituent body has arbitrarily declared the election to be valid. It has been argued that the declaration of validity is not arbitrary and some norms of free and fair elections were applied. But after seeing the cavalier manner in which the elections have been declared valid, no one can say that any norms were applied.'

Justice Chandrachud: The constituent body may have applied its own norms, which were different from the norms of a judicial body. Suppose it was considered that even if the High Court's ruling was substantially correct, the charges were too technical to justify the invalidation of the Prime Minister's election?

Justice Mathew: No, that cannot be, because if the cross-appeal is considered, then the complexion of the charges changes completely.

Counsel: Exactly, my Lord. The cross-appeal contains allegations of bribery, etc. Who can say that bribery is a technical offence?

Bhushan then advanced several reasons which, he said, showed that the constituent body did not apply any norms while validating the election: He said:

1. It does not merely deprive the High Court of its jurisdiction, but also makes the substantive law inapplicable to the election of the Prime Minister. It flatly declares that the election of the Prime Minister could not have been void on any ground on which it was declared to be void. This means that the election has been made invoidable.

2. If the constituent body applied any norms, they would have said so. Neither the preamble nor the statement of objects and reasons give any clue for that.

3. The amendment was moved on the 7 August. It received the Presidential assent on the 10th of August. This means that it was passed by both Houses of Parliament and ratified by a majority of the state legislatures in just three days. The evidence in the case and the issues arising in it could not have been considered by all these people within three days.

Bhushan then referred to the other side's contention that election disputes came within the domain of Parliament and the court's jurisdiction in election matters stood excluded by Article 329(b) of the Constitution. He pointed out that the original scheme of the Constitution was that under Article 324, the power to appoint election tribunals was vested in the Election Commission, and the jurisdiction of this tribunal was amenable to the jurisdiction of the Supreme Court under Article 136. So the Supreme Court retained overall authority on election matters. The Nineteenth Amendment of the Constitution however took away the Election Commission's power to appoint election tribunals and under Article 329(b), Parliament had conferred the jurisdiction to decide election disputes to the High Court with normal appeals to the Supreme Court.

Justice Mathew: Does the power granted by Article 329(b) to Parliament not exclude the jurisdiction of the Supreme Court under Article 136?

Counsel: I submit not. Whichever body is vested with the jurisdiction regarding election disputes becomes a tribunal within the meaning of Article 136, and its decision is subject to an appeal by special leave in the Supreme Court.

In this connection, Bhushan cited a case of the US Supreme Court[1] in which it was held, 'In exercising the power to judge the election returns and qualifications of its members, the Senate acts as a judicial tribunal.'

Regarding the contention of the other side that an election dispute was a political question with which the judiciary could not interfere, Bhushan referred to the American doctrine of political questions, which evaded the issue by saying that the issue raised a political question. 'It was thus a way of avoiding a principled decision which could be damaging to the court, or an expedient decision damaging to the principles of the court.'

Counsel asserted that in any case, the political questions doctrine had been overthrown in the United States, and that in India, however, the political questions doctrine had never held sway and was rejected in the Privy Purse case.[2]

He quoted from the judgment of Justice Shah where he had said:

The only forum under our Constitution for determining a legal dispute is the court, which is by training and experience, assisted by properly qualified Advocates, fitted to perform that task. A provision which purports to exclude the jurisdiction of the court in certain matters and deprive the aggrieved party of the normal remedy will be strictly construed.

Counsel pleaded that according to a strict construction, Article 329(b) could not be interpreted to exclude the special jurisdiction of the Supreme Court under Article 136. 'Your Lordships will have to see which interpretation is more reasonable: whether the legislature itself, which has a vested interest in the outcome of the election dispute, or the judiciary, which is an impartial observer, should have the ultimate say in election disputes.'

Bhushan also referred to May's *Parliamentary Practice* on election disputes in England which says,

Before the year 1870 controverted elections were tried and determined by the whole House of Commons as mere party

---

[1] 73 Lawyers Edition 867, *David S. Barry v. The United States of America*.
[2] AIR 1971, SC 530, *Madhav Rao Scindia v. Union of India*.

questions upon which the strength of the contending factions might be treated. In order to prevent *so notorious a perversion of justice*, the House consented to submit the exercise of its privilege to a tribunal constituted by law, which though composed of its own members should be appointed so as to secure impartiality in the administration of justice according to the laws of the land and under the sanction of oaths.

Bhushan argued that there was no reason why Article 329(b) should be given an interpretation which would lead to such a notorious 'perversion of justice' when an alternative interpretation was possible.

Coming to the scope of the amending power, Bhushan strongly rebutted Sen's contention that the constituent power was an amalgam of legislative, executive and judicial power. 'Mr Sen argued that the constituent power is sovereign and is analogous to the sovereign powers of the native Indian princes which they exercised by firmans. The myth that the constituent power is sovereign or unlimited has been conclusively destroyed by the Kesavananda Bharati case. It has been held that there are limitations on the amending power. An amendment under Article 368 means not only a law but a law on a particular subject. This would be a law of a particular kind dealing with the creation of organs of government and their relation inter se.'

Justice Mathew said that the Indian Constitution was very long, unlike the US Constitution, and contained many things which did not relate to the organs of government and the power distribution between them. Counsel, however, totally disagreed.

Justice Mathew: What about Directive Principles of State Policy?

Counsel: They are directions to the organs as to how they will function.

Justice Mathew: Everything is a subject matter of the State. So every law can be included in the Constitution. You can only say that a judicial exercise is not law at all.

Counsel: That is all I want to establish. A purely judicial or a purely executive power cannot be said to be constituent power.

Justice Beg: Would you say that the judicial authority cannot be vested in Parliament?

Counsel: No, I would not say that. It could be vested in Parliament subject to the limitation of basic structure.

Chief Justice: The principle of law is that if a body can create a power, it can also exercise that power.

Counsel: I submit that it is not correct. Let us take an illustration. The Governor has the power to appoint Judicial Magistrates. Does it mean that he can himself exercise the functions of a Judicial Magistrate?

Counsel submitted that if it was established that constituent power did not include judicial power, the only question which remained was whether deciding a particular dispute was an exercise of lawmaking power or of judicial power. 'Mr Sen has conceded that clause (4) is an exercise of judicial power, although he maintained that judicial power can be exercised by the constituent body. On the other hand, Mr Sinha and Mr Kaushal have submitted that clause (4) retrospectively takes away the jurisdiction of the High Court and makes the substantive laws relating to corrupt practices inapplicable to the election. Even if this were so, the election would not become valid automatically. When a statutory remedy for enforcing a right is removed, the common law remedy remains, specially when an election has already been held and the validity of it is disputed. Even if the High Court judgment became void by the effect of clause (4), the election would still remain disputed and the declaration of validity was clearly an exercise of judicial power.'

Justice Mathew: When the law no longer applies to election petitions, where is the question of election petitions existing?

Justice Khanna: But the complaint against the election still existed, though it may not be in the form of an election petition.

Counsel: Exactly. Even if the legal remedy in the form of election petitions has been taken away, it does not follow that the legal right has also been taken away.

Justice Chandrachud: The sole purpose of clause (4) appears to be to take away the legal right as well as the remedy.

Counsel: If that is so, then it involves shameful destruction of the rule of law.

The Solicitor-General at this point intervened to say that the validation of the election was a legislative function in which a decision was taken after considering the relevant material.

Chief Justice: If the election petition does not exist, which material did the constituent body take into consideration?

Sinha: Material collected by the High Court did not exist 'in law'. But it existed 'in fact'. In addition to these facts, the constituent body applied its own intelligence. It was a question of general appraisal as to whether the election has been free and fair or not. It came to the conclusion that the election was free and fair.

Bhushan then referred to De's contention that there were precedents of election validation in England as well as in India. He told the court that in all the validation cases of England cited by De, only the disqualification of a person for contesting the election was removed retrospectively. It was not that the claims for both parties were gone into and adjudicated upon. Referring to De's contention that the R.P. Act of 1956 had validated about 6000 elections, Bhushan said that it was absolutely wrong. He said that the R.P. Act, 1956 did not validate a single election, but merely removed the disqualification which people might have had, and thus allowed them to contest the 1956 elections. Regarding the other four cases cited by De as examples of specific election validations by the legislature, Counsel said that in none of these, the election as such was declared valid. Only a particular defect of the election was removed by a retrospective change in law.

Counsel labelled as absurd Sinha's arguments that the nature of function depended on the authority which was performing that function. He cited a US Supreme Court case[3] in which it was held that the Senate, though a legislative body, was conferred certain powers which were not legislative, but judicial in character. Bhushan also cited an Indian Supreme Court case[4] in which Justice Bhagwati had stated the fact which distinguished a judicial inquiry from legislation. He had said, 'That question depends not upon the character of the body but upon the character of a proceeding.' Relying on this judgment, Counsel contended that it completely demolished Sen's argument.

Bhushan then came to the second leg of his arguments: that the amendment destroyed several basic features of the Constitution. 'I have tried to show that free and fair elections are necessary for democracy, and for free and fair elections it is essential that a candidate resorting to corrupt practices cannot be declared elected. The other side has argued that this amendment affects only one election and all the other elections were still free and fair. Therefore, democracy cannot be destroyed by it. I submit that it is not a matter of one or two elections,

---

[3] 73 Lawyers Edition 867, *Barry v. United States.*
[4] AIR 1958, SC 578, *Express Newspapers Ltd. v. Union of India.*

it is a matter of principle. If today one unfair election can be declared valid, then tomorrow all the unfair elections can be declared valid.

'The Solicitor-General's argument was that the constituent body while determining the fairness of the election had applied its own norms. My reply is twofold. Firstly, it is quite clear that no norms had been applied. Secondly, even if some norms were applied, the application of different norms for different candidates for the same election is completely destructive of democracy. If Raj Narain had been elected, the validity of his election would have been tested on the norms prescribed by the R.P. Act. On the other hand, because the Prime Minister was elected, the constituent body decides to apply its own norms to such an election. How can we have a free and fair election when opposing candidates are required to maintain different standards of fairness?

'The other side has also submitted that in all democratic countries, election disputes are decided by the legislature itself. Let us see the true position. In Britain, upto 1870, controverted elections were tried and determined by the whole House of Commons, but in order to prevent so notorious a perversion of justice, the House consented to grant this power to the courts of law. Thus today, in England, election disputes are decided by the courts. In America, the power of deciding elections was previously considered a political question, but we find that this too has been rejected. So when the House decides an election dispute, it acts as a judicial tribunal which is subject to the appellate jurisdiction of the Supreme Court.' He cited a few cases in which the Supreme Court had interfered with the determination of the House.

Regarding his challenge on equality, Bhushan said, 'The main argument of the other side on this point was that since Article 31(b) was upheld in Kesavananda Bharati's case, equality cannot be said to be a basic feature. This is not correct because the validity of Article 31(b) was not in question in Kesavananda Bharati's case. Only the Twenty-ninth Amendment was challenged in that case, which merely inserted two Land Reform Acts in the Ninth Schedule. (Article 31(b) provides that any act inserted in the Ninth Schedule could not be challenged as violative of any fundamental right.) Since the Land Reform Acts related only to the property right, which Mr Justice Khanna held not to be a basic feature, the Twenty-ninth Amendment was upheld. Lack of equality in the matter of property might not have the same effect on the basic structure as the lack of equality in the matter of elections. Suppose an Act discriminates against people in the matter of dresses. Suppose it provides that some people will have to wear a particular dress and some other people will have to wear a different dress. Although this Act is discriminatory, it probably does not affect the basic structure of the Constitution. But suppose an Act discriminates in the matter of elections and provides that a Muslim will have half a vote, a Christian will have quarter of a vote, a Harijan will have one-tenth of a vote, a Brahmin will have five votes and a Bhumihar like Mr Raj Narain will have ten votes; would that Act not affect the basic structure of the Constitution? Can anyone say that democracy will still survive if such an Act came into force?'

Counsel further contended that even if Article 14 was not basic, because republican democracy was a basic feature, therefore, equality which flows necessarily from republicanism must be a basic feature of the Constitution.

Justice Mathew: Is not Article 14 the only guarantee of equality?

Counsel: Equality is also guaranteed by the Preamble. Moreover, there could also be an implication of equality in the Constitution. Even if equality in other spheres is not basic, it has to be basic in the matter of status and opportunity, which are mentioned in the Preamble. In this case, the amendment discriminates merely on the basis of status. Just because the person concerned happens to be the Prime Minister, her election is made immune from all attack. I do not dispute that the Prime Minister is a class by herself. But what is the connection between a person being the Prime Minister and his election being immune from judicial scrutiny? Even the Prime Minister contests an election as an ordinary candidate. What kind of contest is that in which one person can cheat and the other cannot?

Counsel then referred to Sinha's argument that the amendment was made to save the country from chaos and anarchy. 'Mr Sinha has advanced a very strange argument. He says that the constituent body found that a change in the Prime Minister in these circumstances would lead to chaos and anarchy in the country. The court cannot take notice of this argument. I will not deal in detail with the merits of his claim. I will only say that a democratic Constitution like ours does not contemplate a situation where a single person can become indispensable to the country.'

Parliament Session Illegal

When Bhushan began his rejoinder on the legality of the Monsoon Session of Parliament, he was immediately interrupted by Justice Khanna.

Justice Khanna: Suppose an illegal order of detention is issued by a District Magistrate to arrest a Member of Parliament. If what you are saying is correct, this would invalidate the session. How can a wrong order of a District Magistrate invalidate a session?

Counsel: Because the President, by suspending the fundamental rights, has become a party to the continued illegal detention of the members. The President convenes the session of Parliament. If he himself becomes a party to an illegal prevention of some Members of Parliament from attending the session, then the session clearly becomes illegal. Otherwise the government can get the whole Opposition arrested and pass whatever it likes without anyone to oppose it.

With this, Bhushan concluded his rejoinder on the validity of the constitutional amendment.

As he was ending his arguments, the five judges were conferring with each other. Two minutes after he had ended, the Chief Justice made a startling announcement. He said, 'After hearing both the sides on the validity of the constitutional amendment, we have decided to hear the counsels of both sides on the merits of the case in order to decide the validity of the constitutional amendment.'

Bhushan was taken aback by this announcement. He was expecting that the judges would first pronounce on the validity of the constitutional amendment before going into the merits of the case. As he was confident that the constitutional amendment would be struck down, he wanted to start arguments on the merits of the case only after the constitutional amendment was struck down, so that the slate was clean at that time. He protested, 'How can the merits of an individual case affect the validity of a constitutional amendment? Its validity should depend solely on the limitations imposed by the Constitution. Moreover, since the amendment ousts the jurisdiction of the court to hear the merits of the case, it would be highly improper to go into the merits before deciding on the validity of the amendment.'

Justice Beg also agreed with the Chief Justice and said that an evaluation of the merits of the case was extremely important in order to decide the validity of the amendment. Bhushan did not persist. Saying that he was duty-bound to obey the dictates of the court, he sat down. So it was on 19 September that Ashok Sen was called upon to make his submissions on the merits of the case.

Giving a historical background of the entire case, Sen started explaining the effect of the election law amendments on the case. As he was explaining this, Justice Mathew interrupted him and pointed out that these amendments, if they be valid, took care of almost all the charges framed in the petition. Therefore, unless their validity is assailed, it would be pointless to go into the merits of the case. He conferred with the Chief Justice who then called upon Bhushan to make his submissions on the validity of the election law amendments.

5

VALIDITY OF THE ELECTION LAW AMENDMENTS

16

Rules of the Game
Changed Retrospectively

Opening his arguments Bhushan told the court that the validity of the election law amendments would depend upon their interpretation. He would advance his interpretations of the amendments and in case they were accepted, he would not challenge the validity of the amendments. He would only assail their validity if his interpretations were rejected by the court.

DEFINITION OF CANDIDATE

Bhushan first read out the change made by the amendment in the statutory definition of candidate in Section 79 of the R.P. Act. The original Section 79(b) of the Act defines a candidate as the person 'who has been, or claims to have been, duly nominated as a candidate at any election, and any such person shall be deemed to have been a candidate as from the time when, with the election in prospect, he began to hold himself out as a prospective candidate'. The amended definition defines a candidate as a person 'Who has been or claims to have been duly nominated as a candidate at any election.'

A Wise and Just Amendment

Bhushan submitted that according to him the original definition involved the identification of the person who was the candidate as well as the time from which he was to be regarded as the candidate. 'The amended definition has done away with the second part of the definition. Now a person would be regarded as a candidate for the purposes of Section 123 (corrupt practices) from any time.' Section 123 provides that a corrupt practice can be committed by a candidate or his election agent or by any other person with the consent of the candidate or his election agent. Counsel argued that previously a candidate could commit a corrupt practice only after he held himself out as a prospective candidate. But after the amendment a corrupt practice can be committed at any time, even ten or twenty years before a person is nominated as a candidate. 'I am very happy that the Parliament has made such a wise amendment which makes the law on corrupt practice extremely just.'

Justice Beg: What you are interpreting could not have been the intention of Parliament.

Counsel: Why not, my Lord? We must assume that Parliament makes fair and just laws.

Justice Beg (smiling): You want us to be legislators.

Counsel: The court never makes the law. It only interprets it.

Justice Mathew: The theory has been discarded long ago. (Citing from his judgment in Kesavananda Bharati's case) 'The dictum that judges do not make law, but only interpret it, is a fairy tale. And nowadays we do not believe in fairy tales.'

Counsel: At least judges are supposed to interpret the law. Your Lordships will see what will happen if my interpretation is rejected. If the phrase 'corrupt practice committed by a candidate' implies that they must be committed after a person becomes a candidate, then on the same logic Section 100(1)(b) which mentions the phrase 'corrupt practice committed by a returned candidate', would mean a corrupt practice by a candidate after he becomes a returned candidate. (Section 100(1)(b) provides that the High Court shall declare the election of the returned candidate void if it finds that any corrupt practice has been committed by the returned candidate or his election agent.) This would render Section 100(1)(b) quite absurd because obviously no person will commit a corrupt practice after he gets elected and becomes a returned candidate.

Justice Mathew: Section 100 cannot involve the concept of time. That is impossible.

Counsel: If Section 100 does not involve the concept of time, why should there be a concept of time in Section 123? Section 123 only provides that a corrupt practice must be committed by that person, who was a candidate at the election or by any other person with the consent of the candidate. Your Lordships will consider what the situation would be if Section 123 really means that the corrupt practice must be committed by a candidate after he becomes a candidate. It would mean that a person can commit all sorts of corrupt practices, bribe all voters, use undue influence, even prevent the rival candidates from filing their nomination papers, before he himself files his nomination papers and he would incur no liability. This would make the provision of the chapter on corrupt practices absolutely redundant. What a candidate would have to do to escape the consequences would just be to file his nomination papers at the very last day. Why should the court give an interpretation which would completely destroy the meaning of the chapter on corrupt practices?

On this point Bhushan made full capital out of the passage read by Justice Mathew from his judgment in Kesavananda Bharati's case where he had said that the view that judges do not make the law was a fairy tale. Bhushan said, 'Your Lordships will be making the law in Justice Mathew's opinion and will have to see whether the law is to be reasonable or absurd.'

OFFICIAL DUTIES MEAN STATUTORY DUTIES

Bhushan then took up the amendment in Section 123(7) of the R.P. Act. The original Section 123(7) provides that if a candidate obtained or procured any assistance from government servants belonging to a specified category for the furtherance of the prospects of his election, it would be a corrupt practice. The amendment adds a proviso to clause (7) saying that 'where any person in the service of Government and belonging to the specified class, in the discharge or purported discharge of his official duty, makes any arrangements, or provides any facilities, or does any other act or thing, for, or in relation to any candidate or his election agent, then such arrangements, facilities, or acts shall not be deemed to be assistance for the furtherance of the prospects of the candidate's election.'

Bhushan's interpretation of this proviso was that 'the official duty' mentioned here would only mean statutory duty (provided by law). He submitted that this interpretation of official duty would not include duty which was assigned by an order of the government.

Justice Mathew: Can a limitation be imposed on official government function?

Counsel: A limitation has to be there. If there is no limitation it would mean that if the government by a circular directed government officials, such as District Magistrates, Secretaries etc., to organize the election campaign of ministers, it would be an official government function and no liability of a corrupt practice would be incurred. It would mean that the government merely by an administrative order could direct that the entire election campaign of the ruling party, including canvassing for votes, giving speeches etc., be carried out by government servants.

Interpretation of the 1974 Amendment

Bhushan's interpretation of the R.P. Amendment Act, 1974 was the same which he had given in the Allahabad High Court. This amendment about election expenses has provided that any expenditure incurred or authorized in connection with the election of a candidate by the political party or friends and supporters of the candidate would not be included in the candidate's election expenses. Counsel told the court that according to his interpretation the amendment only made it clear that any expenses incurred or authorized by a political party or a friend or supporters of the candidate without the authorization of the candidate or his election agent could be excluded from the candidate's election expenses. 'It does not protect expenditure which has been incurred or authorized by a candidate or his election agent. If the correct interpretation is that even if expenditure has been incurred or authorized by the candidate himself, but if it is also authorized by someone else it could be excluded from the election expenses of the candidate, then the limit on expenses would become meaningless. A candidate will only have to ask his party or any other individual to authorize him to spend money and then the candidate can spend any amount of money without being required to show it in his return.'

Justice Mathew: If a candidate is spending his own money, the authorization by any other person has no meaning. An authorization has meaning only when the person intends to reimburse the candidate for the amount authorized by him. The candidate need not get authorization from any other person to spend his money.

Counsel: In Chawla's case it has been held that when a candidate participates in a function organized by his party or any other person, he impliedly authorizes the expenditure in connection with that function. Here though the candidate does not reimburse the party with that amount, he still has authorized that expenditure. So authorization need not always carry with it an idea of reimbursement.

After giving his interpretation, Bhushan told the court that he would not challenge the validity of these amendments if his interpretations were accepted. Then he would only challenge the validity of other amendments for which he had offered no interpretation. But if his interpretations were rejected, he would challenge the validity of all the election law amendments.

Scope of Attack on Ninth Schedule

Bhushan told the court that since the Election Laws Amendment Act, 1975 and the Representation of People Amendment Act, 1974 were included in the Ninth Schedule by the Thirty-ninth Amendment, therefore the scope of the challenge on them would have to be seen. Parliament can include any ordinary law in the Ninth Schedule only by a constitutional amendment. Any law included in the Ninth Schedule is protected from challenge as being violative of a fundamental right. Bhushan submitted that the Acts included in the Ninth Schedule could still be challenged as destructive of the basic features of the Constitution.

Justice Mathew: Mr Bhushan, how can an ordinary law be struck down as violative of the basic features of the Constitution?

Counsel: Once an Act is included in the Ninth Schedule, a challenge on the basis of infringement of fundamental rights is blocked off. Hence an attack on the ground of destruction of basic features of the Constitution is thrown open, because what the constituent body cannot do they cannot do by any means, including the device of the Ninth Schedule. Counsel then read out the judgments of the majority judges in Kesavananda Bharati's case where they had pronounced on the scope of attack on the Ninth Schedule. Six of these judges, Chief Justice Sikri, Justices Shelat, Grover, Hegde, Mukherjea and Jaganmohan Reddy had held that the Acts included in the Ninth Schedule could be struck down, if they violated any basic feature of the Constitution. Justice Khanna had not said anything in his judgment about the scope of attack on any Acts included in the Ninth Schedule.

Bhushan submitted that since Justice Khanna had imposed the limitation of basic structure on the amending power it must be assumed that this limitation was also imposed on Acts included in the Ninth Schedule. 'Let us look at it this way. It is clear that an amendment of the Constitution can be struck down on the basic feature doctrine. Since the inclusion of an Act in the Ninth Schedule is itself an amendment of the Constitution, its validity can be examined on the basic feature doctrine. If it is found that any of the Acts included in the Ninth Schedule violates a basic feature, then that constitutional amendment which gives it the protection of the Ninth Schedule can be struck down.'

Justice Mathew: Can an ordinary law which is not included in the Ninth Schedule be struck down as violative of a basic feature of the Constitution, although it is not in conflict with any specific provision of the Constitution?

Counsel: Suppose an amendment to the R.P. Act provides that Rs 50,000 would have to be paid for the right of casting a vote. This law does not come in conflict with any specific provision of the Constitution, although it would clearly destroy democracy. Can such a law be upheld? The theory behind the basic feature doctrine is that the Constitution as a whole contains an implication that certain features of the Constitution cannot be destroyed in any way.

Justice Chandrachud: The implied limitation, if there is one, is applicable only to the constituent power, and not to the normal legislative powers of Parliament.

Counsel: If there is an implied limitation on the constituent power, it is because certain features of the Constitution are sacred and cannot be destroyed by any means whatsoever. If there is such a mandate in the Constitution then it must apply to all powers granted by it. How can the Constitution which intends to make certain features permanent, allow them to be destroyed by legislative power?

Justice Mathew: Can Directive Principles of State Policy also illustrate the basic features of the Constitution?

Counsel: Yes.

Justice Mathew: One of the Directive Principles is that the State shall strive to bring about social and economic justice. Can a law be struck down as being violative of social and economic justice?

Counsel: If the mandate for social and economic justice is regarded as a basic feature of the Constitution, then certainly such a law can be struck down. Suppose the law provides for regressive income-tax rates so that people with an income of Rs 50 would pay 90 per cent as tax, people with an income of Rs 500 would pay 60 per cent, people with income of Rs 5000 would pay 20 per cent and people with an income of Rs 50,000 would pay no tax. This law would be clearly destructive of social and economic justice and can be struck down.

Justice Khanna: Another Directive Principle is that the State shall endeavour to bring about prohibition. If a law is made to repeal prohibition in a State, can this be struck down as being violative of the basic feature?

Counsel: Sometimes the State may be desperately short of finances, which it needs to provide social security benefits. Therefore, to raise more funds, it might be essential to repeal prohibition in a State. Then it is a question of paramountcy of two conflicting needs. If prohibition is more essential than social security, then a law which repeals prohibition can also be struck down.

Bhushan, while maintaining that it would be in the highest degree absurd to hold that what the constituent body could not do by amending the Constitution it could do by putting the Act in the Ninth Schedule, said that the specific Article of the Constitution with which the election law amendments came into conflict was Article 81. Article 81(1) (a) provides that subject to the provisions of Article 331, the House of People shall consist of not more than 525 members chosen by 'direct' elections from the territorial constituencies in the state. Counsel told the court that the direct elections mentioned here must mean free and fair elections and the election law amendments, as they were discriminatory, did not provide for free and fair elections. Therefore, even if it was held that the basic structure imposes no limitation on the Ninth Schedule, these laws could be struck down as violative of Article 81.

Counsel then told the court that he would make his submissions on the validity of the election law amendments on the assumption that his interpretations were rejected and that they could be struck down as violative of the basic features. He said that although the retrospectivity of the amendments made them worse, he would submit that even in their prospective effect they destroyed the basic structure of the Constitution.

Dealing first with the amended definition of 'candidate', Counsel told the court that it would clearly have the effect of damaging democracy in the country.

Justice Khanna: Suppose this law was made in 1951, could it have been struck down at that time?

Counsel: Yes, it could. As it could have the effect of completely destroying the fairness of the elections.

Justice Chandrachud (smiling): But it gives an equal opportunity to everybody to do all these things.

Counsel: Yes, my Lord. So might will be right and the law of the jungle will prevail.

Dealing with the amendment about religious symbols, Bhushan said that this deeming provision added to Section 123(3) created a legal fiction by which even if a religious symbol were allotted to a candidate, it would be deemed not to be a religious symbol. He went on, 'Even if a symbol like a portrait of Rama or Christ on a Cross were allotted to a candidate, the election would still be valid. In a religious country like India, the allotment of a religious symbol would have an extremely significant effect on the election results. That is why the R.P. Act, 1951, provided that the use of a religious symbol shall be a corrupt practice. But now this provision is more or less abolished by the amendment which would also lead to the destruction of democracy.'

Justice Mathew: But the symbols are allotted by the Election Commission which is an independent body. Why should it allot a religious symbol?

Counsel: The symbol is allotted at the request of the party and it is the normal practice of the Commission to allot symbols which have been asked for by the party. Moreover, the Election Commission is not as independent a body as the judiciary. It is a quasi-judicial body.

Referring to the amendment in Section 123(7) about the discharge of official duties of government servants, Bhushan said that if his interpretation was rejected, the consequence would be that the party in power could use the entire government machinery for their election work and yet there would be no corrupt practice. 'The explanation which has been added to Section 77 (dealing with the ceiling on expenses) that any expenditure incurred by government servants in the discharge of their official duties would not be regarded as an expenditure of that candidate, makes it very easy for the party in power to use the funds of the state exchequer for its election campaign. So they cannot only use all government servants for election purposes, but they can also use all public funds for election purposes without suffering any consequences.'

Justice Beg: But you can complain if this power is misused.

Counsel: A law is bad if it allows easy misuse of power. Since this law permits the violation of the fairness of the election, it militates against democracy.

Bhushan then argued on the validity of the amendment in Section 123(3) which added an explanation about the date of appointment and resignation of government servants. In that, it has been explained that the dates specified in the Official Gazette for the appointment, resignation or termination of service of any government servant shall be conclusive proof of the date of such appointment, resignation or termination of service. Bhushan submitted that this amendment also created a legal fiction by which the government could specify any date it wanted in the Official Gazette, and that would be deemed to be the correct date of appointment or resignation of a government servant. 'This would allow the government to use a government servant for election purposes, and then specify a fictional date as the date of his resignation, which could be even months after the date on which the person had actually resigned.'

Justice Khanna: Can it not mean that if the date is in doubt, the date specified in the Gazette shall be the date which would be taken into account?

Counsel: This does not apply only in doubtful cases. Even if the date of resignation is absolutely beyond doubt, the government can still specify another date in the Gazette and that date will be deemed to be the correct one.

Bhushan then submitted on the validity of the R.P. Amendment Act, 1974. The validity of this Act (regarding election expenses) was also assailed in the High Court, but the judge then had not pronounced on it. Bhushan contended that this amendment would have the effect of abolishing the ceiling on election expenses, and would completely stultify the small man's chance of winning elections, and the small man's chances must be the essence of Indian democracy.

Retrospective Effect of the Amendment

Bhushan then assailed the retrospective operation of these amendments.

Justice Mathew: There is no doubt of the unfairness of retrospective laws about corrupt practices. But can you cite some legal authority to impugn their validity, because retrospective legislation is normally permissible.

Counsel: I submit that there is a great difference between retrospective legislation on ordinary matters and retrospective legislation about rules of a contest. The latter would inevitably lead to discrimination against some candidates. Any law which is discriminatory is void because, as I have submitted, equality is a basic feature of the Constitution.

Justice Khanna: What about retrospective laws removing disqualifications? That was upheld in Kanta Kathuria's case. How do you distinguish it from this?

Counsel: In the Kanta Kathuria case, the rules of the election were not changed. Only Kanta Kathuria's disqualification for contesting the election was retrospectively removed. Therefore, the rival candidate could not complain of any discrimination against him because if Kanta Kathuria had been qualified to contest the election before it took place, the rival candidate could not have done anything more to further the prospects of his election. The only person who could complain would be a person who was similarly situated as Kanta Kathuria before the election took place and was hence unable to contest as he was not qualified. Only he could have challenged the retrospective removal of Kanta Kathuria's disqualification. Here the situation is completely different. If the laws relating to corrupt practices had been different before the elections, Mr Raj Narain could also have taken advantage of those laws. If government servants could render assistance to candidates in performance of their official duties, then Mr Raj Narain could have asked the state government of UP to depute government officers to work for his election.

Counsel further argued, 'If such retrospective legislation was permissible, the party in power could manipulate laws in such a way so as to always remain in power.'

Justice Khanna: Right now we are not concerned about the addition of disqualifications. We are only concerned with the removal of this qualification.

Counsel: No, not now. But if this power is conceded today, then in future such contingencies are bound to arise. If they can retrospectively relax the rules, they can also retrospectively make them stricter. What you are going to lay down in this case will be the law by which the future of such laws will be determined.

Bhushan next contended that the entire Election Laws Amendment Act was meant for a single case and was a colourable piece of legislation. He said, 'The election against Mrs Gandhi contains seven charges of corrupt practices. Five of these have been resolved by these Election Laws Amendment Act. Only two minor ones remain. After seeing the timing of this Act, there could be no doubt that this whole Act is meant just for Mrs Gandhi's election. It is only concerned with validating one single election. It is a legislative plan to secure a particular result in a particular dispute, and in the Liyanage case[1] it has been clearly held that such a plan is impermissible.'

Bhushan's final submission was that since these amendments were also passed in the same Monsoon Session of Parliament in which several Opposition members were illegally detained, therefore, these amendments too were void because of the illegality of the session.

With a final plea that the Election Laws Amendment Act be struck down as destructive of the basic structure of the Constitution, Bhushan concluded his arguments on the validity of these amendments.

After concluding his arguments on the validity of the election law amendments, Bhushan took up the merits of the case on the assumption that none of his interpretations would be accepted by the court and that the amendments would be held valid. He told the judges that if his submissions did not find favour with the court, there would be only three issues surviving in the case: the issues of bribery, conveyance of voters and election expenses. He said that he would not press the issues of bribery and conveyance of voters. Thus the only surviving issue on which he would make his submission was the issue of election expenses.

Actually the issue of election expenses too did not survive if Bhushan's interpretation of the R.P. Amendment Act, 1974 was rejected by the court. Therefore, the reason why he argued only this issue on merits was that the judges seemed to be more inclined to accept his interpretation of this amendment than they were to accept his interpretation of the other amendments.

Making his submissions on this issue, Bhushan said that the expenditure assessed by the High Court was about Rs 32,000 which was only Rs 3000 below the prescribed limit. 'This assessed expenditure did not include the money spent on the twenty-three

---

[1] 1967(1) A.C. 259 *Liyanage v. Queen.*

vehicles which are shown to have been used by the District Congress Committee of Rae Bareli. However little be the expenditure on these vehicles it would certainly add up to more than Rs 3000.' Asked by the court as to why this expenditure was not added by Justice Sinha, Bhushan replied, 'Justice Sinha has held that since one does not know how many of these vehicles were used in Mrs Gandhi's constituency and what expenditure was incurred on them, he would not estimate any expenditure on them. This is wrong according to Chawla's case. In that case, it has been held that if any expenditure is shown to have been evaded in the return of expenses, then it is the duty of the court to make a reasonable estimate of the expenditure and add it to the return. Just because an exact estimate cannot be made, it does not follow that no estimate can be made. The court has to make a reasonable estimate.'

Justice Mathew: You mean to say that the return of election expenses is like an income-tax return?

Counsel: Yes, exactly like that. Once it has been shown that the return is not correct, then the income-tax authority has to make a reasonable assessment of the income.

Justice Beg: But how do we know who incurred the expenditure on the vehicles? The party might have incurred this expenditure, or they might even have been provided by friends and supporters of Mrs Gandhi.

Counsel: In Chawla's case, it had been laid down that even though an expenditure may not be incurred by a candidate, if it is expressly or impliedly authorized by him or his election agent, it would be treated as his election expense. In this case, Mr Yashpal Kapoor himself got the vehicles released. Therefore, he clearly authorized their use.

Justice Beg: But if a friend or supporter of a candidate spends money on his election, how can the candidate prevent him from doing so?

Counsel: Section 171(b) of the Indian Penal Code makes an expenditure greater than rupees ten by any person for a candidate a penal offence. So if a candidate knows that his friend is incurring expenditure on his election, it is his duty to advise his friend that it is a penal offence. But if his friend persists, then it is his duty to publicly disavow this expenditure and not to take any advantage of it.

Justice Beg: If your interpretation is accepted, then it could be almost impossible to fight an election with this limit.

Counsel: Rs 35,000 is not an insignificant amount. In a poor country like India, if the limit is raised further, the results of the election would be significantly distorted in favour of moneyed people. Only the representatives of rich people would be able to get elected to the legislatures. The small man would have no chance.

Bhushan submitted that at the very least, one-third of the expenditure on the twenty-three jeeps would have to be included in Mrs Gandhi's election expenses. (He said one-third because according to the evidence, the twenty-three vehicles were used in the three constituencies of Rae Bareli.) Calculating the expenditure on the maintenance, depreciation, petrol and driver of the vehicle, Bhushan contended that at least Rs 4500 would have been spent on each vehicle during the election. Therefore, on twenty-three vehicles, a total expenditure of Rs 1,03,500 must have been incurred. Even one-third of this figure is almost Rs 35,000, and if this is added to Mrs Gandhi's return, the limit is easily exceeded and a corrupt practice is established. With this, Bhushan concluded his arguments on 26 September.

17

'Rules Not Changed, Merely Clarified'

Since the Attorney-General had not yet recovered from the attack of high blood pressure which he had suffered while making his submissions on the constitutional amendments, L.N. Sinha took upon himself the task of replying to Bhushan's arguments on the election law amendments.

THE SOLICITOR-GENERAL'S ARGUMENTS

Beginning his reply, Sinha said that the first question to be decided was whether the limitation of basic features applied to ordinary legislation too. Arguing that this limitation did not apply to ordinary legislation, Counsel submitted three propositions to support this.

1. The Constitution itself affirmatively creates and negatively restricts legislative power and the only limitation which can be applied to ordinary legislative powers which are specifically granted by the Constitution must be specific limitations, such as the fundamental rights.
2. The limitation of basic features on the amending power has been held in the Kesavananda Bharati case to be ultimately based on the concept and scope of the word 'amendment' used in Article 368 and is wholly irrelevant to test the validity of a statute made in exercise of the legislative power granted by Article 245.
3. The terms of the Preamble which are further amplified in the Directive Principles are the ideals to be achieved and not the conditions of validity for legislation. The Preamble or Directive Principles therefore could not import any restriction on the legislative power. The Preamble only sets out the ends sought

to be achieved. The means, through which such ends are to be achieved, are left entirely to the will of the legislature. Counsel further submitted that if this implied limitation of basic features also applied to ordinary legislation, it would throw the doors open to endless litigation. 'Every Bill will have to be submitted to the judiciary before being voted upon. I submit that the merits of the policy adopted by the legislature cannot be questioned by the judiciary. A law can only be struck down if it is repugnant to a specific provision of the Constitution or to a direct implication of a specific provision.'

Justice Chandrachud: Implied or inherent limitations can arise from the totality of all the provisions of the Constitution.

Counsel: The implication must arise from some specific provision of the Constitution. Limitation cannot be a matter of speculation. Justice Khanna has clearly rejected the implied limitation theory.

Justice Mathew: Would it not be a paradox if the limitation of basic features is applicable to the constituent power which is a higher power and not to legislative power which is a lower power?

Counsel: My Lord, a power which is affirmatively granted by the Constitution cannot be against the basic features. Moreover, the basic feature theory is so vague that it would be almost impossible to apply it to ordinary legislation. It would be a dangerous extension of Kesavananda Bharati's case to hold that laws inserted in the Ninth Schedule must also satisfy the test of basic features. What has been held in Kesavananda Bharati's case should not be extended now just for the sake of consistency. It is much better for law to be certain than to be logical. Imagine the situation which would arise if Mr Bhushan's contention is upheld. There would be endless litigation. All laws made by Parliament would be challenged as violative of some provision of the Preamble or of the Directive Principles, or of something else.

1974 Amendment Merely Restores Earlier Law

Going on to the actual validity of the amendments, Counsel first took up the Representation of the People Amendment Act, 1974 which deals with expenses. He said that in Section 77 of the Act, 'incurred or authorized' means incurred by the candidate or incurred by an authorized agent. 'Whatever expenditure is incurred by any person who is not authorized by the candidate to act as his agent, cannot be included in the return of expenses filed by the candidate. In fact that is the ambiguity which is cleared up by this amendment.'

Counsel submitted that in order to appreciate the provisions of Section 77 of the Representation of the People Act, one must examine the provisions of the Indian Penal Code. 'Section 171H of the Penal Code prohibits people from spending more than a sum of Rs 10 for a candidate's election without his written authorization. It is made a penal offence which is punishable with a fine extending to Rs 500. This provision of the Indian Penal Code prevents any misuse of the law on election expenses. Therefore, the "authority" contemplated by Section 77 is written authority. In my humble submission, authorization can only be there if the rights and liabilities of a person who is authorized are transferred to the person who authorizes him. Otherwise authorization does not make any sense. Every person can act on his own. It is only when I accept the liabilities which a person may incur that I have authorized him. This carries with it the idea of reimbursement. Unless the person authorized is entitled to be reimbursed by the candidate, there is no authorization.'

Justice Mathew: The criminal offence incurred by a person spending money for a candidate under Section 171 of the Penal Code is another matter. The question is whether a person is allowed to spend money for the candidate under Section 77 of the Representation of the People Act.

Counsel: A person who is spending for a candidate without his authority in writing is making himself liable for a criminal offence. If he does not bother about it, it cannot be helped. There is this slight loophole in the law. The law cannot be perfect.

Justice Mathew: Suppose a party sponsors a candidate and spends money for him. Who will be prosecuted under Section 171?

Counsel: The person who is responsible for that expenditure.

Justice Chandrachud: But how can you pinpoint that person?

Counsel: Yes, it would be difficult. But it cannot be helped.

Justice Mathew: So an individual cannot evade Section 171. But a group of persons acting together can.

Chief Justice: Suppose a candidate asks a political party to spend for him. Is that authorization?

Counsel: That is only a request. As long as the political party is acting on its own, there is authorization.

Counsel submitted that the law on election expenses laid down in Chawla's case in 1974 was a clear departure from the law laid down in all the earlier cases. This placed those candidates who had understood the law correctly in 1971 at a disadvantage. That is why Parliament enacted the 1974 Amendment and clarified the position of the law before Chawla's case.

Justice Khanna: Can the court go into the justification behind an amendment? Will it have any effect on its validity?

Counsel: It will have the effect that if the amendment merely clarifies the law as it stood before Chawla's case, then it does not change the law at all. It only disagrees with the interpretation given in Chawla's case.

Definition of Candidate

Sinha then took up the amendment made in Section 79 of the Representation of the People Act, which changes the definition of candidate and defines him as a person who has been, or claims to have been, duly nominated as a candidate at an election, thus abolishing the concept of holding out as a candidate. Counsel argued that this amended definition did away with the legal fiction created by the 'deeming' provision of the earlier definition. 'A person shall no longer be "deemed" to be a candidate from the time he holds himself out as a candidate. So now, either he is a candidate or he is not. Thus the amended definition has removed a lot of unnecessary ambiguity and has made the definition precise and exact.'

Counsel strongly contested Bhushan's argument that the injunction on corrupt practice starts applying before a person becomes a candidate. He contended that the amended definition of 'candidate' will have to be substituted wherever the word 'candidate' occurs. 'Since the chapter on corrupt practices provides that they must be committed by a candidate, therefore they must be committed by that person who has been, or claims to have been, duly nominated as a candidate. So now a candidate cannot commit corrupt practice before he has been, or claims to have been, nominated as a candidate.

'Mr Bhushan has argued that this would mean that a candidate can commit all sorts of corrupt practices and undesirable acts before he is nominated, without incurring the liability of a corrupt practice. That is not correct, because the last date for nomination is about a month before the date of election and most corrupt practices can only be committed after this date.'

Counsel further argued that Bhushan was wrong in contending that a candidate could get away with bribery if it was committed before nomination. He said, 'Section 171(E) of the Penal Code makes bribery at any time a penal offence. Section 8(1) of the Representation of the People Act provides that any person held guilty under Section 171(E) of the Penal Code shall be disqualified from contesting elections for a period of six years from the date of his conviction. Therefore, even though a person committing bribery before nomination does not commit a corrupt practice, he gets disqualified because of Section 8(1) of the Representation of the People Act.'

Counsel thus contended that there were few abuses possible even after the amended definition of 'candidate'. He went on, 'But even if there is a slight infirmity in the law, it cannot be helped. Your Lordships will agree that it is a perfectly valid compromise. How can anyone argue that it destroys democracy?'

Official Duty

Sinha next took up the amendment regarding the corrupt practice of procuring the services of government servants. The amendment provides that any assistance rendered by a government servant to a candidate as part of his official duty would not be deemed to be assistance for the furtherance of the prospects of a candidate's election. Counsel disputed Bhushan's contention that under this amendment, the government could impose all sorts of official duties on government servants to further the prospects of the elections of their party members. He argued that official duty meant duty which could be treated as pertaining to government. This would include the maintenance of law and order and the provision for security of VIPs. Giving speeches or doing other strictly election work for a candidate would not be regarded as official duties, and whenever such a duty is conferred by the government, it could always be struck down by the court.

Justice Mathew: What pertains to the government and what does not, I do not know.

Counsel: Bribery and corruption do not pertain to the government. Law and order pertain to the government. Official duties will be those which could reasonably be regarded as duties which the government has to perform. In fact, the concept of official duty is much less vague than the concept of basic features of the Constitution.

Justice Mathew: Executive power is so wide that you can do anything in connection with the election by conferring an official duty through an administrative order.

Counsel: No, my Lord. A line has to be drawn in between.

Justice Mathew: Where will you draw the line? What cannot be done in purported discharge of official duties?

Counsel: Malafide administrative orders cannot bring into existence official duties.

Justice Khanna: So you mean to say that this law should be upheld and each administrative order should be checked to see whether it is proper or not.

Counsel: Yes.

Date of Resignation

Referring to the explanation added in Section 123(7) of the Act (which provides that the date of appointment or resignation of a government servant specified in the Official Gazette would be conclusive proof of the date of such appointment or resignation), Sinha then submitted that this again provides finality to the law and removes all ambiguity which the law had before this. Rebutting Bhushan's argument that this provision could be misused by the government which could specify fictitious dates of the appointment or resignation of government servants, Counsel said that this was mere speculation, and, in any case, the possibility of abuse of a law was not a ground for striking it down. 'It should be assumed that the government is not mad and will not act in a wholly capricious manner.'

Symbols

Going on to the amendment regarding symbols, Sinha argued that since symbols were allotted by the Election Commission, it was not right that the candidate should be made to suffer for the mistake of the Commission. In any case, he said, the Election Commission was an independent body which would on its own see that no religious symbol was allotted to anyone. He, therefore, did not see anything wrong in this amendment.

Amendments Do Not Change the Law

Arguing then on the retrospectivity which had been conferred on these amendments, Sinha contended that in fact none of these amendments changed the law. 'They only clarified what the law was. Hence it is not a question of changing the rules of the game after the game had been played, but only explaining what the correct rules of the game were.'

Justice Mathew (smiling): So you have only interpreted the law.

(Interpreting the law is the monopoly of the judiciary under the Constitution.)

Counsel further submitted that what had to be seen was whether the corrupt practices were such so as to call for vitiating the election. 'Otherwise, setting aside the election would be undemocratic. These amendments by curing the infirmities existing in the earlier law have only given greater effect to democracy.'

Justice Khanna: Some American judges have described all retrospective laws as repressive laws.

Counsel: My Lord, as I have submitted, these amendments have not really changed the law, but only clarified it.

After arguing very briefly on the validity of the constitutional amendment again, Sinha concluded his arguments. After Sinha concluded his arguments on behalf of the Union, Ashok Sen began his arguments on behalf of Mrs Gandhi.

SEN'S ARGUMENTS

Arguing first on the effect of the amendment in the definition of 'candidate' in the Representation of the People Act, Sen also assailed Bhushan's contention that a corrupt practice could be committed by a candidate even before he fell within the statutory definition of a candidate.

He drew the court's attention to Section 171(C) of the Indian Penal Code which provides that: 'Whosoever threatens any candidate or voter, or any person in whom a candidate or voter is interested, with injury of any kind, shall be deemed to interfere with the free exercise of the electoral right of such candidate or voter . . .'

Counsel also drew the court's attention to Section 171(G) of the Indian Penal Code which provides, 'Whoever with intent to affect the result of an election, makes or publishes any statement purporting to be a statement of fact which is false and which he either knows or believes to be false or does not believe to be true, in relation to the personal character or conduct of any candidate, shall be punished with fine.'

Counsel argued that if Bhushan was right in his contention that the word 'candidate' as it appeared in the chapter on corrupt practices was only used to identify the person who became the candidate, then in the Indian Penal Code too, it should have been used merely to identify the person who became the candidate. If this is so, your Lordships will see what will happen. Suppose a person 'A' makes or publishes a false statement about another person 'B', who ten years later becomes a candidate, then 'A' becomes liable to a penal offence relating to an election under Section 171(G) of the Penal Code, although when he threatened 'B', he had no idea that 'B' would later become a candidate at an election. Thus, in effect, 'A' would be prosecuted for an offence relating to an election, though he had no idea of the election at that time. Such a result could clearly not have been intended by the legislature. Therefore, it is clear that whenever the word 'candidate' occurs in the Indian Penal Code, the definition of 'candidate' given in the Representation of the People Act should be strictly applied so that these would be offences only after a person becomes a candidate.

'Moreover, if the word "candidate" is used merely for identification of a candidate, then the words "election agent" should also have been used merely for identification of the election agent. This would lead to the absurd result that if a corrupt practice was committed by a person with the consent of another person who later becomes the election agent of a candidate, then the election of the candidate would be liable to be set aside. I submit that this could not have been the intention of the legislature.'

Authorization Implies Agency

Making his submission on the interpretation of the term 'authorization' used in the Representation of the People Act, Sen argued, 'There is a vital difference between authorization and consent. The principle of agency is involved in authorization. The authorized person becomes an agent of the candidate.'

While Counsel was making his submissions on the issue, Justice Beg interrupted to ask him whether there was any evidence that

Yashpal Kapoor had acted on the Prime Minister's instructions when
he went to Rae Bareli on 7 January and again on 19 January. Counsel
replied that there was no evidence whatsoever.

This question of Justice Beg related to a finding of fact of the Allahabad
High Court. Though the findings of fact of the High Court were not
in issue at all in the Supreme Court, Justice Beg asked several questions
on them while counsels of either side were making their submissions on
the amendments. He appeared to be reading the paper books (record of
evidence) of the case during the arguments. It is, therefore, not surprising
that part of his judgment in this case was a pronouncement on the
correctness of the findings of the Allahabad High Court.

Arguing further, Counsel said that authorization meant that
the rights and liabilities of the person authorized become the rights
and liabilities of the person who authorized him. 'Unless this was
so, it would lead to a very odd situation. All sorts of people do odd
jobs for the candidates. How can the candidate find out how much
expenditure was incurred on these?'

Justice Khanna: Sometimes people do voluntary work not because
they are friendly with him, but because they hate the rival candidate.

Counsel: Exactly, my Lord. That is why the word 'authority'
has been pointedly used in the Act and not the words 'consent' or
'knowledge'.

Counsel submitted that unless the person authorized also has
a right to be reimbursed for the amount which he spent for the
candidate, there is no authorization.

Justice Mathew: So you mean that the entire expenditure which
is liable to be included in the candidate's return must be spent from
his own pocket?

Counsel: It has to be, my Lord.

Citing a number of cases to support his contention, Counsel
submitted that this was where the decision in Chawla's case was wrong
and made a clear departure from all previous cases. 'Chawla's case laid
down the proposition that mere consent or failure to disavow was
enough to make an expenditure the candidate's expenditure. This is
not a correct proposition according to all previous cases.'

Justice Mathew: According to you, can authorization ever be
implied?

Counsel: Yes, it can. But implied authorization must be an
unequivocal and unambiguous act.

Sen also pleaded that since the amendment did not change the law at all, it had to be valid.

Issue of Expenses

Taking up the issue of expenses, Sen argued that the pleadings in the petition about the expenses alleged to have been incurred by Mrs Gandhi or her election agent were not specific or sufficient. He said that it was not pleaded as to who had incurred and authorized the expenditure, nor had the extent of the expenditure or the things on which it was incurred been specified.

'However, even assuming that their pleading is correct in law, there is hardly any evidence in this case to show that the expenditure exceeded the prescribed limit. The learned judge of the High Court after adding Rs 16,000 on the construction of rostrums, and Rs 1900 on the loudspeakers etc., to the amount shown in the return of expenses, had come to a total of about Rs 32,000. Now, because of the explanation added to Section 77 (that any expenditure incurred by arrangements by a government servant in the discharge of his official duties shall not be deemed to be expenditure incurred in connection with the election of a candidate), this amount added by the learned judge would have to go out of the list of expenses. Rostrums and loudspeakers were arranged by government servants in the discharge of their official duties. So once these expenses are removed from the total reached by the High Court, there would remain a gap of about Rs 22,000 for the ceiling to be reached.'

Bhushan's main argument on the expenses issue was that the twenty-three vehicles used by the DCC of Rae Bareli must have been used in Mrs Gandhi's constituency and the expenditure on these vehicles must be included in her election expenses. Sen submitted that there was a total lack of evidence on the expenditure on these vehicles. 'None of the drivers of the vehicles have been examined. This itself shows that their case was not bonafide. Nor has he given any evidence to show the number of days these vehicles were used, or whether they were used in the Prime Minister's constituency at all.'

Justice Khanna: There are three possibilities of how these vehicles could have been used: (1) they were used wholly in the Prime Minister's constituency; (2) they were used partly in her constituency and partly in the other two constituencies; and (3) that all of them were used in the other two constituencies.

Is there any reason for us to accept the third possibility?

Counsel: In the absence of any evidence as to the number of these vehicles used in the Prime Minister's constituency, how can we estimate the expenditure incurred on them for her constituency?

Justice Chandrachud: If a candidate asks his party to spend money for him, but the party spends money jointly for two or three constituencies, then the question of apportionment of the expenditure would arise.

Counsel: There is no evidence that Mrs Gandhi or Yashpal Kapoor had asked the DCC to use those vehicles in her constituency. The only evidence is that Yashpal Kapoor wrote a letter to the DM to get those vehicles released as they were requisitioned by the DM. This was because the president of the DCC had requested Yashpal Kapoor to get them released as he was unable to find the candidates of the other two constituencies. From just this, we cannot conclude that the vehicles were used in the Prime Minister's constituency.

Giving his interpretation of the amendment about 'official duties', Sen said that this was merely to clarify the actual law. 'Since it was not clear before the amendment whether any assistance provided to a candidate by a government servant in the discharge of his official duties could attract a corrupt practice, the Parliament, by this amendment, decided to make things clear. They have conclusively laid down that if any incidental assistance was provided to a candidate by a government servant in the discharge of his official duties, it would not be deemed to be assistance for the furtherance of the prospects of the candidate's election, and would thus not have the effect of vitiating the election.'

Counsel contended that official duties did not merely mean statutory duties, but would include even administrative duties. He said that in England, procuring the assistance of government servants was not a corrupt practice. Hence, he said, it was in the fitness of things that Parliament had made this amendment in India. He said that in any case, the possibility of abuse of a provision was not a test of its validity.

Issue of Symbols

Explaining the amendment regarding the symbols, Sen said that by this amendment, Parliament had made it clear that if a religious symbol was allotted to a candidate because of the negligence of the Election Commission, the candidate would not have to pay the penalty. He said that even if the symbol was allotted at the request of the party, there was no reason why the poor candidate should be made to suffer for the fault of his party. 'Being the party's candidate, he has no option but to use the party's symbol. In any case, the Election Commission being an independent body will ensure that no religious symbol is allotted to a candidate. But if the Election Commission errs, it cannot be helped. Someone has to take a final decision about whether a symbol is religious or not. If the Commission can make a mistake, so can the courts.'

Sen's submissions on the amendment regarding the date of resignation of government servants were substantially the same as the Solicitor-General's. He said that this amendment had provided finality to the law and removed all ambiguity from it.

Spirit of Constitution a Vague Concept

Coming to the most crucial aspects of the case, Sen also submitted that the test of basic features could not be applied to ordinary laws, even if it could be applied to constitutional amendments. 'The validity of ordinary laws is governed by entirely different provisions like the chapter on fundamental rights. Bhushan has argued that the amendments are against the spirit of the Constitution. What is the spirit of the Constitution? Chief Justice Das had said that the spirit behind anything was a very elusive concept. There is no spirit except what the statute says.'

Justice Mathew: If the text of basic features can be applied to constitutional amendments, why can't it be applied to ordinary laws as well?

Counsel: The other side has argued that the election law amendments are against the ideal norms of free and fair election. Now it may be said that the limit of Rs 35,000 on election expenses is too high for a poor country like ours. This makes the election very unfair and is thus against the norms of free and fair elections. But can this be sustained? I submit that the only norms are the statutory norms incorporated in the Representation of the People Act.

Justice Mathew: If we can proceed on the basis that the concept of free and fair election is a valid limitation for a constitutional amendment, then why is it not a valid limitation for an ordinary law?

Counsel: My Lord, for a statute, it is not possible to apply that test.

Justice Mathew: But for a constitutional amendment, is it possible to apply it? Take a case where an amendment to the Representation of the People Act provides that people with an income above Rs 20,000 will have two votes. Does this not destroy the basic structure of a democratic State?

Counsel: No, it does not. All these rights are statutory and can be changed by amendment of the statute.

Justice Mathew: We must have some concept of our democracy.

Counsel: Then the validity of laws would be left to the likes and dislikes of the judges. This concept of basic structure is very difficult to understand.

Justice Mathew: Then the basic feature theory must go even for a constitutional amendment. If equality is a basic feature of the Constitution, then discrimination in voting is not possible. Do you say that free and fair elections are not a basic feature of the Constitution?

Solicitor-General (interjecting): The dimensions of the basic structure can be changed. The only condition is that it must not be destroyed. The voting age can be increased to twenty-five or reduced to eighteen without destroying the basic structure.

Sen: The only mandate of the Constitution is that there shall be a Parliament elected by the people. The residual norms of how the elections shall be fought and who shall be able to fight the elections is left to Parliament. This lodging of the power to create residual norms is itself a basic feature of the Constitution and you cannot deny this power to Parliament.

Arguing on the retrospectivity which had been awarded to the amendments, Sen submitted that the Parliament's competence to enact laws was not determined by the prospectivity or retrospectivity of the laws. 'If Parliament can enact a law prospectively, it can also enact the same law retrospectively. All that has to be seen is whether the Parliament is competent to enact that law.'

This concluded Sen's reply to Bhushan's arguments on the validity of the election law amendments.

KAUSHAL'S ARGUMENTS

After Sen, J.N. Kaushal, the assisting counsel for Mrs Gandhi, also made brief submissions in defence of the election law amendments.

Kaushal urged that this basic feature limitation should not be extended to ordinary legislation, as it would be a dangerous extension of the Kesavananda Bharati case. He pleaded that even though it may logically follow from the majority view of the Kesavananda Bharati case that this limitation should also apply to ordinary legislation, it should not be applied, because a case is an authority only for what it actually decides, and not for what follows logically from it. He cited a Supreme Court case to support his contention. In that case, Justice Hegde had observed, 'A case is only an authority for what it actually decides. I entirely deny that it can be quoted for a proposition that may seem logical from it. Such a mode of reasoning assumes that the law is necessarily a logical code, whereas every lawyer must acknowledge that the law is not always logical at all.'

Justice Mathew: If other things remained the same what is the harm in law being logical?

Counsel: If this basic feature limitation is applied to ordinary laws as well, it would open the doors to endless litigation. Thousands of writ petitions will be filed challenging various laws on vague grounds like political justice, etc.

Justice Mathew: Article 245, which gives the Parliament power to make laws, uses the words 'subject to the provisions of the Constitution'. Now this must mean subject to the basic structure.

Counsel however maintained that the words 'subject to the provisions of the Constitution' meant subject to the specific provisions of the Constitution.

Arguing on the validity of the amendments, Counsel said that the possibilities of abuse of the amendment suggested by Bhushan were hypothetical. He sought justification for the amendments on the ground that the provisions of the amendment had not been misused in Mrs Gandhi's case at least. 'The construction of rostrums was part of the legitimate duties of the state to provide security for the Prime Minister. The date of Yashpal Kapoor's resignation which was specified in the Gazette was also the correct date and not a fictional date. It is clear that the resignation of Yashpal Kapoor was tendered on 13 January, but the learned judge of the Allahabad High Court has come to the conclusion that the resignation did not take effect till 25 January, because in the eyes of law it does not take effect till it is formally accepted in the name of the President. The very concept of the "eyes of law" sometimes defeats the purpose of law.'

Justice Mathew: Then something must be wrong with the 'eyes of law'.

Kaushal: Yes, my Lord. And that is what has been put right by this amendment.

After briefly reinforcing the submissions of Sen on the expenses issue, Kaushal concluded his arguments.

18

'Parliament Cannot Interpret the Law'

Beginning his rejoinder on the election law amendments, Bhushan said that he would first deal with the other side's contention that the basic feature limitation could not be applied to ordinary legislation. He said, 'I have absolutely no quarrel with Sinha's first proposition that there can be no limitation on the powers of Parliament because of some natural rights of Man. He says that the restriction on the Constituent power flows from the use of the word "amendment" in Article 368. That might be so. But I submit that the basic features of the Constitution certainly cannot be discovered from Article 368. The problem in Kesavananda Bharati's case was to discover the connotation of the word "amendment" used in Article 368. Just by looking at the word "amendment" itself, one cannot say whether it was meant to be used in the wide or narrow sense in Article 368. Therefore, to discover the connotation of "amendment", the judges had to look at the rest of the Constitution to discover the intention of the Constitution-makers. The majority found that there were certain basic features which the Constitution-makers intended to be permanent and unamendable by any means. This is why they read a limited meaning into the word "amendment" used in Article 368.'

Justice Mathew: If you assume that certain features of the Constitution are intended to be permanent, then it is easy to import this limitation on the legislative power, but where do you find this in the Constitution?

Counsel read out some passages from some judgments in the Kesavananda Bharati case in support of his contention that certain features of the Constitution were intended to be permanent. He said, 'This was the premise on which the conclusion that the power under Article 368 is limited rests. The other side thinks that this conclusion can stand without the legs on which it rests.'

Counsel then dealt with the contention that the basic feature doctrine was too vague to be applied to ordinary legislation. He said, 'I fail to understand that if this same vague doctrine can be applied to constitutional amendments, what great difficulty can arise in applying it to ordinary legislation. They say that this will open the gates to a flood of litigation. On the other hand, let us see the consequence of not applying this to ordinary legislation. Does anyone want a law which in the opinion of the Supreme Court is repugnant to the basic features of the Constitution?'

Justice Mathew: Basic features must be there in every Constitution. All legislative power is subject to the Constitution. Basic features are also a part of the Constitution. Why has this argument not been applied to strike down legislation in the USA?

Counsel: Perhaps because of the 'due process' clause in America. The 'due process' clause is sufficient safeguard against any legislation repugnant to the basic feature. (The US Constitution contains a clause that no person shall be denied the 'due process of law'.)

Justice Khanna: In America, a lot of retrospective legislation has been struck down because of the 'due process' clause.

Chief Justice: Mr Bhushan, what is your syllogism in regard to legislative power? How do you reach the conclusion that the legislative power is also limited by the basic feature doctrine?

Bhushan did not know what a syllogism was, so he let it go at that time. In the lunch break, he asked me if I knew what a syllogism was. Having been a student of formal logic, I explained that a syllogism was an argument in which a conclusion is derived from two premises taken jointly. He immediately formed his syllogism and presented it before the Chief Justice right after lunch.

He said, 'Your Lordships asked me the syllogism for deriving the basic feature limitation on legislative power. This is my syllogism. The proposition established by Kesavananda's case is that there are some basic features of the Constitution which are intended to be permanent. This is my first premise. My second premise is that all legislative power is subject to the provisions of the Constitution. From this the conclusion clearly follows that legislative power is also subject to the restrictions imposed by the basic features of the Constitution.'

Chief Justice: But Mr Bhushan, this is *petitio principi* (circular argument).

Bhushan was again out of his depth. He did not know the meaning of this either. He thought it wise to avoid further arguments in formal terms of logic. Trying another line of argument, he said, 'I submit that it would be extremely illogical to hold that the legislature can destroy the basic features of the Constitution, by an ordinary law which can be enacted by a simple majority, while by a constitutional amendment which requires a two-third majority they cannot.'

Counsel submitted, 'To hold that the basic feature limitation does not apply to ordinary legislation would be so illogical that no expediency can sanction it. Mr Sinha stated that illogic had to be restored to in England to confer legitimacy on illegitimate children. I agree with the Solicitor-General that the law can be made illogical for some noble end. Legitimatizing innocent children is certainly a noble end. But in this case what is the innocent illegitimacy, which has to be legitimized? What great end is to be achieved by allowing the legislature to damage or destroy the basic structure of the Constitution? What great purpose is being served by these retrospective amendments, except upholding the election of one individual which had been declared invalid by the High Court?'

Justice Khanna: We must move out of this sensitive region.

Justice Mathew: No, this argument is very vital for your case. Therefore you must argue it this way. Suppose the majority in Kesavananda Bharati had held that there was some basic structure of the Constitution, but the amending power of the constituent body was plenary. What would you say about legislative power in that case? Would that be subject to the basic features?

Counsel: I submit it would. Because basic features would still constitute implied limitations on legislative power.

Justice Mathew: Suppose some people feel that proportional representation is a basic ingredient of democracy, what would happen then?

Counsel: If the judiciary feels that proportional representation is absolutely essential for democracy, then the judiciary must see that a law providing for proportional representation is made by the legislature.

On the amendment in the definition of 'candidate', Bhushan gave a cyclostyled compilation of various election laws of England, Australia and New Zealand. He told the court that in all these countries, the scheme was that the corrupt practice could be committed at any time either before, during or after the election.

Justice Khanna: Mr Bhushan, do you know that no person has been disqualified for corrupt practices in England since 1921? Not even a single election petition has been filed since then.

Counsel: If the laws are applied properly, then people know that their election will be set aside for any violation of the law. It is only when people think that they can get away without any penalty, that they resort to such practices.

Bhushan rebutted the argument that the object of the legislature in making this amendment must have been to reduce the liability of a corrupt practice. He said, 'We must assume that the intention of the legislature was honest and just. Why should we assume that the legislature intended that a candidate could commit all sorts of corrupt practices before filing his nomination papers? The Solicitor-General agreed with me that as far as bribery is concerned, it cannot be condoned even if it was done before the nomination of a candidate. He says so, because of the provisions of the Indian Penal Code. So if a candidate commits bribery before his nomination, his election would still be set aside through a long and circuitous process. Why should we credit the legislature with the intention that to achieve the same result they wanted a long and circuitous process to be followed? If the intention was that the candidate's election should be set aside even if bribery was committed before nomination, then there is no reason why my interpretation should not be accepted. Moreover, bribery is not the only corrupt practice. If the interpretation of the other side is accepted, it would mean that the entire government machinery can be used by a candidate before he files his nomination papers, without incurring any liability.

'Mr Sen referred to Section 171(C) and Section 171(G) of the IPC in order to prove that a corrupt practice could only be committed after the nomination of a person. Let us read Section 171(G). It says,

Whosoever with intent to affect the result of an election, makes
or publishes any statement, purporting to be a statement of
fact, which is false, or does not believe to be true, in relation
to the personal character or conduct of any candidate, shall be
punished with a fine.

'What Sen overlooks here is the effect of the crucial words "Whosoever with intent to effect the result of an election". How does it matter if a false statement is published even ten years before the election? If a person does it with the intention of affecting the result of the election, then why should he not be punished even if it is done twenty years before the election. If Sen's interpretation is accepted, it would mean that a candidate can flood the constituency with defamatory posters of the rival candidate just before filing his nomination paper, and get away without any liability.'

Bhushan said that the scheme of the R.P. Act was that an election should be set aside even if a corrupt practice was committed without the consent of a candidate if it materially affected the result of the election. 'Thus it is clear that the legislature intended the election to be vitiated, if the result of the election was materially affected by any corrupt practice. With this in view, can it be said that a corrupt practice, however serious, should be condoned if it were committed before the nomination of a candidate?'

Justice Khanna: Your contention is that there should be no time limit for corrupt practices. Why is there a time limit for election expenses? (Section 77 provides that a record of election expenses will be maintained from the date of the Presidential Notification calling for the elections.)

Counsel: It is because of practical necessity. It is very difficult to calculate the election expenses unless some time limit is specified. In England too, there is a time limit for election expenses though other corrupt practices can be committed at any time.

On the amendment about official duties of government servants, Bhushan said that the Solicitor-General had tried to limit the scope of official duties. 'He had said that everything cannot come in the category of official duties and the court would have to see whether a duty conferred on a government servant could be classed as official duty or not.' He, however, submitted that any duties for the security of VIPs would be official duties within the meaning of this section. I submit that if the construction of rostrums, as in this case, can be regarded as an official duty, then anything, even if it wholly deals with election work, can be regarded as an official duty.

Justice Mathew: If an act can be conceived to be in public interest, and in the process some benefit accrues to a candidate, can this act be said to be an official duty?

Counsel: Everything can be said to be in public interest. It all depends on the point of view. If a person is considered indispensable for the country, then anything done for his benefit can be in the public interest.

Justice Mathew: Is there anything in this amendment which contemplates these facilities for only one party? How can you say that this is discriminatory? If it is applied with an uneven hand and an evil eye, then perhaps you can complain.

Counsel: The power of imposing duties is conferred on the government. Normally, the government should be presumed to act fairly and if it issues an unfair order, that order can be challenged. But the order can also be a secret order. So it may not be possible to challenge it before it is executed. This is exactly the situation in this case. The Blue Book contained secret instructions not known to the outside world. If an order is executed which gives an unfair advantage to a candidate, what is the use of getting it struck down subsequently?

On the amendment regarding the date of resignation of a government servant, Bhushan referred to Kaushal's argument. He said, 'Mr Kaushal has said that Yashpal Kapoor submitted his resignation on 13 January which was accepted orally on the same date. It had also been accepted in writing with effect from 14 January. But the learned judge of the High Court has found that in the eyes of law the resignation did not become valid till 25 January because it was accepted in writing only on that date. Mr Kaushal said that since the eyes of law had begun to see illusions, the legislature had amended the law and had set the eyes of law right. I wonder when the eyes of law can see all sorts of complicated legal matters, what happens to them when they are determining the date on which a government servant's resignation becomes effective, that the legislature has to supply them with special glasses. The general law about the date of resignation of a government servant is quite clear. This amendment gives government an arbitrary power to specify the date on which a resignation takes effect, however divorced from reality it might be.'

Justice Khanna: The amendment is like a rule of evidence. It only says what the court will have to take into account in deciding the date of resignation.

Counsel: If there are two principles which can be followed when applying the law, the legislature can prescribe as to which principle should be followed by the courts. That is a rule of evidence. But here no principle has been prescribed. A judicially determinable matter has been left entirely to the government.

Going on to the amendment regarding symbols, Bhushan said, 'The argument of the fault being the Commission's is not correct because the symbol is chosen by the party itself. Although this is not a mandatory rule, the procedure followed is that the party submits a list of three symbols and normally the Commission allots one of these. The alternative submission of Sen was that a candidate should not be made to suffer for the fault of his party. This is also a fallacious argument. A party candidate contests on the label of his party and therefore cannot be divorced from it. If his party is at fault, why should he not suffer for it? Moreover, even if the candidate is not at fault, but it is found that the allotment of a religious symbol substantially affected the result of the election, then there is no reason why the election should not be vitiated. Elections are sometimes vitiated when the returning officer has improperly rejected the nomination papers of some persons, which is also not a fault of the elected candidate.

'Another argument of the other side is that someone has to be conferred the final authority to decide whether a symbol is religious or not. The Election Commission has been conferred this authority. Why should the power of deciding whether the symbol is religious or not be conferred to the Election Commission which is a quasi-judicial body instead of the courts? They say that the Election Commission would not allot a religious symbol. Let us look at the peculiar facts of this case. The symbol of cow and calf was the second preference of the Congress party. Their first preference was a mother with a child in her arms. I do not know what objection the Election Commission could have had to the first preference of the Congress. But by a curious process of reasoning, the Election Commission allotted the second. The reasoning was that since the Congress (O) had also been allotted its second preference, therefore, to ensure equality, they were allotting the Congress (R) its second preference too. The only objection to the mother and child symbol could be that children would be attracted to vote on that symbol.'

Justice Khanna: But children have no vote.

Counsel: Precisely.

Justice Mathew (smiling): No, they could perhaps induce their mothers to vote on that symbol.

Arguing on the retrospectivity conferred on these amendments, Bhushan ridiculed the other side's contention that the amendment had not changed the law but merely clarified it. 'They say that when Parliament found that the judiciary was not interpreting the laws according to the Parliament's intention, they had to move in to interpret them for the benefit of the judiciary. I do not know under which provision of the Constitution the Parliament has been given this power to show the judiciary how to interpret a law. The judiciary is the final interpreter of all laws. The law was as the Supreme Court interpreted it. These amendments have clearly altered the law.

'Mr Sen has submitted that Parliament's competence to make laws is not affected by the retrospectivity given to them. If the Parliament can make a law with prospective effect, it can also do so with retrospective effect. I am surprised that Mr Sen could advance such a grossly erroneous proposition. Let us take the simple case of ex post facto laws. The Parliament cannot enhance the penalty for a crime retrospectively, though they can certainly enhance it prospectively. I agree that retrospective legislation is possible where it does not come in conflict with any constitutional provision, but retrospective legislation about the rules of a contest is certainly discriminatory.'

Bhushan then took up the issue of expenses. He strongly contested Sinha's and Sen's contentions that the word 'authorization' used in Section 123 meant a transfer of rights and liabilities of the person who had been authorized, to the candidate who had authorized him.

Counsel said, 'Let us take an example. When a person is authorized by an officer to carry on a business, does it mean that he is carrying on the business on behalf of the officer? Are the rights and liabilities of this person transferred to the officers? If authorization is taken to mean a transfer of rights and liabilities, then a ceiling on expenses would become meaningless. A candidate could get any amount of money spent on his election by his friends and supporters merely by refusing the liability. It is also incorrect to say that authorization implies reimbursement. If that is so, it would mean that a friend or supporter of a candidate could give him a cheque of Rs 5 lakh because most elections are fought on donated money and the candidate would be free to spend this money on his election.'

Justice Mathew: Suppose a person canvasses for his ideals, and his ideals happen to coincide with those of a candidate. If that person spends his money to canvass support for this candidate even though the candidate does not ask for it, will this expenditure have to be included in the candidate's return?

Counsel: It would depend on the facts of the case. If it is found that the refusal of the candidate was a facade and he really consented to the expenditure incurred by that person, then it would have to be included. It could certainly be a difficult question. But just because the application of a particular law can sometimes pose a difficult problem, it does not mean that the law should be given an absurd interpretation.

Justice Mathew: Suppose a juristic person like a company spends money on a candidate. Is it an offence under Section 171(H) of the Penal Code?

Counsel: Yes, it is.

Justice Mathew: How can the company be jailed or hanged?

Counsel: The person responsible for the acts of the company can be punished.

On the expenses issue regarding the twenty-three vehicles used by the DCC in Rae Bareli, Bhushan contested the other side's argument that the petitioner had not discharged his burden by proving the extent of expenditure on the vehicles. He said that once he had shown that these vehicles were used in Mrs Gandhi's constituency with the authorization of Yashpal Kapoor, the burden shifted to the appellant to show exactly how much expenditure was incurred on them. 'In this case, I have shown that at least some of these vehicles were used for Mrs Gandhi's election with Kapoor's consent. The expenses on none of these have been included in the return. Now it is their duty to show the exact expenditure incurred on these. In the absence of that, it is the duty of the court to make a reasonable estimate of the expenses likely to have been incurred and add that to the return. Regarding their allegation that we have not tried to examine any of the drivers of the vehicles, your Lordships will appreciate that in theory, it is easy to say that this should also have been done, but in practice, it can be extremely difficult. When we managed to locate some of the drivers with great difficulty, they were not willing to give evidence in this case. Nobody wants to give evidence against the Prime Minister. They are all afraid. We cannot drive them from their houses and force them to come to court.' Regarding Sen's allegation that the pleading in the petition about the corrupt practice on the expenses issue was not specific, Bhushan said that pleading must be of a corrupt practice. 'The corrupt practice in this case was exceeding the limit of election expenses. The petition has clearly alleged that the appellant exceeded the limit of election expenses. We have also given as many details about the expenses as we could. But I submit that it is not necessary to give the details of every expenditure which was incurred by the appellant. If I can show that the totality of expenses exceeded the limit, then I have proved a corrupt practice.'

Bhushan concluded his rejoinder on the election law amendments just before the court rose on 9 October. At last the long arguments of the Supreme Court had ended. They had worked continuously for thirty-one days.

19

The Supreme Court Judgment

As soon as the Supreme Court arguments concluded, Bhushan was asked by some foreign journalists about the prospects of the amendments being struck down. He said that he was sure that the constitutional amendments would be struck down, and was also confident of the election law amendments being declared invalid. When questioned about the possibility of the judges being pressurized, Bhushan answered in the affirmative. He was then asked whether he thought they would succumb to the pressure. He said that judges were trained to resist pressure, but in these extraordinary conditions it would depend on the kind of pressure that was brought to bear upon them. He said, 'If I was told that I would be jailed for arguing this case, I could have resisted that pressure. But if I was told that my children would be slaughtered, then, perhaps, the situation would have been otherwise. But in any case I do not think that the Supreme Court judges will succumb to any pressure.'

When Bhushan reached Allahabad after the conclusion of the Supreme Court arguments, he heard that Kanhaiya Lal Misra, the former Advocate-General of UP, who had also argued Mrs Gandhi's case at the preliminary stages, was very ill. He took the first opportunity to call on him, at which occasion Mrs Gandhi's case was also discussed. Misra's last words to Bhushan were, 'Democracy is dead in this country.' The very next day he expired.

Incidentally, 9 October, the day the arguments ended, was the last working day before the court recessed for the Dussehra vacations. Since the Chief Justice, at the conclusion of the hearing, had not said that the judgment in the case was reserved, people who had witnessed the case were wondering whether, when the court assembled after the vacations, the Chief Justice would not call upon both the sides to advance their arguments on the merits of the case as they stood before the election law amendments. Everything was possible. They had, after all, decided to hear the case on merits as it stood after the election law amendments, even before deciding the validity of the Thirty-ninth Constitutional Amendment. This speculation, however, was put at rest, when the court assembled after the Dussehra vacations and the Bench began its routine work. Speculation now was about when the judgment would be delivered. Although utmost secrecy was supposed to be maintained, the date leaked out on 2 November. On that day, word went around that the judgment was to be delivered on Monday, 7 November. The official announcement came only when the list of the court for 7 November was published the previous evening.

Meanwhile, on the political scene, things were moving. All the state chief ministers and all the central Cabinet ministers were asked to be present in Delhi on 7 November. On that date, a large number of people had gathered around the Prime Minister's residence where elaborate arrangements had been made for them.

On 7 November, visitors and lawyers started arriving at the Chief Justice's court from 9.30 a.m. Entry, again, was by passes and no one was allowed to stand. By 10.30 a.m. when the judges arrived, the court was filled to capacity. One could almost feel the excitement in the court. This case was being seen as the last chance to overthrow Mrs Gandhi's dictatorship. There was pin-drop silence as the people waited to hear the Chief Justice.

The Chief Justice announced that an equal amount of time would be given to all the judges to read out their respective judgments. He was the first to start reading out his judgment. As it is not the convention in the Supreme Court to first announce the operative portion of the judgment, the people had to wait till the end to know the operative order.

The Chief Justice first dealt with the constitutional amendment. Within twenty minutes it was clear that he had struck down the constitutional amendment. Reporters rushed out in joy to ring up their news services. Their joy was, however, short-lived, as in another fifteen minutes it was clear that the Chief Justice had upheld the election law amendments. He finished reading his judgment in forty-five minutes. He had accepted the appeal and reversed the High Court's decision because of the election law amendments. The people who had witnessed the proceedings were not greatly surprised at the Chief

Justice's decision. They now held their breaths and waited for Justice Khanna to deliver his judgment.

Justice Khanna was decidedly not at his best when he began his ordeal. He looked slightly worried and his face betrayed a tinge of sadness. He read out his judgment slowly. The people were not surprised when he read out that he had struck down the constitutional amendment. They were, however, surprised when he read out that he had upheld the election law amendments and had thus declared Mrs Gandhi's election valid.

The onlookers groaned. All their hopes were shattered. Now it seemed certain that the election law amendments would be upheld by the majority. The fact that the constitutional amendment would be struck down was a poor consolation in these circumstances.

It was next Justice Mathew's turn to read out his judgment. In a bold and clear voice, he too declared this constitutional amendment invalid, upheld the election law amendments and, therefore, reversed the High Court's decision. The two judgments which now remained were of merely academic interest. By now it seemed that the judgment would be unanimous.

But Justice Beg's judgment was not without surprise. In his 231-page judgment, he did not pronounce at all on the validity of the constitutional amendment. By a strange piece of reasoning, he held that the constitutional amendment did not bar the courts from going into the merits of the case. Although he did declare the election law amendments valid, he did not stop there. He went on to discuss the correctness of Justice Sinha's judgment on the basis of the unamended laws. Observing that Justice Sinha's judgment contained 'manifest errors', Justice Beg disagreed with Justice Sinha's findings on the two issues on which he had found Mrs Gandhi guilty. Observing that these amendments were unnecessary and futile, Justice Beg absolved Mrs Gandhi of all blame, even on the basis of the unamended law.

It was lastly Justice Chandrachud who read out his judgment. His was the shortest judgment. In a fifty-five-page judgment he declared the constitutional amendment invalid and the election law amendments valid. Thus, he too upheld the validity of Mrs Gandhi's election.

The Supreme Court judgment was greeted with mixed reaction. While the Opposition was disappointed, though not unexpectedly so, there were jubilant celebrations at Mrs Gandhi's house. The 'rented crowd' there danced with joy and said that the Supreme Court judgment had vindicated Mrs Gandhi and had shown that she was 'innocent' of the corrupt practices declared by the High Court.

The irony of this exercise of back-patting at Mrs Gandhi's house was adroitly brought out by a cartoon published in *Time* magazine. The cartoon depicts Mrs Gandhi sitting on a Judge's desk and saying, 'You have been found guilty of election law violations. Do you wish to say anything to the court before sentencing?' She runs from the Judge's chair to the 'accused's' position and replies, 'Why not get rid of these laws, your honour?', whereupon she moves up again to the Judge's desk to say, 'Sounds good to me. Case dismissed. Not guilty.'

Raj Narain's lawyers were slightly surprised at the Supreme Court judgment. They were half expecting that the election law amendments would also be declared void. But it was Justice Beg's judgment which had really surprised them. Bhushan was very angry, and he immediately decided to file a review application against this judgment. The review was sought on the ground that Justice Beg, by delivering a judgment on the merits of the case without hearing the parties, had given a go-by to the principles of natural justice.

The review application came up for hearing on 18 December. The same five-member Bench was reconstituted to hear this application.[1] It is sufficient to mention here that the review application was dismissed by the five judges on the ground that one of them was of the opinion that there were no sufficient grounds for a review. Justice Beg, giving his separate judgment, set out his reasons for delivering a judgment on the merits of the case.

Thus ended what has been perhaps the most sensational case in India's legal history.

The Judgment of the Chief Justice

In his judgment, the Chief Justice first deals with the validity of the constitutional amendment. Pronouncing generally on the powers of the constituent body and of the legislature, he observes that validation Acts in almost all spheres of legislation are possible in India and the legislature has power to validate a transaction which has been

---

[1] The details of the review application and the judgments on it are given in Appendix 4.

declared void by the judiciary. All the sales-tax validation cases and the election validation cases are illustrations of this proposition.

'Constituent Power Is Sovereign'

The Chief Justice further holds that there is no separation of powers for the constituent body. The constituent power is sovereign. It is the power which creates the organs and distributes the powers.

He further says that judicial review is not an essential feature of the Constitution and not a feature at all when it comes to elections.

On the question of equality, the Chief Justice says that the classification made by the legislature cannot be questioned by the judiciary.

He also rejects the petitioner's contention that free and fair elections was a basic feature of the Constitution. He said that the concept of free and fair elections varied from person to person and the only norms were those provided by the R.P. Act.

The Chief Justice interpreted clause (4) of the constitutional amendment as first, having wiped out not merely the judgment but also the election petition and the law relating thereto. 'Secondly, it has deprived the right to raise a dispute about the validity of the election by not having provided another forum. Third, there is no judgment to deal with and no right or dispute to adjudicate upon. Fourth, the constituent power of its own legislative judgment has validated the election.'

After all that he has observed about the power of the constituent body, it should have seemed that the Chief Justice would uphold the constitutional amendment. But he does not. With a sudden turn, he declares clause (4) of Article 329(A) invalid. The main infirmity in the amendment, according to him, was that no norms were applied by the constituent body in validating the election. He says that the constituent body could adjudicate the election disputes, but it had to apply some law. In this case all the law relating to the election was retrospectively repealed and there was thus no law which the constituent body could apply. Thus he says that the amendment offends the rule of law.

The Chief Justice rejects the petitioner's contention that the Parliament session was illegal. He holds that the legality of the session could only be determined by the Parliament itself. The court is not competent to pronounce on it.

Interpretation of Election Law Amendments

He then discusses the effect of the election law amendments on the case. The amendment about the definition of 'candidate', he says, makes it clear that a person can commit a corrupt practice only after he has been nominated as a candidate. He also rejects the petitioner's argument that the amendment about 'official duties' refers merely to statutory duties of government servants.

Observing that these amendments took care of the two grounds on which the appellant was convicted by the High Court, the Chief Justice proceeds to deal with the expenses issue. About the expenses on the twenty-three vehicles, he observes that the petitioner had not shown how much expenditure was incurred on these vehicles and in what proportion they were used in three constituencies. He says that there is also no proof that they were authorized by Yashpal Kapoor. He also observes that authorization implies reimbursement of the agent by the principal. For these reasons, he holds that Mrs Gandhi had not exceeded the limit of election expenses.

Ordinary Laws Not Subject to Basic Structure

On the crucial issue of whether the limitation of basic features would also apply to ordinary laws, the Chief Justice says that the validity of the exercise of legislative power must be determined by the affirmative grant of that power in the Constitution and the negative restrictions imposed by the Constitution. He observes:

> The contentions on behalf of the respondent that ordinary legislative measures are subject like Constitution amendments to the restrictions of not damaging or destroying basic structure, or basic features are utterly unsound. It has to be appreciated at the threshold that the contention that legislative measures are subject to restrictions of the theory of basic structure or basic features is to equate legislative measures with constitutional amendments.

He further observes, 'The theory of basic structures or basic features is an exercise in imponderables. Basic structures or basic features are indefinable. The legislative entries are the fields of legislation. The pith and substance doctrine has been applied in order to find out legislative competency and eliminate encroachment on legislative entries. If the theory of basic structures or basic features will be applied to legislative measures, it will denude Parliament and state legislatures of the power of legislation and deprive them of laying down legislative policies. This will be encroachment on the separation of powers.'

Coming to the Ninth Schedule, the Chief Justice says that according to the majority view in Kesavananda Bharati, laws inserted in the Ninth Schedule were not open to challenge on the ground of either damage or destruction of the basic features or violation of any fundamental rights. In view of all this, he pronounces the election law amendments valid. Thus, the Chief Justice accepts the appeal, sets aside the judgment of the High Court and dismisses the cross-appeal.

THE JUDGMENT OF JUSTICE KHANNA

In his judgment, Justice Khanna first deals with the second phase of Bhushan's attack on the validity of the amendment; that the Parliament session was illegal. Rejecting the contention, he says that the legality of the detention cannot be gone into collaterally in this case. That can only be determined by a writ of habeas corpus. Moreover, he says that the detention of an MP is a matter which can only be dealt with by Parliament itself which is the sole judge of the lawfulness of its proceedings.

Interpretation of Constitutional Amendment

Giving his interpretation of the Thirty-ninth Amendment, Justice Khanna says that clause (4) of the amendment retrospectively repeals the Representation of the People Act for the PM's election. The consequence of this is that the High Court judgment becomes void. Although this may be the consequence, it does not become void automatically. The judgment would have to be declared void, he says, by some authority. In this case, the constituent body has been declared void. This is clearly not permissible as the constituent body cannot encroach upon the judicial sphere.

He further holds that free and fair elections—which require that the candidates and their agents should not resort to unfair means or malpractices—are a basic feature of the Constitution.

Forum Necessary to Decide Election Disputes

Justice Khanna says that for free and fair elections it was necessary to have a machinery to resolve election disputes and to investigate the allegations of malpractices.

He says that the vice of the constitutional amendment is that 'without even prescribing a law and providing a forum for adjudicating upon the grounds advanced by the respondent to challenge the election of the appellant, the constituent authority has declared the election of the appellant to be valid'. He says that such an arbitrary conferment of validity is destructive of free and fair elections.

Regarding the Solicitor-General's arguments that the constituent body had itself become the forum for deciding the election disputes of the appellant, Justice Khanna observes that there is no material before him which would indicate that the constituent body considered any material in declaring the election to be valid.

He does not pronounce on Bhushan's contention that the validation of an election could not be a subject-matter of a constitutional amendment. Even assuming that it could be, he rejects the arguments of the Solicitor-General that an amendment dealing with but one election could only have the effect of damaging the basic structure of the Constitution. He says, 'If an amendment striking at the basic structure of the Constitution is not permissible, it would not acquire validity by being related only to one case. To accede to the argument advanced in support of the validity of the amendment would be tantamount to holding that even though it is not permissible to change the basic structure of the Constitution, whenever the authority concerned deems it proper to make such an amendment, it can do so and circumvent the bar to the making of such an amendment by confining it to one case. What is prohibited cannot become permissible because of its being confined to one matter.'

In view of all this, he strikes down clause (4) of Article 329A which was introduced by the Thirty-ninth Amendment.

Interpretation of the Election Law Amendments

On the interpretation of the amendment in the definition of 'candidates', Justice Khanna rejects the petitioner's contention that corrupt practices start applying even before a person falls within the statutory definition of a 'candidate'.

Regarding the amendment about official duties of government servants too, Justice Khanna rejects the petitioner's contention that the official duty mentioned in the amendment referred merely to statutory duty.

Validity of the Election Law Amendments

Going on to the validity of election law amendments, Justice Khanna does not pronounce on the preliminary question of whether laws included in the Ninth Schedule were subject to the basic feature limitation.

He, however, rejects the petitioner's contention that even in their prospective operation, the election law amendments damage the basic structure of the Constitution. He says that these amendments merely make the law certain. The possibility of abuse suggested by the petitioner was no ground for striking down the amendment. He says that if the power conferred by the amendment was abused by the government, the courts would not be helpless. So the proper course would be to strike down the action instead of the law.

Dealing with retrospective operation of the amendment, he observes that the legislature is allowed to give retrospective effect to the laws unless some specified provision of the Constitution restricts it. He says that retrospective legislation involving election matters has taken place earlier too. Free and fair elections are not violated by retrospective legislation relating to the elections. Therefore, he says that the amendments did not affect any basic feature of the Constitution and were thus valid.

Expenses Issue

On the expenses issue, Justice Khanna says that there was not enough evidence to hold that the twenty-three vehicles or even some of them were used in Mrs Gandhi's constituency nor was it known how much expenditure was incurred on them. So he holds Mrs Gandhi not guilty of a corrupt practice on this issue.

In view of these findings, he accepts the appeal of Mrs Gandhi and dismisses the cross-appeal of Raj Narain.

THE JUDGMENT OF JUSTICE MATHEW

In his judgment, Justice Mathew first deals with the validity of the constitutional amendment. After discussing its validity in a fair amount of detail, he sums up his findings in this way:

> Our Constitution by Article 329B visualizes the resolution of an election dispute on the basis of a petition presented to such authority and in such manner as the appropriate legislature may, by law, provide. The nature of the dispute raised in an election petition is such that it cannot be resolved except by judicial process, namely, by ascertaining the facts relating to the election and applying the pre-existing law. When the amending body held that the election of the appellant was valid, it could not have done so except by ascertaining the facts by judicial process and by applying the law. The result of this process would not be the enactment of constitutional law but the passing of a judgment or sentence. The amending body, though possessed of judicial power, had no competence to exercise it, unless it passed a constitutional law enabling it to do so. If, however, the decision of the amending body to hold the election of the appellant void was the result of the exercise of an 'irresponsible despotic discretion' governed solely by what it deemed political necessity or expediency, then, like a bill of attainder, it was a legislative judgment disposing of a particular election dispute, and not the enactment of a law resulting in an amendment of the Constitution. And, even if the latter process (the exercise of despotic discretion) could be regarded as an amendment of the Constitution, the amendment would damage or destroy an essential feature of democracy as established by the Constitution, namely, the resolution of election dispute by an authority by the exercise of judicial power by ascertaining the adjudicative facts and applying the relevant law for determining the real representative of the people.

Justice Mathew is thus the only judge who accepted the argument raised by Bhushan that clause (4) of Article 329A introduced by the Thirty-ninth Amendment was not an amendment of the Constitution at all.

Regarding equality, Justice Mathew holds that the majority in Kesavananda Bharati's case did not hold equality to be part of the basic structure of the Constitution and the only logical basis for supporting the validity of Article 31A, 31B and the first part of 31C, was that Article 14 was not a basic feature.

Because of the foregoing observations, Justice Mathew strikes down clause (4) or Article 329A introduced by the amendment.

'Basic Feature Limitation Inapplicable to Ordinary Laws'

On the validity of the election law amendments, Justice Mathew observes:

> I think the inhibition to destroy or damage the basic structure by an amendment of the Constitution flows from the limitation on the power of 'amendment' under Article 368 read into it by the majority in Bharati's case because of their assumption that there are certain fundamental features in the Constitution which its makers intended to remain there in perpetuity. But I do not find any such inhibition so far as the power of Parliament or state legislatures to pass laws is concerned. Articles 245 and 246 give the power and also provide the limitation upon the power of these organs to pass laws. It is only the specific provisions enacted in the Constitution which could operate as limitations upon that power.

Here it seems that Justice Mathew makes a serious error of reasoning. Although he holds that the limitation in the amending power is because the Constitution makers intended certain features of the Constitution to be permanent, he still holds that the ordinary legislative power of Parliament is not limited by these basic features. If the Constitution intends certain features to be permanent, then it is obvious that there is an implied limitation on the power of any organ of the State to damage those features.

Justice Mathew further holds that the Preamble does not set out the essential features of the Constitution. He says that there are no ideal norms of free and fair elections and the norms are made by the legislature itself. These norms, he says, can only be tested by some specific provision of the Constitution or necessary implications from them, but not on the anvil of the concept of free and fair elections in an ideal democracy. He also says that since democracy is a nebulous concept, one cannot test the validity of laws with reference to the essential elements of an ideal democracy. They can only be tested with reference to the principles of democracy actually incorporated in the Constitution.

Ninth Schedule

Justice Mathew holds that because an ordinary law is not subject to the basic features limitation, it cannot become subject to it because of its inclusion in the Ninth Schedule. He says:

> The concept of a basic structure, as brooding omnipresence in the sky, apart from the specific provisions of the Constitution constituting it, is too vague and indefinite to provide a yardstick to determine the validity of an ordinary law.

He says that Acts did not attain the status of constitutional law merely because they were put in the Ninth Schedule. Therefore, they cannot be challenged on the ground of basic features. 'The utmost that can be said is, as I indicated, that even after putting them in the Ninth Schedule, their provisions would be open to challenge on the ground that they took away or abrogated all, or any, of the fundamental rights, and, therefore, damaged or destroyed the basic structure if the fundamental rights or right taken away or abrogated constitute or constitutes a basic structure.' He, therefore, holds that the election law amendments were not liable to be challenged on any ground argued by the petitioner and were thus valid. He also did not agree with any of the interpretations of the amendments advanced by Bhushan.

Parliament Session Not Illegal

Regarding the illegality of the Monsoon Session of Parliament, Justice Mathew says:

> If a statutory authority passes an illegal order of detention and thus prevents a Member of Parliament from attending the House, how can the proceedings of Parliament become illegal for that reason? It is the privilege of Parliament to secure the attendance of persons illegally detained. But what would

happen if the privilege is not exercised by Parliament? I do not think that the proceedings of Parliament would become illegal for that reason.

In view of these findings, he accepts Mrs Gandhi's appeal setting aside the order of the High Court and rejects Raj Narain's cross-appeal.

THE JUDGMENT OF JUSTICE BEG

Justice Beg starts his judgment by taking great pains to explain why he considers it important to go into the merits of the case as they stood before the election law amendments. He says:

The recurring theme of the petitioner's argument was that the constitutional amendment and the election laws amendments were instituted entirely to deprive the petitioner of the remedies which he had under the law against an election vitiated by corrupt practices. It was suggested by the petitioner that the lawmaking powers had been abused by majority in Parliament for the purpose of serving a majority party and personal ends. It was even alleged that the President of India had also become a party to the misuse of the constitutional powers by detaining Members of Parliament and thus disabling them from opposing the amendments.

In the circumstances indicated above, it seemed to me to be absolutely essential for us to call upon the parties defending or assailing the Thirty-ninth Amendment and the Acts of 1974 and 1975, to take us, inter alia, into the merits of the cases, of the two sides and the findings given by the trying judge so as to enable us to see how far these findings were justifiable under the law as it stood even before the amendment by the Act of 1974 and 1975, how they were affected by these amendments, and how they were related to the validity of Section 4 of the Thirty-ninth Amendment.

Going on to deal with the merits of the case, Justice Beg says that he will not disturb the findings of facts of the High Court judge and that he would only deal with the questions on law involved in the case.

Issue of Yashpal Kapoor

Dealing with the first issue, Justice Beg says that there was no evidence to show that Mrs Gandhi had given her consent to Yashpal Kapoor for doing election work for her before 1 February. He also holds that Yashpal Kapoor's resignation became effective in law on 14 January because of the President's retrospective acceptance with effect from 14 January. In any case, he says that the amendment puts these issues absolutely beyond doubt. He further holds that there was no reliable evidence to show that Kapoor had done any election work for Mrs Gandhi before 25 January. Therefore, he finds Mrs Gandhi not guilty of corrupt practice on this issue even on the basis of the unamended law.

Issue of Holding Out

Dealing with the question of when Mrs Gandhi held herself out as a candidate, Justice Beg vehemently disagrees with the High Court's findings that Mrs Gandhi's reply to a question in the press conference on 29 December amounted to holding out as a prospective candidate. He says that what was really relevant was Mrs Gandhi's intention in making that statement, and not what other people understood her statement to mean.

Moreover, he says that all uncertainty about holding out has been removed by the amendment in the definition of 'candidate' and, therefore, Mrs Gandhi only became a candidate on 1 February. He rejects Bhushan's contention that a corrupt practice could be committed even before a person fell within the statutory definition of a 'candidate'.

Issue of Rostrums

Regarding the construction of rostrums and the installation of loudspeakers, Justice Beg says it did not amount to furtherance of the prospects of Mrs Gandhi's election. They were merely security arrangements which are made by every government of a civilized country. Secondly, he says that these arrangements were made almost automatically and Mrs Gandhi did not solicit these arrangements. Therefore, this assistance, if any, was not procured at the instance of Mrs Gandhi. Justice Beg also accepts the validity of the amendment about official duties of government servants, because, he says, that this amendment does not change the law but merely clarifies it.

Dealing generally with the validity of the election law amendments, Justice Beg observes that Acts inserted in the Ninth Schedule are not open to challenge on the basic feature doctrine. Moreover, he says that these amendments do not damage the basic structure of the Constitution nor are they against equality. He says that these amendments made a reasonable classification between the Prime Minister and the other people. The Prime Minister, he says, with all the great hazards and trials, which go with his office, is entitled to certain benefits not available to other people.

About Justice Sinha's findings that Mrs Gandhi was not a very truthful witness, Justice Beg says,

> the learned judge was unduly conscious of the fact that he was dealing with the case of the Prime Minister and he seemed to be anxious not to allow this fact to affect his judgment; nevertheless, when it came to appraising evidence, he applied unequal standards in assessing its worth so as to benefit the election petitioner.

Cross-appeal

Dealing with the issues in the cross-appeal, Justice Beg ignores the issues of bribery and conveyance of voters because they were not raised by the petitioner in the High Court. He also ignores the issue of travel by IAF planes as it was covered by the amendment made about official duties of government servants.

Dealing with the issue of the cow and calf symbol, Justice Beg says that on the evidence produced in the court, it was clear that this was not a religious symbol. Moreover, he says that the amendment, by providing that a symbol allotted by the Election Commission would not be deemed to be a religious, symbol, removed all doubt in the matter.

Dealing with the expenses issue, Justice Beg says that the expenses alleged by the petitioner were incurred by the DCC. Since they have not been shown to be authorized by Mrs Gandhi or Yashpal Kapoor, the limit has not been exceeded. He, therefore, decides this issue in Mrs Gandhi's favour.

Legality of Parliament Session

Regarding the contention of Bhushan that the Parliament Session was illegal, Justice Beg says that the violation of a privilege of Member of Parliament must be considered by Parliament itself. It could not be considered by the court. Moreover, the legality of the detention could not be challenged collaterally in this case. He, therefore, dismisses the attack on the amendment on this ground.

Validity of the Constitutional Amendment

Justice Beg deals last with the validity of the constitutional amendment. This, by itself, is strange, because the amendment on the face of it deprives the Supreme Court of its jurisdiction to go into the merits of this case. Therefore, unless he provided another interpretation to the amendment, or declared it invalid, he was precluded from going into the merits of the case. However, this is not strange enough. The way in which he has dealt with the constitutional amendment is even stranger.

Justice Beg observes that the separation of powers was a basic feature of the Constitution. The constituent power is not an amalgam of legislative, executive and judicial powers. He further says that the constituent body cannot exercise judicial power without changing the basic structure, but he holds that clause (4) was not an exercise of judicial power.

In a judgment punctuated by surprises, Justice Beg goes on to say that the basic feature limitation also applies to ordinary legislation. He is thus the only judge to hold this.

Clause (4) does not Prevent the Court from going into the Merits of the Case

Justice Beg then comes to the most interesting part of his judgment, wherein he gives his reason for believing that clause (4) did not preclude the court from going into the merits of the case. In a benevolent gesture towards the petitioner, he observes:

> It is true that the right which the election petitioner claimed is purely a statutory right. The right to come to this court under

Section 116A of the Act of 1951 is also a creature of statute and can be taken away retrospectively. But, where this taking away also involves the taking away of the right to be heard by this court on a grievance, whether justifiable or not, that a minority party is being oppressed by the majority, can we deny the spokesman of the minority even a right to be heard on merits?

I think that this is a basic consideration which must compel us in the light of the principles laid down by us in Kesavananda Bharati's case to hold that we must look into his grievance and determine for ourselves, where his case stood on the law before it was amended.

He further says that if the amendment was interpreted as barring the jurisdiction of the Supreme Court, then

the original respondent would also be denied an opportunity of asserting her rights under the 1951 Act and of vindicating her stand in the case by showing that there was really no sustainable ground for the findings given by the learned judge of the High Court against her. We would, therefore, be prevented from doing justice to her case as well, if we were to accept the contention that the Thirty-ninth Amendment bars our jurisdiction to hear the appeals under Section 116(A) of the Act on merits. The total effect would be that justice would appear to be defeated even if, in fact, it is not so as a result of the alleged bar to our jurisdiction if it were held to be there. Could it be the intention of Parliament that justice should appear to be defeated? I think not.

Proceeding with his curious reasoning, he further observes:

Undoubtedly, clause (4) of Article 329A could be said to have a political objective, in the context in which it was introduced, and we could perhaps take judicial notice of this context. Even if it was possible to go beyond the statement of objects and reasons and to hold that clause (4) of Article 329A is there essentially for demonstrating the strong position of the government and of the Prime Minister of this country to all inside and outside the country, so as to inspire the necessary confidence in and give the necessary political and legal strength to the government to enable it to go forward boldly to deal with internal economic and law and order problems and international questions. Yet, I fail to see why this could make it necessary to exclude the jurisdiction of this court so as to prevent it from considering a case which would have been over much sooner if we had not been confronted with difficulties, at the very outset, in examining the merits of the case. Speaking for myself, I fail to see what danger to the country could be jeopardized by a consideration and a decision by this court of such a good case as I find that the Prime Minister of this country had on facts and law. Nevertheless, I am prepared to concede that there may be, and was, some very useful political objective to be served by demonstrating the strength and ability of the government to face the difficulties with which it had been confronted. If that is so, we can certainly see that clause (4) of Article 329A had a political objective and utility which has been served.

Observing the principle that out of two possible interpretations of a provision, one which prevents it from becoming unconstitutional should be preferred, Justice Beg says:

> If the purpose of clause (4) of Article 329A was purely to meet the political needs of the country and was only partly revealed by the policy underlying the statement of reasons and objects, it seems possible to contend that it was not at all to oust the jurisdiction of the court. Hence, Article 329A, clause (5), will not, so understood, bar the jurisdiction of the court to hear and decide the appeals when it says that the appeal shall be disposed of in conformity with the provisions of clause (4).

What he probably means by this is that since the amendment directs the court to dispose of the appeal in conformity with clause (4), that is by declaring the election valid, the court is allowed to deal with the merits as long as the final result is that the election is declared valid. This is what he himself has done.

He, therefore, says that he is disposing of the case in conformity with clause (4) of Article 329A by declaring the order of the High Court void and the election valid. He thus accepts the appeal of Mrs Gandhi and dismisses the cross-appeal of Raj Narain.

THE JUDGMENT OF JUSTICE CHANDRACHUD

Dealing first with the validity of the constitutional amendment, Justice Chandrachud gives his interpretation of clause (4). He says clause (4) consists of six parts:

1. The laws made by Parliament prior to 10 August 1975, insofar as they relate to election petitions and matters connected therewith, cease to apply the Parliamentary election of Smt. Indira Gandhi which took place in 1971.
2. Such laws are repealed retrospectively insofar as they govern the aforesaid election, with the result that they must never be deemed to have applied to that election.
3. Such an election cannot be declared to be void on any of the grounds on which it could have been declared to be void under the laws which were in force prior to 10 August 1975.
4. The election shall not be deemed ever to have become void on any ground on which, prior to 10 August 1975, it was declared to be void.
5. The election shall continue to be valid in all respects notwithstanding the judgment of any court, which includes the judgment dated 12 June 1975 of the High Court of Allahabad.
6. The judgment of the Allahabad High Court and any finding on which the judgment and order of that court is based are void and shall be deemed always to have been void.

Constituent Body Can Exercise Judicial Power

On the question of whether the constituent body could pronounce upon private disputes, Justice Chandrachud says that what the Constitution ought to contain is not for the courts to decide. The touchstone of the validity of a constitutional amendment is firstly whether the procedure prescribed by Article 368 is strictly complied with and secondly whether the amendment destroys or damages the

basic structure of the Constitution. The subject-matter of the
constitutional amendments is a question of high policy and courts are
concerned with the interpretation of laws, not with the wisdom of the
policy underlying them.

The Basic Features of the Constitution

Justice Chandrachud then lays down what, according to him, are the
basic features—democracy, equality, secular character of the State,
and rule of law.

He did not agree with Bhushan's contention that the Preamble
held the key to the basic structure of the Constitution. He says
that the Preamble cannot be regarded as a source of any substantive
power or a source of any limitation.

Judicial Review Not Basic

Justice Chandrachud holds that Article 329B of the Constitution
can plainly be used by the legislature to exclude judicial review. He
further says:

> Since the Constitution, as originally enacted, did not consider
> that judicial power must intervene in the interests of purity of
> elections, judicial review cannot be considered to be a part of the
> basic structure insofar as legislative elections are concerned. The
> theory of basic structure has to be considered in each individual
> case, not in the abstract, but in the context of the concrete
> problem. The problem here is whether under our Constitution,
> judicial review was considered as an indispensable concomitant
> of elections to country's legislatures. The answer, plainly, is, no.

Amendment Does Not Destroy Democracy

Justice Chandrachud holds that the amendment does not destroy
democracy. He said that the provisions for election still remain
exactly the same as they were before the amendment. The
amendment had validated only one election. The validation of a
single election does not destroy democracy, he says.

Equality and Rule of Law Negated

Justice Chandrachud, however, accepted Bhushan's contention that the amendment was destructive of equality by discriminating in favour of the Prime Minister. He says that just because a person is a class by herself, it does not mean that the election law should also be different for her. Moreover, since the amendment makes all law relating to elections inapplicable to the Prime Minister's election, it is destructive of the rule of law.

Justice Chandrachud also holds that the amendment had decided a matter of which the courts were lawfully seized. He does not agree that the amending power is an amalgam of legislative, judicial and executive powers.

For these reasons, he strikes down clause (4) of Article 329A introduced by the constitutional amendment.

Election Law Amendments Valid

Dealing with the scope of attack on the election law amendments, Justice Chandrachud rejects Bhushan's contention that ordinary laws must also be subject to the basic feature limitation. He says:

Shri Shanti Bhushan thought it paradoxical that the higher power should be subject to a limitation which will not operate upon a lower power. There is no paradox, because certain limitations operate upon the higher power for the reason that it is higher power. A constitutional amendment has to be passed by a special majority and certain such amendments have to be ratified by the legislatures of not less than one-half of the States as provided by Article 362(2). An ordinary legislation can be passed by a simple majority. The two powers, though species of the same genus, operate in different fields and are, therefore, subject to different limitations.

No objection can accordingly be taken to the constitutional validity of the two impugned Acts on the ground that they damage or destroy the basic structure. The power to pass these Acts could be exercised retrospectively as much as prospectively.

Expenses Issue

Dealing very briefly with the issue of expenses, Justice Chandrachud observes that the limit of expenses is not shown to have been exceeded in this case. He, therefore, holds Mrs Gandhi not guilty on this issue.

On the question whether the Parliament session was illegal, he holds that the legality of the detention of Members of Parliament cannot be questioned collaterally in this case.

For these reasons he holds Mrs Gandhi not guilty on any corrupt practice and accepts the appeal reversing the High Court's judgment.

20

Epilogue: From Court Battle to Electoral Battle

The Supreme Court judgment effectively killed all speculation on the consequences of a verdict against Mrs Gandhi. An adverse verdict by the High Court resulted in the petitioner being jailed. It is indeed difficult to speculate on the fate of the Supreme Court or its judges if the Supreme Court had given an adverse verdict. Mrs Gandhi had at no time said that she would accept an adverse verdict of the Supreme Court. On 13 July 1975, the reporter of *Sunday Times* of London asked her the following question: 'If the Supreme Court upholds the Allahabad High Court judgment setting aside your election, would you step down as Prime Minister?' This was her answer:

> I have sought legal remedy to which every citizen is entitled. The Supreme Court will give its finding. Is it right to speculate on what it will say? It is relevant to note that the government in the state at that time was an Opposition one and the Minister-in-charge of Police belonged to my constituency and was the election agent of my opponent who later filed the petition.

Again, on 1 August, Mrs Gandhi was interviewed by Norman Cousins, editor of the *Saturday Review* of New York. She was asked as to what she planned to do in the event of an adverse Supreme Court verdict. She again hedged and her reply was substantially the same as her last reply.

The questions put to Mrs Gandhi were only as to whether she would accept an adverse Supreme Court verdict. It is difficult to imagine why she could not have said that she would accept an adverse verdict, if she really had intentions of doing so. For her, the appeal to the Supreme Court was a matter of convenience—heads I win, tails you lose.

For the Supreme Court too, the Emergency will remain a lesson for the future. Quite apart from Mrs Gandhi's case, where it ruled that retrospective changes were permissible in the election law,[1] it also passed a highly contentious ruling in the ADM Jabalpur case, also known as the Habeas Corpus case. In this infamous and universally criticized judgment,[2] it held that during an Emergency when fundamental rights are suspended, anyone could be picked up by the police, for any reason, and such a person and their relatives had no recourse in law.[3] The learned Attorney-General of India during the hearing of the case went so far as to say that 'Even if life was taken away illegally, courts are helpless'.[4] One of the judges, the late Mr P.N. Bhagwati, years later expressed remorse about the ruling and said: 'The majority judgment was not the correct judgment. If it was open to me to come to a fresh decision in that case, I would agree with what Justice (H.R.) Khanna did. I am sorry (for the judgment)'.[5]

The sordid story of the remaining months of the Emergency is well known and need not be told here. The people gave their verdict on it in the March 1977 polls by giving a severe drubbing to the Congress party. It seems that the people also had their final verdict on Mrs Gandhi's case at the polls. In another straight fight between Mrs Gandhi and Raj Narain, the people of Rae Bareli turned the tables by defeating Mrs Gandhi by 55,000 votes. In an election where the case had also been made a major issue, this amounted to a verdict of the people's court—'guilty'.

In retrospect, it is now possible to analyse the long-term effects of the case. Although the immediate effect of the case was the imposition of the Emergency, it seems clear now that the nation has learnt much from it, and would ultimately be grateful for it. Democracy in the country has emerged immensely stronger after the traumatic experience. After having lost their rights once, the people of India have learnt to value them much more.

The experience of the Emergency also dealt a possibly mortal blow to a dangerous school of thought which was gaining strength before the Emergency: that dictatorship was the best form of government for India. The sour experience of the short spell of dictatorship strengthened the faith of the people in the democratic process.

Apart from these long-term gains, there was at least one immediately beneficial effect of the Emergency. The Janata Party would not have been formed if Mrs Gandhi had not chosen to crush the Opposition so rudely. The shock greatly hastened the process of unification of the Opposition parties which shed their differences to deal with the common enemy, when their very survival was threatened. Thus the Emergency has helped bring about a two-party system, with each party fully aware of the price of disunity. It is indeed ironical that for all this, the nation has Mrs Gandhi and the Emergency to be grateful for.

References

1. The judgment stated that 'it is permissible for a legislature to make a law with retrospective effect. The power of a legislature to make a law with retrospective effect is not curtailed or circumscribed by the fact that the subject matter of such retrospective law is a matter relating to an election dispute'. AIR 1975 SC 2299, Para 186.

2. See Upendra Baxi, 'Emergency's useful scar', *The Indian Express*, 1 July 2015, http://indianexpress.com/article/opinion/columns/emergencys-useful-scars/ and Fali S. Nariman, 'My Unsolicited Suggestion', *The Indian Express*, 7 September 2016, http://indianexpress.com/article/opinion/columns/supreme-court-judges-appointment-transparency-collegium-working-system-3017291/.

3. The judgment read: 'In view of the Presidential order dated 27 June 1975 no person has any locus standi to move any writ petition under Article 226 before a High Court for habeas corpus or any other writ or order or direction to challenge the legality of an order of detention on the ground that the order is not under or in compliance with the Act or is illegal or is vitiated by malafides factual or legal or is based on extraneous consideration.' *A.D.M Jabalpur v. Shukla*, AIR 1976 SC 1207, Para 596.

4. Jos. Peter D'Souza, 'A.D.M. Jabalpur vs Shukla: When the Supreme Court struck down the *Habeas Corpus*', *PUCL Bulletin*, June 2001, http://www.pucl.org/reports/National/2001/habeascorpus.htm.

5. Maneesh Chhibber, '35 yrs later, a former Chief Justice of India pleads guilty', *The Indian Express*, 16 September 2011, http://archive.indianexpress.com/news/35-yrs-later-a-former-chief-justice-of-india-pleads-guilty/847392/.

Appendix 1

Testimony of Yashpal Kapoor

In the oral deposition of a witness, the counsel asks questions which the witness answers. After that the judge dictates only the answers to the questions. Thus the records of the oral depositions merely contain the answers and not the questions.

In his examination in chief, which was conducted by S.C. Khare, Kapoor stated that he had gone to Rae Bareli on 7 January 1971 with Shri G.L. Nanda, who was then the railway minister. Kapoor said that Nanda addressed a public meeting at Munshiganj because of the Shahid Mela (Martyrs' Day celebration). 'I also went on the platform and paid my tributes to the martyrs. I spoke for only half a minute. I did not mention anything about Respondent No. 1 contesting election to the Lok Sabha from the Rae Bareli constituency, nor any other thing pertaining to elections, as it was not a political meeting.' When asked whether this was a private or an official visit, he replied that it was a private visit and he did not charge any travelling allowance (TA) for it.

About his resignation date, Kapoor said that on 13 January he had conveyed to Mrs Gandhi his final decision to resign from his post. She agreed to it and asked him to meet Haksar, who was then Secretary-in-Charge of the Prime Minister's Secretariat. Kapoor stated, 'Some time during that day, I met Shri Haksar in his office and submitted my resignation letter to him.' After asking Kapoor whether he had informed Mrs Gandhi about his decision, Haksar told him that as far as he was concerned, the matter was all right and that he was relieved from his post.

Giving the reason for putting the date 14 January under his signature, though he signed the transfer of charge report on 13 January, Kapoor said that this was done because in his resignation letter he had requested to be relieved with effect from 14 January.

Kapoor stated that he was sure that Mrs Gandhi decided to contest from Rae Bareli only on 1 February, because on that date while she was at Rae Bareli, members of the DCC met her and requested her to contest from there. After having heard their request, Mrs Gandhi took Shri Kamlapati Tripathi (then president of the UPCC) aside and spoke to him. Kapoor stated that she also consulted him and only thereafter did she announce her decision to contest the election from Rae Bareli.

Kapoor further stated that till 1 February, Mrs Gandhi had not asked him to do any election work for her. Nor did he do any. He, therefore, denied the petitioner's allegation that he had started working for Mrs Gandhi's election much before 1 February.

Kapoor also explained the reason why the return of election expenses showed some items to have been bought in connection with the election before 1 February. He said that these items which included a voters' list were bought by the DCC of Rae Bareli for the benefit of whosoever ultimately become a candidate from there. He had considered it proper to repay the money spent on these accounts to the DCC and had, therefore, included the expenditure on these in the return of election expenses.

CROSS-EXAMINATION

It was then Shanti Bhushan's turn to cross-examine Yashpal Kapoor.

Bhushan first questioned Kapoor about his duration of service in the Prime Minister's Secretariat. Kapoor said that he had been in the Prime Minister's Secretariat since 1951. Counsel then suggested to Kapoor that he had resigned from his post in 1967 in order to work for Mrs Gandhi's election, because he had rejoined the Secretariat just three months later. Kapoor denied that he had resigned in order to work for Mrs Gandhi's election. The reason for his resignation, he maintained, was his desire to enter public life; but he rejoined the Secretariat because Mrs Gandhi was particularly keen about it and she requested him to do so.

Counsel: You resigned in 1967 on the eve of Parliamentary elections. You resigned again in 1971 on the eve of Parliamentary elections. In 1967, you worked in Mrs Gandhi's constituency. In 1971, again you worked in her constituency. Is there any particular reason behind this coincidence?

Kapoor: Everyone wants to get into work which may push him into Parliament or the legislature of any state.

Kapoor was then questioned about the fact that his name appeared in the voters' list of Rae Bareli which was prepared for the 1971 elections. In this connection, he was asked where he was residing in 1970. He replied that although he had been to Rae Bareli six or seven times, he was residing in Delhi.

Counsel: You concede that during the year 1970 you were not a resident of any town or district of Uttar Pradesh. You would then concede that your residence as mentioned in the copy of the electoral roll is wrong?

Kapoor: I will not call it wrong. I remember that when the revision of electoral roll was taking place, I was at Rae Bareli and I was told that my name had been entered in the electoral roll of Rae Bareli.

Counsel: Your answer does not answer the question that was precisely put to you. You still have to answer as to how the description of your residence in the electoral roll is correct when you concede that during that year you were not residing in any town or district of UP.

Kapoor: I will not be able to answer this question.

Counsel: Is it not correct that a person who is not a resident of a particular state cannot be elected a member of the Rajya Sabha from that state? (Bhushan was suggesting that Kapoor had got his name enrolled in the voters' list of Rae Bareli so that he could be elected a member of the Rajya Sabha from UP.)

Kapoor: I don't think so.

Counsel: Would you kindly read Section 197 of the R.P. Act and then answer as to whether a person who is not a resident of any particular state can be an elector of that state?

Kapoor: Since the word used in Section 197 is 'ordinarily resident', I still maintain that a person who is not a resident of a particular state can be an elector of that state. At the time the electoral rolls were revised, I was a person 'ordinarily resident' of Rae Bareli.

Kapoor was then asked as to how he happened to reach Rae Bareli on 15 January if it was a fact that at that time he did not even know whether Mrs Gandhi would be contesting the election from there. He replied that after resigning from his post, he went to Lucknow and met Kamlapati Tripathi who then told him to go to the eastern districts of UP, and since Rae Bareli was one of the eastern districts, it was just by chance that he reached there.

Kapoor was then shown the issue of a newspaper dated 22 January 1971. It carried a news item stating that on 15 January Kapoor reached Rae Bareli with a fleet of seventy cars to launch the election campaign of the Prime Minister. Kapoor denied the report, and said that the correspondent who filed it must have played on his imagination to write it.

Kapoor was then asked as to what he did during the period between 14 January and 1 February? He said that he was in Rae Bareli from 14 January to 17 January, from where he went to Sultanpur and Barabanki to do some organizational work. When asked as to where he stayed at both these places, he said that he could not remember.

He further stated that he was in Delhi between 21 January and 26 January. When asked as to whether he had met the Prime Minister during these five days, he replied that he must have met her twice during this period.

It is interesting to note that in his cross-examination the next day, when Kapoor was asked whether he had met Mrs Gandhi between 13 January and 1 February, he stated that he could not remember.

He was also questioned extensively about election expenses. He said that election expenses were being maintained by Shri Gaya Prasad Shukla (a Congress worker) and he did not know much about them. He was then shown a copy of the receipt obtained for the payment made as remuneration to his driver. The receipt showed that the driver had been paid for the period 15 January to 10 March.

Counsel: According to you, you obtained a jeep only on 1 February. Would you explain the remuneration having been paid to the driver for the period prior to 1 February 1971, if you had obtained the jeep only on 1 February and not prior to it?

Kapoor: I paid a salary to the driver for the period from 15 January because Shri Gaya Prasad Shukla told me that the driver had been hired from that date. (According to Kapoor, the jeep was with the DCC of Rae Bareli from 15 January to 1 February.)

Counsel: You are aware that in the return of election expenses only the amounts spent in connection with the election have to be shown. The amount specified in the receipt, according to you, includes the amount which was not spent on the election. If that was so, why did you include the entire amount shown in this receipt in the election expenses?

Kapoor: I have erred, but I erred on the right side There was a big margin available. I, therefore, saw no harm in including the whole amount specified in the receipt in the election return.

Counsel then asked some questions unconnected with the case in order to damage the credibility of Kapoor. Kapoor answered affirmatively to Counsel's query of whether a property of value not less than Rs 4 lakh had been purchased by his wife in the Golf Links area of New Delhi. When asked as to where the money for this property had come from, Kapoor said, 'When my wife told me that she wanted to purchase the property, I told her that my savings were only Rs 20,000. My father had received Rs 30,000 as gratuity and that amount had also been passed on by him to me, by cheque. I therefore told my wife that I could not make arrangements for the money beyond Rs 50,000. My wife then told me that her mother, who was living with us, had agreed to advance her a sum of little more than Rs 1 lakh. Narang Bank also agreed to advance a sum of a little more than Rs 1 lakh to my wife for purchasing the building. A family friend of ours gave my wife a little more than Rs 1 lakh. It was thus that the amount of Rs 4 lakh and odd was arranged by my wife to purchase the property.'

Counsel then asked him about the conditions on which the loans had been obtained. Kapoor said that he was not aware of them. Counsel further asked him whether the building purchased by his wife had been mortgaged by her in favour of any persons from whom the loan was taken. Kapoor was not aware of this either. He was then asked about the covered area of the building. Kapoor said that he had no idea of the covered area as he claimed that he had been to the house just once and that too for a few minutes only.

In the end, Counsel put the case before Kapoor.[1] He suggested that Kapoor had resigned in January 1971 in order to work for Mrs Gandhi's election, and that he had started working right from 14 January or even earlier. Kapoor denied all these suggestions.

After Bhushan ended his cross-examination, Khare requested the judge to permit him to re-examine Kapoor on one point. Being allowed to do so, Khare elicited from Kapoor that his name was recorded on the electoral roll of Rae Bareli towards the end of 1968 or the beginning of

---

[1] Putting the case before a witness, is suggesting all those facts which the counsel wants the witness to affirm.

1969, and that he had cast his vote in the assembly election that took place in 1969 at Rae Bareli.

In his cross-examination on this point, Bhushan asked him as to how he happened to be in Rae Bareli in 1969 on the date of the assembly polls. Kapoor said that he went to Rae Bareli in 1969 specially to cast his vote.

Counsel: Were you so keen to exercise your franchise that you went all the way from Delhi to Rae Bareli merely in order to cast your vote?

Kapoor: I was not able to exercise my right of franchise in 1957, 1962 or 1967. So when I came to know that my name as an elector was recorded in Rae Bareli, I just went down to Rae Bareli to exercise my right of franchise.

This ended Kapoor's testimony.

Appendix 2

Testimony of Mrs Indira Gandhi

The examination in chief of Mrs Gandhi was led by Khare. He first addressed questions on the facts of the issue of holding out. This was the main issue for which she had been produced in court. What she said on this would be of crucial importance. In reply to his questions, Mrs Gandhi affirmed that she held a press conference after the dissolution of the Lok Sabha in December 1970. She could recollect that at the press conference, a question was put to her to the effect that a short while ago members of the Opposition parties had stated that the Prime Minister was changing her constituency from Rae Bareli to Gurgaon. In answer to this question, she recollected having said that she did not intend to contest from Gurgaon.

Khare: Did you in reply to the question put to you in the press conference say, 'No, I am not'?

Mrs Gandhi: I meant specifically that I was not going to contest from Gurgaon. Since it's been such a long time, I do not precisely remember, but most probably, while replying to the question I used the words 'No, I am not'. I would add that my reply did not necessarily mean that I would not change my constituency. I only meant that I would not contest from Gurgaon constituency.

Being asked whether she had requested or authorized Yashpal Kapoor to announce her candidature from Rae Bareli or to work for her election prior to 1 February, she replied in the negative. 'Since I had not made up my mind until 1 February 1971 to contest the election from Rae Bareli, obviously I could not request or authorize any person to do election work for me in that constituency or to announce or propagate that I was to contest from there.'

On being questioned about Yashpal Kapoor's resignation date, Mrs Gandhi stated that in the second week of January 1971, Kapoor had expressed to her his desire to resign. She had told him to think about it as his decision would be final. On 13 January, he had met her and told her he had made up his mind to resign. She agreed to his being relieved and asked him to contact P.N. Haksar for completion of formalities. She said that according to her understanding, P.N. Haksar as the Secretary-in-Charge of the Prime Minister's Secretariat was competent to accept Kapoor's resignation.

Mrs Gandhi also deposed that she had not issued any specific instructions to the Air Force to place any aeroplanes or helicopters at her disposal for her election tours. Nor did she give any specific directions to the District Magistrate or Superintendent of Police of Rae Bareli to make arrangements for her election meetings.

She said this to repel the charge in the petition that she had 'procured' their services for furthering her election prospects.

CROSS-EXAMINATION

Her examination in chief was over in an hour and she was then cross-examined by Bhushan. After asking some preliminary questions about Yashpal Kapoor's work in her Secretariat, Bhushan decided to make use of the letter which had been procured from the Congress office at Jantar Mantar to impeach her credibility.

Counsel showed her three letters written in May 1959 by the chief minister of Himachal Pradesh to Mrs Gandhi. She was the Congress president at that time. These letters helped her recollect that a by-election had taken place in a constituency in Himachal Pradesh in 1959.

Counsel: Did you ask the Lt. Governor of Himachal Pradesh to help your candidate in winning the election?

Khare shot up from his chair and objected to the question. The judge agreed with the objection and dictated the following order:

> Whether the witness did or did not do so in 1959 does not appear to be relevant for the purpose of this case, as this case relates to an election that took place in 1971. The question is accordingly disallowed.

Bhushan immediately clarified that he had not asked this question because it was relevant for the issues in the case. He showed the relevant provisions of the Evidence Act which allowed the cross-examining counsel to ask questions which did not strictly relate to the issues, but which could have the effect of impeaching the credibility of the witness. It was to impeach the credibility of the witness that he had asked this question.

Counsel then showed Mrs Gandhi a letter addressed to her by the Lt. Governor of Himachal Pradesh in 1959. In that letter, the Lt. Governor had informed Mrs Gandhi that the Congress candidate had managed to win the by-election, and that this was the toughest test that Mrs Gandhi had put him to. Mrs Gandhi replied that the statement of the Lt. Governor that she had put him to any test was incorrect, and added that the word 'test' could mean many things. It could also mean a test of maintenance of law and order during the period of the by-election, which was ultimately the responsibility of the Lt. Governor.

In response to a question about Yashpal Kapoor's resignation before the 1967 elections, Mrs Gandhi denied that he had resigned in order to be able to work for her election. She said that Kapoor had told her that he was resigning because he wanted to do political work, and she also thought that Kapoor had worked for the Congress and not specifically for her in 1967. In response to another suggestion, Mrs Gandhi denied that when Kapoor had resigned in 1967, it was decided that he would be reappointed after the elections were over.

Counsel: Did you not ask Mr Kapoor to rejoin the Secretariat after the elections were over?

Mrs Gandhi: I did.

Counsel: Did Mr Kapoor make any formal application for that purpose?

Mrs Gandhi: I do not think so. But Mr Kapoor was looking for some opportunities which were not available in 1967 and I, therefore, felt that he might be interested in rejoining my Secretariat. It was for this reason that I asked him to rejoin it.

Coming to Mr Kapoor's resignation in 1971, Counsel suggested that he had resigned in 1971 merely in order to organize the election campaign of Mrs Gandhi.

Mrs Gandhi denied the suggestion and said that at the time when Mr Kapoor resigned, she did not even know that she would be contesting the election from Rae Bareli.

Regarding the date of Kapoor's resignation, Counsel asked her whether she had been shown any paper to indicate that Kapoor had resigned on 13 January.

Mrs Gandhi: No. But I had been told that Mr Kapoor was paid his salary only for the period ending on 13 January. Mr P.N. Haksar also told me that Mr Kapoor had resigned on 13 January. There was also the gazette notification regarding the acceptance of the resignation submitted by Mr Kapoor which I had myself seen. Another thing which I would like to mention is that he did not attend my Secretariat from 14 January onwards.

Counsel: How can you remember clearly that Mr Kapoor did not attend the Secretariat from 14 January onwards?

Mrs Gandhi: Because on 13 January he had spoken to me about resigning from the job.

Counsel: Did you see the election petition regarding the date of his resignation?

Mrs Gandhi: Yes, but when I saw the election petition, I did remember that he had resigned on 13 January. In order to make sure, I had also inquired from Shri Haksar about it.

Counsel: Do you remember any particular event which took place on 13 January 1971 or 13 December 1970?

Mrs Gandhi: Not unless some indication of the event is given to me.

Counsel: Do you remember any particular event which took place on 18 February 1975 (exactly one month before the date of cross-examination)?

Mrs Gandhi: No, I do not.

Counsel then questioned her about the acceptance of Kapoor's resignation. He asked her whether she had herself formally accepted his resignation. She replied that she had not.

Counsel: Can you recall any instance in which you have asked any person to take charge of any post before an order appointing him to that post was made in writing and signed by the relevant authority? (He asked this question because Haksar had in his deposition stated that he was appointed Deputy Chairman of the Planning Commission by an oral order of Mrs Gandhi.)

Mrs Gandhi: I do not remember any such instance.

Counsel: Are you aware of any rule authorizing the Secretary-in-Charge of your Secretariat to appoint a person as officer on special duty in your Secretariat?

Mrs Gandhi: I am not aware of any rule investing such authority in the Secretary, but I am also not aware of any rule contrary to it. I have always functioned on the basis that my Secretary was competent to make such appointments.

Being questioned about the date on which she decided to contest from Rae Bareli, Mrs Gandhi said that the final decision in this respect was taken only after she had had talks with Kamlapati Tripathi and the workers of that area. This was done only on 1 February 1971.

Counsel showed her the newspaper report of 15 January 1971 in which it was stated that the Congress parliamentary board had decided that sitting Members of Parliament would contest the elections from their old constituencies. Bhushan was suggesting that since Mrs Gandhi was also a sitting Member of Parliament, this decision would also apply to her, thus fixing her constituency at least on this date. Mrs Gandhi denied that the Congress parliamentary board had taken a decision of this nature, and she said that in any case, for the Prime Minister and other prominent leaders, the matter was left to their own choice.

Counsel then showed her own tour programme, dated 28 January 1971, for Rae Bareli. In this tour programme, 11.30 a.m. was marked out for filing her nomination paper.

Counsel: Was this tour programme issued after obtaining your approval?

Mrs Gandhi: It was. But I do not accept that I decided to file my nomination paper from Rae Bareli on or before 28 January. It was tentatively mentioned in the tour programme so that if I decided to contest from Rae Bareli, the nomination paper could be filed at that time. I was also told that a nomination paper after it was filed could be withdrawn.

Mrs Gandhi was then asked certain formal questions on the issue of Air Force planes and rostrums and barricades. Bhushan then asked her some more questions unrelated to the case to impeach her credibility. These questions related to some gifts which she had received from foreign dignitaries. Most of these questions were disallowed by the judge.

This ended the cross-examination for the first day. It was resumed the next day.

Counsel: When did you see Mr Kapoor next after 13 January 1971?

Mrs Gandhi: I saw him next at Rae Bareli on 1 February 1971.

Counsel: Mr Kapoor had stated before this court that during the period 21 January 1971 to 26 January 1971, he stayed at Delhi and had met you twice. Is that statement incorrect?

Mrs Gandhi: It may be correct. I meet a very large number of people every day, so I have no idea about it.

It was now that Counsel decided to play his trump card. Till now, Mrs Gandhi had vehemently maintained that she had not decided to contest from Rae Bareli before 1 February. Her demeanour suggested that she was quite confident that there was no evidence to suggest the contrary.

Counsel: Did the Congress party take any decision about your constituency?

Mrs Gandhi: The Congress party did not take any decision about my constituency, but once I had taken the decision, it was deemed to be the party's decision because the party had left the matter to me.

Counsel: Did Shri K.N. Joshi, parliamentary secretary to the All India Congress Committee, make any announcement regarding your candidature on 29 January 1971?

Mrs Gandhi: Not within my knowledge.

Counsel then invited her attention to the additional written statement which had been filed by her in August 1972. In the additional written statement, she had averred that K.N. Joshi had informed her about the final decision in regard to her constituency which was announced by the All India Congress Committee on 29 January 1971.

For the first time in her deposition, Mrs Gandhi squirmed. So far she had been exuding confidence, but now she was nervous. She said that she could not recollect that fact that day.

Counsel: Are you quite certain that no announcement was made by the All India Congress Committee on 29 January 1971 about your constituency?

Mrs Gandhi: I do not know whether any such announcement was made.

Counsel: Did you read the additional written statement before signing it?

Mrs Gandhi: I did read it before signing it, and to the best of my ability, I took care to see that whatever was contained in it was true. I must, however, say that the language contained in the additional written statement is legal language which I find difficult to understand.

Counsel had clearly trapped her here and her explanation did not pass muster in the eyes of the audience or the judge. Bhushan made full capital out of this in his arguments.

Counsel finally asked Mrs Gandhi some questions about the Maruti Project of her son, Sanjay Gandhi. Most of them were disallowed by the judge. Nevertheless, he did allow some of them.

Counsel: Was the matter of the grant of Letter of Intent to Sanjay Gandhi considered by a sub-committee presided over by you?

Mrs Gandhi: No.

Counsel: Did the Government of India announce a policy decision that if the project of manufacturing a small car was ever undertaken, it would be in the public sector?

Mrs Gandhi looked hopefully at the judge as if to say 'Do I have to answer this question?' The judge smiled and nodded politely. She would have to answer that question. So she said, 'There was discussion in the government regarding this, but no final decision was taken to that effect.

'In 1962, when this matter was being thought over, no person had submitted any design for the completely indigenous production of a small car. There was, however, later, a proposal in the industries ministry, that if anybody came forward with the proposal to manufacture a completely indigenous small car, it may be considered.'

Counsel: I suggest that the proposal for the manufacture of a small car in the public sector was given up because Mr Sanjay Gandhi got interested in it.

Mrs Gandhi: That is not true. If the government wants to go ahead with the manufacture of a small car in the public sector, the Maruti Project would not prevent the government from doing so.

Counsel: Are you aware that in March 1971, the acquisition of land for the Maruti Project was objected to on behalf of the Indian Air Force on the ground that it would constitute a risk to the security of the Explosive Depot at Gurgaon?

Mrs Gandhi: The land was acquired by the Haryana state for industrial purposes and much construction had come into existence near the Explosive Depot at Gurgaon. Some objection was raised in that connection. But I am not sure whether the objection was raised by the Air Force authorities or by some Parliamentarians. The objection was not sustained.

Counsel: Are you aware that Maruti Ltd, even though it has not gone into production yet, has already acquired dealership deposits amounting to over Rs 2 crore up to the year 1973–74?

This question was disallowed.

Counsel then put his case before Mrs Gandhi. He suggested that she had decided to contest from Rae Bareli right from the time of the dissolution of the Lok Sabha in 1970 and that Kapoor had started working for her election right from that time. Mrs Gandhi denied these suggestions.

This ended Mrs Gandhi's cross-examination. It lasted only ninety minutes the second day.

Appendix 3

The Supreme Court Reviews the Kesavananda Bharati Case

It was some time during the end of October 1975 that Chief Justice A.N. Ray announced the constitution of a thirteen-member Bench (the entire strength of the Supreme Court) for a review of Kesavananda Bharati's case. Ever since the Kesavananda Bharati case had been decided in April 1973, the government had constantly been trying for a review. The government's requests had not been heeded earlier as no Constitution Bench had felt the need to do so. Normally, a case can only be reviewed if its decision creates a serious difficulty in the decision of some other case. Therefore, according to the established procedure, Kesavananda's case could only be reviewed if some Constitution Bench had difficulty in applying its dictum to some other case before them. Mrs Gandhi's appeal was the first occasion when Kesavananda's case became involved in a big way. But even in Mrs Gandhi's case, the Bench did not feel that there was sufficient reason for a review. Therefore, the thirteen-member Bench for review was not constituted in pursuance of any reference by a smaller Bench, but on the oral directions of the Chief Justice.

PALKHIVALA'S OBJECTIONS

The entire Bench assembled in the Chief Justice's courtroom at 11 a.m. on 10 November 1975 for the hearings of the review.

At the very outset, Palkhivala, arguing on behalf of the petitioners, raised some preliminary objections against the reconsideration of the Kesavananda Bharati case. Dividing his objections into two parts, Palkhivala asserted that: (1) the court did not have the legal competence to review the case at that juncture, and (2) assuming that the court has the discretionary authority of reviewing it, it should not exercise its discretion to review it at that juncture.

Elaborating on the first objection, Palkhivala submitted that in the Kesavananda Bharati case, there were six petitions in connection with which the full court had been constituted. He said, 'In all these petitions, some constitutional amendments were challenged. After deciding on the validity of the amendments and the amending powers of Parliament, the thirteen-member Bench had referred the six petitions for disposal to the Constitutional Bench, in the light of the law laid down by the full court. So, none of the original six petitions were disposed of by the full court. In fact, two of those five petitions are listed in today's list.

'Suppose that this court now reviews and reverses the decision of Kesavananda Bharati. What happens then, when the original six petitions come up for hearing. The reversed decision of this court will be res judicata[1] as far as those petitions are concerned. Therefore, those petitions will have to be decided in accordance with the original Kesavananda Bharati decision, the judges knowing fully well that it is an overruled case. Therefore as long as any of those petitions are pending before the court, this court cannot review that case.'

Justice Untwalia: But that means that if in a High Court, a full Bench decides a point of law in connection with a case and asks a Division Bench to dispose of the case, then as long as those cases are not disposed of, a full Bench cannot reconsider the point of law laid down earlier.

Palkhivala: Yes, if the full Bench had said that those cases be decided in accordance with its decision, then as long as those cases are pending, the full Bench cannot reconsider that point of law. However, in such situations, a difficulty might arise; but why should we create a difficulty when we can very easily avoid it. Observe the curious situation that would arise. Suppose this case is overruled. When the original petitions come up for hearing, the judges of the Constitution Bench would be placed in a very peculiar situation. The mandate of

---

[1] Res judicata is a legal principle according to which, if a point of law in a case has been decided, the rest of the case will have to be decided according to that law.

Article 141 commands them to apply the new Kesavananda Bharati, but res judicata commands them to apply the old Kesavananda Bharati. What do they do?

Justice Krishna Iyer: What you mean is that the judges will be tossed between the horns of dilemma—res judicata on one side asking them to apply the old Kesavananda Bharati case, but Article 141 on the other, commending them to apply the new Kesavananda Bharati case.

Palkhivala: Exactly.

Elaborating on his second preliminary objection, Palkhivala said that there were ten different reasons why the court should not reconsider the Kesavananda Bharati case, even if it could, at that juncture. Outlining his reasons, he said: 'Such a request could not have been entertained for a citizen, so it should not be entertained for the government. I have no doubt that if a citizen had asked for a review instead of the government, the request would have been turned down. Thus there is absolutely no reason why this request of the government should be accepted. And it is only an oral request. This Bench has been constituted only on the oral request of the government.'

Chief Justice: No, the request had also come from the petitioners. Ever since the Kesavananda Bharati case, we have been flooded with requests for review from these petitioners.

Palkhivala: I beg your pardon, my Lord. It is impossible that the petitioners had requested a review. Why should they ask for a review which could only damage their case? If the basic feature theory disappears, then no constitutional amendments can be struck down.

Chief Justice: Even the Tamil Nadu government had asked for a review.

Tamil Nadu Advocate-General: I beg your pardon, my Lord. We never even once asked for a review.

Chief Justice: Well, you were all asking for some constitutional amendment to be struck down on the basic features. The government said that it could not understand the theory, so the question arose.

Palkhivala: The question would, of course, arise whenever a constitutional amendment is to be struck down on that theory, but that does not mean that it should be reviewed. If a principle has to be reviewed every time that it arises, then every case of the Supreme Court would have to be reviewed within a few days.

Going on to his second point, Palkhivala submitted that none of the established principles of jurisprudence could justify such a reconsideration. Citing a few cases of the Supreme Court to support his contention, Palkhivala contended that a case could only be reconsidered if (1) the judgment in that case was manifestly wrong, and (2) that the continuance of the judgment of that case was baneful to public interest. These two conditions must coexist, he said. He went on, 'I challenge the government to say that there is a manifest error in the judgment. As far as the second condition is concerned, I can't see how by any stretch of imagination, the judgment in that case can be regarded as baneful to public interest. All it says is that there are certain things which are basic and beyond the Parliament's powers of amendment. It says that the government cannot abolish the rule of law, equality, liberty, etc. Can anyone say that the preservation of these values is baneful to public interest? Let the government tell us which is the amendment which it wants to pass and which is prevented by the Kesavananda Bharati case. In fact, if anything, it will be the overruling of this case which will be baneful to public interest.'

Justice Beg: Mr Palkhivala, how can you assume that we will overrule that case?

Palkhivala: Then are we going to waste five months of the Supreme Court's time merely to reaffirm an old judgment? We are not a debating society that we argue in order to reaffirm a judgment. Therefore, we have to consider the possibility of it being overruled.

Justice Beg: You see, I don't know what these basic features are.

Palkhivala: With the greatest respect, my Lord, it is inconceivable that the Supreme Court cannot understand its own judgment. If the Supreme Court cannot understand its own judgment, then who will? I have absolutely no doubt in my mind as to what the basic features are, and anybody who reads the judgment carefully cannot have any doubt.

Justice Murtaza Fazl Ali: Mr Palkhivala, it seems that the judgment in Kesavananda Bharati is ambiguous, and by reconsidering it, we might only clarify the issues.

Palkhivala: I do not think it is ambiguous, but assuming that it is, we have judges of enough competence to interpret even ambiguous judgments. Ambiguous judgments involving general principles are interpreted every day by this honourable court. What about the dictum that 'the essential powers of legislation' cannot be delegated. What are the essential powers of legislation? Or take the due process clause of America. For 200 years, the US Supreme Court has been interpreting and evolving that principle. Does it have any precise meaning? We can't have cut and dried definitions of general principles. They are not things which can be applied like mathematical formulae.

Citing cases from England, the US and Australia, Palkhivala contended that vagueness or lack of definiteness is not a basis for discarding a sound legal principle.

Justice Beg: But I think every Article in the Constitution is basic.

Palkhivala: If you take that view my Lord, I will be the happiest man, because then the Constitution will remain substantially unchanged throughout.

Justice Beg: No, I mean I cannot tell the difference between basic and non-basic features.

Palkhivala: Suppose Article 368 of the Constitution itself said that the basic structure of the Constitution cannot be damaged or destroyed. The judiciary as the interpreter of the Constitution would have had to interpret it. Could it have said that it did not understand the Constitution?

Justice Untwalia: Suppose there is a manifest error, but we are not sure of the baneful effect on public interest. In that case, can we review a judgment?

Palkhivala: My Lord, if a case goes on for five months, is heard by thirteen judges and literally thousands of authorities are quoted in the judgments, can anyone say that there is a manifest error in the judgment?

Laying the Forty-first Amendment Bill (already passed by the Rajya Sabha) before the judges, Palkhivala read out the provisions of the Bill which was introduced in Parliament in the Monsoon Session. It states that any person who has held the office of either President or Prime Minister or Governor shall have lifelong immunity against all criminal suits for 'personal' acts done either before or during the tenure of office. It also gives immunity while in office against all civil suits to these category of persons. Expressing horror at the provisions of the Bill, Palkhivala said that this was the type of amendment for which the government wanted unlimited powers.

Palkhivala continued, 'When we argued the Kesavananda Bharati case, we were told that the possibility of misuse of power was only hypothetical and we should trust our elected representatives.

Today the misuse of power is no longer a hypothetical possibility. It is a stark reality. The Forty-first Amendment has already been passed by the Rajya Sabha. If this Bill became law, then any person can commit the most heinous crimes, even murder his political opponents, and he has only to have enough political influence to get himself made the Governor of a state even for a day, to get away scot free. With such amendments being passed when Kesavananda Bharati is still good law, consider what will come when it is overruled.

'If the Kesavananda Bharati decision stays, then I have no doubt that this Forty-first Amendment Bill will not be introduced in the Lok Sabha, but if Kesavananda Bharati is overruled, then it is going to be the law of tomorrow. When the Kesavananda Bharati case was being argued, the government said that we had vested interests and wanted to preserve our property. In the Kesavananda Bharati case, it was decided that property right is not basic. We accept the judgment. There are some interested people who want to distort our stand by connecting us with property. We wish to make it clear that we are not fighting for the property right. Let the government take away all our property. But what about liberty, what about equality, what about the freedom of speech and dissent. It is for these values that we are fighting.'

Proceeding further with his arguments against a review, Palkhivala asserted that the court would stultify itself and the judicial process would command no respect if the court struck down a recent Constitution amendment on the basis of Kesavananda Bharati, and, on the immediately following working day, sat to consider whether the Kesavananda Bharati case was correctly decided. Enunciating a well-known principle, Palkhivala said, 'Justice must not only be done but it must also be seen to be done. This was why we have open courts, where people can see justice being done. What respect and confidence will people have in the highest court of the land if they find it behaving in such a capricious way? Judicial discipline demands that cases should not be reviewed just because the constitution of the court changes. What will happen to judicial discipline if the Supreme Court fails to observe it?'

Justice Mathew: You can't say that we didn't observe judicial discipline. We struck down the Thirty-ninth Amendment by respecting the majority decision.

Palkhivala: I never said that you didn't observe judicial discipline. In fact, until now, the Supreme Court has had the most glorious tradition of observing judicial discipline and it would be very sad if this tradition is broken now.

Palkhivala's next reason against review was that nothing had happened since Kesavananda's case to justify reconsideration because all that had happened since then was the passing of some laws which justified to the hilt the wisdom of the Kesavananda Bharati decision.

'Let us see what the situation was when Kesavananda's case was decided. We had individual liberty, equality, rule of law, freedom of speech and dissent. What do we have now? There is no liberty today. Anyone can be put behind bars for no reason at all, so much so that the latest amendment to MISA says that the grounds of detention cannot be "permitted" to be disclosed even to the courts. It expressly says that "no citizen can claim the right of liberty on any grounds of common law, natural law or principles of natural justice". As a result, thousands of people are languishing in jail without trial. Can anyone say that we have equality after observing the various obnoxious constitutional amendments which have been enacted? They expressly say that some people will be above the law. This is the atmosphere in the country today in which the government has the nerve to come and ask for unlimited powers. Can one think of any country where we have such laws as the Forty-first Amendment Bill proposes?'

Justice Mathew: They might be there in some military dictatorships.

Palkhivala: I meant civilized countries. Of course, if the government is ruthless enough it can abrogate the Constitution and have such laws. But then, let them say that they do not respect the Constitution. Let the people no longer be fooled into believing that everything that is being done is constitutional.

Justice Beg: Mr Palkhivala, do you remember that famous US Supreme Court decision which led to the Civil War? Do you want us to be a party to such a decision?

Palkhivala: That is exactly why I am insisting on not having a review. Because if the Kesavananda Bharati decision is reversed, it might very well lead to a civil war. You cannot suppress the people for long.

Palkhivala again pleaded for the judgment to be given with the utmost caution.

Justice Murtaza Fazl Ali: But we might only clarify and lay down as to what the basic feature is.

Palkhivala: We don't need the full court of thirteen judges to lay down what the basic structure is. Each Constitution Bench can come to its own conclusion on that. Moreover, that is not the question referred to this Bench. The question referred to this Bench is whether the Parliament's powers are limited by the basic feature theory. And even if this court does try to clarify, how can we assume that the judgment will be any less ambiguous than in the Kesavananda Bharati case?

Palkhivala then went on to his next point. 'This is the most inopportune time to review the case,' he submitted, 'because only one party is effectively functioning and all Opposition leaders are in jail without trial. With a monstrous press censorship and all dissident voices silenced, how can we have an effective public debate on such an important topic.' Commenting on the extent of press censorship, Palkhivala told the court that even proceedings and judgments of courts were not allowed to be published in the newspapers. In his opinion, that was gross contempt of court.

Justice Krishna Iyer: Are there any written orders about censorship of court proceedings?

Palkhivala: Yes, there are, and we have enough documentary evidence to prove it to the hilt. The Delhi High Court's judgment on the habeas corpus of Mr Kuldip Nayar was not allowed to be published. The only way one heard of it was by tuning in to the BBC which reported parts of it. What I am saying now also will not be reported in tomorrow's newspapers due to censorship. If I say anything about the recent amendments in public, I shall probably be arrested. In fact the only place where there is any freedom of speech in this country is the few hundred square feet of various courtrooms. In fact, I am very grateful to the government for giving me the opportunity of expressing my views in this court.

Justice Krishna Iyer (amidst laughter): You should thank the court for this.

Palkhivala: My Lords, I do thank the court.

Justice Murtaza Fazl Ali: Suppose the Kesavananda Bharati decision had gone against you. Would you not have been entitled to come and ask for a review now? So why should you object to the government asking for a review?

Palkhivala: Let me answer this without any flippancy, my Lord. If the Kesavananda Bharati decision had gone against us, then there would be no Supreme Court today before which I could come for a review. But supposing that by some stroke of good fortune some part of the court survived, I would have perhaps been entitled to ask for a review because of its baneful effect on public interest. But here the case is just the opposite. If the decision is reversed, then it will have a baneful effect on public interest.

Palkhivala's next reason against reconsideration was that it would start a pernicious precedent which would gravely impair the continuity of law, and make law dependent on changes in the composition of the court. In fact, asserted Palkhivala, following the precedent of this case, another full Bench would be justified in reviewing this reconsideration soon after the decision in this case. 'Such a precedent would seriously erode the judicial discipline, the confidence of the people in the Supreme Court. What has happened in these two and a half years which justifies such a reconsideration?'

Justice Mathew: That is why Jefferson said that the Constitution must be changed every twenty years.

Palkhivala: But certainly not every two years, even if that is true.

Reading out the written submissions of the state of Jammu and Kashmir and Tamil Nadu, Palkhivala asserted that these states had no difficulty in identifying the basic features of the Constitution. Pointing out that in the Kesavananda Bharati case, all the states supported the Union government and it was for the first time now that some states were opposing the Union government in its plea for overthrowing the basic feature theory, Palkhivala argued that in these circumstances, a reconsideration would threaten the integrity and unity of the country.

Justice Mathew: How can it affect the unity or integrity of the country?

Palkhivala: Well, there are some parts of India which do not agree with the Union government. Now if the basic feature theory is overthrown, the Union government could and quite likely would abolish some states. This would certainly sow the seeds of disunity and disintegration.

Palkhivala further pleaded that a review would mean reopening and rehearing all that was argued in Kesavananda Bharati. 'That would take another five months. So for five months the entire Supreme Court will hear no other case except this. Can we waste five months of the court's time for reasons which are not absolutely compelling?'

Rounding off his submissions on the preliminary objections, Palkhivala ended with an impassioned plea that the Kesavananda Bharati case should not be reconsidered at that juncture.

TARKUNDE'S SUBMISSIONS

Following Palkhivala's arguments, V.M. Tarkunde, counsel for a detenu, spoke for a few minutes. Supplementing Palkhivala's arguments, Tarkunde said that after examining all the petitions connected with the present case, he had found that all but one of them related to property. Since in Kesavananda Bharati it was made clear that the property right was not basic, the Kesavananda Bharati case could not be invoked in any of those petitions. The only case remaining was a petition challenging the Thirty-second Constitution Amendment which had replaced the High Court's jurisdiction under Article 226 by an administrative tribunal in connection with the service matters of some government servants. Tarkunde contended that the case would only be referred to the full court if the Constitution Bench found that the constitutional amendment in question should be struck down on the basis of Kesavananda Bharati. 'Without the Kesavananda Bharati case creating any difficulty in any case, how could this case be referred to the full court?' Therefore, Tarkunde contended, the Kesavananda Bharati case should not be reconsidered unless it was found to be presenting an unsurmountable difficulty in some cases. With this plea, Tarkunde concluded his brief submissions.

THE ATTORNEY-GENERAL PLEADS FOR A REVIEW

Appearing on behalf of the Union of India, which had asked for a review, the Attorney-General Niren De started by arguing that the so-called preliminary objections of Palkhivala are not preliminary at all. 'A preliminary objection is one which challenges the legal right of the litigant party to come to the court, but here the objection is to a thirteen-member Bench being constituted to review the Kesavananda Bharati case. This is not a preliminary objection at all. The decision to review that case was taken by your Lordships for good or bad, and it cannot be questioned now on any preliminary objection.' Charging that Palkhivala had delivered a political lecture to the Supreme Court, De said that the situation in the country was absolutely 'pell mell' following an incoherent decision in the Kesavananda Bharati case. 'Every constitutional amendment is being challenged in the High Courts all over the country. Everybody was giving a different interpretation to the decision. In these circumstances, it is essential that the court clears up the issues.'

On being asked by the Bench as to whether any baneful effect flowed from the judgment of Kesavananda Bharati, De replied that the question about the limits of the Constitution-amending powers of Parliament surely could not be divorced from public interest.

Justice Khanna: Has the theory of basic features impeded any legislation about socio-economic measures?

De: Socio-economic measures are not the only thing, important as they are. The very structure of government is the fundamental object of the amending process. You don't need the amending power for non-essential features of the Constitution.

Justice Untwalia: Is there any example where the government wanted to amend the Constitution in public interest and has been prevented by the basic feature theory?

De: Take the case of the Thirty-ninth Amendment.

Justice Untwalia: I am talking of amendments in public interest.

De: The point is that the Parliament doesn't know what it can do. It doesn't know where it stands. We must know where we stand.

De pleaded that the case be reconsidered as there were many fundamental issues involved in the case.

Justice Krishna Iyer: The same plea can be advanced the very next day after reconsideration. You can still say that it is very important and must be reconsidered. The point is, what has really happened to justify a second look at the ruling?

De told the court that there was a tremendous amount of uncertainty in the country about the meaning of the basic structure theory.

Justice Krishna Iyer: Are you asking for a clarification of the basic structure, or do you want us to annihilate the theory?

De: Mr Palkhivala has raised a preliminary objection that we can't go into that case. At least the court can go into it to clarify it.

Justice Bhagwati: This is a matter of application of the case. Every judge can have his own view as to what the basic structure is. We need not review the case for that.

De: All over India, litigation is going on, on the concept of basic structure. Are we going to tolerate a situation where different High Courts give different judgments on the same concept?

Justice Krishna Iyer: Are you assuming that after reconsideration we will get a homogenized version?

De said that even amongst the Supreme Court judges, opinion was divided as to what was decided in the Kesavananda Bharati case. Justice Mathew has not held that equality is basic.

Justice Mathew: I have said that I do not know whether the majority in Kesavananda Bharati held equality to be basic.

De: It did not. If the Supreme Court itself cannot find out as to what the judgment was, how do you expect the High Courts to find out.

Justice Chandrachud: There will always be difference of opinion in every case. You cannot prevent that.

On this note, the court rose for the day.

THE BENCH IS DISSOLVED

The next day, that is, 12 November 1975, the visitors' gallery was also allotted to the lawyers because there were insufficient seats for lawyers. However, the visitors did not miss much. As soon as the thirteen judges assembled and the Attorney-General was about to continue, the Chief Justice made a startling announcement. 'This Bench is dissolved,' he said. 'For two days the arguments have gone into the air. These cases will now go to the Constitution Bench.' With a pointed reference to the Andhra Pradesh case about the service matters, the Chief Justice said that the Constitution Bench could refer it back to the full court if it had any difficulty with the Kesavananda case. With this, the court rose and the Bench was dissolved.

Appendix 4

Review Application against Justice Beg's Judgment

The review application against Justice Beg's judgment was heard by the same five judges who had heard the appeal—on 18 December between 3.30 and 4 p.m., the time at which miscellaneous matters are heard.

Appearing on behalf of the applicant, Shanti Bhushan read out the text of the review application. The main grievance was that Justice Beg had dealt with the merits of the case without hearing the arguments on them. After giving a history of the arguments in the Supreme Court, the petition stated, 'On the morning of Friday, 19 September 1975, when the petitioner's counsel concluded his rejoinder on the validity of the constitutional amendment, the court said that before pronouncing judgment on the validity of the constitutional amendment, it would hear arguments on the merits of the appeal. It asked A.K. Sen, counsel for the appellant, to start arguments on the merits which he promptly did. After Sen had given an introduction to the issues arising in the appeal, but before he could make his submissions on these issues, or refer to the evidence on them, or even read the reasonings and findings of the High Court on these issues, Justice Mathew interrupted him and observed that in view of the Election Laws (Amendment) Act 1975, there was no occasion to enter into the merits of the issues decided by the High Court unless the court first heard the arguments on the validity of the Election Laws (Amendment) Act. His Lordship further observed that as the Amendment Act must be presumed to be valid till the contrary was proved by the petitioner, he should be called upon to start arguments on the validity of that.

The court, thereafter, directed the petitioner's counsel to address the arguments on the validity of the Election Laws (Amendment) Act.

'The hearing which continued thereafter was, therefore, confined only to the validity and interpretation of the provisions of the Election Laws Amendment Act and the issue relating to expenses, and it was made clear to the counsel that arguments on the merits of the other issues would be heard, if at all, only at a later stage if the provisions of the Election Laws (Amendment) Act were either held to be invalid or inapplicable.

'It is true that when the validity of the Thirty-ninth Constitution (Amendment) Act was being argued by the parties and the learned Solicitor-General was defending the constitutional amendment on the ground that the same had become necessary in order to prevent any arguments being made on sensitive issues arising out of the allegation of corrupt practices against the holder of the high office of Prime Minister, Hon'ble Mr Justice Beg did make observations that such an argument may not be in the interests of the Prime Minister herself as it may deprive her of an opportunity of getting herself exonerated on the facts. This suggestion was, however, not accepted either by the Solicitor-General or by the counsel who argued the case on behalf of Mrs Indira Gandhi and they continued to defend the impugned clause (4) of the Constitutional (Amendment) Act.

'It was in these circumstances that the petitioner's counsel was not given an opportunity to make any submission on the correctness of the findings of the High Court, or on the merits of the other issues on the basis of the law as it existed at the time when the High Court decided the case.

'While the Hon'ble Chief Justice A.N. Ray, Hon'ble Justice Khanna, Hon'ble Justice Mathew and Hon'ble Justice Chandrachud have only decided the points on which the parties' counsels were permitted to argue, to the surprise of the petitioner, it was found that Hon'ble Justice Beg had entered into the merits of the issues decided by the High Court in contravention of the principles of natural justice, and without giving any opportunity to the parties to address arguments on those questions.

'Hon'ble Mr Justice Beg has also on pages 9 and 10 of his judgment made the following observations:

If that election was not really void and had been wrongly held by the Trial Court to be vitiated, it did not need to be validated at all. In that event, a purported validation would be an exercise in futility before this court had decided these appeals. Could it not be said that the intended validation was premature inasmuch as it proceeded on a basically erroneous premise that the original respondent's election was invalid when the question of its validity was subjudice in this court? How could such a premise be assumed to be correct before this court had gone into the merits and decided the appeals pending before it? Such an inquiry is not irrelevant if the very nature and purpose of the exercise of a power are put in issue by both sides.

'Neither had the petitioner's counsel advanced any contention that the constitutional amendment was invalid on the ground that it was premature, or that it was not necessary at all, nor could the validity of the Thirty-ninth Amendment of the Constitution depend on the correctness or otherwise of the different findings of the High Court.

'In fact, the validity of the amendments to the election laws neither were, nor could be challenged merely on the grounds that they were either not necessary or not justified. As stated earlier, Hon'ble Justice Beg had not persisted in his query relating to the trial court's findings when he was informed by Mr Raj Narain's counsel that it would require going into considerable evidence and a number of witnesses and circumstances, and would require protracted hearing, and that if the same was to be done, it had to be indicated as to whether the appellant's counsel or the petitioner's counsel would be heard first. Hon'ble Justice Khanna after conferring with Hon'ble Justice Beg, had then made it clear that they would not be entering into a discussion of the correctness of the findings of the High Court of the other issues at the stage. It is respectfully submitted therefore that the discussion of the merits of the issues on which counsels were not permitted to argue involves a serious breach of the principles of natural justice and had led to very palpable errors in the various observations made.

'On page 40 of his judgment, Hon'ble Justice Beg has recorded the finding that Shri Yashpal Kapoor had visited Rae Bareli on 7 January 1971, accompanying Shri Gulzari Lal Nanda, railway minister, in connection with his own official duties whereas Shri

Yashpal Kapoor himself in his oral evidence before the High Court had clearly stated that: "On 7th January 1971, I went along with the Railway Minister in my private capacity. I, therefore, did not charge any TA, for these journeys."'

The application, therefore, prayed that the honourable court be pleased to:

a) review its judgment dated 7.11.1975;

b) clarify that the parties were not required or permitted to make their submissions on the merits of the various issues arising in the election petition except those which were not covered by the retrospective provisions of the Election Laws (Amendment) Act, 1975;

c) expunge the findings from the judgment of the Hon'ble Justice Beg from page 19 beginning with the words 'On Issue No. 1 the case set up in paragraph 5 of the petition is . . .' and ending with the sentence 'the learned Judge also cited the following case where it was decided that a cow is not a religious symbol . . .' on page 89;

d) also expunge the other observations from the judgment of Hon'ble Mr Justice Beg which have been set out in the body of the application.

Justice Beg: Your only grievance is that we did not hear complete arguments on the merits of the case.

Bhushan: Yes. It is a total negation of the principles of natural justice to decide on the merits of the case without hearing the arguments of either side. We were asked to restrain ourselves from arguing on the merits by Justice Khanna and Justice Mathew.

Justice Beg: Well, you can submit your written submissions now and we will consider them.

Bhushan: Written submissions would not be enough, oral arguments would be necessary.

Chief Justice: No, we cannot go into it now.

With this, the court rose and reserved judgment on the review application.

The judgment came the next day. The order signed by all the five judges was a very small one. It said: 'In view of the fact that one of us (Justice Beg) is of the opinion that there is no sufficient ground for reviewing the judgment, this review application is dismissed.'

This order is so strange that it invites comment. The order dismisses the review application merely because Justice Beg is of the opinion that there is no ground for reviewing the judgment. This is an obviously erroneous principle of law. If five judges had heard the arguments, it was the duty of each of them to give their individual opinions on the application. It was clearly unjustified to leave the decision to just one of them.

Justice Beg delivered a much longer judgment. In his judgment, he said that he had indicated to the parties that he regarded consideration of the merits of the case essential for a just and proper decision and disposal of the appeals. He further says,

> Indeed, the direction given by His Lordship, the Chief Justice, to the parties to address their arguments on merits, after those on the constitutional amendment, necessarily meant, I think, that a consideration of merits could not be separated from the question of validity of the amendments of the election laws.
>
> It was the contention of the petitioner's counsel that the respondent in the High Court, being in the advantageous and powerful position of the Prime Minister of the country, supported by a large majority in Parliament, had obtained a change of laws in her favour so as to convert a defeat into a victory. It was, therefore, essential for the decision of this issue raised by the learned counsel for the election petitioner himself to convince us that the case of election petitioner, according to the laws as they stood at the time when the election was held, was bound to succeed on merits.

Justice Beg agreed that he had gone into the merits of the case in much more detail than his brother judges. He observes:

> I found that there was no alteration of the election laws, except in one respect, and, therefore, there could be no question of an alteration of 'the rules of the game' to the disadvantage of the election petitioner. Once I had reached this conclusion, it was not possible to avoid considering findings on merits. Learned Counsel for the election petitioner had conceded, no doubt in the interests of his client, that the findings of the learned trial judge were unsustainable if the amendments were rejected. I do

not think that I could possibly decide the case on this concession after reaching a conclusion, possibly not anticipated by the learned counsel for the election petitioner, that the election laws were not really changed except in one respect.

It may be difficult for learned counsel sometimes to anticipate and meet the requirements of every learned judge of this court when there are five of us hearing arguments. It is, however, the duty of counsel who raise issues, which may necessitate consideration of questions of fact and law, to satisfy the requirements of any one of us who may be of opinion, as I am, that these issues could not possibly be decided properly without considering findings of fact and the application of law to them.

It seems, from the petition now before us, that the greatest concern of the election petitioner and his learned counsel is not the result of the election petition or the common conclusions reached by all the five learned judges, with which no fault has been found in this petition, but that the merits of the case, on facts, were examined at all by me. If this is part of a political game, I think that it is high time that it was realized by everyone that courts are not meant for political tactics or propaganda.

In the end, giving a left-handed compliment to Bhushan, he observed: 'Learned counsel for the election petitioner also seemed to complain that my judgment contained some remarks indicating that he did not discharge his professional duties towards his client satisfactorily. If that is so, I would like to remove this grievance by saying that he discharged his duty towards his client so well that he succeeded in averting a closer and more detailed scrutiny by all of us of the pleadings, the evidence, and the patently erroneous conclusions of the trial judge in this case.'

With this, Justice Beg concluded his judgment on the review application.

Appendix 5

The Representation of People Act, 1951
—Part VII, Section 123

'123. Corrupt practices. The following shall be deemed to be corrupt practices for the purposes of this Act:

(1) "Bribery" that is to say,—

(A) any gift, offer or promise by a candidate or his agent or by any other person with the consent of a candidate or his election agent of any gratification, to any person whomsoever, with the object, directly or indirectly of inducing—

- (a) a person to stand or not to stand as, to withdraw or not to withdraw from being a candidate at an election, or
- (b) an elector to vote or refrain from voting at an election or as a reward to—
  - (i) a person for having so stood, or not stood, or for having withdrawn or not having withdrawn his candidature; or
  - (ii) an elector for having voted or refrained from voting.

(B) the receipt of, or agreement to receive, any gratification, whether as a motive or a reward—

- (a) by a person for standing or not standing as, or for withdrawing or not withdrawing from being, a candidate; or
- (b) by any person whomsoever for himself or any other person for voting or refraining from voting, or inducing or attempting to induce any elector to vote or refrain from voting, or any candidate to withdraw or not to withdraw his candidature.

Explanation: For the purposes of this clause the term "gratification" is not restricted to pecuniary gratifications or gratifications estimated in money and it includes all forms of entertainment and all forms of employment for reward but it does not include the payment of any expenses *bona fide* incurred at, or for the purpose of, any election and duly entered in the account expenses referred to in Section 78.

(2) Undue influence, that is to say, any direct or indirect interference or attempt to interfere on the part of the candidate or his agent, or of any other person with the consent of the candidate or his election agent, with the free exercise of any electoral right:

Provided that—
(a) without prejudice to the generality of the provisions of this clause any such person as is referred to therein who—
  (i) threatens any candidate or any elector, or any person in whom a candidate or any elector is interested, with injury of any kind including social ostracism and ex-communication or expulsion from any caste or community; or
  (ii) induces or attempts to induce a candidate or an elector to believe that he, or any person in whom he is interested, will become or will be rendered an object of divine displeasure or spiritual censure,
  shall be deemed to interfere with the free exercise of the electoral right of such candidate or elector within the meaning of this clause;
(b) a declaration of public policy, or a promise of public action, or the mere exercise of a legal right without intent to interfere with an electoral right, shall be deemed to be interference within the meaning of this clause.

(3) The appeal by a candidate or his agent or by any other person with the consent of a candidate or his election agent to vote or refrain from voting for any person on the ground of his religion, race, caste, community or language or the use of or appeal to religious symbols or the use of, or appeal to, national symbols, such as the national flag or the national emblem, for the furtherance of the prospects of the election of that candidate or for prejudicially affecting the election of any candidate.

(3A) The promotion of, or attempt to promote, feelings of enmity or hatred between different classes of citizens of India on grounds of religion, race, caste, community, or language, by a candidate or his agent or any other person with the consent of a candidate or his election agent for the furtherance of the prospects of the election of that candidate or for prejudicially affecting the election of any candidate.

(4) The publication by a candidate or his agent or by any other person, with the consent of a candidate or his election agent, of any statement of fact which is false, and which he either believes to be false or does not believe to be true, in relation to the personal character or conduct of any candidate, or in relation to the candidature, or withdrawal, of any candidate, being a statement reasonably calculated to prejudice the prospects of that candidate's election.

(5) The hiring or procuring, whether on payment or otherwise, of any vehicle or vessel by a candidate or his agent or by any other person with the consent of a candidate or his election agent, or the use of such vehicle or vessel for the free conveyance of any elector (other than the candidate himself, the members of his family or his agent) to or from any polling station provided under Section 25 or a place fixed under sub-section (1) of Section 29 for the poll:

> Provided that the hiring of a vehicle or vessel by an elector or by several electors at their joint costs for the purpose of conveying him or them to and from any such polling station or place fixed for the poll shall not be deemed to be a corrupt practice under this clause if the vehicle or vessel so hired is a vehicle or vessel not propelled by mechanical power:

> Provided further that the use of any public transport vehicle or vessel or any tramcar or railway carriage by any elector at his own cost for the purpose of going to or coming from any such polling station or place fixed for the poll shall not be deemed to be a corrupt practice under this clause.

Explanation: In this clause, the expression "vehicle" means any vehicle used or capable of being used for the purpose of road transport, whether propelled by mechanical power or otherwise and whether used for drawing other vehicles or otherwise.

(6) The incurring or authorizing of expenditure in contravention of Section 77.

(7) The obtaining or procuring or abetting or attempting to obtain or procure by a candidate or his agent or, by any other person with the consent of a candidate or his election agent, any assistance (other than the giving of vote) for the furtherance of the prospects of that candidate's election, from any person in the service of the Government and belonging to any of the following classes, namely:

(a) gazetted officers;
(b) stipendiary judges and magistrates;
(c) members of the armed forces of the Union;
(d) members of the police forces;
(e) excise officers;
(f) revenue officers other than village revenue officers known as lambardars, malguzars, patels, deshmukhs or by any other name, whose duty is to collect land revenue and who are remunerated by a share of, or commission on, the amount of land revenue collected by them but who do not discharge any police functions; and
(g) such other class of persons in the service of the Government as may be prescribed.

Explanation: (1) In this section the expression 'agent' includes an election agent, a polling agent and any person who is held to have acted as an agent in connection with the election with the consent of the candidate.

(2) For the purpose of Clause (7), a person shall be deemed to assist in the furtherance of the prospects of a candidate's election if he acts as an election agent of that candidate.'

Appendix 6

The Representation of People
(Amendment) Act, 1974
—No. 58 of 1974

'An Act further to amend the Representation of the People Act 1951.

BE it enacted by Parliament in the Twenty-fifth Year of the Republic of India as follows:

1. (1) This Act may be called the Representation of the People (Amendment) Act, 1974.

   (2) It shall be deemed to have come into force on the 19th day of October, 1974.

2. In Section 77 of the Representation of the People Act, 1951, in subsection (1), the following Explanations shall be inserted at the end, namely:

Explanation 1: Notwithstanding any judgment, order or decision of any court to the contrary, any expenditure incurred or authorized in connection with the election of a candidate by a political party or by any other association or body of persons or by any individual (other than the candidate or his election agent) shall not be deemed to be, and shall not ever be deemed to have been, expenditure in connection with the election incurred or authorized by the candidate or by his election agent for the purposes of this sub-section:

Provided that nothing contained in this Explanation shall affect—

   (a) any judgment, order or decision of the Supreme Court whereby the election of a candidate to the House of the People or to the Legislative Assembly of a State has been declared void or set aside before the commencement of the Representation of the People (Amendment) Ordinance, 1974;

(b) any judgment, order or decision of a High Court whereby
      the election of any such candidate has been declared void or
      set aside before the commencement of the said Ordinance if
      no appeal has been preferred to the Supreme Court against
      such judgment, order or decision of the High Court before
      such commencement and the period of limitation for filing
      such appeal has expired before such commencement.

Explanation 2: For the purposes of Explanation 1, "political party"
shall have the same meaning as in the Election Symbols (Reservation
and Allotment) Order, 1968, as for the time being in force.'

Appendix 7

The Election Laws
(Amendment) Act, 1975
—No. 40 of 1975

An Act further to amend the Representation of the People Act, 1951 and the Indian Penal Code.

BE it enacted by Parliament in the Twenty-sixth Year of the Republic of India as follows:

Short title.

1. This Act may be called the Election Laws (Amendment) Act, 1975.

43 of 1951
Substitution of
new section for
Section 8A.

2. In the Representation of the People Act, 1951 (hereinafter referred to as the principal Act), for Section 8A, the following section shall be substituted, namely:—

'8 A. (1) The case of every person found guilty of a corrupt practice by an order under Section 99 shall be submitted, as soon as may be, after such order takes effect, by such authority as the Central Government may specify in this behalf, to the President for determination of the question as to whether such person shall be disqualified and if so, for what period:

Provided that the period for which any person may be disqualified under this sub-section shall in no case exceed six years from the date on which the order made in relation to him under Section 99 takes effect.

(2) Any person who stands disqualified under Section 8A of this Act as it stood immediately before the commencement of the Election Laws (Amendment) Act, 1975, may, if the period of such disqualification has not expired, submit a petition to the President for the removal of such disqualification for the unexpired portion of the said period.

(3) Before giving his decision on any question mentioned in sub-section (1) or on any petition submitted under sub-section (2), the President shall obtain the opinion of the Election Commission on such question or petition and shall act according to such opinion.'

Amendment of Section 11.

3. In Section 11 of the principal Act, after the words 'under this Chapter', the brackets, words, figure and letter '(except under Section 8A)' shall be inserted.

Amendment of Section 11 A.

4. Section 11A of the principal Act shall be renumbered as sub-section (1) thereof and—

(a) in the sub-section as so renumbered, clause (b) shall be omitted; and

(b) after the sub-section as so renumbered, the following sub-sections shall be inserted, namely:

'(2) Any person disqualified by a decision of the President under sub-section (1) of Section 8A for any period shall be disqualified for the same period for voting at any election.

(3) The decision of the President on a petition submitted by any person under sub-section (2) of Section 8A in respect of any disqualification for being chosen as, and for being, a member of either House of Parliament or of the Legislative

Assembly or Legislative Council of a State shall, so far as may be, apply in respect of the disqualification for voting at any election incurred by him under clause (b) of sub-section (1) of Section 11A of this Act as it stood immediately before the commencement of the Election Laws (Amendment) Act, 1975, as if such decision were a decision in respect of the said disqualification for voting also.'

Amendment of Section 11 B.

5. In Section 11B of the principal Act, for the words 'any disqualification under this Chapter', the words, brackets, figures and letter 'any disqualification under sub-section (1) of Section 11 A' shall be substituted.

Amendment of Section 77.

6. In Section 77 of the principal Act, in sub-section (1),—

(a) for the words 'the date of publication of the notification calling the election', the words 'the date on which he has been nominated' shall be substituted;

(b) after Explanation 2, the following Explanation shall be inserted, namely:

Explanation 3: For the removal of doubt, it is hereby declared that any expenditure incurred in respect of any arrangements made, facilities provided or any other act or thing done by any person in the service of the Government and belonging to any of the classes mentioned in clause (7) of Section 123 in the discharge or purported discharge of his official duty as mentioned in the proviso to that clause shall not be deemed to be expenditure in connection with the election incurred or authorized by a candidate or by his election agent for the purposes of this subsection.'

Amendment of
Section 79.

7. In Section 79 of the principal Act, for clause (b), the following clause shall be substituted, namely:

'(b) "candidate" means a person who has been or claims to have been duly nominated as a candidate at any election.'

Amendment of
Section 123.

8. In Section 123 of the principal Act,

(a) in clause (3), the following proviso shall be inserted at the end, namely:

'Provided that no symbol allotted under this Act to a candidate shall be deemed to be a religious symbol or a national symbol for the purposes of this clause.';

(b) in clause (7), the following proviso shall be inserted at the end, namely:—

'Provided that where any person, in the service of the Government and belonging to any of the classes aforesaid, in the discharge or purported discharge of his official duty, makes any arrangements or provides any facilities or does any other act or thing, for, to, or in relation to any candidate or his agent or any other person acting with the consent of the candidate or his election agent (whether by reason of the office held by the candidate or for any other reason), such arrangements, facilities or act or thing shall not be deemed to be assistance for the furtherance of the prospects of that candidate's election.';

(c) in the Explanation at the end, the following shall be added, namely:

'(3) For the purposes of clause (7), notwithstanding anything contained in any other law, the publication in the Official Gazette of the appointment, resignation, termination of service, dismissal or removal from service of a person in the service of the Central Government (including a person serving in connection with the administration of a Union territory) or of a State Government shall be conclusive proof—

(i) of such appointment, resignation, termination of service, dismissal or removal from service, as the case may be, and

(ii) where the date of taking effect of such appointment, resignation, termination of service, dismissal or removal from service, as the case may be, is stated in such publication, also of the fact that such person was appointed with effect from the said date, or in the case of resignation, termination of service, dismissal or removal from service, such person ceased to be in such service with effect from the said date.'

Amendment of Section 171A of Act 45 of 1860.

9. In the Indian Penal Code, in Section 171 A, for clause (a), the following clause shall be substituted, namely:

'(a) "candidate" means a person who has been nominated as a candidate at any election;'.

Amendment to have retrospective effect.

10. The amendments made by Sections 6, 7 and 8 of this Act in the principal Act shall also have retrospective operation so as to apply to and in relation to any election held before the commencement of this Act to either House of Parliament or to either House or the House of the Legislature of a State—

(i) in respect of which any election petition may be prescribed after the commencement of this Act; or

(ii) in respect of which any election petition is in any High Court immediately before such commencement; or

(iii) in respect of which any election petition has been decided by any High Court before such commencement but no appeal has been preferred to the Supreme Court against the decision of the High Court before such commencement and the period of limitation for filing such appeal has not expired before such commencement; or

(iv) in respect of which appeal from any order of any High Court made in any election petition under Section 98 or Section 99 of the principal Act is pending before the Supreme Court immediately before such commencement.

Appendix 8

The Constitution (Thirty-ninth Amendment) Act, 1975

An Act further to amend the Constitution of India.

BE it enacted by Parliament in the Twenty-sixth Year of the Republic of India as follows:

Short title. 1. This Act may be called the Constitution (Thirty-ninth Amendment) Act, 1975.

2. For article 71 of the Constitution, the following article shall be substituted, namely:

Substitution of new article for article 71. '71. (1) Subject to the provisions of this Constitution Parliament may by law regulate any matter relating to or connected with the election of a President or Vice-President, including the grounds on which such election may be questioned:

Provided that the election of a person as President or Vice-President shall not be called in question on the ground of existence of any vacancy for whatever reason among the members of the electoral college electing him.

(2) All doubts and disputes arising out of or in connection with the election of a President or Vice-President shall be inquired

into and decided by such authority or body and in such manner as may be provided for by or under any law referred to in clause (1).

(3) The validity of any such law as is referred to in clause (1) and the decision of any authority or body under such law shall not be called in question in any court.

(4) If the election of a person as President or Vice-President is declared void under any such law as is referred to in clause (1), acts done by him in the exercise and performance of the powers and duties of the office of President or Vice-President, as the case may be, on or before the date of such declaration shall not be invalidated by reason of that declaration.'

Amendment of article 329.

3. In article 329 of the Constitution, for the words 'Notwithstanding any thing in this Constitution—', the words figures and letter 'Notwithstanding anything in this Constitution but subject to the provisions of article 329A—' shall be substituted.

Insertion of new article 329A.

4. In Part XV of the Constitution, after article 329, the following article shall be inserted, namely:

'329A. (1) Subject to provisions of Chapter II of Part V except sub-clause (e) of clause (1) of article 102, no election

Special provision as to elections to Parliament in the case of Prime Minister and Speaker.

(a) to either House of Parliament of a person who holds the office of Prime Minister at the time of such election or is appointed as Prime Minister after such election;

(b) to the House of the People of a person who holds the office of Speaker of that House at the time of such election or who is chosen as the Speaker for that House after such election;

shall be called in question, except before such authority not being any such authority as is referred to in clause (b) of article 329 or body and in such manner as may be provided for by or under any law made by Parliament and any such law may provide for all other matters relating to doubts and disputes in relation to such election including the grounds on which such election may be questioned.

(2) The validity of any such law as is referred to in clause (1) and the decision of any authority or body under such law shall be called in question in any court.

(3) Where any person is appointed as Prime Minister or, as the case may be, chosen to the office of the Speaker of the House of the People, while an election petition preferred to in clause (b) of article 329 in respect of his election to either House of Parliament or, as the case may be, to the House of the People is pending, such election petition shall abate upon such person to the office of the Speaker of the House of the People, but such election may be called in question under any such law as is referred to in clause (1).

(4) No law made by Parliament before the commencement of the Constitution (Thirty-ninth Amendment) Act, 1975, insofar as it relates to election petitions and matter connected therewith, shall apply or shall be deemed ever to have applied to or in relation to the election of any such person as is referred to in clause (1) to either House of Parliament and such election shall not be deemed to be void or ever to have become void or has, before such Commencement, declaring such election to be void, such

election shall continue to be valid in all respects and any such order and any finding on which such order is based shall be and shall be deemed always to have been void and of no effect.

(5) Any appeal or cross appeal against any such order of any court as is referred to in clause (4) pending immediately before the commencement of the Constitution (Thirty-ninth Amendment) Act, 1975, before the Supreme Court shall be disposed of in conformity with the provisions of clause (4).

The provisions of this article shall have effect notwithstanding anything contained in this Constitution.'

Index

ein intellektueller Mensch. Der Intellekt ist eine selbstgebaute Scheidewand innerhalb der Seelenkörper, und wer sie einmal — durch fanatische intellektuelle Einstellung seines Denkens — fest errichtet hat, der hat weder Intuition, noch Religion, noch seelisches Erleben, denn es ist ihm unmöglich geworden, sich „nach innen" zum Ich zu vertiefen, er kann n u r noch materiell, also sachlich und real denken, und bekanntlich läßt sich nicht alles mit dem sachlichen Verstande erfassen, wie z. B. Metaphysik, Religion, Kunst. — (Siehe: „Die Seele des Menschen" vom gl. Verfasser.)

Der Geist besitzt aus sich heraus hohe und höchste Erkenntnis, wie sie sich im Genie oft offenbart. — Nicht der Geist ist Widersacher der Seele, wie L. Klages behauptet, sondern der Intellekt ist der Widersacher! Das ist ein sehr großer Unterschied! Der Intellekt ist ein Gegner alles Spirituellen (Geist - Seelischen) und des Erkennens durch Innenschau und ist nur groß im Kritisieren, „Besserwissen". — Erkenntnis ist eine geistige Eigenschaft, Empfinden eine solche der Seele, und Gefühl eine des Körpers. Da ist nichts zu verwechseln!

Chirologie ist die Wissenschaft und Kunst, aus den durch Erfahrung gewonnenen Regeln für die Bedeutung der einzelnen Handmerkmale (Signifixe) und deren Kombinationen ein richtiges Charakter- und Schicksalsbild zu gewinnen und zu konstruieren.

Wissenschaftliche Chirologie und ihre Anwendung.

Urteile nicht über eine Sache, wenn du sie nicht verstehst oder begreifen kannst, sondern meditiere und versuche durch Konzentration deiner Gedanken in die Tiefe der Weisheit und des Geheimnisses des Universums einzudringen! Nur so wird es dir möglich sein, Erleuchtungen zu erlangen und deshalb: Verstehen.

Was ist Chirologie?

Chirologie ist eine alte Wissenschaft, Beobachtung und Erfahrung wie jede andere Wissenschaft der Personenkenntnis — was jemand ist, was er war und was er sein wird. Dies Wissen, so schwer verständlich für jene, die damit nicht vertraut sind, ist für einen wirklichen Chirologen so klar wie Quellwasser. Wie alles Wissen, hat auch dieses seinen Grund in Beobachtung und Erfahrung von Ursache und Wirkung, folglich kann man auch aus der Wirkung die Ursache erkennen. Die Handlesekunst ist nicht von gestern und heute, sondern wird seit Jahrtausenden ausgeübt. Sie ist Meta-Physiologie, also Naturwissenschaft. Jeder gute Beobachter kann nicht umhin, die Verschiedenheit des Charakters zu erkennen an Form und Ausdruck des Kopfes und Gesichts bei Personen, mit denen er in Berührung kommt. Dasselbe wird er bei näherer Betrachtung der Hände finden. Das Gesicht gibt ein klares Bild der Leidenschaften und Neigungen. So auch die Hand, die Form und Haltung des Körpers, der Gang usw. Man erkennt gewisse Menschen schon am Gang, an Klang und Art des Trittes, der Stimme, selbst wenn sein Körper noch nicht sichtbar ist. Ebenso erkennen wir auch den Charakter und selbst Krankheiten aus der Hand, Handschrift, Kopfform (Belastung), dem Auge, der Iris usw., auch ohne Hellseher oder Psychometer zu sein. Wer aber noch mit einer dieser göttlichen Gaben gesegnet ist — sei es von Geburt oder durch Ausbildung —, der sieht oder fühlt noch weit besser und mehr und erkennt sicherer, was er sucht. Das Studium der Chirologie wird jedem Wißbegierigen in dieser Hinsicht ein weites und äußerst interessantes Feld eröffnen, eine Quelle von Wissen bieten zum Nutzen seiner Gesundheit, seines Erfolges — in geistiger und materieller Hinsicht. Viele Ehen werden unglücklich durch späteres Erscheinen oder Hervortreten von Eigenschaften, die man zunächst weder vermutet noch in Betracht gezogen hatte. Manches Kind wurde einer Erziehungsmethode unterworfen, welche seiner Individualität nicht Rechnung trug, dann in einen Beruf gedrängt, der seinen Fähigkeiten nicht entsprach. Wie fremd es auch für manche klingen mag, doch Erfahrung hat gelehrt und bewiesen, daß Chirosophie die Natur und das Alter von Geschehnissen, die das Leben und sein Ende beeinflussen und angehen, entschleiert und oft mit großer Genauigkeit definiert. Sie enthüllt überstandene oder kommende Krankheiten, drohende Unfälle und Gefahren. Sie enthüllt den Grad der Liebesfähigkeit; klärt den Wert von Freundschaften. Sie erkennt, welcher Beruf am besten zu wählen ist, wie man zu Wohlstand kommt und Verluste verhütet.

Sie sagt Bedeutsames aus über die Aussichten einer geplanten Ehe, die Möglichkeit Kinder zu bekommen und über guten oder bösen Charakter der Partner.

Ganzes Interesse, Neigung und Fleiß werden jeden ernsthaft Studierenden mit der Zeit dieses Wissen gewinnen lassen und ihn von seinem Werte überzeugen. Mancher wird evtl. nach dem Lesen dieses Buches sagen, daß er mit einzelnen Dingen des Inhalts wenig anfangen könne. Dem ist aber nicht so. Jedem wird wohl ein wenig bange vor der Fülle des Materials, das er auswendig lernen muß, wenn er ganzes Können erreichen will. Denn es kommen zeitweise Hände vor, die so viele Kombinationslinien haben, daß jede derartige Hand nahezu ein Studium für sich ist. Solche Fälle erfordern

Geduld und ruhiges logisches Denken. Tief nachdenken und genau sich klar werden: wo entspringt und wohin geht die Linie, was streift und kreuzt sie, wo und weshalb biegt sie da oder dort um oder aus, wo ist sie unterbrochen, weshalb ist gerade hier ein Kreuz, da ein Stern, Punkt, eine Insel, ein Fleck, Gitter usw. Dann wird man auch die Antwort finden. Es ist wirklich nicht so schwer, wie es anfangs aussieht, wenn man die Charakteristik des Handtyps, der Berge und Linien kennt. Dies ist Grundbedingung! Viel Übung ist erforderlich, und der ernste Schüler wird jede Gelegenheit zu nutzen wissen, sei es unauffällig in der Straßenbahn, auf dem Ball, im Geschäft oder sonstwo. Zu jedem Studium ist großes Interesse, Liebe, Streben und Ausdauer erforderlich, und Chirosophie bildet darin keine Ausnahme. Die besten wissenschaftlichen Bücher machen im Schrank einen imponierenden Eindruck, sind aber wertlos für jeden, der sie weder benutzt, noch ihren Inhalt im praktischen Leben anwendet.

Gewiß gibt es viele Hände, aus denen man wenig erkennen kann außer den Charaktereigenschaften und Krankheitsanlagen. Das ist so, wenn der Betreffende zu materiell oder nur materiell ist und denkt, oder nur intellektuell eingestellt (reiner Verstandesmensch) ist; denn rein verstandesmäßiges Denken vertreibt das Empfindungsleben! Diese Bestätigung findet man bei solchen Leuten, welche alles Empfinden und Gefühl als „Gefühlsduselei" hinstellen möchten. Sie berauben sich selbst ihrer ideellen und praktischen Werte. Außerdem hemmen sie sich selber dadurch in ihrer Höherentwicklung zum wahren Menschen. Wie sollen sich die unterdrückten seelischen Schwingungen in solchen Fällen zeigen? Auch kommt der Fall vor, daß das Schicksal des Betreffenden es besser findet, den Weg absichtlich dunkel zu erhalten; d. h. der in Frage kommende Mensch soll nicht „wissen" und Prüfungen durchmachen, die für ihn durchaus notwendig sind. Ich sage keinesfalls, daß a l l e s von der Chiromantie heute bekannt ist. Auch ich studiere weiter und lerne Neues — zur Vervollkommnung. Es gibt noch sehr viel, wovon man heute noch nichts G e n a u e s weiß, anderseits vieles, was noch nicht genügend erforscht und erprobt ist. Welche Wissenschaft ist heute vollkommen? Nicht eine! Es handelt sich bei der wissenschaftlichen Chirosophie durchaus nicht um das vielverrufene Wahrsagen, sondern lediglich um die wirklich vorhandenen, ablesbaren Zeichen, welche nach uralten „Regeln der Erfahrung" in unsere Sprache übersetzt werden, die allerdings Vergangenheit, soweit solche Zeichen noch nicht verblichen sind, außerdem Gegenwart und Zukunft enthalten, was jederzeit nachprüfbar ist. Menschen, welche dies bestreiten, fehlt es an Einsicht. Sie glauben aber an Wettervoraussagen u. dgl. Jeder

Arzt, Prediger, Mathematiker, Astronom, Politiker und — Kriminalist deutet die Zukunft! Auch Feldherren, Strategen. Man versuche sich doch klar zu werden über die Frage: was ist Zeit? Ein Menschenalter währt, wenn es hoch kommt, hundert Jahre. „Zeit" ist uns nur durch die Tag- und Nachtunterschiede bewußt geworden. Hätte die Erde dauernd Sonnenschein, wer würde sagen können: „heute", „morgen", „gestern"? Es wäre ein dauerndes Heute. Man betrachte den Sinn „Zeit" vom Standpunkte Gottes, der Natur, des Kosmos, oder wie man will. Dann wird man auch erkennen, daß die Dauer eines Menschenlebens nur ein Augenblick im kosmischen Sinne ist. Wo aber sind Vergangenheit, Gegenwart und Zukunft in solch einem Augenblicke?! Sie sind ein Begriff geworden. Je höher das spirituelle (nicht intellektuelle) Bewußtseinsleben im Menschen ist, desto kürzer erscheint ihm das Leben. Nur ein Mensch, der wenig oder kein Innen-(Seelen-)Leben hat, kennt „Langeweile"!

Die a s t r o l o g i s c h e n Bezeichnungen der Finger, Berge und Linien behalte ich hier bei. Sie haben ihren guten Grund, sind kurz, sachlich und machen es besonders denen leicht, welche mit den Elementen der Astrologie vertraut sind. Anfänger werden sie sich ohne viel Mühe merken können.

Zur leichteren Erlernung möchte ich hier anführen: Sonne für Sonntag, Mond für Montag, Mars für Dienstag, Merkur für Mittwoch, Jupiter für Donnerstag, Venus für Freitag, Saturn für Sonnabend. Das ist durchaus nicht sonderbar oder Spielerei; denn in der Astronomie werden diese Zeichen ebenfalls angewandt und auch in der Medizin, wo das Marszeichen für „männlich" und das Venuszeichen für „weiblich" gebraucht wird. Uranus und Neptun sind leicht zu merken. Man wird diese Zeichen noch besser verstehen lernen, wenn man die esoterische Bedeutung der Symbole kennt. Ich will mich hier kurz äußern über

Symbolik und Geistlehre.

Das Alter der Symbole ist so groß, daß man darüber heute nichts mehr sagen kann. Sicher ist, daß sie auf die ältesten Kulturvölker zurückgehen, weil die meisten Symbolzeichen auf die nordische Runensprache zurückzuführen und in dieser enthalten sind (s. die „Ursprache" und „Bilderschrift der Ario-Germanen" von Guido v. List). Das Ichselbst, das Ego, wird dargestellt durch einen Punkt (der Geist); die Seele durch einen Kreis, das Prinzip der Unendlichkeit. Punkt im Kreis ist das Symbol (auch astronomisches Zeichen) für die Sonne. Der

Mond hat das Zeichen eines Halbkreises oder einer Sichel und bezeichnet die Persönlichkeit, Leidenschaft und Gefühle des Menschen. Der senkrechte Strich stellt das Männliche dar, der waagerechte Strich das Weibliche; das Kreuz: männlich und weiblich, positiv und negativ. Das Kreuz im Ring ist das Glückszeichen (von der Seele umgeben). Anderseits ist das Kreuz das Symbol der Erlösung, also christlich. Dieses Kreuz muß überwunden werden. Das wird dargestellt durch den Kreis mit daraufstehendem Kreuze: das Symbol der Erde. Das Kreuz obenstehend bedeutet hier, daß das Leid noch nicht überwunden ist. Venus hat als Symbol einen Kreis über dem Kreuze: das Kreuz oder die Leiden durch Liebe überwunden. Dasselbe Zeichen mit einem liegenden Halbmonde darüber ist das Merkurzeichen und bedeutet, daß das Kreuz und das Leiden durch Liebe und Vernunft überwunden sind. Die Zeugungsrune, ein Pfeil mit einem Ringe daran, ist das Symbol des Mars. Dieselbe Rune aufrechtstehend mit einem Halbmond im Kreis auf der rechten Seite und dem Punkt in der Mitte ist das Zeichen für Uranus: höchste Erkenntnis durch Geist, Seele, Vernunft und Sexualmysterien. Der Jupiter ist dargestellt durch ein Kreuz, auf dessen waagerechtem Balken ein Halbmond steht: das Kreuz durch Fühlen und Denken, somit Erkenntnis — überwunden. Das Saturnzeichen besteht aus einem Kreuze mit darunterhängendem Halbmonde: das Leid noch nicht überwunden, und da dieser Planet sehr kräftig wirkt, ist er der Erzieher, aber auch der Helfer. Saturn ist auch der Intellekt (Halbmond), überschattet vom Stoffe (Kreuz), also vom Gehirndenken eingeschränkt und gefesselt; deshalb egoistisch. Durch seine Hemmungen wirkt er zur Nachdenklichkeit und Konzentration. Wir wissen, daß alle Ereignisse schwerer Art, alles Leid, uns zum Nachdenken bringen. Wird der Stoff und die Hemmungen, das Leid durch Erkenntnis überwunden, so kehrt sich dieses Zeichen um, und aus dem Saturn entsteht der Jupiter. Die unmanifestierte Gottheit wird symbolisiert durch den Kreis und die sich manifestierende Gottheit durch den Punkt. Die Manifestation im Vollendeten wird dargestellt durch einen Punkt und einen Doppelkreis: die Zentralsonne, der göttliche Wille. Die Swastika bedeutet, mit einigen Worten gesagt: die Bewegung des Kosmos. Es ist das Sonnenkreuz, das Kreuz der alten Magier und Weisen, eines der ältesten Symbole der nordischen Rasse. Mißbrauch der heiligen Runen rächt sich früher oder später immer. Rechtmäßig gehört in das Hakenkreuz ein Punkt (in das Zentrum). Der fünfzackige Stern mit e i n e m Strahl nach oben ist das Symbol der Gottheit; mit zwei Strahlen nach oben ein Symbol des Dämons. So stellt der erste den kosmischen Menschen aufrechtstehend dar, der letzte den göttlichen Menschen auf den Kopf gestellt, (Adam Cadmon) „aufgehängt". Der Sechsstern, auch Siegel Salomonis oder Schild Davids

genannt, bedeutet die Verstofflichung des Geistes und die Ver-
geistigung des Stoffes. Es ist ebenfalls ein nordisches Zeichen und wird
gern von den Juden benutzt. Der Fisch ist das Symbol Christi und
der Wiedergeburt. Das griechische A und O bedeuten Anfang und
Ende. Daher sind sie oft auf Grabsteinen zu finden. Die Runen der
hebräischen Schrift stellen sowohl Zahlen wie Buchstaben dar. Die
Feuerzeichen des Tierkreises werden dargestellt durch aufrechtstehende
Dreiecke, die Wasserzeichen durch Dreieck auf der Spitze stehend;
Luftzeichen durch aufrechtstehendes Dreieck mit waagerechtem Strich
durch den oberen Teil und die Erdzeichen mit derselben, aber
umgekehrten Rune. Jeder Planet hat noch seine eigenen Runenzeichen
dieser oder jener Art, wie ich sie auf Bild 23 unten links gebracht
habe. In jeder Zeile bedeutet das letzte Zeichen ein dämonisches
Siegel und die beiden vorletzten, theonische Siegel. Befinden sich
auf einer Stelle in der Hand ein oder mehrere Planetenzeichen,
so hat man darauf zu achten, w i e sie stehen. Aufrechtstehend,
mit dem Kopf nach den Fingerspitzen zu, haben sie günstige
Bedeutung, umgekehrt stehend ungünstige; liegend sind sie zweifelhaft und wechselartig. Man muß die Bedeutung der Planeten-
charakteristik als Person betrachten und diese Person in Verbindung
bringen mit der Bedeutung der betreffenden Stelle in der Hand, Berg
oder Linie. Aus dieser Kombination ergibt sich, was die Natur damit
sagen will. Für gute und günstige Bedeutungen müssen Runenzeichen
immer aufrecht stehen. Das mag hierüber genügen. Einiges andere ist
beschrieben im Kapitel: „Astrale Symbolik".

In der alten Symbolik ist Wahrheit enthalten. Diese Bezeichnungen
entsprangen nicht dem „Zufall", wie irgendein Sprichwort, sondern sie
entsprachen sowohl den Funktionen der einzelnen Handteile, als auch
den Eigenschaften, mit denen die Götter von den Menschen versehen
wurden. Wenn z. B. der Zeigefinger droht und warnt, so ist sein
Sinn und Ausdruck sehr wohl mit dem donnernden Jupiter zu vergleichen. Wir winken, zeigen, warnen, befehlen mit dem Zeige-
Jupiterfinger; ebenso der Daumen mit der Bejahung bzw. Verneinung
des „Ich", wie dies bei den Römern zu Neros Zeiten gebräuchlich war.
Aufwärts zeigend: ja; abwärts: nein, Tod. Im Daumenballen wird
das Triebleben dargestellt, erotische Liebe, daher Venus; „die Feste
der Venus". Der Mittel- oder Saturnfinger ist der längste und sehr
massiv; wir wissen alle, welchen Einfluß das „Böse" (Saturn — Satan)
oder auch Gewissenhaftigkeit auf die Menschen hat. Das Symbol der
Sonne ist Gold. Am Apollofinger trägt man den goldnen Schmuck;
vor allem aber den Ehering. (Zufällig?) Der kleinste Mensch ist
gewöhnlich der gewandteste. Gewandt muß man sein im Handel und

in der Sprache. Wenn jemand recht „vornehm erscheinen" will, sei es beim Trinken, Rauchen usw., so spreizt er seinen kleinen Finger nach außen und gibt ihm eine besondere Stellung. Dasselbe erfolgt im Gedankenleben als Diplomatie, d. h. Verstellung; alles Attribute des Merkur. — Warum das so ist, hat man bisher nicht besser erklären können, doch die immer wiederkehrenden Erfahrungen beweisen, daß es so ist! — Die Proportionsverhältnisse der Finger zueinander und zur ganzen Hand haben ihre ganz bestimmten Charakteristiken. Sehen wir z. B. eine breite, kurze und gedrungene Hand, so wirkt sie unsympathisch, oft sogar abstoßend auf uns. Wir erkennen sofort (durch bewußtes Empfinden) die brutalen und niederen Eigenschaften des Eigners — wir s e h e n sie — „Das Innere formt das Äußere!" —; weil seine Art und sein Wesen so sind, formt das Äußere sich auch dementsprechend. Man darf deshalb solchen Menschen durchaus nicht verdammen; denn es ist sein Schicksal: den Lebensweg derart zu durchwandern und zu durchleben, wie es ihm von dem Karmagesetz vorgezeichnet wurde. — Die Erziehung und die Eltern können und dürfen niemals für die Qualität und die Eigenschaften eines Kindes oder Erwachsenen und seiner Lebensart verantwortlich gemacht werden! — Wer dies nicht einsieht, ist blind und unwissend.

Ein Kind ist nur leiblich das Kind seiner Eltern, nie aber geistig. Über diese Lehren und Erkenntnisse ist Ausführliches enthalten in meinem Buche „Mein eigner Weg". Der Geist und die Seele des Kindes haben nichts von den Eltern. Das Wesen des Geistes ist Absicht und Zweck! Er ist eine Individualität für sich und bildet sich eine eigene Persönlichkeit. Der Drang und die Kraft zur Verkörperung waren die Macht, welche die Eltern zusammenführte, um jene Kombination von Körper zu schaffen, die dem äußeren Ausdruck der treibenden — sich verkörpernden — Individualität entspricht. Das werdende Kind konnte keine anderen Eltern aussuchen, weil gerade die beiden Körper dieser Eltern in ihrer Kombination wiederum eine neue und ganz bestimmte Kombination Körper hervorbringen. Sie ergibt, zusammen mit den zu einem bestimmten Lebensschicksal erforderlichen astralen Einflüssen und Schwingungen, d a s physische Menschenleben, das wir dann vor uns sehen. Daß der Körper des Kindes von den Eltern evtl. manches Ähnliche hat an Eigenschaften, ist ganz klar. Denn aus vielen dieser Ähnlichkeiten (die nicht allemal sichtbar zu sein brauchen) ergibt sich d i e Vererbung, welche für die „Erfahrungsschule des Lebens" des Betreffenden durchaus erforderlich ist, — seien diese Ähnlichkeiten nun geistiger oder physischer Art. Gaben, Talente usw. werden nicht vererbt, nur die dazu erforderlichen Bedingungen in größerem oder kleinerem Maße. Wenn ein Kind also z. B. sehr stark seinem Großvater ähnelt — geistig oder körperlich —, so

braucht es bzw. der Geist des Kindes — das ein ganz fremdes „Ich"
ist — gar nichts mit dem Großvater noch mit den eigenen Eltern zu
tun zu haben. Seine Ahnen haben nur dazu beigetragen, ihm das für
ihn genau passende und notwendige Gehäuse zu schaffen, weil sie
geistige Ähnlichkeiten mit ihm (dem sich im Kinde neu verkörpernden
Geist) zu d e r Zeit hatten. — Jede Verkörperung ist an bestimmte
Bedingungen und Verhältnisse, Gesetze gebunden, die wiederum ein
ganz bestimmtes Schicksal in sich schließen. — Aus dem Grunde ist
es richtig, wenn man sagt: Deine Kopfform, dein Charakter ist dein
Schicksal. — Es kann nicht j e d e r z e i t ein Christus geboren werden!
Auch er muß sich bei einer Verkörperung den kosmischen Gesetzen
unterwerfen, die genauer arbeiten als das beste Uhrwerk. Alles ist
eben: Ursache und Wirkung. Hierauf beruht auch das Gesetz: Jede
Schuld rächt sich auf Erden! Mit irgendeiner „Schuld" (Sünde)
verstoßen wir gegen die kosmischen Harmoniegesetze und legen
s e l b s t die Ursachen, deren Wirkungen auf uns zurückkommen
müssen. Jede Tat setzt „Gedanken" voraus. Gedanken sind aber
Kräfte, haben Form (und Farbe), und diese Kraftformen sind die
Plagegeister, die wir schufen — oder herbeiriefen — und dann nicht
mehr loswerden, da sie uns folgen wie Schatten, bis der geeignete
Augenblick kommt, wo wir ihre Macht zu erleben haben — im guten
wie im bösen Sinne. — Wir erleben heute in jeder Beziehung das,
was in den letzten Jahrzehnten „gedacht und gewünscht" wurde! —
Weil nun jeder Mensch eine eigene, selbständige Individualität ist, in
einer eigenen Gedankensphäre lebt und in Wirklichkeit keine körperliche Verwandtschaft hat, muß er auch seinen vor sehr langen Zeiten
sich selbst vorgezeichneten Lebensweg allein durchleben. Es kann
ihm niemand dabei helfen; nur er sich selbst — durch sich selbst.
„L e i d e a l l e i n !" lehrt die Yogischule. Darum ist höchste Aufgabe des Erdenlebens: sich selbst zu ergründen und zu erkennen;
dadurch ergründet man gleichzeitig sein Schicksal. Richtiges Denken
ist hierzu erste Bedingung! Lerne richtig denken, richtig wünschen,
richtig wollen, denn daraus fließen deine Handlungen, und diese wieder
bestimmen dein Schicksal. Aus Verkehrtem kann nur Verkehrtes
entspringen! Der erste Schritt zur geistigen Wiedergeburt ist die feste
Überzeugung, die unerschütterliche Erkenntnis, daß unser physischer
Körper nicht unser wahres Selbst (Ich) ist, daß dieser physische Körper
vielmehr — wie die ganze Welt der Erscheinungen — nur die Wirkung,
die Verkörperung geistiger Kräfte ist; daß unser geistiger Wesenskern
der innere unsterbliche Mensch, der wahre Mensch ist. In dem
Maße, wie wir uns als Geistesmenschen fühlen und danach leben,
in dem Maße, wie der göttliche Geistesfunke in uns zur Aktivität

erwacht, genau in dem Maße werden wir Herr über unser Schicksal!*) —
„Alle Dinge, um die ihr beten und bitten werdet, glaubet (d. h. seid
überzeugt), daß ihr sie empfangen werdet, so erhaltet ihr sie auch." —
„Was du denkst, das wirst du!" Eine Kraft, die imstande ist, irgendein
System zu leiten und zu lenken — wie den menschlichen Lebensweg —
oder einem Gegenstand eine zweckentsprechende Form zu geben —
wie dem menschlichen Körper —, eine solche Kraft handelt nicht blind,
nicht automatisch, sondern zielbewußt! Deshalb: Der Geist ist nicht
nur die höchste Form der Energie, er ist mehr als diese, er beherrscht
jede Energie, er leitet und lenkt sie; er ist Herr der Materie, nicht
„Funktion".

Was der Mensch bedeutet, das fängt erst da an, wo er nicht nur
Gattungswesen, sondern wo er Einzelwesen ist. Man kann nicht aus
dem, was zwischen Geburt und Tod liegt, die geistige Gestalt erklären.
Die Verschiedenheit der Menschen in geistiger Beziehung rührt durch-
aus nicht (allein) von der Verschiedenheit ihrer Umgebung, ihrer
Erziehung usw. her. Denn zwei Menschen entwickeln sich unter den
gleichen Einflüssen der Umgebung, der Erziehung in ganz verschiedener
Art, eben weil jeder Mensch geistig ein eigenes, selbständiges Wesen
ist. Meine physische Menschengestalt habe ich von meinen physischen
Vorfahren, die geistige Gestalt von mir selber, durch meine geistige
Entwicklung! — Aus dieser Ursache wiederhole ich die Rassengestalt
und das Blut meiner Vorfahren und die geistige Gestalt meines Selbst.

Ich kann also meine Gestalt von niemandem anders haben als von
mir selbst —, weil „das Äußere der Spiegel des Innern" ist! Weil
ich nicht mit unbestimmten, sondern mit bestimmten Anlagen in die
physische Welt eintrat — da durch diese Anlagen mein Lebensweg,
wie er in der früheren Wesensart zum Ausdruck kam, bestimmt ist —,
so kann meine Arbeit an mir selbst nicht bei meiner Geburt begonnen
haben. Ich muß als Ichheit vor meiner irdischen Geburt vorhanden
gewesen sein. In meinen Vorfahren bin ich sicher n i c h t vorhanden
gewesen; denn diese sind als geistige Menschen von mir verschieden.
Meine Art ist nicht in der ihrigen zu finden, aus derselben auch nicht
erklärbar. Also bin ich als geistiges Wesen die Wiederholung meiner
selbst; denn nur in mir selbst liegt die Erklärung meines Selbst und
des Seins meiner Art und deshalb meines Schicksals. Somit war ich
von Uranfang und bin ewig! — Zu sein heißt: zu wirken. Jede
Wirkung schafft in sich neue Ursachen (gleichgültig, ob uns diese
bewußt sind oder unbewußt), und diese Ursachen müssen und werden

---

*) Das wichtigste Ereignis im Leben des Menschen ist der Augenblick, da er sich seines
Ichs bewußt wird. Die Folgen dieses Ereignisses können die wohltätigsten oder die schreck-
lichsten sein. — Es hängt unendlich viel davon ab, ob sich jemand als Tiermensch oder als
Geistesmensch fühlt und erkennt! Es ist selbstverständlich, daß der Begriff Rasse immer
n u r psycho-physiologisch in Betracht zu ziehen ist! D. V.

sich wieder in Wirkungen auslösen. Dies ist die endlose Kette von Geschehnissen, die erfahren und e r l e b t werden müssen; denn sie sind von uns selbst geistig — somit auch physisch — geschaffen und deshalb in die Sphäre unserer Geistes- und Wirkungsart hineingezogen. Sie bilden unser Karma, unser Schicksal.

Wie wir diese Geschehnisse seelisch und deshalb auch physisch erleben, durchleben und verwerten, davon hängt das weitere Entwickeln neuer Ursachen und Wirkungen der Qualität und Quantität ab, somit auch die Verbesserung oder Verschlechterung unseres Schicksals. — Innerhalb der durch Geburt und Tod bestimmten Grenzen gehört der Mensch den drei kabbalistischen Welten — Physisch, Astral und Mental (oder Körper, Seele, Geist) — an. Die Seele ist das Mittel- und Verbindungsglied zwischen Leib und Geist, indem sie als Seelenleib mit der Empfindungsfähigkeit den physischen Körper durchdringt und als Bewußtseinsseele den Geistleib durchsetzt, beide verbindet. Die Seele hat dadurch während des Lebens sowohl Anteil an dem Leibe, wie an dem Geiste. Dieser Anteil kommt in ihrem ganzen Dasein zum Ausdruck. Von der Organisation des Seelenleibes wird es abhängen, wie die Empfindungsseele ihre Fähigkeiten entfalten kann. Von dem Leben und Schwingen der Bewußtseinsseele anderseits wird es abhängen, wieweit das Geistselbst in ihr sich entwickeln kann. Die Empfindungsseele wird einen um so besseren Verkehr mit der Außenwelt entfalten, je entwickelter der Seelenleib ist. Das Geistselbst wird um so reicher, machtvoller sein, je mehr Nahrung ihm die Bewußtseinsseele durch Erleben zuführt. Das heißt: es werden während des Lebens im Körper die verarbeiteten Erlebnisse als Früchte durch die Bewußtseinsseele dem Geistselbst zur Bereicherung und zum Erstarken zugeführt. Diese gewonnenen Schätze bleiben dem Geiste nicht in unveränderter Gestalt. Vorstellungen, welche der Mensch aus Erlebnissen äußerer und innerer Art gewinnt, entschwinden dem Gedächtnis allmählich. Nicht aber ihre Früchte! Der Geist nimmt Umwandlungen mit den Gedächtnisschätzen vor. Er entnimmt ihnen nur die Kraft zur Erhöhung seiner Fähigkeiten. Auf diese Weise geht kein Erlebnis ungenützt vorüber, besonders kein tieferes. Die Seele bewahrt es als Erinnerung für eine Zeitlang; der Geist saugt aus ihm das, was seine Fähigkeiten, seinen Inhalt und Wert für die Weiter- und Höherentwicklung bereichert. Des Menschen Geist wächst durch die verarbeiteten Erlebnisse. Wenn man sie auch nicht aufbewahrt finden kann, wie in einem Museum, man findet ihre Wirkungen in den Fähigkeiten, die sich der Mensch erworben hat, folglich auch in der Anwendung dieser Fähigkeiten, im Charakter — in seinem Schicksal und Lebensweg. Nur in dieser Hinsicht ist jeder seines Schicksals Schmied, sonst nicht! Für denjenigen, dessen seelisches Schauen erschlossen ist, wirken die obigen Tatsachen genau mit derselben Kraft wie ein Vorgang, welcher sich vor seinen physischen Augen abspielt. Er erkennt sie als klar und selbstverständlich*).

Hat man sich selbst erkannt, dann erkennt man auch Gott und seine Mitmenschen und — kann ihnen helfen. Denn Erkennen heißt auch Liebe und Verstehen. „Wer versteht, wird nie verdammen!", denn er erkennt sofort die Motive, den Urgrund der Handlung. Selbsterkenntnis ist erstes Gesetz für jeden. Sie zu erlangen ist jedes Menschen größte Pflicht (und der Grund seiner Verkörperung auf unserem Planeten) gegen sich selbst und seine Mitmenschen. Wege dazu gibt es mehrere, die später immer auf den einen geraden Hauptweg führen. Doch ist jeder Weg nicht gleich leicht für jeden. Die Chirosophie ist einer dieser Wege und ein guter, klarer, praktischer. Wer andere beurteilen will, muß sich selbst und das Leben kennen! Er muß es verstehen, sich in den zu Beurteilenden hinein zu versetzen, durch dessen Augen die Umwelt zu betrachten und auf sich wirken zu lassen. Es gehört viel Erfahrung und Erkenntnis dazu, ihm dann raten zu können in den überaus vielseitigen Kompliziertheiten dieser oder jener Verhältnisse und Umstände, welche das Leben des einzelnen birgt. Man muß schon viel Lebens- und Welterfahrung besitzen und alle Lebenslagen, alle Verhältnisse kennen, aber auch eine hohe Weltanschauung errungen haben. Die hohe Warte der Betrachtung will erklommen, gewonnen sein! — Der Weg hierzu führt durch Entsagung, Aufopferung, mit einem Worte, durch Selbstbefreiung von der Ichsucht. Das ist erlebte spirituelle Erkenntnis. Es ist durchaus falsch, aus reiner Neugierde die Regeln einer Wissenschaft erlernen oder oberflächlich studieren zu wollen, um das so gewonnene oberflächliche Halbwissen in irgendwelcher Form zu verwerten. Selbsterkenntnis erlangt man durch Oberflächlichkeit nie. Soweit der Weg in den Irrtum hineinging, soweit ist er auch zurück! Gerade die menschliche Natur zu studieren, ist das schwerste, und das gewonnene Wissen macht verantwortlich!

Es ist jedem Menschen selbst überlassen, in der Finsternis oder im Lichte zu wandeln. Da ist kein Zwang; Gott schuf keine Automaten! Wer aber einmal Erkenntnis erlangt hat, der ist von dem Augenblick an verpflichtet, den Weg des Lichts zu wandeln — der besseren Einsicht zu folgen —, oder aber die Rückwirkung ist furchtbar. Nicht die Verhältnisse machen den Menschen, sondern der Mensch macht die Verhältnisse.

---

*) Es gibt sehr vieles für den Durchschnittsmenschen, was sich vorläufig nicht handgreiflich beweisen läßt, eben weil der Durchschnittsmensch und vor allem der rein verstandesmäßig denkende Mensch nicht die seelischen und geistigen Sinne entwickelt hat. Nie darf deshalb ein Mensch sagen: nur das sei wirklich, was er mit den fünf Sinnen wahrnehmen kann, denn es gibt so unendlich viel Wirkliches, für dessen Wahrnehmung ihm die Organe nicht gerade fehlen; aber sie sind unentwickelt. „Wer es nicht fühlt, der wird es nie ergründen!"

43

Sie wirken dann wohl auf den Menschen zurück, doch ist dies gerade das Erziehende zum Besseren und zur Verbesserung. Der Mensch wird dadurch zum Denken erzogen, zur Erkenntnis seines Selbst durch sich selbst.

Ein sehr wichtiger Punkt, der noch zu beachten ist, bleibt das g e i s t i g e N i v e a u !

Wenn zwei dasselbe tun, so ist es nicht das Gleiche! Es kommt auf die Motive des Handelns an, und diese sind bei verschiedener Geistigkeit andere, nicht gleiche.

Ein spiritueller Mensch handelt aus anderen Gründen (Motiven) als ein intellektueller, und dieser aus ähnlichen wie ein materieller. Ganz abgesehen davon, daß es Eigenschaften gibt, die im Grunde keine typischen, sondern zusammengesetzte sind, nehmen wir einmal z. B. Ehrlichkeit. Aus welchen Gründen ist jemand ehrlich? Der eine, weil er es wirklich der Gesinnung nach ist; ein anderer aus Mangel an Gelegenheit zur Unehrlichkeit, ein Dritter aus Angst vor Strafe oder Angst vor üblem Ruf usw. — je nach Geistigkeit oder geistigem Niveau.

Diese Niveau-Unterschiede erkennt man in den Händen an der feinen, mittleren, oder groben Hauttextur. (Bild 1.) Je feiner die Haut und die zarten Hautlinien sind, desto höher ist das geistig-seelische Niveau. Konform damit gehen auch noch der Reichtum oder die Armut an wirklichen Handlinien und Zeichen und deren Unversehrtheit, Klarheit und Farbe.

Im folgenden lege ich die Begründung und die Grundursachen des großen „Wie", „Woher", „Warum" dar.

Die astralen Einflüsse.

„Ich hebe meine Augen auf zu den Sternen, von welchen mir Hilfe kommt. Doch folge ich dem Stern in meiner Brust!"

Die alten Weisen stellten durch tausendfache Erfahrung fest, daß aus der Form der Hand der Charakter und aus den Linien und Zeichen die Vergangenheit und Zukunft zu erkennen ist; jeder kann diese Angaben nachprüfen. Viel von dieser Wissenschaft ist verloren gegangen, genau wie in der Astrologie und allen anderen Wissenschaften; doch wird den Menschen im Laufe der Entwicklung (nicht aber der geistigen und körperlichen Entartung!) alles Verlorene wiedergegeben werden. Keine Berufstätigkeit ändert die Linien, und kein Gewerbe hat bestimmte Linienformationen. Es gibt keine Linien, aus denen man den Beruf (Schneider, Schlächter, Bäcker, Schlotfeger usw.) erkennen kann. Die

Frauen schonen und pflegen ihre Hände, üben keinen Beruf oder schwere Arbeit aus, aber dennoch sind meist solche Hände mit Linien dicht bedeckt. Anderseits haben schwerarbeitende Personen meist in ihren Händen nur die Hauptlinien, keine anderen. Damit ist auch zugleich der Einwand beseitigt, die Linien in den Händen entstünden durch Arbeit. Wenn ein geistiger Arbeiter durch Umstände gezwungen ist, schwere körperliche Arbeit zu tun, werden sich die Handformen und Hauptlinien nicht ändern, sondern nur einige der feinen und feinsten Linien verlieren sich, weil sein seelisches Empfinden durch die schwere physische Arbeit abstumpft und dadurch wiederum das Einströmen der astralen Kräfte gehemmt wird. Mancher wird sagen: der Mensch habe sein Schicksal in der Hand, und jeder habe seinen freien Willen. Dem ist durchaus nicht so! Wahlfreiheit hat er, freien Willen jedoch nicht! „Die Sterne (Kräfte) beherrschen den Menschen, aber der Weise (Spirituelle), weil er erkannt hat und sich bei ihm das Lebenserkennen mit dem Lebenkönnen paart, beherrscht die Sterne (Kräfte)!" Er kann den Fesseln der niederen Welt entfliehen, sich ihr entziehen, nicht aber der Alltags-Durchschnittsmensch der materiellen Welt. Der Weise hat in sich das Geist-Seelische vereint, er ändert sein Schicksal nicht; denn er hat sich dem Universalwillen (kosmischen Willen) untergeordnet zur Erreichung des Endziels der Entwicklung. Er zahlt seine rückständige Schuld im guten wie im bösen Sinne auf einmal und bewußt ab und wird dadurch frei. Der aus der zweiten Welt (des Intellekts) mißbraucht seinen Willen, soweit er ihn besitzt, denn er ist „kalter Verstandesmensch". der, um seine Neugierde (Wissenschaft) zu befriedigen, andere Geschöpfe, Tiere — „manchmal" auch Menschen — quält, lebendig zerschneidet, vergiftet, verbrennt, jammern hört und sieht, aber — nichts empfindet. Wohl kann er verschiedene Wege seines Lebens wählen, doch muß er darum den falschen gehen, weil er soviel wie kein Empfinden besitzt und glaubt, alles mit dem bißchen Verstande begreifen zu können, was allerdings in die Irre führen muß. Bei dem Menschen der dritten (elementaren) Welt (Bild 6, 75) kann man mit großer Bestimmtheit auf die Unveränderlichkeit des Schicksals schließen; denn er steht noch zu sehr unter dem Karmagesetz und kann nur im Wandel der Zeiten die verschiedenen Stufen erklimmen, bis auch für ihn der Tag des Lichtes kommt und er frei wird. Karma ist das kosmische Gesetz der ethischen Wiedervergeltung und ausgleichenden Gerechtigkeit, welches die ewige Ordnung und Harmonie alles Lebenden aufrecht erhält. Jede Störung, die ein Einzelwille auf Kosten der anderen verursacht, indem er gegen die Harmoniegesetze verstößt, wird vom Karma gerächt (Hiob XXXIV, 10 bis 11), nicht als Strafe, sondern, als Wirkung der selbstgeschaffenen Ursache, zur Erziehung. Festgesetzte Schicksalsschläge lassen sich nicht ändern; nur die Wege sind frei, die zum Ziele führen. Wie der Mensch sich beträgt, so wird er behandelt! – Nicht von anderen behandelt, sondern durch die Auswirkung, die sein eigener Geist durch Tat oder Denken veranlaßte. Also: der eigene Geist behandelt den eigenen Körper, wie der Erzieher den Zögling. Geist und Körper sind zwei Dinge, und einer ist des anderen Vermittler. Jede Schuld muß ausgeglichen werden. Der Weise zahlt auf einmal – der Unwissende in Raten. Durch die Kenntnis der Chirosophie können wir unser Schicksal verbessern; denn sie gibt uns Selbsterkenntnis und zeigt jedem Einzelnen seine Reisekarte. Kennen wir sie aber durch tiefes ernstes Studium, so können wir unseren Charakter und damit auch unser Geschick verbessern, weil wir die verschiedenen Gefahren erkennen, die aus Mangelhaftigkeit, Minderwertigkeit und deshalb oft aus Leidenschaft, niederem Verlangen und Wünschen entstehen und drohen, uns zu schädigen. Nicht diese sollen uns überwinden, sondern: wir s i e !

Alle äußeren Einflüsse nehmen wir auf durch Vermittlung unserer Aura, des Sonnengeflechts und des Gehirns. Gedankenwellen nimmt der Geist auf und überträgt sie durch die Funktion der Seele auf das Kleinhirn (Unterbewußtsein). Dieses gibt sie weiter in das Großhirn, wo sie uns dann bewußt werden, als ob wir die Gedanken selbst gedacht hätten. Das Sonnengeflecht (das große seelische Nervenzentrum nahe der Magengrube) nimmt Empfindungen des Erlebens auf, z. B. Traumbilder, Ahnungen, Angst- und Freudegefühle, Schreck usw. Die feinsten dieser Einflüsse aber ziehen wir an und ein durch die Fingerspitzen (Habakuk III, 4), welche Strahlensammler sind für die feinen Nervenzentren (Chakras) der Hände (genau wie bei der drahtlosen Telegraphie). Hier handelt es sich um die Einflüsse von Kräften, die Charakter und Neigungen des Menschen bestimmen. Die für die Aufnahme dieser astralen, elektrischen und magnetischen Fluidströme abgestimmten Empfangsapparate sind die Fingerspitzen (Bild 3). Regulatoren und Akkumulatoren der Ströme sind die Finger, Formen und Berge (Erhöhungen unter den Fingern) der Hände, das Flußbett sind die Linien; die Finger - K n o t e n (natürliche Knoten in den Fingerbeugegelenken) sind die Schotten oder Ventile, welche nur so viel Strom durchlassen, wie ihre Form und Öffnung (Intelligenz, Verstand) zulassen; d. h. je kritischer und logischer, auch fanatischer der Verstand ist, desto stärker bilden sich die oberen Knoten aus, wodurch das größere, vollere Einströmen bzw. Durchströmen behindert wird. Andere Ströme – solche, die ihren Eingang durch Gehirn und Sonnengeflecht nahmen – kommen mit dem Blut- und Nervenkreislauf von innen durch die Handwurzel in die Nervenzentren, wo dann verstärkt oder abgeschwächt wird (je nachdem) und diese astralen Kraftströme sich kristallisieren, materialisieren, in Zeichen erkennbar werden.

Unter „astralen Einflüssen" sind auch diejenigen der Planeten einschließlich der Sonne, welche oft nicht dazu gerechnet wird, zu verstehen: Venus, Jupiter, Saturn, Sonne, Merkur, Mars, Mond, Uranus, Neptun, Pluto, Isis.

Die Kraftströme von Uranus und Neptun finden sich nicht alltäglich in den Händen, sondern deutlicher in linienreichen. Die Kraftströme von Pluto und Isis sind noch sehr selten, und die Bedeutung ist noch nicht gesichert. Es sind erst zarte Anfänge. Einflüsse sogen. „transneptunischer" Planeten in den Händen sind — Phantasien, die jeder Grundlage entbehren!*)

B i l d 1 zeigt die feinen Hautlinien (Niveaustufe) der Hand, B i l d 2 die Muskulatur, Sehnen, Adern zum Teil und die Hautlagen als weicheren Teil, in dem sich schon die feinstofflichen Kräfte und Strahlungen bemerkbar machen durch Harmonie (Gesundheit) oder Disharmonie (Krankheit), verdichten, materialisieren.

Nun könnte ich hier auch noch den Nachweis erbringen, daß sich bei einem Fötus im Mutterleibe zuerst die Hauptlinien und danach erst die feinen Linien der Haut bilden, und daß weder diese jene, noch jene diese in ihrem Wachstum oder in ihrer besonderen Gestaltung beeinflussen. Ich habe dies aber in „Medizinische Hand- und Nageldiagnostik" in Wort und Bild schon eingehend erklärt.

Die A u r a d e s K ö r p e r s und seiner Nervenzentren bedeutet: 1. die geistige Aura des Menschen und 2. die astrale. Hauptnervenzentren sind Scheitel, Augen, Herz, Sonnengeflecht, Sexualorgane und Lumbalgehirn. Die Stärke der geistigen Aura richtet sich ganz nach der geistigen und göttlichen Erkenntnis des Menschen und hat dementsprechend verschiedene Farben. Alles im Kosmos strahlt, solange es lebt, von Geist durchdrungen ist, auch das Erz; besonders stark strahlen Edelsteine sowie Samenkörner. Wenn auch nicht jedes physische Auge diese Strahlungen wahrnimmt, so werden sie doch durch geistseelisch (spirituell) geschulte geistige Augen erschaut. — In der Hand haben wir ein großes Nervenzentrum und sieben kleine Nervenzentren, deren jedes für sich strahlt, aber auch alle sind untereinander verbunden, wie es auf B i l d 3 dargestellt ist. Bei der Strahlung, die auf dem Handprofil zu ersehen ist, habe ich die Strahlz e n t r e n stärker markiert, mit Bezeichnung 2. Bezeichnung 3 ist die Odstrahlung der Innen- und Außenhand. 5 und 6 bezeichnen die Blutbahn und Nervenbahn im Handinnern und 4 die Strahlung beider in Wechselwirkung. — Denken wir uns, stark vergrößert, die Hauttextur der Innenhand in einer

---

*) Siehe auch „Sternenmächte und Mensch" von Dr. med. Schwab; „Transitlehre" von Prof. Dr. Uhle; „Medizinische Astrologie" von dem Wiener Arzt Feerhof; „Periodenlehre" von Dr. Fließ; „Geistesperioden im Leben der Völker" von Ing. Rud. Meewes; „Das Siebenjahr" von Dr. Swoboda usw.; sie alle enthalten Lehren über diese Kräfteeinflüsse.

Darstellung wie z. B. der Lichtreklame an den Häusern. Hier enden die feinsten Nerven, und die Erschütterungen und Schwingungen der Seele und des Körpers zeichnen sich ein. Genau wie man bei der großen Lichtreklame einen besonderen Kontakt berührt, worauf eine ganz bestimmte Formation von Buchstaben erscheint, ein Name, ein Bild, so erscheint auch an der Oberfläche des Handinnern an bestimmter Stelle ein bestimmtes entsprechendes Zeichen durch Einwirkung auf ein entsprechendes Gehirn- oder Nervenzentrum. Das kommt daher, weil bestimmte Teile der Hand mit bestimmten Organen des Körpers und noch besonders mit ihren korrespondierenden Zentren des Gehirns in enger Verbindung stehen. Bestimmte Denkart wirkt auf entsprechende Organe und beeinflußt diese in positivem oder negativem Sinne, erstes zur Aktivität und gesunder Tätigkeit, letztes zur Hemmung und Krankheit. Als Beispiele will ich nur kurz anführen: alles, was mit Sorgen, Gram, Kummer, Trauer zu tun hat, hängt mit der Leber zusammen. Schwermut, Grübelei, Melancholie und Tiefsinn stehen in Verbindung mit der Milz; Ängstlichkeit und Nervosität, Humor sowie Schreck mit dem Herzen; Verbitterung mit dem Magen; Hysterie mit der Überreizung der Sexualnerven des Uterus und Rückenmarks; Anpassungsvermögen mit der Wirbelsäule, usw.

Verschiedenheit und Nuancierung des menschlichen Charakters (z. B. Menschlichkeit oder tierische Instinkte, Härte oder Weichheit, Empfindlichkeit und Indolenz, Feuer und Phlegma, Beweglichkeit und Langsamkeit, Festigkeit und Flüchtigkeit, Eigensinn und Nachgiebigkeit, Herzhaftigkeit und Weichheit oder Feigheit, Standhaftigkeit und Verzagtheit, Verschiedenartigkeit der Laune und des Humors und andere Charaktereigenschaften) sind bestimmt durch den Grad der Assimilation des Nervenäthers, seine größere Annäherung oder Entfernung von der Natur der elektrischen Materie, den Grad der Verbindung desselben mit dem ganzen Nervensystem, die Richtung, Intensität und Stabilität der Strömungen des Nervenäthers, die Struktur und Beschaffenheit der Nerven selbst — soweit sie dadurch zu vorzüglichen Leitern des Nervenäthers gemacht werden. Hierin ist auch der Grund sowohl der naturgemäßen Nervenwirkungen, als auch der Nervenkrankheiten im eigentlichen Sinne enthalten.

Somit ergibt sich hieraus, daß durch physische und geistige Mittel Charaktere umgeschaffen, Nervenkrankheiten und seelische Leiden erzeugt und behoben werden können!

Je konischer, spitzer und glatter die Finger sind, desto mehr Strom saugen sie auf (daher die größere und leichtere seelische Empfänglichkeit — Intuition, Inspiration, innere Weichheit, Stimmungen — der Menschen mit konischen Händen). Je knotiger die Finger, desto mehr Verstandesherrschaft! Der Verstandesmensch läßt sich wenig oder nie von Empfindungen leiten. Die reine Verstandestätigkeit schaltet das Empfindungsvermögen sehr stark aus, weil die Empfindungsbereitschaft mehr oder minder bis zur Vernichtung verdrängt wurde, und läßt es verkümmern, anstatt es zu entwickeln und zu nutzen, mit dem Verstand in Einklang zu bringen, woraus sich dann eben die Vernunft als das Göttliche — weil Harmonische — ergibt.

Da der Mensch ebenfalls kosmischer Natur ist, wird er auch von den Strömen des Kosmos durchzogen, beeinflußt. Die physischen sichtbaren Linien (Bild 21) der Hände sind aber nur die p h y s i s c h e Gemarkung der darin und darunter laufenden astralen Ströme. Die Hauptlinien sind die Hauptkraftströme, die kleinen, feinen und feinsten Linien die Nebenströme und sich durch Kombination ergebenden Flüsse und Bäche. Die Formationen und Kombinationen der Hauptlinien geben so den Hauptcharakter und die der kleinen und feinsten Linien die Neigungen, die teilweise durch die Wahlfreiheit, das jeweilige Maß und die Kraft des eigenen Willens eine Abänderung erhalten. Das Maß des freien Willens richtet sich nach der Höhe der göttlichen Erkenntnis der Seele und der Geisteskraft. Der Geist ist unsterblich; denn er ist der Gottesfunken und besitzt die göttliche Erkenntnis seit Ewigkeit, wie er auch alle Kräfte der Gottheit in sich umschließt; das ist überhaupt die Wahrheit aller Mysterien, diese Kräfte in sich zu erkennen und zum Erwachen zu bringen (das verlorene Meisterwort). Nur ist er durch die materielle Welt zwecks Schulung umschattet, und diesen Nebel kann nur die empfindende Seele in Erkenntnis des Göttlichen und Wahren, also durch bewußt empfindendes Wissen durchleuchten. Dieses bewußt empfindende Wissen kann aber nur eine schwingende, stark vibrierende, strahlende Seele erlangen; eine Seele, die in Harmonie mit dem Unendlichen, also mit und in der höheren Welt schwingt, der spirituelle Mensch! (Bild 48.) Je stärker und bewußter dieses Schwingen und Leben in der göttlichen Erkenntnis ist, desto kräftiger werden die „schädigenden Einflüsse" der Astralwelt ausgeschaltet, weil die Erkenntnis von dem unmittelbaren Zusammenhang alles Lebendigen entfacht worden ist, wodurch die üblen Wirkungen lebensgieriger und vererdeter Ich-Sucht aufgehoben sind; denn das Erkennen der Abhängigkeit des Gesamtwohls vom Wohlergehen des Einzelnen muß die wahre Nächstenliebe betätigen. Die Nächstenliebe verhält sich zur Ich-Sucht ähnlich wie der Segen zum Fluch, wie die weiße zur schwarzen Magie. So wird der eigene Wille dem kosmischen Allwillen untergeordnet, dem Willen Gottes, und Gott will nur Gutes und vollkommene Entwicklung. Je stärker die Seele vibriert, desto mehr erlebt der Mensch, desto bewußter werden die Einflüsse des Kosmos durch die Fingerspitzen wahrgenommen, und desto leichter kristallisieren und zeigen sich die Zeichen in den Händen. Folglich bringt das Empfinden und E r l e b e n d e r S e e l e die meisten Linien und Zeichen in den Händen hervor. Ich sage: bringt hervor, nicht erzeugt! Denn alle Linien, auch die feinsten, sind schon bei der Geburt vorhanden, wenn auch meist nicht sichtbar. Der geübte Chiromant kann oft solche Untergrundlinien schon zum Teil erkennen. Es kommt ganz d a r a u f an, in welcher der drei Welten der Betreffende lebt. Die Hände eines Menschen aus der materiellen (niedrigsten) Welt werden nie viele andere außer den Hauptlinien haben, da die höhere Seele so gut wie nicht entwickelt ist. Und weil diese Seele noch dumpf, unentwickelt ist, wird sie z. B. ein Ereignis, wie Trauer, Kummer, Enttäuschung, Tierquälerei, überhaupt Seelisches, nicht stark erleben und sich dadurch nicht beeinflussen lassen; sie wird sich sehr schnell über derartiges hinwegsetzen, eben weil sie noch stumpf, empfindungslos ist. Wie sollen sich da seelische Erlebnisse — ganz gleich, ob vergangen, gegenwärtig oder zukünftig — in den Händen materialisieren, zeigen?

Jemand aus der intellektuellen (zweiten) Welt, Bild 8, wird stets den Verstand sprechen lassen und damit die Schwingung der Seele hindern, sich zu entfalten. Derjenige aus der (ersten) spirituellen Welt wird mehr bewußt empfinden, mit dem Kosmos im Einklange, geistig und seelisch am weitesten entwickelt (aufnahmefähig) sein, deshalb auch die meisten Linien und Zeichen in den Händen haben. Die Charakteranlage wird angezeigt durch die Formierung der Aufnahmestationen — Finger und Berge. Die am meisten und stärksten einwirkende Kraft, die dann auch dominiert, entwickelt den entsprechenden Platz und erzeugt so eine plastisch hervorragende Stelle, den dominierenden Berg. Die größte Empfangsstation wird folglich auch die meiste Kraft aufnehmen und verarbeiten, somit auch eine bestimmte Richtung des Charakters oder Charakterhaupteigenschaften entwickeln und erkennen lassen.

Es sind vor allem sieben bekannte kosmische (planetare) Kräfte vorhanden und sieben Empfangsstationen, Berge. So treffen sieben verschiedene Kräfte ihre sieben entsprechenden Aufnahmestationen, die dafür vorhanden sind (Offenb. I, 16). Ihre Kombinationen ergeben dann die Unterschiede in Charakteren, die unbegrenzt sind. Einer dieser sieben Kräfteströme ist fast immer der dominierende, und sein Einfluß kann so weit gehen, daß er der Haut die ihm entsprechende Farbe gibt, so daß man an der Hautfarbe oft den Planeteneinfluß oder die vorherrschende Kraft und so das Temperament erkennen kann. Z. B. Mond = blaß und matt = phlegmatisch; Mars = dunkles Rot = heftig, brutal; Venus = helles Rot = leidenschaftlich; Saturn = dunkel = melancholisch; Merkur = gelblich = nervös, beweglich usw.

Die Einflüsse von Uranus und Neptun sind in den ihnen entsprechenden Linien zu erkennen. Für ihre feinere Kraft der Strahlung sind die Menschen noch nicht genügend vorgeschritten, und deshalb ist auch kein Sammler (Berg) dafür vorhanden — bis jetzt.

Bei der Beurteilung der Hände muß also genau in Betracht gezogen werden:

1. Rasse, Artgeschlecht.
2. Was ist krankhaft, erworben oder
3. erbliche Belastung?
4. In welcher der drei Welten lebt der Betreffende (Niveau)?
5. Welche der sieben kosmischen Kräfte sind vorherrschend?
6. Was ist als Karma anzusehen?
7. Die Stärke des eigenen Willens (Grenze des Erreichbaren).

Die einströmenden astralen Kräfte sind die Vollzieher des karmischen Gesetzes. Sie laufen, sammeln, arbeiten in den unsichtbaren Bergen und Linien, sind Manometer (Uhren), nach denen sich der Mensch selbst zu richten hat. Jesaias XLIX, 16: „Siehe, in die Hände habe ich dich gezeichnet, deine Mauern (Hindernisse und Kampf) sind immerdar von mir."

Hieraus ist schon der Wert dieses Wissens zu ermessen. Doch: „Unwissenheit ist das Grundübel allen Elends in der Welt, und nur Wissen allein zeigt den Weg zur Erlösung!" Z e i g t den Weg; gehen muß ihn jeder selbst — durch sich selbst! (Parsifal: Durch Mit — leid w i s s e n d d e r r e i n e T o r.) Hierauf baut sich alles andere in seiner Wirkung auf, und verkehrte Berechnungen und Voraussetzungen (Ursachen) ergeben falsche Schlüsse (Wirkungen, Taten).

Die Linien ändern sich nicht. Sie sind alle vorhanden bei der Geburt, vom Karma vorgeburtlich geschaffen und reguliert. Wenn sie auch oft nicht gleich erkennbar sind, sie sind da, erscheinen früher oder später, alles zu seiner Zeit. Sind die Einflußwege: Fingerspitzen, Knoten, Linien = Schotten, Ventile, Flüsse eingeengt, verstopft, gebrochen, zerrissen, gewunden usw., so entsteht naturgemäß auch Stockung, Störung, Hindernis für astrale Einflüsse, und hieraus ergibt sich wiederum — kristallisiert — ein physisches, sichtbares oder fühlbares Geschehnis, das sich in der Handfläche erkennen und — da die Linien usw. in Zeitmaße eingeteilt sind — für einen gewissen Zeitpunkt ausmessen, bestimmen läßt. „Alles im Universum ist geregelt nach Maß, Zahl und Gewicht, und die Gesetze sind ohne Wandel!" Wie im Makrokosmos, so im Mikrokosmos. (Wie oben, so unten! Wie innen, so außen!) Alles ist Wechselwirkung, Evolution (Entwicklung) des Seins; die menschliche Verkörperung ist das Werkzeug, durch das solches erreicht wird. Jeder sieht — wenigstens zeitweise — einen Teil seines Weges vor sich; einer mehr, der andere weniger; der aus der Vogelschau, d. h. von dem universalen oder kosmischen Standpunkte Betrachtende, am meisten. Der geübte Chirosoph und Okkultist oder Metaphysiker betrachtet alles aus der Vogelschau und wird deshalb am weitesten für sich und andere sehen und — wo es nottut — raten können. Ich behaupte hiermit durchaus nicht, daß sich des Menschen Schicksal n u r a l l e i n durch die Hände bzw. in den Händen offenbart. In j e d e m Körperteil ist die ganze Persönlichkeit verborgen, wie es u. a. psychometrische Experimente beweisen und bewiesen haben. Deshalb kann man auch aus Schädelform und Ausdruck, aus dem Gesicht, aus dem Auge, Haar, überhaupt aus dem ganzen Körper entziffern wie aus der Hand. Es ist nichts Einseitiges in der Natur. In der Physiognomie prägen sich diejenigen Ereignisse mehr aus, welche Vergangenheit betreffen. In den Stirnlinien und dem Auge auch betreffs der Zukunft; in der Regenbogenhaut des Auges kann man sehr deutlich Krankheitserscheinungen wahrnehmen, die erst im Entstehen begriffen sind, also noch gar nicht bemerkbar, fühlbar zu sein brauchen.

Ob nun jemand für oder gegen die Dreiteilung der Natur (Geist, Seele, Körper oder Mental, Astral, Physisch) ist, bleibt ihm überlassen. Der Gegner dieser Prinzipien wird die Handlesekunst auch erlernen können. Der Anhänger wird es jedoch in seinen Kenntnissen und Erkenntnissen viel weiter bringen, soviel ist sicher. Die Symbolik der Astralwelt ist kein leichtes Studium, doch sie nutzt sehr viel und gibt Aufschluß über das „Warum" und „Woher". Ohne sie wird niemand ein Meister der Chiromantie. Einiges dieser Symbolik gebe ich zur Erleichterung des ganzen Überblicks in Bild 19, anderes an den betreffenden Stellen über Handberge, Finger, Hauptlinien.

Das menschliche Leben kann man sehr zutreffend mit einer Seefahrt vergleichen. Vielleicht erleichtert dieser Vergleich dem angehenden Chirologen und Chiromanten die Übersicht im Studium; ich erkannte dies bei meinen Schülern jedenfalls. Der Mensch wird geschaffen (meist leider unbewußt, und diese Ursache bleibt nicht ohne Wirkung!), so auch das Schiff. Das Kind (Körper = Fahrzeug) wird geboren, das Schiff läuft vom Stapel. Das Kind bleibt noch lange in der Obhut und erhält Anweisung und Erziehung; das Schiff bleibt gleichfalls noch lange im Dock und Hafen, erhält Takelwerk, Vervollkommnung. Die Reife kommt für beide; das Kind soll hinaus ins Leben, das Schiff auf die große Reise, auf den Ozean des Lebens. Der Körper (Schiff) ist so weit gediehen, daß der Verstand (Kapitän) ihn mit Vernunft (Erkenntnis) gebrauchen, führen soll. Die Seekarte ist in beide Hände gezeichnet vom Karma (Schiffahrtsgesellschaft) und mit Zeichen (Leuchtfeuern, Klippen, Tiefen usw. d. h. Sternen, Kreuzen, Punkten, Ecken usw.) versehen, damit das Schiff (Körper) keinen Schaden erleidet. Wenn aber der Kapitän betrunken (unwissend) ist, so wird sein Schiff bald zerschellen. Klarer Verstand (Kenntnis, Wissen) ist deshalb erforderlich. Ist das Schiff (Körper) auf dem hohen Meere (im Strudel des Lebens), so hat der Kapitän (Verstand) wohl acht zu geben, wie und wohin er seinen Weg nimmt. Weicht er von seiner rechten Fahrstraße ab und beachtet die Bojen und Leuchtfeuer (Warnung vor Gefahren und Verführungen) nicht, so muß er selbst und sein Schiff die Folgen tragen, wird Schiffbruch (Krankheit, Unglück) erleiden und die Reise erneut (im nächsten Leben) antreten, bis er die vom Schicksal (Karma) vorgezeichnete Reise gut aus- und zu Ende führt, am Bestimmungsorte den sicheren Hafen (Gotteserkenntnis, die göttliche Welt) gewonnen hat. — Eine Schule der Erfahrung und der Entwicklung ist das Leben. Die Chiromantie ist der Lotse (Wegweiser), kennt jedes Seezeichen und jede Warnung. V o r g e b u r t l i c h sind die Linien und Zeichen in der Hand des Menschen eingegraben, wie längst erwiesen; sind sie aber vorgeburtlich, so beweisen sie das Vorhandensein der Seele und deren Wirken, beweisen das Gesetz, das sie grub.

Des öfteren fand ich Zeichen für Todesfall eines Blutsverwandten auf der Lebenslinie, die als Zeitpunkt zwei, drei, auch vier Jahre v o r der Geburt des Betreffenden anzeigte, und deren Tatsächlichkeit auch bestätigt wurde. D a s beweist allein schon, daß wir unsere physischen Eltern Jahre v o r der Geburt gekannt haben müssen, ebenso, daß wir v o r der Geburt als geistiges bewußtes Wesen existierten; beweist das Karma, das ewige ausgleichende Gesetz der göttlichen Gerechtigkeit, das nichts mit dem vom beschränkten Menschenverstande gemachten gemein hat. W o K a r m a i s t, d a i s t R e - i n k a r n a t i o n (Wiederverkörperung). Dies beweist hiermit auch die Chirosophie. Zeitweise wird bemerkt, daß es wohl anginge, Ereignisse der Vergangenheit in den Händen zu erkennen, daß es aber doch zweifelhaft sei, solche der Zukunft zu erkennen. Die Antwort darauf ist schon im obigen Hinweise „Was ist Zeit?" gegeben und auch in der wissenschaftlichen Begründung der Chirologie! Sollte das nicht genügen, dann wird folgendes die Antwort ergänzen. Warum kann man denn die Veranlagung und deshalb das Sichentwickeln und Näherrücken einer Krankheit aus den Händen erkennen? Weil sie geistig schon vorhanden ist. Erst muß sie aber geistig vorhanden sein, um sich physisch zu entwickeln, bemerkbar zu machen*). Wenn ich ein Haus bauen will, muß ich es z u e r s t geistig bauen; in Gedanken, in der Phantasie, wie man es nennen will, dann

---

*) Aus dem Grunde ist es verkehrt, wenn ein Arzt eine Krankheit „örtlich" beseitigen will und dies versucht, ohne sich um den „geistigen" Sitz der Krankheit zu kümmern (siehe Paracelsus!). Ein Übel kann nicht beseitigt werden, es sei denn, daß es mit der Wurzel vernichtet wird. Bei der Behandlung eines Organs wird der Organismus zumeist vergessen, obgleich dieser wichtiger ist, weil in ihm die Ursachen zu suchen sind. Nicht Organtherapie, sondern Konstitutionstherapie sollte mehr angewendet werden.

kommt die Verdichtung des Gedankens, das näher Erkennbare, Formulierende (astrale Prinzip), der Plan auf Papier, und d a n n erst das Materialisieren des Gedankens: das greifbare Physische. So geschieht alles in der Natur im Großen wie im Kleinen.

Handform und Karma.

Betrachten wir viele Hände, so fällt uns die Verschiedenheit der Form oder des Typs mitunter recht drastisch auf. Weil nun der Mensch schon im achten Lebensjahr eine ganz bestimmte Handform aufweist und diese wieder meistens verschieden ist von denen der Eltern — also von direkter Vererbung im geist-seelischen Sinne keine Rede sein kann —, folgt hieraus: daß die Handform eines jeden Menschen durch bestimmte Veranlagung naturgesetzmäßig ist, deren Bedingungen durch die Präexistenz festgelegt, geschaffen, s e l b s t geschaffen wurden. Was „geistige Vererbung" genannt wird, ist in Wirklichkeit nichts anderes als die Anziehung von Geistwesen, die den Eltern entsprachen. Reinheit der Art ist also eine religiöse Forderung. Daß der Mensch nicht nur einmal lebt auf diesem Planeten, sondern eine lange Kette von verschiedenen Daseinsstufen durchleben und erfahren muß, um dem Ziele der Vervollkommnung näher zu kommen, ist jedem Tieferdenkenden selbstverständlich. In e i n maliger Verkörperung kann er niemals die Vervollkommnung erreichen, die in einer immer engeren Vereinigung mit dem göttlichen Ideal im eigenen Herzen besteht; denn die Zeit eines normalen Erdenlebens (also im Durchschnitt 60 bis 70 Jahre) ist viel zu kurz, lächerlich kurz, und das Medium (Vermittler) des Geistes, der menschliche physische Körper, zu sehr beschränkt (durch den derzeitigen Stand der Erdentwicklung), um diese Titanenarbeit zu bewältigen. Alles im Kosmos entwickelt sich ganz allmählich. Sprünge gibt es nicht, weder im Großen (für Planeten), noch im Kleinen (für die Menschheit und den Einzelmenschen). — Beispiel: Man stelle sich einen hochrassigen Menschen von 30 Jahren vor. Daneben einen Menschen im selben Alter, Lemurier, Eskimo oder Neger. Wenn der Erdenmensch nur einmal lebt — wie dies gedankenlose Leute gern behaupten —, was hat der Fremdartige „verbrochen", daß er in bezug auf Geist, Seele und Körper (infolgedessen auch in Art, Charakter und Kultur) anders ist im Verhältnis zum Hochrassigen? — Ungerechtigkeiten gibt es im Kosmos nun aber nicht. Während einer Verkörperung kann aus einem Neger oder sonst einem Andersrassigen aber auch nie ein Feinrassiger werden. Diese Tatsache beweist schon, daß eine Höherentwicklung nur in einer langen Kette von Daseinsstufen erfolgen kann. Ziehen wir nun noch die vielen verschiedenen Abstufungen der geistig-seelischen Qualitäten in ein und derselben Rasse in Betracht, die in e i n e m Erdenleben auch nicht erlauben, von niederer Geistesstufe zum Genie zu kommen, so wird es noch klarer, wie viele Erdenleben notwendig sind, vom Unterrassigen zur Hochzucht zu gelangen, vom primitiven Handtyp zum philosophischen oder idealen. Bei Tieren ist es das Gleiche. — Gewiß wird man auch bei einem Negerstamm Hände finden, die Unterschiede aufweisen vom niederen bis zum höheren Handtyp. Trotzdem wird der Neger mit konischem Handtyp n i c h t dieselben Qualitäten aufweisen wie ein Weißer mit konischem Handtyp. — Hier kommen die Rassenunterschiede als e i n Merkmal. Das innere Erleben ist ein ganz verschiedenes, da die physische Basis und das Blut (als Mittler der Seele, der Aura und deshalb des Empfindungsvermögens) eine andere Beschaffenheit aufweisen. — Beweis: Bluttransfusionen von Negern, Mongolen (Andersrassigen) auf Weiße wirken verderblich auf diese. — Ein anderer Beweis: Bei Mischmenschen zwischen Ariern und dunklen Rassen läßt sich nach vielen Generationen durch chemische Blutprobe immer noch nachweisen, w e l c h fremdrassiger Einfluß die „physische Imprägnation" hervorrief, und zwar ganz genau von welcher Art! — Phreno-physiognomisch läßt sich dies ebenfalls nachweisen, wenn auch nicht mit ganz derselben Sicherheit wie durch die chemische Blutprobe. Ich habe auf meinen weiten Reisen den Weg einiger Männer gekreuzt, die mit Sicherheit auch nach der Hand (ohne den Körper zu sehen, wohlverstanden!) die Mischung analysierten. — Da die Form der Hand sich nicht verändert (so daß aus einem niederen ein hoher Handtyp werden kann), ist es klar, daß der Entwicklung bestimmte Grenzen gesetzt sind: Grenzen der erreichbaren Möglichkeiten. Diese „Grenzen des Erreichbaren" sind in jeder rechten Hand erkennbar, und zwar durch die Handform und in weiterer Analysierung durch die Hauptlinien. Also muß diese Wirkung (als feststehende Tatsache der Begrenzung) eine Ursache haben. „Ursache und Wirkung" sind aber die Gesetze des Karma, sind die beiden Faktoren, aus welchen unser Schicksal besteht, sich gegründet hat und weiter sich bildet. Gedanken sind lebende und formende Kräfte. Sie können aufbauend oder verderbend wirken. W a s und w i e wir denken — d a s sind wir! Der Mensch ist in bezug auf Charakter und Krankheit das Produkt seiner Weltanschauung und Erfahrungen, also — s e i n e s D e n k e n s ! Wirken Gedanken aufbauend oder zerstörend nach außen (wie z. B. bei Liebe, Segen, Wunsch, Haß, Fluch), dann wirken sie auch nach innen, d. h. auf unseren Organismus; erst geistig und durch Vermittlung der Seele auf den Körper und die Organe. „Sünde ist Krankheit" sagt schon die Bibel, und so ist es. Beispiel: Bekannt ist, daß man durch bestimmte Experimente in der ausgeatmeten Luft Farben feststellen kann. So hat der Atem eines wütenden Menschen graue Farbe und wirkt giftig nach außen u n d nach innen. Ärgerliche und wütende Menschen vergiften sich selbst, denn diese Gifte greifen die Organe an. Seelische Liebe wirkt positiv, aufbauend, gesundend. Hat und betätigt man eine falsche (un- oder widernatürliche) Weltanschauung durch verkehrtes Denken, so wird sich dies im Organismus notgedrungen bemerkbar machen, weil die Organe negativ beeinflußt werden und dementsprechend arbeiten: Gedanken — Tat; Ursache — Wirkung. Eine gefestigte Anschauung und deren konsequente Betätigung nennt man Charakter. Somit sind Krankheit und Charakter die Polaritäten, die dauernd in uns arbeiten und nach außen verlegt — verwirklicht — in die Tat umgesetzt werden. J e d e Tat hat somit Motiv, Ursache und in der Wirkung neue Ursachen, die wieder Wirkungen auslösen — m ü s s e n , weil jede Tat materialisiertes Denken ist. Der Gedanke oder das Wort werden durch den Willen zur Tat. Taten schaffen neue Umstände und diese wiederum veränderte Verhältnisse. Neue Verhältnisse schaffen veränderte Bedingungen, diese wieder neue Gedanken, diese wieder andere Taten. So ergeben sich die „Ketten", welche wir schleppen. Dieser verwickelt sich in ihnen, jener läßt sie an sich vorüberziehen. Je feiner ein Apparat, desto feiner seine Schwingungen, im geistigen Sinne sowohl wie im physischen. Ein feinnerviger Mensch nimmt (als bessere und feinere Antenne — Aufnahmestation) auch feinere Einwirkungen auf, als ein physisch robuster vermag, und verarbeitet sie in seinem Denken. Die robuste Natur ist noch zu unreif hierzu. Das „Reifen" erfordert Zeit — ist Entwicklung. Infolgedessen ist der feinnervige Mensch älter (verfeinerter) in der Entwicklung, hat mehrere Leben (Daseinsstufen oder Verkörperungen) durchlebt (ein höheres Niveau erlangt). Die Folge davon ist, daß er in seinen Händen auch mehr Linien und Zeichen (Sprachrunen) aufweist und diese m e h r Auskunft geben. — Auf jeden Fall ist die Handform, der Typ, ein höherer und die Höhe der Entwicklung erkennbar. Von einem Fakir erfuhr ich, daß die Zahl der stattgefundenen Verkörperungen innerhalb seiner Rasse an bestimmter Stelle in der linken Hand erkennbar sei. Ich erwähne dies nur und überlasse es jedem, über die Möglichkeit nachzudenken. Im allgemeinen haben Frauen mehr Linien und Zeichen in ihren Händen als Männer, weil sie seelisch empfindungsfähiger, daher Instinkt-Menschen sind. Wie oft finden wir unverstandene Frauen, wie selten unverstandene Männer im Eheleben! Warum? Weil fast jedes Weib Gefühls- und Empfindungsmensch ist und deshalb auch meist blind liebt, anstatt bewußt, indem es erkennt: w e n und w a s es liebt. Wer mit vielen Menschen in Berührung kommt, kann sich leicht davon überzeugen. Es ist selbstverständlich — weil natürlich —, daß sich eine Frau mit vielen Handlinien (feinere Seelenschwingung) auf die Dauer nicht glücklich fühlen kann bei einem Manne mit wenigen Handlinien (mangelhafte Seelenschwingung), weil er nicht mitschwingt, deshalb ihre Schwingungen (ihre Empfindungen) nicht versteht, nicht verstehen k a n n ! Sie leben in verschiedenen Welten und können nicht in Harmonie kommen. Unharmonische Ehen = auseinander-leben. Ein Weib kann sich n u r dann glücklich fühlen, wenn es (und sein Empfinden) verstanden und gewürdigt wird. Seelische Liebe ist: harmonische Schwingung. Die Ehe zwischen zwei so verschiedenen Menschen als Ursache hat stets die entsprechende Wirkung zur Folge. Auch hier greift das Karma ein und — zeigt sich in der Hand. Anderseits hat aber auch jede unglückliche Ehe eine Ursache, die durch Handlungen in der Präexistenz begründet ist. Menschen, die ihre „Ketten" gegenseitig mit solchen tiefgreifenden Ereignissen verbinden und verwickeln, haben sie auch wieder zu entwirren, ob in diesem oder im nächsten Erdenleben, d a s hängt von der Erkenntnis und Gelegenheit ab. Wie es mit den Ursachen und Wirkungen der Verkettung bei den Ehekameraden ist, so ist es auch mit den größeren und kleineren Verkettungen zu anderen Mitmenschen. — Wer mordet, der soll wieder gemordet werden. Denn: „Es kommt niemand von dannen, bis er den letzten Heller (seiner Schuld-Ursache und Wirkung s e l b s t geschaffen) bezahlet hat" oder die Auswirkungen der selbstgeschaffenen Ursachen v e r arbeitet hat. Dies gilt sowohl für geistige Dinge (Gedanken-Weltanschauung, Charakter), als auch für physische (Krankheiten, Taten).*)

> Wenn der Jüngste Tag kommt, läßt der Herrgott sich die Hände zeigen. Wer von Arbeit und Mühe harte, rauhe Hände hat, darf sich im Himmel ausruhen; wer aber feine, weiße Hände hat, muß Gott noch erst sein Herz zeigen.   Friesischer Spruch.

Für den ernsthaften Studenten der wissenschaftlichen Chirologie und Lebensberater ist es erforderlich, den bisherigen Teil des vorliegenden Werkes sehr eingehend durchzuarbeiten, bis er ihn restlos verstanden hat. Ohne die Erkenntnis des Wirkens der feinstofflichen Kräfte bleibt vieles unklar, und Mißdeutungen können dann leicht unterlaufen. Es ist nun einmal so, daß alles, was vom Geistigen her kommt, auch nur von jener Sphäre aus verstanden werden kann.

Es folgt nun der praktische Teil, und ich weise nochmals darauf hin, daß dieser sehr genau, langsam und gründlich, Teil für Teil, erarbeitet werden muß, um ein vollständiges Wissen auf diesem Gebiet zu gewährleisten.

---

*) Siehe vom gleichen Verfasser: „Kosmische Religion."

Und noch eine Warnung, die nicht oft genug wiederholt werden kann:

Für lange, viel zu lange Zeit, war es das Schicksal der Graphologie, weder ernst genommen, noch anerkannt zu werden. Nicht zum wenigsten lag der Grund darin, daß mit ihr zu oft ein Gesellschaftsspiel getrieben und nach einigen Schriftmerkmalen „etwas gesagt" wurde, zum Amüsement. —

Der Chirologie ergeht es nicht anders, und es gibt auch heute noch ungezählte Leute, die mein vorliegendes Lehrbuch — genau so wie früher die Lehrbücher der Graphologie — als „Kochbuch" verwenden, um „jemand etwas sagen zu können", ohne sich in dieser Richtung ein zuverlässiges Wissen zu schaffen.

Abgesehen davon, daß damit diese Wissenschaften immer nur geschädigt und in schlechten Ruf gebracht werden, ist es nicht ohne seelische Gefahren, in solcher Weise nach einigen Zeichen ein Charaktermerkmal oder eine Eigenschaft jemand zu nennen, die er vielleicht gar nicht besitzt. Man entfacht in ihm seelische Konflikte, die jahrelang haften und ihn belasten können.

Gerade auf dem Gebiet der Charakterkunde sind ganz besondere Vorsicht und größte Gewissenhaftigkeit nötig, und sie lassen sich nur durch intensives und gründliches Studium und durch den immer gegenwärtigen Gedanken erreichen, daß es sich dabei in jedem Fall um einen M e n s c h e n handelt, um eine Seele, die in den allermeisten Fällen nur wenig Halt und Kraft besitzt, um solche Erkenntnisse bzw. Diagnosen zu ertragen. Außerdem ist es auch gefährlich, überhaupt solche Diagnosen und Gutachten in Anwesenheit dritter Personen zu geben, da diese leicht ausgenutzt werden können. V e r s c h w i e g e n - h e i t ist hier noch mehr vonnöten als beim Arzt. Darum Vorsicht vor seelischen Schädigungen!

Zweiter Teil.

Chirognomie oder Handformenlehre.

Der G e i s t baut den Körper!
Nicht der Körper den Geist!
Das Äußere ist Form und Ausdruck des Innern.
Wie oben, so unten; wie innen, so außen!
Der Mensch ist das Maß aller Dinge!

Proportions- und Formgesetz der Hand.

Bild 4 zeigt die elementare und die geistige Hand extrem dargestellt. Während die eine Hand in der Form nahezu ein Quadrat bildet, formt die andere ein langes Rechteck. Aus diesem gesetzmäßigen Maß der Form und Proportion erkennt man schon, wann eine Hand als höhere und wann als niedere Form erkannt und betrachtet werden muß, und zu welcher Seite die Zwischenstufen von Handformen mehr neigen. Dieser Punkt ist bei der Beurteilung aus der Innenfläche immer in Betracht zu ziehen; denn wenn ein Ereignis in Betracht kommt, so werden die Dispositionen und Begleitumstände bei beiden Formen verschiedene sein, obgleich das Ereignis das gleiche sein kann oder ist. Ein geistiger Mensch wird immer anders erleben als eine Durchschnittsnatur. Für die höhere sensible Bedeutung der Hand bestimmt die Größe des menschlichen Gesichts, in dem die höchsten Sinnesorgane zum feinsten Ausdruck zusammenwirken, das „Normalmaß" der Hände. Beide Handflächen bedecken die volle Breite des Gesichts. Die Länge — Wurzel bis Spitze — des Mittel-(Saturn-)Fingers soll die Länge der Stirnhöhe haben und eine Hand mit angelegtem Daumen die Wange (Nase bis Ohr) bedecken.

Die Frauenhand ist meist im Verhältnis kleiner, schmaler und zarter, in den Fingern rundlicher, schmiegsamer gebaut, auch meist mit zarterer Haut bedeckt als die Männerhand, die stets breiter, kräftiger, auch größer, mit rauherer Haut und oft mit Haaren versehen ist (vgl. Bild 11, 12, 13).

Ist die Handfläche größer, d. h. breiter und länger als die Finger, so ist mehr materieller Charakter vorhanden; doch kann ihr Eigner trotzdem ein energischer und „Weiß was er will"-Mensch sein.

Auf Bild 5 bringe ich einige A f f e n h ä n d e und eine primitive oder elementare Hand eines Trinkers. Man sieht sofort an dem tief-angesetzten Daumen des Pavians, um wieviel er gegenüber dem Schimpansen „geistig minderwertiger" ist. Bei beiden sowohl wie auch bei der Hand des Orang fällt auf, daß die Finger v i e l kürzer sind als der Handteller. Bei dem Pavian sind keine Linien in der Innenhand, wohl aber schon Anfänge bei dem Schimpansen und Orang, ebenso bei dem Gorilla.

Die Anthropoiden oder Menschenaffen haben unterschiedliche Hand-formen. Hier meine ich nicht die Unterschiede in den Handtypen-Formen, sondern eher in der Art des Baues, des Formniveaus, ähnlich wie es bei den Handformenunterschieden der verschiedenen Menschen-rassen ist.

Die Hände der Neger, im allgemeinen der niederen Stämme, haben eine gewisse Ähnlichkeit mit den Händen des Gorilla, die Hände der Mongolen mit denen des Orang-Utang und die Hände der weißen Rasse — wenn auch weit entfernter — mit den Händen des Schimpansen. (Diese Meinung des englischen Gelehrten Crookshank teile ich nicht. D. V.) Besonders gut beobachten kann man diese Ähnlichkeiten zwischen Orang-Händen und denen von mongoloiden Idioten. Aber die von jugendlichen mongoloiden Idioten sind sehr bezeichnend und sehr verschieden von den langen, mageren, flachen und eher schim-pansenartigen Händen von Personen, die an jugendlichem Irresein leiden. Die Beugefläche der Hand ist bei jenen mehr viereckig und plump und, wenigstens in den ersten Monaten des Lebens, mit an der Handfläche befindlichen vorgewölbten bläulichen Polstern versehen, die den Handflächenpolstern junger Affen gleichen. Die Daumen sind kurz, zumeist auch tiefer angesetzt (geistige Minderwertigkeit), die Finger-enden stumpf (keine Einfühlung, kein inneres Erleben), die Zeigefinger mehr oder minder unausgebildet (Mangel an Selbstbewußtsein und Persönlichkeit), der kleine Finger kurz und krumm (Mangel an normal-gesunder Denkart, Intelligenz und normalem Geschlechtsempfinden).

Gleiche Handformationen findet man bei reinrassigen Mongolen (siehe auch Sir Will. Lawrence „Lectures on comparative anatomy", p. 279. — 9. ed. London, und weiter W. H. B. Stoddart „Mind and its disorder", pp. 312—313, 3rd. ed. 1919). Diese Hände gleichen also, wenn auch verkürzt, den Händen eines jungen Orang-Utang. Schim-pansenhände gleichen eher den langen Händen des Ägypters oder Bengalen (Inders); die massige, an der Basis der Finger mit schwimm-hautähnlichen Gebilden versehene Gorillahand in vielem derjenigen eines Negers niederer Art. (Siehe hierüber auch die Forschungen des englischen Gelehrten F. G. Crookshank „Der Mongole in unserer Mitte", wo er eine allgemeine Fingerformel mongoloider Idioten im Vergleich zu der gelben Rasse mit 3 4 2 5 2 aufstellt.) Der englische Gelehrte Dr. Reginald Langdon-Down beschreibt in „British medical Journal", 1909, II. 665, eine Hauptlinienkonstellation der Innenhand: Eine lange, quer über die Handfläche verlaufende Herzlinie, die in den Anfang der Lebenslinie mündet, bei fehlender Kopflinie, wird bei den meisten Händen von mongoloiden Idioten und auch oft bei mongoloiden Personen gefunden, und diese Hauptlinienkonstellation weist auf eine bestimmte geistige Entwicklung und einen bestimmten Gehirnbau hin. Er nennt diese extrem lange Herzlinie auch „mongolische" Linie, die zuweilen auch, aber doch nur bei e i n e m Affen gefunden wird, beim Orang-Utang*).

Diese Linienkonstellation, mit Kopflinie, bedeutet immer, daß gewaltsamer Tod und Lähmung in der Familie waren. Diese Bedeutung scheint dem genannten Gelehrten aber unbekannt zu sein. Es mag die Möglichkeit bestehen, daß Personen wie mongoloide Idioten oder auch solche mit mongoloidem Rasseneinschlag aus noch nicht bekannten Gründen, die sich aber evtl. erklären ließen, mehr Dispositionen für gewaltsamen Tod haben. Aber der Schluß des Gelehrten in seiner Abhandlung, daß alle jene Menschen, die solche Linienformation in ihren Händen aufweisen, einen mongoloiden Rasseneinschlag besitzen, ist falsch. Sehr interessant dagegen sind die Feststellungen, die die beiden genannten Gelehrten in bezug auf sonstige Ähnlichkeiten der Körper- und Organbeschaffenheiten zwischen Neger und Gorilla, Mongolen und Orang, der weißen Rasse (?) und Schimpansen machten. Nähere Ausführungen darüber würden aber hier von meinem Thema abführen.

In allen diesen Fällen, wie überhaupt im Tierreiche, schlummert das geistige Bewußtsein noch. Eine Pflanze empfinde nichts, wenn sie abgeschnitten wird, sagen w i r. Mangel an Nachdenklichkeit **)! Wenn ein Tier ein Messer sieht, weiß es auch nichts über seine Wirkung, fühlt aber schon den Schmerz, wenn es in Aktion tritt. Der Mensch braucht nur ein Messer zu sehen, dann weiß er sofort, wozu es da ist, und kennt die Eventualitäten. — Hier haben wir zuerst ein geistiges Bewußtsein, ein Denkvermögen. Das Tier hat dafür einen Instinkt, ein Vorfühlen, um geleitet zu sein. Das Tier empfindet schon v o r dem Schlachthause, was bevorsteht. Im Schlachthause bemerkt man bei ihm Angstausdrücke, die sehr deutlich sprechen.

---

*) Hierfür liegen besondere Gründe vor, die dem betr. Forscher anscheinend nicht bekannt sind, die näher zu erklären jedoch hier nicht der Platz ist.
**) Siehe: Bose, „Pflanzenschrift und ihre Offenbarungen".

Bei uns Menschen ist der gute Instinkt zum allergrößten Teile verlorengegangen, zum Teil ausgetrieben worden durch die Verhältnisse, durch unnatürliche Lebensart, durch verkehrte Erziehung, vor allem aber durch die Schulung des rein intellektuellen Denkens! Besser wäre es sicherlich, wenn wir den Instinkt wieder entwickelten, denn er nutzt jedem im täglichen Leben in vieler Hinsicht und bei allen Gelegenheiten.

Eine sehr schmale und sehr zarte Hand bezeichnet ein kraftloses, weiches Wesen; mit laschem Temperament, wenn sie weich ist. Die Phantasie ist sehr mangelhaft (kleiner, flacher Mondberg), das Denken schlaff und mühsam. Mangel an Kraft, Ausdruck und Zähigkeit, Eigenschaften, die mehr in der festen und harten Hand mit gutem Daumen vorhanden sind. Der Verstand ist fein wie die Art, jedoch nicht groß und tief. In den Händen gelangen auch die Altersgrade zum Ausdruck, ein Beweis dafür, daß die Veränderung (Entwicklung) der Hand mit dem geistigen und körperlichen Entwickeln bzw. Verfall übereinstimmt. Im allgemeinen sehen wir dies sofort, wenn wir die Hände von Persönlichkeiten verschiedener Altersstufen nebeneinander haben; z. B. von 2, 7, 14, 21, 28, 35, 42, 48, 70 Jahren (vgl. Bild 12, 13, 14). Der Grundtyp bleibt derselbe, ob Kind oder Greis. Im Alter und bei langer Krankheit (langem Ruhen) verändern sich die Hände ein wenig im Ausdruck (nicht im Typ). Alter läßt das Gehirn (Gedankenkraft) einschrumpfen, so auch die Hände im allgemeinen (Bild 14). Man ist weniger unternehmungslustig, biegsam, anpassungsfähig, romantisch, poetisch, zart usw. und mehr den prosaischen, materiellen, irdischen Dingen geneigt. Es kommt die sog. „Philosophie des Realen" mehr zum Ausdruck. Krankheit und Ruhe machen eine feste Hand weicher, weil weniger Willen und Kraft angewandt wird für Tätigkeit, Bewegung, wodurch wiederum der Körper geschwächt wird und Phantasie — bewußt oder unbewußt — sich mehr entwickelt. Aus diesem Grunde mit sind Kranke beeinflußbar durch Suggestion jeder Art. Die geistige und seelische Tätigkeit beeinflußt, gestaltet das Physische in Form und Wesen. Auch ein Gradmesser der physischen Widerstandskraft, Charakterfestigkeit und des sinnlichen Genußlebens ist die Hand. Sie ist — als ein Nervensammelzentrum — ein kleiner Reflexspiegel des Lebens im Blut- und Nervenkreislauf.

Man findet verschiedene Temperatur und Merkmale bei Fieber, Lungenleiden, Asthma, Ohnmacht: heiß, trocken, feucht, klamm, schweißig usw.

Handtypen.

1. Die elementare oder primitive Hand.
2. Die Spatelhand oder praktische Hand.
3. Die eckige oder nützliche Hand.
4. Die knotige oder philosophische Hand.
5. Die konische oder künstlerische Hand.
6. Die psychische, ideale oder mediale Hand.
7. Die gemischte Hand.

Charakteristik*).

Die elementare Hand (Bild 6).

Große Handfläche, dick, hart; Finger kurz, steif, dick, Daumen kurz, formlos, klobig, gerade und abstehend. Phlegmatisch, primitiv, tierisch in Art, Wesen und Instinkt. Unentwickelte Nerven, brutal in Kraft und Verlangen.

Personen mit solchen Händen haben besondere Vorliebe für Feldbau und ähnliche grobe Arbeit, für welche physische Kraft und wenig Geist genügen. Diese primitiven Menschen sind nicht überflüssig, sondern zum Fortschritt der Kultur notwendig. Sie sind schwerfällig und träge im Geiste, gleichgültig und apathisch, aber körperlich zähe, stabil und meist stark abergläubisch. In ihrer Anspruchslosigkeit begnügen sie sich mit dem Allernotwendigsten und stellen keine großen Anforderungen an die Welt. Rein findet man diesen Handtyp nur bei Eskimos, Tataren und anderem auf niedriger Kulturstufe lebenden Volke.

Die Spatelhand (Bild 7 und 12).

Mittelgroß bis groß; Knöchel entwickelt oder nicht. Fingerspitzen breiter als das erste Glied (Ballen-, Froschfinger-Form). Daumen meist mittel bis groß.

Energisch, zähe, rastlos, aktiv, beweglich, spekulierend, imitierend und erfinderisch; fleißig, strebsam, resolut und selbstvertrauend. Weniger konventionell und romantisch, mehr praktisch und materiell; evtl. etwas tyrannisch. Ist die Hand weich, wird vieles von diesen Eigenschaften abgeschwächt und durch Sinnlichkeit, Genußliebe ersetzt. Personen mit diesen Handformen sind immer unternehmungslustig und für Neues zu gewinnen. Sie versuchen alles materiell zu nutzen und praktisch zu verwerten, eignen sich sehr gut für feine,

---

*) In diesem Kapitel über Charakteristik der Handformen habe ich Hinweise betr. Berufseignung bzw. Berufsrichtung der einzelnen Typen nur vereinzelt eingestreut. Ausführlich beschrieben und erklärt befindet sich der Spezialteil „Berufseignungsprüfung" im „Lexikon der Chirologie, Berufseignungsprüfung und Fachliteratur". (vergriffen)

akkurate Arbeit, Feinmechanik usw., aber auch für große Unternehmungen, Kolossalbauten, Landwirtschaft, Schiffahrt, Jagd, Handel, Pionierarbeit für Kultur und Instrumentalmusik. Sie haben eine gewisse natürliche Intelligenz (siehe den entwickelten, geistigen Teil der Finger). Ihnen imponiert das Massenhafte, Große, Kolossale; mehr das Gewichtige, Wuchtige in der Ausdehnung, nicht die Zierlichkeit und Feinheit. Spatelhände haben viel Sinn für das Regelmäßige, Symmetrische und ziehen lieber Land-, Bezirks-, Provinz- und Staatengrenzen mit dem Lineal, weil es praktischer und einfacher ist. Sie haben jedoch nur wenig übrig für Philosophie, Poesie und Metaphysik; sie sind zu materiell denkend, aber gute, praktische Lebenskünstler, die besten Kulturpioniere für unerschlossene Länder, Menschen, die sich in allen Lebenslagen zu helfen wissen. Am meisten findet man diesen Typ in Nordamerika.

Spatelhänder neigen mehr zu Protestantismus, weil Mangel an Romantik, die mehr dem Katholizismus entspricht und konischen oder spitzen Händen. Darum ist es auch schwer, den Katholizismus nach Norden zu bringen, wo der Spateltyp viel mehr vertreten ist. Unter allen großen Sportsleuten und jenen Menschen, die mit aktivem Wettstreit oder auch angewandten Wissenschaften zu tun haben, finden wir Spatelhände, die Tat, Energie, Bewegung, Zähigkeit und Zielstrebigkeit zur Charakteristik haben. Diese Handform mit Knoten in den oberen Fingergliedern bzw. Beugegelenken finden wir mit mehr Logik begabt. Solche Menschen lieben Unabhängigkeit im Regieren und im aktiven Verfolgen der eigenen Pläne. Sie sind sehr skeptisch betreffs Zärtlichkeiten und Zuneigung, bis ihnen der Beweis erbracht wird, daß von der Gegenseite wirklich Neigung vorhanden ist. Sie sind intolerant betreffs Fanatismus und abgewandt allen Vorstellungen und allem Exzentrischen. Sie lieben politische Freiheit der Massen und haben Geist für den Zusammenschluß. Mit Knoten in beiden Beugegelenken aller Finger werden diese Leute ihre physische Tätigkeit, exakte Wissenschaft, praktisches Studium, kombinieren; denn sie sind allen mechanischen, konstruktiven Künsten und Wissenschaften, wie Navigation, Geometrie, Architektur usw., ergeben.

Beachte:

Jupiterfinger sehr lang: Große Vorliebe für das Mysteriöse, Neigung zu Irrtum und Fanatismus.

Saturnfinger sehr lang: Aktive Einbildungskraft, Neigung zu Literatur über Okkultismus und Wissenschaft, auch zu Depression. — Zu lang: Neigung zu sehr großer Melancholie.

Apollofinger sehr lang: Talent für Imitation, Darsteller von Personen; Gedanken, Gefühl; Vorliebe für Hindernisse.

Merkurfinger sehr lang: Innige Beredsamkeit, wenn auch nicht immer kluge Handlungsweise; als Redner: kraftvolle Ausdrucksart. Neigung zu Mechanik, Elektrizität usw.

Ist einer dieser Finger sehr kurz, so besagt dies: Mangel an den betreffenden Eigenschaften oder Qualitäten.

Die eckige Hand (Bild 8).

Mittelgroß bis groß; zum Teil entwickelte Knöchel und eckige Fingerspitzen (Bild 17). Mehr oder weniger gefühlvoll, zäh, eigensinnig und kleinlich im Denken und Tun. Ruhig, strebsam, gewissenhaft, pflichttreu. Mehr Verstandesmenschen mit gewisser Selbstbeherrschung. Sie lieben Ordnung, Methode, System, Symmetrie und Pedanterie (Bürokraten, Lehrer usw.). Der Daumen ist meist groß und mit ebensolcher Wurzel (Venusberg), die Handfläche derb und fest. Personen mit diesen Händen haben Vorliebe für die moralischen, politischen und sozialen Wissenschaften, Erziehung, Lehrtätigkeit, Geometrie, Sprache für das Traditionelle, Autoritäten, für das Praktische und Solide. Die Besitzer dieses Handtyps geben gute, aber auch leider zu pedantische Beamten und Bürokraten, strenge Lehrer ab. Sie lieben das Herrschen. Sie bevorzugen meist das Reale dem möglicherweise Unrealen, praktische Talente den Fähigkeiten, die der Phantasie entspringen. Eigner dieser Hände hegen die Anschauung, daß das Gute besser als das Schöne, das Nützliche jedoch das allerbeste sei. Sie arten meist aus in Pedantismus und wollen zäh an Regeln, engen Begriffen usw. hängenbleiben, in der Kunst, im Wissen, in allem. Daher kleben sie meist an Form, Manier, Wort und Althergebrachtem, sind pünktlich wie eine Uhr und Gegner aller Freiheit und Großzügigkeit. Sie haben viele gute Eigenschaften, hindern sich selbst aber in der Entwicklung zum Höheren, da zu kleinlich. Man findet diesen Typ überall, vorwiegend jedoch in Nordeuropa.

Eckige Hände mit Knoten besitzen jene Menschen, die vorsichtig sind, durchhaltend und ordnungsliebend. Sie sind gleichmäßig in ihrer Art. Sie haben Disposition zum Organisieren, Arrangieren, Klassifizieren und Gleichmachen in Form und Annehmen von Dingen, die man beschreiben und erklären kann. Sie gehen immer von dem Grundsatz aus: „Es muß alles passend sein!" Sie finden leicht Unterschiede außen und innen, sind romantisch, wenn es vernünftig ist, sie sind treu in der Liebe, aber nicht wegen der Tiefe der Gefühle, sondern weil es sich so gehört, und damit der gute Ruf nicht geschädigt wird: „die Leute könnten darüber reden"; „was sagen die Leute?" Sie arrangieren die Bücher nach dem Titel, nicht nach dem Format oder Aussehen in der Farbe, wie es jene Menschen mit konischen Fingern tun, obgleich diese gern gleiches Format hätten. Sie sind immer gebürstet und adrett und wahren „Etikette". Sie haben Disziplin. Alles ist vorbedacht und vorbereitet. Auch haben sie Gesicht und Lachen in Gewalt, ebenso Sprache und Blicke. Sie sind sehr unangenehm berührt, wenn das Wetter sich ändert, oder wenn Wohnungswechsel kommt. Sie sind komplette Meister für Intrigen, mißtrauisch und schlau im Geheimen. Sie haben wenig Freude, weil sie sich diese nicht gönnen und zu sehr im Real-bewußtsein verstrickt sind. Sie lieben den langsamen Fortschritt und sind im allgemeinen allen Neuerungen plötzlicher Art abgeneigt. Wenn die Knoten an allen Fingern stark ausgeprägt sind, so ist dieser Typ schon etwas besser. Sie haben Vorliebe für elegante Wissenschaften, wie Botanik, Archäologie, Psychologie, Jurisprudenz, Orthographie, Geschichte und Politik, weniger Metaphysik. Etwas Unaufrichtigkeit wird man bei ihnen immer finden.

Beachte:

Jupiterfinger sehr lang: Wahrheitsliebe, Stolz.

Saturnfinger sehr lang: Sehr ernst und nachdenklich.

Apollofinger sehr lang: Vorliebe für Studien und Nachdenken in der Kunst.

Merkurfinger sehr lang: Vorliebe für wissenschaftliche Studien und gute Darstellungskraft.

Wenn einzelne Finger zu kurz sind, ergibt dies eine etwas impulsive Natur, voll Ungeduld in Begründung und Argumenten.

Die konische Hand (Bild 9).

Schöne symmetrische und angenehme Form. Konisch (schmaler werdend) verlaufend mit konischen (zugespitzten) Fingern (Bild 50 b u. 59). Hier drei Unterarten:

a) Geschmeidige kleine Hand, schmaler Daumen, bezeichnet Vorliebe für Schönheit, speziell in Form (geht an jede Sache mit Begeisterung). Bild 10.

b) Große Hand, kurz, dick mit großem Daumen, verrät großes Verlangen nach Reichtum und Pracht (sucht seine Pläne mit Schlauheit auszuführen). Bild 45.

c) Weiche oder wenig feste große Hand mit sehr entwickelter Innenhand (Berge), die Neigung zu Sinnengenuß gibt (sucht sein Ziel mit Selbstzufriedenheit zu erlangen). Bild 50 b.

Alle drei sind wertlos für mechanische und physische Arbeit, da alle drei von Inspiration bzw. Stimmungen regiert, geleitet werden. Sie sind je nachdem weniger oder mehr Gefühlsmenschen, sentimental, instinktiv, impulsiv, eindrucksfähig, nervös, launisch, romantisch, poetisch, träumerisch, lebensfreudig und begeistert, bescheiden und empfindlich, besonders gegen Lächerlichkeit, ideal, daher keine sog. „Geschäftsleute". Man findet diesen Handtyp viel bei Künstlern, doch muß ein Künstler nicht unbedingt solche Hände haben. Das Gefühls- und Empfindungsleben ist hier viel stärker als die Verstandestätigkeit. Solche Menschen hängen gern an Äußerlichkeiten und versuchen auch fälschlicherweise, danach zu beurteilen. Personen dieses Handtyps sind große Anhänger von Freiheitsideen, lieben die Abwechslung in bezug auf alles, Aufenthalt, Personen, Beschäftigung sowohl wie in der Liebe. Sie sind sehr von Stimmungen abhängig; begeistert, exzentrisch, lustig bis zum Überschäumen, morgen traurig, launisch, melancholisch, gereizt, und deshalb wird man auch verstehen können, daß diesen Menschen Einschränkungen und geregeltes Leben weniger gut liegen. Sie sind Bohémiens. Da sie (als Künstler) außerdem noch oberflächlich und leicht veranlagt sind und (mit weichen Händen) noch viel Sinnlichkeit und Flatterhaftigkeit dazukommen, kann man treue, tiefe Liebe nicht gut erwarten, weshalb die Ehen solcher Menschen selten von langer Dauer und innigem, wirklich festem Glücke sind. Eine f e s t e Hand verbessert die Eigenschaften und macht fester im Charakter und Wesen, doch kommt viel auch auf den Daumen an. Sehr weich (schwammig) ist der Typ des „Nur-Genuß"-Menschen, weshalb man in solchem Falle von einer „Vergnügungshand" spricht (Bild 9, 50 b).

Die weichen Hände verraten immer eine große Portion Sinnlichkeit, Hang zum Schwelgen und Genießen, Trägheit, Beschaulichkeit, Vergnügungssucht und Mangel an höherer Verstandeskraft. Auch oft Neigung zur Lüge und Heuchelei. Menschen, welche zu faul und sinnlich sind, um ernst und physisch zu arbeiten, hängen sich oft an die Kunst. Dieser Typ ist überall zu finden, mehr jedoch im Süden und in den Tropen.

Die erste Art tut alle Dinge mit Begeisterung, die zweitgenannte Form tut alles mit Schlauheit, der letztgenannte Typ mit Selbstsucht und Eigennutz. Die erste liebt das Schöne mehr als das Praktisch-Nützliche; doch sind diese Personen immer ängstlich vor evtl. Lächerlichkeit. Sie sind begeistert und äußerlich bescheiden, impulsiv. Sie haben wenig Gewalt oder Zähigkeit in der Durchführung von Plänen, auch wenig Entschlossenheit. Sie sind unfähig zu befehlen, besitzen aber viel Ergebenheit. Diese Personen mögen gern gezogen werden, aber nicht getrieben. Wandelbar in Liebesangelegenheiten, da kühl, haben sie aber warme Vorstellung. Wenn diese Hände noch mehr entwickelt sind, der Handteller größer, die Finger feiner und zarter, so ist solch ein Mensch noch mehr Sklave der Leidenschaft und hat weniger Selbstzucht oder Kraft. Sie machen gern Schulden und ver- schwenden mit Freunden, sind sehr empfindlich gegen Verdächtigungen und Blamagen, anderseits aber sehr gerührt bei Güte und Freundschaft. Die Naturen dieser Typen neigen zu Sinnlichkeit, Faulheit, Egoismus, zu Raffiniertheit, Falschheit, Übertreibungen und Mangel an Konzentration, können leicht exzentrisch und zynisch sein. Sie sind keiner geistigen Liebe fähig.

B e a c h t e bei konischen oder psychischen (idealen) Händen in b e i d e n Handtypen Charakteristik ähnlich, nur bei dem idealen Typ überbetont, verfeinert.

J u p i t e r f i n g e r s e h r l a n g : Große Vorliebe für Religion mit dem Verlangen, führend darin zu wirken.

W e n n s o l a n g w i e S a t u r n f i n g e r : Das Leben wird durch Ehrgeiz regiert.

S a t u r n f i n g e r s e h r l a n g (selten!): Streiche und Frivolitäten. (Das Gegenteil von dem schweren eckigen oder Spatel-Saturnfinger.)

A p o l l o f i n g e r s e h r l a n g : Starke Intuition in Kunst und Inspiration in bezug auf Personen. Wenn jedoch das 3. Glied das längste ist: Ausnutzung der Kunst usw. zu materiellen Zwecken.

M e r k u r f i n g e r s e h r l a n g : Intuition in bezug auf Okkultismus, Mystik, Medizin. Ebenso Beredsamkeit.

Wenn einer dieser Finger s e h r k u r z ist, deutet dies auf Egoismus, Impulsivität, die durch Unbesonnenheit zu Unglück führen kann.

Die psychische, ideale oder mediale Hand (Bild 10 und 47).

Auffallend schön in Form; schlank, zart und zugespitzt. Sie ist die verfeinerte, veredelte Form der konischen Hand, wie man sie auf den Heiligenbildern sieht. Wie die geistige Anschauung dieser Menschen nicht irdischer Art ist, so sind auch die Hände unbrauchbar für jede physische Arbeit, und ihre Art ist zu unpraktisch und wertlos für irgendwelche materiellen Dinge. Sie werden regiert von Herz und Seele, sind sehr feinnervig und medial, lieben alles Große, Schöne, Hohe, Reine, Ideale, Sittliche und Göttliche. Sind schwärmerisch, reich an Phantasie, sind Spiritualisten und Mystiker. Dies ist der schönste Typ der Menschenhand, durchgeistigt, im Volksmund „Hände mit Spinnenfingern" genannt. Diese Handform ist an keine Gegend gebunden, man findet sie überall, jedoch recht selten — leider. Alle die minderwertigen Eigenschaften der konischen Hand sind hier harmonisch vereint und veredelt, zu Tugenden geworden. Meist sind die Finger ohne Knoten und glatt (Bild 47). Sind Knoten und ein entwickelter Daumen vorhanden, so kommt Geisteskraft und Kombinationsvermögen hinzu, doch auf Kosten der Milde und Weichheit. Je feiner, zarter diese

Hand, desto zarter ist die physische Kraft des Besitzers. Sie ist solchen Persönlichkeiten zu eigen, bei denen das seelische Leben das leibliche in jeder Beziehung weit überragt, welche sich im Reiche der Phantasie, des Idealen, des Jenseitigen wohler und mehr zu Hause fühlen als im Irdischen. Sie verabscheuen alles Gemeine, Niedrige, Selbstsüchtige, Unschöne, Ungerechte, Ehrgeizige, Materielle, besitzen aber meist einen festen und zähen Willen, der ihnen die Kraft gibt, für edle, ideale Zwecke und Ziele einzutreten, wie es die vielen Märtyrer taten. Ihr Drang nach Wahrheit und Vernunft (nicht nach menschlichen Begriffen, sondern nach der höchsten, reinsten, göttlichen Vernunft und Wahrheit) ist wohl das Stärkste in ihnen. Da sie so wenig für das Materielle und das Alltagsleben geschaffen sind, werden sie meist von anderen Menschen ausgenutzt und betrogen; aus dem Grunde ist es notwendig, daß Personen mit diesem Handtyp gute, treue Freunde zur Seite haben, falls sie in unserer egoistischen Zeit nicht verkommen sollen.

Dieser Handtyp ist nicht das ausschließliche Erbe edler Geburt. Seele ist ihnen alles. Sie werden fast nie verstanden, und das sollte gewürdigt werden. Man sollte dankbar dafür sein, daß so feine, hohe Einflüsse und reine Intuitionen dieses Types zwischen uns leben. Mit den oberen Knoten haben wir einen mehr oder weniger wechselvollen Charakter, der etwas exzentrisch, fanatisch und unzuverlässig ist. Mit beiden Knoten in allen Fingern ergibt sich mehr Kalkulation und Intellekt; bei Männern positive und fruchtbare erfinderische Gedanken, aber ein anderer (eckiger oder Spateltyp) muß die Ausführung übernehmen. Ohne großen Daumen zeigen diese Hände an: Neigung zu Unzufriedenheit, Zweifel, Furcht, Niedergeschlagenheit wegen des eigenen Unvermögens. Bei Menschen mit „idealer Handform", worin sich nur die drei Hauptlinien und keine Ereignislinien noch Zeichen befinden, sei man sehr vorsichtig. Meistens sind sie falsch, intrigant, lügnerisch.

Viel seltener als diesen idealen Handtyp (mit spitzen oder konischen Fingern) findet man die i d e a l e e c k i g e H a n d. Sie ist die wirklich schönste aller Hände in Gestalt, Harmonie, in allem; leider aber auch ebensowenig für das praktische Alltagsleben geeignet wie die ideale Hand. Was dieser Handtyp mit dem ideal-konischen gleich, aber doch noch im v e r s t ä r k t e n - M a ß e hat, sind: Inspirationen, die anderen, Künstlern, Schriftstellern, wirklichen Wissenschaftlern, in hohem Maße nützen können.

Die knotige oder philosophische Hand (Bild 11).

Der charakteristische Ausdruck dieser Hand kann nicht verwechselt werden. Sie ist mittelgroß oder kleiner: Fingerspitzen oval-keulenförmig (der Länge nach). Es ist der Gegentyp zur konischen oder künstlerischen Hand (welche jedoch mit Kunst nicht viel gemein hat), auch in den Eigenschaften.

Hier müssen wir zwei Arten unterscheiden, nämlich den einen Menschen, der seine Ideen von außen und äußeren Einflüssen empfängt und bei dem die unteren Knoten stärker ausgeprägt sind; bei dem anderen Typ kommen die Ideen von innen, von inneren Strömungen und vom Unterbewußtsein, bei den kleineren Händen ist Herzdenken vorhanden, bei den großen Herz- und Gehirndenken. Beide haben aber die gleichen Resultate. Bei beiden Typen finden wir als Haupteigenschaft Synthese und Analyse. Persönlichkeiten mit diesem Handtyp überhaupt propagieren gern soziale und religiöse Freiheit, sie sind die besten Religionslehrer (hier ist die große Verschiedenheit von den eckigen Typen).

Der Daumen ist meist groß und stark. Menschen mit diesen Handformen lieben Unabhängigkeit im Tun und Denken, Begründung, Logik und Beweis, Ergründen von Ursache und Wirkung, Wahrheit, Gerechtigkeit, das Ideale. Sie bevorzugen die Wahrheit dem Schönen gegenüber, sind Moralisten, Ethiker und meist sehr philosophisch, gerechtdenkend, gute, tiefe Menschen. Die Vernunft ist der Leitstern für sie; sie läßt sie rück- und vorwärtsblicken und erwägen, berechnen und betrachten; sie macht sie unabhängig von dem Gegenwärtigen und der Meinung anderer. Was ein solcher Mensch tut, tut er mit Selbstbewußtsein und Begründung. In der ihm eigenen Gründlichkeit denkt er über alle Möglichkeiten, Folgen und Zwecke nach. Die Regel wird ebenso studiert wie die Ausnahme. Das Interesse für den einzelnen ist ebenso groß wie das für die Familie, Nation, Rasse, Menschheit. Er läßt sich nie vom bloßen Glauben oder verkehrter Liebe und Mitleid beherrschen, sondern vom Wissen und Erkennen, von der Vernunft; deshalb die Vorliebe für das Ethische und Ästhetische. Anschauung und Gewohnheit gelten nicht, sondern nur tieferes Erkennen des Wahren und Wirklichen. Auf religiösem und sozialem Gebiete kämpft er für Unabhängigkeit und Höherentwicklung, für die Vervollkommnung. Vermöge des großen Ordnungssinnes und der Fähigkeit, das Wesen (den inneren Wert) der Dinge zu erkennen, klassifiziert er mehr der Natur entsprechend, nicht nach Form, Größe, Eigenschaften und äußerem Anschein. Man trifft diesen Handtyp überall, doch nicht oft; in der alten Welt jedoch mehr als in der neuen, wo der reine und wahre Idealismus noch seltener geworden ist als hier. In kleinerer, reinerer und feinerer Form findet man diesen Handtyp öfter in Indien, besonders bei den Yogis. In dieser Hand wird das Intellektuelle und Spirituelle in Harmonie zur wahren (d. h. göttlichen) Vernunft vereinigt. Ich sage: „wird"; ob das „wird" ein „ist" ist, muß von Fall zu Fall heraus erkannt werden.

Die gemischte Hand (Bild 54 b).

Die gemischte Hand enthält Kombinationen der verschiedenen Hand- und Fingerformen und deshalb auch gemischte Charakteristik und Vielseitigkeit. Sie wird am häufigsten angetroffen; doch ist nicht jede Hand, die etwas vom reinen Typ abweicht, eine gemischte. Man muß schon Übung besitzen, um nicht z. B. eine etwas konische Elementar- hand oder eine knotige konische Hand usw. mit einer gemischten Hand zu verwechseln. Hierauf kommt sehr viel an bei der Beurteilung. Was die Eigenschaften der gemischten Hand betrifft, so muß in Betracht gezogen werden, aus welchen Typen die Mischung hervorging, welche die Hand aufweist. Hiernach hat man zu kombinieren. Meist wird ein bestimmter Typ als Grund zu erkennen sein, wovon dann auch die Charakteristik am stärksten vertreten ist. In der Hauptsache haben alle gemischten Hände zu eigen: Vielseitig in Kenntnissen und Können, große Anpassungsfähigkeit in jeder Beziehung, Sinn für praktische und nützliche Verwertung; sie sind besitzliebend, schlau, hart, eigensinnig. Oft ist jeder Finger verschieden, so daß man jeden erst einzeln und dann mit der Hand im Zusammenhange kombinieren muß.

Die Intelligenz, die durch diesen Handtyp repräsentiert wird, ist eine gemischte und setzt sich zusammen aus d e n Geistesrichtungen, welche die einzelnen verschiedenen Finger darstellen. O h n e diese gemischte Intelligenz (und daher ohne die „gemischte Hand"), die eine gewisse säureartige geistige Schärfe enthält, würde die sog. „Gesellschaft" sich nur mit Hemmungen, Kampf und in Sprüngen entwickeln. Der g e m i s c h t e n Hand gehört die Intelligenz für gemischte Arbeiten und verbindende Ideen; für Wissenschaften, die nicht ausschließlich reine Wissenschaften sind, wie Administration, Handel und Verkehr; für Künste, die nicht das Resultat von Poesie sind, und für die Schön- heiten und die relativen Wirklichkeiten der Industrie. E s s i n d d i e H ä n d e , w e l c h e d e n w e l t l i c h e n u n d g e i s t i g e n F o r t - s c h r i t t t r e i b e n u n d m e h r o d e r w e n i g e r m a c h e n !

Wenn konisch-elementare Form, weicher und etwas kleiner als die Elementarhand, Finger dick und glatt, Daumen konisch und groß, dann sind als Charakteristik Egoismus und Geiz vorherrschend. Solche Personen sind wenig geeignet für Handwerk und Industrie und leben sich aus in Verhandlungen, Plänen und Selbstlob.

Personen, deren Hände einen bestimmten reinen Typ repräsentieren, besitzen weniger oder mehr einen Intellekt, der kraftvoller in einer bestimmten Richtung ist. Der Intellekt der gemischten Hand ist anpassungsfähiger und praktischer. Dieser Handtyp ist meist unter den Autodidakten zu finden, die ja bekanntlich immer Bestes leisteten, wie die allermeisten Erfindungen und Entdeckungen bewiesen haben und noch beweisen. Personen mit bestimmtem reinen Handtyp arbeiten wohl intensiver in e i n e r Richtung, aber darum auch eben einseitiger, beengter.

Der Spatelhänder genießt aus praktischen Gründen die raffinierten Speisefeinheiten, in denen die konischen Handeigner mit Leichtsinn schwelgen, und die sich solche Leute mit eckigen Händen aus Geiz nicht leisten, wohl aber zu schätzen wissen, wenn sie nichts kosten.

Der Mensch mit eckigen Händen kauft quantitativ vorsichtig ein, immer nur soviel, wie er ganz sicher verantworten kann; jener mit konischen Händen kauft die doppelte Quantität (und Schein-Qualität), weil er leichtsinniger, großzügiger und auch leichter zu beeinflussen ist. Aber der Spatelhänder kauft das Dreifache, weil er schon zur Zeit des Einkaufes instinktmäßig weiß, wo und wann er das alles mit Nutzen wieder absetzen kann.

Menschen mit konischen Händen sind begeistert für eine Sache; der Spatelhänder nutzt sie, und jene mit eckigen Händen wehren ängstlich ab, weil sie immer Bedenken haben.

Besitzer konischer Hände haben eine Vorliebe für Dinge, die schön oder elegant aussehen, sie kaufen auch eher auf Abzahlung, ohne viel darüber nachzudenken, ob die Qualität dem Kaufpreis entspricht, oder ob sie die Abzahlungsraten einhalten können. Leute mit eckigen Händen machen nicht gern Schulden und sind daher viel schwerer zu einem Kauf zu überreden; es müßte dann schon ein billiger Gelegenheitskauf, dauerhafte und praktische Ware sein, während der Spatelhänder dem Wert entsprechend kauft, was praktisch und haltbar ist, und was er unter Umständen zu gegebener Zeit selbst wieder vorteilhaft weiter abgeben kann. Der Besitzer gemischter Hände würde sich durch Prospekte oder Preislisten eher „auf dem Laufenden" halten, um überall mitreden zu können und bei guter Gelegenheit auch praktische Dinge zu erwerben, dann aber daran herumzumäkeln, damit der Preis noch etwas herabgesetzt wird, da er ja gern wieder bei Weitergabe etwas verdienen will.

Frauen mit knotigen oder idealen Handformen gehen nicht gern aus einem Geschäft heraus, ohne etwas gekauft zu haben, weil sie sich „genieren" und auch durch ihre Sensivität die Gedanken des Geschäftsmannes unangenehm und belastend empfinden. Bei erhaltenen Geschenken werden sie sich oft wundern, wie jemand etwas verschenken kann, was gar nicht zu dem Beschenkten paßt. Das würde ihnen selbst weniger oder gar nicht passieren.

Um die Unterscheidung der Handtypen zu erleichtern, betrachte man Bild 74. Hier ist außen der Spatelfinger, schraffiert der eckige und innen der konische Finger übereinandergelegt sehr leicht zu erkennen.

Es ist leicht zu unterscheiden, was an dem einen Typ fehlt, um den anderen darzustellen.

Gleichzeitig zeigt das Bild die Dreiteilung Geist, Seele, Körper in der Zoneneinteilung an Kopf, Gesicht und Finger, als Sphäre der Entsprechung, was bei der Analysierung des Charakters und Wesens zu berücksichtigen ist.

Beachte:

Die meisten Hände sind gemischte. Reine Typen findet man weniger, außer (in Nordeuropa) in reichlichem Maße die eckige Hand oder doch wenigstens eckige Finger. Auch unter den Frauen, obgleich sehr viele konischen Typ besitzen, der natürlicher ist. Der Spateltyp ist schon seltener zu finden, besonders bei Frauen. Der ideale Typ kommt dann und wann vor. Viel seltener aber ist der knotige Typ. Meist ist die Mischung so, daß Jupiter- und Merkurfinger konisch oder spitz sind und die beiden anderen — Saturn- und Apollofinger — einem und demselben Typ angehören: eckig oder spatel.

„Konisch" und „spitz" ist nicht dasselbe. Man achte auf diese Verschiedenheit!

Jupiter und Merkur spitz, Saturn und Apollo konisch (Analyse: 1., 4., 2., 3. Finger). In guter Hand: Hohes Streben, Liebe zur Wissenschaft um ihrer selbst willen; gesunde Religiosität; edle Auffassung der Kunst. — In schlechter Hand: Krankhafter Stolz; viel unehrliches Planen; Aberglauben; Kunst unangebracht.

Jupiter und Merkur spitz, Saturn und Apollo eckig. In guter Hand: Hohes Streben, sehr gute Beredsamkeit; kluge Vorsicht; wahrhaft in künstlerischen Bemühungen. — In schlechter Hand: Krankhafter Stolz; Meisterschaft in Diplomatie; Menschenhaß; Gebrauch der Kunst zu schlechten Zwecken.

Jupiter und Merkur konisch, Saturn und Apollo eckig. In guter Hand: Vorliebe für wertvolle Romane; Fähigkeiten für Wissenschaft und Erfindung; Vorliebe und Klugheit für Landwirtschaft; starke Neigung zu Kunst, Musik, Literatur. — In schlechter Hand: Eitelkeit, Nichtigkeit; kaufmännische Unehrlichkeit; falsche Ideen über Religion; Praktizieren der Kunst aus Gewinnsucht.

Jupiter und Merkur konisch, Saturn und Apollo spatel. In guter Hand: Vorliebe für Reisebeschreibungen; Spekulationen in entfernten Ländern; dauernde Aktivität, Tätigkeitsdrang; Maler, Literaten usw. für historische Dinge. — In schlechter Hand: Großsprecher, Prahler; Finanz-Napoleon; Irr-Religion; Realismus in Kunst. —

Eine Veränderung der Handform von einem Typ zum andern ist ausgeschlossen. Man mag durch Massage in der Hinsicht erreichen, daß die Finger ein schlankeres Aussehen erhalten — für kurze Zeit. Sie werden aber immer wieder in die frühere Form zurückkommen. Wie man durch starkgeistiges Schaffen an sich selbst, also strenge Selbstzucht und Selbstveredelung im geistigen Sinne, u n d auch körperlich die Kopfform etwas ändern, die Nasenform und Mundform verbessern, den Augenausdruck veredeln kann, so kann man auch jedoch n u r durch diese Art im v e r s t ä r k t e n Maße, nur ein w e n i g auf die Handform einwirken. Der Ausdruck der Hand wird sich verfeinern, die Form aber n i c h t ! — Der Zeitraum, in dem dieses geschehen kann, beträgt nach meiner persönlichen Erfahrung etwa 15 Jahre. N i e aber wird eine „eckige" zur „Spatelhand"; nie eine „eckige" zur „konischen" oder umgekehrt; oder eine gemischte zur philosophischen Hand! Gegenteilige Behauptungen sind falsch und beweisen absolute Unkenntnis in dieser Hinsicht.

Die natürliche Entwicklung geht vom primitiven über den intellektuellen zum spirituellen Typ, nie umgekehrt.

Um für die Praxis einen klareren Begriff von verschiedenen Mischungen zu erhalten, habe ich mehrere Abbildungen beigefügt (Bild 45, 46, 47, 49, 50) mit der Bezeichnung der Mischung. Mit einigem Unterscheidungsvermögen wird jeder sehr bald die Unterschiede auf den Bildern und dann auch in der Wirklichkeit erfassen, wenigstens soweit sie die Handform betreffen. Die Unterschiede im Hinblick auf die verschiedenen oder einzelnen Finger zu erkennen, gelingt danach dann ebenfalls in kurzer Zeit. Selbstverständlich muß man für Beurteilung der Hand- und Fingerform die A u ß e n hand benutzen, weil in der Innenhand die Rundungen und Wölbungen irritieren, wenn die Form nicht gerade s e h r gut markiert ist. Man arbeite dies Buch von Anfang an langsam und sicher durch, dann wird alles verständlich. Ich warne vor Sprüngen. Alles muß gelesen und beobachtet werden, denn ich habe nichts Nebensächliches oder Nutzloses beschrieben. Nur wer mit Geduld langsam vorgeht, wird dieses Buch ganz in sich aufnehmen und verstehen, deshalb auch praktisch anwenden können. Man studiere nur soviel, wie man mit einem Male erfaßt. Zuerst muß unbedingt die Handformenkunde erfaßt und verstanden sein, und erst h i e r n a c h darf die Handlinienkunde folgen, sonst bleibt alles nur Teilwissen, das richtige Auswertung verhindert. Bei den Handabdrücken der Innenhand, die ich hier beifüge, wolle man weniger auf die Form u m r i s s e geben; denn sie werden sehr selten genau sein können. Man erkennt sie nur an Handphotographien oder Handmodellen (Gips usw.).

74

Etwas über Frauenhände.

Es ist selbstverständlich, daß man bei der Beurteilung einer Frauenhand die Verschiedenheit der weiblichen Konstitution von der männlichen in Betracht ziehen muß. Gerade in der Verschiedenheit der Konstitution der beiden Geschlechter liegt ja der Grund der verhältnismäßigen Disposition, in der die Geschlechter zueinander stehen. Ohne diese Differenzierung des männlichen und weiblichen Geistes kann weder eine gute Kombination noch eine richtige Analyse stattfinden. Die physische Energie des Mannes verlangt direkt die passive Einstellung und den instinktiven Takt des Weibes, um ihm die Verwendung und Anwendung zu zeigen. Das Weib hat oft eine Idee, und der Mann setzt sie in die Wirklichkeit um, in die Tat. Die Idee des Mannes ist oft undefiniert, grob und kraftvoll. Geht sie aber durch das Hirn des Weibes, dann wird sie klarer und definierter. Ein Man kann niemals den Takt eines Weibes sich ganz aneignen, auch nicht die instinktive Intelligenz, ohne von seinen feinsten Lebenskräften zu verlieren. Viele Mißerfolge der Männer haben ihre Ursache darin, daß sie nicht genügend den Instinkt des gesunden Weibes befragen. Die Idee des Weibes ist oft wild, unpraktisch und verworren, doch sind die Grundprinzipien der Idee immer genau und richtig. Die größten Männer aller Zeiten hatten immer kluge Frauen. Den besten Beweis für die obige Tatsache finden wir im Orient, wo die Frau gar nicht befragt wird, sondern mehr als Haustier oder „Lieblingstier" betrachtet wird. Das Resultat ist, daß jene Nationen zum großen Teil an Wichtigkeit verlieren und schließlich aussterben werden. Der Mann regiert und bestimmt, das Weib verwaltet und verlangt. Diese Tatsachen sind bei dem Lesen von Frauenhänden in Erwägung zu ziehen. Die Charakteristik der spatelförmigen und der eckigen Frauenhand wird immer etwas weniger markant entwickelt sein als bei dem Manne. Der knotige Typ ist bei Frauen viel seltener zu finden. Das Resultat ist Mangel an physischer Kombination und Kalkulation, die gewöhnlich ihre Beweglichkeit charakterisieren. Der Mann schafft, das Weib entwickelt. Männer machen Gesetze, aber Frauen machen die Moral. Der Mann ist echter als das Weib, aber das Weib ist flacher als der Mann. Ein altes Wort sagt, daß der Mann der Geist des Weibes ist und das Weib die Seele des Mannes. Käme dieses treffliche Wort nur mehr zur Anwendung! Das Weib denkt mit dem Herzen, der Mann mit dem Gehirn. Die Sinne des Mannes sind grob; die Frau ist sensitiv; ihre Empfindung und ihr Instinkt sind zumeist und im allgemeinen richtiger als die vorsichtige Logik des Mannes, weil sie das Sinnen und die Begriffe des Mannes mit Intuition und kraftvoller Analyse aufnehmen. Frauenhände haben viel seltener Fingerknoten, ein Zeichen dafür, daß sie mehr mit Instinkt und Diplomatie, weniger mit Wissen, mehr mit der Schnelligkeit des Kleinhirns (Unterbewußtsein) als mit Schnelligkeit der Tat, mehr mit Phantasie und Vorstellung als mit Schätzung arbeiten. Wenn ein Weib knotige Finger hat, dann ist es weniger eindrucks- und vorstellungsfähig, dafür geschmackvoll, phantastisch und mehr vernünftig. Hat ein Weib einen großen Daumen, dann ist es mehr intelligent (intellektuell) als intuitiv schnell. Hat es einen kleinen Daumen, so ist es schneller in der Ausführung als intelligent in der Tat. Das erste wird mehr Vorliebe für Historie haben, das zweite für Romantik. Mit einem langen Daumen ist ein Weib feinfühlig und vorsichtig in Herzensangelegenheiten, denn Liebe ist ihm ein göttlicher Zustand, nicht Leidenschaft. Es wird daher die Ehe nach Auswahl und Überlegung eingehen (was bei einem Weibe mit kleinem Daumen viel seltener geschieht). Es ist nicht leicht zu gewinnen, auch sonst unnahbar; ein Mittelding gibt es bei ihm nicht, weil es nie herabsteigt zur Koketterie oder Eifersucht. Eine Frau mit kleinem Daumen ist mehr kapriziös, kokett, leicht geneigt zu Eifersucht, vielleicht auch mehr faszinierend und verführerisch. Bei ihr ist Liebe Leidenschaft, ein kraftvolles und heißes Gefühl. Sie verlangt ungeteilte Heiterkeit und Freude und eine sentimentale, romantische Form von Anbetung und von der Liebe. Die elementare Hand ist nie (oder fast nie) unter Frauenhänden zu finden. Ihre natürliche Intelligenz, die Sorge der Mutterschaft und die komplizierte physische Konstitution des Weibes erfordern einen höheren Instinkt, eine größere intuitive Intelligenz, als für den weniger komplizierten männlichen Körperbau erforderlich ist. Die Folge davon ist, daß, wenn in einer Gegend bei den Männern der elementare Handtyp vorherrscht, die Frauen die Oberhand haben und alle Angelegenheiten ihrer Männer und jene anderer dirigieren. Jene Frauen, die ein zielloses Schmetterlingsleben der Freude, Liebe und Verschwendung leben, haben zumeist kleinere, konische Hände, die mehr weich und dick sind; Frauen mit Spatelfingern und kleinem Daumen sind wahre Freunde, herzlich und etwas impulsiv, weniger reserviert und tätig. Sie lieben Bewegung und Sport, Tiere und Kampfveranstaltungen. Ihre Nadelarbeit ist eher brauchbar und vollständig als künstlerisch und ausdrucksvoll. Sie arrangieren gern Spiele für die eigenen und auch für fremde Kinder. Bei eckigen Frauenhänden haben wir Pünktlichkeit, Ordnung bis zur Kleinlichkeit und Pedanterie und gute Zusammenstellungen, Verordnungen im Haushalte, wenn der Daumen k l e i n ist. Ist der Daumen an derselben Hand groß, finden wir den „Haustyrannen", der ewig zu nörgeln weiß, ungeduldig wird, wenn kontrolliert, und ein Verschwender der eigenen Kräfte ist. Frauen mit eckigen Händen erfordern Höflichkeit, Ordnung und „Regulierungen" in Herzensangelegenheiten. Sie lieben Männer von Bildung, doch dürfen diese nicht exzentrisch sein, geistvoll, aber nicht weitschweifig, ruhig, selbstbewußt, aber unberührbar von Eifersucht und Unzuverlässigkeit. Sie sind sehr vorsichtig, extra vorsichtig in der Beobachtung „gut bürgerlicher" Sitten und Gebräuche und fliehen das Außergewöhnliche oder was mehr ist — das Vulgäre.

Eine kleine rosige, elastische, zarte Hand, dünn, aber nicht knochig, mit sehr fein entwickelten Knoten, läßt eine redegewandte, sprühende Weiblichkeit erkennen. Um sie zu gewinnen, muß man heiter, klug, belustigend und voll plötzlicher Einfälle sein. In der „grande passion" muß man schnell und sprühend sein, weniger sentimental oder romantisch als bei den konischen Fingern. Bei diesen wieder muß der Mann innig, zurückhaltend, ergeben, selbstbewußt, erklärend, entschuldigend und gerecht sein gegen alle Dinge. Sie sind indolent, phantastisch und meist sinnlich. Mit schmalen, zarten spitzen Fingern, einem kleinen Daumen und schmaler Handfläche haben wir die Frau vor uns, die höchste Romantik und Idealismus in weltlichen Dingen liebt. In bezug auf Liebesleben, Freude ist sie mehr für eine Sache des Herzens und der Seele als für körperliches Gefühl und Empfinden. Bei diesem Typ sind Indolenz und Innigkeit kombiniert. Konventionen sind ihr verhaßt, ebenso alle realen Seiten des Lebens. Sie neigt mehr zur Pietät und auch etwas zu Aberglauben als zu wirklicher Ergebenheit. „Genius" steckt in ihr weit mehr als Alltagsverstand, und von der Höhe ihres idealen Standpunktes schaut sie herab auf alles Schöne in vergeistigenden Gedanken und erschaut daher mehr und schöner als andere Handtypen.

Die Darlegungen dieses Kapitels und die Tatsache, daß Charakter und Denkart von Mann und Weib grundsätzlich von Natur aus verschieden sind, lassen klar erkennen, daß es keine gemeinsame Psychologie für beide Geschlechter geben kann, wenn sie ernsthaft und von Wert sein soll. Die Psychologie des Weibes ist eine andere und muß daher auch gesondert erkannt und gewertet werden. Dementsprechend muß auch eine Handanalyse von Frauenhänden anders erarbeitet werden als eine solche von Männerhänden. Das ist zu beachten.

Chiromimik oder die Sprache der Hand.

Oft hört man das Wort Chiromimik, gesprochen von Personen, die sicher gar nicht wissen, was es bedeutet; auch wenn sich mancher „Chirologe" nennt. Chiromimik ist das Wissen von der Bewegungssprache der Hand, also wie man die Hand im ganzen, wie man die einzelnen Finger hält, bewegt, oder wie man mit ihnen „spricht", um der Sprache weiteren Ausdruck zu verschaffen, oder w i e man mit den Fingern spricht, wenn man sich ohne Worte verständlich machen will, wie es bei der Zeichensprache und bei Stummen geschieht; diese Bewegungsarten werden immer ganz bestimmte Schlüsse auf Charakter und Wesen des Betreffenden zulassen. Letztes in Verbindung mit erstem: d a s ist Chiromimik. Literatur hierüber gibt es sehr wenig. Man findet Stücke dieser Wissenschaft hier und dort, aber sehr selten etwas Brauchbares. Vor Jahren wurde mir aus zuverlässiger Quelle berichtet, daß ein Richter in England ein Meister dieses Wissens sei und Angeschuldigte auf Grund dieses Systems ergründete und überführte. Ohne Zweifel ist dieses Wissen wertvoll, und es wäre wünschenswert, wenn man mehr darüber erfahren könnte. Wenn jemand sehr viel Zeit und eine sehr gute Beobachtungsgabe hat, so kann er schon manches, vielleicht auch viel von dieser Lehre gewinnen. Gelegenheit gibt es im täglichen Leben genug zu solchen Studien. Leider scheint es aber wenig Persönlichkeiten mit obigen Fähigkeiten und der hierzu sehr erforderlichen Ausdauer zu geben. Einiges über die „Sprache der Hand" in folgendem:

Beweglichkeit des Daumens. Es ist auffallend, daß mancher Daumen sich von den Fingern um 90° entfernen kann, andere wieder um 30° oder noch weniger. Je weiter der Daumen sich abwenden kann (ohne Anstrengung), desto mehr ist vorhanden: Unabhängigkeitsliebe und freiere Betätigung des eigenen Willens, leichte Erledigung eigener Angelegenheiten und Hilfe bei denen anderer. — Personen, die ihren Daumen nicht oder schwer über etwa 45° abwenden können, zeigen Mangel an freier Betätigung des eigenen Willens und sind deshalb mehr Sklaven ihrer Umgebung. (Selbstverständlich kommt das nicht für Gichthände in Betracht!)

Verstecken des Daumens unter den anderen Fingern: Verstecken oder Ausschalten des Verstandes finden wir bei kleinen Kindern, in denen der Intellekt noch schläft, unentwickelt ist; bei Idioten oft, weil der Intellekt ausgeschaltet ist; bei teilweiser Paralyse und veraltetem Rheuma, weshalb man also auf krankhafte Zustände achten muß. Auch beim Sterbenden finden wir oft, daß er den Daumen verbirgt. (Er zieht sich in sich zurück.) Der Verstand schwindet! — Bei einem gesunden Menschen darf es nicht sein, oder es ist immer ein Verstecken der Gedanken — des Verstandes — vorhanden; aber auch Feigheit. Der Betreffende wird nur mangelhaft seine Angelegenheiten dirigieren können.

Ein dauernd weit abstehender Daumen in steifer Haltung zeugt von einer Person, die ihr Ich zu sehr betont und aus dem Grunde dreist, frech, unverfroren ist, unter Umständen gewalttätig und brutal sein kann (Bild 63 b).

Lässig und schlaff herunterhängende Hände beweisen: Lässigkeit, Schlendrian, augenblickliche Schlaffheit des Geistes und gewisse Willenslosigkeit. — Geschlossene Hände zeugen von Verschlossenheit des Gedankenlebens; auch von großer Vorsicht, Wachsamkeit. Letztes mehr, wenn der Daumen abseits liegt.

Das Verbergen der Hände auf dem Rücken (bekannte Haltung Napoleons) oder unter dem Rock, zeugt davon, daß der Betreffende seine derzeitigen Gedanken vor anderen zu verbergen sucht.

Spricht jemand mit erhobenen Händen, so will er mehr Eindruck erreichen. Manche versuchen, durch den Schlag mit der Faust auf den Tisch noch mehr zu erwirken.

Je nachdem, wie lose und weit das Ellenbogengelenk sich vom Körper entfernt (bis zum geraden Strecken), soviel Mut oder Ängstlichkeit ist bei dem Sprecher in der Zeit vorhanden.

Ebenso ist es bei dem Händedruck! Je freier und loser die Hand ausgestreckt wird, desto ehrlicher die Meinung. Nur zwei oder drei Finger geben, das deutet auf Versplecktheiten, Unaufrichtigkeiten, evtl. Hinterlist.

Auch die Handhaltung spricht, die gezeigt wird, wenn jemand etwas gibt oder entgegennimmt. Dies sowohl bei dem Gebenden wie auch bei dem Nehmenden.

Man achte auf die Haltung und Lage der Finger, wenn die Hand in Ruhe ist, d. h. wenn sie auf einem Gegenstande flach aufliegt. Sind hierbei der Daumen und der Zeigefinger geschlossen, ebenso die drei anderen Finger, so deutet dies auf Unabhängigkeit im Denken.

Liegen Merkur- und Apollofinger für sich zusammen, so zeugt das von Unabhängigkeit im Tun.

Unabhängigkeit und Eigenart des Denkens und des Handelns, sowie außerhalb dieses noch Betrachtungen für dritte Dinge im besonderen, solches zeigt die Haltung der Hand auf Bild 63 b.

Das Abspreizen nur des Merkurfingers allein, wie man es öfter beobachten kann, bedeutet: momentane Bereitschaft der Gedanken, gemischt mit ein wenig Verstellung. (Der Betreffende ist in solchen Augenblicken nicht ganz natürlich in seinem Wesen oder Sichgeben.)

Das Nichtbieten oder -geben der Hand bei einem Gruße hat verschiedene Gründe. Es kann sein, daß der Betreffende nicht mit der Aura des anderen in Berührung kommen will, um anderer Menschen Gedanken aufzunehmen (z. B. Tagore); oder es kann Reserve sein, welche den Betreffenden dazu veranlaßt. Jedenfalls bedeutet es nicht Unhöflichkeit. Das können nur jene behaupten, welche für die feineren Schwingungen im Kosmos keinen Sinn und deshalb auch kein Verständnis dafür haben.

Am Druck und der Festigkeit der Hand erkennt man die Verläß-
lichkeit des Menschen. Ein schlaffer Händedruck, der eher ein Vorbei-
wischen ist, als daß er den Namen Händedruck verdient, zeugt von
laschen, gleichgültigen, oft auch von haltlosen Personen; auf jeden
Fall von unzuverlässigen.

Der Händedruck bester Bedeutung ist: ein sanftes, doch festes Zu-
fassen, leiser, fester Druck für einen Moment und ein sanftes Lösen. —
Er schließt alles Gute in sich, besonders wenn sich beide Parteien dabei
offen und gerade in die Augen schauen.

Mit einiger Beobachtung und Einfühlung kann man die Nuancierungen
dieser Sprache sehr bald verstehen lernen.

Die Haut und die Hautfarbe.

Töne und Farben sind Schwingungen; folglich
sind Farben Musik und Musik Farben. Somit sind
Stimmungen auch Farben und aus der Farbe die
Stimmungen erkennbar!

Die Haut gehört in der Beurteilung zu den Nebenmerkmalen und
gibt bei sehr genauer Beobachtung Aufschluß über das augenblickliche
Befinden und das Temperament.

Feine, zarte und glatte Haut ist immer ein Zeichen für große
Empfänglichkeit durch seelische Einflüsse, große Empfindsamkeit, Zart-
gefühl und: lange Jugendlichkeit, körperlich wie auch im Temperament.
Ist die Haut von Natur aus spröde und grob, so ist wenig Fein-
empfinden, und wenn sie derbe und stark ist: mehr oder weniger
„Dickfelligkeit" vorhanden.

Die gesunde Haut hat ein helles Rosa zur Farbe mit einem schwachen
Ton ins Hellbraune (Bild 12, 13).

S t a r k e s   R o s a bedeutet: Sanguinisch, hoffnungsvoll und freu-
diges Wesen.

R o t : Robust in Gesundheit und Gemüt; leidenschaftlich, heftig,
evtl. brutal, wenn sehr dunkel. (Vollblütige Menschen sind immer
kraftvoll und heftig.)

G e l b l i c h e   F ä r b u n g ist ein Zeichen von Gallen- oder Leberstörung. Solche Menschen sind melancholisch und auch schwermütig,
neidisch, gereizter Stimmung. Die Seelenschwingung ist dann stark
gehemmt, und wenn die Haut sehr starkes oder dunkleres G e l b
zeigt, durch Gallenstörung, dann kommen gereiztes Wesen in verstärktem Maße, Heftigkeit und Zank (galliges Wesen) zum Ausdruck.

B l ä u l i c h e   F ä r b u n g ist ein Mangel an guter Blutzirkulation.

G r ü n l i c h e s   W e i ß : Böses Temperament und rachsüchtig. Diese
Farbe findet man meist nur bei stark brünetten oder schwarzhaarigen
Personen.

Natürliches Blaß besagt: Weiches, weibliches Wesen; geistiges und körperliches Phlegma.

Wenn die Innenhandflächen blaß oder weiß sind, so kommen Egoismus und unsympathisches Wesen in Betracht.

Ist der Handrücken behaart, so ist ein zu kraftvolles Temperament vorhanden und infolgedessen Unbeständigkeit in den Gefühlen. (Hierzu muß man auch die Innenhand und den Daumen beurteilen, um zu ersehen, wie weit Selbstzucht geübt werden kann.)

Wenig Haare auf männlichem Handrücken: Klug, vorsichtig, Liebe für Luxus.

Haare an allen Fingergliedern: Reizbares, cholerisches Temperament.

Haare an den dritten (unteren) Fingergliedern: Warmherzigkeit.

Haarige Frauenhand bedeutet allemal Grausamkeit; vergleiche Daumen.

Starke Behaarung ist immer ein Zeichen für fremdrassigen Einschlag.

Die Fingernägel.

Mannigfaltigkeit ist das Wesen der Natur. Die Nägel sind ebenso wie Haare, Knochen, Blut, Fleisch aus demselben Urstoff entstanden und haben ihre Bedeutung.

Aus den Fingernägeln läßt sich in bezug auf Charakteristik wissenschaftlich wenig sagen. Hauptsächlich bieten die Nägel Krankheitsmerkmale. Folgendes dürfte aber als sichere Richtschnur dienen:

Kurze Nägel sind immer ein Zeichen dafür, daß die betreffenden Persönlichkeiten ein gereiztes, nörgelndes, kritisierendes, skeptisches und analysierendes, aber auch oft zänkisches Wesen haben. Sie sind schnell erregbar und rasch im Temperament, haben aber auch ein schnelles Begriffsvermögen. — Diese Eigenschaften haben alle ihre physiologischen Gründe, die leicht zu erkennen sind, wenn man alles das in Betracht zieht, was über Krankheitsdiagnosen aus den Nägeln gesagt ist. „Kurze" Nägel sind natürlich nicht kurzgeschnittene, sondern kurzgewachsene, d. h. solche Nägel, deren angewachsene Fläche breiter als lang ist.

Lange Nägel sind solche, deren angewachsene Fläche länger als breit ist. Langnagelige Personen sind immer umgänglicher, weniger kritisch, aber eindrucksfähiger, ruhiger in den Gedankengängen, resignierter und idealer.

Harte Nägel sind ein Zeichen dafür, daß auch die Knochen sehr stabil sind, was zu einer guten Körperbeschaffenheit und zum Erfolge gehört. Materielle Denkart.

Weiche oder dünne Nägel besagen, daß die Knochen ebenfalls nicht stark sind und deswegen auch die Körperbeschaffenheit eine schwächere ist. Keine Kampfnaturen.

Klauenartig gebogene Nägel sind ein Zeichen von Habsucht und Geiz, Unduldsamkeit, Intoleranz.

Weiteres über Charakteristik möchte ich hier nicht bringen, um nicht den Anfänger in dieser Wissenschaft zu verwirren. Es ist durchaus nicht so leicht, den charakteristischen Teil von der Krankheitsdiagnostik zu trennen; denn eines ist vom andern abhängig. Beide gehen ineinander über. Durch Übung und Beobachtung kommt jeder zu dieser Erkenntnis und wird dann auch das Richtige finden. Es ist ganz ohne Zweifel, daß ein blutarmer Mensch wenig Kraft zur Ausführung von Plänen und Unternehmen hat, anderseits auch eine gewisse Zurückhaltung und Schlaffheit zum Ausdruck bringt. Menschen mit Gallenleiden werden immer eine mehr oder weniger gereizte Stimmung und Unzufriedenheit zeigen. Das sind ganz natürliche Folgeerscheinungen.

Die Konsistenz der Hand.

Um die Konsistenz (Gehalt, Festigkeit) der Hand zu erkennen, preßt man die Finger in die Innenfläche des Handtellers und fühlt mit dem Daumen auf den Handrücken. Man wird dann finden: ob die Hand fest, hart, dünn, weich, schwammig, klamm oder lose ist.

Die weiche Hand besagt Neigung zu künstlerischen Dingen, Eindrucksfähigkeit, Naschhaftigkeit und Abneigung gegen schwere Arbeit, Sinnlichkeit.

Ist sie schwammig, speziell wenn sie weiß und ein großer Venusberg vorhanden ist, besagt dies: Faulheit, Liebe zu Genuß und Schwelgerei.

Bei einer festen Hand sind die Muskeln auch fest, aber die Haut ist weich. Dies zeigt Energie und Liebe zur Beweglichkeit, Intelligenz; eine Person, die Kinder- und Tierliebhaber ist. In Summa: Meist gutherzige Leute, speziell wenn die Farbe der Haut rot (nicht dunkel) oder fleischfarbig ist; nicht weiß.

Die harte Hand mit gutem Venusberg und guter Herzlinie zeigt große Vorliebe für Außensport und Außenarbeit, wenn auch das dritte Fingerglied des Saturn-(Mittel-)Fingers lang ist. Die Besitzer haben meist philosophischen Sinn, sind gerade und offen in Rede und Wesen.

Ist die Hand sehr hart und sind die Finger sehr krumm nach der Innenseite gebogen (einwärts), so besagt dies: Mangel an Intellekt, Brutalität, Aberglaube, Geiz.

Sind die Hände außen sehr zart und l i n i e n r e i c h : Feinfühligkeit und Wohlwollen.

Innen sehr faltenreich, so muß auch hier die Konsistenz in Betracht gezogen werden.

In einer w e i c h e n Hand besagt dies: Eindrucksfähigkeit.

In einer h a r t e n jedoch: Reizbarkeit, Streitlust. (Beachte Daumen und Nägel!)

Launenhaft und hochnervös: falls dazu kurze und zerbissene Nägel.

Wenn die Hände sich gut und weit öffnen, die Finger sich separieren: Herzlichkeit, Generosität und Natürlichkeit im Wesen.

Wenn die Finger sich nach innen biegen: Unnatürlichkeit im Wesen und Geiz.

Rückbiegen der Fingerspitzen: Große Feinfühligkeit und tiefes Empfinden, Neugierde (oder Wissensdrang).

Allgemeine Regeln.

K l e i n e   H ä n d e : Neigung für große Pläne und Ideen, für alle großen Dinge.

K l e i n ,   b r e i t   u n d   k n o t i g e   F i n g e r : Routinierte, schlaue polemisierende Menschen.

M i t t e l m ä ß i g e   H ä n d e : Anpassung und Sinn für Kalkulation, Kombination und das Einzelne in den Dingen.

G r o ß e   H ä n d e : Vorliebe und Neigung für kleinliche und feine Arbeit, Genauigkeit (Feinmechanik, Juwelierkunst, Uhrmacher usw.).

G r a d   d e r   H ä r t e : Grad der Charakterfestigkeit und physischen Widerstandskraft.

K r u m m e   H ä n d e   u n d   F i n g e r (gedreht, entstellt von Natur aus): Ebensolche Charaktere.

D ü n n   u n d   h o h l , ledern und flach: Sehr beschränkter Intellekt, schwaches Denken, Mangel an Gemüts- und Charaktertiefe, Energie und moralischer Kraft.

K u r v e n a r t i g   z u r ü c k g e b o g e n e   H ä n d e   u n d   F i n g e r : Anpassend und angenehm, sympathisch und elastisch in Umgang und Gesellschaft, doch meist neugierig und extravagant im Wesen.

H o h l e   H ä n d e (Gruben): Tiefe Höhlungen bedeuten ungünstige Verhältnisse (durch äußere Einflüsse, welchen man nicht aus dem Wege gehen kann), Unglück im guten Sinne, wie Hindernisse, Misere, Verlust an materiellen Werten, Gefahr für Gelingen, Erfolglosigkeit.

B e a c h t e   L a g e : Unter Lebenslinie: Mißerfolge in häuslichen Angelegenheiten. Unter Saturn-(Schicksals-)Linie und Marsfeld: Mißerfolge durch derzeitige Verhältnisse und Umstände (äußere stärkere — astrale — Einflüsse).

B e a c h t e : a) Im Alter werden Hände härter und fester, so auch das Gemüt (Bild 14, 100jährige Greisenhand). Man wird ruhiger, ernster und philosophischer, mehr logisch, weniger romantisch. b) Während Krankheit und langer Ruhe können Hände für die Zeit weicher werden. Solche Zeit macht Menschen weicher, eindrucksfähiger und nervöser, auch phantastisch und Suggestionen zugänglicher.

D i e „G u t e H a n d" : ist fest, ohne hart zu sein, elastisch, ohne schwammig und weich zu sein.

T r e u e : Besitzer weicher Hände können zärtlicher, inniger und diplomatischer (d. h. heuchlerischer) sein als treu und fest in der Liebe. Harte Hände: Können fester und treu sein in der Liebe und weniger zärtlich in Ausdruck und Tat, da ihre Natur ernster, gerader, fester und aufrichtiger ist.

D u r c h s i c h t i g e (transparente) Hände und glatt im Ausdruck: Indiskretion, Klatscherei, oft auch Falschheit.

(Treue kann man nur zu sich selbst haben, d. h. e c h t sein. Daher Motive für Treue oder Untreue ergründen!)

Der Daumen (Bild 15, 16, 17 d).

> Die Individualität ist der göttliche Kern der inneren Persönlichkeit. Das Äußere ist der Ausdruck des Innern. Art und Ausdruck des „Ich" haben wir im Daumen.

Der Daumen ist als Ausdruck und Darstellung der betreffenden Persönlichkeit zu betrachten; als Ausdruck des „Ich-Selbst" — alles andere der Hand als das Material der Begleitumstände der Verkörperung und somit des Schicksals. Das erste (Nagel-)Glied zeigt das Maß und die Kraft des Willens an; das zweite Verstand, das dritte — das zugleich den Venusberg darstellt — das Maß des Trieblebens im Menschen. Wir ersehen daraus, daß das dritte Glied im Verhältnis zu den anderen beiden reichlich bemessen ist. Wir wissen aber auch, daß das Triebleben im Menschen eine recht große Rolle spielt und sehr oft, sogar zu oft, die festen Entschlüsse zum Wanken bringt. Beispiele hierfür anzuführen erübrigt sich, da solche von jedermann täglich und stündlich beobachtet werden können, wenn ein wenig Sinn dafür vorhanden ist. Man beobachtet Menschen mit wenig oder schwachem Willen und mehr Vernunft und Trieb (Impuls) (Bild 15/6); solche mit nur Trieb (Impuls, Sinnlichkeit). Anderseits wieder solche, bei denen nur verstandesmäßige Vernunft vorherrscht, ohne genügenden Willen, diese durchzusetzen. Noch andere Personen, bei denen ein harmonischer Ausgleich besteht zwischen Wille und Vernunft (Bild 15/1). Endlich solche, wo der Wille in brutaler Form in Erscheinung tritt, ohne Vernunft und Logik (Bild 15/3, 5). Diese Formationen ergeben in ihrer mannigfaltigen Verteilung schon die vielen Verschiedenheiten der Persönlichkeiten und deren Charakteranlage. Dazu kommt das Beugegelenk zwischen dem ersten und zweiten Daumenglied mit mehr oder weniger ausgeprägten „Knoten der Unabhängigkeit" (Bild 16/6). Knoten im zweiten Daumengelenk: Sinn für Symmetrie, Musik (s. S. 78, 2. und 3. Absatz).

Der Daumenausdruck ist bei jeder Betrachtung und Beurteilung in Betracht zu ziehen; denn der Wille des Menschen vermag sehr viel — mehr noch, wenn er richtig entwickelt ist. Ein Mensch mit starkem und großem Willen kann Dinge anders gestalten und ausführen, also auch besser zum Erfolge führen, als jemand mit schwachem oder unentwickeltem Willen. Ebenso können schlechte Eigenschaften zurücktreten, wenn der starke Wille zum „Nichtaufkommenlassen" vorhanden ist, mit der nötigen Zähigkeit und von guter Vernunft geleitet wird. — Verliert jemand den Daumen, so wird er auch an Willenskraft verlieren; diese Tatsache ist von altersher bekannt.

S t e i f e r D a u m e n : Starrer, eigenwilliger Mensch. (Der Grad der Steifheit läßt das Maß des Eigensinnes im guten wie im bösen Sinne erkennen.) (Bild 18.)

E i n w ä r t s g e b o g e n e r D a u m e n : Extreme Vorsicht, Argwohn, Reserve; hiermit ist gleichzeitig ein Grund für Feigheit gelegt. (Bild 67 a.)

A u s w ä r t s g e b o g e n e r D a u m e n : Anpassungsfähigkeit, je nach Grad, bis zur Waschlappigkeit, d. h. bis zur Aufgabe der eigenen Wesensart, der Persönlichkeit; großzügig. (Bild 15/8, 38 unten.)

A u s w ä r t s g e b o g e n e D a u m e n s p i t z e : Etwas Anpassung, aber zähes Wollen und eine Anlage, sich in Dinge hineinzudenken, falls der Daumen spitz ist. (Bild 44 b.)

D a u m e n k u r z u n d d i c k : Schnelle Erregbarkeit, egoistisch und sinnlich. (Bild 44 b.)

B r e i t e r , s t a r k e r D a u m e n : Starker Eigensinn, Zähigkeit im Wollen, evtl. auch grausame Neigungen. (Bild 16/2, 3.)

L a n g e r , s t a r k e r D a u m e n : Selbstbewußtsein, zielbewußt und energisch. Stabiler Charakter. (Bild 44 a.)

S e h r k l e i n e r D a u m e n : Mangel an jedem Willen und Selbstbeherrschung, unsicher und zaghaft. (Bild 26—29, 68 d.)

K e u l e n d a u m e n , erstes Glied dick, breit keulig (ähnlich wie beim Frosch) oder auch gleichmäßig stark, aber sehr dick und breit (kleine Banane): Brutal, herrschsüchtig, sehr leicht erregbar, impulsiv, zänkisch, jähzornig, wütend bis zur Tobsucht (Bild 15/5). „Männer, die man nicht heiraten soll!" Bei Frauen kommt dieser Typ sehr selten vor; wenn doch, dann Vorsicht! (Bild 16/1 und Bild 46!).

Zweites Daumenglied schmaler als das erste (wespen-artig): Eigensinn, evtl. selbst unter Außerachtlassung der besseren Einsicht. Auch Verstellungskunst (Diplomatie). (Bild 16/6, 68 A.)

Erstes und zweites Glied gleichlang: Harmonischer Ausgleich; zuverlässig, verträglich. (Bild 15/1, 68 a.)

Erstes Glied kurz, zweites lang: Überlegung und Ver-nunft, aber nicht die Kraft zur Ausführung (da das dritte Glied — Venus-Triebe stark entwickelt und den geringen Willen noch hemmt). Läßt sich leiten. Anlehnung. (Bild 15/6, 67 a, 72 b.)

Erstes Glied lang, zweites kurz: Rechthaberisch, un-überlegt, unvernünftig, zielstrebig. Will um jeden Preis Erfolg ge-winnen. (Bild 15/7 u. 50 a.)

Ein schmaler, fester und gerader Daumen hat die Eigenschaft, Temperament durch den Willen zügeln zu können. (Bild 66 c.)

Ein stark ausgebildetes erstes Daumengelenk be-deutet: Intelligenz und starke Unabhängigkeitsliebe sowie große Zähigkeit in der Ausführung von Plänen. Hartköpfig, unberechenbar, rechthaberisch. (Bild 15/3, 7, 54 b.)

Kleiner Daumen bei verschiedenen Handtypen.

Auf Bild 17 d sind die Längenmaße für den Daumen gezeigt. Die normale Länge reicht bis zur Hälfte des unteren Gliedes des Zeige-fingers, wie der Pfeil andeutet. Es gibt kürzere und auch längere Daumen, je nachdem, welches Maß von Willen und Durchsetzungskraft veranlagt ist.

Elementarhand: Schwäche der ohnehin kleinen intellektuellen Kraft. Deshalb werden diese Naturen nur durch ihre tierischen Instinkte beherrscht. Daher wenig Selbstbeherrschung.

Spatelhand: Unzuverlässig. Diese Personen werden viel anfangen und nichts zu Ende führen.

Eckige Hand: Vorliebe für Ordnung, Formalitäten, Zeremonien und Genauigkeit, doch fehlt die Kraft zur Durchführung dieser Dinge.

Konische Hand: Verstärkte Impulsivität. Diese Personen sind sehr verliebt in ihre Arbeit und verlieren dadurch an praktischer Lebensbetätigung und Verstehen. (Ein großer Daumen würde hier mehr praktischen Sinn hineinbringen und extravagante Ideen abschwächen.)

Philosophische Hand: Abschwächung der Verstandeskräfte und Logik.

Eine Frau mit großem Daumen wird in der Liebe auch viel Verstand zeigen und vorsichtig sein; mit kleinem Daumen wird sie impulsiv und leichter erringbar sein. Ist der Daumen sehr biegsam, so wird auch sie selbst sich biegsam und anschmiegend zeigen, aber auch beeinflußbar sein. Ist der Daumen klein, das erste Daumenglied kurz und biegsam, so wird solche Frau jedem starken Ansturm unterliegen und nicht die Kraft zum Widerstand aufbringen, weil sie diese nicht gar hat. (Aus dem Grunde wird von den Eltern grundverkehrt verfahren, wenn die „besiegte und gefallene" Tochter dazu noch getadelt wird.) Die Liebe einer Frau mit geradem, festem und langem Daumen wird, wenn sie sehr tief ist, zu einer großen Leidenschaft; diese Frau wird treu sein aus tiefer Liebe u n d Charakter.

Fingerregeln (Bild 17),
Fingerlänge.

J u p i t e r - (Zeige-)Finger so lang wie Saturn-(Mittel-)Finger: Überwiegen des herrschenden Prinzips, Neigung zum Dominieren.

A p o l l o - (Ring-)Finger so lang wie Saturnfinger: Überwiegen des Prinzips, alles zu materiellen Zwecken auszunutzen.

A p o l l o f i n g e r so lang wie Jupiterfinger: Ideales und Materielles gleich stark.

M e r k u r - (kleiner) Finger fast so lang wie Apollofinger: Große Beredsamkeit und Routine, Übersicht, große geistige Anpassung und schnelles Begreifen.

K n o t i g e F i n g e r : Starke Logik und Sinn für Ordnung (Bild 17 a und 71 b).

do., erstes Glied konisch: Praktischer Sinn für Kunst.

do., erstes Glied eckig: Neigung zur Genauigkeit bis zum Fanatismus.

do., erstes Glied spatelförmig: Berechnend, aktiv energisch (stets mehr oder weniger berechnend).

G l a t t e F i n g e r : Weniger Ordnung und wenig Gedankentiefe (Bild 17 c und 68 b.)

do., erstes Glied konisch: Idealität, Begeisterung, Sinn für Schönheit.

do., erstes Glied eckig: Schnelle Ausführung der Gedanken; in Literatur u. dgl.

do., erstes Glied spatelförmig: Neigung für Nützliches und Praktisches aus materiellen Gründen; Sinnlichkeit. Stets mehr oder weniger lasch und sich gehen lassen!

H a r t e F i n g e r : Ökonomisch und zähe Natur.

W e i c h e F i n g e r : Impulsiv, wechselnde Stimmungen, empfindliche, sinnliche Naturen. (Bild 50 B, 70 c, 72 B).

Ballen an der Innenseite der Fingerspitzen: Feinfühligkeit des physischen Körpers und Empfindungsfähigkeit des seelischen, feinstofflichen Körpers. Diese Ballen nennt man auch die Augen der Blinden, weil Blinde mit diesen feinnervigsten Stellen der Finger die Blindenschrift fühlend lesen und Unbekanntes abtastend zu erkennen versuchen. Sehr feinnervige Personen fühlen mit diesem zarten Ballen durch leichtes Abtasten Qualitäten von Stoffen, Papieren, die Figuren auf Spielkarten und ähnliches heraus und können solche ungesehen genau bestimmen. Diese feinen Ballen der Fingerspitzen sind an bestimmte Handtypen nicht gebunden. (Bild 72 A u. B).

Kombinationen.

Jupiterfinger:

Spitz: Neigung zu Schönheiten in Natur, Kunst, Religion.

Zu lang: Übergroßer Stolz und Hochmut, Anmaßung, befehlende Art.

Eckig: Forschen nach Wahrheit in Natur und Dingen.

Spatel (selten): Extreme Neigungen zu Mystik, Religion, Phantasie und unter Umständen Ausnutzen des erlangten Wissens zu materiellen Zwecken.

Saturnfinger:

Spitz (selten): Nicht leicht melancholisch; frivol, oft hartherzig.

Breit und schwer: Melancholie, schwermütig, tiefsinnig.

Eckig: Melancholisch, praktisch, resigniert.

Apollofinger:

Spitz oder konisch: Künstlerisch, mehr seelischer Art; notwendig für Sänger.

Eckig: Schaffende Kunst, auch Theorie (Unterricht).

Spatelform: Praktische, materielle Kunst, Plastik, Rednertalent, Kraft für Sensation, Schauspieler, Dramatiker.

Merkurfinger:

Spitz: Neigung zu Mystik und Okkultismus.

Eckig: Ergründung der Ursachen und Gründe, Wissenschaft, Handel, Organisationsgabe.

Spatelform: Studien betr. des Wechsels der Dinge, besonders Handel, Gewerbe, Spekulation.

So lang wie Apollofinger: Kraft und Einfluß in Sprache und Unterhaltung, philosophischer Sinn, große Gaben.

Beachte: Aufschluß betr. dieser Neigungen und Anlagen gibt die Innenhand.

Bedeutung der Fingergliedlängen.

Jupiterfinger:

Erstes Fingerglied am längsten an:

Spatelhand: Neigung zu Rastlosigkeit, Vorliebe für Mystik.

Eckiger Hand: Interesse an sozialen Dingen, soweit Formalitäten und Zeremonien in Betracht kommen.

Konischer Hand: Nachdenklichkeit in Religion und spirituellen Dingen.

Zweites Fingerglied am längsten an:

Spatelhand: Großer Ehrgeiz und Kraft, ihn zu betätigen.

Eckiger Hand: Ehrgeiz, aber nicht die nötige Verwirklichungskraft, weil Fortschritt gehindert wird durch übermäßige Ordnung, Genauigkeit, Kleinlichkeit.

Konischer Hand: Ehrgeiz, jedoch macht er sich mehr geltend in Verlangen und Wünschen nach Verwirklichung der Ideale.

Drittes Fingerglied am längsten an:

Spatelhand oder auch eckiger Hand: Ehrgeiz und Verlangen nach Herrschen über andere, Scheinehre, Hängen am Materiellen, Irdischen.

Konischer oder idealer Hand: Möchte gern die durch Intuition empfangenen Ideen und Gedanken im täglichen Dasein verwirklichen. Neigung zu Bequemlichkeit und Genuß.

Saturnfinger:

Erstes Fingerglied am längsten an:

Spatelhand: Neigung zu Grübelei, Schwermut. Immer nur das Traurige und Schmerzvolle sehen wollen und damit die Umgebung vergiften. Neigung zu Lebensüberdruß evtl. Selbstmord.

Eckiger Hand: Das Denken ist mehr harmonisch mit dem Realen, jedoch nüchtern, ernst und fest.

Konischer oder idealer Hand (selten): Oberflächlichkeit, Schein und Frivolität.

Zweites Fingerglied am längsten an:

Spatelhand: Ausnutzen der Talente und Fähigkeiten für mechanische Tätigkeit, Sport und Außenarbeit.

Eckiger Hand: Spekulatives und abstraktes Sinnen in bezug auf Wissenschaft oder Mechanik.

Konischer oder idealer Hand: Tieferes Fühlen und Empfinden mit etwas Leichtigkeit und Frivolität.

Drittes Fingerglied am längsten an:

Spatelhand: Ausnutzen der Talente und Fähigkeiten für egoistische Zwecke.

Apollofinger:

Erstes Fingerglied am längsten an:

Spatelhand: Vorliebe für Tat in der Wiedergabe in Kunst und dramatischer Darstellung.

Eckiger Hand: Wahrheitsliebe im Ausdruck in Kunst und Literatur. Gesunde Kritik.

Konischer oder idealer Hand: Intuition und Fähigkeit, mit gutem Verständnis, geschmackvolle Dinge auszuwählen.

Zweites Fingerglied am längsten an:

Spatelhand: Schaffensfreude um des Erfolges willen.

Eckiger Hand: Nachdenklichkeit in künstlerischen und literarischen Dingen.

Konischer Hand: Weniger Intuition, mehr Sinnen.

Drittes Fingerglied am längsten an einer dieser Typen: Künstlerische oder literarische Betätigung werden nur wegen materieller Erfolge bezweckt.

Merkurfinger:

Erstes Fingerglied am längsten an:

Spatelhand: Tatkraft in Wissenschaft, erfinderisch und sehr praktisch, sowie kraftvolle Ausdrucksart in Sprache und Schrift.

Eckiger Hand: Vorliebe für Studien und Forschungen wissenschaftlicher Art.

Konischer Hand: Dasselbe, mit Intuition und um der Sache selbst willen.

Zweites Fingerglied am längsten an:

Spatelhand: Gute Ausführung geschäftlicher Angelegenheiten.

Eckiger Hand: Ähnlich, nur weniger aktiv (wegen der Hemmungen zum Fortschritt durch Kleinigkeiten).

Konischer Hand: Gutes Sprachtalent.

Drittes Fingerglied am längsten bei einer dieser Typen: Neigung zu Schlauheit und Unwahrheit.

Zweites und drittes Glied gleich lang: Gleiches Maß von Können für Wissenschaft, Geschäft und Handel.

Dickes drittes Glied an konischen Händen: Bedeutet stets, daß Bequemlichkeitsliebe vorhanden ist. Bei fleischigen, mehr noch bei weichen Händen geht die Bequemlichkeit in Faulheit, Genuß und Sinnlichkeit über. Solche Personen sind deshalb unzuverlässig und zu nichts gut verwendbar. Sie gehen von einem Vergnügen ins andere, um an den Lebensgenüssen möglichst ausgiebig teilzuhaben.

Fingerknoten

nennt man die von Natur aus verdickten Gelenke (rheumatische Ver-
dickung; Gichtknoten müssen hiervon unterschieden werden, da sie
nicht gemeint sind). Die Knoten an den ersten Fingergliedern (Finger-
spitze) sind die geistigen Knoten, jene zwischen zweitem und drittem
Gliede die physischen. Bild 50 a, 54 a, 68 B. Knoten sind Hemmungen,
Siebe für die feingeistigen Ströme aus dem Kosmos. Das Hemmen und
Sieben wird veranlaßt durch das Gehirndenken. Durch letztes allein
werden diese Knoten entwickelt. Daher auch die Bezeichnung „philosophische" Knoten. Bei dem knotigen oder philosophischen Handtyp
finden wir sie sehr stark ausgeprägt. Sie sind also ein Merkmal für
Bedachtsamkeit, Ordnung in Gedanken. Die physischen Knoten
hemmen das Denken in materieller Hinsicht (Materie, Sache) und
bedeuten Sinn für Ordnung in materiellen Dingen. Nichtknotige Finger
können durch geistige Arbeit sehr wohl zu knotigen entwickelt werden,
nicht aber zum knotigen Typ. Nie werden knotige Finger zu glatten
werden, denn die Natur arbeitet nie rückwärts.

Entwickelte Knoten an verschiedenen Handtypen.

Bei der philosophischen Hand sind sie selbstverständlich vorhanden.
Ohne sie wäre dies kein knotiger Typ. Hier geben die Knoten das
angeborene Verlangen, allen Dingen durch Nachdenklichkeit und
Intuition auf den Grund zu gehen (erstes Glied). Diese Erkenntnisse
werden übertragen und verarbeitet für die intellektuelle und physische
Sphäre (zweites und drittes Glied); daher die Bezeichnung „philosophisch". (Bild 56, 57, 11, 72 a.)

S p a t e l h a n d : Unruhe und Gedanken. Ein Drang hin und her
zwischen Erkenntnis und ihrer Ausführung einerseits und Verwendung zur praktischen Seite des Lebens anderseits. Wenn Spatelhand weich: Liebe zur Bequemlichkeit. Die Weichheit nimmt von
der Aktivität viel. Deshalb viele Pläne, aber weniger praktisch und
wenig Energie zur Verwirklichung (Bild 7, 16/3, 71, 74).

E c k i g e H a n d : Zuverlässigkeit, Vorliebe und Verlangen nach
Gerechtigkeit unter allen Umständen. Alles Für und Gegen wird
mit großer Bedachtsamkeit erwogen (Bild 8, 16/5, 40).

K o n i s c h e H a n d : Nachdenklichkeit, wo sonst Impulsivität wäre, in
Verbindung mit unpraktischer Phantasie. In bezug auf Religion und
Liebe ein Kampf zwischen Glauben und Frage nach Begründungen
(Bild: 38, 9, 13, 66 d, 69 b.)

I d e a l e H a n d : Exzentrisch und skeptisch im Moment. Doch durch
Empfindung und Intuition sowie Inspiration richtig geleitet, kehren

solche Menschen stets zu tiefen Empfindungen zurück (angedeutet: Bild 10, 47, 49 a, 66 c).

Entwickelte zweite Knoten an verschiedenen Handtypen.

Gilt der erste Knoten in geistigen Dingen, Gedanken, so zeugen die zweiten Knoten von denselben in physischen, materiellen Dingen. Beide Knoten an idealer Hand verändern die Inspiration und Intuition zu einer Mischung mit intellektuellem Denken. Diese gibt Begabung für Erfindungen und gute Pläne, doch fehlt das praktische Ausführen, weil solche Hand nicht zum praktischen Typ zählt, da Besitzer nicht zur praktischen Arbeit prädestiniert ist.

Die Handberge.

(Bild 18)

Wo Form ist, da ist Gesetz. Aller Formausdruck
ist Gesetzmäßigkeit.

In der Hand findet man unter jedem Finger und am Handrand entlang hervortretende und meist klarumzeichnete Erhöhungen, die Handberge genannt werden. Auf Bild 3 und 18 habe ich diese punktiert und mit den astrologischen Zeichen derjenigen Planeten, die ihnen entsprechen, angedeutet (s. Bild 18). Unter dem (Zeige-)Jupiterfinger findet sich der Jupiterberg, unter dem (Mittel-)Saturnfinger der Saturnberg, unter dem (Ring-)Sonnen- oder Apollofinger der Apolloberg, unter dem (kleinen) Merkurfinger der Merkurberg, darunter am Handrand entlang, zwischen Herz- und Kopflinie, der Marsberg, darunter bis zur Handwurzel der Mondberg; auf der anderen Seite der Handballen: der Venusberg. Ihre verschiedenen Eigenschaften und Einflüsse sind in den entsprechenden, die einzelne Berge behandelnden Abschnitten angegeben. Siehe auch die große Tafel „Die astrale Bedeutung der Hand" (Bild 19), worauf die einzelnen Eigenschaften zur leichteren und schnelleren Übersicht symbolisch eingezeichnet sind. Manche Berge sind entwickelt, manchmal sogar extrem. In anderen Fällen wieder sind sie flach oder eingesunken; öfter findet man sie verschoben, so daß ein Berg von den Eigenschaften des andern annimmt und beide verschmelzen. Ist ein Berg groß, so sind auch die betreffenden Eigenschaften in verstärktem Maße vertreten; ist er versunken, so verliert er nicht nur seine guten Eigenschaften, sondern verschlechtert noch die verbliebenen minderwertigen. Man nehme als Beispiel zur besseren Erklärung ein weites Feld, auf dem Berge von verschiedenen Größen sind. Das Bild sagt uns auf den ersten Blick, daß der größte und an Masse wuchtigste

Berg die größte Kraft und Macht in sich birgt, während der kleine dagegen schwächlich wirkt und es auch ist. So auch in der Hand. Anderseits erklärte ich schon weiter oben, daß die Berge Akkumulatoren, Sammler von astralen Energieströmen sind, welche den Strom an die Linien abgeben, und daß jede Linie, die einen Berg berührt, auch von ihm beeinflußt wird.

Auch hier wiederhole ich: Man kann weder Berge noch Linien in eine Hand hineinarbeiten oder durch Arbeit entwickeln, sondern nur Schwielen bekommen.

Diese haben aber mit Bergen nichts gemein, werden bei der Deutung auch nicht als Berge betrachtet.

Die Eigenschaften desjenigen Berges, welcher am meisten entwickelt ist, sind auch im Besitzer der Hand hervorragend und beeinflussend.

B e a c h t e   f ü r   C h a r a k t e r i s t i k :

Bei Spatelfingern wird stets die Neigung zu den materiellen Auswirkungen der Qualitäten bestehen.

Bei eckigen Fingern werden die kräftigen Einwirkungen der Berge mehr durch Verstandestätigkeiten verarbeitet.

Bei konischen und idealen Fingern wird die Charakteristik mehr dem Intuitiven und Phantasievollen zuneigen.

Gefestigter ist eine Charakteristik in dem Betreffenden, wenn die Bergeshöhe unten liegt (nach der Handfläche zu). Mehr im Werden begriffen ist die Festigkeit, wenn die Bergeshöhe dicht unter den Fingern liegt. Daher auch mehr beeinflußbar. Auch hier ist das Normale besser.

Wenn alle Berge gleich gut entwickelt sind, ergibt das Harmonie in der Kombination der Charakteristik. Hier sind wieder weniger Reibungsflächen für den Charakter vorhanden. Daher wirkt selbst das Negative ruhevoller, gleichmäßiger und zeugt von Gleichmut.

V e r s c h o b e n e   B e r g e . Das Starke zieht das Schwächere an! So auch bei den Handbergen. Der Venusberg steht und strahlt für sich — scheinbar. Der obere Venusberg ist der kleine, positive Marsberg, der oft vom Venusberg durch eine tiefe Furche (nicht Linie) getrennt ist. In anderen Fällen sehen wir aber auch beide vereinigt. Venus und Mars sind die beiden Faktoren der Sexualliebe und -triebe. Venus ist das weibliche, Mars das männliche Prinzip.

Die Plätze der Berge (Bild 18) habe ich g e n a u begrenzt und hier durch scharf markierte Felder angezeigt. Man präge sich diese Grenzen genau ein. Wenn auch die meisten Hände „verschobene Berge" aufweisen, d. h. Berge, deren Wölbung oder Plastik sich nach links oder rechts hinüberneigt, so bleiben die genauen Grenzen für den Stand oder die Bestimmung eines darauf befindlichen Zeichens oder Linie maßgebend. In anderen Worten ausgedrückt: Die Wölbung oder Plastik eines Berges kann sich verschieben, die Grenze jedoch nie. In diesem Bilde habe ich nochmals die Benennung der Fingerglieder mit I., II., III. angegeben, wie sie im Text oft benannt sind.

Eigenschaften der Berge.

♀ **Venusberg** (Liebe): Liebe, Sinnlichkeit, Leidenschaft, Geschlechtsleben, und was damit zusammenhängt, auch Verirrungen im Geschlechtsleben, Perversität; Gefühl, Harmonie, Frohsinn; Sinn für Rhythmus, Ton und Farbe. Häusliche Angelegenheiten. (Leidenschaftliches Temperament.) — Alles, was sich in der Hand zeigt, wiederholt sich auf dem Venusberg in irgendeinem Ausdruck oder Zeichen, weil fast alles seinen Grund in den Sexualmysterien hat.

♃ **Jupiterberg** (Macht): Geist, Streben, Ehrgeiz, Protektion, Ehren, Stolz, Erfolge (im weltlichen Sinne). Sanguinisches Temperament.

♄ **Saturnberg** (Verdichtung, Erde): Schicksal — gut oder böse — (das erzieherische Prinzip), tiefe Gedanken, Grübelei, Schwermut, Religion, Mystik; Gefahren, Unfälle, Körperverletzung. Melancholisches Temperament.

☉ **Apolloberg** (Sonne): Seele (Schönheit, Feingefühl, Schönheitssinn, inneres Erleben, Toleranz, künstlerisches Fühlen, Sinn für Veredelung und Gerechtigkeit), Ehren, Wohlstand; materielle Gewinne. Sonniges Temperament.

☿ **Merkurberg** (Luft, verstandesmäßiges Denken): Intellekt, Schlauheit, Falschheit, Routine, Handel, Gewerbe; Okkultismus, Wissenschaft, Erwerbstrieb. Nervöses Temperament.

♂ **Marsberg** (Feuer, Hitze): Mut, Jähzorn, Selbstkontrolle, Geistesgegenwart; Durchführungskraft. Galliges, cholerisches Temperament.

☽ **Mondberg** (Wasser, Säfte): Gefühl, Stimmungen, Laune, Phantasie, Sensitivität, Intuition, Medialität, Mystik, Musik; Veränderungen, Reisen, Abenteuer, Extravaganzen äußerlich wie auch im Gefühlsleben (Perversität). Phlegmatisches, lymphatisches Temperament.

Dies sind nur Stichworte. Die Eigenschaften der Berge lassen sich noch erweitern und verfeinern, wenn man über die Stichworte nachdenkt, sinnt und alles in Betracht zieht, was mit den betreffenden Dingen im engen Zusammenhange steht. Um auch hierfür eine Erleichterung zu geben, führe ich nachstehend für die einzelnen bestimmten Berge positive und negative Eigenschaften auf.

94

Positive und negative Eigenschaften der Berge.

Venus:

Lebenskraft	Ausschweifung
Sinnlichkeit	Blasiertheit
Lebensgenuß	Verschwendung
Herzensgüte	Hartherzigkeit
Zärtlichkeit	Kaltherzigkeit
Mitgefühl	Herbheit
Heimliebe	Bohéme
Aufopferung	Berechnung
Milde	Gefühlsroheit
Leidenschaftlichkeit	Gefühlskälte
Harmlosigkeit	Egoismus, Koketterie
Sinn für Kunst	Interesselosigkeit
Sexuelle Eigenart	Perversität
Rhythmus	Laschheit

Lebensbejahung, Sexualleben, Degeneration.

Jupiter:

Streben	Gleichgültigkeit
Religion	Scheinheiligkeit
Gerechtigkeitsliebe	Anmaßung, Herrschsucht
Güte	Niedertracht
Gleichmut	Heftigkeit, Jähzorn
Lebensfreude	Geltungsdrang
Genußliebe	Schwelgerei
Kameradschaft	Prahlerei
Freundschaft	Phantasterei
Protektion	Diktatur
Naturliebe	Ehrgeiz

Kopf, Lunge, Blase, Blut, Haarausfall.

Saturn:

Festigkeit	Ängstlichkeit
Nachdenklichkeit	Mißtrauen, Argwohn
Konzentration	Berechnung
Selbstzucht	Hinterlist
Gewissenhaftigkeit	Selbstsucht
Erkenntnis	Haß, Rachsucht
Beobachtung, Vorsicht	Blödheit
Zurückgezogenheit	Einsamkeit
Besinnlichkeit	Grübelei
Zähigkeit, Ausdauer	Depression

Materielle Interessen	Habsucht, Geiz
Das Konservative	Frivolität

Materielle Erfolge, Mißerfolge, Mißgeschick, Unfälle (schicksalhafte Erziehung), Leid.
Knochen, Zähne, Krampf, Verkrüppelungen, Lähmung, Irrsinn, chron. Leiden, Epilepsie, Krebs.

Apollo:

Ethik, Ästhetik	Verkommenheit
Ideale	Ideale aus Berechnung
Toleranz	Intoleranz (rechthaberisch)
Aufrichtigkeit	Überschwenglichkeit, Komplimente
Hoffnung	Enttäuschungen (= Selbsttäuschung)
Begeisterung	Fanatismus
Freiheitsliebe	Philister („gut bürgerlich")
Großzügigkeit	Verschwendung
Inneres Erleben	Hohlheit
Weistum	Torheit, Narrheit
Natürlichkeit	Etikettesucht
Selbstbewußtsein	Überhebung
Erfolg (Ruhm)	Gewinnsucht

Augen, Herz, Sonnengeflecht, Nieren, Beine.

Merkur:

Wissenschaft	Ausbeutung
Handel	Wucher
Erwerb	Dieberei
Spekulation	Betrug
Klugheit	Verschlagenheit
Umsicht	Routine
Intelligenz	Schlauheit
Kritik	Kritizismus
Erfindung	Nachahmung
Beredsamkeit	selbstsüchtige Suggestion
Einsicht	Verstellung, Diplomatie, Falschheit

Nerven, Schultern, Arme, Sexualorgane, Hände.

Mars:

Mut	Feigheit
Tatendrang	unbeherrschte Leidenschaft
Disziplin	Laschheit
Kampfsinn	Jähzorn, Tobsucht
Aufbau	Zerstörung

Zielsicherheit	Grausamkeit
Aufopferungsfähigkeit	Herrschsucht
als Idealist (Kämpfer)	Sadismus
Gattenliebe, Kinderliebe, Heimfanatismus.	

Mond:

Gemüt	Schwärmerei
Phantasie	Lügenhaftigkeit
Gemütsruhe	Unruhe
Träumerei	Faulheit
Versonnenheit	Verstiegenheit
Medialität	krankhafte Zustände
	(Besessenheit, Wahn)
Romantik	Hysterie, Mondsucht usw.
Reiselust, Wechsel	Abenteuerlust
Okkultismus (Metaphysik)	**Mystizismus**
Ideale	Irrtum, Täuschungen

Säfte, Milz, Fall, Gemütsleiden, Einbildung, Wahn, Salze, Rheuma.

Berge: Normal, groß, eingefallen
sind die Bezeichnungen für den Grad der Plastik. Eingefallen heißt,
wenn die Fläche an der Stelle flach oder vertieft ist; normal, wenn eine
fleischige Erhöhung, und übergroß oder extrem entwickelt, wenn diese
fleischige Stelle im Vergleich mit anderen Bergen zu stark hervorragt.
Bei Vergleich mehrerer Hände wird man diese drei Unterschiede sehr
bald erkennen. Natürlich muß man immer eine Harmonie der Plastik
der ganzen Hand beachten. Spezielles hierüber einige Seiten weiter!

Kombinationen der Berge.
In der Einführung wies ich schon darauf hin, daß der ausdrucksvollste
Berg die ausdrucksvollste oder hervorragendste Charaktereigenschaft
erkennen läßt. Es kann aber vorkommen — und das ist meist der Fall —,
daß mehrere Berge groß und entwickelt sind. In solchen Fällen
werden sich die Eigenschaften der größeren Berge stark vereinigen und
ein ganz besonderes Gemisch sehr stark zum Ausdruck bringen.
Beispiele:
Ist die Innenhand flach und nur der Venusberg — der meist stärker
entwickelt ist, weil das Triebleben in unserem Evolutionsstadium
noch immer eine Hauptrolle spielt — stark ausgeprägt, so tritt das
Trieb- und Sinnengenußleben am stärksten hervor. Es wird in
solchem Falle alles nur deshalb getan, um sich materielle und sinnliche Genüsse zu verschaffen. Im Liebesleben ist hier die Erotik
die Hauptsache. — Gleich hier möchte ich einschalten, daß „Sinnlichkeit" durchaus keine böse oder zu verdammende Eigenschaft

ist. Im Gegenteil! Es kommt nur darauf an, w i e sie ausgelebt und ausgewertet wird. Es gibt keine große Warmherzigkeit, keinen Familiensinn, keine Heimliebe o h n e Sinnlichkeit! Es gibt keine Kunst und kein künstlerisches Empfinden und Schaffen ohne Sinnlichkeit, Erotik! — Ist ein Weib nicht sinnlich, so hat es schon an Weiblichkeit verloren, weil Sinnlichkeit ein großer und bedeutender Teil der Natur und des Wesens des Weibes i s t.

V e n u s b e r g u n d M o n d b e r g stark entwickelt, ergibt starke Sinnlichkeit mit viel Phantasie, Abenteuerlust und Unzuverlässigkeit in bezug auf Treue. Stimmungen und Launenhaftigkeit mit den Gedanken, „was sein könnte, wenn ...", dazu die Phantasie mit Schmieden von Plänen, die meist unerreichbar sind, ergeben ein Schwanken und deshalb Unzuverlässigkeit im Charakter. Anderseits lassen sich Rhythmus und Phantasie, wenn gut geschult, in der Ausübung der Tanzkunst verwerten, wenn die Finger nicht zu kurz sind.

Entwickelter Venus- und Marsberg ergibt ein Wesen, das recht brutal in der Liebe ist; also mit Neigung zu Sadismus, wenn sehr stark ausgeprägt und der Daumen (der immer in Betracht zu ziehen ist!) dick ist. Ist der Daumen fest, schlank, harmonisch, so ist der Betreffende heftig in der Liebe, aber auch fest und treu, verläßlich. Auf jeden Fall wird der Eigner sich in der Werbung nicht leicht abweisen lassen, sondern mit Mut und Zähigkeit sein Ziel zu erreichen suchen.

Ein entwickelter V e n u s - u n d M e r k u r b e r g läßt erkennen, daß der Betreffende in allen Liebessachen die Berechnung und das verstandesmäßige Denken nicht vergißt. Alles wird vom Nützlichkeitsstandpunkt aus betrachtet, auch wenn es sich nicht gleich um eine Ehe handelt. Die Herzensgüte wird deshalb betätigt, weil sie „etwas einbringen" soll; sie ist also in dem Falle keine echte Herzensgüte. Der Inhaber ist Idealist aus Berechnung; denn alles wird vom „kaufmännischen" Standpunkt aus betrachtet. Er wird z. B. den Wert eines schönen Bildes erkennen und auch verstehen, aber er wird es verkaufen. Man findet diesen Typ unter den Heiratsvermittlern.

Entwickelter V e n u s - u n d A p o l l o b e r g gibt Aufrichtigkeit und natürliches Wesen; wahres künstlerisches Gefühl und Erleben, Schauen und Schaffen. In der Liebe wird alles veredelt und vom ästhetischen Punkt aus betrachtet. Es sind Menschen mit idealer Richtung und Tiefe in der Liebe. Wieweit das Ideale geht oder entwickelt werden kann, ist aus den anderen Merkmalen, Fingern, Linien, Zeichen erkennbar.

Entwickelter V e n u s - u n d S a t u r n b e r g ergibt ein Liebesleben aus einer Mischung von Egoismus, starker Sinnlichkeit, Eifersucht und Melancholie mit mehr oder weniger Berechnung. Es kommt auch hier auf den Typ der Hand und die Entwicklung der anderen Eigenschaften an, also ob das Erleben und die Auswirkung auf höherer oder niederer Bewußtseinsebene erfolgt.

Entwickelter V e n u s - u n d J u p i t e r b e r g ergibt die Liebe, die aus Liebe und Freundschaft besteht, wahre Kameradschaft und Eigenschaften, die eine glückliche, zufriedene Ehe, Harmonie und Freude gewährleisten. Es sind Menschen mit aufrichtiger und anständiger Gesinnung.

Man muß immer die g a n z e Handqualität in Betracht ziehen, dann findet man auch das Richtige. Nicht gefühlsmäßig, sondern nur mit vorhandenen Tatsachen arbeiten, dann ist Irrtum ausgeschlossen! Diese Kombinationen lassen sich fortsetzen, soweit Material vorhanden ist. Zu berücksichtigen ist, daß auch drei Berge und mehr in Betracht kommen können.

Z. B. entwickelter S a t u r n - , M e r k u r - u n d M a r s b e r g ergibt in einer schlechten Hand die niederen Eigenschaften kombiniert. Saturn: Egoismus, Habsucht, Geiz; Merkur: Erwerbstrieb, Routine (evtl. Verschlagenheit, Falschheit) und Gewandtheit; Mars: Mut, Kraft, Zorn; zusammengenommen Eigenschaften, wie sie Räuber und Einbrecher haben (niederer Typ). Der „bessere" und etwas höher entwickelte Typ wäre der Schieber und Hochstapler. Die Eigenschaften zum Besten veredelt — Wissen, Erkenntnis, bewußte Hilfsbereitschaft, geschultes, verstandesmäßiges und intuitives Denken, dazu Mut, Kraft und Selbstbeherrschung — ergeben in der Kombination den besten Typ eines Geistlichen und Wissenschaftlers.

Entwickelter S a t u r n - u n d M o n d b e r g in primitiver Hand ergibt Träumerei, Schwermut, Aberglauben; in einer guten eckigen oder knotigen Hand einen guten Pastor oder Okkultisten.

Ist der J u p i t e r b e r g a u c h noch stark hervortretend und der Venusberg klein, so ergibt dies eine Mönchsnatur.

In den Händen des Lustmörders (Bild 46) sind folgende Berge sehr stark ausgeprägt: Venus-, Mond-, Mars-, Merkur- und Saturnberg. Der Typ dieser Hände ist gemischt aus primitiver, spatelförmiger und eckiger Form. Der Daumen ist groß, dick, bananenartig. Die Kopflinie gut, gerade und sehr lang, dazu gegabelt, wie die Kopflinienform, welche auf Irrsinn deutet. Die Kombination ergibt folgendes Bild (hier nur oberflächlich gegeben): gute Intelligenz und Gedankenkraft mit Routine, Schlauheit und Verschlagenheit, großer Vorsicht. Irrsinnsanlagen ererbt von der mütterlichen Linie. Sehr stark entwickelte Phantasie und perverse Anlagen, großer Erwerbstrieb und Habsucht mit Geiz, sowie Berechnung und Kaltblütigkeit. Geschicklichkeit und Genauigkeit; Ordnungssinn. Starke physische Widerstandskraft. Heftigkeit und Brutalität mit Anlagen zur Tobsucht. Was ist von einem gereiften, alten Menschen mit diesen stark entwickelten Eigenschaften und ererbten Anlagen anderes zu erwarten?!

Verschobene Berge.

Jene Hände sind selten, in denen die Berge alle genau unter den Fingern liegen. Zumeist wird man eine Verschiebung des einen oder mehrerer Berge finden. Dementsprechend ist auch die Charakteristik zu lesen. Man muß sich nur vor dem Fehler hüten, ein Zeichen zu der Bergerhöhung zu rechnen, anstatt zu dem Platz des Berges, auf dem es steht. Ich muß wieder darauf hinweisen, daß die Grenzen der Berge genau zwischen den Fingern liegen, wie sie durch die senkrechten Linien auf Bild 18 angezeigt sind. Wenn nun der Jupiterberg zum Saturnberg hinüberragt, so ist anzunehmen, daß das stärkere Prinzip immer das schwächere an sich zieht, daß also in diesem Falle die Strebsamkeit (Jupiterberg) auf das häusliche Leben, auf die Nachdenklichkeit und das Sinnenhafte (Saturn) übergeleitet und von der Charakteristik des Saturnbergs mit aufgenommen wird.

Ist der Saturnberg zum Jupiterberg hinübergeschoben, so werden die Saturneigenschaften auf das Jupiterprinzip übergeleitet. Die Strebsamkeit wird also stark mit Bedachtsamkeit, vielleicht auch stark mit Melancholie durchsetzt sein. Der Apolloberg bildet zumeist mit dem Merkurberg ein Ganzes. Wenn der Apolloberg den Merkur aufgenommen hat — man erkennt das daran, daß der Merkur flacher erscheint und eine sanfte Erhöhung gegen den Apolloberg anzeigt —, so werden die Empfindungen, das innere Erleben stark durch das verstandesmäßige Denken beeinflußt. Umgekehrt, wenn der Apollo von dem Merkurberg angezogen ist und mit ihm vereint, wird das verstandesmäßige Denken, das Nützlichkeitsprinzip — wenn verdorben, auch die Unehrlichkeit — durch das Einfühlen und Empfindungsleben gesteigert bis zur Raffiniertheit. Raffiniertheit nennt man die Eigenschaft, die verstandesmäßiges Denken, Instinkt und Schlauheit kombiniert. Für einen schaffenden Wissenschaftler und Künstler ist erstes (Merkurberg vom Apolloberg angezogen) günstiger; für einen Kaufmann das andere, nämlich der vom Merkur angezogene Apolloberg.

Zwischen dem Merkur- und Marsberge beginnt die Herzlinie. Hier ist also schon von der Natur eine Stromgrenze gezogen, die nie ganz verschmelzen kann. Dennoch kann diese Grenze manchmal erhaben, also mehr flach vorhanden sein. In dem Falle kombinieren sich die Kräfte des Merkur und Mars etwas. Dies ist günstig für Strategie, für Fechtkunst und für Kampfnaturen, die sich schriftstellerisch betätigen.

Marsberg und Mondberg werden immer etwas ineinander verlaufen. Die Grenze findet man durch Abschätzung: Teile die Fläche von der Wurzel des Merkurfingers bis zum Handgelenk, also bis unter den Mondberg, in vier Teile! Der erste Teil oben bis zur Herzlinie ist der Merkurberg. Die restlichen drei Teile entfallen zu zwei auf den Mondberg, von unten gerechnet, und der verbleibende vierte Teil — zwischen Herz- und Kopflinie — ist der Marsberg. Wenn die Kopflinie sehr leicht nach abwärts geneigt ist, also nicht genau gerade verläuft, zeigt sie die Grenze zwischen Mars- und Mondberg. Verbindungen zwischen Mars- und Mondberg geben eine kraftvolle Phantasie, evtl. auch etwas gesteigerte Gestaltungskraft. Sie ist aber immer hauptsächlich vom Verlauf der Kopflinie i n den Mondberg angezeigt, d. h. eine Kombination von Phantasie und verstandesmäßigem Denken.

Diese Anleitungen und Hinweise mögen genügen. Jeder kann sie bei einiger Übung und Beobachtung weiter ausbauen und nutzen.

Auf die bis hierher gebrachten Lehren baut sich die Chirognomie oder Handformenkunde auf, woraus die Hauptcharakteristik eines Menschen zu erkennen ist. Besondere Zeichen auf einzelnen Bergen, besonders Planetenzeichen, werden natürlich verschiedenes verstärken oder abschwächen. Um die A r t eines Menschen zu erkennen, dazu genügen die Handform und die Berge, die ja auch zur Form gehören. Die Linien und Zeichen geben nur den weiteren Aufschluß über Neigungen, Lebensrichtung, Denkart und Ereignisse. Da aber eines in das andere über- und hineingreift, läßt sich eine ganz genaue Scheidung der Lesearten nicht machen.

Bis hierher geht die Chirognomie oder Handformenkunde. Anderseits greift das Gebiet der B e r g e aber auch in die Chiromantie oder Handlinienkunde über; denn es kommt sehr oft vor, daß die Bedeutung eines bestimmten Berges eine einschneidende Veränderung erfährt durch das Vorhandensein eines oder mehrerer bestimmter Zeichen auf ihm *). — S o m i t   i s t   b e w i e s e n ,   d a ß   s i c h   d i e   H a n d - f o r m e n k u n d e   v o n   d e r   H a n d l i n i e n k u n d e   n i c h t   s c h a r f   s c h e i d e n   l ä ß t ,   w e n n   g u t e   u n d   r i c h t i g e   R e s u l t a t e   e r - z i e l t   w e r d e n   s o l l e n . — Aus dem Grunde vereinige ich hier die beiden Gebiete. Im folgenden bringe ich nun eine Anleitung zur Kombination der Berge, die in der Praxis zu berücksichtigen unbedingt notwendig ist.

---

*) Wenn in der „Arbeitsstätte für Menschheitskunde" von Prof. Dr. H. Friedenthal in Berlin auch nur die Handformenkunde Eingang gefunden hat, so will dies weiter nichts bedeuten, als daß man den Anfang gemacht hat für die Aufnahme der Chirosophie. Mit der Zeit wird auch die Handlinienkunde dazu kommen müssen, weil sich eines durch das andere erst ergänzt. Besonders dann wird man das ganze Wissen erfassen wollen, wenn der große Wert der „Krankheitsdiagnosen aus den Handlinien und -zeichen" erkannt wird, was nicht mehr allzulange dauern kann. Heute arbeiten schon sehr viele Ärzte und Heilkundige überaus erfolgreich mit meiner Handdiagnostik. (Seit 1933 existiert die A. f. M. nicht mehr, da sie von der Hitlerregierung verboten und enteignet wurde.)

Kombinationen der Finger und Berge

	normal	extrem groß	mangelhaft
Jupiterberg			
mit spitzen Fingern	religiöse Ideale	Aberglauben	Mangel an Verehrung
mit konischen Fingern	feiner Stolz	Schein, eitel, Extravaganz	Respektlosigkeit
mit eckigen Fingern	alltäglicher Stolz	dummstolz, selbstherrlich rechthaberisch	Mangel an Selbstachtung
mit spatelförmig. Fingern	große Unternehmungslust	Übertreibung	Niedrigkeit, Gemeinheit
Saturnberg			
mit spitzen Fingern	poetisch und melancholisch	Schwermut und Lebensüberdruß	Mangel an Sinn für Übersinnliches, keine besonderen Ereignisse, Unschlüssigkeit
mit konischen Fingern	sorgenvoll und Grübelei, Empfindsamkeit	Kunst-Pessimist, Melancholie, unschlüssig	Künstler rein materieller Art
mit eckigen Fingern	gedankenvoll und einsamkeitsliebend, ernsthaft, Genauigkeit	Menschenhaß, kleinlich, geht eigenen Weg	absolute Gleichgültigkeit, ödes Leben
mit spatelförmig. Fingern	Sinn für alle solide Arbeit, Bedachtsamkeit	tätlicher Haß gegen andere	liebt harte Arbeit und keine Geselligkeit
Apolloberg			
mit spitzen Fingern	Schwärmer und ausgesuchter Träumer, liebt Eleganz	Genius, grenzt an Wahn, unzuverlässig	keinen Sinn für Kunst, wenig Ethik
mit konischen Fingern	ideale Künstler, Schriftsteller usw. liebenswürdig, heiter	überschätzt sein Talent, Ruhmsucht	klug, aber weniger talentiert
mit eckigen Fingern	feiner Künstler, aber praktisch, Güte	Verliebtheit zerstört vorhandene Talente	keinen Sinn für geistige Freuden, materielles Denken
mit spatelförmig. Fingern	liebt Aufregung und Geräusche als Anregung	Prahler ohne Talent, dauernd auf der Suche, übertriebener Schein	Feind aller Kunst und Herzkultur

	normal	extrem groß	mangelhaft
	M e r k u r b e r g		
mit spitzen Fingern	intuitives Erfassen von Wissenschaften	Träumer für neue Religion, aber schlau, veränderlich	gute Gedanken für üble Zwecke mißbrauchend, unehrlich
mit konischen Fingern	göttliche Beredsamkeit, Witz, liebt Diskussion, Abwechselung	Erfinder für praktische Dinge, Habsucht	Beredsamkeit gestört durch körperliche Fehler, unbegabt
mit eckigen Fingern	große Erfinder, liebt Ausnutzung	gefährliche Planmacher, Falschheit, Intrigen	weder Talent für Handel noch für Wissenschaft, Mangel an Intellekt
mit spatelförmig. Fingern	große Entdecker, Tatendrang, Anpassung	Abenteurer, der über Leichen gehen würde, List, Schlauheit, Anpassung	aktiv in minderwertigen evtl. niederen Dingen, Betrug
	M a r s b e r g		
mit spitzen Fingern	Mut zum Märtyrer, passive Resistenz	Heftigkeit eines religiös. Verfolgers	Feigling in seiner Religion
mit konischen Fingern	Mut zum Patrioten, mehr passiv	Heftigkeit einer verletzten Eitelkeit	Feigling in der Öffentlichkeit
mit eckigen Fingern	Bestimmtheit, Energie, Mut eines Kriegers, angriffslustig	Grobheit, Tyrannei, Heftigkeit eines enttäuschten Planmachers	Feigling im Alltäglichen
mit spatelförmig. Fingern	Mut eines Entdeckers oder Spions, resolut, Führer, Geistesgegenwart	Heftigkeit eines Wüterichs oder Mörders, unbeherrscht quälerische Natur, Härte	Feigling im Kriege, ungeeignet zum Führen
	M o n d b e r g		
mit spitzen Fingern	Vorliebe für Mystik, Mitleid, beste Einbildung	launenhaft, Gereiztheit, Unsinnigkeit	Mangel an Einbildung und Poesie
mit konischen Fingern	begabter Künstler, sentimental, Träumer	närrischer Stolz (Eitelkeit), fanatisch	Imitation in Kunst, Schauspieler
mit eckigen Fingern	gesunder Sinn für Poesie usw., Phantasie	Mangel an Durchschnittsverstand	nutzlose Existenz sehr prosaische Natur
mit spatelförmig. Fingern	Naturliebe, Intuition, romantische Natur	unberechenbares Denken (Anfälle), Vorliebe für Gram und Schmerz	Mangel an Übersicht und Höherstreben, innere Hemmungen

103

	normal	extrem groß	mangelhaft
V e n u s b e r g			
mit spitzen Fingern	ideale Liebe, liebt Vergnügen	verdorbene Einbildung, unbeständig, verdorbener Geschmack	ohne Sinn für Liebe, Gefühlskälte, geschmacklos
mit konischen Fingern	materielle Liebe mit poet. Charakter, verträglich	wechselartig, Genießer und Schwelger	Künstler mit seiner Kunst verheiratet, geizig
mit eckigen Fingern	ehrliche Familienliebe, Geselligkeit	Sinnlichkeit, Langlebigkeit	gleichgültig geg. das andere Geschlecht, wenig Lebenskraft
mit spatelförmig. Fingern	wünscht in seiner Ehehälfte einen geschäftstüchtigen Kameraden	Neigung zu Flirt bei jeder Gelegenheit	findet im anderen Geschlecht nur Hemmungen im Fortschritt, Egoist
K l e i n e r M a r s (oberer Venusberg)			
mit spitzen Fingern	Entsagung	ungesunde Selbstquälerei	sensitive Seele, ängstlich
mit konischen Fingern	Standhaftigkeit	Hartherzigkeit	leicht beleidigt, feige
mit eckigen Fingern	Geduld, resolut, unternehmungslustig	passive Quälerei (seelisch quälen)	sehr empfindlich gegen körperl. und seelischen Schmerz
mit spatelförmig. Fingern	rücksichtslos gegen Schmerz	aktive Quälerei, grob	Feigling, prahlt in der Ferne

Die astrale Symbolik der Hand und ihre Bedeutung.

Um dem Anfänger der Chiromantie eine bessere und schnellere Übersicht in bezug auf die Bedeutung der einzelnen Plätze in der Hand zu geben, zeichnete ich die Symbole in ihrer Bedeutung auf die hierfür in Betracht kommenden Stellen ein (Bild 19). Im folgenden will ich sie erklären, damit die Einzelheiten noch leichter verständlich sind. Es ist nahezu unmöglich, a l l e s einzuzeichnen, was an Bedeutung in Betracht kommen kann; deshalb sind die Bedeutungen in den speziellen Beschreibungen der Handberge und Handlinien hiermit zu kombinieren, um Vollständigkeit des Wissens zu sichern.

D e r D a u m e n : Erstes Glied; der befehlende Mann symbolisiert den Willen.

Zweites Glied: Der Mann mit dem Sprachrohr ruft die Warnung: „Was tust du?!", symbolisiert Vernunft, Logik, Überlegung.

Das dritte Glied (Venusberg): Das Liebes- oder Tänzerpaar symbolisiert: das Liebes- und Geschlechtsleben und den Rhythmus und Tanz; außerdem Perversität, Genußliebe, Gatten-, Kinder- und Nächstenliebe. Die Palette und Harfe bedeuten: Sinn für Farbe und Ton; das Haus: häusliche Angelegenheiten und den eigenen Körper.

Die Lebenslinie bildet die Grenze des Venusberges und stellt dar: die Zufuhr, Umwandlung und Verwertung der Lebenskraft. Am Anfang der Linie erkennt man eine Wiege (Geburt), weiter nach unten das Kind, den Jüngling, den Mann, den Greis und das Grab als Abschluß der Linie; das Ganze auch als Zeiteinteilung.

Jupiterberg und -finger: Der König symbolisiert Protektion, Stellung, Beruf, Gunst; Ehren und Wohlstand die Münze. Auch Ehrgeiz oder Streben und Wohlleben gehören hierher. Die Brandfackel an der Seite symbolisiert: Gefahr durch Umgang mit Feuer.

Saturnberg und -finger: Auf dem ersten Fingergliede symbolisiert das Wasser: Gefahr durch Wasser und Schwermut, Lebensüberdruß. Die Sense ist das Symbol für Landwirtschaft; der Förderkorb für Minenbetrieb; der Galgen, das Gefängnis und die Mörderhand für Gefahren durch Überfall, Mord, Körperverletzung und Gefängnis. Die Swastika ist das astrologische Zeichen für Karma, Schicksal, und der Miner oder Erdarbeiter symbolisiert Dinge, die hiermit in Verbindung gebracht werden können, wie z. B. Mineralien, Erze, Erde, Grund- und Hausspekulation. Das zerbrochene Automobil gilt als Warnungszeichen für Gefahren durch Unachtsamkeit, Verletzung durch Metall, Baumaterial, Erde (Eisenbahn, Straßenbahn, Auto, Verkehrsmittel, Steine, evtl. auch Gas und große Tiere). Der Saturnfinger ist der längste, und der Einfluß des „Bösen" auf den Menschen ist dementsprechend groß.

Apolloberg und -finger: Der Mund und die Noten deuten Gesang an; die Violine Instrumentalmusik und die Palette Malerei; die Maske symbolisiert Bühnenkunst, die Büste Skulptur und Sinn für Plastik überhaupt (wozu das dritte Glied lang sein muß). Die Lyra und die Münze deuten allgemein auf Schönheitssinn, Kunst und Wohlstand.

Merkurberg und -finger: Hier finden wir folgende Symbole: Den geflügelten Merkurstab für Handel, die Waage für Gewerbe und Unruhe; Buch und Feder für Literatur; Äskulapstab und Blume für Arzneikunde, die Retorte für Chemie und Physik; das Auge für Intelligenz, Beobachtungsgabe und okkulte Fähigkeiten; den Fuchs mit Vogel für Diebstahl (zu starker Erwerbstrieb!) und List; den Redner für Sprache und Beredsamkeit; darunter den Satyr an der Herzlinie für Witz. — Die Herzlinie symbolisiert die ideale, ethische Seite der Liebe.

Der Marsberg: Zwei verbundene Ringe und ein Baby gehören eigentlich an die Seite des Merkurberges als Symbol für Ehe und Liebesneigungen, doch habe ich sie hier plaziert aus Platzmangel, und weil man hier Zeichen für Feinde (geheime) und Neider findet, die ebenfalls auf diese Dinge Bezug haben. Der Krieger symbolisiert Mut, Willen, Kraft, Selbstkontrolle, Geistesgegenwart, Streitigkeiten, evtl. Brutalität; Verwundung durch Metall (Körperverletzung, Operation usw.), Strategie.

Der Handtisch oder das große Viereck mit der offenen Hand läßt erkennen, wie das Wesen seinen Mitmenschen gegenüber offenbart wird, also Toleranz.

Die Marsebene: Das Streitfeld symbolisiert Streit und hitzige Einflüsse (auch Krankheiten fiebriger Art, wie Grippe, Influenza, Fieber). Die Formation der Grenzlinien des Marsfeldes geben Aufschluß über Gesundheit und Denkweise

Der Mondberg: Das Wasser symbolisiert das Wässerige (Blut, Säfte und die Drüsentätigkeit im Organismus), außerdem Phantasie, Mystik, Intuition, Melancholie; Schiffe bedeuten Reisen, Abenteuer, Veränderungen. Andere Einflüsse des Mondes sind: Stimmungen, Laune, Feinfühligkeit, Medialität, Musik. Auf dem unteren Mondberge finden sich noch folgende Symbole: Die Eule für Mystik, das versiegelte Buch für Geheimwissenschaft (Okkultismus), das Auge für Hellsehen; Hexenkessel und Tarnkappe für Magie, der Sechsstern für Kabbalistik und Sympathie. In dieser Gegend entspringt die Uranuslinie, die sich auf die ebengenannten Dinge bezieht. Auf der gegenüberliegenden Seite, auf der Neptunslinie sind als Symbole für Gift zu finden: die Likörflasche, Medizinflasche, Zigarre, Rauchgefäß.

Der auf der Handwurzelmitte gezeichnete Stammbaum gibt zu erkennen, daß hier die Zeichen für Herkunft, Geschlecht, Art zu suchen sind.

Die drei Armbänder (Raszette) bezeichnen ererbte Lebenskräfte.

Diese Auslegungen und Andeutungen mögen phantastisch anmuten, sind es aber durchaus nicht. Sie lassen sich psychologisch und physiologisch begründen. Jeder sollte durch tieferes Denken selbst zu der Erkenntnis kommen.

Die kabbalistische Einteilung der Hand.

An anderen Stellen dieses Buches wies ich schon darauf hin, daß „das Äußere der Ausdruck des Innern" ist, daß alles seinen geistigen Grund und seine Ursache hat, daß z. B. Krankheitsanlagen geistig schon vorhandene Krankheiten sind, kurz, daß alles an Anlagen,

Neigungen, Talenten, Eigenschaften, Krankheiten usw. eine geistige Ursache hat. Ist dies so, dann muß auch für solche geistigen Ursachen ein Sitz und Betätigungsfeld vorhanden sein, an dessen Ausdruck und Form wir die Kraft und Beschaffenheit und das Arbeiten dieser geistigen Ströme und Kräfte erkennen und beurteilen können. Zum Zwecke der besseren Erklärung bringe ich Bild 20: „Kabbalistische Einteilung der Hand". Es zeigt eine genau bestimmte Einteilung der Hand, eine waagerechte und eine senkrechte Linie, den Handteller in vier Plätze teilend. — Als Grundeinteilung der Anlagen — von oben nach unten — gilt bei der Innenhand — wie überall — die kosmische Dreiteilung. Die Finger: der geistige Teil; die Fläche vom Fingeransatze bis zur Kopflinie: der seelische Teil; die Fläche unterhalb der Kopflinie bis zur Handwurzel: der physische Teil.

Die Finger in ihrer Länge, ihre Proportion zur Handlänge und -breite lassen die geistigen Anlagen und deren Stärke erkennen. Die Formen der Finger lassen erkennen, welcher Art diese Kräfte sind und wie sie genutzt werden können. Die Finger haben — jeder für sich — eine verschiedene Art der Bedeutung und werden nochmals in drei Unterbedeutungen geteilt — geistig, seelisch, physisch. Der Daumen stellt die Persönlichkeit — das „Ich-Selbst" — dar; das erste Glied: das Maß und den Ausdruck des Willens; das zweite Glied: das Maß und den Ausdruck der Vernunft und Überlegung. Das Knotengelenk zwischen diesen beiden Gliedern läßt in seinem Ausdruck das Maß der Zähigkeit — und Durchführungskraft — erkennen. Das dritte Glied: Ausdruck des Trieblebens, bildet einerseits das dritte Daumenglied: Maß des Betätigungstriebs in der physischen Sphäre, andererseits — und gleichzeitig — als vierter Teil des Handtellers das Maß der produktiven Schöpfungskraft. (Hier liegen Erklärungen für die Sexualmystik!) Je nachdem wie der Daumenausdruck, so die Persönlichkeit selbst. Die Haltung des Daumens zeigt die geistige Haltung des Besitzers. Hält jemand den Daumen immer abseits gespreizt — für sich alleinstehend —, so wird der Betreffende bei jeder Gelegenheit für sich selbst stehen w o l l e n , also über viel Mut, Tatkraft und Unabhängigkeitsliebe verfügen. Ob er es kann, das hängt von dem Ausdruck (Form und Plastik) des Daumens ab. Daß eine allgemeine Harmonie in der Form zu beachten ist, braucht nicht erst erwähnt zu werden; dies ist natürlich und selbstverständlich. Ich meine hiermit, daß man durchaus nicht von dem Gedanken ausgehen darf, daß eine Eigenschaft um so stärker vorhanden ist, je stärker, dicker der betreffende Finger ist. Die L ä n g e der Fingerglieder ist ausschlaggebend z u s a m m e n mit der Stärke und Dicke (Form und Plastik). — Wenn etwas unharmonisch verteilt ist in der physischen Sphäre — d. h. an der sichtbaren Formproportion der Hand —, dann sind auch die entsprechenden Eigenschaften unharmonisch in der geistigen Anlage vorhanden.

B e i s p i e l : Jemand hat eine mittelgroße, massive, gut entwickelte Hand von mittlerer Breite; der Jupiterfinger ist im Verhältnis zu den anderen Fingern klein, dünn und spitz, der Jupiterberg mit flach zu bezeichnen, so ist in dem Eigner dieser Hand nicht viel Ehrgeiz und Strebsamkeit, noch weniger aber die Kraft, sie in kurzer Zeit zu erlangen. Auch ist dieser Mensch nicht in der Lage, anderen ein Führer oder guter Aufseher zu sein, da ihm die Qualitäten dazu (praktische Tat als Beispiel, Persönlichkeit, Erwägen) fehlen; dies um so mehr, wenn der Daumen klein und schmal ist. Der spitze Finger mag ihm eine gewisse intuitive Erkenntnis geben, die er jedoch für sich geistig wenig oder nicht, körperlich gar nicht verwerten kann.

Wie die Proportion (Form und Plastik) des einen Finger g l i e d e s zum anderen und zu dem ganzen Finger, und wie die Proportion des einen betreffenden Fingergliedes zu allen anderen Fingergliedern der Hand ist, danach hat man zu urteilen: w a s für Anlagen und w i e sie vorhanden sind; z. B. für Außenarbeit und Sport muß das dritte Glied des Saturnfingers lang und gut entwickelt sein.

Für Skulptur (Bildhauerkunst) muß das dritte Glied des Apollofingers lang und gut entwickelt sein; dazu das erste Glied des Apollofingers eckig oder spatenförmig.

Rednertalent ist vorhanden, wenn der Merkurfinger über das erste Beugegelenk (zwischen dem ersten und zweiten Gliede) des Apollofingers hinausragt. Auf die Form der Spitze dieses Fingers kommt es an bei der Entscheidung darüber, welcher Art der Ausdruck des Talentes ist. Die Rednergabe desjenigen mit eckiger Merkurfingerspitze wird mehr oder weniger derbe Ausdrucksart haben, während Menschen mit konischer oder spitzer Merkurfingerspitze eine tiefsinnige, von mehr Findigkeit und Routine (Gewandtheit und Raffinesse) zeugende Ausdrucksart besitzen. Organisationstalent erfordert eckige Merkurfinger.

Spitze Finger zeugen von Intuition. Die hohe Kunst des Gesanges fordert Intuition, ein Sicheinfühlen der Seele, ohne welches wahre Kunst unmöglich ist; aber auch Gestaltungskraft (Dramatik), Streben zur höchsten Vollendung und eine gute Portion Findigkeit, um unter Umständen einen kleinen Fehler sofort zu verschleiern. Deshalb sind für Gesangskunst alle Fingerspitzen verschieden, der Apollofinger jedoch immer konisch oder spitz, der Daumen gerade, harmonisch, Spitze etwas nach außen gebogen. Gute Leistungen setzen stets gute Anlagen voraus, hier wie überall.

Im Hinblick auf die Gesangskunst ist zu bemerken, daß eine Reflexwirkung zwischen Stimme und Sexualorganen besteht. Ein Kenner wird am Gesang einer Frau erkennen, ob sie Jungfrau ist oder nicht. Eine

Jungfrau hat keinen Schmelz, keine Sinnlichkeit in der Stimme; es „fehlt die Wärme", das Erotische.

Wie ich oben sagte, wird der Handteller durch die Kopflinie in einen oberen und unteren Teil geteilt, und diese beiden Flächen werden durch eine senkrechte Linie (Saturnlinie) nochmals geteilt, so daß vier Flächen vorhanden sind, vier Kraftfelder. Unter dem Jupiter- und dem Saturnfinger: das Feld der geistigen; unter dem Apollo- und Merkurfinger: das Feld der seelischen Kraft. Darunter wieder: der Mondberg als Feld der physischen Widerstandsfähigkeit, und links davon: der Venusberg, das Feld der physischen Schöpfungskraft. Die Kraft des geistigen Schaffens hängt von der Beschaffenheit des Blutes und Gehirns ab. Zeichen für evtl. Störungen sind auf diesem ♃ ♄ -Felde zu finden. Die Ausdruckskraft der Seele ist von der Stärke der Nerven abhängig, die auf diesem ☉ ☿ -Kraftfelde zu erkennen ist.

Die persönliche Strahlkraft (persönlicher Magnetismus) oder Sex-Appeal ist abhängig von der Stärke der Venuseigenschaften, also von der Sinnlichkeit. Ebenso auch die künstlerische Begabung. Es gibt keine lebendige und wirkliche Kunst ohne Sinnlichkeit; andernfalls ist sie keine Kunst. Darum sind bei entsprechender Begutachtung immer auch diese Eigenschaften genauestens zu beachten und zu werten.

Eine gute Widerstandsfähigkeit des Körpers setzt gute Verdauungsorgane und geregelte Drüsentätigkeit voraus, alles Dinge, die auf dem Mondberge zu erkennen sind. Die sexuelle Schöpfungskraft hängt mit dem Triebleben und der Sinnlichkeit zusammen. Sie sind auf dem Venusberg zu erkennen. — Obgleich dies nun schon in den medizinischen Teil der Chiromantie hineingreift, ist es doch für die „Handformenkunde" wertvoll und notwendig. Es ist überhaupt sehr schwer, die medizinischen von den anderen Bedeutungen zu trennen, da alles zueinander oder ineinander Beziehungen hat, wie Temperament und Krankheit, Charakter, Neigungen usw.

Dritter Teil.

Chiromantie oder Handlinienlehre.

Das menschliche Leben ist nur e i n e Episode
in dem großen Zyklus kettengliedrig aufeinander-
folgender Lebensbewußtseinsstufen, in der sich
alle Ereignisse von Zeit zu Zeit — periodenweise
und gesetzmäßig — wiederholen.

Wie ich schon weiter oben (unter „astrale Einflüsse") beschrieb, sind
die Linien der Hand als Fluß- oder Strombetten der ein- und durch-
fließenden astralen Kräfte zu betrachten. Alle kleinen und kleinsten
Abzweigungen von den Hauptlinien sind Nebenflüsse und sehr zu
beachten. Man vergleiche mit der Natur: Jeder Nebenfluß — sei er noch
so klein — nimmt dem Hauptstrom einen Teil der Ganzkraft, gibt ihm
aber zu gleicher Zeit ein größeres Wirkungs- oder Interessenfeld, je
nachdem, durch und über welchen Boden er seinen Lauf nimmt. Zum
Beispiel, kommt ein Nebenfluß über ein Feld, das durch Dünger usw.
verdorben ist, so wird das Wasser folglich auch Elemente von der verdorbenen Erde in sich aufnehmen oder Gifte annehmen, falls solche in
dem Boden liegen. Dasselbe finden wir in den Händen. Jede Teilung
einer Linie teilt und vervielseitigt ihre Eigenschaft, nimmt Eigenschaften
an von dem betreffenden Berge, der durchquert oder berührt wird, oder
beeinflußt andere Linien, die von dieser berührt, gekreuzt oder geschnitten werden. Derartige Beispiele finden wir in der Natur tausendfach,
wenn wir nur sehen wollen.

Bei den Hauptlinien werde ich ihre Charakteristik (astrale Bedeutung) an den entsprechenden Stellen obenan stellen. Es ist gut, wenn
der Student der Chirologie auch gleichzeitig — für den Anfang wenigstens — die bildliche Darstellung der astralen Bedeutung der Berge
damit vergleicht und in Zusammenhang bringt.

B e a c h t e : Eine gute Linie soll klar, gut gezeichnet, von guter
Länge und Farbe sein. Sie soll nicht kettig oder knotig sein, nicht
Punkte, Flecken, Insel, Ring, Kreuz oder Stern enthalten. Auch soll sie
nicht zu sehr gegabelt, mißformt, gedreht sein, noch Bruch oder dicke
Querlinien enthalten. Jedes Zeichen muß erst für sich allein und dann
in Kombination beurteilt werden. Je mehr Linien vorhanden sind,

110

desto tiefere Empfindungskraft der Seele ist vorhanden, obgleich manchmal unbewußt bzw. ungeweckt. Eine „zerrissene" Seele bedingt zerrissene Linien. Man vergesse nie die Farbe der Linie.

Bei der Beobachtung des Verlaufs der einzelnen Linien dürfte es auffallen, daß die Kopflinie in e n t g e g e n gesetzter Richtung zur Herzlinie verläuft; ebenso die Lebenslinie entgegengesetzt zur Saturnlinie. Das ist kein Zufall. Es ist ein scheinbarer Widerstreit der Kräfte, der jedoch für die persönliche Entwicklung erforderlich ist. — Nur durch Arbeit an uns selbst können wir zur Klarheit und zum Aufstieg gelangen.

Handlinien. Allgemeines und Besonderes.*)

Bild 21 zeigt die normale Lage der

H a u p t l i n i e n.

L e b e n s l i n i e , beginnend zwischen Daumen und Zeigefinger und um den Daumenballen verlaufend. Sie gibt Auskunft über den Strom der Lebenskraft; Zufuhr, Umwandlung, Verwertung derselben, sowie über den Verlauf des Lebens, Körper- und Blutbeschaffenheit, über den Zeitpunkt der Ereignisse und die Lebensdauer.

K o p f l i n i e , beginnend nahe am Anfang der Lebenslinie und quer über die Handfläche nach dem Mars- oder Mondberge verlaufend. Sie gibt Auskunft über das Gehirn und alles, was damit in Verbindung steht, Denken, Gedanken r i c h t u n g , Pläne, Krankheiten des Gehirns und der Augen.

H e r z l i n i e , beginnend am Handrand unter dem kleinen Finger und in waagerechter (aber der Kopflinie entgegengesetzter) Richtung verlaufend nach Saturn- oder Jupiterberg. Sie gibt Aufschluß über alles, was mit dem Herzen zusammenhängt: Krankheiten, Herzgefühle, Liebessachen und Ethik.

M a g e n - o d e r G e s u n d h e i t s l i n i e , beginnend nahe dem Handgelenk und in der Richtung zum kleinen (oder Merkur-) Finger verlaufend. Aus dieser Linie ist zu ersehen: der Gesamtnervenzustand und die Drüsentätigkeit, Störungen der Verdauungsorgane sowohl, als auch Geschäftsangelegenheiten, Stimmungen.

---

*) In dem Buch „Hand und Persönlichkeit" von Steindamm-Ackermann werden nur drei Handlinien gebracht und auch nur einige Berge. Diese Unvollständigkeit und das bewußte Vertauschen der geistigen und seelischen Einteilung sind irreführend und darum praktisch unbrauchbar.

Die Nebenlinien.

Saturn- oder Schicksalslinie, beginnend nahe der Handwurzel und nach dem Saturn- oder Jupiterberge verlaufend. Diese Linie bedeutet mehr ein Barometer für den Lebensweg, Ablauf des Lebens in bezug auf Tätigkeit, Beruf und Störungen darin, sowie Veränderungen.

Apollo- oder Sonnenlinie, beginnend nahe der Handwurzel oder Handmitte, verlaufend nach dem Apolloberge. Sie läuft fast immer parallel mit der Saturnlinie und gibt dieser eine Stabilisierung. Aus ihr erkennt man die seelische Empfindungsfähigkeit; das innere Erleben durch das Sonnengeflecht. (Nur in **dieser** Hinsicht hat der Name „Kunstlinie", der sonst ein Mißbrauch ist, eine Bedeutung.) Ob jemand musikalisch ist, also über Musik- und Farben **sinn** wirklich verfügt, läßt sich aus der Hand **nicht** ersehen, auch nicht materieller Wohlstand des Handeigners.

Venusgürtel; das ist eine Linie, die — wenn vorhanden — zwischen Jupiter- und Saturnfinger beginnt und halbkreisartig, zwischen Apollo- und Merkurfinger, verläuft. Diese Linie zeigt die Konstitution der Sexualnerven des Rückenmarks an; somit Feinnervigkeit, Neurasthenie und Hysterie.

Uranus- oder Intuitionslinie, wenn vorhanden, beginnend in der unteren Ecke des Mondberges und im Bogen in die Magenlinie verlaufend, bedeutet Intuition, Einfühlung, evtl. Hellsinnigkeit.

Neptun- oder Giftlinie, wenn vorhanden, aus dem unteren Venusberg oder der Handmitte kommend, nach dem mittleren oder oberen Mondberge verlaufend. Bedeutung: Vorhandensein von Medizinalgiften im Körper, sowie Leid in der Liebe durch Irrtum.

Isislinie (selten!), verläuft senkrecht am Handrande vom Mondberge hoch bis nach dem Herzlinienanfang; Lebensernst, Enthaltsamkeitsneigungen.

Raszette oder Armband verläuft, unter dem Venusberge beginnend, über das Armgelenk (wie ein Armband) in ein bis drei, seltener vier Linien. Sie bedeutet: das Maß der ererbten Lebenskraft, evtl. eine zarte Lebenslinie verstärkend, ergänzend.

Ehelinien befinden sich auf dem Handrande des rechten Merkurbergs und zeigen an, in welchen Lebensjahren (der eigenen Entwicklung nach) eine Verbindung mit dem anderen Geschlecht für längere Zeit günstig oder ungünstig ist.

Die Zeichen (Bild 23).

> Wo ein Eindruck, ein Zeichen, eine Linie ist, muß eine Kraft tätig sein, durch welche jene hervorgerufen werden. Hat das Zeichen aber eine bestimmte Form, einen bestimmten Ausdruck, so arbeitet diese Kraft bewußt und ist vom göttlichen Geist beseelt.

Den Zeichen und den Linienformationen ist genaueste Beachtung zu schenken! Um sich von ihnen keine falschen und unklaren Vorstellungen zu machen, füge ich hintenstehend ganz klare Abbildungen bei. Manche Zeichen können durch Linien geformt sein, sie m ü s s e n es aber nicht; auch brauchen sie durchaus nicht allein zu stehen. Beides kommt aber oft vor. Es ist nicht die Beachtung des Zeichens allein notwendig, sondern auch, mit welchen Linien und Bergen es in Verbindung steht. Aus der Form der einzelnen Zeichen ersehen wir schon eine ganz bestimmte Gesetzmäßigkeit, und wer tiefer über die Entstehung nachdenkt, wird auch die Ursache erkennen. Es ist selbstverständlich, daß diese ganz bestimmten Zeichenarten nicht zufällig und zwecklos an den bestimmten Stellen stehen. Ein Kreuz besteht immer aus zwei kleinen Linien. Linien sind, wie ich schon sagte, Flüsse astraler Energien. Wenn eine solche kleine Linie auf einer Stelle erkennbar wird, m u ß an dieser Stelle auch etwas ganz Bestimmtes von einer Auswirkung vorhanden sein. Wieviel mehr noch, wenn sich zwei Linien in einem Kreuz oder einem Stern schneiden! Ein Ring ist wieder ein anderes Zeichen und muß dementsprechend auch wieder eine andere ganz besondere Bedeutung haben. Physiologisch ist die Ringlinie — die ja nicht allein auf der Haut liegt, sondern viel tiefer greift — eine Begrenzung, ein Abschließen von einem kleinen Platze, von vielen kleinen Zellen, die naturgemäß auch eine Anzahl Nervenenden enthalten. Ein Gitter ist nichts weiter als ein Zusammenschluß sehr vieler Kreuze. Siehe hierzu das eingeklammerte Bild 23/5. Für die Art der Zeichen ist keine Grenze gesetzt. Es gibt deren mehr, als man allgemein annimmt. Man muß auch in Betracht ziehen, daß alle Zeichen Symbole, Zeichensprache des Kosmos sind. Auf Wunsch vieler Zuschriften bringe ich auch diese verschiedenen Zeichen. (Bild 23.) Machen wir uns klar, w i e ein Zeichen entsteht, was es ist, und wie es konstruiert ist, so kommen schon die Gedanken der Erklärung von selbst. Nehmen wir eine gegebene Linie. Es bildet sich durch eine bestimmte Kraft oder einen Kräfteeinfluß eine zu dieser senkrecht verlaufende Linie. Hat letzte die erste geschnitten, so entsteht ein Schnittpunkt und damit ein Kreuz. Schneidet nun noch eine Linie dieses Kreuz im Schnittpunkte, so entsteht ein Stern; das Kreuz also aus zwei Kräften, der Stern aus drei. Damit beweist sich, daß der Stern in seiner

Wirkung stärker ist. Daß ein Kreuz oder Stern nicht an einer Linie zu hängen brauchen, sondern auch selbständig stehen können, wurde erklärt. Die alleinstehenden Sterne und Zeichen haben stärkere Wirkungen, als wenn sie mit Linien verbunden sind. Betrachten wir die Genauigkeit und Symmetrie bei Stern, Dreieck, Viereck, Buchstaben, Rune, Symbol, so muß man unbedingt zu der Überzeugung kommen, daß hier bewußte Kräfte und Gesetzmäßigkeit arbeiten. Es ist n i c h t gleichgültig, an welcher Stelle der Hand ein solches Zeichen erscheint. Denn da auch sie wieder mit einem bestimmten Organ verbunden ist, und dieses wieder durch Gedankenkräfte mehr oder weniger beeinflußt wird — Denkart, daher Anschauung, Charakter —, so ergibt sich von selbst d i e Erkenntnis, daß Krankheit und Charakter, Lebensanschauung in Wechselwirkung stehen, voneinander abhängig sind und sich gegenseitig beeinflussen. — Das beschrieb ich schon in der Einführung: Verkehrtes Denken ergibt Krankheit, und Krankheit ist verkehrtes Denken.

Ein roter Punkt z. B. zeigt eine allerfeinste Ansammlung von Blut, eine Verletzung im kleinsten Sinne. Weil die Stelle, an der der rote Punkt erscheint, mit einem bestimmten Organ in Verbindung steht, aber auch mit einer bestimmten Stelle des Gehirns, so ergibt sich hieraus, daß in dem betreffenden Organ eine — wenn auch sehr kleine — Veränderung eingetreten ist; ebenso auch, daß die betreffende Stelle im Gehirn — wenn auch nur sehr minimal — eine Beeinflussung erlitten hat. So wirkt sich der rote Punkt einmal organisch (als Leiden, Krankheit) aus, zum andern durch das Gehirn, im Denken oder Handeln. Mit dem blauen und braunen Punkt ist es ebenso, nur daß sie nicht mit einer Verletzung, sondern mit den Nerven, mit Fieber oder auch Krampf zusammenhängen.

Ein Ring ist eine Abgrenzung eines bestimmten Teiles der Oberfläche der Innenhand, muß also auch eine Abgrenzung innerlich haben. Da Inseln in den Hauptlinien schon bei der Geburt mitgebracht werden, so sind sie Zeichen der Vererbung. Inseln sind ebenso wie Kreise, aber in verstärktem Maße, Abgrenzungen, jedoch hier in den feinstofflichen (astralen) Flußströmen (Hauptlinien) und wirken deshalb zumeist das ganze Leben hindurch auf den Körper ein. Wenn Ringe auch wieder gelegentlich verschwinden, Inseln verschwinden — wenn sie in den Hauptlinien vorhanden sind — selten oder n i e. — In kleinen Linien können sie verschwinden und tun es oft. Stehen sie allein, d. h. unabhängig von Linien, so sind sie Zeichen für körperlichen Eingriff (Verletzungen, Operationen). Was symmetrisch und scharfkantig ist (Dreieck u. dgl.), wirkt positiv, was rund, weich ist, wirkt mehr negativ. Deshalb zeigt auch die viereckige Insel in der Kopflinie eine stärkere Kraft in der Auswirkung als die runde.

F l e c k e dürfen nicht mit Punkten verwechselt werden. Ein Punkt ist so groß, als wäre eine Stelle mit einer Stecknadel gestochen; ungefähr 1/4 so groß wie der Kopf solcher Nadel, also etwa 0,5 mm.

F l e c k e sind größer, 3, 4, auch 5 mm. Sie haben wieder eine ganz andere Bedeutung, die ich hier nicht weiter erklären will, da die Beobachtungen noch nicht abgeschlossen sind. — Ebenso ist es mit Warzen. Diese Dinge werden genauer in meinem Ergänzungsband erklärt *).

P u n k t e können verschiedene Farben haben. Rote Punkte sind ein Zeichen für Verwundungen oder Verletzungen; dunkle für Krankheiten der Nerven, Fieber, auch für Krampf.

F l e c k e sind verschieden groß, meist aber nicht größer, als auf Bild 23 ersichtlich ist. Die Farben sind auch hier verschieden: Rot, blau, braun.

R i n g e sind immer ungünstig, mit Ausnahme auf dem Jupiterberg.

K r e u z e haben verschiedene Bedeutung, sind aber meist ungünstig. Das liegende oder Andreaskreuz (das letzte auf dem Bilde), auch Sägebock genannt, ist sehr ungünstig, besonders auf dem Jupiterberge.

S t e r n e sind meist bösartig, mit Ausnahme auf Apollo- und Jupiterberg. (Die eingeklammerten Zeichen zeigen, wie solche entstehen.)

I n s e l n , in Linien, sind allemal Zeichen von Leiden oder Schwächen vererbter Art. Alleinstehend zeigen sie Verletzungen durch Operation an.

D r e i e c k e sind mit einer Ausnahme in jedem Falle ein sehr günstiges Zeichen und deuten auf geistige Dinge und Wissen hin.

Q u a d r a t e sind immer ein gutes Zeichen und bedeuten Schutz. Hoch- und alleinstehend mit gekreuzten Ecken ist das Quadrat ungünstig (Mondberg).

G i t t e r sind immer ungünstig. (Die eingeklammerte Figur zeigt, wie ein Gitter entsteht.)

H a l b s t e r n e , manchmal am Ende einer Linie zu finden, sind ungünstig (Augen).

R u n e n , verschiedene Zeichen, worunter auch Symbole und Buchstaben kommen, sind auf Bild 23 gezeigt.

Die zuletzt, unten links, aufgeführten sind solche Runen, die einer Zugehörigkeit zu dem betreffenden Planeten (am Anfang der Zeile) unterstehen, infolgedessen auch mit ähnlichen Eigenschaften wirken. W i e sie an den einzelnen Stellen der Innenhand wirken, ist noch nicht genau festgestellt, da sie verhältnismäßig selten vorkommen. Ich füge sie hinzu, um den Fortgeschrittenen neue Anhaltspunkte in bezug auf Zeichen zu geben. Symbole wie Hakenkreuz, Fünfstern, Sechsstern usw. haben mehr eine rein geistige Bedeutung. Dementsprechend sind sie

---

*) Siehe: „Charakterologische Tatsachen und deren Merkmale." Neudruck wird vorbereitet.

auch in der Lesung zu werten. Ein Hakenkreuz bedeutet nicht etwa „Antisemit". — Das Hakenkreuz oder Swastika hat mit der jüdischen Frage ursprünglich nichts zu tun, sondern ist eine uralte Heilsrune und hat vielmehr eine tiefreligiöse Bedeutung. Ein Mißbrauch solcher Heilsrunen kann für die Bedeutung im wahren Sinne nie verantwortlich gemacht werden. — Ebensowenig hat der Sechsstern mit den Juden zu tun; er ist ein Symbol tiefgeistiger Bedeutung — selbstverständlich im ethischen Sinne. — Bei den Planetenzeichen auf der Tafel (unten links) fügte ich in jeder Zeile noch die beiden vorletzten Runen hinzu: göttliche Siegel, und als letztes Zeichen: dämonisches Siegel der betreffenden Planeten (nach Paracelsus u. Agrippa v. N.). —

Buchstaben zwischen oder an den Linien oder auf den Bergen sind keine Seltenheit. Besonders oft sind sie auf dem Apolloberge zu finden und klar erkennbar. Sie sind ebensowenig wie sonstige Zeichen zufällig, sondern haben ihre Bedeutung. Meist sind es Anfangsbuchstaben von Vornamen (selten von Geschlechtsnamen, denn im Namen steckt Gesetz), und zwar von Menschen, mit denen man in engere Berührung kam oder noch kommen wird. Mag mancher dies auch als Spielerei betrachten, es tut nichts; Tatsachen lassen sich nicht leugnen. Sie werden ja fast immer von den Betreffenden, welche diese Buchstaben haben, bestätigt. Dieser Beweis gilt mehr als alle Vorurteile. Ob Buchstaben günstig stehen, erkennt man daran, daß sie nach oben (nach den Fingern zu) offen sind. Umgekehrt sind sie, wie die dadurch repräsentierten Personen, ungünstig. Liegend bedeuten sie Hemmungen durch jene Personen. — Manchmal erkennt man vollständige Namen. Auch Zahlen kommen in derselben Art vor.

Kreuz (Größe ¼ bis 1 cm).

Jupiterberg (günstig): Günstige Bekanntschaft in dem Jahre, wo der Schnittpunkt liegt (Bild 27/15).

Saturnberg: Warnungszeichen für Körperverletzung durch Stein, Erde, Ziegel, Baugerüst, Einsturz, Eisenbahn, Straßenbahn, Auto, Gefährt, Zusammenstoß (durch Hemmungen) usw. (Bild 29/28).

Apolloberg (günstig): Günstige Zeit (zu messen ist der Kreuzpunkt) für Bekanntschaften mit Personen von freigeistigen Berufen: Künstlern, Wissenschaftlern (Bild 24/26).

Merkurberg: Günstig, wenn keine schlechte Handform oder sonstige Zeichen von Minderwertigkeiten vorhanden sind, für Literatur und Unternehmen im Handel. In schlechter Hand: Niederes Denken und Handeln (Bild 27/16).

Marsberg: Streit und evtl. dadurch Körperverletzung, Überfall, Anrempelung (Bild 28/2).

116

M o n d b e r g , oben: Melancholische Anwandlungen (Bild 29). Unten, nahe Raszette: Geschenke im späteren Alter (Bild 27 links); neben der Saturnlinie: Warnung vor Verlust durch Diebstahl und Spekulation (Bild 27 rechts).

V e n u s b e r g : Liebesangelegenheiten, die Ungünstiges in sich bergen (Bild 27).

In der L e b e n s l i n i e : Gefahr durch Krankheit oder für das Leben, je nach der mehr oder minder starken Markierung (Bild 27/25).

In der K o p f l i n i e : Kopf- oder Augenverletzung (Bild 29/8).

Dicht neben der Herzlinie: Verlust einer nahestehenden Person (Bild 29/23).

In der M a g e n l i n i e : Kränklichkeit (Bild 26 rechts).

Dicht an der L e b e n s l i n i e (außen): Streitigkeiten, Prozesse (Bild 25/3).

Im M a r s f e l d : Streit (Bild 27).

Dicht über der K o p f l i n i e , unter Apolloberg: Warnt vor Beinverletzung (Bild 29). Unter Merkurberg: Warnt vor Armverletzung (Bild 29 rechts).

In d e n F i n g e r n : Meist ungünstig.

In d e r R a s z e t t e : Sorge, Verlust, Ärger (Bild 28).

S t e r n (Größe 0,5 bis 1 cm).

Sterne verstärken die Bedeutung des Kreuzes.

A m H a n d r a n d e n a h e J u p i t e r b e r g : Gefahr für Brandschaden (Bild 29 rechts).

I m H a n d t i s c h : Gunst bei dem anderen Geschlecht (Bild 28/12).

V i e l e k l e i n e S t e r n e oder Kreuze im Handtisch (oder „G r o ß e n V i e r e c k"): Gefahr für Körperverletzung durch Feuer, Dampf; Verbrennen oder Verbrühen (Bild 28/12).

A u f d e r S a t u r n l i n i e , mehr nach dem Anfang zu: Finanzielle Verluste zur Zeit, da der Betreffende noch jung war (Bild 27/7).

In d e r L e b e n s l i n i e : Starkes Ereignis, wie schwere Krankheit; wenn sehr tief markiert, evtl. Tod i n d e m Jahre, wo der Schnittpunkt liegt, falls in beiden Händen. Immer ist die R e c h t e ausschlaggebend (Bild 27/25).

N a h e L e b e n s l i n i e (innen): Gram durch Verlust einer nahestehenden Person. Außen: Streitigkeiten, Prozesse (Bild 27).

I n d e r K o p f l i n i e : Augenschaden durch Verletzung oder Operation (was dasselbe ist); wenn am Ende der Kopflinie: Augenschaden durch Entzündung (Bild 29/8).

In e i n e r R e i s e l i n i e : Gefahr für Körperverletzung auf Reisen (Bild 25 links).

In einer Ehelinie: Ungünstig.
In den Fingern: Zumeist ungünstig.
(Wenn alte Chiromanten solche Zeichen für „Ruhm", „Ehre" usw. werten, besonders solche, die soviel Stolz auf minderwertiges „Zigeunerwissen" legen, so sind das Fabeln. Ruhm und Ehre sind leere Begriffe, Schein, und werden durch Kreuze oder Sterne n i c h t angezeigt.)

Dreieck (Größe 0,5 bis 1 cm).

Dreiecke sind immer Zeichen, die mit Wissen in Verbindung stehen. Sie müssen nicht allein stehen, doch ist ihre Kraft größer, wenn sie allein stehen. In Verbindung mit Linien hängen auch die Eigenschaften mit den betreffenden Linien zusammen. — Sie bedeuten auf dem:

Jupiterberg: Neigung zu Politik, soweit diese nicht mit Lügen zusammenhängt oder mit Verschleierung (Bild 28/18). Bei minderwertigem Handtyp wird beides verbunden.

Saturnberg: Gibt Neigung zu Religionsphilosophie und magnetischen Wissenschaften, wenn die Hand gut ist. Bei einer minderwertigen Hand macht sich die Neigung bemerkbar, diese Wissenszweige zum Schaden anderer im Mißbrauch auszunutzen oder anzuwenden (Bild 28/29).

Apolloberg: Ethik und Ästhetik als Neigung oder Interesse (Bild 28).

Merkurberg: Klugheit, Routine in geschäftlichen Angelegenheiten oder Auswerten von wissenschaftlichen Gedanken und Dingen, auch Diplomatie (Bild 28/37).

Marsberg: Sinn für Strategie; auch sich aus Affären ziehen können, also Strategie im Kleinen (Bild 28/33).

Mondberg: Sinn für Studien metaphysischer oder okkultistischer Art; auch, daß solche Kenntnisse praktisch oder wissenschaftlich ausgewertet werden: Symboldeutung (Bild 29).

An der Magenlinie: Verstärkt magnetische Kräfte; pharmazeutische Begabung (Bild 28 links).

An der Uranus- oder Intuitionslinie: Gute okkulte Fähigkeiten (Bild 27 rechts).

Am Ende der Kopflinie: Telepathie (Gedankenübertragung) (Bild 24/B). Dieses Dreieck entsteht durch Kombination von Kopflinie (Verstand), Magenlinie (Nervenkraft im allgemeinen und gute Drüsentätigkeit), Apollolinie (Vibration des Sonnengeflechts).

Nahe Anfang der Herzlinie: Sinn für Elektro-Biologie und Magie (Bild 27/47). Dieses Dreieck entsteht durch Kombination der Herzlinie (Herzkraft, Mut), Magenlinie (siehe oben) und Sonnenlinie (siehe ebenda).

In oder an der R a s z e t t e : Ruhiges Alter (Bild 27/14).
A u f r e c h t s t e h e n d e s Dreieck (mit der Spitze nach oben, nach den Fingern zu), macht mehr geneigt zur Betätigung des Wissens.
U m g e k e h r t   s t e h e n d (mit der Spitze nach unten), macht mehr geneigt, über das Wissen nachzudenken, zu meditieren, zu sinnen.
Beide zusammen, ähnlich einer $\overline{\times}$, kombinieren beides günstig.
Ein D o p p e l d r e i e c k , eines i m anderen (Bild 25/10), kommt sehr selten vor und nach meiner Beobachtung nur im Marsfelde: Gibt Neigung zu Mord.

V i e r e c k   o d e r   Q u a d r a t (Größe 0,5 bis 1 cm).

Vierecke sind immer günstig und bedeuten Schutz in der betreffenden Sache, mit der sie in Verbindung oder in deren Nähe sie stehen.
Ungünstig ist das Zeichen nur, wenn auf dem Venusberg, a n der Lebenslinie. Hier bedeutet es: Abgeschiedenheit, Asyl, Internat, Gefangenschaft (Bild 27 rechts).
Ungünstig ist es noch, wenn es hoch steht mit gekreuzten Ecken, wie liegendes Andreaskreuz (das letzte auf dem Bild), auf Mondberg: Nierenstörung (Bild 26/6).

R i n g (Größe 3 bis 5 mm).

Ringe haben in den Linien immer eine ungünstige Bedeutung, und ihre Einflüsse sind nicht gut zu umgehen. Einzeln stehend kommen sie seltener vor, und die Bedeutung ist dann verschieden — zumeist aber ungünstig. Auch dieses Zeichen ist mehr für medizinische Diagnostik zu verwerten und zeigt an verschiedenen Stellen Augenschaden an.
A u f   d e m   A p o l l o b e r g (nahe dem Beugegelenk des Apollofingers), auf der K o p f l i n i e , auf der L e b e n s l i n i e , auf der M a g e n - l i n i e bedeuten sie Augenschaden (Bild 29/10, 25/16, 25/25).
Auf der H e r z l i n i e : Warnungszeichen für Gifte (Bild 26 rechts).

I n s e l n (Größe verschieden, von 0,5 bis 3 cm lang,
mitunter sogar länger).

Dieses Zeichen kann man mit einem zusammengedrückten Kreis oder Ring vergleichen. Bedeutung ist i m m e r ungünstig!
I n   e i n e r   E r e i g n i s l i n i e bedeutet eine Insel: Enttäuschung (Bild 31/52, Linie 19—19; 31/41, 30/38.)
I n   e i n e r   H a u p t l i n i e : I m m e r   V e r e r b u n g von Krankheits- dispositionen. O b und w a n n sich diese Leiden auslösen, bemerk- bar machen, ist eine Frage der Zeit. Manchmal kann man sie aus- messen, manchmal nicht (noch unsicher).

Alleinstehend sind Inseln Zeichen von Verletzung des Körpers durch Operation. In diesem Falle sind sie nicht auszumessen.

In einer O p e r a t i o n s l i n i e (Linie von der Lebenslinie oder aus dem Venusberge nach dem Marsberge, quer über die Hand laufend) lassen sie sich genau ausmessen, aufs Jahr (Bild 31/19—19).

Also auch dieses Zeichen ist rein medizinisch zu werten; doch will ich die Vererbungszeichen hier erklären, um den Interessenten auch in diesen besonders wertvollen Wissenszweig einen Einblick zu geben (Bild 32).

I n s e l 1: Körperliche Erbmasse, die in der Kindheit eine Schwäche des Körpers gibt.

I n s e l 2: Vererbung von Dispositionen für Schwäche im mittleren Alter.

I n s e l 3: Vererbung von Krebskonstitution, die ein Vorfahr hatte, die derjenige aber, der dieses Zeichen hat, nicht auch bekommen muß.

I n s e l 3 u n d 18 : Vorfahr hatte Magenkrebs.

I n s e l 3 u n d 19: Vorfahr hatte Hals- oder Brustkrebs.

I n s e l 3 u n d 20: Vorfahr hatte Leber- oder Darmkrebs.

I n s e l 3 u n d 21: Vorfahr hatte Blasen- oder Unterleibskrebs.

I n s e l 4: Vorfahr hatte Brustkrankheit.

I n s e l 5: Vererbung von Disposition für Augenschwäche.

I n s e l 6: Vererbung von Disposition für Gehörschwäche.

I n s e l 7, 8 (in der Kopflinie): Vorfahr hatte Verkalkung. Bei allen, die diese Insel haben, werden sich früher oder später Kopfschmerzen bemerkbar machen: Migräne!

I n s e l 9, 10: Vererbung von Disposition zu Herzleiden (Bild 41).

I n s e l 11: Vererbung von Disposition zu Lungentuberkulose (Bild 43 links).

I n s e l 12: Vererbung von Disposition zu Leberleiden.

I n s e l 13: Vererbung von Disposition für Nierenleiden (Bild 37).

I n s e l 14: Vererbung von Disposition für Gallenleiden (Bild 41).

I n s e l 15: Vererbung von Disposition für Magenleiden (Bild 41).

I n s e l 16: Vererbung von Disposition für allgemeine Feinnervigkeit.

I n s e l 17: Vererbung für Störungen im Solar plexus (Sonnengeflecht), vorgeburtlicher Einfluß durch die Mutter: Scheu, Lampenfieber.

I n s e l 23: Vererbung von Disposition für Hysterie usw.

I n s e l 25: Vererbung von Feinnervigkeit für Hellsinnigkeit. (Uranus-L.)

I n s e l 25: Vererbung von allgemeiner Schüchternheit, Erröten (seelische Belastung von seiten der Mutter in der Zeit der Schwangerschaft durch Leid). Apollo-L. unter Herzlinie.

I n s e l 25: Unter Merkurfinger: Gehirnnervenschwäche.

Gitter.

Gitter sind Liniengebilde aus Senkrechten und Waagerechten und können verschiedene Größe haben, von 0,5 bis 2 cm im Quadrat. Die Größe kann man nicht genau festlegen, denn viele Kreuz- und Querlinien ergeben schon Gitter. Sind senkrechte Linien gut als Längsströme, so sind alle Querströmungen Hemmungen; sie stören und verderben. Es gibt genaue Gitterformationen, die wie am Lineal gezogen erscheinen. Diese sind dann von obenerwähnter Größe. Auch kann, wie es bei allen Zeichen der Fall ist, ein Gitter selbständig stehen oder durch andere Linien in Kombination konstruiert sein. Erstes hat mehr Kraft in der Auswirkung, da es eine positive Krafterscheinung ist. Wo immer sie erscheinen, verderben sie die Stelle und deren Einfluß. Man kann sagen, ein Gitter besteht aus sehr vielen Kreuzen (siehe Zeichentafel). Denken wir uns zwei Linien waagerecht und zwei senkrecht die ersten durchschneidend, dazu eine Umrandung, dann haben wir dreimal drei kleine Felder: das Quadrat des Saturn (Bild 23/6). Nebenbei bemerkt sei, daß dieses Zeichen in der Gaunersprache Gefängnis bedeutet. Ein Gitter besonderer Art gibt es noch, das nur mitunter auf dem Apolloberg erscheint. Diese Linienformation ist mehr auf die Spitze gestellt (Bild 23/4) und bedeutet: Disposition zu Besessenheit. Sie ist eine rein astrale — sehr selten eine diesseitige — Angelegenheit. Personen, die niederen Spiritismus treiben, können von solchen Einflüssen angegriffen werden. Diese Art Einflüsse zu leugnen oder abzustreiten, beweist nur Unwissenheit auf diesem Gebiete.

Es gibt noch andere Zeichen, Runen und Symbole, die man nicht in eine bestimmte Ordnung bringen kann. Ich habe sie auf Bild 23 auf der unteren Hälfte gebracht. Die Wertung und Ausdeutung ist in d i e s e m Falle eine mehr esoterische und intuitive, die abhängt von dem Ort, an dem solch ein Zeichen steht, wie auch von der Umgebung anderer Zeichen und Linien. Aus dem Grunde kann ich hier auch nicht näher darauf eingehen. Man kann solche Ausdeutung nicht als wissenschaftlich bezeichnen, weshalb sie den rein objektiven Inhalt des vorliegenden Werkes überschreitet.

Über die Zeichen auf den einzelnen Fingern.

Bei besonders linienreichen Händen oder solchen mit sehr zarter Haut findet man auf den Fingerflächen der Innenhand mitunter verschiedene Zeichen, wie Querlinien, Kreuze, Sterne, Gitter, Haken, Quadrate usw., die selbstverständlich auch ihre besonderen Bedeutungen haben.

Bisher brachte ich über diese Zeichen auf den Fingern sehr wenig, da ich nur einige beachte und in ihrer Bedeutung auswerte. Es kommt noch dazu, daß ich diese Zeichen nicht immer mit den angegebenen Bedeutungen übereinbringen konnte, soweit es sich um alte Literatur handelte. Dennoch will ich aber Interessenten dieser Wissenschaft nicht vorenthalten, was Comte de Saint-Germain, einer der besten Chirosophen vergangener Jahrzehnte, darüber schreibt. Jeder mag dann mit Nachprüfungen beginnen oder seine Beobachtung darin machen. Für die Richtigkeit a l l e r dieser Ausdeutungen kann ich keine Garantie übernehmen, da meine Nachprüfungen dieser Zeichen noch nicht abgeschlossen sind. Ich gebe sie also ausdrücklich mit Vorbehalt wieder.

A m D a u m e n. E r s t e s G l i e d seitliche Längslinien: Die Willenskraft ist klarer und markanter. Wenn zu viele Linien vorhanden sind, wird die Willenskraft durch Zersplitterung verringerte Resultate ergeben. Sind diese Längslinien durch Querlinien gestört, bedeutet dies, daß sich Hindernisse im Verlauf des Erfolges zeigen werden.

Ein Kreuz an der Innenseite des ersten Daumengliedes, dazu viele Linien auf dem Venusberg: Untugenden im Sexualleben. Zwei Kreuze: Liebe für Luxus.

Ein Stern an derselben Stelle; dazu viele Linien auf dem Venusberg: Wie bei einem Kreuz, aber verstärkt.

Zwei Sterne (in der Nähe des Nagels): Dauernörgler.

Ein Dreieck: Die Willenskraft und Aufmerksamkeit ist konzentriert im wissenschaftlichen und sonstigen tiefen Denken.

Ein Ring: Gute Erfolge durch einen sich gleichbleibenden, ruhigen Willen.

Ein Quadrat: Die Willenskraft ist in einer bestimmten Richtung konzentriert; oft auch Disposition zu Tyrannei.

Ein Gitter in der Nähe des Nagels: Gefahr für schwere Körperschäden oder Tod durch den eigenen Lebenskameraden (Gatten oder Gattin).

Z w e i t e s G l i e d. Längslinien bedeuten klare gesunde Logik.

Querlinien: Falsche Logik, wenig Realbewußtsein.

Eine Gabellinie: Hemmungen in der Durchführung von Dingen.

Ein Kreuz: Eine leicht zu beeinflussende Natur.

Ein oder zwei Sterne: Eine Natur, die leicht auf schlechte Wege gebracht werden kann, aber sonst eine liebenswürdige Art hat.

Ein Dreieck: Anlagen für tieferes und philosophisches Denken.

Ein Quadrat: Eine nicht leicht zu erschütternde Logik; wenn aber negative Zeichen, Querlinien usw. vorhanden sind: Hartköpfigkeit bis zur Dummheit.

Ein Kreis: Scharfes Denken und beste Logik.

Ein Gitter: Mangel an Sinn für Moral und ehrliches Nachdenken.

122

Eine lange Linie aus dem zweiten Daumenglied bis zur Lebenslinie: Unannehmlichkeiten usw. im Eheleben.

An allen Fingern. Zarte kleine Ballen an den ersten Gliedern: Große körperliche Feinfühligkeit und Empfindlichkeit.

Kleine kurze senkrechte Linien über alle Fingergelenke: Plötzlicher Tod. (Hierzu muß man auch noch möglichst andere Zeichen beobachten!)

Lange durchgehende Linien von der Spitze bis in das dritte Glied: Strenger Sinn für Ehre und Ehrenhaftigkeit.

Viele kleine Querlinien an allen Fingerspitzen: Geschwächte Gesundheit (Bild 25/32).

Wenn diese kleinen Querlinien wellenartig sind: Gefahr durch Wasser (Bild 25/33 u. 55).

Dreiecke an allen zweiten Gliedern: Neigung zur körperlichen Schwäche und Krankheit.

Am Zeigefinger. Längslinien im ersten Glied: Religiöser Fanatismus.

Querlinien auf dem ersten Glied: Religiöser Wahn.

Ein Kreuz auf dem ersten Glied: Gefahrvoller Wahn durch Visionen; oft auch Zeichen für plötzlichen Tod.

Ein Dreieck: Neigung für Religionsstudien, alte Magie und Okkultismus.

Ein Kreis (Ring): Der Glaube übertrifft die Logik.

Ein Gitter: Abgeschiedenheit wie Gefängnis, Kloster; ein Zeichen für ausführenden (aktiven) Fanatismus (Bild 29/55).

Zweites Glied. Längslinien: Edle Bestrebungen des Betreffenden finden gute Mithilfe.

Krumme Linien: Die Bestrebungen sind von minderwertigem Charakter.

Querlinien auf dem zweiten und dritten Gliede: Neidische und betrügerische Instinkte (Bild 25/26 u. 27).

Eine Gabellinie im zweiten Gliede: Mißerfolge.

Ein Kreuz auf dem Beugegelenk zwischen erstem und zweitem Gliede: Erfolg in Literatur.

Ein oder zwei Kreuze auf dem zweiten Gliede: Protektion durch Höhergestellte (Bild 25/53).

Ein Stern mit einer senkrechten Linie zu beiden Seiten: Keuschheit.

Ein Stern mit Mond zur Seite: Unbescheidenheit; Unverschämtheit.

Ein Dreieck: Politiker. Ein Quadrat: Zähigkeit in der Zweckverfolgung.

Ein Ring: Erfolgreiche Bestrebungen. Ein Gitter: Treulos und verräterisch.

Auf dem dritten Gliede. — Gerade Längslinie: Sichere Kontrolle über andere. Krumme Linien: Vorliebe für gute Dinge und Genuß regieren.

Senkrechte Linien und aufsteigende Äste an der Lebenslinie: Reichtum.

Querlinien: Hindernisse bei Unternehmen; kleine Rente; schlechte Verdauung.

Eine Gabellinie: Unternehmungen haben Mißerfolg.

Ein Stern: Schlechteste Angewohnheiten und böse Instinkte.

Ein Gitter: Eine verkommene Natur; oft auch Gefängnis.

Eine Linie aus dem Venusberg kommend und das dritte Beugegelenk schneidend: Heftiger Tod; andere Zeichen müssen mit in Betracht gezogen werden!

Am Mittelfinger. — Langdurchgehende senkrechte Wellenlinien, dazu Querlinien auf dem Saturnberg: Anhäufung von fatalen Ereignissen.

Erstes Glied: Längslinien: Selbstmord. (?)

Querlinien: Selbstmordgedanken.

Ein schwarzer Punkt oder Fleck: Chronische Malaria.

Ein Kreuz: Krankhafte Einbildungen, die oft zum Wahnsinn führen — manchmal auch Neigungen zu Verbrechen oder Selbstmord (Bild 25/31).

Ein Stern: Eine außergewöhnliche Existenz für Gut oder Böse. Wenn in beiden Händen: Gefahr, ermordet zu werden. — Wenn aber seitlich stehend: Tod im gerechten Sinne (Bild 25/30).

Ein Stern, dazu ein Dreieck auf Saturnberg: Verdorbenheit.

Ein Stern je im ersten und zweiten Gliede: Tod durch Hinrichtung.

Zweites Glied. Eine Längslinie, die das erste und zweite Beugegelenk schneidet: Dummheit und Narrheit.

Querlinien: Unwissenheit und Hartköpfigkeit (Bild 25/56—58).

Eine dicke Querlinie: Tod durch Gift (Bild 25/57).

Ein Kreuz: Gefährliche Zufälle.

Ein Stern: Für gewöhnlich unvermeidliche Katastrophe, evtl. Verbrechen (Bild 25/29).

Ein Quadrat: Ein weiteres Zeichen für unvermeidliches Unglück.

Ein Dreieck: Neigung zu okkulten Studien.

Ein Gitter: Unglück; oft Leiden der Beine, Ohren oder Nerven.

Drittes Glied. — Eine oder zwei Längslinien vom zweiten ins dritte Glied: Weisheit.

Eine einzelne starke senkrechte Linie im dritten Glied: Erfolg beim Militär.

Wenn diese Linie schräg verläuft: Tod im Kriege.

Viele kleine Längslinien: Erfolg durch Minenarbeit, Bergwerk usw.

Viele Querlinien: Ein verdorbenes Leben in Einsamkeit, von Freunden verlassen (Bild 26/34).

Ausnahmsweise und mit glattem erstem Glied: Erbschaft.

Eine Gabellinie: Eine unglückliche Natur, die anderer Leute Gesellschaft haßt und unbeliebt ist.

Ein Kreuz (in Frauenhand): Unfruchtbarkeit. Ein Kreuz mit je einer waagerechten Linie über und unter sich: Diebische Neigungen.

Ein Stern: In guter Hand bedeutet die Möglichkeit des Ermordetwerdens.

In einer schlechten Hand mit anderen Zeichen bedeutet er, daß der Betreffende selbst Mörder ist (Bild 25/28).

Ein Ring: Großer Fortschritt im Studium der Naturphilosophie.

Ein Dreieck: Eine schlechte Natur, die auch vom Unglück verfolgt ist.

Ein Quadrat: Unbarmherzige und geizige Natur.

Ein Gitter: Typischer Wahnsinn der Geizigen (Bild 26/34).

Am Ringfinger. Erstes Glied. Längslinie: Künstlerische Talente führen zum Wahnsinn.

Querlinien: Hindernisse der künstlerischen Laufbahn verursachen Wahnsinn (Bild 29/54).

Ein Kreuz: Außergewöhnliche Keuschheit. Der Betreffende geht in seiner künstlerischen Arbeit ganz auf. Manchmal Wahnsinn durch übergroße Aufregungen in bezug auf künstlerische Bestrebungen.

Ein Stern: Wenn das vorher Gesagte nicht entwickelt ist, des Eigners Talente brechen durch zu Pracht und Glanz.

Ein Dreieck: Wissenschaft des Schönen. Ein Ring: Erfolg.

Ein Gitter: Wahnsinn schlimmster Art.

Zweites Glied. Eine starke Längslinie, durch das zweite ins dritte Glied: Große Berühmtheit.

Querlinien: Mangel an Talent, Eifersucht (Bild 25/59).

Eine Gabellinie: Bestrebungen sind geteilter Art und daher öde.

Ein liegendes Kreuz: Der giftige Neid des unvermögenden hinterlistigen Wettbewerbers.

Ein Stern: Außergewöhnliche Talente.

Ein Dreieck: Das Wissen und Erkennen der wahren Kunst reicht bis zu den göttlichen Mysterien.

Ein Quadrat: Ein auf bestimmtes Feld beschränktes Talent.

Ein Ring: Großer Erfolg. — Ein Gitter: Größte Disposition zu Neid.

Drittes Glied. — Viele Längslinien, die auch das zweite Beugegelenk durchschneiden: Ungehöriges Benehmen gegen das andere Geschlecht.

Eine tiefe Längslinie, ohne die Beugegelenke zu berühren: Glücksgefühl.

Querlinien: Dauerndes Unglück und beharrliche Armut.

Eine Gabellinie: Vergebliche Versuche für Berühmtheit und Reichtum.

Ein Halbmond: Unglück. — Ein Kreuz: Gestörter Beruf oder Geschäft.

Ein Stern: Außergewöhnliche Vorliebe für Lob, und Gefahr für Wahn aus diesem Grunde (Größenwahn).

Ein Dreieck: Klug und routiniert, sich ins rechte Licht zu bringen.

Ein Ring: Berühmtheit und Glück.

Ein Gitter: Armut; neidische Disposition; verdient Erniedrigung (Bild 25/60).

K l e i n e r   F i n g e r.   E r s t e s   G l i e d. Längslinien: Mischt sich in alle Angelegenheiten. In einer sehr guten Hand: Beredsamkeit und Gewandtheit.

Querlinien: Ein leerer Sprecher, oft auch Lügner und Dieb.

Eine Gabellinie: Wenig Erfolg in Geschäften.

Ein Kreuz, in guter Hand: Medialität; in schlechter Hand: Ein Diebstahl, der dem Dieb sehr zu schaffen macht.

Ein Stern: Erfolg als Redner, Mißerfolg in Geschäften.

Ein Dreieck: Neigung zu okkulten Wissenschaften, zu Beschwörungen usw.

Ein Quadrat: Ein kaufmännisches Genie.

Ein Gitter: Stotterer; schwarze Magie, diebische Neigungen und sonstige schlechte Merkureigenschaften (Bild 25/62).

Z w e i t e s   G l i e d. Krumme Längslinien: Betrügerische Neigungen.

Eine Gabellinie: Mangelhafte Ordnung verhindert jeden möglichen Erfolg.

Querlinien: Eine buntfarbene Lebensbahn.

Ein Kreuz: Große Schwierigkeiten; oft Gefängnis.

Ein Stern: Bekanntwerden durch Anwendung der schlechtesten Merkureigenschaften.

Ein Dreieck: Erfolg im praktischen Okkultismus.

Ein Quadrat: Hemmungen in der sonst guten Rednergabe; oft Gefängnis.

Ein Gitter: Gefängnis; Dummheit in eigenen Angelegenheiten.

D r i t t e s   G l i e d. Krumme senkrechte Linien: Diebische Neigungen.

— Eine dicke Linie, Querlinien oder Kreuz: Dasselbe.

Ein Stern: Gewandtheit und Witz.

Zwei Sterne: Unehrenhafter Tod als Folge von Diebstahl.

Quadrat: Schlechtes Betragen.

Gitter: Dieb mit großer Dummheit (Bild 25/61).

Der Venusberg. ♀

S c h w a c h   e n t w i c k e l t: Mangel an Seelengröße, Talent für Kunst, Energie, Herzlichkeit. Ist selbstsüchtig und gemütskalt.

N o r m a l: Sympathische Natur mit Anmut, Sinn für Schönheit in Farbe und Ton; auch Liebesbedürfnis und etwas Eitelkeit.

E x t r e m   s t a r k   u n d   r o t: Leichtsinn und Koketterie, zügellos (und evtl. grausam und wild) in Sinnlichkeit, infolgedessen treulos.

Fein gefurcht: Lebhaft und leidenschaftlich (in der Liebe nicht ohne Raffiniertheit) (Bild 24/20).

Stark gefurcht: Starkes sinnliches Verlangen, derbe Leidenschaft, gemütstief.

Voll und weich: Mildtätig, hilfsbereit, zart und kinderlieb, Zärtlichkeitsdrang.

Glatt, ohne Linien: Wenig Liebestrieb, leidenschaftslos, kühl bis kalt.

Gut entwickelt, mit weichen Fingern: Frohsinn, sonnig, leichtsinnig, zart und herzlich. Sinn für Genüsse des Lebens, Talent für Musik, Malerei, Poesie (ob Talente entwickelt oder nicht). Lieben Heiterkeit, Schönes, Tanz und Vergnügen.

Beachte: Ein guter Venusberg mildert böse Einflüsse in der Hand.

Zeichen auf Venusberg ♀.

• (Dunkel): Neigung zu Gehörstörung; rechte Hand: rechtes Ohr (Bild 30/56); linke Hand: linkes Ohr.

⊘ Verletzung: Vorsicht in geschlechtlicher Beziehung (Bild 30/22).

∂ Vorteilhafte Heirat verpaßt (Bild 30/14).

∂ Nahe der Lebenslinie: Skandalaffäre (Bild 30/13).

+ Nahe der Lebenslinie: Zank mit Verwandten (Bild 25/2).

+ Nahe der Mitte: Meist eine unglückliche Liebe, wenn nicht + auf ♃ Berg (Bild 27).

▦ Laune, Ausschweifung und zu starke evtl. verdorbene Sinnlichkeit (Bild 30/54).

✲ Einfluß des anderen Geschlechts: Gefahr oder Erfolg (Bild 30/23, 26/2).

✲ An Linie bis Lebenslinie: Verlust einer lieben Person (Bild 30/24).

✲ An der Basis des zweiten Daumengliedes: Unglückliche Ehe mit vielen Leiden (Bild 27/23).

△ Ruhe und Berechnung in der Liebe; Kraft zur Enthaltsamkeit (Bild 25/35, 25/5).

☐ Selbstverschuldete Gefahren durch und in Liebessachen (Bild 27).

☐ Nahe Lebenslinie, berührend: Gefahr für Abgeschlossenheit (Bild 30/32). Internierung, Klausur, Gefängnis.

Viele feine Linien: Sinnlichkeit verfeinerter Art (Bild 30/41).
Starke, tiefe Linien: Undankbarkeit; in schlechter Hand: Sehr sinnlich (Bild 30/55).
Querlinien (zu den Sinnlichkeitslinien): Hindernisse in der Liebe durch äußere oder ethische Einflüsse (Bild 24/21).

Vergleich mit Bild 30.

Gerade der **Venusberg** ist der Hauptplatz in der Hand, auf den wir besonders und genaueste Beachtung zu legen haben. Um dem Anfänger diesen Platz mit seinen vielen Wirkungen recht klar zu machen, sei mir gestattet, diese Erklärung bildlich darzustellen:

Betrachten wir den **Venusberg** als einen großen Hügel, auf dessen höchstem Punkt wir unser Haus (Heim) bauen. Die Lebenslinie, welche den Berg abgrenzt, sei die Grenze, der Zaun um unser Grundstück. Die dazwischen liegenden vielen kleinen und größeren Linien (Sinnlichkeitslinien) betrachten wir als die Wege in unserem Garten. Gehen wir einen dieser Wege entlang, so kommen wir, wenn er nicht an den Zaun (Lebenslinie) heranreicht, auch nicht an ihn heran, bleiben für uns in Ruhe. Führt aber einer dieser Wege bis an den Zaun (nahe der Straße), so bedeutet das (mit Bezug auf die Ströme und Kräfte, die außen vorbeilaufen): Eine Bekanntschaft. Wir stehen am Zaun und plaudern mit jemand drüben. (Bild 30, Zeichen 40). Natürlich kann solches Zeichen auch weiter oben liegen, je nachdem, in welchem Alter das Ereignis stattfindet.

Führt solch ein Weg aber über den Zaun hinaus und endet in der Marsebene, die Einfluß und Heftigkeit und Hitzigkeit hat, so bedeutet dieses Zeichen (Bild 30/26) Streit mit der Bekanntschaft.

Querlinien zu den Gartenwegen bedeuten Hemmungen im Liebesleben (Zeichen 42). Diese Hemmungen können selbst gesetzt sein aus ethischen oder moralischen Gründen; sie können auch durch äußere Umstände bedingt sein.

Winkellinien (wie Zeichen 15) teilen etwas ab von den allgemeinen Kräften, deshalb: Gefahr für Körperverletzung. Auswirkung erfolgt immer in dem Jahre, wo die Ereignislinie die Lebenslinie berührt.

Können wir auf einer solchen Ereignislinie weitergehen bis in die Kopflinie, so hat das wieder zu tun mit Eigenschaften des Kopfes, Gehirns (Verstandes oder Unverstandes). Sterne an solchen Linien verstärken den Einfluß bedeutend. Aber auch darauf kommt es sehr an, **woher** die Linie kommt, wo sie entspringt. Vergleichen wir hier die Linie mit einer Pflanze, die mit der Wurzel an einer bestimmten Stelle verankert ist; oder auch mit einer elektrischen Verbindungsschnur, die einen Kontakt hier, den anderen dort einschaltet und dadurch beide Stellen verbindet. Dann wird alles klar.

Der obere Teil des Venusberges, der „kleine Mars", hat hitzige Einflüsse. Deshalb ist die kleine Linie 6 (am Anfang der Lebenslinie) auch mit dieser hitzigen (fiebrigen) Kraft geladen. Sie wirkt sich hier aber nicht aus oder zumindest erst zu einer späteren Zeit, was man beobachten muß. Die kleine Linie 2 führt bis in die Lebenslinie (an den Zaun) heran oder hinein. Da kommt eine Auswirkung zustande durch Eintreten einer fieberigen Krankheit in d e m Alter; ganz jung, in diesem Fall zu Anfang des Lebens. Wir kennen diese Krankheiten als Masern, Influenza, Scharlach, Diphtherie, Rippenfellentzündung, Lungenentzündung, Typhus usw.

Beginnt solche Linie schon mit einem Stern in diesem Teile der Hand, so sind starke Kräfte mitbeteiligt. Linie 8 zeigt solche in die Kopflinie gehend und besagt: In diesem Jahr ist der Kopf in Gefahr für Verletzung. Ich habe dieses Zeichen oft bei solchen Personen gefunden, die sich zu erschießen versuchten oder durch Unfall Verletzungen starker Art hatten. — Bei Linie 9 ist es ähnlich; da wird ebenfalls der Kopf eine Verletzung erleiden, mehr aber das Auge (linke Hand: linkes Auge). Bei Linie 12 finden wir im Verfolg der Linien einen dunklen Punkt in der Kopflinie, was mit Kopfnervenfieber zusammenhängt. Ob diese Dinge sich nun halb oder ganz auswirken, ist eine andere Sache; das läßt sich an der Stärke des Punktes erkennen. Linie 13 enthält eine Insel, welche die Lebenslinie berührt oder überschreitet. Dieses Zeichen hängt mit körperlichen Leiden zusammen, wie Geburten, wenn bei Frauen zu sehen.

Zeichen wie 20, 21, 22, oder Gitter 54 hängen zusammen mit negativ angewandter Sinnlichkeit, Ausschweifung usw. — Eine lange, quer durchlaufende Linie (wie 46) bedeutet Lebensgefahr durch eine feindlich gesinnte Person.

Durch Kombinationen oder Querlaufen, Schräglaufen von anderen Linien ergeben sich auch Zeichen, wie Dreiecke (55). — Ein kleines Viereck an der Lebenslinie (32) bedeutet Abgeschiedenheit. Das kann sein: Kloster, Klausur, Internat, Asyl, Gefängnis, Gefangenschaft u. ä.

Die anderen Zeichen und Linien, die mit der Lebenslinie mehr zu tun haben, beschreibe ich im Abschnitt „Lebenslinie".

Erklärungen des Bildes Nr. 30: Venusberg ♀ und Lebenslinie.

1. Babykrankheiten.
2. Krankheiten in früher Jugend mit fiebrigem Einschlag.
3. Protektion in ganz frühen Jahren.
4. Krankheiten des Kopfes oder Kopfverletzung durch heftige Ursachen.
5. Blutarmut.

6. Eine latent gebliebene Krankheit, z. B. unterdrückte Grippe.
7. Chronische Krankheit, da diese Linie im Bogen vom oberen Marsberg zum Saturnberg verläuft.
8. Ein Unfall mit leichter Verletzung des Kopfes. Die Ursachen sind
   heftig, da am Anfang der Linie ein Stern steht.
9. Durch heftigen Einfluß schwere Verletzung des Kopfes oder des
   Auges. Bei Nr. 8 ist Heftigkeit die Ursache, bei Nr. 9 ist Heftigkeit die Auswirkung, wie der Stern an der Kopflinie anzeigt.
10. Diese Linie geht vom oberen Marsberg über die Lebenslinie, die
    Kopflinie und die Schicksalslinie in die Herzlinie. Diese eine Linie
    hat mehrere Bedeutungen und zeigt mehrere Ereignisse an, die
    entsprechend der Kreuzung mit anderen Linien an verschiedenen
    Stellen auszumessen sind. Sie bedeutet vom Beginn bis zur
    Kreuzung der Lebenslinie eine Krankheit, von der Kreuzung der
    Lebenslinie bis zur Endung in die Herzlinie aber im selben Zeit-
    punkt Gram oder Trauer wegen eines Todesfalls in der Bluts-
    verwandtschaft oder auch Gram aus anderen Gründen. Zur selben
    Zeit (Kreuzung mit der Lebenslinie) formt ein kleiner Teil gerade
    an dieser Stelle mit einem später aufsteigenden Ast (Nr. 16) ein
    kleines Dreieck, dessen obere Linie durch seine Konstruktion
    dieselbe Zeit anzeigt, in der die Krankheit und der Todesfall bzw.
    Gram vorkommen, eine Liebesangelegenheit. Sie ist in diesem
    Falle als günstig zu werten, weil die obere Linie waagerecht oder
    auch schräg hoch verläuft. Ginge sie schräg abwärts, so wäre die
    Liebesangelegenheit ungünstig. — Dieselbe Linie, deren Kreuz-
    punkt man in der Kopflinie ausmißt, würde an dieser Stelle für
    ein anderes Jahr einen Plan anzeigen. Bei der Kreuzung der
    Schicksalslinie zeigt sie, in einem wieder anderen Lebensjahr, eine
    Freundschaft oder Bekanntschaft an, und ihre Endung in die Herz-
    linie wird nochmals als Ast von der Herzlinie aus gemessen, als
    rückwärts laufende Linie, sie zeigt in diesem Schnittpunkt noch-
    mals eine günstige Herzensangelegenheit an.

    Aus der Lage aller dieser Linien ergibt sich folgendes: Je früher
    die Ereignislinie die Lebenslinie kreuzt, um so später das Ereignis-
    jahr in der Herzlinie. Je später diese Linie die Lebenslinie kreuzt,
    desto früher das Ereignisjahr in der Herzlinie.

    Um aber bei der Ausdeutung dieser Ereignislinien nicht durch-
    einanderzukommen, zerlege man sie bei ihrer Zeitfeststellung in
    Abschnitte und betrachte nur die einzelnen Abschnitte unter
    Berücksichtigung der ganzen Konstellation. Z. B. wenn man bei
    einer Handanalyse zum Schluß (wegen ihrer vielen Daten) die
    Lebenslinie abmißt, würde man am praktischsten in diesem Falle
    den Kreuzpunkt auf der Lebenslinie für die Ereignisse, die Krank-

heit, die Liebesangelegenheit und den Todesfall, feststellen. Bei Abmessung der Schicksalslinie nehme man nur den zweiten Teil zwischen Kopf- und Herzlinie und stelle den Schnittpunkt nach Lebensjahren auf der Schicksalslinie für Zeit, für Freundschaften oder Bekanntschaften fest. Beim Ausmessen der Herzlinie benötigt man zur Ausdeutung nur den Schnittpunkt bei der Herzlinie und das Inbetrachtziehen des Verlaufes dieser Linie bis zur Kopflinie.

11. Eine Marslinie. Sie verstärkt als Parallellinie der Lebenslinie die Lebenskraft, soweit sie mit dieser parallel verläuft.

12. Ist ähnlich zu werten wie Nr. 9, nur daß hier ein Punkt in der Kopflinie anzeigt, wenn er rot ist = Kopf- oder Augenverletzung, wenn er blau ist = Kopfnervenfieber, Kopfgrippe usw.

13. Ist wieder eine Krankheit, die sich nicht immer genau definieren läßt, oft aber eine Geburt oder eine ähnliche Operation anzeigt.

14. Eine verpaßte, gute Ehegelegenheit.

15. Diese Linie zeigt zumeist einen kleinen Unfall an.

16. und 17. sind aufsteigende Linien, die materiellen Erfolg anzeigen; Nr. 16 ist eine frei endende Linie, wo der Erfolg sich gut durchführen läßt. Linie 17 endet in der Kopflinie, die in diesem Falle für die aufsteigende Linie eine Querlinie bedeutet, also diesen Aufstieg hemmt, und zwar durch verkehrtes Denken. Es wäre günstiger, wenn diese Linie kurz vor der Kopflinie stehengeblieben wäre oder, wie bei Nr. 16, darüber hinaus ginge.

18. Liegt schon außerhalb des Bereiches der fiebrigen Einflüsse des Marsberges und befindet sich bereits auf dem Venusberg. Deshalb bedeutet die Linie in diesem Falle eine Bekanntschaft mit Streitigkeiten, also ungünstig.

19. hat dieselbe Bedeutung wie Nr. 10. Auch in diesem Falle bildet diese Ereignislinie mit der aufsteigenden Linie Nr. 27 ein Dreieck und zeigt auch eine Liebesangelegenheit in diesem Jahre an, unter Umständen auch mehrere, da es sich hier nicht nur um ein Ereignis, sondern um die günstige Zeit hierfür handelt.

20., 21. und 22. sind sehr üble Zeichen und bedeuten verdorbene Sinnlichkeit und mit anderen Merkmalen zusammen auch Perversität. Besonders Nr. 21 und 22 sind sehr schlechte Zeichen.

23. Ein Stern, Traurigkeiten in Liebesangelegenheiten. Die Zeit hierfür kann man nur schätzen nach der Einteilung des Berges von oben 0 Jahre bis unten 60 Jahre, hier also ungefähr 28 Jahre.

24. Ein Kreuz an der Innenseite der Lebenslinie: Eine Gramangelegenheit.

25. ist wie Nr. 19 zu werten, nur daß hier noch der Stern in der Kopflinie eine Kopf- oder Augenverletzung für dasselbe Jahr anzeigt

wie bei Nr. 9, aber auch eine günstige Zeit für Liebesangelegenheiten.

26. Streitigkeiten mit Bekannten, weil diese Linie im Marsfeld endet, im selben Jahr aber Liebesangelegenheiten anzeigt durch das Dreieck.

27. wie Nr. 17.

28. Eine sehr starke Linie mit Richtung auf den Marsberg: Körperverletzung durch Unfall oder Streit. Ein gefährliches Jahr für die Gesundheit.

29. Eine Bogenlinie nach abwärts zum Mondberg zeigt Lebensüberdruß, evtl. Versuch zu Selbstmord.

30. Ein Kreuz außerhalb der Lebenslinie: Streitigkeiten oder Prozeß.

31. wie Nr. 36: Günstige Zeiten für große Reisen.

32. Ein Quadrat an der inneren Lebenslinie: Gefahr für Abgeschiedenheit durch Gefängnis, Internierung oder Krankenhaus.

33. und 34. Kritische Zeitpunkte für Gesundheit, deren Zeit gleichzeitig die Lebensdauer von zwei Blutsverwandten aus der betreffenden Generation angibt. Diese scharfen Linien zeigen auch an, daß jene einen plötzlichen Tod hatten. Es ist aber nicht festzustellen, ob es Vater, Mutter, Onkel, Tante oder Großeltern waren, die hier starben.

35. Ein Ring in der Linie bedeutet Gefahr für das Augenlicht der entsprechende Seite.

36. siehe Nr. 31.

37. Ein kettiger Verlauf der Lebenslinie zeigt stark geschwächte Gesundheit und Ruin der Konstitution an. Falls die Lebenslinie, wie in diesem Falle, hier endet, ist diese Krankheit von tödlichem Ausgang. In solchem Falle gelten die weiteren Zeichen auf der Lebenslinie nicht mehr.

38. Eine Insel zeigt geschwächte Konstitution für die Länge der Zeit an, wie sie abmeßbar ist.

39. Endung der Lebenslinie in dünnen Fasern bedeutet Siechtum.

40. Eine Liebesbekanntschaft, die mit starker Erotik in Zusammenhang steht.

41. Die vielen dünnen Längslinien besagen Temperament und Leidenschaftlichkeit in der Erotik.

42. sind Querlinien zu den vorhergenannten, die allemal Hemmungen in der Erotik bedeuten. Viele dieser Querlinien zeigen ein so großes Maß von Hemmungen an, daß der Ehepartner leicht das Interesse verlieren kann und sich abwendet. Diese Hemmungen sind, wenn die Linien sehr dünn sind, mehr eingebildeter Art (Bedenken usw.), und wenn sie sehr stark sind, seelischer Natur.

43. Eine Insel an dieser Stelle oder ein Dreieck (Nr. 44) zeigt stets an, daß bei den Vorfahren Krebskrankheit vorgekommen ist.

45. ist keine Reiselinie, weil sie nicht nach dem Mondberg zeigt, sondern abwärts. Sie bedeutet also in diesem Falle ungünstige Zeiten für Geschäftsunternehmen, außerdem leichter Beginn der Körperschwäche (Herznerven).

46. Eine Linie quer durch den Berg zum zweiten Daumenbeugegelenk zeigt Verfolgung an.

47. Plötzliches Aufhören der Lebenslinie: Plötzlicher Tod.

48. und 49. ebenfalls plötzlicher Tod, und auch hier wieder die Lebensdauer von blutsverwandten Vorfahren angebend.

50. Zerfall der Kräfte.

51. Erbstreitigkeiten.

52. Eine Inselkette zwischen dem zweiten Beugegelenk des Daumens und dem Venusberg, deren Bedeutung ich hier vorbehaltlich gebe, und die ich von einem Fakir mitgeteilt erhielt, die man aber nicht objektiv kontrollieren kann: So viele Kettenglieder hier abzählbar sind, so oft hat der Betreffende sich in der derzeitigen Rasse inkarniert.

53. Ein Punkt in der Lebenslinie (neben Nr. 39) bedeutet, wenn er blau ist, eine Krankheit, und wenn rot, eine Verletzung.

54. Ein Gitter auf dem Venusberg zeugt von verdorbener Sinnlichkeit.

55. Ein Dreieck: Bedachtsamkeit oder auch Berechnung in Liebesangelegenheiten.

55a. Sehr kleine Punkte in den Kreuzungen der Längs- und Querlinien von rötlicher Farbe zeigen Störungen des Unterleibs an (manchmal durch Onanie, wie ich beobachtet habe).

56. Ein brauner Fleck: Gehörschaden.

57. Ist eine Giftlinie, und zwar zeigt diese Linie e r w o r b e n e Medizinalgifte an, z. B. Impfgift usw.

58. Ein Stern in der Raszette, jedoch seitlich stehend: Mißerfolge im späteren Alter. Noch mehr seitlich: Körperverletzung durch Unfall. Ein Leberfleck an dieser Stelle warnt vor Verstümmelung des Armes.

Der Jupiterberg ♃

F e h l t o d e r f l a c h : Egoismus, Faulheit, Berechnung, Interesselosigkeit, Gemütskälte, Mangel an Achtung.

N o r m a l : Gesunder Ehrgeiz, Ehrgefühl, Liebe zu Natur und Frohsinn.

S t a r k : Zuviel Ehrgeiz, Einbildung, Dummstolz, Hochmut, Genußsucht im Essen und Trinken, Lebensgenuß, Neigung zu Haarverlust.

Extrem stark: Selbstüberhebung, Größenwahn, bzw. Geltungsdrang.

Glatt, ohne Linien: Ruhiges Leben mit mäßigen Erfolgen.

Gefurcht mit starken Linien: Unruhiges Leben und Erfolge.

Zeichen auf Jupiterberg ♃.

- • Fall in Position, Stellung, Ärger im Beruf (Bild 26).
- ○ Freude und Ehre (Bild 26).
- + Eine Liebesangelegenheit, Gelegenheit zur Ehe; oben später, unten früher (Bild 27).
- ✴ Erfolgreicher Ehrgeiz, günstig für Unternehmen aller Art (Bild 24/27).
- ✴ An der Seite auf Handrand: Vorsicht bei Umgang mit Feuer (Bild 25/50).
- △ Diplomatische und politische Fähigkeiten (Bild 28/18).
- ☐ Innere Kraft und Zähigkeit, Schutz vor zuviel Streben (Bild 29).

▦ Fremder, erfolgverderbender Einfluß von äußerer Gewalt (Bild 26/8).
Kein Erfolg bei Prozessen (evtl. Neigung zu Selbstsucht, eben deshalb).

↙ Vom Saturnberg: Leid, Betrübnis und Gefahr (Bild 26).

𝑁 Glück im Handel (Bild 27/15).

═ Störungen im Erfolge (Bild 25/22).

‖ Zwischen Jupiter- und Saturnfinger: Rheumatismus, mit kleinen Linien auf Berg (Bild 27/35 und Bild 29/29).

⟶⟩⟩ Zwischen Finger und Berg: Neigung zu Leberleiden. Folge: Gram, Sorge (Bild 28 und Bild 26/30).

| Von Berg bis über die erste Beugefalte: Warnt vor Kopfverletzung (Bild 29).

)) Über den Berg nach außen laufend: Warnt vor Abtreibung des keimenden Lebens, Fehlgeburten und Unterleibsoperationen bei Frauen (Bild 25/22), bei Männern: Blasenleiden.

♃ Jupiterzeichen: Sehr günstige für alle Dinge, besonders für Protektion (Bild 28).

♀ Venuszeichen: Sehr günstig für Herzensangelegenheiten (seltenes Zeichen, Bild 28/28).

♄ Saturnzeichen: Erfolg in okkultistischen Studien (Bild 24).

☽ Mond: Kranke Phantasie zerstört Strebsamkeit (Bild 27).

Der Saturnberg ♄.

F e h l t o d e r f l a c h : Bei schlechter Saturnlinie: Freudloses, ödes, melancholisches Dasein. Eine gute Saturnlinie verbessert viel.

G l a t t , o h n e L i n i e n : Wenig Freude, wenig Leid.

N o r m a l u n d g u t e n t w i c k e l t : Tiefes Denken, liebt Unabhängigkeit, Einsamkeit, ist mehr beständig und treu.

S t a r k e n t w i c k e l t : Sparsamkeit bis zum Geiz, Hartnäckigkeit (siehe Daumen).

E x t r e m s t a r k : Traurigkeit, Verschlossenheit, innere Unruhe, häufig Schwermut bis zum Lebensüberdruß und Selbstmord.

G e f u r c h t m i t m e h r e r e n s e n k r e c h t e n L i n i e n : Viel Lebenskampf und Erfolg, besonders, wenn oben offene Gabel.

Q u e r l i n i e n , evtl. bis durch den Venusgürtel: Hindernisse äußerer Art, wenig Erfolg, saturnbeeinflußte Menschen ungünstig.

S a t u r n r i n g (Halbkreis den Berg einschließend): Hindernisse in jeder Beziehung in verstärktem Maße.

Z e i c h e n a u f S a t u r n b e r g ♄.

• Rot und langes erstes Fingerglied: Neigung zu schlechten Zähnen (Bild 27).

• Dunkel: Ungünstiges, böses Ereignis.

○ Gewinn durch Mineralien und Erz (Bild 27).

Von Lebenslinie oder Venusberg kommend: Liebessachen, Verführung (Bild 27).

+ Große Gefahr durch Unachtsamkeit, Straßenbahn, Auto, Pferde usw., auch andere Unfälle und Ärger (Bild 58)

✳ Böses, unruhiges Geschick, Gefahr durch Körperverletzung Mord usw. (Bild 25/15).

✳ Auf drittem Fingergliede: Warnt vor Gefahr durch Mord und Anfälle (Bild 25/28).

✳ Auf zweitem Fingergliede in weiblicher Hand: Unfruchtbarkeit (Bild 25/29).

△   Neigung zu okkulten und religiösen Studien, Magnetismus (Bild 28/29).

☐   Schutz vor und in Gefahren (Bild 26).

▦   Unglück, starke Melancholie (Bild 26/17).

Ψ   Guter Erfolg, Wohlstand im späteren Leben (Bild 28/30).

≫≫≫   Zwischen Berg und Finger: Neigung zu Epilepsie (Bild 29).

·) ໄ   Verstärkte Schwermut, unruhiges Alter (Bild 24).

〜〜   Im ersten Fingergliede: Lebensunmut, evtl. Selbstmord-gedanken, mit selben Zeichen auf erstem Daumen-glied (Bild 26).

⊤   Linie mit Stern bis ins dritte Fingerglied: Gefahr für Mord, Gefängnis (Bild 25/52), besonders, wenn an Saturnlinie.

||| Senkrechte gute Parallelen: Günstig (Bild 29/28), Stabili-sierung des Lebensweges im Alter.

Querlinien: Sind immer Hindernisse und sehr schwer überwindbar (Bild 25/12, 13).

卍   Intuitives Erfassen in Mystik und Philosophie.

☽   Schwermut (bis zum Irrsinn) (Bild 26).

Der Apolloberg ☉

Fehlt oder schwach: Prosaische Natur, materiell, ohne Sinn für Ideales.

Normal: Durchschnittsinteressen für diese Dinge.

Stark: Prahlerei, Leichtfertigkeit, Verschwendung.

Extrem stark: Geldsucht, Ruhmsucht, großmäulig, frivol, ver-schwenderisch.

Glatt, ohne Linien: Zufriedenstellender bescheidener Lebens-lauf.

Querlinien, vom Saturnberg kommend: Hindernisse aus eigenem Hause, Verwandten (Bild 25).

Querlinien, vom Merkurberg kommend: Heimliche Neider und Feinde (Bild 28).

Eine senkrechte Linie, kurz: Erfolge später, lange Linie: früher, gutes Talent (Bild 29/26).
Mehrere senkrechte Linien: Vielseitigkeit im Können, Neigung zu Zersplitterung (Bild 25/47).

Zeichen auf Apolloberg ⊙.

☽ Im ersten Gliede des Apollofingers: Misere, unangenehme Zeit (Bild 27).

• Rot, und Ende der Kopflinie zweigartig: Augenkrankheit (Bild 29).

• Dunkel: Unannehmlichkeiten und Ärger.

○ Durch gefahrvolle Erfolge zum Wohlstand (Bild 29).

⑂ Ungünstige Verhältnisse, Wechsel in Geschäften, Skandal usw. (Bild 29).

+ Ohne Sonnenlinie: Enttäuschungen.

+ Mit guter Sonnenlinie: Erfolg durch andere, mehr indirekter Art.

✻ Erfolg und Gelingen, meist ohne Freude (wenn ohne Sonnenlinie).

✻ Mit guter Sonnenlinie: Wohlstand.

△ Pietät, praktisch in Kunst, innere Ruhe, Sinn für Literatur (Bild 28).

□ Schutz vor Verlust.

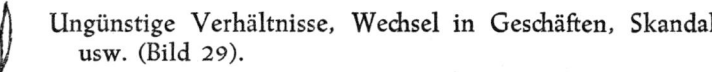 Verlangen nach Ruhm und Erfolg hat Mißlingen, verdirbt gutes Gelingen (Bild 26).

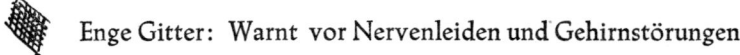 Enge Gitter: Warnt vor Nervenleiden und Gehirnstörungen.

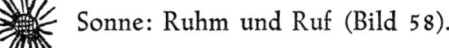 Sonne: Ruhm und Ruf (Bild 58).

⅄ Sehr günstig für Spekulation und Unternehmen (Bild 27/38).

|× Gute (materielle) Ehe.
|×

Senkrechte Linien, nach unten sich zersplitternd: Vielseitige Anlagen werden verdorben durch Zersplitterungen, die zu nichts führen (Bild 26/20).

☿ Merkurzeichen: Außergewöhnliches Händlertalent.

☽ Mond: Gefahr für krankhafte Phantasie in Ausübung von Kunst (Bild 27).

♀ Venuszeichen: Idealisierung bester Art in künstlerischen Berufen.

Der Merkurberg ☿

Fehlt oder schwach: Mangel an Fähigkeiten für Handel und Wissenschaft.

Gut entwickelt: Handelstalent, Neigung zum Studium, Witz, Schlagfertigkeit, Rednertalent (wenn Merkurfinger lang), Routine, Sinn für Mystik, Literatur und geistiges Schaffen.

Extrem stark: Heuchelei, List, lügenhaft, unverschämt und dreist, große Routine, evtl. auch mit anderen Zeichen: Dieberei.

Man muß die Güte der Hand im ganzen in Betracht ziehen, denn in einer guten Hand können diese minderwertigen Eigenschaften zum guten Teil oder ganz verbessert, veredelt worden sein.

Zeichen auf Merkurberg ☿.

≡ Im ersten Gliede des Merkurfingers: Schwäche der Gesundheit (Bild 25/32).

• Auf Berg: Mißerfolg in Geschäften infolge Irrtums und Krankheit (Bild 25).

○ Nervenleiden, evtl. nervöser Zusammenbruch (Bild 25).

+ Erfolg in Geschäften, Diplomatie und Literatur, in schlechter Hand: Neigung zu Unehrlichkeiten (Bild 25).

+ Unter Merkurberg: Wechsel in Geschäften (Vorsicht geboten) (Bild 29).

✻ In guter Hand: Erfolge in Wissenschaft und Handel, Literatur usw. (Bild 25/18).

✻ In schlechter Hand: Unehrlichkeit und Dieberei.

✻ Im dritten Gliede des Merkurfingers: Somnambule Fähigkeiten (Bild 27/41).

△ Innere Ruhe, sehr günstig für Wissenschaft, Politik, Handel (Bild 28).

□ Schutz vor Verlusten, vermindert außerdem die Rastlosigkeit des Merkurtemperaments (Bild 25).

	Mangel an Prinzipien und Verläßlichkeit, lügen und stehlen (Bild 26/15).
⊃	Warnt zur Vorsicht auf Reisen usw. (Bild 25).
	Zuviel Zersplitterung in Streben und Studien (Bild 26/31).
	Talente für Handel, Studium, Drogen- und Heilkunde (Bild 28/15).
──	Störungen und Intrigen durch andere (Bild 29).
‖‖	Durch den ganzen Finger: Talente für Medizin, Krankenpflege (Bild 29).
☀	Sonne: Erfolge als Arzt oder Chemiker.
♂	Marszeichen: Zu großer Erwerbstrieb, mit Gewalt.

Der Marsberg ♂.

Flach: Mangel an Mut und Energie.

Stark: Mut, Energie, Eigensinn, gute Metallarbeiter und Sportsmenschen.

Extrem stark: Zänkisch, leicht wütend und evtl. brutal.

Linien am Handrande des Marsberges: Feinde oder feindlich gesinnte Personen.

Linie von Lebenslinie oder Venusberg bis in Marsberg: Operation oder andere Verletzung des Körpers durch **Metalle** (Bild 31/17—17, 19—19).

Linie von Kopflinie bis Marsberg: Verletzung oder Operation am Kopfe (Bild 31/30).

Linie mit Stern in Venus- oder Marsberg: Verletzung oder Operation ist mit großen Gefahren verbunden (Bild 31/33).

Zeichen auf Marsberg ♂.

● **Dunkel:** Warnt vor Krankheit der Därme (Bild 26).

● **Rot:** Warnt vor Verwundung und Wundfieber als Folge.

+ Zänkisch, halsstarrig; wenn dazu Kreuz in Marsfeld: Gefahr für Körperverletzung oder Mord durch Streit (Bild 25).

✳ Gefahr für Mord und schwere Körperverletzung (Bild 25/44).

△   Große Ruhe, Selbstbeherrschung, Geistesgegenwart, Strategie, sich aus Affären ziehen können (Bild 28/33).

☐   Schutz in Gefahr durch Feinde und Waffen.

▬   Heftiger Tod und sonstiges böses Geschick (Bild 26/28).

Der kleine Marsberg oder „Obere Venusberg"

Wenn gut und stark entwickelt: Gattenliebe; eine weitere (zweite) kleine Erhöhung ganz nahe dem Anfange der Lebenslinie: Kinderliebe.

Auch ist aus der Entwicklung dieser beiden Stellen das Maß der aktiven Kraft zu ersehen und mit den korrespondierenden Zeichen hierfür zu vergleichen (♃ ♆ ☌ ♀ Gürtel).

Dünne Linien aus dem kleinen Marsberge kommend: Einflüsse des anderen Geschlechtes (siehe Herzlinie, Ehelinien, Mondberg).

Zeichen auf kleinem Marsberg.

✳   Bösartiger Streit; nahe Lebenslinie: Prozeßsache (Bild 27).

P   Schutz in Feuersgefahr, wenn weiter unten liegend; Schutz bei Fieber, wenn weiter oben liegend (Bild 27).

斗   Eine Marslinie endigt im Winkel in die Lebenslinie: Streit mit Verwandten (Bild 30/15), evtl. Körperverletzung.

Der Mondberg ☽.

Für Kunst jeder Art, Musik, Malerei, Skulptur, Theater, Literatur sowie Mystik, Religion, Okkultismus ist ein gut entwickelter Mondberg erforderlich, d. h. die Eigenschaften des Mondberges müssen vorhanden sein.

Fehlt oder flach: Mangel an Phantasie und Schönheitssinn, materielle, kalte Natur.

Wenig entwickelt: Ziemlich reale und materielle Geistesrichtung.

Normal: Normale Phantasie mit Sinn für Schönheit und Kunst.

Stark: Gute Phantasie, Talent für Kunst, Literatur, Harmonie und mehr oder weniger Intuition (die sich aber entwickeln läßt), Neigung für praktischen Okkultismus, Religionsstudien und Mystik.

Extrem stark: Starke Einbildungskraft, Neigung zu Träumerei,

Poesie und Launen, auch Neigung zu verdorbenen Säften und Rheumatismus.

Unten stark, oben schwach entwickelt: Ausnutzung der Empfindungen und Gaben zu materiellen Zwecken.

Gute senkrechte Linien verstärken Intuition und okkulte Fähigkeiten.

Kleine abgerissene Linien: Sehr sensitiv, Neigung zu Rheuma, Gicht (Bild 29/19).

Linien vom Mondberg kommend, zur Handmitte laufend, sind immer fremde Einflüsse von Bedeutung und müssen entsprechend in Betracht gezogen werden.

Solche Linie, die Saturnlinie berührend, geht den Beruf, Lebensweg an.

Solche Linie, die Kopflinie berührend, geht Gedanken und Pläne an.

Solche Linie, die Herzlinie berührend, geht Herzenssachen an.

Solche Linie, die Lebenslinie berührend, geht Körper und Veränderung an.

Solche Linie, die Gesundheitslinie berührend, geht Gesundheit, Blut, Säfte usw. an.

Solche Linie nach Jupiterberg betrifft Position und Wohlstand durch Reise oder durch das andere Geschlecht.

Solche Linie nach Saturnberg betrifft Unglück und Verlust auf Reisen.

Solche Linie nach Apolloberg betrifft Wohlstand durch Reisen und das andere Geschlecht.

Solche Linie nach Marsberg, ungünstig, betrifft Streit, evtl. Mord.

Solche Linie berührt Saturnlinie, erfolgbringende Reisen.

Solche Linie, neben Saturnlinie laufend, Finden von Freund oder Gatten auf oder durch Reisen, Nutzen dadurch.

Solche Linie in die Kopflinie: Lebhaftes Wesen, beunruhigende fremde Einflüsse.

Wirre und zerrissene Mondlinien: Eine tief im Innersten unruhige und unglückliche (weil zu empfindsame) Persönlichkeit.

Man braucht nur zu beobachten, woher solche Linie kommt, was sie streift, wo sie evtl. ausbiegt, und dies in Betracht zu ziehen, wohin sie geht, welche Linie und welcher Berg berührt, geschnitten oder verletzt werden. Dann das Ganze kombinieren. Ruhiges, sachliches und tiefes Denken und Üben lassen jeden die Sache ganz klar ersehen. Phantasie ist dazu nicht notwendig, sonst würden die Beurteilungen nicht nachzuprüfen, also unbestimmt sein; das muß aber verhindert werden. Was einer aus der Hand liest, muß auch ein anderer lesen können, und was man heute liest, muß man auch nach einem Monat lesen können, soweit keine kleinen Änderungen eingetreten sind, was nach vier Wochen schon (frühestens) sein kann, aber nicht notwendig sein muß.

• Dunkel: Warnt vor Krankheit der Säfte und Verdauungsorgane (Bild 27).

Rote, kleine Flecke: Irregeleitete, krankhafte Phantasie, perverse Neigungen usw., die nicht immer praktische Ausübung voraussetzen.

Warnt vor Gefahr auf Wasser und durch das andere Geschlecht (Bild 27).

⊙ Warnt vor Gefahr auf Wasser; dieses sowie vorhergehendes Zeichen geben Neigungen zu okkulten Studien (Bild 27).

An Uranuslinie: Anlage zum Hellsehen (Bild 27).

+ Melancholie (Bild 29).

+ Nahe Raszette: Legat oder Geld spät im Leben (Bild 25).

+ An Kopflinie oder Zweig derselben im Mondberge: Gefahr für Kopf- oder Gehirnnervenkrankheit, Unfall auf Reisen (Bild 26).

✳ Tiefe Melancholie, Gefahr für Irrtümer und zu große Phantasie bei großem Mondberg und dadurch entstehende Neigungen zu Heuchelei, Lügen (Bild 27).

✳ Am Ende der Kopflinie im Mondberge: Gehirnnervenkrankheit (Irrsinn), oft mit Selbstmord (durch Ertränken) verbunden (Bild 26/26).

✳ Unten auf Mondberg: Fallsucht (Epilepsie), wenn mit anderen Zeichen verbunden (Bild 26/26).

△ Wissenschaftliche Methodik in phantastischen Ideen und große, gute Neigungen zu Mystik und Okkultismus, Magie usw. (Bild 25/7).

☐ Schutz vor Übermaß in Phantasie und Unfällen auf Reisen (Bild 27).

Übersensitiv, verdorbene Phantasie, Laune, krankhafte Neigungen; wenn dazu noch Venusgürtel vorhanden: Hysterie; dies extra stark: wenn Venusgürtel zerrissen oder gebrochen und kettige Kopflinie (Bild 26/27).

Reise längerer Art (Bild 25).

Reise mit Wechsel.

Reise unterbrochen oder plötzlich endend, evtl. mit Erlebnis.

142

———✗ Reise mit Gefahr für Tod auf Wasser.

⤳ Reise mit Rückreise.

——— Reise mit Ärger und Verlust, Enttäuschung.

———◁ Reise mit Bereicherung des Wissens, sehr günstiger oder okkulter Art.

~~~~ Warnt zur Vorsicht auf Reisen zu Wasser (Mondberg).

———▱ Schutz vor Gefahr auf Reisen.

Sehr sensitiv: Zeichen für Rheumatismus und Leberleiden, wenn sehr weit unten, nahe Handwurzel: auch Milzleiden (Bild 25).

♄ Saturnzeichen: Neigung zu religiösen Wahnideen (Bild 29).

♃ Jupiterzeichen: Neigung zu Wahrträumen (Bild 29).

☿ Merkurzeichen: Neigung zu krankhaften Spekulationen.

♂ Marszeichen: Neigung zu Jähzorn (Bild 29).

Die Lebenslinie (Vitalis).
(Bild 21.)

Liebe, häusliche, körperliche Angelegenheiten, Krankheiten, Unfälle, Gefahren, materielle Erfolge und Mißerfolge, Alter, Krisen, Lebensdauer.

Fast jedes größere Ereignis registriert sich (mit den anderen korrespondierend) auch auf der Lebenslinie.

Lebenslinie blaß und breit: Kränklichkeit, Neid, böse Neigungen.

Dick und rot: Gewalttätige, robuste Natur, siehe Daumen usw.

Kettig: Zarte Gesundheit, siehe Nägel.

Verschiedene Stärke: Wechselnde Stärke der Gesundheit, launisches Wesen.

Je kürzer die Linie, desto kürzer die Lebensdauer. Dies besagt aber nicht, daß eine lange Lebenslinie ein langes Leben bedeutet, wie allgemein angenommen wird; denn eine kurze Kopf- oder Herzlinie kann das Leben sehr stark verkürzen, ebenso gebrochene Kopflinien usw. Man muß gerade hierfür noch mehrere Punkte bzw. Zeichen in Betracht ziehen, die oft schwer sichtbar sind.

Die Lebensdauer findet man, falls keine anderen Anzeichen vorhanden und beide Hände gut sind, indem man ausmißt, wo die Lebenslinie scharfe Querstriche aufweist (Bild 30/48, 49, 57 und Bild 37/62, 63, 64). Diese kleinen Querschnitte zeigen das Alter an, das die Vorfahren (mütterlicher Generation in der linken, väterlicher in der rechten Hand!) erreichten. Da nun die Lebensdauer schon bei Beginn der Lebensbahn durch die Körperkonstitution festgelegt ist (nämlich durch die Kraft und Konstitution des väterlichen Samens, nicht etwa durch das mütterliche Ei!), die väterliche Konstitution und deren Rhythmus also von ausschlaggebender Bedeutung ist, so ist auch die rechte Hand bzw. deren Lebenslinie der Ort, wo die am schärfsten oder tiefstgeschnittene Querlinie die Lebensdauer des Handeigners recht genau zu erkennen gibt. — Ein solch scharfer Ab-Schnitt, wie ihn eine scharfe Querlinie zeichnet, kann auch nur ein plötzlicher Tod sein. Wenn sich aber die Endung der Lebenslinie langsam, fadenartig verliert, ist es kein plötzlicher, sondern ein langsamer Tod, dessen Zeit festzustellen ein sehr geübtes Auge und lange Erfahrung erforderlich sind. — Es sollen, wie vorher gerade schon gesagt wurde, auch andere Merkmale in Betracht gezogen werden. — Ich warne also sehr davor, „aus Spaß" oder „zur Unterhaltung" die Lebensdauer eines anderen feststellen zu wollen. Derartige Dinge sind sehr ernst zu behandeln. Und ich erkläre hier die Angelegenheit n u r deshalb, um mir nicht den Vorwurf machen zu lassen, daß ich mein Wissen verheimliche.

Z e i c h e n f ü r T o d in der Lebenslinie müssen korrespondierend in b e i d e n Händen zu sehen sein.

B r u c h ist allemal Krankheit und Lebensgefahr, sofern nicht die Bruchstelle durch eine feine Linie verbunden oder ein Viereck als Umrahmung der Bruchstelle vorhanden ist (Bild 27 und 29).

A u f h ö r e n d e r L e b e n s l i n i e mit kurzem Querstrich (i n b e i - d e n H ä n d e n): Plötzlicher Tod (Bild 29).

A u f h ö r e n d e r L e b e n s l i n i e a l l m ä h l i c h : Langsames Ende des Lebens (Bild 29/50).

O f t g e k r e u z t von kleinen Linien: Viele Störungen verschiedener Art (Bild 27).

S c h w e s t e r n l i n i e : Wirkt erhaltend und stärkend (Bild 28).

L i n i e n a u s V e n u s b e r g über die Lebenslinie hinaus: Sorgen, Ereignisse, müssen beachtet und ausgemessen werden.

L e b e n s l i n i e a n f a n g e n d a m J u p i t e r b e r g : Strebsamkeit und Wohlstand dadurch; siehe evtl. Störungen und Hindernisse hierfür (♀ Berg, ♭ und ☉ Linie usw.) (Bild 28/22).

Lebenslinie mit Kopflinie verbunden: Je länger beide verbunden, desto langsamer ist die Entschlußkraft (Bild 26 und 27). **Je weiter beide voneinander** am Anfang entfernt liegen, desto schneller und unbedachter, wagemutiger handelt der Betreffende (Bild 26 und 28).

Verbindung beider am Anfange für 1 cm ist normal (Bild 29).

Verbunden mit Kopf- und Herzlinie: Karmisch bestimmter, gewaltsamer Tod. (Falls nur in der linken, nicht in der rechten Hand, so hat der Betreffende schon einen Teil dieses Karmas ausgelöst und verbessert; die Gefahr bleibt, nicht immer aber die Auswirkung.) Man beachte genau den Rest der Hand (Bild 26/24). Selbstmord ist bei Vorfahren vorgekommen.

Lebenslinie zu nahe dem Daumen: Gibt zu kleinen Venusberg, Kaltherzigkeit und evtl. Unfruchtbarkeit (Bild 25 rechts).

Ende einwärts gebogen: Gefahr durch Ersticken.

Ende aufwärts gebogen gegen Saturnberg: Gefahr durch Gift und Ansteckung.

Plötzlich abbrechend: Tödliche Krankheit oder Tod, Schlaganfall usw. (Bild 27).

Langsam verschwindend: Schleichende, zehrende Krankheit (Bild 29/50).

Linie von Lebens- bis Marslinie: Gefahr durch Zank und Wut (Bild 31/6).

Linie von Lebenslinie in den Jupiterberg: Ehrgeiz und Pläne (günstig) (Bild 31 und 30/3).

Linie aus Venusberg bis Lebenslinie: Angelegenheiten der Sinnlichkeit (Bild 30/40).

Linie aus Venusberg bis Kopflinie: Angelegenheiten Kopf und Denken betreffend (Bild 31/16).

Linie aus Venusberg bis Herzlinie: Angelegenheiten das feinere Empfinden betreffend (Trauer, Gram usw.) (Bild 31/1, 4, 10).

Aufsteigende Linien von der Lebenslinie: Materielle Erfolge (Bild 31/9, 18 und Bild 30/16, 17).

Absteigende Linien von der Lebenslinie: Materielle Mißerfolge und Verlust (Bild 30/36, 45 und Bild 31/21).

(**Zeichen auf der Lebenslinie** siehe unter „Zeichen".)

Für die Markierungen der Ereignislinien, die die Lebenslinien schneiden, ist noch folgendes zu beachten:

Auf Bild 30 sind Linien für seelische Erschütterungen (durch Todesfall, Gram in Liebesangelegenheiten usw.) durch die Zeichen 10, 19 angegeben. Diese Linien entspringen auf dem Venusberg und enden in der Herzlinie oder nahebei. Auf Bild 30 sind sie für etwa das 15. und das 30. Lebensjahr angezeigt. Es kommt nun auch vor, daß sich solche Ereignislinie an der Stelle befindet, die auf demselben Bilde mit 1 bezeichnet ist, oder noch etwas früher. Das würde also ein Ereignis im zweiten, dritten oder gar vierten Jahre v o r der Geburt sein. Dies besagt dann, daß ein Blutsverwandter (linke Hand = mütterlicher, rechte Hand = väterlicher Generation) zwei, drei bzw. vier Jahre v o r der Geburt des Handeigners gestorben ist.

Abgesehen davon, daß diese Zeichen und die Tatsachen des Ereignisses beweisen, daß wir schon Jahre v o r unserer Geburt unsere Vorfahren gekannt haben müssen und deshalb unsere Geburt b e w u ß t herbeiführten (uns körperlich schaffen l i e ß e n !), fand ich noch ein weiteres heraus. Nämlich, angenommen, der Verwandte starb im 63. Lebensjahre, dann wird man auf der Lebenslinie dort, wo man das 63. Jahr durch Abmessung erkennt, finden, daß hier ein Strich quer zur Lebenslinie vorhanden ist, wie z. B. auf Bild 30 mit Bezeichnung 57 und 48 angegeben ist. Das ist aber ein Zeichen dafür, daß der Eigner der Hand an der Stelle (nach obigem Beispiel also im 63. Jahr) einen kritischen Zeitpunkt für seine Gesundheit oder sein Leben hat. — Meine Nachprüfungen haben ergeben, daß die betreffenden Jahre auf der Lebenslinie, die mit der Bedeutung „kritischer Zeitpunkt für Gesundheit" in Verbindung stehen, wozu auch solche Linien und Zeitpunkte gerechnet werden, die eine schwere Verletzung (auch Operation wie Linie 28 auf Bild 30) anzeigen, Todesjahre von den Blutsverwandten sind. — Immer aber kommt für Lebensdauer der tiefste Querschnitt — auch stark markierter Stern, Punkt — auf der Lebenslinie in der r e c h t e n Hand in Betracht. Also hierfür ist die Erbmasse und der Blutrhythmus der väterlichen Erbmasse — Generation — maßgebend, wie ja auch der Stammbaum väterlicher- oder männlicherseits ausschlaggebender ist.

Zieht man hierzu noch in Betracht, daß sehr oft, wenn ein Großvater, Onkel, eine Großmuter oder Tante stirbt, die Nichte oder ein Neffe zur selben Zeit erkrankt, dann beweist dies alles, daß jeder Mensch bei seiner Geburt einen ganz bestimmten Rhythmus für sein Leben und die Ereignisse desselben mitbringt oder aufnimmt, und daß die Ereignisse seines Lebens sich gesetzmäßig abrollend ergeben. — Jeder bringt also von Geburt her sein „Schicksal" mit! — Nebenbei bemerken möchte ich noch, daß ich des öfteren beobachtet habe, daß, wenn zwei junge Leute heiraten, im selben Jahre einer von den vier Eltern stirbt. — Mit w e l c h e m Großvater, Onkel oder w e l c h e r Großmutter, Tante ein bestimmter Neffe oder eine bestimmte Nichte nun so eng im Rhythmus verbunden ist, das zu finden ist viel schwieriger und wird von mir noch weiter verfolgt.

146

Die Marslinie auf Venus- und kleinem Marsberg.

(Bild 21.)

Hier ist zu unterscheiden, ob „die Marslinie", d. i. eine gut markierte Linie, die aus dem Daumenwinkel oder dem kleinen Marsberg entspringt und kurz oder lang sein kann, oder eine Mars - E i n f l u ß - linie vorhanden ist.

Erste gibt in einer schlechten Hand, d. h. einer Hand, welche aus der Form der Konstellation der Linien böse oder niedere Eigenschaften des Betreffenden erkennen läßt: hitziges, gewalttätiges Temperament und Wesen, besonders wenn die Lebenslinie dick und rot ist.

In einer guten Hand gibt sie Willensstärke, verstärkt die Kraft der Lebenslinie und Gesundheit.

Andere dünne und feine Marslinien sind Einflüsse des anderen Geschlechts oder aber Einfluß von Freunden, was allerdings seltener ist.

Eine ganz lange, dünne Linie, die den Anschein erweckt, eine doppelte Lebenslinie zu sein: gibt Liebe zu Luxus und Extravaganzen.

Eine doppelte Lebenslinie verstärkt die Gesundheitsverhältnisse sehr.

Zum Abmessen benutzt man immer die äußere, weitere Linie, welche in 90 Grade (meist Millimeter) zu teilen ist; siehe Meßkarte Bild 34.

Allgemeines über die Kopflinie.

Die Kopflinie teilt die ganze Hand in einen oberen — geistigen — und einen unteren — materiellen — Teil. Dies ist bei der äußeren und inneren Beurteilung der Hände in Betracht zu ziehen, da das Verhältnis den Handtyp beeinflußt, was ich sogleich erklären werde.

Bei einer eckigen, knotigen und spatelförmigen Hand geht die Kopflinie naturgemäß der Charakteristik entsprechend geradeaus auf oder in den Marsberg, die materielle bzw. intellektuelle Art des Denkens kennzeichnend. Sie zeigt auch Mangel an Gestaltungskraft.

Verläuft sie in solcher Hand tiefer herab in den oberen oder gar unteren Mondberg, so verändert sie bei dem Betreffenden die materielle Denkart in eine mehr oder weniger idealistische oder phantasievolle. Es liegt nicht in der Art desjenigen mit eckiger Hand, melancholisch oder reich an Phantasie zu sein, sondern real und materiell zu denken, entsprechend der Kopflinie dem Marsberge zustrebend. Dringt die Kopflinie aber — ich nehme hier zum leichteren Verständnis das Extrem an — tief in den Mondberg, so wird der sonst nur materiell Denkende eine große Neigung zum Grübeln, Träumen und Phantasieren haben, wird evtl. sogar (was er sonst nicht tun würde) intuitiv denken und, was wieder bezeichnend ist, das auf solche Art Gewonnene praktisch und materiell verwerten. Aus diesem Grunde wird ein Musiker, der Lieder schaffen (komponieren) will, stets eine Kopflinie haben müssen, welche in den Mondberg hineinreicht, wenn er Empfindung, Gestaltung in das zu Schaffende hineinbringen, wenn er, wie man sagt: Seele in die Musik legen will. Bei Malern verhält es sich ebenso.*) Der Künstler mit eckiger Hand, Kopflinie in den Marsberg, wird mehr geneigt sein, Stilleben, Landschaften, Blumen usw. in dem schönen, aber alltäglichen Ausdruck zu schaffen, während der andere (mit der Kopflinie im Mondberge) den Bildern mehr einen mystischen, übersinnlichen oder „phantastischen" Sinn und Ausdruck geben wird. Konische, ideale oder mediale, zum Teil auch schmale knotige Handtypen haben naturgemäß eine Kopflinie, die in den Mondberg verläuft. Bei diesen Händen würde eine gerade, dem Marsberge zustrebende Kopflinie einen Einfluß von Materialismus und Berechnung haben, was solchen Naturen nicht entspricht, vielmehr meist sogar zuwider ist.

Wer die ausschlaggebende Formation der Kopflinie in seinem Studium nicht beachtet und in der Praxis nicht in Betracht zieht beim Lesen der Hände, wird genaues und wissenschaftliches Handanalysieren weder erlernen, noch gewissenhaft ausüben können. Gerade diese Linie läßt die Denkrichtung des Menschen erkennen. Die Denkart beeinflußt aber die Handlungen, und ein Ereignis kann verschiedenartigen Ausgang nehmen, je nachdem w i e einer an eine Sache herantritt und sie handhabt.

Die Kopflinie (Cerebralis).
(Bild 24/9, 14 und Bild 21.)

Gedankenkraft und Denkrichtung, Willen, Pläne, Krankheit und Unfälle des Kopfes, der Augen, Gehirn- und Kopfnerven, Melancholie, Delirium, Irrsinn, Phantasie.

D o p p e l t e K o p f l i n i e : Vielseitiger Intellekt, materielle Erfolge und Doppelnatur. Mehr oder weniger rätselhafte Personen (Bild 28/6, 7 und Bild 63). Alkoholismus bei Vorfahren.

L a n g e , g u t e L i n i e : Guter Intellekt, besonders wenn Venusgürtel und feste Hand vorhanden (Bild 24/9, 14).

E x t r e m l a n g , v o n R a n d z u R a n d : Guter Kopf, zuviel Logik und Wortfechterei, Egoismus, neigt meist zu Geiz und Selbstüberschätzung; Rechthaberei, materielle Ausnutzung.

K u r z e K o p f l i n i e : Evtl. kurzes Leben; dazu kurze Lebenslinie: plötzlicher Tod.

Anfang im kleinen Marsberg: Unbeständig, unzuverlässig, hitzig, zänkisch, Nörgler (Bild 27/1).

Anfang getrennt von Lebenslinie: Schnelle Entschlußfähigkeit, Wagemut (Bild 26 und Bild 43); voreilig, zu offen.

Anfang zu weit verbunden mit Lebenslinie: Mangel an Entschlußkraft, überlegt zu lange (Bild 27/24, 25/36). Verschlossenheit.

Bruch: Meist Kopfverletzung (Bild 27/3, 27).

Endet unter Saturnberg: Warnt vor Überanstrengung des Kopfes, evtl. Tod in jungen Jahren (Bild 27/1—3). Egoismus.

Endet im oberen Mondberge: Neigung zu Idealismus, Träumerei, Mystik, Poesie, Literatur (Bild 26/13). Gestaltungskraft.

Endet mit Stern im unteren Mondberge: Neigung zu Wahn; wenn mit Insel: ererbt (vergleiche: Stern im Venusberge, Saturnberg und Bild 25/40, 26/25).

Insel im Anfang oder Ende der Kopflinie sind Zeichen von erblicher Belastung; in linker Hand: von der Generation der Mutter; rechts: von der des Vaters. Augenschwäche (Bild 26).

Kopflinie endet in einem Berge: Zuviel Einfluß von dessen Eigenschaften.

Endet knotig in der Herzlinie: Böses Geschick in Herzensangelegenheiten.

Zurückbiegend nach dem Daumen: Großer Egoismus und Unglück dadurch. Belastung.

Endet unter Mondberg: Gefahr durch Wasser, Ertrinken (Bild 25/40, Bild 37 und Bild 42). Wahn bei Vorfahren.

Endet im Marsberg: Fester Wille, Berechnung, Neigung zum Ausnutzen anderer (Bild 24/14).

Endet ein Ast im Mars- und ein Ast im Mondberg: Inneren Einflüssen zugänglich, äußeren nicht oder sehr wenig. Gehirnschwäche.

Knotig: Neigung zu Verbrechen, evtl. Mord. (In guter Hand wird dies etwas abgeschwächt, bleibt aber trotzdem eine Warnung). Krankhafte Veranlagung.

Allgemeines über die Herzlinie.

Die Herzlinie beginnt am Handrande unter dem kleinen Finger und verläuft als oberste waagerechte Linie quer über die Hand in Richtung zum Zeigefinger. Selbstverständlich ist der Verlauf dieser Linie in allen Händen verschieden. Schon mancher hat sich darüber gewundert, weshalb die Herzlinie über der Kopflinie liegt, da doch sonst beim menschlichen Körper der Kopf sich über dem Herzen befindet. Das ist phrenologisch leicht zu begründen. Wir haben oben in der Mitte des Kopfes, am Scheitelpunkt, den Sitz der Sinne für Moral und Ethik, Angelegenheiten des Herzens; ebenso auch den Sinn für Religion. Erst weiter unten an der oberen Stirn befinden sich die Zentren für den Intellekt und für den Verstand. Schließlich ist ja auch im Leben das Herzdenken das Richtigere; denn wir werden oft finden, daß der Intellekt durchaus nicht immer das Richtige trifft und daß sogar logische Schlüsse falsch sein können. Was der Mensch aber mit dem Herzen erfühlt und zugleich mit dem Sonnengeflecht empfindet, ist immer das Richtige. Besonders die Frau ist nicht von Natur aus dafür geschaffen, Verstandeskräfte auf die Höhe einer männlichen Intelligenz zu trainieren, sie wird es auch rein physiologisch nicht dazu bringen können. Auch das spirituelle Zentrum wird bei ihr nie in dem Grade erweckt sein können, daß es schöpferisch wirkt. Die Tatsache beweist, daß wir bisher selten schöpferische Frauen erlebt haben, diese sind Ausnahmen. Da sie aber bei dem Vergleich gar nicht in Betracht kommen, kann man sagen, daß es nicht vorkommt. Selbst auf dem ihr eigensten Gebiete der Musik hat die Frau auch dieselben Grenzen. Anderseits werden wir immer finden, daß z. B. bei Erfindungen intellektuelle Arbeit oder rein verstandesmäßiges Denken wohl die Vorarbeit tätigen, das Herzdenken aber und die Intuition die letzte Lösung bringen.

Daher ist auch Herzdenken u n d Gehirndenken zusammen dasjenige, was wir mit Vernunft bezeichnen. Natürlich ist es nicht in dem Sinne zu verstehen, daß jemand bei einer Herzensangelegenheit nur den Verstand sprechen lassen soll. Es gibt auch solche Leute, die mit dem Verstand lieben; das ist aber keine Liebe, sondern Gehirnakrobatik. Liebe ist reine Herzenssache, die man durch den Verstand weder ein- noch ausschalten kann. Das kann man nur mit der Sinnlichkeit, die zum Teil zur Liebe gehört, aber nicht die Liebe selbst darstellt. Natürlich ist die heute in manchen Leuten verkrampfte Anschauung, daß der Asketismus das Höchste sei, mehr als eine Krankheit aufzufassen; denn man wird bemerken können, daß diese Leute dementsprechende Gesichtszüge tragen, schmale Lippen bekommen und überreizte Sexualnerven haben. Was durch Jahrhunderte bei unseren Vorfahren in natürlichem Maße gebräuchlich war, läßt sich nicht so leicht plötzlich abbrechen oder zu stark verringern. Daß bei sinnlichen Erregungen das Herz ebenfalls eine Rolle spielt und dadurch auch stark in Mitleidenschaft gezogen werden kann, ist allbekannt. Wir sehen an einer sehr breiten Herzlinie einerseits eine stark veranlagte Sinnlichkeit, die zumeist auch in bezug auf dieses Zeichen konform geht mit einer Erweiterung des Herzens oder der Venen. Anderseits steht aber auch das Herz mit dem Gehirn in enger Verbindung, wie der Umstand beweist, daß Herzklopfen eintritt, wenn jemand Unrechtes gedacht hat. Die Wechselwirkung ergibt, daß durch das Gefühl des Herzens und die Erkenntnis dieses Unrechts der Betreffende im Gesicht errötet. Allerdings ist diese Eigenschaft des Schamgefühls und des Errötens nur dem Nordländer eigen und nicht den niederen Rassen. Ebenso ist das Herzdenken besonders markant bei dem Nordländer, weshalb er auch viel tiefer liebt als der Südländer oder der Niederrassige, bei dem sich wohl plötzliche Aufwallungen wie Strohfeuer bemerkbar machen bzw. nur Sinnlichkeit. Wenn einige englische Autoren den Anfang der Herzlinie unter den Jupiterberg verlegen, ist und bleibt das ein Irrtum. Wer sich die Herzlinie genau betrachtet, wird immer finden, daß der breitere Anfang unter dem kleinen Finger liegt und die Endung im Jupiterberg, die zu allermeist zart aufläuft. Wir können in der Natur einen Baum auch nicht auf den Kopf stellen, um dann zu sagen, er beginne mit den Zweigen an der Erde, und das dicke Ende sei oben.

Je länger die Herzlinie ist, d. h. möglichst bis in den Jupiterberg hineinreichend, um so größer ist auch das herzliche Gefühl oder die Herzlichkeit. Selbstverständlich gilt auch hier wieder, wie überall: Extreme sind krankhaft.*) Die gute normale Herzlinie soll möglichst bis in die Mitte des Jupiterberges gehen und dort aufhören. Geht sie weiter, bis an den jenseitigen Rand, also quer hinüber von Rand zu Rand, so ist das schon nicht mehr normal und bedeutet in dem Fall, daß bei den Vorfahren Lähmungserscheinungen vorgekommen sind; auch hier muß wieder beachtet werden: linke Hand mütterliche Generation, rechte Hand väterliche. Man darf auch nie vergessen, stets beide Hände zu betrachten; denn die linke Hand zeigt gewissermaßen Jugend oder erste Hälfte des Lebens an, die rechte Hand die zweite Hälfte. Der Übergang von der linken zur rechten Hand in d i e s e r Beziehung liegt zwischen dem 28. und 30. Jahre. Wenn z. B. die Herzlinie in der linken Hand von Rand zu Rand verläuft, und noch mit der Kopf- und Lebenslinie verbunden ist, so bedeutet das, daß die Gefahr für gewaltsamen Tod für den Betreffenden nur bis zum 30. Jahre gilt, vorausgesetzt, daß diese Linienkonstellation in der rechten Hand nicht vorhanden ist. Ist diese Linienführung, wie beschrieben, nur in der rechten Hand vorhanden, besagt sie wieder, daß die Gefahr für den gewaltsamen Tod bis zum 28. Jahre nicht vorliegt, sondern erst später, außerdem daß die Lähmungserscheinungen in der väterlichen Generation vorhanden waren. Diese Linienkonstellation als Merkmal für „Mongolismus" zu kennzeichnen ist Phantasie!

Die Verbindung von Herz-, Kopf- und Lebenslinie ist in jedem Falle ungünstig, da die verschieden gerichteten Ströme zu irgendeiner Zeit eine Art Kurzschluß ergeben müssen. Wenn die Herzlinie aber von den

---

*) Veranlagung zu Nymphomanie, bzw. Satyrismus.

anderen Linien getrennt ist, so kommt ein heftiger Tod nicht in Frage oder braucht nicht vorzukommen. Es muß einem ja schließlich auffallen, daß der Verlauf der Richtung der Herz- und Kopflinie ein entgegengesetzter ist, wie zumeist auch im täglichen Leben das Herz- und Kopfdenken ebenfalls gegensätzlich ist. Wenn diese Linie zwischen dem ersten und zweiten Finger endet, bedeutet das, daß der Betreffende in seinen Liebesangelegenheiten, wozu auch die Ehe gehört, Bitternisse haben wird. Auch in diesem Falle vergesse man nicht zu beachten, wie die Endung in der linken und rechten Hand vorhanden ist.

Da Herz-, Kopf- und Lebenslinie die drei Haupt- oder auch karmischen Linien sind, erkennt man sofort daraus, daß die Gründe oder Ursachen dieser Traurigkeiten aus einem früheren Leben datieren. Der Beweis hierfür ist dadurch erbracht, daß die Formationen der Hauptlinien sich niemals ändern und daß sie schon lange vor der Geburt genau festgelegt sind, wie die Hände des vor der Geburt aus dem Mutterleibe entfernten Fötus zeigen. Außerdem verlaufen zumeist die Linien bei den Eltern anders als bei den Kindern; deshalb kann von Vererbung keine Rede sein. Die Gründe der Auswirkung der Traurigkeiten können zweierlei sein, nämlich Nichtverstandenwerden, also Entfremdung, oder aber früheres Ableben des Ehepartners. Um festzustellen, was von beiden in Frage kommt, muß man natürlich das Übrige der Hand genau betrachten. Man darf auch nicht vergessen, daß Egoismus zumeist eine Rolle hierbei spielt, weil die Herzlinie zu nahe am Saturn (Prinzip für Egoismus oder Ichsucht) endet. Da, wo eine Linie endet, nimmt sie auch Kraft auf oder die Einflüsse der betreffenden Stelle. Meist gehen ja alle Liebesverhältnisse durch den Egoismus des einen oder des anderen in die Brüche. Der Grund hierfür dürfte wohl darin liegen, daß die meisten Menschen keinen richtigen Begriff von der wahren Liebe haben. Hingabe, Aufopferung, das Leben im Du, für den anderen, das ist wahrhafte Liebe. Nur muß man darauf achten, daß der andere Teil nicht in den Egoismus verfällt, den Ersten auszunutzen. Es gibt wohl mehr Frauen, die wahrhaft lieben k ö n n e n , als Männer. Sie beweisen es dadurch, daß sie in der Liebe ganz aufgehen, nicht für sich denken, sondern auch für den Mann und i n ihm leben. Hierdurch sind diese Frauen auch sehr leicht in die Lage versetzt, ihre Hellsinnigkeit zu nutzen und für den anderen alles zu erfühlen, was ihn angeht. Der Mann anderseits hat sich zu sehr auf den Kampf des Lebens einzustellen, soll für das materielle Dasein sorgen und seine fünf Sinne in dieser Richtung beisammen haben. Hieraus folgt schon, daß er vielmehr mit dem Verstande arbeitet, ihn oft übermäßig nutzt und dadurch vom Gefühlsleben des Herzens abkommt. Es ist wohl jedem verständlich, daß demnach die Zahl der Männer, die — ich möchte sagen — an ihrer Liebe sterben können, nicht so groß ist. Dennoch, es gibt auch solche.

Je egoistischer ein Mensch denkt, desto engherziger ist er auch. Die Bezeichnung „Engherzigkeit" sagt es schon: kleines Herz. In der Herzlinie bemerken wir keine Breite, sondern eben nur eine fadenartige Linie ohne irgendwelche kleinen Seitenäste. Bei diesen Leuten wird man nicht besonders viel Warmherzigkeit finden. Auch nicht das, was man allgemein als Verliebtheit bezeichnet, was ich übersetze mit: recht lange ein junges Herz behalten. Die Fähigkeit für Verliebtheit oder Herzensjugend erkennt man sehr leicht daran, daß vom Anfang der Herzlinie an nach der Mitte zu hinaus, rechts und links kleine Linien rückwärts abgehen, Widerhaken ähnlich. Da auch die Herzlinie in einer mittelmäßig großen Hand mit 1 mm pro Jahr gemessen wird, läßt sich sehr leicht feststellen, wie viele Jahrzehnte solche Herzensjugend bei den Betreffenden vorhanden ist. Mit dem Aufhören dieser kleinen rücklaufenden Häkchen beginnt bei ihm das Realbewußtsein und daher die Abschwächung der Warmherzigkeit.

Findet sich ein Bruch in der Herzlinie, so ist auch eine organische Störung vorhanden, die aber nicht gefährlich sein muß. In bezug auf Liebesangelegenheiten bedeutet dies, daß sich einmal im Leben eine besondere Traurigkeit in Herzensangelegenheiten einstellen wird, die schicksalsnotwendig ist, wie alles andere; (karmische Linie). Diese Herzenstraurigkeit hat selbstverständlich auch ihre besonderen Gründe und Begleitumstände. So wird sie zusammenhängen mit Selbstüberhebung und Fahrlässigkeit, wenn der Bruch in der Herzlinie sich unter dem Sonnenfinger befindet; mit Egoismus, Berechnung usw., wenn der Bruch unter dem Saturnfinger vorhanden ist. In einigen alten Büchern wird die Herzlinie oft Gedärmlinie genannt, auch Drüsenlinie, da in ihr Zeichen vorkommen für Gallen-, Nieren-, Blasensteine und Unterleibsleiden. Man muß hier auf die Färbung der Linie Obacht geben. Gelbliche Färbung bedeutet immer, daß Galle und Leber nicht gut arbeiten; kleine Pünktchen oder Vertiefungen — ähnlich wie Nadelstiche — sind die Zeichen für Steine oder Gries. Blasensteine: Vertiefungen unter dem kleinen Finger; Nierengries: Vertiefungen unter dem Sonnenfinger; Gallensteine: wenn die Vertiefungen gelblich oder bräunlich sind. Dieselben Punkte unter dem Mittelfinger in der Herzlinie bedeuten schadhafte Zähne. Alle in der Linie befindlichen Inseln sind Anzeichen dafür, daß hier Vererbungen von Herzstörungen vorhanden sind. Eine Ausnahme bildet nur die Insel am Ende der Herzlinie, die aber jedesmal unter dem Jupiterberg oder Jupiter- und Saturnberg liegt. Sie bedeutet, daß in der Familie Lungentuberkulose vorhanden war. Es ist aber nicht gesagt, daß der Betreffende, bei dem sich dieses Zeichen befindet, dasselbe Leiden bekommen müsse. Größere absteigende Äste der Herzlinie nach der Kopflinie zu, kann man in vielen Händen beobachten und sie haben mehrfache Bedeutung. Einmal ist die Stelle, wo solche Astlinie die Hauptlinie verläßt, als ein günstiger Zeitpunkt dafür anzusehen, daß sich Herzensbekanntschaften zeigen oder genutzt werden könnten. Sind die Äste aber verbunden mit der Kopflinie, so bedeuten sie noch dazu günstige Jahre für Freundschaften und Bekanntschaften (nicht nur für Herzensangelegenheiten, sondern auch für Teilhaberschaft u. dgl.). Diese Zeitpunkte werden aber nicht an der Herz- und Kopflinie, sondern auf der Schicksalslinie abgemessen, die von diesen Linien durchkreuzt wird. Gehen die Linien, die als Ereignislinien zu bezeichnen sind, weiter herüber nach der Lebenslinie und schneiden sie, so haben dieselben Linien, deren Zeitpunkt man bei der Lebenslinie abmißt, zur Bedeutung: Kummer, Trauer und Depressionen, mit einem Worte: seelische Erschütterungen, worunter auch gerade und besonders Todesfälle in der Familie zu rechnen sind. Auf die Ereignislinien in diesem Sinne komme ich später noch zurück.

Die Herzlinie (Cardialis).
(Bild 24/8, 13 und Bild 21.)

Herzensgüte, Flirt, Herzensaffären und Enttäuschungen, Kummer, Eifersucht, Freundschaft; die idealere Seite der Liebe (zum Unterschied von der sinnlichen, die durch den Venusberg dargestellt wird). Blut und Zirkulation, Störungen im Kreislaufe, Steinleiden, Herzkrankheiten.

A n f a n g der Herzlinie ist am Handrande; nicht im oder am Jupiterberg!

D i e G r ö ß e d e r H e r z l i c h k e i t entspricht der Länge und Stärke der Linie.

E x t r e m l a n g , v o n R a n d z u R a n d : Übermaß an Liebe, Eifersucht, Laune, z u v i e l Herz (Bild 26/24 und Bild 43). Nymphomanie.

D ü n n e , r o t e , f a d e n a r t i g e L i n i e : Böse Neigungen, tierische Art.

D ü n n e , b l a s s e , f a d e n a r t i g e L i n i e n b e i F r a u e n : Verstandes-betonte Liebe; nur materiell.

D ü n n e , b l a s s e , f a d e n a r t i g e L i n i e b e i M ä n n e r n : Blasiertheit, Lebemann; schwacher Körper.

K e t t i g : Neigung zu Herzkrankheiten (Bild 25/20).

S e h r k e t t i g u n d a s t i g : An Illusionen und Enttäuschungen reiches Leben (Bild 29 und Bild 27/37).

K e t t i g , b r e i t u n d b l a ß : Kaltherzig und blasiert; schwacher Körper.

B r e i t u n d r o t : Heftige Neigungen, gewalttätig in der Erotik.

G e l b l i c h : Leberleiden; Depressionen.

Kleine, blasse Punkte in der Linie: Schwäche der Konstitution zu der Zeit (Bild 29/22).

Herzlinie nahe der Kopflinie: Neigung zu Geiz, Heuchelei. Diese Formation erzeugt ein schmales Rechteck. Man beachte Nägel, betr. Asthma = Intoleranz. Engherzigkeit.

Hohe Lage, nahe den Fingerwurzeln: Sonniges, glückliches Naturell (Bild 26).

Plötzlich endend: Tod durch Herzschlag (Bild 24/13).

Endet unter Saturnberg: Materielle Art in Herzensangelegenheiten (Bild 24/13).

Endet zwischen Jupiter- und Saturnberg: Glück bei dem anderen Geschlecht ist sehr beschränkt (Bild 25/21).

Immer werden sich hier Bitternisse im Liebesleben zeigen, früher oder später! Deshalb darf man ihnen aber nicht ausweichen. Sie sind kosmisch bedingt.

Endet in zwei Ästen im Jupiterberge: Sehr günstig, Wohlstand, aufrichtiges und anständiges Wesen (Bild 29 links). Fingerlinien verstärken die Bedeutung, wenn senkrecht.

Ein Ast im Jupiter-, ein anderer im Saturnberg: Ungünstig für Eheangelegenheiten (Bild 29 rechts).

Endet als ein Ast, den Saturnberg berührend: Mißerfolg, wenn nicht eine gute Sonnenlinie.

Keine Herzlinie: Selten. Heuchelei, wenn nicht sehr gute Magenlinie. Gottlos, herzlos.

Brüche in der Linie: Herzleiden, schwere Geburten, evtl. Unfruchtbarkeit (♀, ♄); angeboren (Bild 26 und Bild 28).

Kreuzende kurze Linien: Herzleiden, bei Frauen schwere Geburten; erworben (Bild 28/31).

Viele senkrechte, kurze Linien: Herzleiden durch Herz- und Leberschwäche.

Herzlinie mit Kopf- und Lebenslinie zusammenlaufend (Bild 25/49): gewaltsamer Tod; außerdem: große Leiden in der Liebe und Neigung zu Genuß und Eifersucht; sind die Hände hart, so wird der Betreffende zur Erlangung seiner Wünsche in der Liebe Hindernisse zu überwinden wissen.

Ende unter Jupiter- oder Saturnberg astig verwirrt: Für Frauen große Geburtsschmerzen (Bild 27/13).

Am Anfang ein Ast abwärts in den Marsberg gebogen: Gefahr durch Feinde und Tiere (Bild 25/45).

Am Anfang eine Linie in den Mondberg gehend: Neigung zu Verbrechen (Bild 25/8).

Linie vom Stern in Venusberg nach Herzlinie: Trauer um eine nahestehende Person (Bild 31/7).

Insel in der Herzlinie und diese kettig: Neigung zu Herzleiden, ererbt; Liebesenttäuschungen.

Große Verästelung der Linie: Viele und tiefe Herzensenttäuschungen (Bild 27/37).

Sehr breite Herzlinie: Venenschwellung; großes Herz (Bild 27/11).

Die Saturn- oder Schicksalslinie.
(Bild 24/ ♄ 1, 2, 3, 4, 5 und Bild 21.)

Die Formation und der Verlauf der Saturnlinie sind Hauptpunkte bei der Beurteilung. Aus ihr erkennt man die Stellung oder das Verhältnis zur Umwelt, den Lebensweg, Erfolge oder Mißerfolge und den betr. Zeitpunkt, z. T. auch Berufsrichtungen. Sie wurde auch Kulturlinie genannt.

Dabei ist zu bedenken, daß z. B. Neger, Mongolen, Indianer, teilweise auch Inder keine Saturnlinie besitzen oder nur kleine Teile davon. Es ist daher notwendig, die Rassenzugehörigkeit des Handeigners immer in Betracht zu ziehen, wenn Beurteilungen vorgenommen werden.

Die Saturn- oder Schicksalslinie zeigt in ihrem Verlauf „unser Barometer für den Lebensweg", unseren Weg oder auch unser „Auf und Ab", außerdem Wechselfälle, die wirklich solche sind und nicht nur so genannt werden. — Wenn alle Leute nur mehr Menschen wären, dann würden sie nicht so großen Wert auf allerlei lächerliche Nebensächlichkeiten des Alltagslebens legen. — Da wird gefragt, ob man einen Stellenwechsel im Beruf habe; ob man einen „neuen Artikel aufnehmen" soll im Geschäft, um es dadurch zu „heben". Ob man „die größere Reise antrete" (von Berlin nach Hamburg), oder ob es „einem gut gehen wird", oder: „Bessert sich nicht bald meine Lebenslage?" — Wenn man diese Fragen immer wieder hört, dann möchte man sich irgendwo an einen schönen waldigen Ort oder ans Meer flüchten, wo keine solchen Leute sind, die das Leben und seinen Sinn weder erkannt noch begriffen haben, die weder Religion, Gottvertrauen, noch Selbstvertrauen haben und sich ängstlich an eingebildete Ereignisse klammern, die in Wirklichkeit nur Schein und Nebensachen sind. — Dazu ist die Chirologie (wie auch die Astrologie) nicht da! — Man sollte mehr die geistige Bedeutung der Ereignisse werten und danach handeln. Was macht es denn aus, ob ich heute oder in einem Monat eine Stellung wechsle? Ich für meine Person würde sagen: so oft wie irgend möglich, damit man mehr Überblick erhält und mehr und Neues lernt. — Die lebenden „Klebemarken", die so gern ein Leben lang auf einer Stelle, einem Posten, bei einer Tätigkeit hocken, wollen natürlich nichts davon wissen, weil sie an der Materie kleben und an geistigen Dingen keinen

Anteil nehmen, sondern nur so tun. Diese Leute werden immer Automaten bleiben. Bei ihnen bedeutet Höherentwicklung: „Aufstieg in Stellung und Beruf". Weltliche „Erfolge" sind keine, sondern nur jene, die Ewigkeitswerte in sich tragen und deshalb nicht verloren gehen können. Das sollte bedacht werden. Aber für den, der keine Religion (ich meine nicht Konfession!) besitzt, der die Wiedergeburts-Gesetzmäßigkeit nicht bedacht und begriffen hat, ist jede Beratung unnütz. Solche Leute sollen erst Mensch werden und die göttlichen Eigenschaften in sich entfalten, damit sie den Zweck des Lebens erfassen. D a n n erst werden sie Nutzen von diesen Wissenschaften haben. Unter dem Begriff „bessere Zeiten" verstehen diese Leute Zeiten, in denen sie mehr Geldmittel zur Verfügung haben. Es ist Schwindel und Betrug, wenn jemand nach der Hand eine Auskunft gibt wie diese: Sie kommen zu Wohlstand, oder Sie werden reich! — In keiner Hand steht ein Zeichen dafür, ob der Betreffende bald 3 Mark oder 600 Mark oder Tausende erhalten wird. Ist eine Linie für Erbschaft (aus der Lebenslinie kommend, in die Apollolinie mündend) vorhanden, so steht nicht dabei geschrieben, ob es Geld sein wird und wieviel, oder ob es ein alter Großvaterstuhl, sonstige Möbel oder Wertgegenstände sein werden. Man muß die Frechheit bewundern, mit der es manche wagen, dem Ratsuchenden solchen Schwindel einzureden. (Kann man sich da über die Feinde der Handlesekunst wundern?) Außerdem können solche günstigen Zeiten angezeigt sein, und der Betreffende vernachlässigt die Gelegenheiten, was dann? Er hätte die Zeit nutzen können und zu Gewinn kommen, aber er — unterließ es. Diese Ereignisse m ü s s e n nicht eintreten, wenn man sie nicht beachtet, aber sie k ö n n e n eintreten und sollten genutzt werden. —

Wir haben eine Wahlfreiheit, aber keine Willensfreiheit! Wir sollen unseren von Gott erhaltenen und selbst entwickelten Verstand anwenden. D a s vergessen die meisten Leute — „nur nicht denken!"

Wo keine Schicksalslinie vorhanden ist, werden sich im Leben des Betreffenden keine großen Ereignisse besonderer Art zeigen. Sein Leben ist ziemlich gleichmäßig, öde oder auch leer. Ist die Linie aber gutgezeichnet, d. h. gerade oder gebogen (nicht gewunden), dazu von normaler Breite, $1^{1}/_{2}$ mm, von guter Farbe, gerötet, dann wird auch der Lebensweg gut, gerade sein, d. h. wenig markante negative Störungen aufweisen. Querlinien beeinflussen diesen Weg selbstverständlich mehr oder minder, und dies ist einer besonderen Betrachtung zu unterziehen. Außerdem müssen bei Unternehmungen u. dgl. noch Zeichen an der Lebenslinie (auf- oder absteigende Äste) genau in Betracht gezogen werden. Beginnt die Saturnlinie im Handgelenk, so nimmt sie viel Kraft aus der ererbten Lebenskraft (Bereich der Raszette), und aus diesem Grunde werden sich immer Selbständigkeitsdrang und auch mehr oder minder Persönlichkeitsgefühl bemerkbar machen. Liegt der Anfang aber in der Lebenslinie, so wird der Betreffende zumeist erst später auf eigenen Füßen stehen oder doch mindestens Hemmungen von seiten der Eltern oder Verwandten aufzuweisen haben. (Einfluß der Lebenslinie zusammen mit negativen Einflüssen des Venusberges.) Entspringt die Saturnlinie im Venusberg, so erhält sie auch hieraus ihre Kraftströme, wie jeder Baum seine Hauptkräfte aus dem Bereich zieht, in dem sich seine Wurzeln befinden. In dem Fall ist der Einfluß des anderen Geschlechts sehr fördernd, daher auch: Aufstieg durch positive Mithilfe des anderen Geschlechts. Auswirkung bei einem Mann: Er wird Frauen finden, die ihm durch Geld oder andere Mittel tatkräftige Unterstützung zuteil werden lassen, damit er seine Pläne verwirklichen kann. Es muß nicht mit „Ehe" zusammenhängen, kann es aber. Bei einem Weibe: Männer werden sich bemühen, ihm den Weg des Aufstiegs zu erleichtern (siehe Geraldine Farrar). Über die Zeit läßt sich nicht immer Genaues angeben. Das schadet weiter nichts; denn jeder Mensch muß warten lernen. Die Auswirkung kommt i m m e r   d a n n , wenn es schicksalmäßig paßt und für die eigene Entwicklung am günstigsten ist. Nicht vom kleinlich-egoistischen Standpunkt aus betrachtet, sondern von hoher kosmischer Warte aus gesehen! Auf die geistige Führung, die ja jeder Mensch hat, kann man sich ganz sicher verlassen; sie ist immer richtig; das erkennt man erst viel später.

Beginnt die Saturnlinie im Mondberg, so sind die Einflüsse wieder andere: Aufstieg durch indirekte Mithilfe des anderen Geschlechts; d. h. Verbindungen und Beziehungen sowie Bekanntschaften sind günstig zur Förderung im Aufstieg. Das andere Geschlecht wird sich immer irgendwie darin bemerkbar machen (Mond), aber da sind auch undefinierbare Einflüsse, so der Wechsel der Dinge, „Laune des Schicksals", Mode und Konjunktur, Reisen, Ausland, Ausländer, und was sonst noch unter den Begriff „Zufälligkeiten" (die es in Wirklichkeit nicht gibt!) fällt. Alles Mondeinflüsse: das Mysteriöse, Wechselartige, Stimmungs- und Launenhafte, Unvorhergesehene. Eine gute lange Linie, aus dem Mondberg kommend nach Saturn- oder noch besser nach dem Jupiterberg gehend, macht günstig für Reisen und Aufenthalt in Übersee und gibt zumeist auch Neigung zu Naturwissenschaften. Verläuft diese Saturnlinie aber nur in der rechten Hand, wie beschrieben, und hat sie in der linken Hand andere Formation, so bedeutet dies, daß die günstige Zeit für Ebengenanntes erst mit dem 28. Jahre beginnt. Man darf aber nicht eine Saturnlinie aus dem Mondberg kommend als ein ungünstiges Zeichen auffassen. Ich persönlich schätze sie als eine der besten Konstellationen, wenn auch die Auswirkung nicht immer angenehm ist. Doch das macht wenig aus. Man lernt durch diese „undefinierbaren" Einflüsse und „Zufälligkeiten", sich besser auf das Leben und seine

Vielseitigkeiten einzustellen. — Die Bezeichnungen „gutgehen" und „schlechtgehen" sind nur Einbildung. Es g e h t ! Wie? Das kommt auf die Auffassung des Betreffenden an und auf das Maß seiner erworbenen Lebenskunst. Hat man es zu einer kosmischen Weltanschauung gebracht, hat man vor nichts Angst. Nichts kann überraschen, weil man auf allerlei schon vorher gefaßt ist oder alles mögliche in der Hinsicht erwartet. Wer dann mit Sorgen und Ärger beginnt, der ist schon von seinem inneren Selbst gerichtet und schadet sich nur selbst. Das nenne ich seelischen Selbstmord. M i t dem Schicksal gehen und die sich bietenden Gelegenheiten benutzen zum Weiterkommen, das ist Lebenskunst. Sich gegen das Schicksal auflehnen, das ist Dummheit und schadet nur. — Eine Saturnlinie aus dem Marsberg kommend gibt Lebenskampf, gibt aber auch das Maß von Mut, sich durchzusetzen, und zwar durch seelische Kraft oder passive Widerstandskraft. Diese Konstellation findet sich z. B. in den Händen der ehemaligen Opernsängerin Claire Dux. Sie war in ihrer Jugend Kontoristin und brachte es durch Fleiß und Aufbietung aller Kräfte zur Kammersängerin. Meist endet die Schicksalslinie im Saturnberg; denn bei den meisten hängt das Leben und der Lebensweg doch stark mit der Materie oder dem Materiellen (d. h. dem Irdischen und Vergänglichen — Saturnprinzip) zusammen; daher auch mit Erde, Grund und Boden, Haus, Heim, Landwirtschaft; Verdichtungsprinzip, das Solide. — Endet die Saturnlinie im Jupiterberg, so wird sich in der Auswirkung folgendes zeigen: entweder wird der Betreffende sich um eine Staatsstellung, Beamtentätigkeit bemühen, oder — falls es ihm nicht gerade „gut" geht und er scheinbar in Not gerät, es findet sich immer unvorhergesehen eine „rettende Hand" (Prinzip für Protektion, Schutz, Fürsprache). Endet die Saturnlinie aber in die Anfangslinie des Venusgürtels, so ist das ein bedenkliches Zeichen. Kommt das in den Händen eines jungen Mädchens vor, so mag sie gut auf der Hut sein vor Entführung, Verschleppung oder Mädchenhandel. Ich fand dies Zeichen oft und erhielt auch bestätigt, daß derartige Versuche tatsächlich vorgekommen sind. Gerade die letzte Bedeutung zeigt wohl zur Genüge, wie sehr die Benennung dieser Linie berechtigt ist. Nur Dumme haben dafür ein Lächeln, um die eigene Lächerlichkeit zu verbergen. Sie werden nur durch die harte Schule der Erfahrung klug werden. Ich gönne ihnen das von Herzen, denn es dient ihnen zum Guten, und der Entwicklung eines Menschen darf man nie im Wege stehen, auch dann nicht, wenn „Schaden" notwendig ist. Das Enden der Saturnlinie im Apolloberg weist einen Lebensweg mit künstlerischer Richtung an. Hierbei muß aber die Apollolinie selbst in Betracht gezogen werden als „Berufsbahn des Künstlers". — Entspringt die Schicksalslinie innerhalb des „Großen Dreiecks", dann berührt sie weder Lebenslinie noch Magenlinie, d. h.

der Träger dieses Zeichens hat einen härteren Lebenskampf zu erwarten. Dazu benötigt man Mut und Ausdauer (siehe Daumen). Ist aber genügend Heiterkeit des Herzens vorhanden, dann ist der Lebenskampf bedeutend erleichtert und wirkt nicht deprimierend oder verbitternd. Es liegt immer an der persönlichen Einstellung zu den Dingen und Verhältnissen. Einer nennt etwas Glück oder gut, was dem anderen Unglück oder Böses bedeuten würde. Alles nur Begriffe, denn es gibt weder Glück noch Unglück, weder Gut noch Böse in d e r Hinsicht. Alles ist nur Ereignis! Was man darin erkennen will, das ist es uns.

F e h l t : Nicht notwendig böse. Ein Lebensweg, der eher öde und unruhig ist; der Handeigner will sich nicht seiner Umwelt einfügen, sondern wird oft versuchen, sich ihr zu widersetzen.

D o p p e l t   u n d   g u t : Günstiges Schicksal; kann mehrere Berufe nebeneinander haben, wenn gute Kopflinie vorhanden. Eine zweite Saturnlinie, vom Mondberge kommend, gibt Neigung zu Erfindungen durch Intuition (Bild 24/4).

D o p p e l t   u n d   g e w u n d e n : Unannehmlichkeiten, Neigung zu Schwelgerei und Krankheiten dadurch (Bild 26/9).

E i n e   L i n i e   g e b r o c h e n   u n d   w e l l e n a r t i g : Störungen in der Gesundheit, Neigung zu Fieber und Zank; viel Wechsel im Leben (Bild 26/9).

B e g i n n t   i n   L e b e n s l i n i e : In der Entfaltung durch Verwandte gehindert, Erfolg erst später, da Abhängigkeit nachwirkend ist (Bild 24/2).

B e g i n n t   i n   R a s z e t t e : Selbständigkeitsdrang, guter Erfolg durch sich selbst; wird oft eine Persönlichkeit, kommt auf die Menschenart an (Bild 56 und Bild 24/3).

B e g i n n t   i m   V e n u s b e r g   (links): Verliebte Natur; wenn auch rechts: Bedient sich seiner Macht bei dem anderen Geschlecht (Bild 24/1 und Bild 59). Aufstieg durch das andere Geschlecht.

A n f a n g   i m   M o n d b e r g : Erfolg hängt stark von anderen Menschen, evtl. vom anderen Geschlecht ab. Auch indirekte Erfolge durch das andere Geschlecht (Bild 24/4). Reisen, Wechsel.

A n f a n g   u n t e r   M o n d b e r g , klar bis Saturnberg: Mediale Anlagen, Psychometrie (Bild 53). Erfolg in Übersee.

A n f a n g   i n   M a r s f e l d : Leben und Streben mit viel Kampf (Bild 25/11).

B e g i n n t   i m   M a r s b e r g : Durchsetzung und Verwirklichung durch eigene Kraft und Mut (Bild 24/5).

B e g i n n t   i m   M o n d b e r g   u n d   m i t   d e r   H e r z l i n i e   v e r -
k n o t e t , endend im Jupiterberge: Reiche gute Heirat.

A n f a n g   g e h t   d u r c h   d i e   R a s z e t t e : Viel Sorgen, Ärger und Elend.

A n f a n g n a h e R a s z e t t e , e n d i g t i n H e r z l i n i e : Unglück durch Herzensaffären, Hemmungen (Bild 27 rechts).

A n f a n g n a h e R a s z e t t e , e n d i g t i n K o p f l i n i e : Irrtum und falsche Einschätzung verhindern Erfolge (Bild 27/8).

B e g i n n t a n d e r K o p f l i n i e : Erfolg spät im Leben, viel Arbeit und Sorgen, auch gefährdete Gesundheit (Bild 26).

B e g i n n t a n d e r H e r z l i n i e (aufwärts): Ruhigere Zeiten erst nach dem 40. Jahre; außerdem: der Lebensweg wird vom anderen Geschlecht in späteren Jahren fördeind beeinflußt (Bild 24/12).

B e g i n n t i m H a n d t i s c h : Sorgen, Unglück, evtl. Gefängnis, wenn nicht kleines Viereck auf Saturnberg (Bild 26).

E n d e t i m J u p i t e r b e r g : Viel Erfolg, Protektion, Ehrgeiz, Wohlstand (Bild 24/11).

E n d e t i m S a t u r n b e r g : Erfolg in Dingen, die mit Erde zusammenhängen, Landwirtschaft, Obst, Blumen, Metall, Minen, Stein, Forst, Häuser, aber auch in Religion (Bild 28/10).

E n d e t i m z w e i t e n G l i e d e d e s S a t u r n f i n g e r s : Große Erfolge zum Guten oder Bösen, sehr launisches Glück.

E n d e t i m d r i t t e n G l i e d e d e s S a t u r n f i n g e r s : Trauriges, böses Geschick, Gefahr für Mord, Gefängnis usw. (Bild 25/52).

E n d e t i m A p o l l o b e r g : Erfolg in Kunst, Spekulation, Wohlstand (selten).

E n d e t i m M e r k u r b e r g : Erfolg in Handel, Industrie, Wissenschaft und Reden (selten).

E n d e t i n d e r K o p f l i n i e : Verhältnisse werden durch Unklugheit und Irrtum nicht ausgenutzt.

E n d e t i n d e r H e r z l i n i e : Viele günstige Verhältnisse werden durch Herzensaffären und Leidenschaften verscherzt (Bild 27/29).

E n d e t i m S c h w u n g e v e r l a u f e n d i m V e n u s g ü r t e l (Teil zwischen Jupiter- und Saturnfinger): Warnt vor Verschleppung (Opfer des Mädchenhandels usw.), evtl. Adoption.

Die Apollo- oder Sonnenlinie ☉.
(Bild 24/10 und Bild 21.)

Ruf, Ehren, Erfolg, Geld. Kunstbegabung, Wohlstand, Erbschaft, Gunst. Solar plexus.

Eine gute Sonnenlinie ist notwendig, um eine „glückliche Hand" zu haben; sie stärkt eine schlechte Saturnlinie und beeinflußt alles in günstiger Weise.

Anfang in der Lebenslinie: Erfolg durch sich selbst.

Anfang nahe der Raszette, im ersten Fingerglied endend: Intuition: Ahnendes Erkennen. Genie, weltberühmt. Solche Sonnenlinie hatten Lord Roberts, Goethe, Napoleon I.

Lange Apollolinie gibt Bekanntwerden. Verstärkt wird dies durch Sonne auf Apolloberg (Bild 58). Eine lange gute Apollolinie besagt auch, daß die Vorfahren wohlhabende, begüterte Personen waren. In der rechten Hand: väterliche, in der linken: mütterliche Generation.

Anfang im Mondberg: Erfolg abhängig von anderen, von der Laune des Schicksals, Erfolg durch andere Menschen, direkt sowie auch indirekt (Bild 29/35 und Bild 58). Phantasievolle Intuition.

Anfang im Venusberg: Erfolg durch das andere Geschlecht (Bild 59) durch direkte Hilfe. Schöpferische Intuition.

Anfang im Marsfeld: Erfolg kostet sehr viel Streben und Mühe, Ärger (Bild 25).

Anfang im Marsberg: Erfolg durch viel Fleiß und Energie; evtl. wird auch Rücksichtslosigkeit und viel Egoismus angewandt, um das ersehnte Ziel zu erreichen, was aber aus der ganzen Hand erkannt werden muß (Bild 28/7—17).

Gebrochen innerhalb des Handtisches: Mißerfolge, die guten Ausgang haben (Bild 26/20).

Kurze Sonnenlinie: Wenig Erfolge und erst später (Bild 29/26).

Mehrere kurze Parallelen: Vielseitig und exzentrisch (Bild 25/47). Sinn für Musik und Zeichnen.

Querlinien: Hindernisse (vom Saturnberg kommend): Neid oder Armut der Verwandten oder häusliche Hindernisse; vom Merkurberg kommend: durch Intrigen und Neid verdorbene Pläne und Unternehmen (Bild 25/39).

Krumme Finger und hohle Hände sind selbst für die beste Sonnenlinie große Hindernisse und besagen oft, daß Gedanken und Pläne sich in schlechten Bahnen befinden.

Sonnenlinie, vom Venusgürtel geschnitten, bedeutet immer: Hindernisse im allgemeinen, welche sehr schwer zu überbrücken sind (Bild 26).

Wenn der Venusgürtel von der Sonnenlinie geschnitten wird und an derselben Stelle plötzlich aufhört, so ist Gefahr vorhanden, daß der Betreffende, zu Leichtsinn und Genußsucht neigend, dadurch seinen Wohlstand verliert. Leichten Sinn im guten oder schlechten Sinne.

Eine Linie, vom Venusberg kommend, in die Sonnenlinie mündend: Geldzufluß, evtl. Erbschaft.

Ist am Anfange der Linie im Venusberg ein Stern, so bedeutet das: Geld- oder Wertzuwachs durch Erbschaft und Tod eines nahestehenden Menschen (Bild 31/7—7).

Schneidet dieselbe Linie aber die Sonnenlinie und geht über sie hinaus, so warnt sie vor materiellem Verluste.

Die Magen-, Leber- oder Merkurlinie ☿ (Hepathica).

(Bild 27/6, Bild 24/25 und Bild 21.)

Die Magen- oder Leberlinie, auch Gesundheitslinie genannt, entspringt entweder in der Lebenslinie, im Venusberg, in der Handwurzel oder auf dem unteren Teile des Mondbergs und verläuft in der Richtung zum Merkurberge.

Aus dem Gesamtbild dieser Linie, ihrer Beschaffenheit, ihrem Verlauf und ihrer Farbe lassen sich sehr gute Schlüsse auf den allgemeinen Zustand der Nerven, der Verdauungsorgane und Drüsentätigkeit ziehen. Die Linie soll entweder ganz und gut oder gar nicht vorhanden sein.

Eine g u t e M a g e n l i n i e v e r b e s s e r t die Bedeutung einer schlechten Saturnlinie (Bild 41).

Zu einer „erfolgreichen" Hand gehört eine gute Magenlinie; d. h. eine Linie, die in ihrem Verlauf gut gezeichnet ist und auch eine gute Farbe hat. (Der „Erfolg" des Menschen hängt mehr als man glaubt von guter Stimmung und gesunden Nerven ab. Wenn die Funktion der Drüsen, die Beschaffenheit der Nerven keine guten sind, dann k a n n auch keine gute „Stimmung" vorhanden sein, weil die Basis hierfür fehlt.)

Ein g u t e r A s t i n d e n S a t u r n b e r g : Sehr günstig für Beruf verbunden mit Erde.

G u t e r Z w e i g v o n M a g e n l i n i e n a c h A p o l l o b e r g : Sehr günstig für die Ausübung der Heilkunde durch Naturmittel, Magnetismus u. dgl. (Bild 41).

E i n g u t e r A s t i n d e n M e r k u r b e r g : Sehr günstig für die Ausübung der Medizinalkunde, Chemie, Pharmazie.

E i n g u t e r A s t i n d e n M a r s b e r g : Ist günstig zur Ausübung eines Berufes, der mit Metallen verbunden ist; außerdem macht dies Zeichen mutig und heftig (Bild 28/8).

Entspringt die Magenlinie zu weit auf dem Mondberge, dann ist die Milz beeinflußt — was nicht immer krankhaft zu sein braucht. Dies gibt Neigung zu Sonderbarkeiten im Gedankenleben, was sich dann auch mehr oder weniger im Handeln zeigt. Man spricht von Menschen, die einen „Spleen" haben. Spleen ist aber der (englische) Name für Milz! (Bild 24/25-25).

Die allermeisten Bedeutungen der Magenlinie sind gesundheitliche, weshalb ich sie im besonderen in Band II „Medizinische Hand-Diagnostik" bringe.

Eine gute, bis tief in den Merkurberg hineinreichende Magenlinie ergibt gute Begabung für fremde Sprachen (Bild 27). Warum? — Eine Linie von derartiger Beschaffenheit zeugt von guter Verdauungstätigkeit und guter Beschaffenheit der Drüsen und der Gesamtnerven; außerdem ist sie ein Zeichen von großer Lebenszähigkeit. Wer diese guten physischen Qualitäten aufweisen kann, der hat auch die Grundlage für das Sprachenstudium.

Zähigkeit der körperlichen Widerstandskraft setzt ebenfalls gesunde Nerven und eine gute Drüsentätigkeit, sowie gutes Arbeiten der Verdauungsorgane voraus. Hier wie überall braucht man nur logisch nachzudenken, um die Basis zu finden, worauf alles beruht.

Der Venusgürtel ♀ (Cingulum veneris).
(Bild 21, Bild 27/16 und Bild 25/48.)

B e a c h t e , ob er in guter, schlechter, harter oder weicher Hand ist.

I n g u t e r H a n d : Intelligenz und Feinfühligkeit.

I n s c h l e c h t e r H a n d : Liebe zu Genuß; mehr noch, wenn doppelt oder gebrochen (Bild 25/48).

I n h a r t e r H a n d : Energie und Rastlosigkeit; mehr noch, wenn gebrochen.

Der Venusgürtel gibt passive Kraft und Neigung zu Poesie und Literatur. Feinnervigkeit der Sexualorgane.

V e n u s g ü r t e l zerrissen, Mond- und Venusberg stark entwickelt und evtl. dazu noch eine Uranuslinie: Starke Neigung zu Hysterie.

E r w i r k t ü b e l , wenn in dicken, sehr weichen Händen, die sehr weiß sind (ohne die Farbe bei Hitze oder Kälte zu wechseln), ein großer Venusberg, rosa Nägel und Intrigenlinie auf Merkurberg vorhanden.

E n d e t g e s c h l o s s e n a u f M e r k u r b e r g : In schlechter Hand: Neigung zu Unaufrichtigkeiten.

E n d e t i n e i n e r E h e l i n i e : Der andere Eheteil wird der Führende sein. (Bild 27/16). Schwaches Rückgrat.

N i c h t u n g ü n s t i g : Wenn nur der Anfang vorhanden ist und vor der Saturnlinie endet, auch wenn er sonst die Stellen frei läßt, wo die Saturn- und die Sonnenlinie durchläuft (Bild 28/16); unterdrückte Sexualität.

G e s c h n i t t e n durch Ende der Apollolinie: Verluste durch Leichtsinn.

Geschnitten durch senkrechte Linien: Nervenleiden. Wenn ein halber Venusgürtel, Nähe Jupiterberg, vorhanden ist, der in einem Schwunge in die Saturnlinie verläuft, so warnt dieses Zeichen vor Entführung (Mädchenhandel), Adoption.

Die Neptun- oder Giftlinie ♆ (Linea toxica).
(Bild 21 und 30/57.)

Sie entspringt aus der Lebenslinie oder im Venusberge (was ungünstiger ist) und strebt dem Mondberge zu. Sie gibt Neigung zu Genüssen schädlicher Art, Liebe zu narkotischen und nebelhaften Dingen (Tabak, Haschisch, Opium, Morphium, Kokain, Parfüm usw.). Am Ausdruck der Linie erkennt man, wieviel von solchen Giften im Organismus schon enthalten ist. Auch zeigt sich derselbe Ausdruck, wenn das Impfgift den Organismus schädigte oder sonst Arzneigifte im Körper lagern und ihn schädigen. (Auch in der Iris gut erkennbar!)

Von Lebenslinie bis hoch in den Mondberg: Frühes Altern durch Gifte (Vergiftung des Organismus) (Bild 30/57).

Aus Venusberg kommend: Arznei- oder Impfgift tiefer in den Organismus eingedrungen.

Verläuft sie waagerecht vom Venusberg in den Mondberg, und ist sie sehr stark: dann sind Giftstoffe schon durch die Erbmasse übertragen, welche schwache Nerven geben (Bild 27/22—20); z. B. durch Spritzen bei der Entbindung.

Insel in dieser Linie: Ein tiefes Leid in der Liebe.

Die Milchstraße oder via lasciva.
(Bild 30.)

Diese Linie ist nicht sehr oft anzutreffen. Sie entspringt in oder nahe der Raszette und verläuft in paralleler Richtung mit der Magenlinie. Gewöhnlich ist sie nur kurz, einige Zentimeter, selten 4 bis 6 cm lang.

Gut und gerade verlaufend, gibt sie Neigung zu Beschaulichkeit und Innigkeit. Sie gibt angeborene Lebensklugheit und zeigt, wie die alte Literatur sich ausdrückt: Personen, die „mit Hilfe der Frauen und der Pfaffen vieles vollbringen können."

Ist diese Linie gedreht und zerrissen, zeigt sie eine innerlich sich quälende Natur an; eine unglückliche, „zerrissene" Seele, voll Unzufriedenheit, die am Schmerzlichen hängt.

Eine sehr lange Linie, bis an den Mars- oder Merkurberg reichend: Glück in entfernten überseeischen Ländern.

Ein Stern in dieser langen Linie: Gefahren in solchen Gegenden.

Zerrissen in viele kleine Linien und Parallelen: Nervosität oder Hysterie infolge gewaltsam unterdrückter oder absonderlicher Leidenschaft.

Die Temperenz- oder Isislinie.
(Bild 27/20)

ist eine senkrechte gerade Linie, die (wenn auch selten genug) auf dem Handrande zu finden ist. Sie gibt Lebensernst und Anlage zur Enthaltsamkeit (Temperenz).

Das ist alles, was ich in bezug auf diese Linie beobachtet habe. Sie fehlt in der ganzen Literatur und wird nur sehr selten, ohne nähere Erklärungen erwähnt.

Die Uranus- oder Intuitionslinie ♅ *)
(Bild 21)

entspringt im unteren Mondberg und verläuft bogenartig zum Merkurberg oder als gerade Linie parallel zur Magenlinie, was aber selten ist. Sie darf mit einer doppelten Magenlinie nicht verwechselt werden. (Bild 42.)

Man findet sie in den Händen mehr oder weniger sensitiver Personen (nach dem Kriege bedeutend öfter als früher), und sie besagt: passive Kraft, Intelligenz, gute Intuition und mediale Fähigkeiten, Anlage für Gedankenlesen und Empfinden, Psychometrie, Symboldeuten, Graphologie, Astrologie, Chiromantie, Psychoanalyse usw. (Obgleich Intuition für die Wissenschaften n i c h t erforderlich ist, leistet sie doch in der Ausübung sehr gute Dienste.)

Eine Uranuslinie nach dem Apolloberg strebend ist sehr günstig für eigene Erkenntnisse durch Forschungen, Erfindungen.

Eine Insel am Anfang der Linie: Anlage zum Hellsehen oder Hellhören.

Eine offene Insel am Anfang der Linie: Neigung zu Launen, übertriebene Phantasie und evtl. Leichtsinn.

Eine Insel am Ende der Linie: Neigung zu Schlafwandeln und gefährlichem Somnambulismus.

---

*) Die Neptun-, die Uranus- und die Isislinie wurden erstmalig von mir benannt und gewürdigt. Sie fehlten in der bisherigen Literatur.

Ein Stern auf der Linie : Warnt vor Verlusten, besonders wenn gebrochene Saturnlinie.
Stern nahe der Linie auf Mondberg : Warnt vor Gefahr für Schiffbruch.

Raszette oder Armband (Restrictica).

(Bild 21)

werden die Linien genannt, welche um die Handwurzel liegen und die Grenze zwischen Hand und Arm bilden. Sorgen, Arbeit, Maß der physischen Kraft, Stammbaum (Abkunft).
Drei Ringe (nicht zerrissen): Stärken eine schwache Lebenslinie (Bild 25).
Der erste Ring kettenartig : Arbeitsreiches Leben (Bild 24/23).
Nach der Zahl der Ringe das Lebensalter bestimmen zu wollen, ist unzuverlässig; man kann nur die Zahl der Ringe und ihre Güte für die Lebenskraft in Betracht ziehen bei der Beurteilung der physischen Kraft und Zähigkeit.
Schlecht geformte Linien : Sorgen, Neigung zu Extravaganzen.
Schlecht, dünn und schwach : Kränkliche Körperkonstitution (Bild 28), darum wenig Durchsetzungsvermögen und Verwirklichung.
Sehr blaß und breit : Schwäche, Kränklichkeit und Melancholie.
Aus der Raszette eine Linie nach Mondberg : Lange Reisen (Milchstraße Bild 30).
Dieselbe Linie nahe dem Rande in den Mondberg: Warnt vor falschen Freunden (Bild 26/5).
Linie in den Venusberg : Günstige Ehe (Bild 26/4). Freunde.
Linie nach Merkur : Wohlstand durch Handel, Wissenschaft usw.
Linie nach Saturnberg : Wohlstand durch Dinge aus dem Boden.
Endet solche Linie in einem Stern, so ist immer Gefahr mit den Dingen verbunden.
Linie, die Magenlinie schneidend : Leid, Lebensüberdruß und Schwermut.
Ein Punkt in der Raszette : Mißerfolg und Sorgen.
Die erste Raszettelinie nach der Handmitte hochgewölbt : Ein Zeichen für schmerzhafte, schwere Geburten (Bild 27/29).
Die Studien betr. Stammbaum, Abkunft sind noch nicht abgeschlossen, weshalb ich sie hier noch nicht bringen kann.

Locus matrimonialis und Ehelinien.

Die Zeichen für Ehe und eheähnliche Verhältnisse befinden sich auf dem rechten H a n d r a n d e d e s M e r k u r b e r g s. Zu beachten und in Betracht zu ziehen hierfür sind auch Inseln in der Saturnlinie, ferner der Venusberg, unter Umständen auch der Jupiterberg. Außerdem: Linien aus Mondberg kommend zur Saturnlinie laufend, die Herzlinie und Flirtzeichen, und Linien, die von der Herzlinie nach einem der oberen Berge oder dem Venusberge führen, und solche nach der Kopflinie.

Z e i c h e n a u f L o c u s m a t r i m o n i a l i s.

Kleine, kurze Herzaffären, in nichts endend (Bild 27/17).

Ein Merkmal für größere Herzensneigung, Ehegelegenheit (Bild 24/7).

Eine Herzenssache dicht vor der Ehe.

Viele verschiedene Liebesaffären, meist in Händen, in denen auch Flirtzeichen auf der Herzlinie zu erkennen sind (Bild 29/20).

Streit in der Ehe, wenn die senkrechten Linien s e h r f e i n sind.

Plötzlicher Tod des anderen Teiles, Witwenschaft, Kummer. (Roter Punkt in der Linie!)

Zank und Enttäuschungen in der Ehe (meist durch eigene Schuld) (Bild 24/17).

Trennung der Ehe plötzlich (Bild 24/18).

Trennung durch Auseinanderleben, Verlieren der Empfindungen zueinander (Bild 24/16).

Parteien sehr ungleich im Alter (Bild 24/19).

Ehe verläuft in Gram; wenn die Linie in die Herzenslinie einmündet und dort einen winzigen Punkt zeichnet, stirbt der andere plötzlich (und daher Gram) (Bild 24/6).

Opposition gegen die Verbindung; wenn die Gabel nach der Seite der Innenhand liegt: von den Verwandten der eigenen Seite; die Gabel nach dem Handrücken zu: von Verwandten der anderen Partei.

Kinder, a) Knabe (starke Linie), b) Tochter (dünne Linie).

a) Schwach in der Kindheit, b) schwach später, in mittleren Jahren (Bild 27/39).

a) Immer kränklich, b) Krüppel an Gesundheit, sollte nicht gezeugt werden (Bild 27/40).

(Merkmale für Kinder sind nur als Möglichkeiten zu werten!)

Fehlgeburten oder herausgenommen durch Operation (s. auch Bild 25/51 und 27/33, 34).

Krankheit wird mit in die Ehe gebracht.

Natürlich steht in der Hand nicht, ob oder daß man zum S t a n d e s - a m t geht. Schließlich ist d a v o n eine Ehe auch nicht abhängig. Weiter sind diese Zeichen Angaben von E h e m ö g l i c h k e i t e n ; wenn eine Ehe- oder Herzenssache angezeigt ist, braucht sie nicht eingegangen zu werden, wenn man nicht will. Zur Zeitbestimmung teile man ein: Herzlinie 10 Jahre; Fingerbeuge des Merkurfingers: 60 Jahre; eine Linie auf der Mitte: 30 Jahre usw. Eine Linie von der Ehelinie zur Lebenslinie ist Trauer. Der Zeitpunkt ist an der Lebenslinienkreuzung abzumessen.

Diese Zeichen müssen mehr in geistiger Bedeutung gewertet werden. Eine wahre Ehe ist immer eine Herzens- u n d Wirtschaftsgemeinschaft, wobei die Dauer keine Rolle spielt. Das tägliche und praktische Leben beweist uns, daß eine Ehe einen Tag, ein oder dreißig Jahre oder länger dauern kann. Das Prinzip ist und bleibt in j e d e m Falle dasselbe.

Die Ehelinien zeigen hauptsächlich an, wann der Mensch seiner Entwicklung entsprechend und daher schicksalsmäßig die günstigste Zeit zur Wahl eines Ehepartners hat.

Das große Dreieck, Triangel.
(Bild 24 A, B, C)

wird gebildet durch die Lebens-, Kopf- und Magenlinie. Es wird auch Marsfeld genannt.

Ist das große Dreieck recht groß in der Fläche, und sind alle drei Hauptlinien gut und klar gezeichnet, die drei Winkel ebenfalls klar, so sind gute Gesundheitsverhältnisse vorhanden (Bild 24 links), auch gutes Gedächtnis (wenn der Blinddarm noch vorhanden).

Sind die Linien aber unklar, wellenartig, unsicher oder schlecht gezeichnet, so hat der Betreffende niedrige Eigenschaften und ist niedriger Dinge fähig.

Wenn statt der Magenlinie die Sonnenlinie den Abschluß bildet: Kleinlich und arg im Denken, aber große Individualität und meist starke Resolution.

Zu beachten sind die verschiedenen Winkel a, b, c.

Winkel a: L e b e n s - u n d K o p f l i n i e ; s p i t z , k l a r , e b e n :
Kultivierte Gedanken, Feinsinnigkeit und Klarheit des Geistes, klug.
d o. s t u m p f : Stumpfer Selbstverständlichkeitssinn, kein Takt,
materiell.
d o. s t u m p f u n d w e i t : Ungeduldiges, hastiges Wesen.
Winkel b:
K o p f - u n d M a g e n l i n i e , k l a r u n d g u t : Gute Gesundheit,
schnelles Begreifen.
d o. s e h r s c h a r f : Zarte Gesundheit, nervöses Wesen.
d o. s e h r s t u m p f : Stumpfsinn, Arbeiten ohne Interesse.
Winkel c:
L e b e n s - u n d M a g e n l i n i e , s e h r s c h a r f : Schwache Gesundheit, Neigung zu Geiz.
S t u m p f : Starke Natur, großzügiges Denken.
(Man vergleiche und kombiniere mit anderen bezüglichen Stellen der
Hände!)

Das kleine Dreieck.
(Bild 24 D, B, E.)

Geformt durch Magen-, Kopf- und Saturnlinie (oder Sonnenlinie).
Ein geistiger Arbeiter sollte ein gutes „kleines Dreieck" haben oder
keine Studien aufnehmen, die tiefdringende Geisteskraft erfordern. Es
wäre gut, dies bei der Bildung und Erziehung von Kindern zu beachten.
Das „H o h e D r e i e c k" wird geformt von Herz-, Sonnen- und
Magenlinie und gibt gute Befähigung zum Studium der Elektro-Biologie
und Magie (Bild 27/47).

Der Handtisch, großes Viereck oder Quadrangel.
(Bild 24 B, D, F, G)

wird geformt von Herz-, Kopf-, Saturn-, Magen- oder Sonnenlinie.
R e p r ä s e n t i e r t : Disposition gegenüber den Mitmenschen.
W e n n g u t u n d e b e n : Ruhiges Denken und Klugheit (Bild 24/15).
Z u s c h m a l : Sorge betreffs guten Rufs (Bild 27). Asthma.
Z u w e i t u n t e r M e r k u r b e r g l i e g e n d : Großzügigkeit ändert
sich in große Ökonomie.
S c h l e c h t g e z e i c h n e t : Sorge, Unglück, schlechte Neigungen.
S e h r s c h m a l i n d e r F o r m : Mangel an Toleranz; rechthaberisches
Wesen, Asthmadisposition.
V i e l e k l e i n e H a a r l i n i e n enthaltend: Geschwächte Kopfnerven
(Ursache: Magen).

Viele kleine Kreuze: Warnt vor Brandschaden und Verletzung dadurch (Bild 28/12).

Ein großer Stern: Materielle Güter zu erwerben ist sehr schwer, dagegen sind Bekanntschaften mit dem anderen Geschlecht leichter und von Vorteil.

Verschiedene Zeichen.

die nicht immer unter eine bestimmte Bezeichnung zu bringen sind und doch vorkommen, so auch auf einigen Bildern vorhanden sind, will ich hier nach der Bilderreihe aufführen:

Bild 24.

28: Strich durch Beugegelenk warnt vor Verletzung; bei Merkurfinger: Armverletzung.

29: Apollofinger: Beinverletzung; 31: Saturnfinger: Leibverletzung; 32: Jupiterfinger: Kopf- oder Halsverletzung.

30: Viele feinere Linien im Beugegelenk des Saturnfingers 3./2. Glied: Warnt vor Vergiftung durch verdorbene Lebensmittel, Konserven, Fleisch-, Käsegift, Pilzgift usw.

Bild 25.

Linke Hand.

6: Störung der Sexualorgane (Ovarien- bzw. Hodenschwäche).

8: Linie aus der Herzlinie kommend: Merkmal für Mord oder Unfall.

12, 13: Querlinien in der Saturnlinie: Hemmungen in dem Jahre, Messen notwendig.

14: Hängt mit religiösen Erkenntnissen zusammen.

19: Soviele Linien hier, soviele Kinder — möglich. (Dies Zeichen ist nur bei Frauen und dort an der linken Hand zu werten. Die Anzahl der Linien geht meist konform mit der Zahl der Kinderlinien, welche sich auf der oder den Ehelinien befinden.)

24: Linie abwarts im stumpfen Winkel von der Kopflinie: Jähzorn.

26: Heftigkeit und dadurch Schaden im Berufe.

27: Diplomatisches Wesen.

28: Stern im 3. Glied des Saturnfingers: Warnt vor Überfall, Körperverletzung.

29: Stern im 2. Glied des Saturnfingers: Warnt vor Lebensgefahr durch Fahrlässigkeit.

30: Stern im 1. Glied des Saturnfingers, seitlich: Warnt vor Lebensgefahr durch Waffen.

31: Kreuz im 1. Glied des Saturnfingers, seitlich: Warnt vor Lebensgefahr, abgeschwächt.

32: Kleine Querlinien an den Fingerspitzen: Schwächliche Gesundheit.

R e c h t e   H a n d.

33 und 55: Schwermut, evtl. bis zum Lebensüberdruß.

34: Tod durch Erhängen. (Dies muß nicht Selbstmord sein!)

37: Beginn der Körperschwäche.

38: Zerfall der Körperkräfte.

39: Zerrüttete Nervenkonstitution, angeboren.

41: Krankhafter Somnambulismus veranlagt. Warnt vor medialer Betätigung, wie Trance und Hypnose (die immer eine Vergewaltigung ist, außer als Narkose).

42: Ungünstiges Auslaufen medialer Bestrebungen.

43: Ungünstiges Zeichen betreffs Reisen auf Wasser.

46: Verliebtheit solange, als diese Äste reichen.

48: Hysteriedisposition, angeboren.

49: Eifersucht (Biegung der Herzlinie nach unten).

51: Bei Frauen: Unterleibsleiden, oft Fehlgeburten, Gewächse.

52: Lebensgefahr und Gefängnis.

56: Warnt vor Gasvergiftung.

57: Warnt vor Medizinalgiften.

58: Warnt vor Körperverletzung durch Unfall.

59, 60: Gehemmtes Empfindungsleben.

61, 62: Hemmungen im ehrlichen Denken, evtl. Unehrlichkeiten.

63: Gehässigkeit.

64: Heftige Angriffe.

B i l d   2 6.

L i n k e   H a n d.

1: Herzstörung.

3: Störungen im Unterleib (Ovarien oder Hoden).

4: Gute Ehegelegenheit.

5: Feinde auf Reisen, falsche Freunde.

6: Nierenstörung.

7, 8: Nierenstörung.

9: Pausen im Berufsleben.

10: Ein gehässiger Feind (weil die Kopflinie bei 13 schneidend).

11: Allgemeine Feinde.

12: Feindliches Ehepaar (zwei gekreuzte Linien).

16: Bruch in der Linie, Bruch in Herzenssachen, durch Überheblichkeit.

17: Leute vom Saturntyp sind dem Betreffenden nicht günstig.

19: Gekrümmter Nagel: Asthma, Engherzigkeit, Intoleranz.

Rechte Hand.

21, 22: Zeichen für sexuelle Ausschweifung.
23 (Beginn der Lebenslinie): Langsame Entschlußkraft.
26: Stern hier, macht immer geneigt zum Fallen.
27: Unaufrichtigkeit, Leberstörung.
29: Zerrissene Linie: Leberstörung. Ebenso 30.
31: Mit starkem Mondberge: Rheuma in Arm und Schulter.
32: Disposition zur Besessenheit (Dämonismus).
33: Saturnring, gibt viele Hindernisse auf dem Lebensweg.
34: Melancholie.
35: Lebensgefahr.

Bild 27.

Linke Hand.

6, 6: Doppelte Magenlinie, stabilisiert Körper- und Nervenkonstitution. Begabung für Arztberuf.
7: Finanzielle Verluste der Eltern des Betreffenden (Jugendzeit).
8: Gehemmter Aufstieg, 18. Jahr.
9, 10: Veränderungen, kleine Pausen. Evtl. Wechsel im Berufe.
11, 12: Schwellung des Herzens.
13: In Frauenhänden: Schwere Entbindung, in Verbindung mit Zeichen 14.
15: Günstiges Zeichen für Handel und Geschäft.
16: Venusgürtel bis in die Ehelinie: Der andere Ehepartner regiert (Grund: Schwaches Rückgrat angeboren, daher keine Kampfnatur!)
19: Ein K-Zeichen: Anfangsbuchstaben des Namens einer nahestehenden Person.
20: Isislinie. Lebensernst, Neigung zu Enthaltsamkeiten.
21: Zarte Anfänge von Intuitionslinien. In dieser vielfachen Zahl sind sie aber ungünstig und als gestörte Milz zu werten.
22: Enttäuschung in Liebessachen ist die Bedeutung der Insel in der Linie. Die Linie selbst ist eine Giftlinie, die vererbte Gifte anzeigt. (Metaphysische Einflüsse derselben Quelle!)

Rechte Hand.

23: Viel Bitternis in der Ehe.
27: Kopfverletzung durch Fahrlässigkeit.
28: Verkehrte Strebsamkeit.
30, 31: Aufstieg zu der Zeit, bessere Verhältnisse. (Selbstverständlich muß man die Zeit bewußt nutzen. Von allein kommt nichts.)
32: Hemmungen durch das andere Geschlecht.
33, 34: Zeichen für Fehlgeburten, die kommen oder waren.

35: In Verbindung mit großem Mondberg: Rheuma.

37: Viel Leid in der Liebe.

38: Buchstaben an der Apollolinie: K, H, E, A; sie deuten Namen an.

39, 40: Kranke Kinder (Zeichen dafür).

41: Stern im dritten Gliede des Merkur: Mediale Veranlagung.

42: Stern im zweiten Gliede des Merkur: Verdirbt Merkureigenschaften.

43: Kurzer Nagel: Gereiztes Wesen (durch Herzstörungen).

44: Gehörstörungen; brauner Fleck oder Punkt.

46: Blinddarmleiden.

47: Das „hohe" oder magische Dreieck.

Bild 28.

Linke Hand.

1: Bronchialleiden.

2 (auf Marsberg): Verstärkt die Bedeutung von 1.

3: Lebensgefahr, aber Schutz darin.

4: Eine Bekanntschaft in dem Jahre.

5: Latente, fiebrige Krankheiten.

8: Darmleiden, nicht bösartig.

11: Verlust durch eine Bekanntschaft auf Reisen.

13: Eine starke und gleich darauf eine schwächere Liebesangelegenheit in der Auswirkung. (Selbstverständlich „verpflichten" diese Zeichen nicht dazu. Es zeigen sich Gelegenheiten.)

14: Kurze Liebesangelegenheit.

15: Linien für Studien oder Literatur.

16: Anfänge vom Venusgürtel; evtl. Disposit. zu Onanie.

17, 17: Ein Bruch in Herzensangelegenheiten durch Intrigen, ein zweiter Fall durch Fahrlässigkeit.

18: Sehr ungünstiges Zeichen ist der Tannenzweig. Dreieck sehr gut.

19, 20, 21: Planetenzeichen in Verbindung mit Mondcharakteristik.

Rechte Hand.

22: Strebsamkeit.

23: Irrsinnveranlagung, in Verbindung mit 24/24.

25: Mondeinfluß, für große Reise oder Reisebekanntschaft.

31: Erworbene Herzstörungen; Neigung zu schweren Geburten.

32: Verdorbene Gesinnung.

37: Ehelinie mit rotem Punkt: Der Ehepartner verunglückt plötzlich.

38: Verpaßte gute Ehegelegenheit.

39, 40: Hemmungen im Liebesleben.

Bild 29.

Linke Hand.
2: Fiebrige Krankheit.
3: Kopfverletzung.
4: Gram und dadurch Nervenfieber, wenn mit 15.
5: Störungen im Berufe durch Verwandte.
6: Bekanntschaft mit Streitigkeiten.
7, 8, 10: Roter Punkt zeigt Augenschaden an.
9: Jähzorn.
11, 13, 14: Günstige Pläne.
12, 17: Ungünstige Pläne.
18: Beinverletzung.
23: Verlust einer nahestehenden Person.
24: Ungünstige Herzensangelegenheiten.
25: Verdirbt den ehrlichen Sinn.
29: Zweig aus dem Beugegelenk: Unterleibsstörungen bei Frauen.
30: Eifersucht.
31: Trennung einer Herzensangelegenheit oder Ehe.

Rechte Hand.
33: Hemmungen in der Handlung.
34: Herzstörungen (Herzklappenfehler).
38: Bitternisse in Liebes- und Ehesachen.
39: Überreizte Kopfnerven.
40: Schwächt viel von der Bedeutung von 38 ab.
43: Kopfverletzung durch Unfall.
44: Überreizung der Kopfnerven, gestörtes Denken. Ursache: Magen.
45: Vererbung von Kopfschmerzen, durch Arterienverkalkung bei Vorfahr.
50: Zerfall der Lebenskräfte.

Bild 30.

Es wurde schon an anderer Stelle (Venusberg) beschrieben.

Bild 31.

1—1: Todesfall und Krankheit in den ersten Lebensjahren.
2—2: Chronische Krankheit.
3: Kopfverletzung.
4: Wie 1; dazu Liebesaffäre.
5—38: Wie 4.
5: Viereck an der Linie: Abgeschiedenheit, Internierung.
5—36: Kleines Dreieck an der Linie: Herzensaffäre.

6: Winkellinie, warnt vor Körperverletzung.

7—7: Herzensangelegenheit; außerdem: Todesfall mit Erbschaft (weil die Ereignislinie in die Apollolinie verläuft).

8: Roter Punkt: Verletzung. Dunkler Punkt: Krankheit mit Fieber.

9: Bekanntschaft.

9—9: Günstige Zeit für Unternehmungen; evtl. eins durch das andere, da beides auf den gleichen Zeitpunkt fällt.

10 sowie 20: Depressionen durch Gram, Todesfall usw.

11: Bekanntschaft mit Streitigkeiten oder Prozeß.

12: Wie 11; dazu: kritischer Zeitpunkt für Gesundheit (einschneidende Linie!).

13: Günstige Zeit für Reise.

14—14: Bekanntschaft und Liebessache mit Streitigkeit im selben Jahre.

15: Selbstmordanwandlungen, wenn die Linie bis 28 verläuft.

15: Kleines Dreieck an der Lebenslinie: Liebessache, ungünstig.

16: Liebessache und ein Ärger oder Gram mit Krankheit.

17, 19: Gefährliche Zeit für Verletzungen, Operationen. 19 ist gefährlicher.

18: Gute Zeit für Unternehmungen. Sie werden aber gehemmt durch das andere Geschlecht (weil die aufsteigende Linie an der Herzlinie endet).

20: Trauer, Depression. Mit 21: Finanziell ungünstige Zeit.

22: Günstige Zeit für Reise.

23: Altersschwäche und ungünstige Zeit für Unternehmen.

24, 25: Kritische Zeitpunkte für Gesundheit und Leben.

26: Kränklichkeiten.

27: Finanzielle Verluste der Eltern in der Jugendzeit der Person.

33 und 52 verstärken die Gefahr bei Operationen (in Zeichen 19).

39: Ehe mit Traurigkeit auslaufend.

40: Ehe mit Streit, Scheidung ausgehend.

44: Kinderlinien senkrecht zur Ehelinie: Erst Knabe, dann Mädel.

46: Leichtsinn (Unbedachtsamkeit) in geschäftlichen Angelegenheiten.

48: Hemmungen durch Intrigen (Merkureinfluß).

49: Hemmungen durch Verwandte (Saturneinfluß).

1, 4 (an der Herzlinie): Abzweigungen sind günstige Zeiten für Herzensangelegenheiten in d e m Jahre, da die kleinen Zweige die Herzlinie verlassen.

Die Zeiten, in welche die Schnittpunkte der Linien 1—1, 4—4, 5—38, 7—7, 40, 10, 14, 17, 19 auf die Saturnlinie fallen, sind günstige Zeiten für Bekanntschaften und Freundschaften.

Bei Linie 5—38 sehen wir, daß eine Verbindung teilweise fehlt. Für diese Ausdeutung gehen uns die Linien nur so weit an, als sie zwischen Herz- und Kopflinie liegen. (Herz = Liebe, Kopf = Verstand: Freundschaft.) Bei Linie 5 liegt die „eigene Seite" (Seite des Daumens), bei der Linie 38 liegt die Seite der anderen Partei. Sie ist länger als die eigene. Dies zeigt: daß bei der anderen Seite mehr Zuneigung sich zeigt oder vorhanden ist als auf der eigenen; Versuch, ohne Zustandekommen der Angelegenheit. — Die Zeit bei Linie 4 und 7 und 10 ist dagegen sehr günstig und gut auslaufend.

*　　*　　*

Ich glaube, mit diesem Abschnitt vielen Fragen begegnet zu sein, viele Fragen beantwortet zu haben, und will hoffen, daß alles klar genug ist, um es ganz zu verstehen. — Einige Merkmale in den anderen Bilderbeilagen habe ich weiter am Schlusse berücksichtigt.

Das Messen der Ereignisse.

Kann man Zyklen, Entfernungen und Ereignisse im Weltenraume messen, dann kann man es auch in der Hand. Wie oben, so unten.

Bild 33 gibt einen Gesamtüberblick der Maßeinteilung, wie sie von Kennern dieses Wissens angewandt wird. Man findet in der alten Literatur sehr oft, daß die Lebenslinie wohl bis 90 Grad oder Jahre gemessen werden kann, aber auch, daß die verschiedenen Dezennien verschiedene Größe in der Fläche haben. Da eine derartige Messung keine Genauigkeit ergeben kann, verbesserte ich die Maße so, wie sie auf den beigefügten Meßkarten (Bild 34) angegeben sind. Um ein Ereignis bzw. die Ereignisse zu messen, suche man eine Ereignislinie auf dem Anfang der Lebenslinie. Nehmen wir an: im 15. Lebensjahre war ein Trauerfall oder eine sonstige seelische Erschütterung eingetreten, welche sich dann auch als eine Linie anzeigt, die von der Lebenslinie — nicht weit vom Anfange — nach der Herzlinie führt (weil Herzensempfindungen in Betracht kommen!). Auf den Schnittpunkt dieser Ereignislinie mit der Lebenslinie legen wir die Zahl 15 der Meßkarte (Lebenslinienmaß), halten fest und lesen dann die anderen Schnittpunkte der weiteren Ereignislinien auf der Lebenslinie ab. Falls Erfolgslinien, das sind von der Lebenslinie nach den Bergen aufsteigende Linien, vorhanden sind, stellen wir auch deren Schnittpunkt mit der Lebenslinie und so das in Betracht kommende Jahr fest. Um „günstige Zeiten für Beruf und Geschäft" zu erkennen, mißt man die eben beschriebene Erfolgslinie und kontrolliert mit dem „Barometer des Lebenswegs", der Saturnlinie. Z. B. steigt die Erfolgslinie aus der Lebenslinie mit dem 35. Jahr. Auf der Saturnlinie haben wir dann das 35. Jahr zu finden; das ist der Punkt, der auf dem Dreiviertel der Länge der Saturnlinie, zwischen den Schnittpunkten der Herz- und Saturnlinie und Kopf- und Saturnlinie liegt. Ist die Saturnlinie in dieser Gegend gut markiert, gut in der Farbe, so ist allgemein günstige Zeit vorhanden. Ist am bestimmten Zeitpunkt aber noch eine aufsteigende Gabellinie, so ist die Zeit besonders günstig. Ein weiteres Kontrollzeichen wäre evtl. die Apollolinie. Andere Dinge abzumessen, z. B. günstige Zeiten für gute Bekanntschaften und Freundschaften, ermöglicht uns die Saturnlinie ebenfalls. Um hierüber ausführlich Klarheit zu gewinnen, nehme man Bild 22 mit der Tafel über die „Linienformationen" zur Hand. Am Schlusse dieser Tafel (h) finden sich die betreffenden Zeichnungen hierfür. Ich will sie der Reihe nach erklären. Die Konstellation „A" zeigt eine senkrechte Linie, welche ich hier als den Teil der Saturnlinie annehmen will, der zwischen dem 20. und 40. Jahr liegt — also zwischen den beiden Schnittpunkten der Herz- und der Kopflinie. Pfeil 1 zeigt hier eine aufsteigende Gabellinie, ein Zeichen dafür, daß günstige Zeiten für Beruf oder Geschäft vorhanden sind. Der Anfang dieser Zeit wäre das 36. bis 37. Jahr. — Pfeil 2 zeigt einen waagerechten Strich, eine Querlinie. Alles, was quer liegt, ist eine Hemmung, ein Hindernis. Die Stärke des letzten ist nach dem Ausdruck der Querlinie zu erkennen. Ist diese Linie nur sehr fein, so ist das Hemmnis nur leicht und wird bald übergangen; ist die Linie sehr dick, so ist das Hemmnis stark und von nachwirkender Dauer. Ist die Linie aber gleich der mit Pfeil 5 bezeichneten, daß sie von der Herz- bis zur Kopflinie führt, so ist die Formation ähnlich einer Gabel und muß Gutes mit sich bringen. Diese Linie bedeutet auch, daß diese Zeit — hier z. B. das 26. Jahr — günstig für Freundschaften, evtl. Herzensbekanntschaften. Pfeil 3 und 4 zeigen kleine Ereignisse an, die erst im Werden begriffen sind. Die Konstellation „B" zeigt wieder die aufsteigenden Gabellinien in starker und schwacher Form (8). Pfeil 7 deutet auf eine sich evtl. bildende günstige Zeit. Noch ist sie es nicht! — Bei „C" zeigt Pfeil 9 eine unten offene Gabellinie. Kommt die Linie 9 von der Lebenslinie, so ist sie eine aufsteigende Linie, welche die Saturnlinie im 25. Jahre trifft und für diesen Zeitpunkt einen guten Einfluß zeigt. Ebenso Linie 10, wenn sie aus dem Mondberge kommt. Sie zeigt an: Geschäfts- oder Berufseinfluß guter Art. Schneidet sie aber die Saturnlinie, so ist der Einfluß kein guter bzw. „vorteil"hafter. — Bei „D" sehen wir bogenartige Querlinien. Diese sind in allen Fällen Zeichen nachwirkender Hemmnisse, genau wie im großen der Venusgürtel solches Allgemeinhemmnis darstellt, wenn er die Saturnlinie und Sonnenlinie schneidet, um die Zirkulation der Kräfte zu binden. — „F" zeigt eine Saturnlinie, die mehrere Male gebrochen ist, um gleich nebenher weiterzugehen in ungeschwächter Stärke. Pfeil 15 zeigt Veränderung im Beruf oder sonst merklicher Art. Pfeil 16 ebenso, doch nicht ganz so drastisch, da die Bruchstücke verbunden sind. Pfeil 17 zeigt eine Lücke (Pause) und Linie 18 einen Einfluß oder ein Ereignis, das in der Bildung begriffen ist. Bei „G" haben wir eine schöne starke Linie. Pfeil 19 zeigt eine Einflußlinie, vom Mondberge kommend, sich in eine starke Parallele verwandelnd, welche Stabilisierung des Lebenswegs bedeutet, und dies durch Bekanntschaft, die auf Reisen gemacht wird, oder durch eine Person des anderen Geschlechts. Diese Konstellationen gelten jedoch nur für die Schicksals- und Apollolinie. — Für die Magenlinie und Lebenslinie kommen sie nicht in d i e s e r Art zur Ausdeutung, sondern müssen da zusammen mit physiologischen Merkmalen in Betracht gezogen werden. Jede Linie, jeder Berg, jeder Handteil hat seine eigene und bestimmte Bedeutung. Ein Bruch in der Saturnlinie wird eine Pause, unter Umständen auch eine Veränderung der Verhältnisse bedeuten; in der Lebenslinie kann derselbe Bruch Todesgefahr heißen; in der Kopflinie: Kopfverletzung.

Zum Messen besonders notwendig sind die Maße der Lebenslinie und die der Saturnlinie, weil sich auf diesen beiden Linien hauptsächlich die einschneidendsten Daten ergeben. Die Fläche auf der Saturnlinie, die zwischen den Kreuzpunkten der Kopflinie (20. Jahr) und der Herzlinie (40. Jahr) liegt, ist in verschiedenen Händen meist verschieden. Einmal sind es 2 cm, ein andermal 2,5 cm, wieder in einer anderen Hand vielleicht nur 1,5 cm. Immer sind es 20 Jahre, und diese in der Hand einmal bestehende Entfernung muß, für die Zeit nach dem 40. Jahre, von der Herzlinie aufwärts übertragen, weiter gemessen werden. Gewiß gibt es auch hier Ausnahmefälle, jedoch kommen sie selten vor. Unter dem Kreuzpunkte der Kopflinie kam ich immer mit 0,5 cm für jedes Jahr (bis zum 15. Jahre) zurecht. Weiter abwärts ist die Zeit nicht genau an der Schicksalslinie zu bestimmen.

Bei der Lebenslinie trifft j e d e r Grad zu. Hier ist nur die Hauptsache, den Nullpunkt g e n a u festzustellen. Ihn findet man ungefähr, wenn man sich eine senkrechte Linie, ein Lot, von der Spitze des Jupiterfingers bis auf die Lebenslinie gezogen denkt. Der Schnittpunkt auf der Lebenslinie läßt den Nullpunkt dann ziemlich genau erkennen. Um ihn aber dann zu „korrigieren", findet man in dieser Gegend ein Ereignis heraus. Z. B. haben die meisten Leute in den ersten Lebensjahren einen Todesfall zu melden, vielleicht den des Großvaters, der Großmutter, eines Onkels oder einer Tante; seltener von Geschwistern oder Eltern. Wenn auch als Kind die „seelische Erschütterung" dieses Ereignisses nicht bewußt durchlebt wird, wenigstens in den meisten Fällen, so ist die Linie (von der Lebenslinie zur Herzlinie) d o c h eingezeichnet. Warum? Weil wir gerade mit den sechs angeführten Personen in einer magnetischen und blutsrhythmischen Verbindung stehen. Daß dies tatsächlich so ist und nicht etwa ein herangezogener

Gedanke, wird durch folgendes bewiesen: Beobachten wir bei Bekannten oder Verwandten, daß ein Onkel oder eine Tante stirbt, dann werden wir auch finden, daß in den allermeisten Fällen zur s e l b e n Zeit ein Neffe oder eine Nichte der oder des Verstorbenen krank wird. Es kann sich um Tage oder Wochen handeln, welche den Zwischenraum der Geschehnisse ausfüllen. In der Hand erkennen wir dieses Doppelereignis daran, daß wir auf der Lebenslinie in dem betreffenden Jahre die Trauerlinie finden (zwischen Lebenslinie und Herzlinie), aber auch: daß von dem Schnittpunkt in der Lebenslinie desselben Jahres d i e - s e l b e Linie eine Verlängerung in den oberen Venusberg, den kleinen Mars, aufweist. Einflüsse dieses Marsbergs sind (hitzige) Krankheiten fiebriger Art. Es sind oft die sog. „Kinderkrankheiten", denen wir dann ausgesetzt sind.

Weiter herunter an der Lebenslinie treffen wir auf andere Doppelereignisse: Eine Trauerlinie, die gleich beim Verlassen der Lebenslinie sich mit einer kleinen senkrechten, aus der Lebenslinie aufsteigenden Linie trifft (und darüber hinausgeht), so ein kleines Dreieck formend. In d i e s e m Jahre treffen zusammen: Ein Todesfall, eine Herzensbekanntschaft (oder Gelegenheit für Ehe) u n d , wenn die Trauerlinie noch die Saturnlinie schneidet, ein Jahr für günstige Bekanntschaften, das aber meistens ein a n d e r e s Jahr ist und auf der Saturnlinie abgemessen wird. Das sind d r e i Ereignisse, durch dieselbe Linie dargestellt oder angezeigt. Ein v i e r t e s kommt hinzu, wenn die Trauerlinie in die Herzlinie mündet. Hier wird nun der Punkt an der Herzlinie gemessen und ergibt: eine günstige Zeit oder ein Ereignis, das mit Liebessachen in Verbindung steht. S o spart die Natur und zeigt mit e i n e r Linie drei, vier oder, wie in diesem Falle, fünf Ereignisse an: zwei negative (Tod eines anderen und Krankheit) und zwei bis drei positive, günstige Ereignisse. Und da jammern die Leute über den „Verlust einer Person", wenn ihnen auf der anderen Seite doppelte oder dreifache Vergütung zu teil wird! — Welche Undankbarkeit gegen das Schicksal, gegen Gott, — weil sie nicht den Zweck des Lebens erkennen w o l l e n .

Die Kopf- und auch die Herzlinie mißt man mit derselben Maßeinteilung, die bei der Lebenslinie Anwendung findet. Die hier gebrachten Maße (Bild 34) sind für eine mittelgroße Hand bestimmt. Für größere oder für Kinderhände sind die auf dem nächsten Blatt befindlichen vier Maße bestimmt. Die mit L. L. bezeichneten Bogenlinien werden in der Weise an der Lebenslinie angelegt, daß der Innenteil des Bogens den Venusberg (Daumenballen) bedeckt. Auf diese Weise erspart man sich das Anheben des Maßes und kann sofort die Schnittpunkte der Ereignislinien auf der Lebenslinie (Ereignisse) erkennen und den Linienverlauf verfolgen, was bedeutend erleichtert. Es ist streng darauf zu achten, daß die Abstände der Dezennien (von zehn zu zehn Jahren) immer g l e i c h g r o ß e sind und in diesen ebenso die einzelnen Längen der Jahre. Wird dies genau beachtet, dann wird sich niemand über Ungenauigkeiten zu beklagen haben.

Mißt man an fremden Händen Ereignisse aus und fragt dabei nach einem Ereignis (um einen Anhaltspunkt für den Nullpunkt zu haben), so kommt es vor, daß jene Personen von keinem Ereignisse wissen wollen, weil sie es vergessen haben. Ein wenig Übung läßt bald zu, daß man den Nullpunkt ziemlich genau an der Lebenslinie schätzen lernt. Wenn dann z. B. im fünften Jahr eine Ereignislinie zu sehen ist, lasse man sich nicht abweisen. Das Ereignis m u ß in der Gegend liegen, es i s t tatsächlich dagewesen, denn sonst wäre die Linie nicht da! — Also kann es sich nur darum handeln,- daß das Ereignis ungefähr im fünften Jahre war. Es kann im vierten oder sechsten Jahre gewesen sein. Wenn man auf diese Art etwas nachhilft, besinnt sich mancher darauf. Tut er es dennoch nicht — manche Menschen sind in der Tat sehr vergeßlich —, nun, dann behalte man den Punkt 5 auf dem geschätzten fünften Jahre der Lebenslinie und korrigiere an einem Ereignisse, das in d e n Jahren liegt, welche der Betreffende gerade hinter sich hat, also in den letzten vergangenen Jahren. Da ergibt sich dann schon eine Bestätigung. Hierauf schaut man nochmals nach Punkt 5, der sich durch die Korrektur vielleicht auf das dritte, siebente oder sechste Lebensjahr verschoben hat. D a n a c h hält man an diesem letzten Meßpunkte fest und rollt so das Leben, die Lebenslinie des Betreffenden ab und notiert die Ereignisse, eines nach dem anderen (wie sie folgen). Stimmen zwei bis drei Ereignisse mit dem Maße bzw. der in Anwendung stehenden Maßeinteilung, dann stimmen sie a l l e. Auch für die Zeit n a c h dem Lebensjahr, in dem der Betreffende steht. Zuerst linke, dann rechte Hand!

Da die meisten Leute (aus Religionslosigkeit und Mangel an seelischer Kraft als Folge davon) nicht vertragen können, daß sie erfahren, wie lange sie ungefähr zu leben haben, warne ich vor solchen Diagnosen. Man spreche bei solchen als für das Leben einschneidend eingezeichneten Zeichen von: „kritischen Zeitpunkten für Gesundheit". D a s sagt genug für d e n, der seinen Verstand gebrauchen w i l l.

In letzter Zeit wird von einigen Verfassern neuerer Schriften über Chirosophie zu erklären versucht, daß man Lebensereignisse aus den Handlinien n i c h t ausmessen könne. Einige versuchen sogar eine abnorme Meßart — Verschiedenheit der Größe der Dezennien — zu bringen. Man lasse sich jedoch durch derartige „eigene Systeme" nicht beirren. Wie schon gesagt, müssen die Abstände der 10-Jahreszyklen g l e i c h groß bleiben, da sonst Ungenauigkeiten eintreten. Meine heute über 45jährigen praktischen Erfahrungen haben m e i n e Maßeinteilung — 90 g l e i c h e Teile für die Lebenslinie — immer noch als richtig durch Beobachtung und Bestätigungen in mehr als einigen 100 000 Handuntersuchungen bewiesen. D a s bedeutet praktisch mehr als die „Meinung" von Anfängern oder von Unbegabten. Ich habe Handanalysen von Menschen angefertigt, die ich persönlich nie gesehen habe, und von denen mir n u r Handphotographien und Handabdrücke, sowie die Daten etwa zweier Ereignisse aus der Jugendzeit zur Korrektur zur Verfügung standen. Sie haben dann bestätigt, daß alles, auch die Ereignisse und Zeiten, genau übereinstimmten. Dies ist wohl der beste objektive Beweis.

Handabdrücke.

stellt man am besten auf folgende Weise her: Mit einem nicht zu trockenen schwarzen Stempelfarbkissen streiche man über die Innenhandfläche und Finger, bis alles ganz gleichmäßig geschwärzt und feucht ist. Besser noch, weil leichter abwaschbar, ist die Verwendung von „Japan Aqua Schwarz". Dieser Farbstoff ist in Tuben in Geschäften für Künstlerbedarf zu haben. Es wird ein wenig davon aus der Tube gedrückt und auf den Innenhandflächen gleichmäßig, aber nicht zu reichlich verrieben. Dann spreize man die Finger ein wenig und drücke fest auf ein Blatt tintenfähiges weißes Papier, das man vorher auf eine gute Unterlage (etwa fünf einmal zusammengefaltete Zeitungen) gelegt hat. Damit nun auch die unter Umständen hohle Stelle der Innenhand gedruckt wird, senke man den Ellenbogen bis zur waagerechten Lage mit der Hand. Dann drücke man mit der freien Hand auf das Druckblatt dicht vor die Finger und rolle die geschwärzte Hand nach hinten (über das Handgelenk) ab, die Finger zuerst in die Höhe hebend. Mit einiger Übung werden die Abdrücke fein sauber und genau sein.

Stempelfarben in violett, rot und grün sind sehr schwer zu entfernen, diese Farben sind auch giftig.

Wer die Absicht hat, viele Handabdrücke herzustellen, der tut besser den genannten Farbstoff in kleiner Menge auf eine dicke Glasplatte, walzt ihn mit einer Gummiwalze dünn aus und rollt ihn dann mit der Gummiwalze auf die Innenhand auf. Hierdurch wird der Farbstoff gleichmäßig aufgetragen, und der Abdruck ist klar. Außerdem sind aber immer für j e d e Analyse gute, d. h. scharfe Fotos der Handf o r m e n erforderlich, eine von der linken Innen- und eine von der rechten Außenhand; denn diese bilden die Grundlagen der Handanalyse. Ohne die Wertung der Handformen bleibt jede Handanalyse ungenau und daher unzuverlässig.

Für eine Sammlung oder Einsendung zur Begutachtung und Analyse müssen die Abdrücke ebenso gut in der Ausführung sein wie das hier beigefügte Bild 64, damit man die einzelnen Linien und Zeichen auch wirklich erkennen kann. Bei verwischten Abdrücken läßt sich nichts erkennen, und deshalb sind sie das Aufheben nicht wert.

Es ist immer wertvoll und lehrreich, wie auch interessant, solche Handabdrücke von seiner ganzen Familie oder seinem Stammbaum zu haben. Da kann man sehr gut herausfinden, woher die einzelnen Krankheiten vererbt sind und deshalb auch einzelne Charakterrichtungen. Ich beschrieb schon, Krankheit und Charakter stehen immer in Wechselwirkung, sind Polaritäten im menschlichen Leben, deshalb auch im Schicksal der Familie und des einzelnen.

Gewiß kann man diese Sammlung der Handabdrücke noch vervollständigen, indem man dem Abdruck hinzufügt: Geburtsdatum, möglichst mit genauer Stundenangabe, Kopfphotographie und Autogramm.

Solche Sammlung nützt jedem einzelnen Menschen im moralischen und ethischen Sinne sehr; denn er erkennt seine Zusammensetzung, sein Material und die Grenzen des Erreichbaren auf Grund dieser höheren Physiologie.

Ich lasse hier die Deutung eines Handabdruckes folgen und hoffe, daß sich der Schüler gut in die Materie hineinfindet. Um dies zu erleichtern, nahm ich einen Handabdruck mit sehr wenig Linien. Wer seine Augen etwas an die Runenschrift der Hände gewöhnt hat, der wird noch mehr finden, als ich aufgeführt habe. Ich habe mit den Abdrücken und den Erklärungen nur zeigen wollen, w i e die einzelnen Zeichen in Natur aussehen, weil man mir oft mitteilte, daß man sich bei Zeichnungen nicht das richtige Bild von den wirklichen Zeichen machen könne. Man sieht hier wohl, daß die Zeichen mit denen, die ich auf den Handzeichnungen brachte, übereinstimmen.

Nach dieser Analyse will ich noch auf einige beachtenswerte Zeichen und Konstellationen der anderen beigefügten Bilder hinweisen. Die Erklärungen soll der Schüler aber s e l b s t durch Nachdenken erarbeiten. Anhaltspunkte bieten ihm die Analyse von Bild 36, die Musteranalyse und das ganze Buch.

Die Praxis.

Analyse von Bild 36.

Dieses Bild zeigt den Abdruck einer Innenhand, die einem anscheinend eckigen Handtyp angehört. Nehmen wir für diesen Fall an, sie s e i eckig. Bei einem Abdruck ist die Form und Plastik nicht zu bestimmen, weshalb ich hier diese Dinge — leider — fortlassen muß.

Zuerst die Bedeutung der eckigen Hand:

Kleinlichkeit, Genauigkeit, Pflichtbewußtsein und Nützlichkeitsprinzip, sowie konservatives Denken. Da die Hand groß ist und die Finger einen Eindruck der Schwere machen, kommt der Eigner mehr für sehr kleine Arbeiten, Feinmechanik in Frage. Der Daumen ist kurz, aber gut entwickelt, ebenso der Knoten im ersten Gelenk, nicht biegsam: Eigener Sinn und Hartköpfigkeit, sogar Grobheit ist vorhanden. Das Maß des Willens ist nicht groß, und daher sind Energie und Durchsetzungskraft nur gering, wenn auch Eigensinn und Hartköpfigkeit einen kleinen Ausgleich zu bieten vermögen, der jedoch nur Schein darstellt. Aus diesen Gründen können Pläne, Unternehmungen auch nur teilweise durchgeführt werden. Da der Daumen sich nicht im rechten Winkel abbiegen läßt, kann die Unabhängigkeitsliebe nicht betätigt werden. Der Merkurfinger ist normal lang und ziemlich eckig: weniger Rednertalent, jedoch Sinn für Organisation und Geschäft. — Alles zusammen: Ein Mann, der ganz auf das Praktische und Nützliche eingestellt ist und sich im täglichen Leben auch durchsetzen könnte, wenn er nicht zu sehr an der Kleinlichkeit und dem Althergebrachten hinge.

Die Plastik der Berge ist auf diesem Bilde nicht ersichtlich, weshalb ich zu den Linien übergehe. Die Herzlinie ist im allgemeinen kraftvoll, hat nahe ihrem Anfang durch Insel zu große Breite, was eine Disposition zu organischem Herzfehler bedeutet und dadurch auch Nörgelei. Sie endet mit (2) einem Aste zwischen Jupiter- und Saturnfinger, was Bitternisse in der Ehe bedeutet, jedoch abgeschwächt wird durch den zweiten Ast (16). In der Linie unter dem Saturnfinger sind kleine Punkte enthalten; sie weisen auf schadhafte Zähne hin (6). Eine kurze und abgebrochene Apollolinie zeigt Schönheitsempfinden an, und da sie in der Saturnlinie entspringt, kommt der Mann durch seinen Beruf auf jenes Gebiet. Diese Interessen setzen für eine Zeit (30. bis 50. Jahr) aus und beginnen dann erst im späteren Alter wieder stärker hervorzutreten.

Die Kopflinie (17—12) beginnt im Anfang (17) ein wenig getrennt von der Lebenslinie (18—18), um sich später (20) nochmals mit ihr zu vereinigen. Solche Leute sind zeitweise hastig im Entschluß, ein andermal wieder sehr schwerfällig. Die Linie ist aber kraftvoll und gut (ungestört), und dies sagt: guter Intellekt (verstärkt durch 5), gute Gehirnnerven. Die Gedanken- oder Denkrichtung (Richtung der Kopflinie!) geht wohl nach der phantasievollen und idealeren Seite des Lebens, neigt aber auch schon stark zu Grübelei (12). Das ist immer gefährlich, und da hier der Mondberg (Säfte) stark entwickelt erscheint, was schon aus der Fläche zu ersehen ist, gibt dieses eine Neigung zu Schwindelgefühl und Fall durch Blutandrang zum Kopf (bei roten

Nägeln und gewölbtem Mondberg) oder Blutleere (bei blassen Nägeln und flachem Mondberge).

Die Magen- oder Merkurlinie ist wohl vorhanden, aber etwas gewunden (Krampf) und gebrochen (Nierenstörung) (13). Es lagert eine Menge von Medizinalgiften im Körper (14). Intuition (15) zeigt sich hier sehr gut im Werden begriffen an, technische Fähigkeiten durch die Ecke im unteren Handgelenk bei der Raszette.

Die Saturnlinie kommt ungefähr aus der Handmitte nahe der Raszette, und das gibt Streben nach Selbständigkeit und Sichdurchsetzen. Da diese Linie nur ein wenig hin- und hergebogen ist, aber nicht schlecht im Ausdruck, wird der Eigner auch einen ziemlich geraden Lebensweg haben, der kleine Abwechslungen in Veränderungen zeigt, die aber nicht schwierig verlaufen. An der Kreuzstelle mit der Herzlinie erleidet die Saturnlinie eine Unterbrechung: Hemmung durch Frauen oder Gutherzigkeit im 42. Jahre. Gleich danach ergibt sich aber schon eine neue Bahn, die gut und stabil ist. Günstige Zeiten für Bekanntschaften und Freundschaften sind (auf den Querlinien der Saturnlinie abzumessen): Lebensjahr: 17., 19. (bei 9), 25., das am besten und günstigsten in dieser Hinsicht ist.

Lebensjahre für Gram, Kummer, Depressionen (Linien vom Venusberge nach der Herzlinie): 27., 34. (20), 40. (schwach zu erkennen), 45. (23), 51. (24), 65. (26); im 71. Jahre macht sich ein absteigender Ast (allgemeine Körperschwäche) bemerkbar, und 79. und 83. Jahr sind sehr kritische Jahre für die Gesundheit und das Leben (27).

Die mit 19, 19 bezeichneten dicken Linien im Venusberge sind solche für stärkere Sinnlichkeit (und dadurch zumeist Undankbarkeit). Linien 1 in den Fingern sind gute Ströme. Linie 3 und 4 gehen durch die Beugegelenke und verletzen sie. Ihre Bedeutung: Warnt vor Verletzung der Beine (3) und der Arme (4).

Um die Hauptlinien besser herauszukennen, habe ich sie mit Planetenzeichen beschrieben. Ich glaube, daß dieser linienarme Abdruck für den Anfänger eine klare Übersicht gibt. Für den Fortgeschrittenen bringe ich das viel reichhaltigere Bild 37, in welchem ich die Hauptlinien ebenfalls wieder mit den betreffenden Planetenrunen bezeichnet und sonstige Zeichen durch einen Strich mit einer Nummer an der Grenze der Hand markiert habe.

Erklärung der Zeichen auf Bild 37.

1. Linie im zweiten Gliede des Jupiter: Diplomatie.
2. Im dritten Gliede Querlinien: Heftigkeit, die im beruflichen Leben Schaden bringt.
3. Ein Hauptast der Herzlinie endet hier: Bitternisse im Eheleben.
4. Dreieck auf Saturnberg: Sinn für Religion und Magnetismus.

5. Kreuz auf Saturnberg: Neigung zu Unfall durch Körperverletzung.
6. Querlinien im dritten Gliede des Saturnfingers: Grübeleien.
7. Warnungs(quer)linien im zweiten Gliede des Saturnfingers: Vergiftung durch Medizinalgift.
8. Ebenso: Gasvergiftung.
9. Senkrechte Linien durch das zweite Beugegelenk: Warnt vor giftiger Speise, Pilzgift usw.
10. Linie von Saturn kommend, die Apollolinie schneidend: Hemmungen in der Betätigung auf künstlerischem Gebiete durch Verwandte.
11. Senkrechte Linien im Apollofinger (wie überall): Gute Ströme.
12. Querlinien: Hemmungen im Empfindungsleben.
13. 14. Dreiecke auf dem Apolloberge: Sinn für Ethik und Ästhetik.
15. Insel in der Herzlinie: Herzfehler, Disposition vererbt, mütterliche Linie.
16. Dreiecke auf Merkurberg: Routiniert, klug in Wissenschaft und Handel.
17. Querlinien im Merkurfinger, erstes Glied: Verdirbt das ehrliche Denken.
18. Querlinien im Merkurfinger, zweites Glied: Verdirbt Ausführungen durch Hemmungen seelischer Art.
19. Zahl der Kinderlinien im Merkurbeugegelenk. Die Zahl der Möglichkeit, nicht der Tatsächlichkeit. Diese Zeichen sind zu vergleichen mit den auf den Ehelinien (21, 22) senkrecht stehenden Kinderlinien.
20. Endung der Magenlinie auf Merkurberg: Sprachtalent.
21. Eheangelegenheiten im 35. Lebensjahre. Ausgang: Entfremdung, Mißverstehen, Trennen.
22. Eheangelegenheit im 27. Lebensjahre. Ausgang: Plötzlicher Abbruch.
23. Eheangelegenheit im 24. Lebensjahre mit traurigem Ausgange.
24. Stern auf Apolloberg: Günstig ist das 28. Jahr für Bekanntschaften mit Angehörigen der freien Berufe. Betreffender wird klug, aber herzleidend sein und im Aussehen Sonne-Merkurtyp mit etwas Saturn im Wesen.
25. Verästelungen an und in der Herzlinie: Traurige Herzensaffären.
26. Marslinie: Feindlich gesinnte Person; oder soviele Linien: Personen.
27. Stern im Marsberg: Körperverletzung. An einer Linie, die aus der Herzlinie kommt: Unfall durch große Tiere. Derselbe Stern hängt an Operationslinie 51, 52. Dreieck: Strategie. (Aus den unter 27 bezeichneten Punkten läßt sich schon das Ereignis gut kombinieren und konstruieren, wenn man die umliegenden Zeichen noch in Betracht zieht.)

28—41 ist die Kopflinie mit zwei Ausläufern 28, 28 als Gabel: Vielseitigkeit.

28, 28 und der Beginn von 25 ergeben fast die Formation einer vier-
eckigen Insel in der Kopflinie: Sie ist noch nicht vollständig, doch
kommt dies noch nach. In diesem Falle: Folgeerscheinung nach
vererbter Disposition für Gehirnerweichung, starke Kopfschmerzen.

29. Insel in der Magenlinie. Diese Stelle: Disposition zu Gallenleiden.

30. (und auch neben 29) Dreiecke in der Magenlinie. Magnetismus.

30. Im unteren Winkel dieses Dreiecks kreuzen sich Saturn- und
Magenlinie.

31. Neptun- oder Giftlinie: Medizinalgifte im Körper. Die Insel in
dieser Linie gibt: Enttäuschungen in Liebessachen. Siehe 21, 22, 23.

32, 65, 40 bis neben 10: Saturnlinie, gut, lang und stabil. Diese
Linie gibt einen guten, geraden Lebensweg. Weil sie unten aus
dem Mondberge kommt, nicht beschädigt ist, wird der Betreffende
auch Glück in Übersee haben, außerdem auf Reisen, mit Reisenden
und solchen Bekanntschaften, mit dem anderen Geschlechte, mit
Dingen, die mit „Mode und Konjunktur" in Verbindung stehen.
Ein wechselvolles, aber doch schönes Leben. — Diese lange gute
Linie vom unteren Mond- bis zum Saturnberge gibt auch eine
vererbte Anlage zu Wahrträumen.

33. Uranus- oder Intuitionslinien geben Einfühlung und guten Instinkt,
Vorfühlen.

34 ist eine Linie, die ihren Anfang in der Lebenslinie (60) hat und
sich von dort in Bogen nach der Handwurzel zieht: Neigung oder
Versuch zu Selbstmord, starke Depressionen. Zeit festzustellen
durch Messen der Lebenslinie.

35. Linien im Jupiterbeugegelenk aufwärts: Leberstörung.

36. Schräge Linie, welche dies Gelenk schneidet, bei Frauen: Fehl-
geburt.

37. Dreieck auf dem Jupiterberge: Sinn für Politik.

38, 39. Zwei schräg über den Berg laufende Linien: Blasenschwäche.

40. Kleine Insel in der Saturnlinie, nahe Herzlinie, in Verbindung mit
dem Dreieck (oder- Insel) in der Lebenslinie unten (63): Vorfahr
hatte Magenkrebs. Mütterliche Generation.

41, 42. Linien aufsteigend aus Anfang der Lebenslinie, Strebsamkeit.

43 ist eine Strahllinie eines Sternes im Anfange der Kopflinie: Augenverletzung.

43, 44 zusammen ergeben eine kleine Insel, die mit diesem Sterne
zusammenhängt und deshalb Operation bedeutet.

43, 44 als zwei Linien weiter verfolgt, enden sie gegen den Merkurberg mit einer kleinen Biegung in der Herzlinie: Todesfälle oder
Depressionen in Verbindung mit materiellen (Merkur) Verlusten.

45. In diesem (20.) Lebensjahre Trauer starker Art. Linie endet in Herzlinie.

45 ist auch die waagerechte Abschlußlinie an einem kleinen Dreieck an der Lebenslinie, das durch die aufsteigende Linie (46) gebildet wird: Im selben Jahre Liebessache oder günstige Gelegenheit für Ehe.

46. Ein aufsteigender Ast von der Lebenslinie: Günstige Zeit für Unternehmen im Berufe oder Geschäfte. Da diese Linie bis hoch in den Jupiter geht, eine Gelegenheit, die sich zum allerbesten ausnutzen läßt. Auszumessen an der Lebenslinie (22./23. Lebensjahr).

47, 48, 49. 50. Jede Linie ein Fall von Depression, Gram, Trauer.

50. Noch ein Ereignis, den Verstand oder Kopf betreffend: Ärger, Streit.

51 endet am Mondberge: Günstige Zeiten für große Wasserreisen. Die bei 41 in der Lebenslinie anliegende Insel deutet auf Leiboperation.

52 (und 51). Zwei sehr feine Linien, welche in eine stärkere münden, die in der Richtung des Marsberges läuft: Verletzungen durch Metall, evtl. Operation.

53. Linie um das zweite Daumenglied laufend: Hemmungen in der Erkenntnis. (Läuft diese Linie rund um das Glied: Tod durch Erhängen; dies braucht n i c h t Selbstmord zu sein, sondern kann auch durch Unfall geschehen.)

54. Zwei Dreiecke, deren gemeinsame Basis die Linie 53 konstruiert: Hinweis, daß diese Person nach Erkenntnis durch Sinnen u n d Tat streben soll.

55. Querlinien im ersten Daumengliede (wenn sie auch im ersten Gliede des Saturnfingers vorhanden sind): Melancholie; bis zum Lebensüberdruß sich oft auswirkend.

56. Diese Linie bildet mit der aus 51 kommenden hier einen Stern in der zweiten Saturnlinie: Finanzielle Verluste der Eltern.

57 formiert mit 51 und 59 einen Stern neben der Saturnlinie im Marsfelde: Zeigt Streitigkeiten mit Heftigkeit an.

57 geht zum Schluß in die Magenlinie und zeigt damit an: Störung in der Gesundheit.

58. Eine Linie, nach dem Mondberge zeigend: Günstige Zeit für weite Reise.

59. Aufsteigende Linie in Saturnlinie mündend: Günstige Zeit für Unternehmen.

A. Dreieck auf Venusberg: Berechnung und Vorsicht im täglichen Leben, besonders bei Herzensangelegenheiten.

60. Saturnlinie. Daneben aufsteigende starke Linie in die Magenlinie

mündend: Besserung der Gesundheit und günstige Zeit im allgemeinen.

61. Absteigende Linie aus der Lebenslinie kommend: Abnehmen der Körperkräfte.

62. Beginn und Aufstieg der Apollolinie. An derselben Stelle scharfer Schnitt in die Lebenslinie: Kritische Zeit für Gesundheit und Leben.

63. Kritischer Zeitpunkt für Gesundheit und Leben.

64. Wie 63, mit Linie nach Marsberg: Plötzlicher und heftiger Tod.

Die Jahre der Ereignisse lassen sich leicht mit der Meßkarte an der Lebenslinie abmessen. Das geschieht in der Weise, wie sie im Anfang dieses Abschnitts beschrieben worden ist. — Zu diesen Ereignissen kommt noch die Handformanalyse, und dann wird beides miteinander verbunden. Die Art des Erlebens der Ereignisse ist von Charakter, geistigem Niveau und Lebenskunst abhängig und sollte bei einer ausführlichen Analyse in Betracht gezogen werden.

Je nachdem, wieviele Linien in den Händen vorhanden sind, wird die Handanalyse klein oder umfangreich. Selbstverständlich kommt nach der linken noch die r e c h t e Hand in derselben Weise zur Betrachtung, und beides wird verglichen, reduziert oder ergänzt, bis das vollständige Lebensbild ausführlich vorhanden ist. Auf der r e c h t e n Hand liegt der H a u p t w e r t. Sie ist die positive!

Zu solch einer vollständigen Handanalyse benutze man die listenartige Aufstellung, wie ich sie hier in drei Formularen folgen lasse.

Der Reichtum an Handlinien und Zeichen darf nicht verwirren. Immer eines nach dem anderen, wie ich es in dieser Erklärung des Abdrucks Bild 37 getan habe, oder, wenn weniger Linien, wie mit Bild 36.

Bei jeder Handanalyse werden die einzelnen Merkmale gesammelt, und zwar zugleich aus beiden Händen derart, daß man also zur gleichen Zeit z. B. die Herzlinie links u n d rechts vom Beginn bis zur Endung aufmerksam und genau absucht und jedes Merkmal notiert. So auch bei den anderen Linien und den Bergen. Die Reihenfolge ist auf folgenden Formularen angegeben. Natürlich ist und bleibt die B a s i s zur Begutachtung immer die äußere Hand - F o r m !

Nachdem die Vorarbeiten fertig sind, wird aus den Merkmalsgruppen das Gesamtbild zusammengestellt. Begonnen wird die Analyse mit dem, was bei der Betrachtung der Hände zuerst oder stärkstens ins Auge fällt. Daran wird angeknüpft, und die weiteren Ergebnisse werden wie Bausteine eingefügt, so daß ein Lebensbild entsteht, ein Gesamtüberblick bei einer großen Analyse. Wenn nur eine Analyse in bestimmter Richtung erwünscht ist, wird nur von Merkmalen und Merkmalsgruppen verwendet, was hierfür erforderlich ist.

Um auch das genau zu wissen, folgt hier im Anschluß eine entsprechende Aufstellung. Danach lasse ich die e r s t e Arbeit einer meiner Schülerinnen folgen: eine Handanalyse mit den Vorarbeiten. Sie möge als Arbeitsmuster dienen. — Bei Analysen ist zu beachten, daß negative Angelegenheiten nicht zu stark betont werden. Dagegen sind Optimismus, Lebensmut, Selbstgefühl und vor allem die s e e l i s c h e K r a f t zu stärken!

Die Reihenfolge der Merkmale zur Ausarbeitung von Handanalysen.

G e s a m t - C h a r a k t e r i s t i k d u r c h :

Handform, Fingerformen, Daumen und Berge kombiniert mit den Hauptmerkmalen der Linien. Ändernde Einflüsse durch Kopflinien, Nebenlinien, Zeichen und Nägel.

B e r u f d u r c h :

Handform, Fingerformen, Daumen und Berge. Saturnlinien-Verlauf, Apollolinien, Kopflinien. Lebenslinien-Ablauf.
Konjunktur des Berufes zur Zeit der Beratung oder Feststellung.

B e r u f s - W e g d u r c h :

Handform und Fingerform für die Eignung. Daumen wegen der Durchführung. Saturnlinien-Verlauf in beiden Händen, so auch die Apollolinien. Zeiten der Aufstiegslinien an der Lebenslinie und das augenblickliche Jahr auf der Saturnlinie; hier die Konstitution der Linie und deren Farbe feststellen.

P s y c h o - A n a l y s e , s e e l i s c h e S t ö r u n g e n :

Grundbild der Hand- und Fingerformen, Berge, Daumen.
Alle Hauptlinien, besonders die Kopflinie, genau beachten.
Venusgürtel, Apollolinie, Vorgeburtslinien, Mondlinien, Uranus- und Neptunlinie, Milchstraße genau nachsehen. Inseln, Punkte, Ringe, Sterne, Quadrate suchen. Evtl. Merkmale für Lähmung oder gewaltsamen Tod in der Familie. Als Ergänzung: Gesichtsausdruck, auch Handschrift hinzunehmen.
(Dieses Kapitel ist in Band II ausführlich behandelt.)

K r a n k h e i t s b i l d d u r c h :

Handtyp, Fingerformen und deren evtl. Deformationen, Nägel, Zeichen auf den Bergen und die Berge, wenn sehr hoch, Daumen. A l l e Hauptlinien nachsehen auf Farbe, Vererbung (Inseln), Punkte, Sterne, Ringe, Gitter, Quadrate. Unterschiede: was vererbt, angeboren oder erworben. Operationen oder Verletzungen, kritische Zeitpunkte. Lebensdauer gibt man nicht bekannt!

Kriminalistik:

Hand-Typ, und Fingerformen. Besonders aber Kopflinien-Verlauf und ob doppelt. Saturn-, Merkurberg und Finger, Mondberg nach Gittern und Querlinien absuchen. Merkmale für Brutalität physisch und geistig, für Unaufrichtigkeit, Raffsucht und „Diplomatie", krankhafte Phantasie und ebensolche Medialität. Daumen, Handwurzel; evtl. Mangel an Linien in guter Hand. Merkmal für gewaltsamen Tod in der Familie. Erbliche Belastungen.

Esoterik durch:

Hand-Prä-existenz, Beinform für jetziges, Kopf für folgendes Leben. Handform, Fingerform und Daumen als Gesamtbild. Deformationen und deren metaphysische Bedeutungen. Hauptlinien-Konstitution und Verlauf. Alle „schlechten" Eigenschaften. Ereignislinien, besonders Herz-, Saturn- und Kopflinie beachten; Venusgürtel in Betracht ziehen und karmische Zeichen.

Chirognomisches Schema für linke Hand.

Handtyp.

Rasse (Art) und kabbalistische Welt.

Daumen.

1. Glied.
2. Glied.

Finger.

1. Finger.
2. Finger.
3. Finger.
4. Finger.
Länge der Hand.
Länge der Finger.
Länge und Breite des Handtellers.

Konsistenz.

Knotig oder nicht
1. oder 2. Knoten.
Glatt.
Weich.
Hart.
Fest.
Trocken.
Aktiv.
Passiv.
Haut.
Farbe.
Nägel.
Niveau.
Besonderes.

Chirognomisches Schema für rechte Hand.

Handtyp.

Rasse (Art) und kabbalistische Welt.

Daumen.

1. Glied.
2. Glied.

Finger.

1. Finger.
2. Finger.
3. Finger.
4. Finger.
Länge der Hand.
Länge der Finger.
Länge und Breite des Hand-
    tellers.

Konsistenz.

Knotig oder nicht.
1. oder 2. Knoten.
Glatt.
Weich.
Hart.
Fest.
Trocken.
Aktiv.
Passiv.
Haut.
Farbe.
Nägel.
Niveau.
Besonderes.

Chiromantisches Schema.

Handtyp.

Daumen (Wille).

1. Glied.
2. Glied.

Welche der drei kabbalistischen Welten.

Spirituell.
Intellektuell.
Materiell.

Berge.

1. Venusberg.
2. Jupiterberg.
3. Saturnberg.
4. Apolloberg.
5. Merkurberg.
6. Marsberg.
7. Kleiner Marsberg.
8. Mondberg.
9. Der regierende Berg.

Linien (evtl. Länge in cm und mm).

1. Kopflinie.
2. Lebenslinie.
3. Saturnlinie.
4. Herzlinie.
5. Sonnen- (Apollo-) Linie.
6. Magen- (Leber-) Linie.
7. Venusgürtel.
8. Uranuslinie.
9. Neptunlinie.
10. Marslinie.
11. Temperenzlinie.
12. Raszette.

Zeichen (Sterne, Kreuze, Punkte usw.).
Karmische Zeichen.

„Swastika" Arbeitsstätte für Charakterologie.

Spezialfach: Wissenschaftliche Chirologie und Krankheits-Diagnostik
aus Hand und Nägeln. — Berufs-Eignungsprüfung.

E. ISSBERNER - HALDANE, BERLIN

Folgende Daten zeigen den Rhythmus der betreffenden Persönlichkeit
an, wie er von Geburt an festgesetzt ist und sich auch in Ereignissen
auswirkt.

Daten nach Lebensjahren (aus den Händen gemessen). Ausgangsdatum vom ... Jahre, in dem ein Ereignis bestätigt ist (Nullpunkt).	Tag der Diagnose: ....

1. Jahre mit seelischen Erschütterungen, Trauer, Gram, Depressionen:

2. Jahre für Bekanntschaften,   } günstig:
3. Freundschaften, evtl. auch für Teilhaberaufnahme: } ungünstig:

4. Günstige Jahre für Herzensangelegenheiten:
5. Ehebekanntschaften günstig nur:

6. Jahre für Unternehmungen,   günstig:
7. Erfolg, Aufstieg,   ungünstig:

8. Jahre für große Reisen und   }   günstig:
9. Veränderungen: }   ungünstig:

10. Kritische Jahre für Gesundheit, leichterer Art:
11. Zeiten für Schwermut, Depressionen:

12. Jahre für Lebensgefahr, Verletzung
(auch Operation, Eingriff usw.):

13. Rhythmus der Todesjahre: väterl. Generation:
14.   mütterl. Generation:

15. Todesart (plötzlich, heftig, langsam):

16. Mögliche Kinderzahl: | 17. Dispos. zu Leiden:

18. Anfangsbuchstaben markanter Namen für das Leben:

19. Erbliche Belastungen:

20. Ungünstige Menschentypen:

Unterstrichen: verstärkte Bedeutung; eingeklammert: abgeschwächt.

Besonderes:

Vorarbeiten zur Handanalyse: Frau W. K.
(Schüler-Analyse von W. Fahnert) *)

Handform:

Handtyp: Eckig mit zarten Knoten und konischem Einschlag. (An der rechten Hand ist zu beachten, daß die Knoten durch Gicht verursacht sind.)

Besitzer solcher Hände sind vorwiegend Verstandesmenschen. Bei der zarten, feinen Haut jedoch kommt hier viel Empfindungsfähigkeit der Seele hinzu. Auch der konische Einschlag schwächt etwas das rein Intellektuelle ab. Die Handform zeigt, daß diese Persönlichkeit gewissenhaft, pflichttreu, zuverlässig, sehr ordnungsliebend und etwas konservativ eingestellt ist.

Fingerform:

Der Daumen ist lang, rechts noch länger als links, die Spitze etwas nach außen gebogen. Das erste Glied ist genau so lang wie das zweite. — Ein Mensch mit einem starken Willen, guter Durchsetzungskraft, feiner Einfühlungs- und Anpassungsfähigkeit. Letztes schwächt hier den starken Willen ab und macht die Frau anschmiegsam und beeinflußbar. Nach dem 28. Lebensjahr wird der Selbstbehauptungstrieb stärker, sie wird eigenwilliger und nicht mehr ganz so nachgiebig.

Zeigefinger: An der linken Hand verhältnismäßig kurz, das 1. Glied nach dem Mittelfinger zu gebogen. — Das Persönlichkeitsgefühl ist in der Jugend nicht sehr stark; es treten dadurch Minderwertigkeitsgefühle auf. Viele Traurigkeiten wurden erlebt, viel Kummer und Sorgen. (Leber.)

Der rechte Zeigefinger ist viel länger, weshalb auch das Persönlichkeitsgefühl nach dem 28. Lebensjahre stärker ist.

Der Saturnfinger ist an beiden Händen normal lang, eckig. — Das Verantwortungsbewußtsein ist groß, die Handeignerin ist vorwiegend ernst und nachdenklich und hat Sinn für wissenschaftliche Themen. Das 3. Glied ist links ziemlich lang, was auf Vorliebe für Arbeit im Freien hindeutet, auch auf Sinn für Sport. An der rechten Hand ist das nicht mehr so augenfällig.

Der Apollofinger ist links viel länger als der Zeigefinger: der Idealismus ist in der Jugend sehr ausgeprägt. Es ist in der Handeignerin ein ständiges Suchen nach dem Ideal, dem man nachstreben kann. Rechts ist er so lang wie der Jupiterfinger. Nach dem 30. Jahre

---

*) Die Unterlagen zu dieser Schüleranalyse gingen durch die Kriegsereignisse verloren. Doch zeigt die Arbeit die Art des Aufbaues einer Handanalyse klar genug, um als Beispiel zu dienen.

ist mehr innere Harmonie vorhanden. Der Idealismus hat etwas nachgelassen, und diese Persönlichkeit versucht nunmehr, sich durch eigene Kraft und Reife zu vervollkommnen, als durch das träumende Streben nach Idealen, die doch nicht erreicht werden können.

Der Merkurfinger hat eine normale Länge. Da er etwas konisch ist, wird die Redeart dieser Handeignerin feinfühlig und nicht verletzend sein.

Da die ersten Fingerglieder alle gut ausgeprägt sind, ist auch viel Sinn für geistige Arbeit und eine gute Intelligenz vorhanden.

Was von all diesen Eigenschaften nun ergänzt, abgeschwächt oder gar aufgehoben wird, das zeigt uns die Innenhand.

Innenhand:

Die Berge:

Sie sind verhältnismäßig schlecht zu erkennen, weshalb ich hier nicht sehr viel näher auf sie eingehe. Man sieht, daß der Venusberg voll und kräftig ist. Es ist viel Sinnlichkeit, Leidenschaftlichkeit, Hingabefähigkeit, Sinn für ein nettes Heim, für die Kinder und den Gatten vorhanden. Ein guter Venusberg gibt auch viel Gutherzigkeit und warmes Mitempfinden.

Der Jupiterberg ist auch gut zu erkennen. Es ist viel Strebsamkeit vorhanden, auch Sinn für Kameradschaft.

Der Saturnberg scheint vom Apolloberg angezogen zu sein. Das Empfindungsleben ist mit sehr viel Ernst, Nachdenklichkeit und auch etwas Melancholie durchsetzt.

Mars und Mondberg sind sehr gut entwickelt. Deshalb ist auch Mut vorhanden und sehr, sehr viel Träumerei, auch Phantasie. Der gute Saturnberg und der gute Mondberg zusammen geben viel Träumerei und melancholische Romantik. Gut ausgeprägte Berge zeigen immer Sinn für Lebensgenuß an. Das ist hier sehr wertvoll, weil Menschen mit eckigem Handtyp leicht zu Geiz neigen; denn alles, was das Leben verschönt, jeglicher Genuß, erscheint ihnen als Verschwendung. Deshalb wird dieser negative Charakterzug hier verbessert, und die Handeignerin gönnt sich hin und wieder schon eine Lebensfreude, allerdings wenn sie es verantworten kann.

Linien.

Kopflinie:

l.: Verläuft etwas gewellt bis an die Grenze zwischen Mars und Mondberg. Sie ist zu Beginn 1 cm mit der Lebenslinie verbunden. —

Die Denkrichtung geht in das Intellektuelle. Die Entschlußkraft ist normal. Eine Insel in der Linie warnt vor Kopfschmerzen.

r.: Die Kopflinie ist länger geworden und im Intellektuellen geblieben. Dadurch ist der Eigensinn gewachsen. Die Entschlußkraft ist genau so geblieben, gut.

Herzlinie:

l.: Ziemlich breit, bis an den Jupiterberg heranreichend: Viel Herzlichkeit, Gutmütigkeit, Herzensjugend, aber auch etwas Egoismus ist vorhanden, da die Linie nicht in den Berg läuft. Die Inselbildung deutet auf einen organischen Herzfehler und eine große Liebesenttäuschung.

r.: dasselbe.

Venusgürtel:

l.: Nur am Anfang vorhanden: Starke sexuelle Unterdrückungen.

r.: dasselbe.

Apollolinie:

l.: Stückweise vorhanden, eine Inselbildung: Das Innenleben ist zerrissen. Es besteht die Gefahr der inneren Zersplitterung. Die Insel zeigt Schüchternheiten.

r.: Die Linie ist schon wesentlich besser. Ein harmonisches Innenleben wird gefunden. Allerdings zeigt eine kleine Insel immer noch Schüchternheit an. Die Linie beginnt im Marsfeld. Es wird viel Mühe, Kampf und Energie kosten, um das ersehnte Ziel zu erreichen.

Magenlinie:

l.: Etwas zerrissen, aber stückweise gut. Darm- und Leberstörungen. Das Stück Magenlinie auf dem Merkurberg gibt Sprachentalent.

r.: Die Linie ist hier besser, doch gewunden. Das gibt eine Disposition zu Krampf. Hier sieht man sehr gut, wie die Magenlinie aus dem Venusberg kommt. Es ist dadurch eine leichte Empfänglichkeit für Sexualkrankheiten gegeben. Anderseits zeigt solch eine Linie eine vorgeburtliche Belastung der Betreffenden durch Leid der Mutter während der Schwangerschaft. Auch die Apollolinie, die teilweise aus dem Venusberg kommt, zeigt diese vorgeburtliche Belastung.

Schicksalslinie:

l.: 2fach: Eine sehr gute Linie, die bei der Raszette beginnt, klar gezeichnet ist bis an das dritte Glied des Saturnfingers, wahrscheinlich sogar da hineingeht. Das gibt meist ein trauriges Schicksal. Die 2. Linie beginnt auf dem Mondberg, geht bis in den Handtisch und setzt sich dann stückweise bis in den Saturnberg fort. Dies gibt eine Tendenz zum Reisen, zum Aufstieg durch indirekte Mithilfe des anderen Geschlechts. Der Stern zu Beginn der Linie sagt, daß die Eltern in der Jugend der Handeignerin einen finanziellen Verlust hatten.

r.: Kommt die Linie mit einem Ast aus der Raszette, mit einem aus dem Mondberg. Eine Insel ist zu Beginn vorhanden. Diese Insel gibt Hellfühlen, auch Disposition zu Wahrträumen. Mehrere Seitenlinien münden vom Mondberg her in die Schicksalslinie ein. Es machen sich also immer mehr äußere Einflüsse wirksam geltend. Diese Linien vom Mondberg geben aber auch eine innere Ruhelosigkeit, ein ständiges Suchen und Ringen nach Harmonie.

Lebenslinie:

Über die Lebenslinie ist hier nicht mehr viel zu sagen, da auf ihr alle markanten Ereignisse des Lebens sichtbar sind, die ausgemessen werden. Da die Linie aber stabil ist, zeigt sie eine gute, körperliche Widerstandskraft. Links geht sie zum Mondberg hinüber. Es sind Eierstockstörungen links vorhanden.

Sonstige Zeichen:

Linke Hand: Aus dem Beugegelenk des Jupiterfingers gehen zwei kleine Linien in den Berg: Zwei Fehlgeburten. Im 1. Glied des Saturnfingers sind Querlinien: Lebensüberdruß.

Querlinien im 1. Glied des Apollofingers: Überreizte Kopfnerven.

Kreuz neben der Saturnlinie auf dem Mondberg: Warnung vor Verlust durch Diebstahl.

Kreuz auf dem Jupiterfinger: Warnung vor Brandschaden.

Rechte Hand: Querlinie im 2. Glied des Jupiterfingers: Diplomatie. Querlinie im 3. Glied desselben Fingers: Heftigkeiten.

Ein kleines Viereck im 2. Glied des Saturnfingers: Unvermeidliches Unglück.

Dreieck auf dem Jupiterberg: Sinn für Politik, auch Diplomatie.

Gesundheitliches:

Disposition zu folgenden Leiden: Blasenleiden, lange Querlinie über den Jupiterberg. Überreizung der Sexualnerven durch Unterdrückungen. Gebärmutterstörungen: Insel am Venusgürtel zwischen Jupiter- und Saturnfinger.

Eierstockstörungen links: Ast an Lebenslinie zum Mondberg. Schilddrüsenleiden: Kleine Kreuze zwischen Kopf- und Lebenslinie. Ebenfalls Bronchialkatarrh Disposition.

Disposition zu Krampf, Gicht (Magenlinie gewunden).

Schüler-Handanalyse für Frau W. K. 1937.

Die Handeignerin ist eine innerlich vornehme, sehr zart empfindende Persönlichkeit. Man kann sich auf sie verlassen; denn was sie tut, tut sie mit ihrer ganzen Kraft. Ein starkes Verantwortungsbewußtsein läßt sie alles nach bestem Wissen und Gewissen ausführen. Sie tut alles genau, korrekt, manchmal ein wenig zu kleinlich.

Ihre Denkrichtung ist vorwiegend konservativ. Sie hängt an der Tradition, an alten Sitten und Anschauungen und kann sich innerlich nicht so schnell umstellen, wenn etwas Neues kommt. In der Jugend war das nicht so ausgeprägt. Da war sie empfänglich für alles Neue, war sehr anpassungsfähig und konnte sich gut in jede neue Situation hineinfinden. Dadurch war sie innerlich aber auch nicht sehr gefestigt; sie wußte nicht recht, wohin mit sich selber, und ließ sich deshalb leichter beeinflussen als später, wo sie nicht mehr so überaus anpassungsbereit ist, sondern den Willen hat, ihr Schicksal selber so gut wie möglich zu gestalten.

So besitzt sie in der Jugend eine sehr empfindliche Seele, zu wenig Selbstbewußtsein, nimmt alles, was ihr begegnete, viel zu ernst, macht sich viel zu viele Gedanken und Sorgen um das Leben, so daß sie schwer zu einer inneren strahlenden Heiterkeit kommt. Dabei kann sie sehr lebhaft, temperamentvoll, lustig sein. Aber solche Hochstimmungen dauern nie allzulange an. Es ist ein steter Kampf gegen Depressionen und Minderwertigkeitsgefühle.

Die ethische Seite des Lebens zieht sie besonders stark an, obwohl sie auch sehr für alle irdischen Genüsse zu haben ist. Aber sie schwelgt nicht gern darin, nur vorübergehend, um sich dann wieder intensiv ihrer Arbeit zu widmen. Sie sieht ein, daß alles Materielle lebensnotwendig ist, auch alle materielle Arbeit. Doch in ihren Mußestunden sehnt sie sich danach, den inneren Menschen zu entwickeln. Obwohl sie religiös veranlagt ist, wird ihr der Weg zum inneren Frieden doch sehr schwer. Ein ständiger Konflikt ist vorhanden zwischen Verstand und Gefühl, zwischen Herz und Kopf. Intuition ist vorhanden und kann ihr den rechten Weg zeigen, aber sie hört nicht darauf. Die Seele ist bereit zu einem großen Schwingen, ist bereit zu starkem Erlebnis, doch hemmt der Intellekt noch sehr. Dadurch entsteht dann die innere Disharmonie, dieses Nicht-Wissen, was man tun soll. Nach dem 28. Lebensjahr wird dies besser. Das Selbstbewußtsein wächst, ein größerer Durchsetzungswille macht sich dann geltend, und dadurch, daß sie sehr viel um die eigene Reife kämpfen muß, erkennt sie ihr wahres Ich, ihr Ziel.

Es ist schicksalsbedingt, daß sehr viele traurige Erlebnisse ihre Seele berühren müssen, und man sieht auch, daß sie sich deshalb schon sehr,

sehr viel gegrämt, gesorgt hat. Solange man sich aber noch dermaßen viel sorgt und grämt, hat man keine wahre Religion. Erst wenn man sich nicht mehr über das Schicksal beklagt, erst wenn man erkennt, daß alle auch noch so traurigen Ereignisse gottgewollt sind zur Erziehung, dann kommt man in Harmonie mit dem All. Und gerade hier ist ersichtlich, daß das Schicksal sie durch eine Schule führen will, damit sie die große, führende Macht erkenne und freudig ja sage zu allem, was geschieht.

Die Phantasie ist groß, und bis zum 28. Lebensjahr wurde viel geträumt, vieles sich wunderschön ausgedacht und ausgemalt, und in Gedanken wurde an schöne, glückliche Tage gedacht. Es wurde alles zu ideell angesehen, in der Phantasie zu bunt ausgemalt, so daß das Leben dann oft sehr entsetzte. Weil die Handeignerin selber ein guter Mensch ist, deshalb sah sie in anderen Menschen dasselbe. So gab es manche Enttäuschung. Erst nach dem 28. Jahr kommt zu der Phantasie und Träumerei die Tatkraft, kommt der Wille, sich nicht mehr vom Schicksal treten zu lassen, sondern sein Leben selber in die Hand zu nehmen. Die Überempfindlichkeit wird abgestellt, die Durchsetzungskraft wächst, und die Nachgiebigkeit ist nicht mehr so groß.

Hemmend für eine innere höhere Entwicklung sind auch die vorgeburtlichen Einflüsse, die von traurigen Erlebnissen der Mutter während der Schwangerschaft herrühren. Dadurch macht sich eine gewisse Menschenscheu geltend, eine eigene Unsicherheit, Schüchternheit, die ein freies, ungehemmtes Auftreten verhindert. Auch über diese seelischen Hemmungen hilft der Wille hinweg.

Ein normales und natürliches Maß von Sinnlichkeit ist vorhanden, und auch auf diesem Gebiet machen sich unterdrückte Regungen geltend. Dadurch werden die Nerven überreizt, die innere Ruhe, die noch nicht vorhanden ist, wird noch schwerer gewonnen. Da eine Anlage für Heftigkeiten vorhanden ist, die aber im allgemeinen nicht hervortreten, kann es durch diese Unterdrückungen zu plötzlichen Heftigkeitsausbrüchen kommen. Auch die Depressionen, die sich manchmal bis zum Lebensüberdruß steigern, nehmen dadurch zu. Gerade die erotische Seite darf bei dieser Persönlichkeit nicht vernachlässigt werden, weil durch sie viele angeborenen Schwächen geheilt werden können. So war auch in der ersten Zeit die Sinnlichkeit etwas verkrampft durch innere Hemmungen. Doch kann das leicht gut werden, sobald von beiden Seiten Liebe und Verstehen vorhanden sind. Schicksalsmäßig sind in der Liebe keine Traurigkeiten angezeigt, wohl aber in der Ehe. Daher wird die betreffende Persönlichkeit wahrscheinlich eine falsche Wahl treffen und wird einen Partner heiraten, der ihr doch nicht der Lebenskamerad wird, der er zu versprechen schien.

Da sie selber ein guter Kamerad ist, sich gern in das Los des Partners fügt, viel Weiblichkeit besitzt, werden die Eheschwierigkeiten wahrscheinlich mehr von der anderen Seite herrühren. Ich sagte ja schon, daß sie dazu neigt, alles zu idealisieren, weshalb sehr leicht eine Enttäuschung entsteht. Soll sie nicht seelisch verhungern, so muß sie trotz einer ersten wahrscheinlich traurigen Ehe versuchen, den Menschen zu finden, den sie liebt. Schicksalsmäßig müßte sie ihn finden. Und da ihr Karma ja sonst für dieses Leben viel Traurigkeiten birgt, wäre hier die Quelle, wo sie sich Kraft und Mut holen kann. Es ist gut, daß sie trotz der Empfindsamkeit seelisch so widerstandsfähig ist; denn sonst wäre sie schon innerlich zerbrochen. Doch steckt die Kraft in ihr, sich über alles hinweg zu setzen. Harmonie wird auch später gefunden, eine innere Ruhe aber nicht leicht. Damit muß die Handeignerin sich zufriedengeben. In ihr stecken so viele Entwicklungsmöglichkeiten, daß sie ihr Leben lang bestrebt ist, sich höher zu entwickeln, und deshalb nie zur Ruhe kommt.

Sie besitzt gute, geistige Fähigkeiten, aber, da die Kopfnerven zart und durch viele Grübeleien und quälende Gedanken sehr angegriffen sind, ist es nicht gut, sich allzuviel geistig zu beschäftigen. Die Nerven müssen sich erst einmal wieder erholen. Jetzt ist es besser, die seelische Seite zum Schwingen zu bringen durch Beschäftigung mit Kunst, Musik, Natur usw. Sie besitzt Naturliebe, ist gern im Freien, wandert gern und kann dabei Erholung suchen. Ihrer Veranlagung nach besitzt sie viel natürliche, weibliche Intelligenz, gemischt mit Diplomatie, so daß sie es nicht einmal dringend nötig hat, ihr Wissen aus Büchern zu schöpfen, sondern, in sich hineinlauschend, selber richtige Schlüsse ziehen kann. Gerade einem Manne könnte sie mit ihrem weiblichen Empfinden gut zur Seite stehen. Aber sie muß wirklich mit der Seele erfühlen wollen, was sie wissen will; denn der Intellekt kann irren und wirkt oft hemmend, wie auch hier. Nach dem 30. Lebensjahr macht sich eine feine Hellfühligkeit bemerkbar, eine Anlage auch zu Wahrträumen, und es liegt an ihr, diese zu entwickeln oder nicht.

Trotz der großen Gutherzigkeit und Warmherzigkeit macht sich manchmal ein wenig Egoismus breit. Dieser ist zu bekämpfen!

Es ist ein Warnungszeichen vorhanden vor Brandschaden, und auch vor Diebstahl. Vorsicht ist anzuraten.

Gesundheitliches: Disposition zu folgenden Leiden: Blasenstörungen, Überreizung der Sexualnerven durch Unterdrückungen; Gebärmutter- und Eierstockstörungen links, Schilddrüsen- und Bronchialleiden, Disposition zu Krampf, zu Gicht. Schwache Kopfnerven und leichte Kopfschmerzen, auch Milzstörungen. Ein undefinierbarer organischer Herzfehler. Dies sind Dispositionen, die sich früher oder später bemerkbar machen können, aber sie müssen es nicht! Jede Krankheit hat eine geistige Ursache und danach löst sie sich früher oder später oder auch gar nicht physisch aus.   W. F.

Zu den Bildbeilagen

Im voraus muß darauf hingewiesen werden, daß aus den Lichtbildern der Innenhände nur sehr wenige und gänzlich unzureichende Auskünfte gegeben werden können, da — durch Licht und Schatten verhindert — die Linien zumeist nur teilweise erkannt werden können. Nur klare gute Handabdrücke sind geeignet. Infolgedessen werde ich bei solchen Abbildungen auch nur soweit auf die Innenhand eingehen, wie Merkmale deutlich ersichtlich sind. —

Bild 38 (oben): Eine konische weibliche Hand mit einem Einschlag zum eckigen Typ. Die mehr zarten Formen zeigen, daß es sich hier um eine feinnervige, sensitive Person handelt, deren Vorfahren auf gute — entsprechende — Auswahl eines mehr geistig entwickelten Ehepartners hielten. Daher das schmale Handgelenk. Minimale Anflüge zur Spatelform an einigen Fingerspitzen weisen auf Sinn für größere Pläne hin und auf Anlagen zu feinen Handarbeiten kunstgewerblicher Art. Die fehlenden Nagelmonde zeigen Herzneurose, und die auffallend kleine Form des Fingernagels am linken Merkur deutet an, daß organisches Herzleiden in der mütterlichen Generation vorhanden war.

Bild 38 (unten): Die mehr fleischige Hand weist auf eine freudige Genußfähigkeit dieser weiblichen Person (gute Entwicklung aller Berge). In der linken Hand zeigt die Kopflinienrichtung noch Neigung zu idealistischem, phantasievollem und romantischem Gedankenleben. In der rechten Hand (nach dem 28. Lebensjahr) erfolgt jedoch eine Umstellung zum intellektuellen, d. h. verstandesmäßig-materiellen Denken. Diese Hand ist — im Gegensatz zu der oberen — physisch und psychisch kraftvoller, die Konstitution des Körpers stabiler (dickere Handgelenke!). Doch weisen die ersten Fingerglieder in ihrer beachtlichen Länge auf gute geistige Veranlagung hin. Ist die obere Hand mehr das Merkmal eines feinnervigen Empfindungsmenschen, der feinste Ströme aufzunehmen imstande ist, aber weniger kraftvollen Magnetismus ausstrahlt, so ist die untere Hand mehr die eines gesunden und kultivierten Triebmenschen mit starker magnetischer Anziehung und kraftvoller Erotik.

Bild 39 (oben): Man beachte genau — da sehr wichtig! — die vom Handgelenk abgebogenen Hände. Diese Verschiebung in der Länge des Zeigefingers im Verhältnis zu den anderen muß schon eine falsche Begutachtung ergeben. Das wird an dem Bilde der rechten Hand deutlich. Hier erscheint durch die Schiefhaltung des Armes naturgemäß der Zeigefinger länger als der Apollofinger. Läge der Arm in gleicher Richtung, d. h. in einer geraden Linie, die von der Mittelfingerspitze bis zum Ellenbogen verläuft, dann wären die beiden genannten Finger gleich lang. Die linke Hand dieses Bildes zeigt die Situation nicht so auffällig.

Auch an dieser Hand sind die ersten Fingerglieder (mit den unteren) in gleicher Länge, so daß eine geistige Begabung vorhanden ist. Da aber die Kopflinien, wie klar ersichtlich, parallel mit der Herzlinie zum Marsberg verlaufen, ist diese Begabung mehr verstandesmäßig. Hierdurch ergibt sich — trotz guten aber nicht mit ihm verbundenen Mondberges — ein Mangel an Gestaltungskraft. Die vollen Berge zeigen bei diesen eckigen Händen den Genießer an, der nur mit dem Verstande, nicht mit der Seele genießt und egoistisch ist.

Bild 39 (unten): zeigt den konischen Handtyp eines Mannes. Ein leichter eckiger Einschlag macht sich in den Fingern bemerkbar und weist auf eine

Mischung von gemüthafter Einstellung zur Umwelt mit dem Versuch, alles verstandesmäßig zu verwerten. Infolgedessen ist er nicht kleinlich und konservativ, sondern hat immerhin noch eine angenehme Mischung von beidem. Der Zeigefinger der linken Hand ist etwas kürzer, doch nur um einige Millimeter, während der Apollofinger reichlich lang ist und den Idealist aus Berechnung anzeigt. Gleichzeitig zeigt der verkürzte Zeigefinger auch Mangel an Persönlichkeit an.

Sind in der oberen Hand die Daumen biegsam und deuten Anpassungsvermögen, sowie etwas Nachgiebigkeit an, so sind die Daumen der unteren Hand steif, ohne Biegsamkeit; daher erscheint der Handeigner ohne Anpassungswilligkeit.

Bild 40: zeigt die Hände der Malerin Käthe Kollwitz (1929). Der Ausdruck allein dieser Hände ist der einer sehr gütigen und klugen Mütterlichkeit, in der sich das Gehirn- und Herzdenken harmonisiert hat.

Bild 41: Die linienreiche Hand einer Sängerin weist auf starke Erlebnistiefe. Die gerade verlaufende Kopflinie — genau auf der Grenze Mars — Mondberg endend — weist auf sachliches Denken und wenig Gestaltungskraft und Einfühlung. Daher ist hier auch der innere Zwiespalt zwischen Kopf- und Herzdenken und somit keine ganze Harmonie im Wesen gekennzeichnet. Die durch Querlinien gestörte Apollolinie zeigt, daß die berufliche Laufbahn als Künstlerin durch Intrigen (Linien vom Merkurberg), aber auch durch Zersplitterung des seelischen Erlebens (Splitterung der Linie selbst), sowie durch Lampenfieber (Insel in der Apollolinie oberhalb der Herzlinie) zu leiden hat. Der Ansatz des Venusgürtels endet in der Apollolinie: Leichtsinn (Unbedachtsamkeit) in Liebesangelegenheiten.

Bild 42: Hier ist die plötzlich und ganz tief abfallende Kopflinie mit hakenförmiger Endung in den Mondberg auffällig. Diese Kopflinienformation weist auf starke Tendenz zum Selbstmord durch Wahnanfälligkeit des Betreffenden selbst, sowie auch darauf, daß Ähnliches bei den Vorfahren dieses Mannes geschehen ist. Die sehr schmale und in ihrer Konstitution sehr schwache Handstruktur weist auf eine sehr schwache und dekadente Körperlichkeit durch Überzüchtung. Der Stern auf dem Saturnberg disponiert zu körperlicher Katastrophe — wahrscheinlich durch eine Frau. Die Intuitions-(Uranus-)linie ist gut in ihrer Formation, jedoch stark zersplittert und weist auf krankhafte Medialität, — üble astrale Einflüsse.

Bild 43: konische, materielle Mädchenhände. Der linke Daumen zeigt in der Form des ersten Gliedes: Neigung zu Jähzorn bis zum 30. Jahre. In der rechten Hand fällt die lange gerade Herzlinie auf. Da diese aber nicht mit der Kopf- und Lebenslinie verbunden, ist eine Disposition zu gewaltsamem Tod nicht gegeben. Doch waren bei den Vorfahren väterlicherseits (rechte Hand!) Lähmungserscheinungen vorhanden, die hier als Nachwirkungen zeitweise Platzangst zeitigen können. Im übrigen zeigt die Länge der Herzlinie Nymphomanie — als Veranlagung, die bei der vorhandenen Verliebheit (siehe Herzlinie) und der genießerischen Sinnenfreudigkeit (mollige Hand) leicht zur Entfaltung kommt.

Bild 44 A (links): Diese auch in ihrer Fülle schöne Frauenhand hat konische Form. Die sonst bei konischen Händen vorhandenen Stimmungsschwankungen und oft auch Haltlosigkeit charakterlicher Art fallen hier ganz fort durch den geraden, festen Daumen (Selbstbewußtsein und Eigenwilligkeit), sowie durch den leichten eckigen Anklang der Fingerform bei Saturn- und Apollofinger. Dennoch zeigt diese Hand ein hohes Maß von Gemüt, Hingabefähigkeit, Fraulichkeit und Zärtlichkeitsbedürfnis (Fülle, Weichheit, Grübchen).

Bild 44 B (rechts): zeigt die ziemlich primitive, aber praktische Hand eines 15jährigen Mädchens. Die Fingerformen sind eckig; das Gedankenleben ist daher nur materiell-verstandesmäßig ohne tiefere Gemütswerte. Der Daumen ist kräftig und etwas biegsam, wenn auch nicht ganz in normaler

Länge. Also: obgleich eigenwillig und stur, kann sich die Handeignerin anpassen und ist auch nicht ohne Beeinflußbarkeit und Nachgiebigkeit, wenn der angeborene Egoismus dieses Types seine Vorteile erkennt. Die ersten Fingerglieder sind kurz; daher keine besondere geistige Begabung.

Bild 45: zeigt elementar-konische Mischung. Großer, breiter Handrumpf, kurze, konische Finger, feste Hand. Instinktiv und praktisch, und da die Hand groß und plump ist: starkes Verlangen nach materiellem Besitz. Die sehr kompakte Basis der Hand (Venus- und Mondberg mit dicken Handgelenken) zeigt eine sehr feste und widerstandsfähige Körperlichkeit, die jedoch leicht zur Verschlackung neigt. Die Kopflinie verläuft in rein intellektueller Richtung (wie auch die Kopfform zeigt), daher vollkommene Unterdrückung des seelischen Erlebens, wie es die linienarme Innenhand beweist. Die Daumen sind stark und starr. Eigenwilligkeit und Herrschlust, keine Anpassung, starrköpfig.

Bild 46: Elementar-eckiger Handtyp mit der Daumenform, die Jähzorn (bis zur Tobsucht) anzeigt. Verstärkt wird diese Reizbarkeit zum Jähzorn noch durch die starke Behaarung der Hände und Arme, sowie durch die kurzen Fingernägel (organische Herzstörungen, daher leichte Erregbarkeit). Es sind die Hände eines bekannten Lustmörders von 1924. Die eckige Handform weist auf Genauigkeit, alles andere auf Rohheit und Brutalität. (In jungen Jahren Fleischer, später Anatomiediener, zuletzt Mörder von — nachgewiesenermaßen — 16 Frauen, die er sehr „sachgemäß" zerteilte und als Fleisch und Würstchen ausbot. In seiner Behausung hielt er peinlich Ordnung. — Die Aufnahme ist technisch leider nicht gut, aber lehrreich.

Bild 47: Idealer Handtyp. Es sind die schönsten Hände in Bau und Ausdruck. Die Handeignerin ist eine vornehme, feine und kultivierte Natur mit einer guten Einfühlung und Feinspürigkeit (wie die schlanken, langen Finger zeigen). Die leichte Aufwärtsneigung der Fingerspitzen bedeutet Wißbegierde und Großzügigkeit. Diese Naturen sind zwar keine „guten Hausfrauen" in bezug auf Wirtschaftlichkeit, aber sie verstehen es, das Heim wohnlich, anheimelnd und künstlerisch zu gestalten und dem Ehepartner mit ihrem besonders feinen Instinkt beste Hinweise zu geben. Die Form der Nägel weist auf Nierenstörungen hin.

Bild 48: zeigt eine Mischung von einem schlanken eckigen Handtyp mit einem Einschlag zum idealen Typ. In genauer Einteilung: spirituell als Basis, intellektuell als zweite und materiell als dritte Unterteilung. Es ist eine harmonische und darum gute Hand, die als schön zu bezeichnen ist. Da der Daumen nur an der Spitze leicht gebogen ist und sonst gerade und fest, sind damit angezeigt: fester Charakter und geistige Anpassung. Die etwas angedeuteten Mittelknoten der Finger zeigen einen Ordnungssinn an, der nicht überaus kleinlich ist im Selbstordnen, wohl aber solches von anderen verlangt.

Bild 49: zeigt drei Männerhände in der Unterschiedlichkeit von spirituell, intellektuell und materiell — oder erkennen, begründen, ausführen — oder erfinden, berechnen, herstellen usw.

Bild 50: a) Eckig mit Knoten; b) konische weiche Genießerhand, weich und innig, ganz Weib; c) guter schlanker konisch-eckiger Typ einer Künstlerin (Sängerin).

Bild 51 oben: Die Pianistenhand von Liszt (eckig-spatel in Form), daher Virtuosität.

Bild 52: Die Hände des weltbekannten Schriftstellers und Kenners der okkulten Medizin G. W. Surya. Die Handform ist eine Mischung konisch-eckig. Intuitives Erkennen, vernunftmäßiges Erfassen und sachliche Bearbeitung der Probleme und Erkenntnisse. Verfasser von „Okkulte Medizin", 12 Bände, 1922.

Bild 53: Die rechte Hand des bedeutenden Anthropologen, Sprachen- und Religionsforschers, Cisterzienserpriesters Dr. Jörg Lanz v. Liebenfels. Handtyp eckig mit leicht konischem Einschlag, geistig und auch praktisch, gut geformter Daumen, 1937.

Bild 54 links: Die Hand des bedeutenden schwedischen Kunst- und Bild- nismalers Ivar Kamke. 1930. Handtyp konisch-eckig mit leichter Knoten- bildung in den mittleren Fingergliedern.

Rechts: Die gemischte Hand eines weitgereisten Wissenschaftlers, 1930. Handtyp gemischt: Zeigefinger und kleiner Finger konisch, Mittelfinger eckig, Ringfinger spatelförmig. Eine feste kräftige Hand mit feiner Haut, geradem, kräftigem Daumen ohne Biegung. Mischung spirituell-materiell (geistig-seelisch und körperlich harmonisiert).

Bild 55: Die Hände des deutschen Kunstmalers Professor Fahrenkroog. 1927. Handtyp schmal eckig mit leichter Bildung der Mittelknoten und kräftigem, etwas biegsamem Daumen.

Bild 56: Die rechte Innenhand des bekannten indischen Philosophen, Yogalehrers und Schriftstellers Swami Vivekananda.

Bild 57: Die rechte Innenhand der ehemaligen Präsidentin der Theo- sophischen Gesellschaft Anni Besant. Schmaler knotiger Handtyp, über- mäßiger Linienreichtum; zersplitterte intellektuelle Kopflinie in Verbin- dung damit zeigt seelische Disharmonien in hohem Grade. Rissige Herz- linie verstärkt noch.

Bild 58: Die rechte Innenhand der weltbekannten Schauspielerin Sarah Bernhard. Handtyp schmal und konisch. Gerader fester Daumen. Man beachte die lange Apollolinie mit der Sonne auf Apolloberg (Berühmtheit); die Saturnlinie entspringt im Handgelenk (der Lebensweg wird aus eigener Kraft gestaltet); Einflußlinie vom oberen Mondberg zum Saturnberg mit Kreuz für Katastrophe des Körpers (Unfall auf einer Fahrt und Verlust eines Beines dadurch); scharfer Querstrich schneidet die Lebenslinie im 80. Lebensjahr (ihr Ableben).

Bild 59: Die linke Hand der berühmten Opernsängerin Geraldine Farrar, 1904. Saturn-, Apollo- und Merkurlinien beginnen im Venusberg in dieser guten konischen Hand. (Aufstieg durch das andere Geschlecht). Drei gute Raszetteringe weisen auf ein hohes Alter. Der spitze, aber gerade Daumen zeigt eine einfühlende und eigenwillige Persönlichkeit mit guter Durch- setzungskraft.

Bild 60: Die eckig-konische Hand einer begabten Sängerin, 1920. Die Finger besonders auch ihr erstes Glied sind etwas kurz; daher eine mehr verstandesmäßige und materielle Einstellung. Grübchen weisen auf viel Zärtlichkeitsbedürfnis; der steife, unbiegsame und etwas kurze Daumen zeigt Eigenwilligkeit, Mangel an Anpassung und Energie. Hier muß Eigen- willigkeit die fehlende Energie ersetzen. Zarte Haut: lange Jugendlichkeit und großes Feingefühl.

Bild 61: Handbild von Strindberg, dem weltbekannten Schriftsteller. Man beachte die typische Kopflinie für Depressionen und Schwermutten- denz. Der Daumen ist sehr lang und kräftig: Energie und Zähigkeit; Eigenwilligkeit und wenig Anpassung (entsprechend seinem geistigen Niveau). Der starke Jupiterberg weist auf Ehrgeiz. Der Handtyp ist sehr ähnlich dem von Bild 54, rechts.

Bild 62 (links): Die in ihrer Proportion sehr gut ausgeglichene Hand des Schriftstellers Mac Manus.

Rechts: Die sehr disharmonische und materielle Hand des Malers Eugen Carriere. Die Fingerlängen im Verhältnis zum Handteller sehr kurz, der Daumen sehr tief angesetzt. Die unteren Fingerglieder verdickt, die Hand fleischig: Bequemlichkeit, materieller Schlemmer, ungeistig, lasch.

Bild 63 (links): Handbild des Schriftstellers Emile Zola. Eine konische, fleischige Genießerhand mit nach aufwärts gerichteten Fingerspitzen. Durch die intellektuelle Kopflinie als Gemüts- und Empfindungsmensch disharmonisch. Rechts: Handbild (und Handhaltung!) des Staatsmannes Clemenceau. Man beachte die doppelte Kopflinie und den starren kraftvollen Daumen!

Bild 64: Das Handbild des britischen Staatsmannes Gladstone. Ein klarer guter Handabdruck, wie er für Studien und für Fernbegutachtung sein muß! Handtyp geistig, knotig, mit kraftvollem, etwas biegsamem knotigem Daumen. Eine besonders gute und auch feine Hand mit guten, klaren Linien. Studienhand.

Bild 65: zeigt die außerordentlich linienreichen Hände einer 24jährigen Stenotypistin. Dieser in seiner Reichhaltigkeit interessante und klare Abdruck sei hier als ein — auch für einen Könner — komplizierter Fall zum Studium und Üben beigegeben. Ein Photo der Handform, die der Umrandung ziemlich genau entspricht, konnte leider nicht beigebracht werden.

Bildtafeln 66 bis 73: bieten Gelegenheit für Studien und Übungen zur Charakterisierung von Hand-F o r m e n. Es ist dem Studierenden zu empfehlen, von jeder dieser Handformen eine Charakteristik auszuarbeiten. Das wird ihm mit der Zeit und bei fleißiger Übung die nötige Sicherheit geben, genaue und reichhaltige Analysen zu fertigen. In diesen Fällen fällt allerdings die Betrachtung der Kopflinie fort, was zu Fehlern Veranlassung geben kann. Dennoch sind diese Übungen sehr wichtig. Als Beispiel wähle ich das Handbild Tafel 70 A, die Hand eines bedeutenden Reform-Arztes:

Diese gemischte Männerhand setzt sich aus dem konischen und dem eckigen Typ zusammen. Daher ist der Handeigner eine Persönlichkeit, die viel Genauigkeit und Gründlichkeit besitzt, was aber durch den konischen Einschlag nie zur Pedanterie ausartet. Er wird eher oft großzügig, schwunghaft, aber auch etwas Stimmungsmensch sein.

Treibt die erstgenannte Veranlagung zu Tätigkeit und gewisser Rastlosigkeit, so die andere zu Gemächlichkeit und Ruhe des Körpers, nicht aber zu Ruhe der Gedanken. Die zarte Haut zeugt von Einfühlung, Empfindungsfähigkeit, langer Jugendlichkeit, körperlich und auch im Temperament.

Da auch der Daumen gute und starke Form (Persönlichkeit) zeigt, wird sich der Handeigner in jeder Richtung durchzusetzen wissen und dies mit kraftvoller Betonung unterstreichen, worauf die kraftvolle Handform im ganzen und der Ausdruck des Daumens und der Finger im einzelnen hinweisen.

Die hier in der Länge stärker ausgebildeten mittleren und unteren Glieder des Zeige-, Mittel- und Ringfingers zeigen an, daß diese Persönlichkeit besondere Begabungen für mehrere Berufe besitzt: Der Zeigefinger, konisch mit eckigem Einschlag (Mystik) und langem 3. Glied, als Geistlicher. Sinn und Liebe für Natur und einfühlende Naturwissenschaft sind hierdurch ebenfalls betont.

Der Mittelfinger, mehr eckig und mit langem 3. Glied: Verantwortungsfreudigkeit, Gewissenhaftigkeit, ausgeprägtes Gerechtigkeitsgefühl und Betätigung praktischer Art in Richtung Landwirtschaft und leichterer körperlicher Sport.

Der Ringfinger, leicht konisch und mit leiser Andeutung für Spatelform, langes 3. Glied: gute Intuition in jeder Richtung, Gedanken für praktische Dinge und Vorausschau, Begabung für Kunst (Musik) und Literatur.

Der kleine Finger zeigt Rednergabe an; das 1. Glied lang und konisch weist nochmals auf Intuition, gewählte Ausdrucksart, Sinn für spirituelle Studien.

Der untere Teil der Hand ist fleischig und voll, kräftig. Dies zeigt eine stabile körperliche Widerstandskraft, gute, gesunde Erbmasse, starken Magnetismus und eine besonders freudige Genußfähigkeit, sowie Lebensbejahung.

Es ist somit die Hand eines verläßlichen, gütigen, vielseitig begabten und anziehenden Mannes mit inneren Werten. Da er, wie oben bemerkt, auch sehr religiös ist, kann er nur Natur- und Priesterarzt sein. Begabung für Chirurgie sei nebenbei bemerkt.

Bild 66 A zeigt eine Photoaufnahme mit Selbstbelichtung durch Auflegen der Hand auf die Platte im dunklen Raum. Die Ausstrahlungen, besonders der Finger, zeigen den menschlichen Magnetismus, die Strahlkraft der Aura, die nicht nur den Fingern, sondern dem ganzen Körper eigen ist.

Etwas über medizinische Hand-Diagnostik.

Da a l l e physischen Geschehnisse primär geistige und sekundär psychische Ursachen haben, ist es selbstverständlich, daß sich Dispositionen zu körperlichen und seelischen Leiden lange vor Erscheinen (Auswirken) zumeist auch körperlich irgendwie bemerkbar machen. Es ist jedoch ein Irrtum zu glauben, daß bei einem im Werden begriffenen oder vorhandenen Leiden sich auch gleichzeitig Schmerzen bemerkbar machen müssen. Wie oft kommt es vor, daß jemand gar nicht weiß, daß er z. B. ein Magengeschwür hat. Wenn man ihn aber an den hierfür in Betracht kommenden Schmerzzentren der Bauchdecke berühren würde, dann würde er Unbehagen oder Schmerzen fühlen. So ist es auch mit vielen anderen Leiden. J e d e r Mensch bringt schon bei der Geburt Dispositionen zu bestimmten Leiden mit. Sie können ererbt oder auch angeboren sein; später kommen evtl. erworbene noch hinzu. Und diese Dispositionen lassen sich teilweise schon rein äußerlich erkennen durch die Konstitutions-Typologie, die Merkmale der Vorder-, Rücken-, Seitenbelastung (Kuhne), durch Haltung, Gang usw. Erbliche Belastungen lassen sich z. T. im Gesicht, am Ausdruck der Augen, an Ohren, Hasenscharte u. a. erkennen. Nicht nur da, sondern auch in den Händen! Erkennt man in der Iris den augenblicklichen Zustand von Gesundheit und Krankheit, so in den Händen mehr die Dispositionen, sowie erbliche Belastungen, was prophylaktisch von besonderem Wert ist; denn Vorbeugen ist immer besser als Kurieren! Gerade die Möglichkeit, die die Handdiagnostik durch ihre zuverlässigen objektiven Merkmale zur Verhütung von Erbkrankheiten bietet, hebt sie über andere Methoden hinaus. Als Forscher und Schöpfer dieses Spezialgebietes (seit 1905) fand ich bisher etwa 150 medizinisch-diagnostische Merkmale, davon allein 42 Merkmale an den Fingernägeln. Diese handdiagnostischen Merkmale werden bereits von einer sehr beachtlichen und ständig wachsenden Zahl von Ärzten und Heilpraktikern in ihrer Praxis mit allerbestem Erfolg verwendet.

Um Wiederholungen zu vermeiden, verweise ich auf mein Werk (das erste dieser Art überhaupt) „M e d i z i n i s c h e H a n d - u n d N a g e l - D i a g n o s t i k", 5. Aufl., mit Vorwort von Dr. med. R. Steintel und im besonderen auf die darin ebenfalls erstmalig veröffentlichten Kapitel „Seelenheilkunde und Handdiagnostik" und „Merkmale zur Verhütung von Erbkrankheiten".

Chirosophie und Astrologie.

Jede Religion unter der Sonne hat eine astrologische Grundlage, und jede Wissenschaft, die der menschliche Geist zu bearbeiten fähig ist, nimmt ihren Usprung von den Sternenhimmeln Uranias. Dahin kehrt sie zurück, darin versinkt sie wieder.

„Alles ist geordnet nach Maß, Zahl und Gewicht, und die Gesetze sind ohne Wandel!"

Es besteht kein Zweifel, daß die Ergebnisse und Bedeutungen, die auf Grund astrologischer Berechnungen und chiromantischer (erfahrungsmäßiger) Ausdeutungen und Messungen gewonnen werden, sich vollkommen decken. Es kommt hier nur auf das Wissen des Betreffenden an. Ich habe sehr viel Gelegenheit gehabt und genutzt, Horoskope und Chiroskope zu vergleichen; ich tue es oft heute noch, soweit es meine Zeit erlaubt. Charakter, Talente, Fähigkeiten, Neigungen, Ereignisse, alles deckt sich übereinstimmend, auch die Krankheitsanlagen und -erscheinungen. Besonders dies letzte dürfte viele interessieren, die sich mit Heilkunde beschäftigen. Auf die Krankheitsdiagnosen auf astrologischer Grundlage kann ich hier nicht weiter eingehen und verweise die Interessenten auf die hervorragende Arbeit von G. W. Surya, Bd. 4 der „Okkulten Medizin" (Verlag Karl Rohm, Lorch/Württbg.), sowie auf das grundlegende Werk des Wiener Arztes Feerhow „Medizinische Astrologie". Gewiß gibt es noch vieles, was in der Chiromantie heute noch nicht ganz wiedergefunden worden ist in bezug auf manche Ereignisse, da ein vielhundertfaches Nachprüfen außerordentlich schwierig ist. Warum ist das so? — Weil sehr viele Menschen nicht wissen, ob dieses oder jenes Leiden, Ereignis usw. bei den Voreltern vorgelegen hat. Andere Dinge, die augenblicklich zu bestätigen wären, werden oft aus Prüderie, Verschlossenheit u.dgl. nicht eingestanden, obgleich man weiß, daß es so und nicht anders ist. Doch mit der Zeit wird das besser werden. Das Wissen der alten Weisen ist immer noch vorhanden, es ist nicht verloren; an uns liegt es, es wieder zu finden. Es gibt — wenn auch sehr selten — hier und da in den verschiedenen Ländern Menschen, die noch etwas über die Astro-Chiromantie wissen, auf deren Basis sich auch Ereignisse auf kleinere Zeitperioden als Jahre, also auf Monate und Wochen berechnen lassen, ja selbst auf Tage. Leider erfährt man zu wenig davon. In diese verfeinerte Wissenschaft einzudringen, ist sehr schwer; die Studien sind sehr langwierig. Aber die Möglichkeit besteht, das habe ich praktisch erlebt.

Kunstbildhauer W. Th. Wulff, Hamburg, ist auf d i e s e m Gebiete der Astro-Chiromantie erfahren, sowohl durch Begabung intellektueller und spiritueller Art, als auch durch Studien in Anatomie usw. und nicht zuletzt dadurch, daß i h m sehr alte und äußerst seltene Schriften zugänglich waren, von denen die allermeisten Astrologen nicht die geringste Ahnung haben, und in denen andeutungsweise sehr wertvolle Hinweise vorhanden sind, die wiederum nur von jenen verstanden werden können, welche schon ein tiefes Wissen in verschiedenen Richtungen besitzen. Wulff war so gütig, mir seine „Tierkreisverteilung in der Hand" zur Veröffentlichung zur Verfügung zu stellen. Bild 76 zeigt diese Einteilung, und ich habe sie für diejenigen zur besseren Anschauung hier beigefügt, welche mich verschiedentlich gelegentlich meiner Vorträge und Kurse danach fragten. Da ich die Astrologie nicht ganz beherrsche, habe ich in der Astro-Chiromantie bis jetzt zu wenig Erfahrung.

Für die Kundigen der Astrologie gebe ich nachstehend eine Gegenüberstellung zum Vergleich. Obgleich sich bei der Astrologie ein kleiner Mangel zeigt, ist ihr großer Wert durchaus nicht zu unterschätzen. Alle unsere heutigen Wissenschaften sind sehr mangel- und lückenhaft, und man arbeitet auf jedem Gebiet weiter auf Vervollkommnung hin, wenn auch nicht immer in richtiger Weise. Wenn die Menschen selbst erst reiner vom Materialismus und Intellektualismus und deshalb vollkommener sind, wird es auch die Wissenschaft sein. Der Grund liegt also nicht in der Lehre, sondern im Menschen selbst.

Eine Beurteilung des vorhandenen Maßes des Willens, seiner Stärke und Zähigkeit ist bis heute astrologisch nicht gelungen. Es läßt sich die Veranlagung nach dieser Richtung wohl erkennen, nicht aber die Entwicklung, wie man sie aus Form und Ausdruck des Daumens erkennen kann. Gewiß, der gewöhnliche Mensch hat keine Willensfreiheit, sondern nur Wahlfreiheit, doch sind das Maß und die Zähigkeit des Willens, der Energie immer die Hauptsache bei allen Handlungen und Unternehmen. Wer in der Zähigkeit bei der Verfolgung seiner Pläne und Ziele nachläßt, stellt den Erfolg in Frage.

Ebenso ist es mit der Verstandes- und Gedankenrichtung, beides Dinge, die am Daumen und an der Kopflinie zu erkennen und zu beurteilen sind. Einige Astrologen bestreiten die Wirkungen der Planeten Uranus und Neptun. Dessenungeachtet kann man aber die

Wirkung ihrer ihnen entsprechenden Eigenschaften deutlich — und mitunter recht drastisch — wahrnehmen nach dem Horoskop sowohl als auch nach der Hand. Warum auch nicht? Ihre Kraft- und Lichtausstrahlungen sind dieselben wie die der anderen Planeten, und eine genaue Grenze der Kraftwirkungen aufzustellen, erscheint mir beschränkt und anmaßend; gibt es doch andere Körper und Körperkomplexe im Kosmos, die in derselben Entfernung auch ihre Wirkung haben. Auch hier kann man wieder vergleichen mit der drahtlosen Telegraphie.

Chirosophie:	Astrologie:
1. Größe der Willenskraft.	1. „Stern in der eigenen Brust". (Ererbte Rassen-, Körper- und Geistesmerkmale.)
2.⎫ Einfluß ⎧(spirituellen) ⎫ Welt. 3.⎬ der kabba- ⎨(intellektuellen)⎬ 4.⎭ listischen ⎩(materiellen) ⎭	2. fehlt. 3. fehlt. 4. fehlt.
5. Einfluß von Jupiter	5. Jupiter.
6. „ „ Saturn ⎫	6. Saturn.
7. „ „ Sonne ⎪ Erste	7. Sonne.
8. „ „ Merkur ⎬ Reihe der	8. Merkur.
9. „ „ Mars ⎪ Kräfte.	9. Mars.
10. „ „ Mond ⎪	10. Mond.
11. „ „ Venus ⎭	11. Venus.
12. „ „ Uranus ⎫ Zweite	12. Uranus.
13. „ „ Neptun ⎬ Reihe der	13. Neptun.
14. „ „ E. (Isis) ⎭ Kräfte.	14. (Pluto oder Isis?)
15. Die Hauptlinien. Karma.	15. Durch Planetenstand zur Geburtszeit am Geburtsort (Radixaszendent). Saturn!
16. Nebenlinien und Siegel.	16. Tierkreiseinfluß und Verhältnis von Planeten zu Fixsternen.
17. Die Farbe der Haut.	17. Einfluß für Temperament.
18. Zeichen und Nebenmerkmale.	18. Fortschreiten der Planetenstände, Transite.
19. Rasse, Art, Geschlecht*).	19. fehlt.
20. Grad d. spirituell. Bewußtseins.	20. Feuer- und Luftzeichen.
21. Lebensdauer.	

Wenn die Entfernung zwischen zwei Stationen zu groß ist, um Wirkungen und Resultate zu erzielen, wird eine dritte Station dazwischengebaut. Wissen wir denn, ob im großen Universum nicht auch solche Zwischenstationen vorhanden und wirkend sind? Ein Weltall, das so wundervoll gesetzmäßig bis ins kleinste arbeitet — ich erinnere hier nur an das Karmagesetz, das Vererbungsgesetz und die Periodengesetzmäßigkeit großer Ereignisse im Leben der Völker wie des einzelnen —, sollte Dinge, die oft über unseren beschränkten Verstand hinausgehen, nicht betätigen? Das zu bestreiten, überlasse ich jenen,

---

*) Da dies aus einem Horoskop nicht ersichtlich, ist es für den Astrologen erforderlich, ein Lichtbild von dem zu sehen, dessen Horoskop berechnet werden soll. Ein gewissenhafter Astrologe wird auch die Handschrift verlangen, um daran den erreichten Stand der Entwicklung zu erkennen. Daher sind Schrift und Lichtbild erforderlich. Das muß beachtet werden!

die ihren mitunter recht unschöpferischen Verstand als die höchste intellektuelle Instanz des unermeßlichen Weltalls betrachten und anmaßend genug sind, behaupten zu wollen, daß einzig und allein auf unserem kleinen Weltkörper Menschen vorhanden seien. Die Grundzüge des Lebensweges sind jedem Menschen vorbestimmt. Dies erkennt man sowohl am Geburtshoroskop wie auch an der Formation der Hauptlinien der Hand. Solche durch kosmische Gesetze festgelegten Grundzüge des Lebensweges — und somit Schicksals — sind weder durch den Willen noch durch die Wahlfreiheit zu ändern; sie sind das konzentrierte Programm, das w i r s e l b s t im vergangenen Lebenszyklus schufen, indem wir die Resultate früherer Ursachen auslebten, die jedoch neue Ursachen in sich trugen und sich nun wieder auslösen müssen. — W i e sie sich auslösen und in Erscheinung treten, das zeigen uns — wie im Horoskop die Direktionen und die Transite — in der Hand die Nebenlinien und Ereignislinien, anderseits die Zeichen. Je feiner ein Instrument gebaut ist — z. B. Seismograph, Chronometer u. dgl. —, desto genauer zeigt es an. So ist es auch mit dem Menschen. Je feiner seine Seelenschwingungen und deshalb auch seine Nerven, desto zahlreicher, feiner und klarer zeigen sich die Linien in seiner Hand, weshalb man bei solchen Personen, die einen spirituellen Einschlag haben, m e h r lesen und erkennen, also auch m e h r ausdeuten kann, als bei einem primitiven, materiellen oder unschöpferisch intellektuellen Menschen. Daß die Astrologie von heute vollkommen ist, hat keiner behaupet; ebensowenig kann man das von der Chiromantie sagen. Aber das angesammelte Material aller Geisteswissenschaften ist derart reich, daß man auf dem besten Wege zur Vollkommenheit ist. Anderseits ist es aber gut so; denn gerade in der heutigen Zeit beweisen die Menschen in ihrer Lebensart und Weltauffassung, daß sie wirklich weder reif noch wert sind, das ganze Wissen zu besitzen. Es ist eine sehr weise göttliche Vorsicht, daß nur e i n z e l n e M e n s c h e n (nicht Leute!) — immer ihrem i n n e r e n Wert entsprechend! — tiefe Erkenntnis und darum tiefes Wissen erlangen. Für die Beurteilung von Fähigkeiten und Talenten zur Berufswahl ist es ziemlich einerlei, ob dies auf astrologischer, graphologischer, chirognomischer oder phrenologischer Basis erfolgt. Bei der phrenologischen Leseart kann man sehr gut die Fähigkeiten und Anlagen, nicht aber die Hindernisse erkennen, die sich durch Verhältnisse, Umstände usw. ergeben. Alles das kann man aber sehr gut bei der Anwendung der Astrologie und der Handkunde ersehen. Bei der Astrologie langsamer, wegen der Berechnungen; bei der Handkunde s o f o r t, weil alles klar vor Augen liegt. Natürlich müssen alle Analysen übereinstimmen. Sie tun es auch, wenn wirkliches Können

vorhanden ist. Alle vier Wissenschaften von einer Person beruflich ausgeübt, ergeben nur bei allerbester Begabung keine Zersplitterung, weil
jede dieser Wissenschaften ein sehr weites Feld ist, viel Gewissenhaftigkeit und Verstand, aber auch Verantwortlichkeit erfordert, dazu ein
sehr gutes Gedächtnis.

Im Interesse des einzelnen Menschen und des Allgemeinwohls wäre
es wünschenswert und richtig, wenn jeder sich betreffs seiner Fähigkeiten und Anlagen durch diese Wissenschaften informieren ließe. Jeder
würde dann den für ihn richtigen Beruf (entsprechend seinen Fähigkeiten) wählen und nicht erst einen verkehrten nach dem anderen, um
nach vielen sorgenvollen Enttäuschungen durch Unfähigkeit nochmals
einen verkehrten, oder wenn es gut geht, endlich den rechten Beruf
zu ergreifen.

Zur Vervollkommnung des tieferen Studiums der astralen Einflüsse
auf den Menschen und die Hand bringe ich in folgendem die r e i n e n
speziellen Einflüsse der einzelnen Planeten. Jeder der dabei beschrie-
benen Menschentypen stellt den reinen Typ dar, d. h. einen Men-
schentyp, der von dem einen Planeten den g a n z e n Einfluß hat, —
ohne andere starke Einflußmischung.

Bei der Beurteilung einer „Personenlinie" oder „Personeneinfluß-
linie" hat man genau, sehr genau zu beachten, von welchem „Berge"
(Planeten) diese Linie kommt. Sie ist in den allermeisten Fällen nur
haarfein gezeichnet; deshalb braucht sie auch nur sehr kurze Zeit, um
in Erscheinung zu treten oder zu verschwinden. Ist sie nur in oder
durch einen Berg gehend: dann kommt ein Personeneinfluß dieses
Planeten (Menschentyps) in Frage. Verläuft die Einflußlinie jedoch im
Anfang zwischen zwei Bergen, so kommt ein Personentyp in Frage,
welcher die gemischten Eigenschaften und das Aussehen hat, das sich
aus der Mischung der beiden betreffenden Planetencharaktere ergibt . . .
D i e s e Art des Ausdeutens — des Lesens der Handlinien — ist sehr
schwer, und man muß wirklich schon ein großes Wissen und sehr viel
Praxis haben, um sich hierin zurechtzufinden. Man muß sich sozusagen
in die Hand hineinleben und sich sehr stark konzentrieren, was nicht
jedem gelingt. Ein sehr geübtes Auge, eine gute starke Lupe und gutes
Licht sind hierfür unbedingt notwendig. Aus diesen Gründen ist
d i e s e Art der Deutung nicht mehr wissenschaftlich zu nennen, soweit
sie eben d i e s e n Teil betrifft. — Sie ist ein Hilfsmittel, wie es jede
Wissenschaft hat, das von Nichtkennern und Pfuschern benutzt, die
wissenschaftliche Chirologie nur in bösen Ruf bringen kann. Ich warne
deshalb sehr zur Vorsicht und empfehle die Benutzung dieses Teiles
nur den weit fortgeschrittenen Chirologen für Studien und Weiter-
bildung.

Planeten-Menschentypen.

1. Die Signaturen der Venus (Bild 77).*)

Figur: die unter dem Venuseinfluß geborenen Menschen haben eine
große physische und moralische Ähnlichkeit mit jenen, die unter dem
Jupitereinfluß geboren sind; nur ist die Schönheit der Venusgeborenen
mehr weiblich. Sie haben schöne, helle, weiche und rosige Haut, sind
von gutem Wuchs und schöner Figur. Ihre Haare sind lang, dicht, geschmeidig, blond oder braun und dauerhaft in der Farbe. Die Augenbrauen sind schön, gutgeformt und dicht. Ihre Stirn ist rund, eher
klein als groß; die Wangen sind rundlich und mit Grübchen versehen.
Die Gesichtsknochen sind kaum bemerkbar. Die Nase ist gerade,
etwas fleischig und doch schön oder fein. Ihre Augen sind groß, freund-
lich, feucht und sehr angenehm durch ihren Ausdruck, hellbraun oder
blau, sehr magnetisch und auch sinnverwirrend, „streichelnd"; die
Augenlider rund und schwer. Ihr Mund ist klein bis mittel, frischrot.
Die Lippen sind voll und schön geschwungen; die Zähne gut. Das
Kinn ist rund, etwas voll und hat ein Grübchen. Die Ohren sind meist
klein, das Ohrläppchen fleischig. Ihr Hals ist weiß, rund und von
mittlerer harmonischer Länge; die Schultern sind rund und voll, ab-
fallend. Die Brust ist meist schmal, doch fleischig; der Busen der
Frauen voll und rund — wie bei der antiken Venus. An den runden
schönen Armen stehen keine Knochen hervor. Die Hüften sind gut
entwickelt, die Lenden wohlgeformt und die Schenkel voll, schlank
und elegant. Die Knie sind ebenfalls voll und etwas nach innen
geneigt, die Beine kräftig, die Waden schöngeformt und die Fesseln
rund und dünn. Die Füße sind klein.

Eigenschaften: Der Venustyp liebt Eleganz und Harmonie in Klei-
dung und Äußerlichkeiten. Er neigt sehr stark zur sexuellen Liebe, da
die Sinnlichkeit eine der stärksten Eigenschaften ist. In der Liebe ist
er gut und sanft, zärtlich und willenlos. Besonders stark ist die Vorliebe für Blumen, Düfte, Musik, Plastik, Farbe und alles Schöne in
Form und Farbe. Der reine Venustyp ist immer Künstler; nicht umgekehrt! Gefallsucht macht sich meist bemerkbar, wenngleich oft nur
ganz leise und diplomatisch. Das träumerische Wesen im Verein mit
der Sinnlichkeit, wird hier oft zum Schaden. Das harmonische und
deshalb verträgliche, gütige Wesen läßt ihn allen mit Wohlwollen
begegnen. Dem Zank und Lärm ist er abgeneigt, da sein Wesen stets
heiter, frohsinnig, humorvoll ist. Venus gibt dem Menschen weibliche

---

*) Zum Studium der Charakteristik der Planetentypen empfehle ich das vorzügliche Werk
von Stein: „Charaktertypen". (Aszendenten-Typen!) Die Kopfzeichnungen der Planetentypen sind dem großen Werk von Carl Huter: „Physiognomik" mit Erlaubnis entlehnt, in
dem sie als Farbentypen gebracht wurden.

Formen und daher auch weibliche Neigungen. Männer dieses Typs tragen gern Frauenschmuck.

Der Venuseinfluß begabt Künstler, Redner, Komponisten usw., durch das Dargebrachte zu rühren, oder „Seele" in die Musik, in die Malerei, in die Skulptur, in die Rede zu legen; also das tiefe vibrierende Schwingen der Seele. Es gibt keinen Künstler, der nicht starken Venuseinfluß hätte. Gibt es dennoch mal einen solchen, so ist das von ihm Dargebrachte nur ein Produkt des Könnens ohne Empfinden, also ein Produkt verstandesmäßiger Imitation. Je mehr Venuseinfluß, desto mehr schöngeistiges Empfinden.

Hände: Die Hände des reinen Venustyps sind voll, etwas weich und mit Grübchen versehen (Oberhand). Die Finger sind glatt, von normaler Länge oder ein wenig kürzer. Die Haut ist weißlich bis weißrosa. Der Daumen ist etwas kurz, der Venusberg sehr voll und stark und reichlich mit Linien versehen.

Venus regiert die Nieren, das Seelische, die Erotik. Metall: Kupfer; Farben: hellgrün, hellblau, rosa; Stein: Achat. (Typ Mozart.)

2. Die Signaturen des Jupiter (Bild 77).

Figur: Menschen, die unter dem ganzen Einfluß des Jupiter geboren sind, haben folgende Merkmale: Die Figur ist groß und stark, manchmal auch etwas über mittelgroß. Die Haut ist hell und farbenfrisch, guter Teint, ihre Stimme ist klar. Sie haben große, feuchte, freundliche Augen, blau oder hellbraun; lange Augenwimpern. Die Augenbrauen sind etwas gelockt und dicht. Die Nase ist mittelgroß und gerade, der Mund ziemlich groß; die Lippen sind stark. Die Oberlippe ist meist etwas überragend. Die Zähne sind groß und gut; die Backen derb und fleischig; das Kinn ist etwas lang und voll. Ihre Ohren sind etwas anliegend, der Hals ist wohl proportioniert. Die Schultern sind groß und fleischig; der Rücken ist fest und dick. Im Alter neigen sie zu Fettleibigkeit und zu Haarverlust. Füße und Hände sind dick und ziemlich fest, die Beine behaart. Kopf und Stirn schwitzen leicht.

Eigenschaften: Ihr Gang ist gelassen, ruhig. Sie lieben das Bequeme, die Vergnügungen, Feste und Gastmähler. Sie haben religiöses Empfinden (Zeremonien, wenn möglich mit Pomp); Familiensinn, großes Selbstvertrauen; sie sind anziehend, sehr sympathisch, stolz, großzügig, ehrgeizig und tüchtig. Auch sind sie lebhaft, zeitweise zornig aufbrausend, aber nicht nachtragend. Sie lieben die Ruhe und den Frieden; sind höflich, gütig, edelherzig, leichtsinnig im guten Sinne, gefällig, beliebt und sinnlich. Im allgemeinen ist ihr Leben glücklich (weil sie schon im Gedankenleben darauf hinarbeiten). (Jupitertyp sind: Albr. Dürer, Friedrich III.)

Jupiter regiert Blut, Leber. Metall: Zink; Farben: purpur, blau; Stein: Saphir, Türkis, Lapis.

3. Die Signaturen des Saturn (Bild 77).

Figur: mittelgroß oder klein. Die Haut ist bräunlich, erdfarbig, mitunter blaß, trocken und runzelt leicht. Das Haar ist schwarz, glatt und grob, fällt aber meist früh aus oder lichtet sich. Der Kopf ist lang (nur bei bestimmten Rassen mehr rund). Die Augen sind sehr dunkel, hohl, traurig und verdunkelt, jedoch durchdringend und listig bei Verdacht, Argwohn oder Zorn. Das Weiße des Augapfels ist mehr gelblich, die Augenbrauen sind schwarz, evtl. über der Nase zusammengewachsen. Die Ohren sind groß, die Nase ist mittel oder lang, mit der Spitze mehr oder weniger abwärts geneigt. Die Nasenlöcher sind mittel bis groß. Der Mund ist groß, die Lippen sind dünn — bei bestimmten Rassen wulstig oder wurstähnlich —, wobei sich die Unterlippe etwas nach vorn schiebt oder sich über die Oberlippe hebt. Die Zähne sind in der Jugend gut, meist weißlich und zuweilen doppelt, verderben aber schnell. Das Zahnfleisch ist blaß. Der Bart ist schwarz; das Kinn lang, unten breit und vorspringend. Der Hals ist hager, zuweilen dünn, mit starken Muskeln und ausgeprägten Adern. Der „Adamsapfel" ist bei diesem Typ sehr stark und deutlich. Im allgemeinen sind diese Menschen mager, haben aber starke Knochen. Die Brust ist schmal und behaart, die Schultern sind hoch; die Arme knochig und muskulös.

Hände: Die Hände sind oft mager, die Finger lang und zum Teil knotig. Der Saturnfinger hat Spatelform. Der Daumen ist meist stark und groß. — Die Adern der Füße sind stark sichtbar, und die Neigung zu Krampfadern ist ausgesprochen. Die Beine werden frühzeitig schwach und im Alter träge, daher meist der gebeugte Körper und unsichere Gang, was diese Menschen prädisponiert, Unfälle des Körpers zu erleiden, besonders aber der Beine. Man findet unter diesem Typ viele Rheumatiker, Gelähmte und Hinkende, Bucklige und Krüppel. Auch Taubheit ist ein Einfluß des Saturn.

Eigenschaften: Saturnbeeinflußte Menschen sind stark melancholisch, neugierig, innerlich unruhig, mißtrauisch, grübelnd. Sie lieben die Einsamkeit, das Spielen aus Gewinnsucht und Kombinationslust. Sie sind tüchtig im Berg- und Ackerbau, in Wissenschaft, Musik, sind sehr arbeitsam und meist geizig, weniger vergnügungssüchtig. In der Musik leisten sie bisweilen Großes. (Saturntypen sind: Paganini, Mephisto.)

Der echte Saturnier verbringt meist einen Teil seines Lebens in Abgeschiedenheit, Einsamkeit, im Gefängnis usw., da dieser Einfluß oft zu Schlechtigkeiten geneigt macht.

Saturn regiert die Knochen, Milz. Metall: Blei; Farben: schwarz, Dunkelgrün, braun; Stein: Onyx, Smaragd.

4. Die Signaturen der Sonne (Apollo) (Bild 77).

Figur: Mittlerer Wuchs und glatte Körperproportionen. Die Farbe der Haut ist gesund, leicht bräunlich. Die Haare sind lang, voll, wellig, geschmeidig, fein blond oder braun. Die Stirn ist mittelhoch, gewölbt; die Augen sind groß, glänzend, etwas feucht; das Weiße ist rein und klar. Der Augenausdruck ist streng und sanft zugleich und die Irisfarbe hellbraun oder blau, die Wimpern sind voll und geschwungen. Die Brauen sind dicht und glatt, sanft gewölbt. Die Wangen fleischig und fest; die Nase ist gerade und fein, jedoch nicht scharf. Der Mund ist von mittlerer Größe, die Lippen sind von normaler, gleichmäßiger Fülle. Die Zähne sind gut und etwas gelblich. Die Stimme ist stark, angenehm und voll, wohlklingend. Das Kinn ist rund und etwas hervorstehend. Die Ohren haben mittlere Größe — eher klein als groß; das Ohrläppchen ist fleischig und von guter Farbe. Der Hals ist mittelstark, muskulös, ohne daß die Muskelformen hervortreten. Der Körper ist unbehaart. Die Brust ist groß und stark, gewölbt. Die Sehnen der Glieder sind dünn und kräftig, die Schenkel von eleganter Form, die Beine schön. Das Sehvermögen ist leicht der Schwäche, Augen und Beine einem Leiden ausgesetzt.

Eigenschaften: Die von der Sonne stark beeinflußten Menschen sind angenehm, weil natürlich und ungezwungen; immer sympathisch und magnetisch, bescheiden, strebsam, verläßlich. Sie sind beliebt und gute, treue Freunde durch ihre aufrichtige Gesinnung. Sie sind etwas heftig, jedoch sofort wieder ruhig, sehr liebenswürdig und haben angeborene Höflichkeit und Herzenstakt; ein heiteres, sonniges Wesen, Humor. Sie haben angeborene innere Würde, übervorteilen nie, sind edelherzig und beredsam. Sie besitzen Scharfsichtigkeit durch ihre Intelligenz u n d ihre Intuition, die sie alles richtig erkennen und beurteilen läßt. (Dies ist ihre hervorragendste Eigenschaft.) Sie sind religiös, doch basiert ihre Religion mehr auf der inneren Betrachtung, Verehrung und Erkenntnis, auf der geistigen Idee, dem inneren Sinn und Wert (Esoterik), nicht auf Aberglauben und Orthodoxie. Von der Sinnlichkeit (Erotik) werden sie stark beeinflußt und sind leicht jemandem zugeneigt. Die Sonnebeeinflußten sind Erfinder und Ausübende aller möglichen Unternehmungen, da sie sehr vielseitig sind. Sie erfinden ungezwungen, mehr durch Inspiration, weniger durch besondere Studien, hauptsächlich in der Kunst und Wissenschaft. Sie sind oft Künstler, Literaten; immer aber Kunstliebhaber.

Hände: Der Sonnentyp hat gemischte Finger, leicht knotig; der Daumen ist mittelgroß, stark und harmonisch. Der Knöchel der Unabhängigkeit (zwischen erstem und zweitem Daumenglied) ist gut entwickelt; der Apolloberg gut ausgebildet und mit einer guten Sonnenlinie oder Parallelen durchfurcht.

Die Sonne regiert das Herz, Rückgrat, die Augen, solar plexus; Metall: Gold; Farben: Gold, orange; Stein: Rubin, Karneol.

5. Die Signaturen des Merkur (Bild 78).

Figur: Die unter vollem Merkureinfluße stehenden Menschen sind klein bis mittelgroß, schlank, angenehm. Sie bewahren ziemlich lange ein kindliches Wesen und erscheinen infolgedessen immer jünger, als sie sind. Ihre Hautfarbe ist zart und etwas blaßgelb; die Haare sind braun und zum Kräuseln geneigt. Die Stirn ist hoch und gewölbt, der evtl. Bart kurz und dunkel, die Augenbrauen sind schmal, lang gewölbt. Ihre Augen sind grau oder braun (seltener blau), unruhig, lebhaft, scharf und durchdringend. Das Weiße der Augen ist gelblich und der Gesamtausdruck verschmitzt, klug. Die Nase ist gerade oder leicht gebogen, lang und gut geformt, evtl. scharf, die Spitze etwas rund und oft mit kleinem Grübchen. Ihre Lippen sind dünn; die Oberlippe tritt etwas hervor über die nach außen gesenkte Unterlippe. Das Kinn ist lang und spitz. Der Kopf ist an der Seite oben, wo die Organe des Erwerbssinns liegen, stärker entwickelt, weshalb bei dem Merkurtyp das Talent für Handel und Erwerb stets von Natur aus stark hervortritt. Der Hals ist stark und wohlgeformt, die Brust mittelgroß, fleischig; die Lenden sind wohlgeformt, biegsam; die Arme dünn, jedoch kräftig. Ihre Stimme ist gut, doch nicht sehr stark.

Eigenschaften: Die unter dem Einfluß des Merkur geborenen Menschen sind körperlich und geistig lebhaft, gewandt, geschickt in körperlichen Übungen sowie in Handfertigkeiten. Sie besitzen lebhafte Intelligenz, schnelle Auffassung, sind intuitiv und witzig; alles Eigenschaften, welche List und Schlauheit ergeben. Sie lieben alle Wissenschaften, besonders die okkulten und metaphysischen Studien; sind gewissenhaft in allen Sachen, beharrlich und schätzen das Vergeistigen aller Genüsse. Sie besitzen eine gute und natürliche Beredsamkeit. Man findet unter ihnen Philosophen, Physiker, Ärzte, Sprachlehrer, Geometer, Akrobaten, Tänzer, Händler. Durch ihr schnelles und großes Fassungsvermögen und die schnelle Übersicht, Liebenswürdigkeit und Vielseitigkeit sind sie die „geborenen Geschäftsmenschen". Aber auch Neid ist eine ihrer Eigenschaften. Der schlecht beeinflußte Merkurtyp mißbraucht seine guten Eigenschaften, und deshalb ist dieser Typ — in niederer Entwicklung — sehr gefährlich, beim Manne sowohl wie bei dem Weibe. („Merkur, der Gott der Diebe und Huren", heißt es in der alten Mythologie: ebenso „Hermes" — ein anderer Name für

Merkur —, d. h. der dreifache Meister des Wissens.) Vermöge der ausgezeichneten Rednergabe, Intelligenz und Intuition ist es ihm leicht, Menschen, mit denen er zu tun hat, schnell zu erkennen und sie mit passenden Redensarten und Wortschwall einzuwickeln und zu beeinflussen. Vom Merkur stark beeinflußte Frauen haben dieselben Eigenschaften, und wenn sie nicht auf einer sehr hohen seelischen (ethischen) Entwicklungsstufe stehen, sind sie immer habsüchtig und nützen alle Gelegenheiten, die „etwas einbringen". Sie sind sehr gute „Schauspieler", faszinierend stark, berauschen und sind leidenschaftlich bis in ein hohes Alter. Ebenso wirken sie sinnlich erregend, was für jüngere, unwissende Leute ohne festen Willen, die unter Mond, Venus oder Jupiter geboren sind, gefährlich werden kann.

Hände: Die Hände des Merkurtyps sind lang; bei Frauen klein. Die Finger sind meist glatt und ungleich — gemischt. Der Merkurfinger ist meist spitz oder eckig und lang. Die Hand ist im allgemeinen geschmeidig, der Daumen lang und biegsam.

Merkur regiert die Nerven, die Arme, die Lungen, das Denken; Metall: Quecksilber; Farben: gelb, grau; Stein: Jaspis, Topas, Bergkristall.

6. Die Signaturen des Mars (Bild 78).

Figur: Die unter diesem Einfluß geborenen Menschen sind mittelgroß bis groß, von derbem Wuchs und starker Körperkonstitution. Der Kopf ist kurz und dick, die Stirn niedrig bis mittelhoch. Ihr Gesicht ist rundlich bis breit, die Haut fest, hart, von dunklerem Rot, mitunter rotbräunlich. Die Haare sind kurz, dick und borstig, evtl. kraus; in der Farbe rot, rotblond oder schwarz. Die Augen sind ziemlich groß, glänzend, kühn; ihre Farbe dunkelbraun, grau oder graurötlich bis rostfarben. Das Weiße des Augapfels ist oft gerötet. Der Mund ist groß, die Lippen sind etwas schmal, die Unterlippe ist etwas wulstig. Ihre Augenbrauen sind dicht, meist struppig, und neigen zur Vereinigung über der Nasenwurzel. Ihre kräftige — gerade oder gebogene — Nase macht einen „hervorragenden" Eindruck; die Nasenlöcher sind weit, das Kinn ist hervorspringend. Der Bart ist meist kurz, struppig. Ihre Ohren sind mittelgroß bis groß und etwas abstehend, die Backenknochen etwas hervorstehend. Der Hals ist kurz, dick, muskulös und rot, die Brust breit, die Schultern und der Rücken sind stark, fleischig; die Beine grobknochig und muskulös.

Eigenschaften: Die Marsbeeinflußten sind immer mutwillig, streitsüchtig, rechthaberisch, herrschsüchtig, meist auch brutal und roh. Die Stimme ist stark, laut, etwas metallisch. Sie schreien und befehlen gern, zu Hause wie auch sonst. Sie stellen das kriegerische (und deshalb zumeist das vernichtende) Prinzip dar. Sie können großmütig sein;

doch kommt dies weniger von Herzen als von der Selbstverherrlichung und dem Bewußtsein ihrer Macht (Kraft). Sie sind mutig und kaltblütig in Gefahren, jedoch sehr hitzig im Wortstreit, da sehr reizbar und rabiat bis zum Haß. Sie lieben starke Getränke, Spiel und Orgien. Starke Sinnlichkeit und brutale Kühnheit machen sie bei manchen „Damen" anfangs beliebt; doch die Streitsucht läßt die Harmonie nicht von Dauer sein. Sie essen gern viel und sind Liebhaber des rohen Fleisches und der scharfen Gewürze, renommieren und übertreiben gern. Sie beschäftigen sich gern und vorwiegend mit Dingen, die aus Metall sind oder damit zu tun haben. Deshalb findet man sie auch meist als Fleischer, Soldaten, Chirurgen, Schlosser, Schmiede, Zahnärzte usw. Als Redner haben sie eine derbe, kraftvolle Ausdrucksart, im Gegensatz zu der Feinheit und Gewandtheit der Merkurbeeinflußten.

Hände: Ihre Hände sind fest bis hart; die Finger grob, stark und im dritten Gliede dick (Genußliebe). Das erste Daumenglied ist groß, breit, meist mehr oder weniger Ballenform, keulenartig. Der Mars- oder Venusberg ist stark entwickelt, die Marsebene ist oft mit vielen kleinen Linien und Kreuzen belebt.

Mars regiert die Geschlechtsorgane und die Kraft des Trieblebens, Därme, Galle; Metall: Eisen; Farbe: rot; Stein: Diamant.

7. Die Signaturen des Mondes (ähnlich Bild 77 — Jupiter — aber weicher).

Figur: Die unter dem Mondeinfluße geborenen Menschen haben einen runden Kopf und ein volles, weiches Gesicht. Die Stirn ist nicht hoch, sondern mehr breit und rund. Ihre Hautfarbe ist matt, blaß oder wenig gefärbt. Durchschnittlich sind sie klein bis mittelgroß, dick, fleischig und schwammigweich. Der Körper ist wenig behaart. Die Haare sind fein, weich, lang und blond. Ihre Nase ist etwas kurz, flach und breit. Der Mund ist mittelgroß, die Lippen sind fleischig und stark, die Zähne groß und fehlerhaft. Die Augen sind groß, rund, klar, etwas hervortretend; ihre Farbe ist blau oder blaugrau. Die Augenlider sind ziemlich dick, die Brauen dünn, blond und sehr glatt anliegend. Das Kinn ist dick, voll und fett; die Ohren sind anliegend. Der Hals ist fleischig, dick und weiß. Brust, Hüften, Lenden und Beine sind stark fleischig, aber dabei weich. Es ist stets Neigung und Anlage zur Fettleibigkeit vorhanden. Ihre Füße sind dick und groß.

Eigenschaften: Die Mondbeeinflußten sind unbeständig, unruhig, egoistisch, wenig kriegerisch, deshalb unzuverlässig. Sie sind kalt, matt, faul, gleichgültig und schwerfällig; weniger der ethischen Liebe, mehr aber der Sinnlichkeit und dem Genuß zugeneigt. Sie lieben, in den Tafelfreuden zu schwelgen. Sie trinken und sprechen viel und haben viele weibliche Eigenschaften. Sie sind mehr mystisch als religiös, haben eine große Einbildungskraft, Phantasie und oft gute Intuition, Wahr-träume, Ahnungen, besonders wenn sie in der Einsamkeit leben. Sie lieben Reisen, Wasser und Bequemlichkeiten, die Künste, alles Schöne und romantische Literatur. Sie sind groß im Wortemachen, nicht aber in der Tat. Gute Redner findet man sehr selten unter ihnen. Ihre Unbe-holfenheit und ihr Phlegma lassen sie schnell ermüden, weshalb sie keine guten Fußgänger sind und gern „Station" machen. Es fehlt ihnen an Ausdauer, Zähigkeit und Wollen. Die vom Monde stark beein-flußten Frauen geben sich leicht hin; nicht aus Liebe, sondern mehr aus Neugierde, meist aber aus Mangel an Widerstandskraft. Mondbeein-flußte ziehen immer Leute im gereiften Alter den jüngeren vor.

Hände: Die Hände sind meist weich, fleischig; der Mondberg ist gut entwickelt, die Finger sind glatt, kurz, spitz oder spatelförmig. Der Daumen ist mittelgroß, das erste Glied kurz.

Mond regiert das Wässerige, die Säfte des Körpers, das Gefühlsleben, Stimmungen, Magen, Gehirn; Metall: Silber; Farben: alle hellen und blassen Farben; Stein: Mondstein. Katzenauge, Koralle.

8. Die Signaturen des Uranus (Bild 78).

Die Figur läßt sich nicht ganz genau beschreiben; denn einmal sind Uranustypen nicht alltäglich, zum anderen findet man sie s e h r selten — viel seltener als die anderen Typen — rein, weil wir noch gar nicht die Auswirkungen des Uranus in d e m Maße kennen wie die der anderen Planeten unseres Systems. Das Uranuszeitalter hat erst be-gonnen.

Im Umriß läßt sich aber über das Äußere des Uranustyps soviel sagen: Meist über mittelgroß, vollschlank oder schlank. Haare sind meist dunkelblond oder dunkler, die Augen dunkelblau oder hell-braun, groß, mit scharfem, sicherem Blicke. Die Augenbrauen sind dicht und breit, in der Farbe sehr dunkel oder schwarz; meist aber schwarz, auffällig. (Dies ist das beste Kennzeichen für den starken Einfluß des Planeten.) Die Farbe der Haut ist eher hell als dunkel, das Gesicht markant, die Stirn frei und hoch. Die Nase ebenfalls markant und kräftig. Die Hände sind näher dem intellektuell-spirituellen Typ, wie auf Bild 49. Die Finger konisch-eckig mit Knotenbildung. Die Lippen sind eher schmal als dick. Das Kinn ist gut markiert und stark. — Wenn ein Vergleich hier überhaupt erlaubt ist, könnte man sagen; eine Kombination von Sonne, Merkur, Mars und Venus. Goethe und Para-celsus waren starke Uranustypen, wenn auch keine reinen. Eckige Be-wegung des Körpers.

Eigenschaften: Die stark Uranusbeeinflußten haben vor allem eine sehr gute und schnelle Auffassungsgabe, rasches Begreifen. Sie sind sowohl intellektuell (verstandesmäßig) als auch spirituell (intuitiv-inspirativ) im Denken. Ihre Interessen liegen meist auf Gebieten, die eigenartig und originell sind, und die man als „ausgefallen" bezeichnet. Sie sind gute Erfinder und Techniker, gute Ingenieure und Elektriker, Aviatiker, Altertumsforscher, Antiquitätensammler und -kenner. Im Wesen anfangs reserviert und innerlich beobachtend, vorfühlend, später mehr auf die Dinge eingehend und sie geistig verarbeitend. Sie können sehr plötzlich heftig werden, wie denn überhaupt Plötzlichkeiten Auswirkungen des Uranus sind; Blitz, Explosionen, Kurzschluß.

Zeitweise sieht man Frauen mit feinerem Gesicht und starken, breiten, dunklen Augenbrauen. Diese haben starke Uranuseinwirkung und Uranuscharakteristik. Besonders blonde Frauen mit breiten, schwarzen Brauen. Typ-Leonardo.

Uranus regiert das feinere Nervensystem, die Drüsen, gibt inneres Erkennen der tiefsten Zusammenhänge, Hellsinnigkeit, starke Neigung zu Studien und Beschäftigung mit Okkultismus, im besonderen mit Kosmologie. Metall: Radium, Uran; Farbe: blauviolett, harmonische Farbenkombination bestimmter Art: Blauviolett mit Gold, mit Silber, mit Gelb; Edelstein: Alexandrid, Bernstein, Magnetstein, Scarabäus.

9. Die Signaturen des Neptun („Eros", nach Schopenhauer).

Hierüber läßt sich nur sehr wenig sagen, da seine Schwingungen noch feiner sind als die des Uranus. Infolgedessen läßt sich auch der Neptuntyp in bezug auf die Person nicht gut beschreiben. Einige Merkmale sind: sehr hohe, oben breite Stirn; Haarfarbe verschieden, mittelblond bis dunkel; Augen (bei reinem Typ) stark hellblau, hellblau-grau, groß, klar, strahlend und doch etwas verschleiert; Nase fein und schmal (Jakob Böhme); der Mund gut; mittelvolle Lippen. (Oft bringt dieser Einfluß sehr viele Falten in den oberen Teil des Gesichts.) Neptun beeinflußt die Aura.

Eigenschaften: Meist etwas verworrene Anschauungen und Gedankengänge. Hochgeistiges Schauen. Jedoch — bei gutem Typ — starker künstlerischer Einschlag und starke Medialität. Bei schlechtem Typ — Einfluß — sexuelle Irrwege und Perversität, Liederlichkeit.

Farbe: ultrarot, rotviolett (lila), blasse Farben; Stein: Amethyst.

10. Verbrecher- oder dämonischer Typ.

Er ist auf Bild 78 dargestellt in zwei gänzlich unharmonischen Köpfen. Man erkennt auf den ersten Blick das satanische Prinzip, das sich hier verkörpert hat und sich ausprägt, weshalb ich das entsprechende Symbol beifügte; denn unter einen bestimmten Planeten kommen beide Typen nicht! Sieht man ein solches Gesicht, einen solchen Kopf, mit d e r Plastik, dann weiß man sofort, was i n solchem Geschöpfe steckt. Daß von ihm nichts Gutes, Edles zu erwarten ist, ist selbstverständlich; denn: Wie innen, so außen, wie außen, so innen, das ist ein uraltes Naturgesetz, das wir Menschen nicht umstoßen, auch nicht mit dem so oft mißbrauchten „Mantel der Nächstenliebe" zudecken können. Wer Augen hat zu sehen, der s e h e !

Alles was häßlich ist, ist dämonisch, weil nicht gut (göttlich). Dämonische Wesen m ü s s e n sich in Häßlichkeit verkörpern, wie sich göttliche Wesen in Schönheit verkörpern. Man darf nur nicht „schön" mit „pikant" oder „interessant" verwechseln. I m m e r , in j e d e m Falle kommt es auf die Plastik des Kopfes, des Gesichts, der Hand an, nicht auf das, was sie s c h e i n e n , oder was durch „Hilfsmaterial" hinzu- oder hinaufgelogen wird. In dieser Zeit der Täuschungen ist es Pflicht des einzelnen, auf diese Unterschiede zu achten, oder — er täuscht und enttäuscht sich.

Chirosophie und Kriminalwissenschaft.

Fingerabdruckmuster.

Die Fingerabdrücke auf Bild 79, A, B, C, D, E und F stellen die Fingerabdruck-Muster dar, wie sie in der Daktyloskopie vorkommen. A ist das sog. Bogen- oder A-Muster ohne Delta. B und C sind Schlingen- oder Schleifenmuster mit Delta, und zwar einmal links und einmal rechts. Die Deltas sind durch kleine Pfeile kenntlich gemacht. D ist ein Tannen- oder T-Muster, ebenfalls mit einem Delta. E ist ein Wirbel- oder W-Muster mit zwei Deltas. F ist ein Doppelschlingenmuster. — Die ersten vier zählen alle unter die Kategorie Schlingenmuster, die beiden letzten unter die der Wirbelmuster.

Alle Fingerabdrücke kommen immer in diesen Zeichnungen vor, nur mit mehr oder weniger großen Abweichungen in bezug auf die Anordnung der Papillarlinien. Die gleichen Muster finden wir auch auf der Innenhand (!), und zwar vorwiegend auf dem Mond- und Venusberg. Zwischen Jupiter-, Saturn-, Apollo- und Merkurberg findet man in der Regel nur die Schleifenmuster; mitunter kommt es auch vor, daß ein Wirbelmuster anzutreffen ist, dies jedoch nur in vereinzelten Fällen.

Das Deltamuster kommt unter allen Fingern auf den Bergen vor, und zwar h i e r in allen Händen. Die anderen Muster k ö n n e n noch nebenher an diesen Stellen vorkommen, doch immer mit Unterschieden.

Wie weit die Kriminalpolizei für den Erkennungsdienst zur Zeit die Zeichen der Innenhand, im besonderen die Delta- und Schlingenmuster benutzt, ist mir nicht genau bekannt. Sicherlich ist dies doch ein sehr wertvolles Gebiet, und es würde der deutschen Polizei von größerem Nutzen sein, wenn sie nicht nur die Papillarlinien, sondern auch die übrigen Handlinien in ihrer Bedeutung zu Rate zöge, wie es z. T. im Auslande schon geschieht.

Ein System, nach dem man aus den verschiedenen Formationen der Fingerabdrücke Charaktereigenschaften herausfinden kann, ist in Europa bisher nicht bekannt.

Die chinesischen Chiromanten haben sich nicht nur auf die Ausdeutung der Handlinien beschränkt, sondern haben auch noch die Formen der Papillarlinien an den Fingerspitzen herangezogen. Sie haben 2 Typen von Papillarlinienbildern aufgestellt: die Wirbelmuster (wie auf Abb. E, chinesisch tou oder lo = Schnecke genannt) und die Schleifenmuster (Abb. C, chinesisch ki = wörtlich Sieb).

Die lo oder tou bedeuten Glück, die ki das Gegenteil. A. H. Smith sagt in „Proverbs and common sayings from the Chinese", Shanghay 1902, p. 314: Ein alter, in China allgemein geläufiger Spruch heißt: Ein Wirbelmuster = arm, 2 Wirbelmuster = reich, 3 Wirbel, 4 Wirbel = eröffne ein Pfandleihgeschäft, 5 Wirbel = werde Kommissionär (gemeint ist das sehr einträgliche und im chinesischen Handel so wichtige Amt des Compradors), 6 Wirbel = ein Dieb, 7 Wirbel = Unglückswurm, 8 Wirbel = friß Stroh, 9 Wirbel und eine Schleife = brauchst nicht zu arbeiten, hast zu essen, bis du stirbst.

Dieser Spruch zeigt, wie die Kenntnis von den verschiedenen Mustern der Fingerlinien in die breitesten Schichten des chinesischen Volkes gedrungen ist.

Die physiognomischen Schriftsteller in Hellas und im alten Rom beschäftigten sich eingehend mit der Rolle, die die Hand und die Finger in der Wahrsagekunst spielten, aber über die Bedeutung der Papillarlinienbilder ist bei diesen Autoren nichts zu finden.

Nach p. 740 des „Picture writing of American Indians" von Mallery erscheint es auch nicht unwahrscheinlich, daß die Steinzeichnung der Mic-Mac-Indianer im Zusammenhang mit der Chiromantie steht. Eine andere Deutung des Petroglyphen wäre folgende: Auf prähistorischen amerikanischen Töpferwaren ist auffallend häufig das Auge als Ornament verwendet. Nach einem Bericht in den „Verhandlungen der Berliner Gesellschaft für Anthropologie, Ethnologie und Urgeschichte" vom 20. März 1886, S. 209, gab ein hierüber befragter Bella-Coola-Indianer (Nordwestamerika) folgende Erklärung: „Er zeigte auf die Volarflächen seiner Fingerkuppen und auf die feinen Lineamente, welche die Haut an denselben bietet; nach seiner Meinung bedeute ein rundliches oder längliches Feld, wie es gewöhnlich zwischen den gegeneinanderstoßenden oder parallelen Linien erscheint, gleichfalls ein Auge, und das komme daher, daß ursprünglich jeder Teil des Körpers in ein Sinnesorgan, und zwar speziell in ein Auge ausgegangen und erst später auf derartige rudimentäre Zustände zurückgebildet sei." Die ganze Natur stellt sich also, wie es scheint, in der Vorstellung dieses Indianers als belebt und sinnlich veranlagt heraus, nur daß im Laufe der Zeit ein großer Teil der Anlagen bis auf bloße Andeutungen verschwunden ist. Das vorerwähnte Zeichen zeigt, wie die Indianer im äußersten Norden Amerikas schon auf der primitivsten Kulturstufe, in der Periode der Bilderschrift, Kenntnis der Papillarlinienmuster und sogar ihrer charakteristischen Unterschiede hatten.

Die japanischen Chiromanten nannten die Tastrosetten an den Fingerspitzen: Hamon, wegen der gerollten Form und lehrten, je regelmäßiger sie seien, desto glücklicher werde ihr Träger sein. Je nachdem dieser oder jener Finger regelmäßige oder unregelmäßige Wirbel trage, zeige dies Glück oder Unglück verschiedener Art an.

Auch die Malaien scheinen den Papillarlinien ihre Aufmerksamkeit nicht versagt zu haben. W. Skeat bemerkt in „Malay Magic", daß bei den malaiischen Chiromanten Wirbelmuster an den Fingerspitzen als Zeichen von Schlauheit betrachtet wurden.

Fragen und Antworten aus der chirologischen Praxis.

1. Welche äußeren und inneren Merkmale muß ein guter Charakterologe aufweisen?

Der indische Gelehrte Varaha Mihira (siehe: Das große Buch der Nativitätslehre „Brihat Jataka" des V. M., deutsch von Wilh. Wulff, Atair-Verlag, Hamburg) schreibt über das Aussehen und die Beschaffenheit eines guten Astrologen — was auch für den Chirosophen und andere Charakterologen gilt — folgendes: „Ein Astrologe muß von guter Herkunft sein, ein angenehmes, freundliches Aussehen, einen ebenmäßigen Körper, edlen Wuchs und wohlgeformte Gliedmaßen haben, er darf nicht durch einen Körperfehler verunziert, und seine Hände, Füße, Nägel, Augen, Zähne, Ohren, Augenbrauen, Stirne und Kinn müssen wohlgestaltet und schön proportioniert sein, überhaupt muß er eine gute Konstitution und eine helle, klare, wohlklingende Stimme besitzen, kurz, ein stattlicher Mann sein; denn in der Regel besteht ein Zusammenhang zwischen den guten und schlechten moralischen Eigenschaften eines Menschen und seinem Aussehen.

Weiter wird von ihm Sittenstrenge, Wahrhaftigkeit, Edelmut, Schlagfertigkeit, Scharfsinn, Wissen, Milde und Güte verlangt, er darf weder aufgeregt noch boshaft sein und muß durch sein Wissen seine Standesgenossen überragen, damit er durch seine erfolgreiche Tätigkeit den Ruhm der Wissenschaft vermehrt. Er muß nicht allein befähigt, sondern auch frei von Lastern sein, muß die Sühneopfer kennen, Heilkunde und die weiße Magie beherrschen, fromm und gottesfürchtig leben, fasten und sich Bußübungen auferlegen. Er muß einen hervorragenden Geist besitzen, um in hinreichender Weise jede Frage beantworten zu können, ausgenommen in solchen Fällen, wo seinen Kenntnissen durch übernatürliche Einflüsse Grenzen gesetzt sind . . ." Diese Forderung ist durchaus gerechtfertigt. — Personen, die äußerlich übel aussehen, sind auch übel im Innern. Die bekannte Warnung im Volk „Hüte dich vor dem Gezeichneten!" ist kein Vorurteil, sondern hat Berechtigung. — Es geht auch deutlich genug aus obiger Vorschrift hervor, daß ein guter Charakterologe nicht minderrassig sein darf. Denn: „Wie außen so innen, wie innen so außen", so heißt eine alte Regel in der Geheimlehre, die sich auch hier bestätigt. Auch damals hat es sicherlich viele Pfuscher gegeben, davon zeugt die Stelle: „Einen angeblichen Astrologen (Chirosophen) ohne wissenschaftliche Vorbildung darf man nicht um Rat befragen. Wer ohne wissenschaftliche Vorbildung den Beruf eines Astrologen (Chirosophen) ausübt, ist ein Bösewicht und eine Schande für die menschliche Gesellschaft."

Wenn heute auch im allgemeinen diese Vorschriften bei uns in Europa nicht beachtet werden, weil die Leute zu gedankenlos und zu „tolerant" geworden sind, so wird sich doch in jedem Falle die Nichtbeachtung von Seiten des Publikums rächen. Daher auch meine immer wieder betonte Forderung: Fragt den Charakterologen (Chirosophen, Astrologen, Graphologen usw.) nach einem Zeugnis und schaut ihn euch v o r h e r an, bevor ihr ihn um Rat fragt! — Habt den Mut, ihn evtl. abzulehnen, wenn ihr kein Vertrauen zu ihm habt, oder wenn er den obigen Vorschriften nicht entspricht!

2. Gilt eine Handanalyse für das ganze Leben?

Bleibt die Diagnose eines Arztes für das ganze Leben gültig? Nein! Alles ist dem Wandel unterworfen; auch der menschliche Körper. Da Krankheit und Charakter Polaritäten sind, die in ihrer Wechselwirkung das Schicksal ausmachen, und da wir täglich weiter und Neues denken und damit die Körperorgane positiv oder negativ beeinflussen, ändern sich Denkrichtung, Ursache und Wirkung wieder und wieder. So auch das Wohlbefinden, die Gesundheit, somit auch das Schicksal im alltäglichen Sinne. So können Zeichen und kleine Linien in den Händen kommen und gehen, — sie müssen es nicht. Wenn sich dann neue Ereignislinien zeigen (durch neue seelische Einwirkungen), so muß man sie erneut absuchen, lesen und auswerten. Alles ist Wandel und Wechsel, Werden und Vergehen, um wieder zu werden. Eine große, ausführliche Handanalyse hat denselben Wert wie ein gutes Horoskop. Die festgelegten und erklärten Eigenschaften und Ereignisse bleiben so. Nur was sich durch das Erkennen und Auswirken der Ereignisse als Folge und neue Kombination bildet, kann sich später durch entsprechende Wandlung etwas anders gestalten und durch neue Linien zeigen. Schriftliche Analysen sind Lebensweiser!

3. Ist die Chiromantie eine Wissenschaft?

Ja, weil sie auf Ursache und Wirkung von Erfahrungstatsachen beruht und von jedem mit gutem Verstande begabten Menschen nachgeprüft werden kann. Sie ist eine höhere Art der Physiologie und genau wie diese und alle Naturwissenschaften eine Wissenschaft, die gelehrt werden kann. In Frankreich (Paris) wurde die Chiromantie 1913 wieder als Wissenschaft anerkannt.

4. Kann man auch aus den Fingerabdrücken der Daktyloskopie, wie sie die Kriminalistik benutzt, etwas erkennen oder herauslesen?

Gewiß wird es auch das geben, doch ist hierüber wenig bekannt. A l l e s am Körper spricht!

5. Haben Kinder auch schon Handlinien und -zeichen, an denen man Ereignisse des Lebens erkennen kann?

Gewiß, mitunter sogar sehr stark und klar, ein andermal weniger ausgeprägt.

6. Bedeuten die Linien und Zeichen in den Fußsohlen auch etwas?

Gewiß haben auch diese Formationen ihre Bedeutung, nur ist das System, sie zu lesen, verschieden. Reichliche Linien auf dem Fuße siehe Bild 35. Ein Schweizer erforscht sie heute.

7. Kann der Mensch sein Schicksal ändern?

Darüber spricht die Einführung dieses Buches ganz ausführlich.

8. Warum wird in den verschiedenen Lehrbüchern nie eine Aufstellung der alten Literatur mit Kommentar zu den einzelnen Werken gebracht, so daß der Schüler einen genauen Überblick über den Wert aller Werke hat?

Diesen Mangel habe auch ich erkannt und habe ihn abgestellt, indem ich im „Lexikon der Handlesekunst, der Berufseignungsprüfung und der Literatur" eine lexikalische Aufstellung mit entsprechendem Kommentar brachte.

9. **Sind die Handlinien nicht Zufall, oder entstehen sie nicht durch Falten wie bei Tuch und Papier?**

Nein! Die Linien sind ebensowenig Zufall wie alles andere, was wir in der Auswirkung zu erleben haben, weil wir es selbst veranlaßten. Was der Mensch säet, das wird er ernten! — Man wird doch nicht glauben, daß ein neugeborenes Kind oder ein über fünf Monate alter Fötus, die mitunter mehr Linien in den Händen aufweisen als ein alter Mensch, dauernd die Hände auf- und zugemacht haben. Außerdem: versuchen Sie dieses Experiment selbst! Es wird sich n i e bestätigen. Alle Linien sind von kosmischen, seelischen Kräften durch frühere Ursachen zur Auswirkung (Materialisation) gelangt.

10. **Kommt es vor, daß Hände mehrerer Personen gleich sind?**

Ähnliche Menschen werden ähnliche Charaktere und ähnliche Hände haben, aber dennoch nicht g a n z gleiche!

11. **Kann der Chiromant in jedem Falle Zeitpunkte nennen?**

Nur dann, wenn dafür die Linien und Zeichen vorhanden sind. Hände mit wenig oder nur den drei Hauptlinien bedeuten für den Chirosophen ungefähr dasselbe, was für jeden anderen eine Zeitung ohne Buchstaben bedeutet, d. h. in bezug auf Zeitpunkte. Es lassen sich aber nur J a h r e ausmessen, nicht Monate usw.

12. **Warum hat die Chiromantie im allgemeinen Feinde?**

Weil sie durch die verwässerten Überlieferungen zu einer Scheinwissenschaft wurde, die gewissenlosen Personen viel Material bot, um Pfuscherei zu treiben und falsche Diagnosen zu stellen. Außerdem sind gewisse kirchliche Kreise daran interessiert, daß Wissenschaften, welche das Erkennen des Menschen ermöglichen (wie Chirologie, Astrologie), weil sie mit dem Göttlichen und den Geisteswissenschaften zusammenhängen, also wahre Religion sind, nicht ins Volk dringen. Daß diese Wissenschaften in den Händen von Pfuschern und Nichtskönnern viel Schaden anrichten, ist selbstverständlich.

Die meisten Anfeindungen aber stammen von jenen Leuten, die von diesen Dingen nichts verstehen oder nichts verstehen wollen. Jeder, der tiefer in Dinge und Geschehnisse, wie auch tiefer in Personen hineinschauen kann, ist ihnen unbequem. Man darf nicht vergessen, daß es manchen Leuten durchaus nicht recht ist, daß man sie erkennt und durchschaut.

13. Kann man die Zukunft voraussagen?

Ja, soweit es sich um Ereignisse handelt, die nicht mit Formalitäten zusammenhängen. Es gibt keine Vergangenheit und keine Zukunft, sondern alles ist ein laufendes Jetzt. Man kann sagen: Alle Ereignisse im Weltall, so auch bei Menschen, wiederholen sich periodenweise in ähnlicher Art, doch mit kleinen Änderungen. Siehe „Periodenlehre" von Fließ, desgleichen von Swoboda, Meewes, Reichenbach u. a. Lebensdauer ist erkennbar.

14. Warum gibt es soviel Schwindler und Pfuscher auf diesem Gebiet?

Weil bisher die ganze erreichbare Literatur der Handlesekunst nicht zuverlässig und nicht von Praktikern geschrieben war. Wenn nun ein Interessent ein solches Buch in die Hand bekam, so mußte er folglich falsche Lehren in sich aufnehmen. Versuchte er, sie an den Händen seiner Mitmenschen anzuwenden, so konnte das Resultat nur Schwindel sein. Besonders viel Unheil auf diesem Gebiete brachten Geßmanns Katechismen usw. Die Handformenkunde stimmt fast in allen alten Büchern, nur die Handlinien- und Zeichenkunde nicht. Sie wurde erst später in zuverlässiger Art veröffentlicht; in kleinem Maße von Ottinger, in größerem vom Verfasser. Jeder kann helfen, dem Pfuschertum zu steuern: Wer zu einem Chirologen geht, der keinen bekannten Namen hat, verlange stets die Vorlage eines Zeugnisses. Wer etwas kann, wird sich nicht scheuen, eine Prüfung zu machen. Vorläufig ist dies die einzige Selbsthilfe gegen betrügerische „Chirologen".

15. Kann man, wie in der Physiognomik, Iriskunde, auch aus der Hand Krankheiten erkennen?

Ja! Soweit es sich um Krankheitsdispositionen, Vererbungen, evtl. auch um überstandene Krankheiten und Operationen handelt. Solche können allerdings von Geburt aus bestehen oder auch vererbt sein; die Unterschiede kann man sehr leicht und sicher erkennen. Die Sicherheit der Hand- und Nageldiagnosen beträgt 98 v. H. Das ist mehr, als die klinische Diagnostik aufweisen kann. Diese Diagnostik wird seit einiger Zeit schon von sehr vielen Ärzten mit gutem Erfolg benutzt. Alle diese Diagnosen bestätigen sich gegenseitig, wie die Praxis seit langen Jahren bewies. Siehe „Medizinische Hand- und Nageldiagnostik" (5. Aufl.).

16. Warum benutzen Ärzte diese Diagnose nicht?

Sie benutzen sie schon vielfach, wenn auch heimlich. Es gibt heute eine neue Strömung, auch bei den jungen Studenten der Medizin, und jeder versucht irgendwo und irgendwie, sich mit dem Wissen zu bereichern, das auf Hochschulen nicht geboten wird. In Zukunft werden Ärzte sich viel mehr mit den neuen (und doch uralten) Arten der Diagnostik praktisch beschäftigen. In England, Amerika, Indien, in der Schweiz und anderen Ländern tut man es längst. Ich gab Ärzten Unterricht.

17. Kann man aus der Hand auch den Beruf erkennen?

Es gibt keine Schneider-, Schuhmacher-, Bäcker- oder Lehrerlinien; deshalb kann man auch nicht erkennen, welchen Beruf jemand hat. Viele Menschen haben einen falschen Beruf gewählt und wechseln später oft mehrere Male. Man kann aber sehr gut und genau die Anlagen und Talente, mit einem Worte, die technischen und geistigen Möglichkeiten einer Person auf Grund der Handform (Struktur und Plastik) erkennen und daraufhin mit Sicherheit angeben, für welche Berufe der Betreffende in Frage kommt. Man darf hier nicht Talent mit Interesse verwechseln; das sind verschiedene Dinge. Es kann Interesse vorhanden sein und doch kein Talent, oder Talent und kein Interesse. Eines allein führt zu nichts oder nur zu Halbheiten. Beides zusammen ergibt den Erfolg für den betreffenden Beruf.

18. Schadet das Beschneiden der Nagelhaut?

Es schadet sogar sehr! Es ist eine Fahrlässigkeit der Manikure, die Nagelschutzhaut zu verletzen oder abzuschneiden. Die Nagelhaut ist zum Schutz der Nagelwurzel gewachsen. Verletzt man sie, dann entsteht dadurch eine — wenn auch fast unsichtbare — Wunde, durch die die magnetischen Kräfte, helle Säfte ebenfalls, ausströmen. Außerdem wird der Nagelwurzel der nötige Schutz genommen und Unreinigkeiten haben Zutritt. Hierdurch kann als Folge eine sehr schmerzhafte Nagelwurzelentzündung entstehen. Die Behauptung, daß die Nagelhaut überwächst oder hart wird, hat keinen Bestand. Sie kann durch Einfetten weich gehalten und überflüssige Teile mit heißem Seifenwasser und Nagelbürste entfernt werden. — Bei der Anwendung der Kapillar-Diagnostik werden die Nagelhäute mit Öl eingerieben und durch ein Mikroskop genau betrachtet. Man sieht dann deutlich die Säfte kreisen. Verdickte Flußstellen zeigen an, wo ein Leiden zu suchen ist. Diese Art Diagnostik ist an der Stelle unmöglich, wo die Nagelhaut entfernt wurde. Aber — der Mode wird ja viel geopfert, selbst die Vernunft!

19. Kann man aus den Papillarlinien der Finger etwas erkennen?

Sicherlich ist das möglich; doch gibt es darüber m. W. in europäischen Sprachen keine Lehrbücher, ausgenommen über die Daktyloskopie. Im Chinesischen hat man allerdings einige Regeln über die Bedeutung einer Anzahl von „Schnecken" und „Schlingen". Was darüber bekannt ist, habe ich im Kapitel „Chirosophie und Kriminalwissenschaft" im vorliegenden Werk schon beschrieben. Die feinen Hautmuster zeigen jedoch das geistig-seelische Niveau des Handeigners und werden auf dem Mondberg am besten gefunden.

20. Welche Hand bezeichnet man als gut?

Gute Hände sind solche, die in ihrer Form und Plastik sowie in den Linienformationen harmonisch und nicht durch schlechte Zeichen, rohes Aussehen und ähnliche Merkmale verdorben sind. Eine gute Hand mit einem Mörderdaumen ist k e i n e gute Hand; ebenso ist es mit einer guten Hand, die in der Innenfläche viele Gitter aufweist.

21. Ist zu ersehen, welche Menschentypen für den Betreffenden ungünstig sind?

Ja, dies erkennt man an bestimmten Zeichen auf den Bergen, die wieder ihrerseits bestimmte Planetentypen (physiognomisch) darstellen. Siehe Abbildungen Nr. 77 und 78.

22. Kann man durch die Chirosophie sein Schicksal verbessern?

Ja! Indem man sich diese Wissenschaft zu eigen macht, lernt man das kosmische Wirken kennen, sich selbst, andere Menschen und die Urkraft — Gott. Wenn man sich, seine Schwäche und Stärke erkannt hat, kann man ihnen besser begegnen, sie besser abstellen bzw. anwenden. Dann beginnt das bewußte Arbeiten. Wenn jemand aber weiß, was er tut und tun soll, ist ihm schon viel geholfen. Er stellt sich dann mehr darauf ein und unterläßt vieles, was er unwissentlich sonst getan hätte. Oder er stellt sich darauf nicht ein, schlendert seinen Gang weiter, wie früher, und wird noch mehr vom Schicksal getreten, bis er sieht, daß größere Kräfte g e g e n ihn arbeiten, wenn er nicht m i t ihnen arbeitet. So verbessert sich der Mensch erst geistig, dann materiell. Umgekehrt wäre es unnatürlich.

23. Was ist von den verschiedenen psychologischen Typenlehren zu halten?

Die Typenlehren sind zumeist nur in der Benennung verschieden, je nach der Wissenschaft, die einer vertritt. Einige dieser Richtungen sind unvollkommen, andere weisen Parallelen miteinander auf. In neuerer Zeit tauchen Anfeindungen gegen die Typenlehre auf, ganz zu Unrecht. Typen sind Klassifizierungen und erleichtern die Erklärungen jedem bedeutend, der einigermaßen Toleranz besitzt und sich ihrer bedient. — Man lasse sich nicht von Nörglern verleiten, eine Sache zu verwerfen, die in Wirklichkeit naturgegeben ist. Am weitesten kommt man immer noch mit der ältesten Typenlehre: Spirituell, Intellektuell, Materiell, da sie der kosmischen Dreiteilung: Geist, Seele, Körper genau entspricht. — Wenn neuerdings versucht wird, in der Handlesekunst anstatt der v o r h a n d e n e n sieben Typen (Handformen) nur drei zu benutzen, so ist das unvollständig aus Mangel an besserer Beobachtung. —

24. Ist die Chirologie eine Basis für Psychoanalyse?

Man muß sich wundern, daß moderne Nervenärzte noch nicht darauf gekommen sind, die Handlesekunst als eine Basis für ihre psychischen und psychologischen Behandlungen aufzunehmen. Einige dieser Ärzte benutzen schon die Astrologie zu diesem Zweck und erreichen erklärlicherweise damit sehr viel mehr als andere, die zu voreingenommen sind, sich dieses alten Wissens zu bedienen. Die Handlesekunst bietet objektiv die beste Basis zur Erkennung körperlicher und seelischer Zustände und ihrer Ursachen. Das ist ihr besonderer Wert. In „Medizinische Hand- und Nagel-Diagnostik" brachte ich bereits einen Abschnitt über die Verwendung der Chirologie zur Erklärung seelischer Leiden und ihrer Aufdeckung. — Wen es interessiert, der mag dort nachlesen. —

25. Kann man aus der Entfernung (brieflich) Handanalysen erhalten, und wie macht man das?

Gewiß ist das möglich. Als Unterlagen müssen hierfür eingesandt werden: ein Photo von einer Außen- und einer Innenhand, dazu Abdrücke beider Innenhände mit Fingern und Daumen. Die Photos können klein, 6 × 9 cm, müssen aber scharf und die Abdrücke klar und genau sein, nicht zuviel, nicht zuwenig Farbe. Als Farbe benutzt man „Japan Aqua schwarz" (leicht abwaschbar) oder, wo nicht zu haben, schwarze oder blaue Stempelfarbe. Rot, grün, violett sind schwer zu beseitigen. — Ferner ist die Angabe einiger Sterbe-Daten von Onkel, Tante oder Großeltern aus den väterlichen und mütterlichen Generationen erforderlich. Außerdem ein Paßbild, um die Rassen- oder Stammeszugehörigkeit festzustellen, was aus der Hand nicht ersichtlich, aber zu wissen notwendig ist, da jede Rasse ihre besondere seelische Struktur hat.

Eine ausführliche Handanalyse ist ein guter Lebensweiser. Günstig ist es auch, wenn besondere Fragen dazu gestellt werden, auf die man dann genauer eingehen kann. Jedoch können keinerlei Angaben über Eltern, Kinder usw. gemacht werden, da dies nicht aus den Händen zu erkennen ist. Eine solche Handanalyse umfaßt etwa vier Seiten Maschinenschrift, wenn die Hände viele Linien aufweisen. —

26. Erteilt Verfasser Unterricht in Chirologie?

Verfasser gab viele Unterrichtskurse, hat aber die berufliche Ausbildung auf besonders gut Begabte beschränkt. Bei Anfragen betr. Unterricht ist stets Lichtbild einzusenden. Ablehnung vorbehalten. — Eine berufliche Ausbildung als Chirologe gebe ich nur; doch mache ich darauf aufmerksam, daß diese allein nicht zur Ausübung des Berufes genügt. Da Chirologie ein Zweig der Charakterkunde ist, der Charakterologe aber auch beraten muß, ist es erforderlich, außer medizinischen im besonderen auch psychologische und physiognomische Kenntnisse und Lebenserfahrung zu besitzen, um wirklich ein guter und zuverlässiger Berater sein zu können. Darum glaube niemand, daß er durch das Studium der Chirologie allein eine ausreichende Existenz findet. Selbst wer alles Wissen und Können besitzt, muß sich erst einmal einen Namen und Ruf schaffen, der von Können und Erfolg abhängig ist. Das dauert Jahre, wie bei jedem anderen ernsten Studium. —· Darum meine kritische Auswahl!

27. Ist es richtig, wenn der Chirologe ungünstige Ereignisse oder Veranlagungen verschweigt?

Nein, es ist nicht richtig; denn jeder hat das Recht, genaue Tatsachen zu erfahren, soweit es ihn selbst betrifft. Man kann a l l e s sagen, es kommt nur darauf an: w i e und w e m ! Die Sprache ist reichhaltig genug, um gefährliche Dinge sehr deutlich zu umschreiben. Ein gewissenhafter Chirologe wird immer die Nervenkonstitution und das geistige Niveau des Besuchers in Betracht ziehen und sich seelisch auf ihn einstellen. Er muß versuchen, mit seinem Geist in den anderen einzutauchen und durch d e s s e n Augen die Welt zu betrachten, zu durchleben, um dessen Einstellung zur Umwelt zu erfassen. Dann wird er dem Klienten gerecht. — Es ist jedoch nicht angängig oder richtig, seine Kenntnisse über Andere dritten Personen mitzuteilen. Dadurch kann viel Schaden für jeden Beteiligten entstehen. Bei jedem gewissenhaften Charakterologen und Psychologen werden Besucher nur einzeln empfangen, auch dann, wenn sie sich in Begleitung von „Verwandten" befinden. Verschwiegenheit ist erstes Gesetz für jeden Berater; hier noch mehr als beim Arzt! —

28. **Was ist nötig, um ein außergewöhnlich erfolgreicher Charakterologe und Berater zu werden?**

Diese verschiedentlich an mich gerichtete Frage sei mit folgendem ausführlich und mit ganzer Ehrlichkeit beantwortet.

Machen Sie Reisen, wenn es geht bis in die äußersten Winkel der
Welt! Arbeiten Sie alles, was Ihnen in den Weg kommt! Lernen
Sie das Leben in allen Situationen kennen und so auch die Menschen, ihre Charaktere, Leiden und Sorgen! Dann studieren Sie
die Physiognomik aller Völker und auch ihre Sitten, Gebräuche
und ihre Religion. Dann studieren Sie, soweit sich Gelegenheiten
bieten und finden lassen, Krankheiten und deren Merkmale (So-
matologie). Dann folgen Psychologie, metaphysische Zusammenhänge von Charakter und Krankheit; ferner Graphologie, Astrologie und Chirologie. Zwischendurch müssen Sie sich aber immer
über alle Möglichkeiten der verschiedensten Berufe informieren.
— Haben Sie das alles getan, d a n n sind Sie — Begabung vorausgesetzt — ein guter, zuverlässiger, gewissenhafter Berater und
l e b e n s n a h e r Charakterologe, der nicht n u r den Suchenden
analysiert, sondern ihm auch helfen kann: sich selbst zu finden
und das, was für ihn geistig, seelisch und körperlich nötig ist. —

Trotz allerbesten Könnens werden Sie auch dann noch — wenn
auch selten — feststellen: daß es leere Schriften, schweigende
Horoskope und stumme Hände gibt, weil wir irdischen Menschen
eben — manchmal! — dem Suchenden (schicksalsmäßig!) nicht
helfen dürfen und er seinen Weg allein finden soll und muß.
Sonst aber werden Sie, wenn Sie den geschilderten Weg gehen,
eine bedeutende Kraft dieses priesterlichen Berufes sein. — Das
ist m e i n e genaue Antwort auf obige Frage. —

29. **Chirologie und Ereignisdeutung.**

Es besteht im weiten Publikum immer noch eine irrige Auffassung über das: „Was in den Händen steht." Das kommt daher,
weil sich unzählige Personen mit der Handlesekunst befassen, die
diese Wissenschaft nie gründlich studiert haben und nur einmal
darüber etwas gelesen haben und n u n ihre persönliche Einfühlung
hinzu nehmen. — Sie arbeiten mit einer mehr oder minder guten
Intuition und berichten z. B. über das Ergehen der Eltern, der Ge-
schwister, Erhalten einer neuen Stellung, Nachricht von Freunden,
oder „d a ß" der Betreffende heirate. D a s alles steht aber n i c h t
in den Händen und ist daher auch nicht — objektiv — erkennbar,
sondern: erfühlt! — Es ist nun nicht an dem, daß ich jede Intuition
verwerfe! Ich will und muß nur darauf — auch an dieser Stelle —
darauf hinweisen, daß n u r das als zuverlässig in der wissenschaft-

lichen Chirologie zu betrachten ist, was man an den entsprechenden Merkmalen objektiv erkennen und zeigen kann. Und was diese Ereignisse betrifft, so sind es deren wenige. Ich nenne: 1): Merkmale für seelische Erschütterungen (Trauer, Gram), Todesfälle in der mütterlichen (linke Hand) und väterlichen (rechte Hand) Generation. Allerdings sind diese Ereignisse, die in diesem Fall „Verluste von Blutsverwandten" anzeigen, gekoppelt mit 2): Ereignissen, die eine Begegnung mit außergewöhnlich sympathischen Personen anzeigt (Liebesbekanntschaften), so daß das Schicksal hierdurch einen Ausgleich für den „Verlust" bietet. 3): Es sind mit diesen beiden Ereignissen noch gekoppelt: Zeitpunkte für Begegnungen, die mehr Bekanntschaften, Freundschaften oder Partnerschaften geschäftlicher Art anzeigen und — evtl. 4): Zeitpunkte für körperliche Krankheiten. Alle Zeitpunkte können nach Jahren genau ausgemessen werden, nicht aber nach Monaten, Wochen oder Tagen, wie es manche „Wahrsager" angeben!

Da nun die oben genannten v i e r oder drei Ereignisse durch e i n e Ereignislinie angezeigt werden, ist damit auch die Gewißheit für bestimmte Rhythmen in der Sippe und der Einzelpersönlichkeit festgelegt! Es gibt noch andere Rhythmen, die sich in den Ereignissen der Handmerkmale zeigen.

Z. B. machen sich die in der eigenen Sippe von Onkeln, Tanten (besonders stark), von Großeltern, weniger von den Eltern erreichten Lebensdauer in den Händen der Nachfahren als gesundheitliche Krisen deutlich bemerkbar. Eine dieser Krisenzeiten ist DIE Krise: die Dauer des eigenen Lebens (in der rechten Hand zu suchen!), was wieder mit der Lebensdauer eines bestimmten väterlichen Vorfahren in engster Verbindung (Rhythmus-Ähnlichkeit) steht.

Was sonst noch an Ereignissen zu erkennen ist, ist folgendes: 1): Zeiten, in denen die Wahl des Ehepartners schicksalsmäßig (d. h. der eigenen Entwicklung entsprechend) am besten ist. 2): Zeiten für materiellen Aufstieg, — oder Verlust, sowie günstige Zeiten für Protektion (Prüfungen, Examen). 3): Zeiten, die kritisch für die Gesundheit sind, wie Operationen. 4): Evtl. Zeiten günstig für große Reisen. 5): Evtl. Jahre, in denen besonders kritische Depressionen (Lebensüberdruß) auftreten. Damit aber haben sich alle Ereignisse objektiv (!) offenbart, soweit die bis heute abgeschlossene Zuverlässigkeit gediehen ist. — Alles andere ist unzuverlässige Einfühlung.

Die medizinische Hand- und Nageldiagnostik

von Prof. h. c. Ernst Issberner-Haldane

In diesem Lehrbuch der medizinischen Handlesekunst werden die Eigenschaften der Berge, Linien und Zeichen der Hand nur so weit behandelt, wie sie für die Erkennung von Krankheiten in Betracht kommen.

Die modernen wissenschaftlichen Untersuchungsmethoden der neuzeitlichen Medizin haben ohne Frage einen hohen Grad der Vervollkommnung erreicht, und doch lassen sie in so vielen Fällen im Stich. Hier kommen dann die Untersuchungsmethoden zu Hilfe, die aus dem uralten, Jahrtausende überdauernden Schatze der Geheimwissenschaften geschöpft werden können und zu denen vor allem auch die Handlesekunst zählt.

An Hand vieler Beispiele und Abbildungen zeigt der Verfasser, welche Merkmale in der Hand auf welche Krankheit schließen lassen.

Aus dem Inhalt:

Zur Einführung in die wissenschaftliche Handdiagnostik — Wie und wodurch entstehen die Zeichen — Die Nageldiagnose — Erklärung der Bezeichnungen der einzelnen Handteile — Die Haut — Handform — Handlinien — Lebenslinie — Kopflinie — Herzlinie — Magen-, Leber- oder Gesundheitslinie — Venusgürtel — Sonnen- und Apollolinie — Uranus- oder Intuitionslinie — Neptun- oder Giftlinie — Raszette oder Armband — Verletzungs- und Vererbungszeichen — Chirologische Drüsenmerkmale — Liste der Krankheitsdiagnosen aus der Hand — Alphabetisches Verzeichnis der Krankheitszeichen — Chirosophie und Psychoanalyse — Psycho-Diagnostik — Der Organismus der Seele (Schichten) — Über die Psychoanalyse und ihre Systeme — Die Chirologie als Hilfsmittel für die Seelenheilkunde — Psycho-Diagnosen — Handdiagnostische Merkmale bei erblicher Belastung.

Dr. med. Feldmann schreibt über dieses Buch:

„Die Handlesekunst und Handdiagnostik aus Hand und Nägeln möchte ich in meiner Praxis nicht mehr entbehren, da sie nicht nur als Hilfsmittel in der Diagnostik an erster Stelle steht, sondern auch erst im Entstehen begriffene Krankheiten anzeigt."

6. Auflage, 180 Seiten, 64 Abbildungen, Ganzleinen

DIE WISSENSCHAFTLICHE
HANDLESEKUNST

Von

ERNST ISSBERNER-HALDANE

ANHANG

80 Abbildungen auf 48 Tafeln.

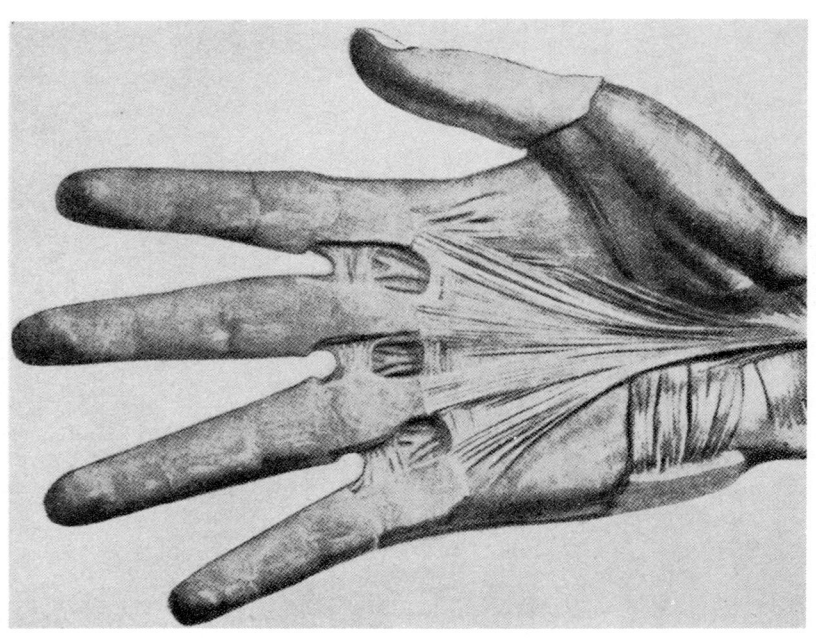

Bild 2. Das Innere der Hand bloßgelegt,
Muskeln, Sehnen, Adern, Häute.

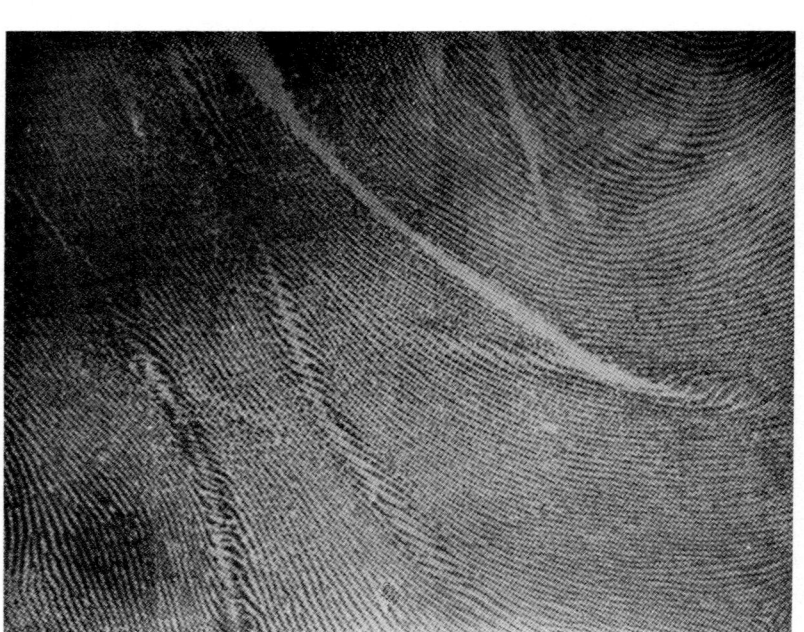

Bild 1. Unabhängig vom Verlauf der Hand-Linien bildet sich
die Haut-Textur und zeigt das geistig-seelische Niveau.

2

Die Berg-Höhe

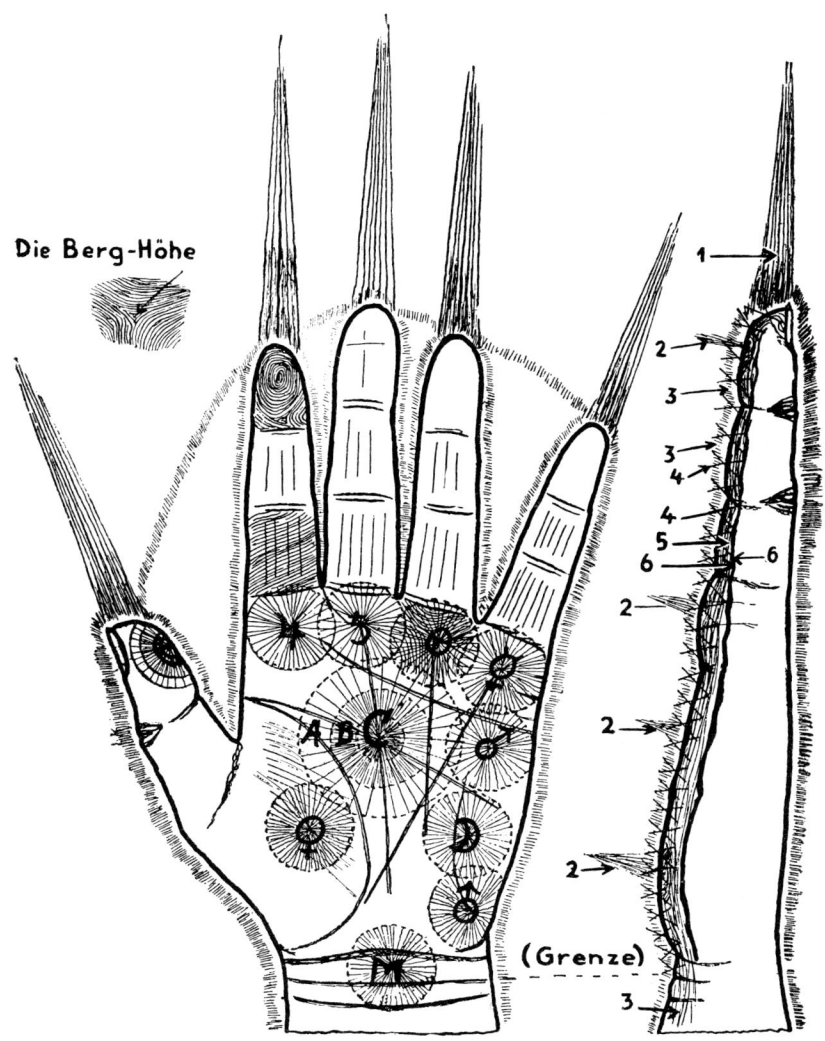

Bild 3. Die Strahlen, Aura und Nervenzentren der Hand

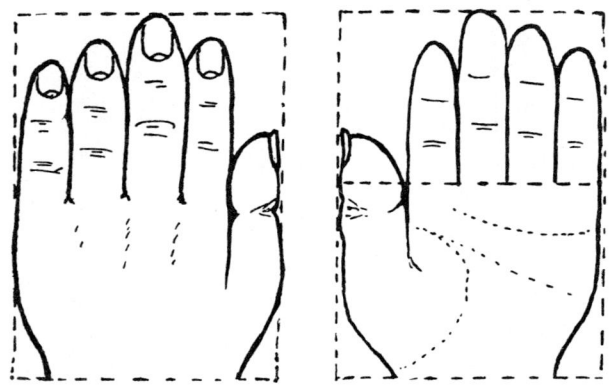

**Extrem elementare Form - fast quadratisch -
nur materiell**

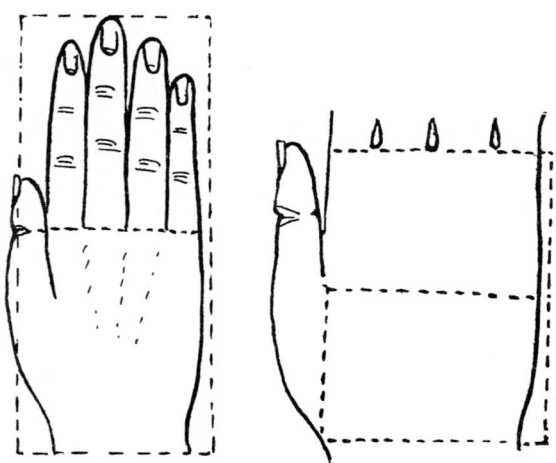

**Extrem geistige Form - hohes Rechteck -
nur geistig**

Bild 4. Extreme Handtypen.

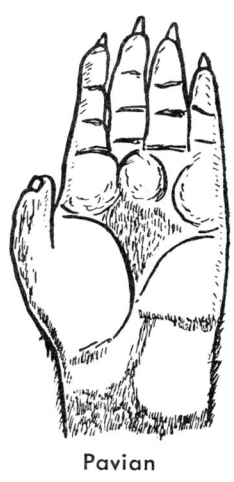

Pavian

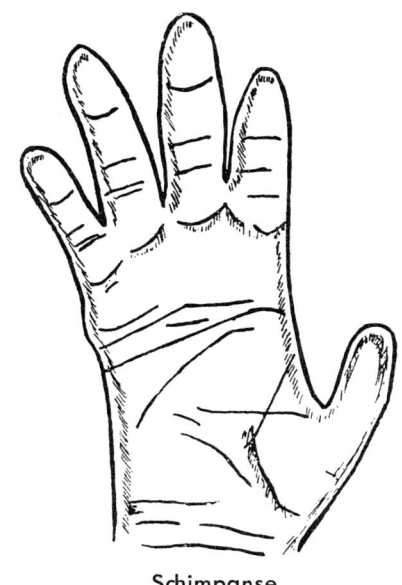

Schimpanse

Orang-Utang

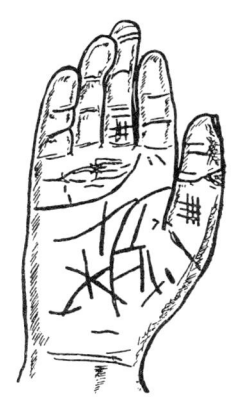

Elementare (Primitive) Hand

Bild 5. Niedere Handtypen: Pavian, Schimpanse, Orang-Utang, Mensch.

5

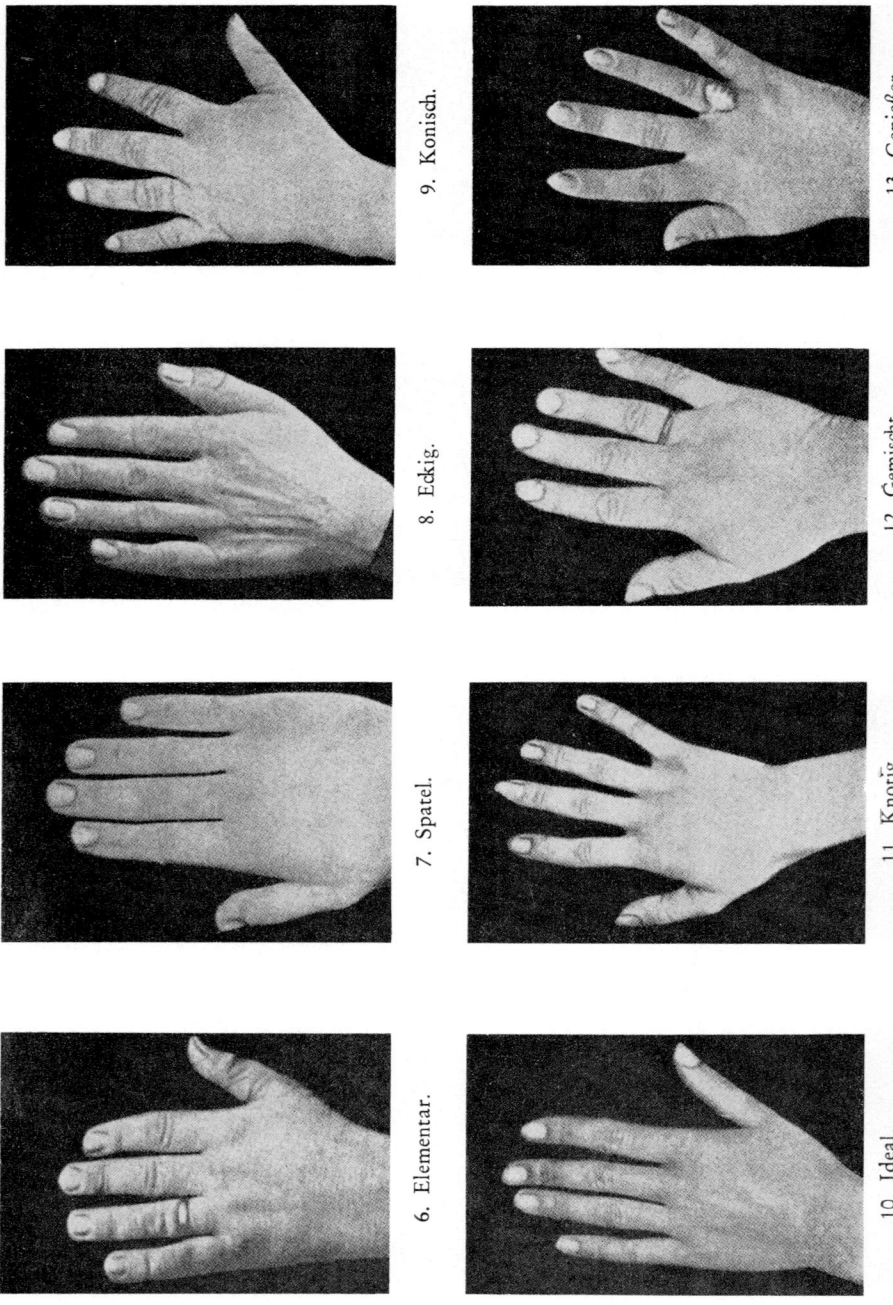

9. Konisch.

13. Genießer.

8. Eckig.

12. Gemischt.

7. Spatel.

11. Knotig.

Bild 6—13

6. Elementar.

10. Ideal.

6

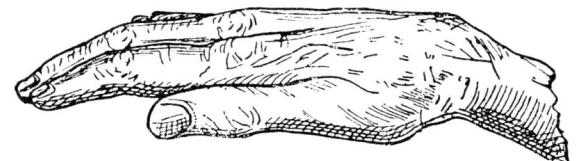

Bild 14. Greisenhand.

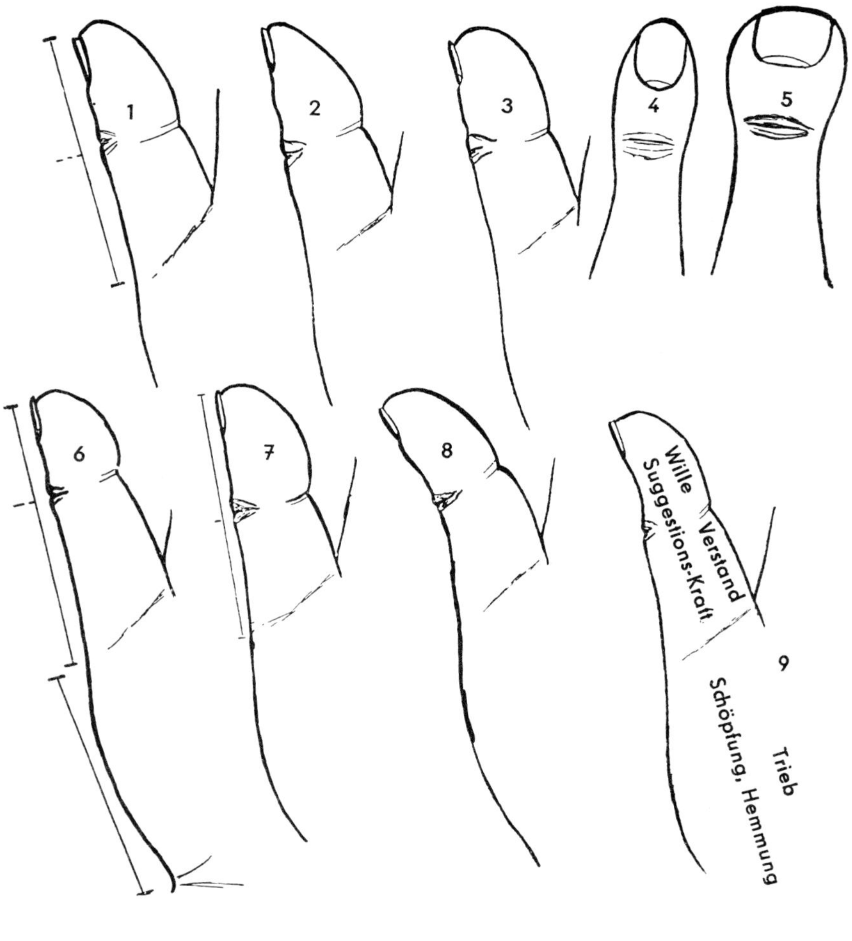

Bild 15. Daumen-Proportionen. Verschiedene Daumen im Profil.

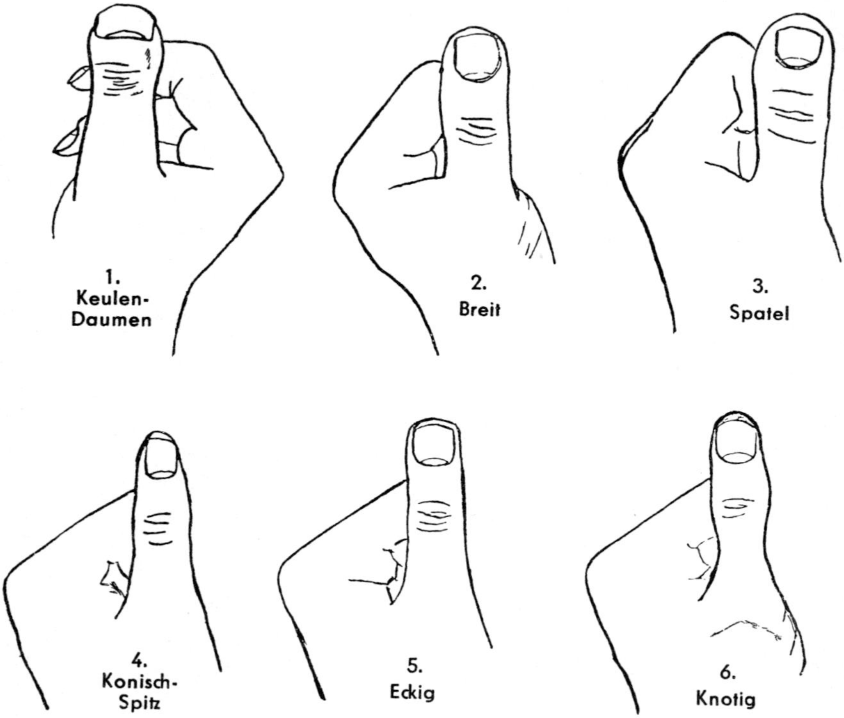

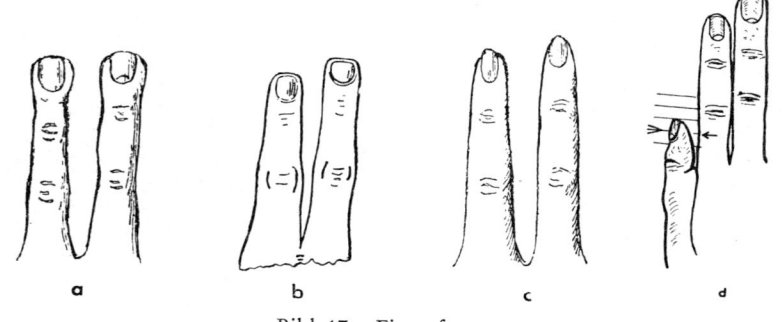

1.
Keulen-
Daumen

2.
Breit

3.
Spatel

4.
Konisch-
Spitz

5.
Eckig

6.
Knotig

Bild 16. Daumenformen. Verschiedene Daumen en face.

a   b   c   d

Bild 17. Fingerformen.

a) Spatelförmige Finger, b) Eckige Finger, c) Konische Finger, d) Daumenlängen.

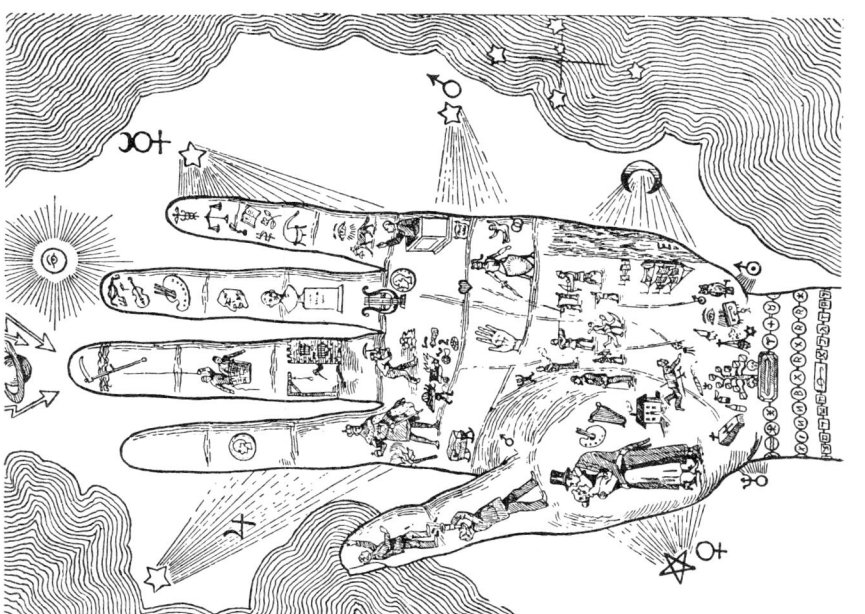

Bild 19. Die astrale Bedeutung der Hand.

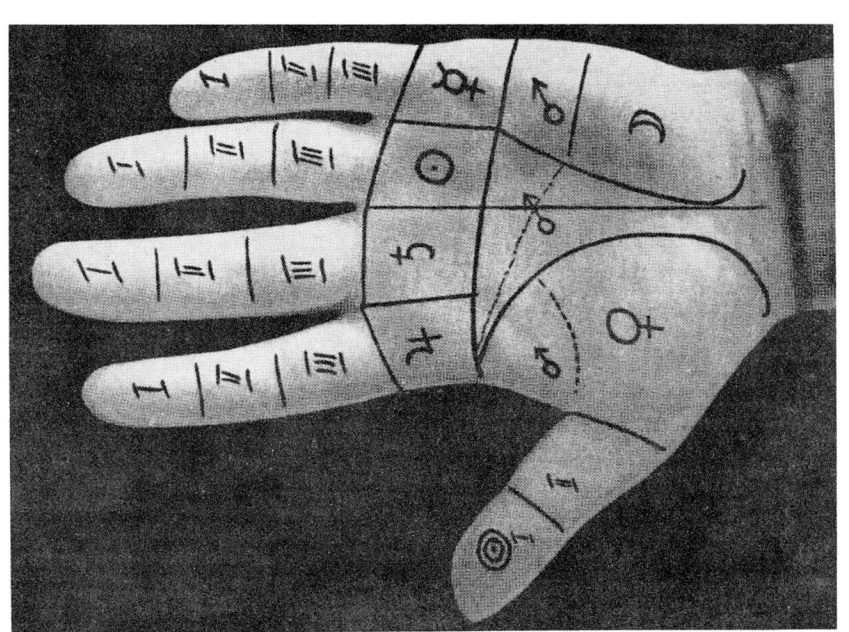

Bild 18. Handberge, genaue Begrenzung.

9

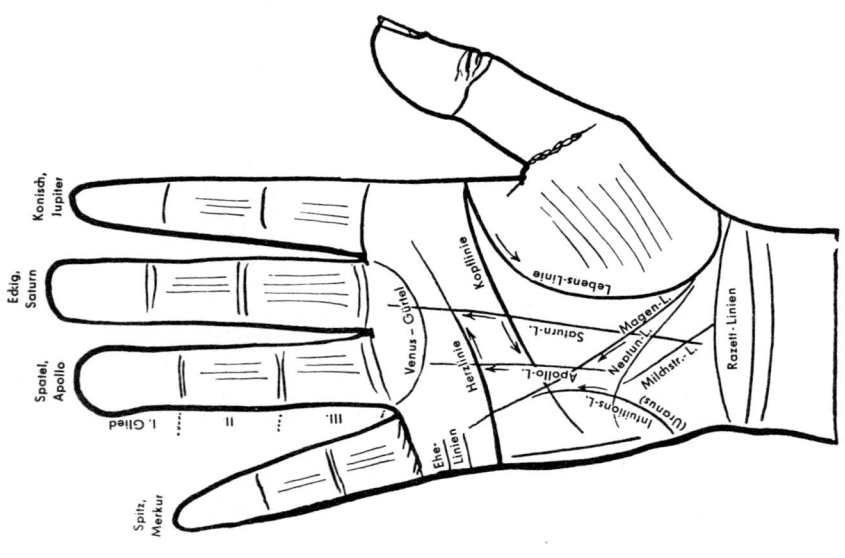

Bild 21. Hauptlinien der Hand und ihre Lage.

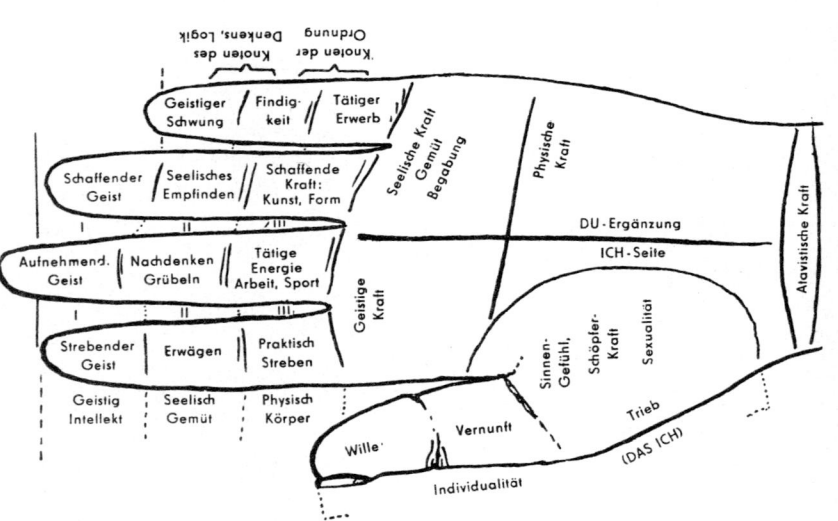

Bild 20. Kabbalistische Einteilung (Ur-arisch).

10

LINIEN-FORMATIONEN:

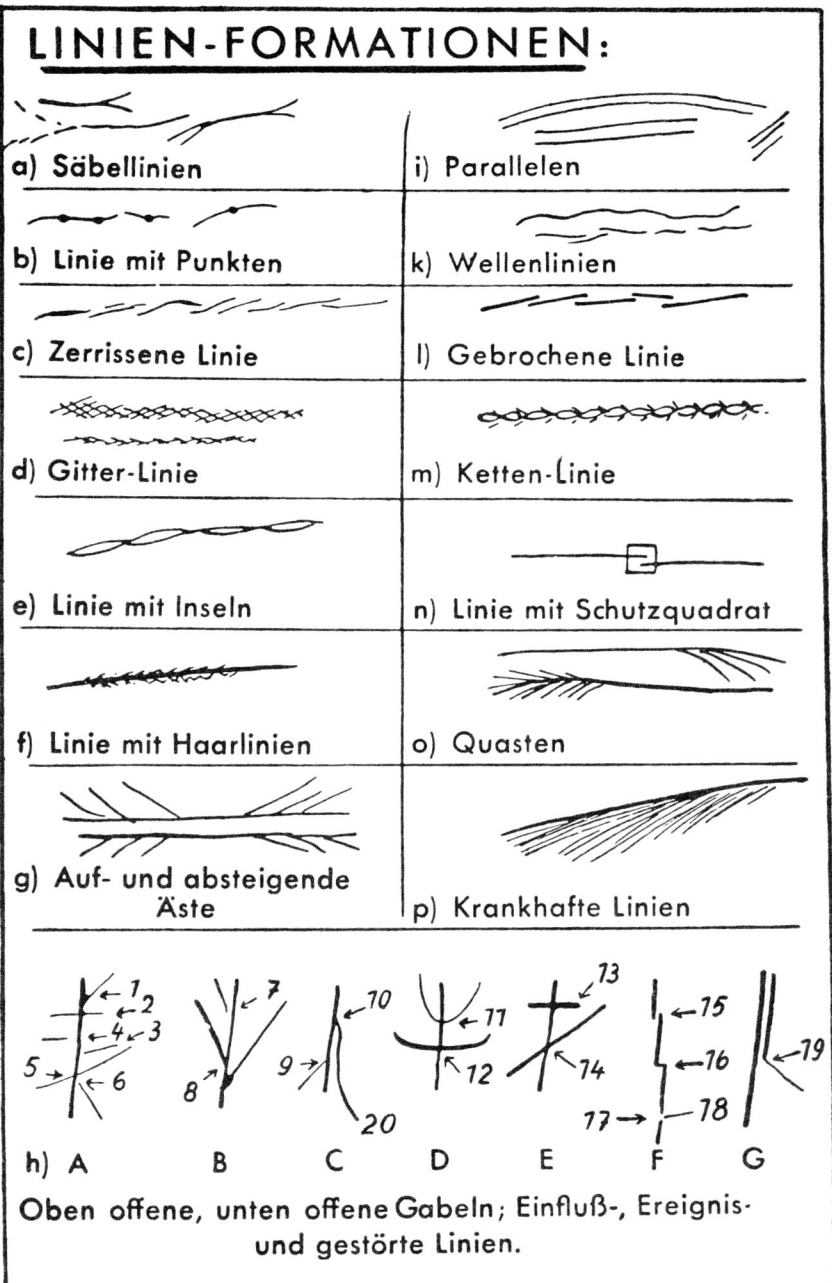

a) Säbellinien	**i) Parallelen**
b) Linie mit Punkten	**k) Wellenlinien**
c) Zerrissene Linie	**l) Gebrochene Linie**
d) Gitter-Linie	**m) Ketten-Linie**
e) Linie mit Inseln	**n) Linie mit Schutzquadrat**
f) Linie mit Haarlinien	**o) Quasten**
g) Auf- und absteigende Äste	**p) Krankhafte Linien**

h) A B C D E F G

Oben offene, unten offene Gabeln; Einfluß-, Ereignis-
und gestörte Linien.

Bild 22.

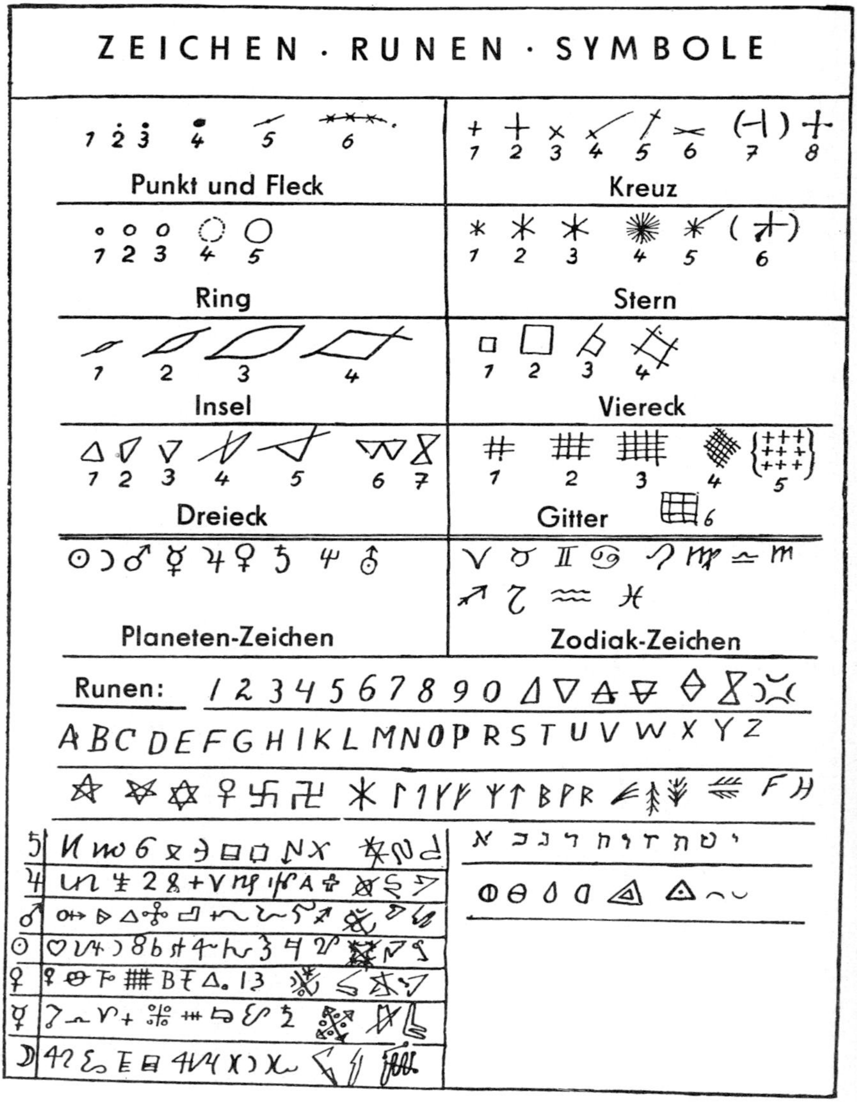

ZEICHEN · RUNEN · SYMBOLE

Punkt und Fleck	**Kreuz**
Ring	**Stern**
Insel	**Viereck**
Dreieck	**Gitter**
Planeten-Zeichen	**Zodiak-Zeichen**

Runen: 1 2 3 4 5 6 7 8 9 0 △ ▽ ⊕ ⊽ ◇ ⊗

A B C D E F G H I K L M N O P R S T U V W X Y Z

Bild 23.

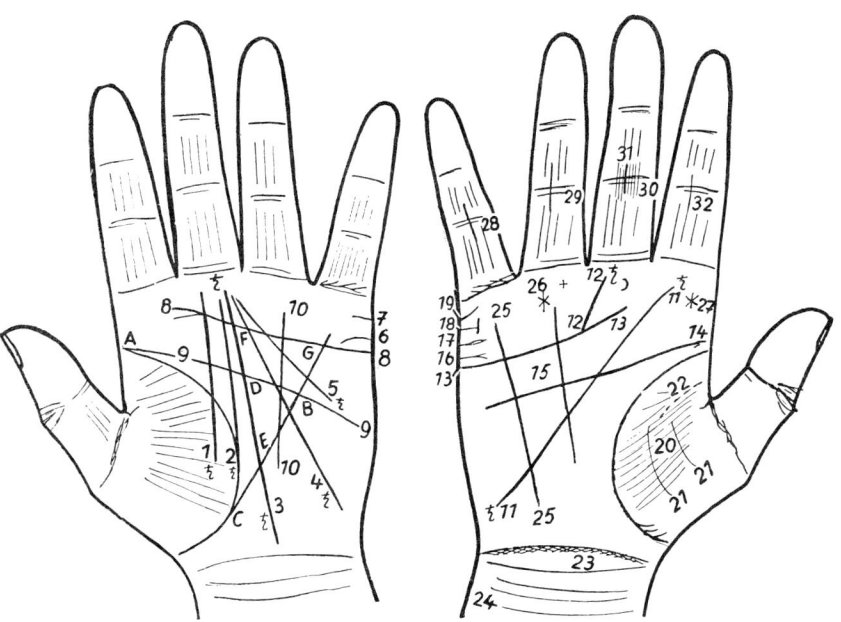

Bild 24. Verschiedene Linienkonstellationen und Zeichen.

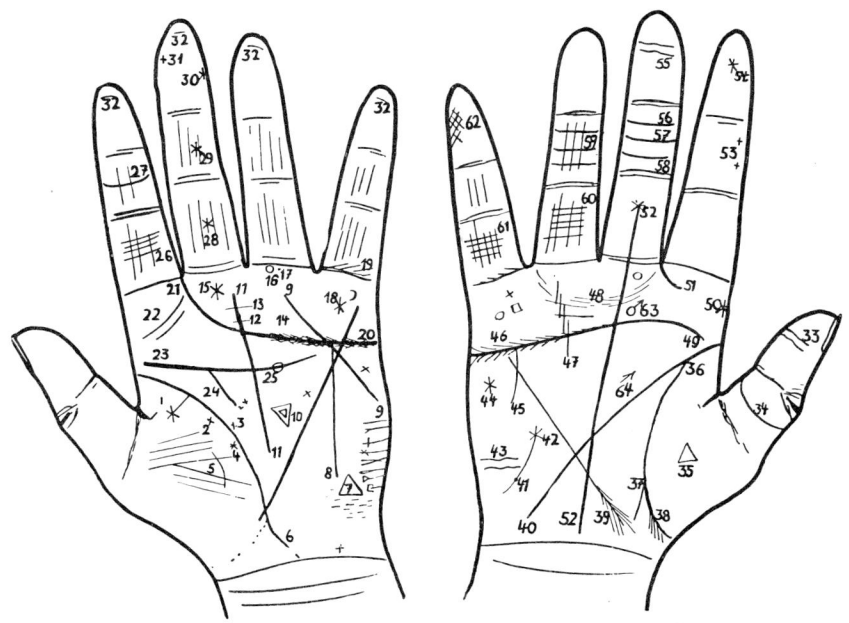

Bild 25. Verschiedene Linienkonstellationen und Zeichen.

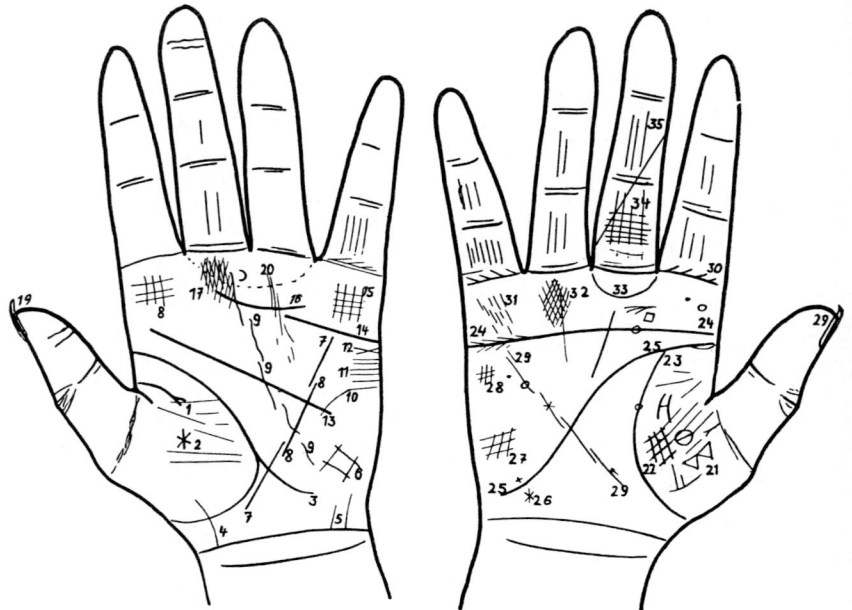

Bild 26. Verschiedene Linienkonstellationen und Zeichen.

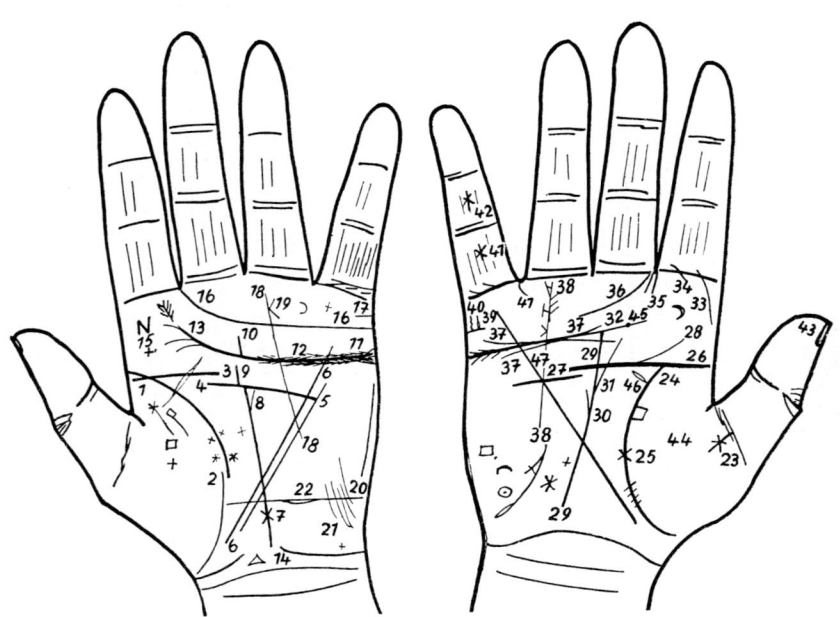

Bild 27. Verschiedene Linienkonstellationen und Zeichen.

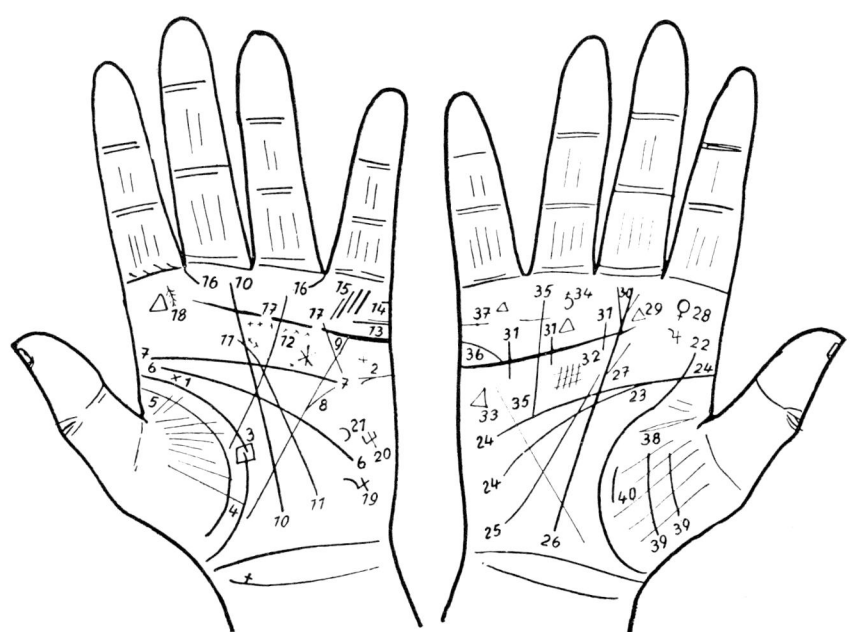

Bild 28. Verschiedene Linienkonstellationen und Zeichen.

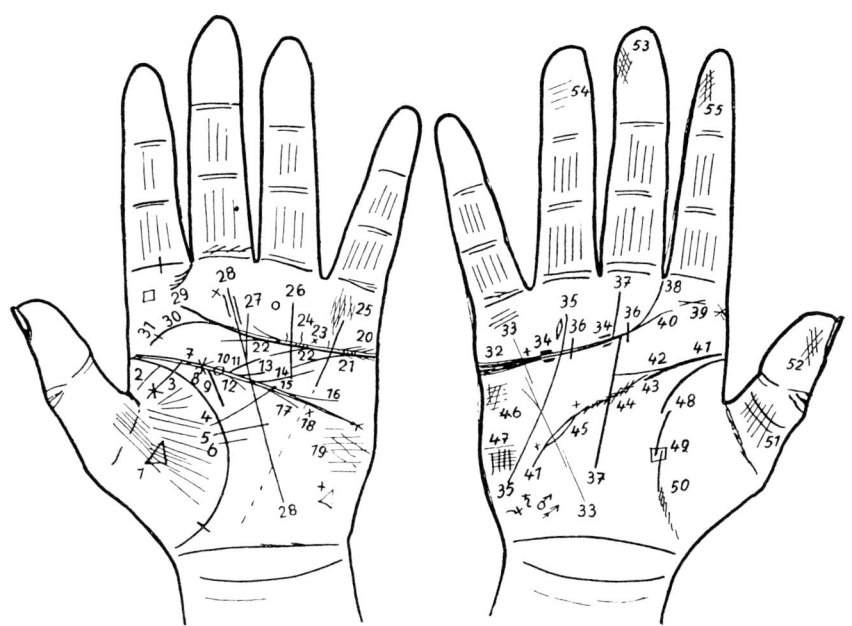

Bild 29. Verschiedene Linienkonstellationen und Zeichen.

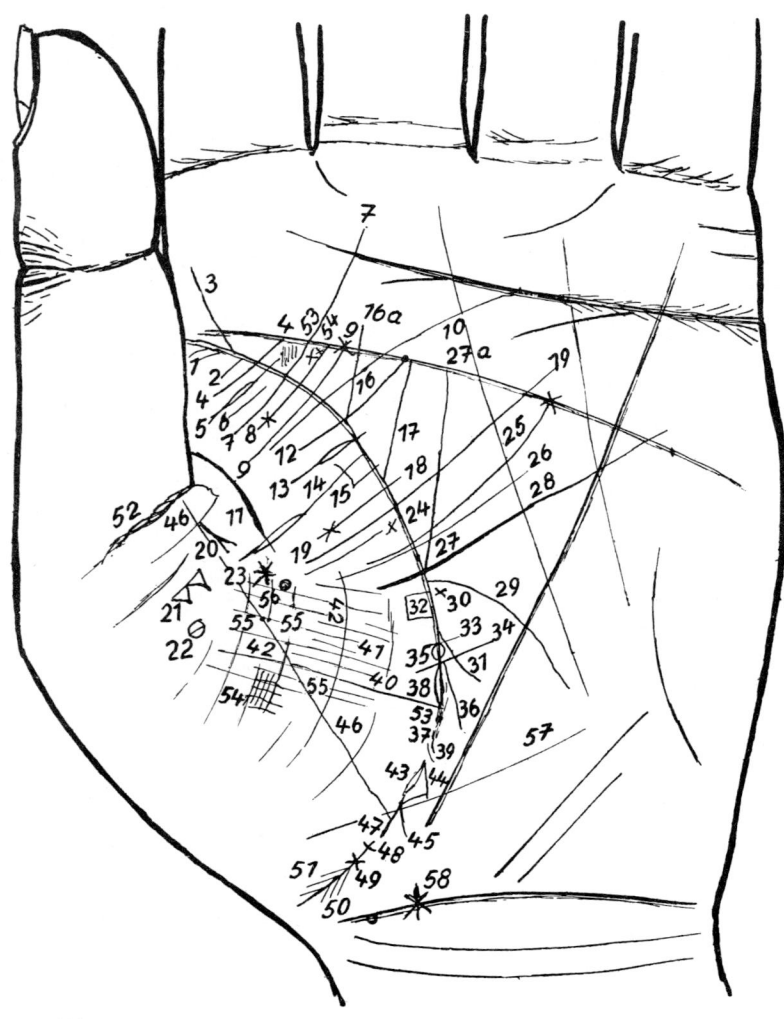

Bild 30. Linien- und Zeichenkombinationen in Verbindung mit Venusberg, Lebenslinie und Kopflinie.

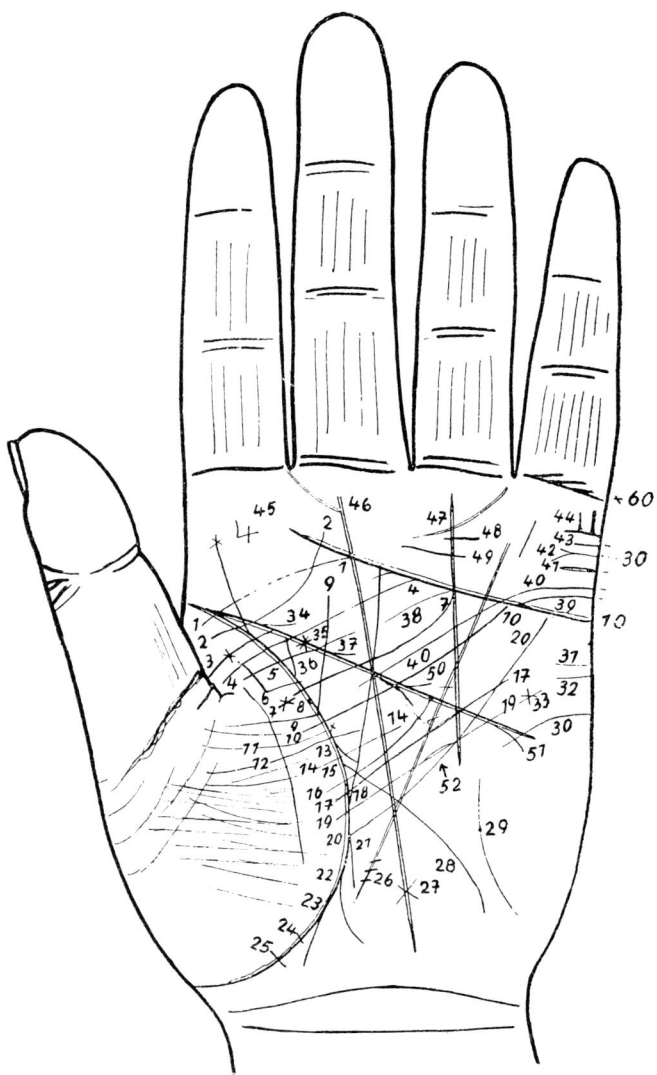

Bild 31. Ereignislinien und deren Kombinationen.

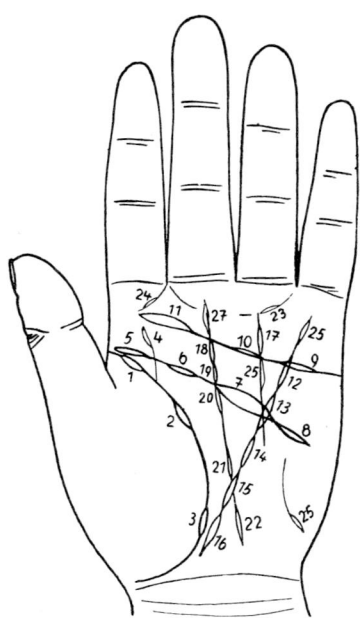

Bild 32. Vererbungszeichen für Krankheiten in den Hauptlinien.

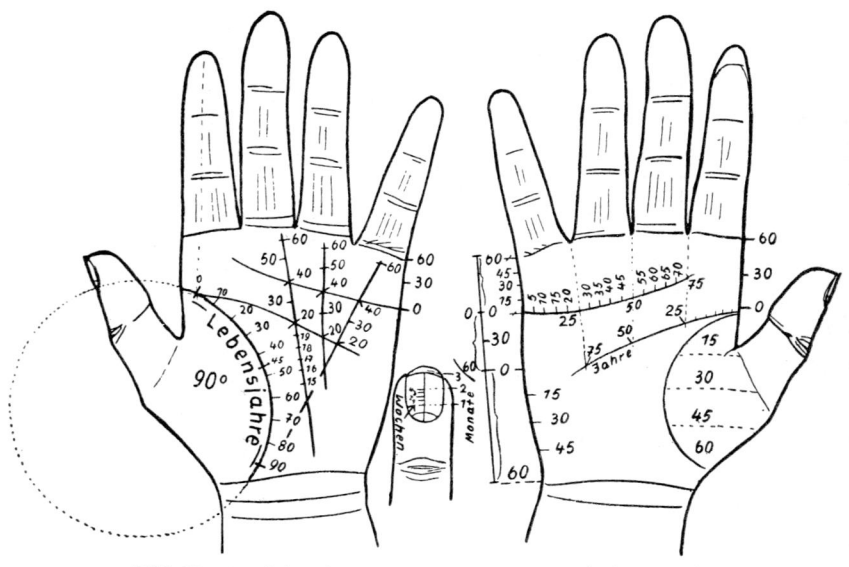

Bild 33. Maßeinteilung der Linien, Berge und des Nagels.

18

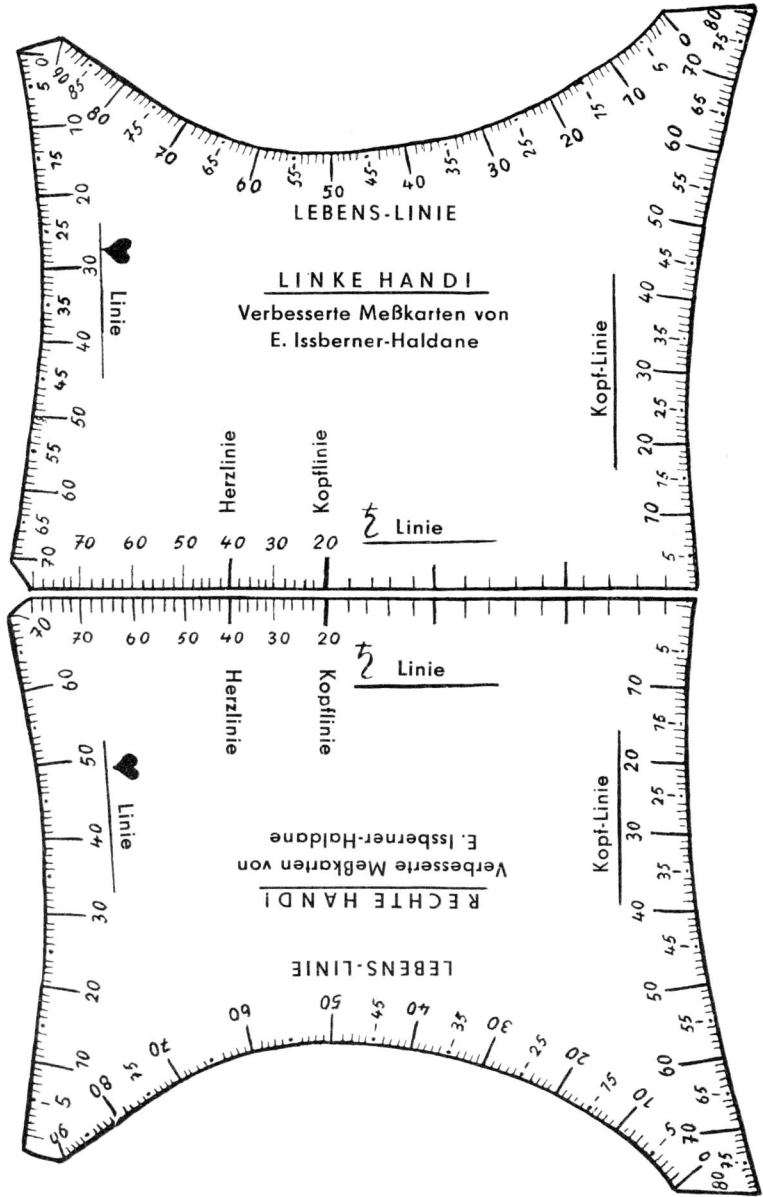

Bild 34. Meßtafeln für die Handlinien.

19

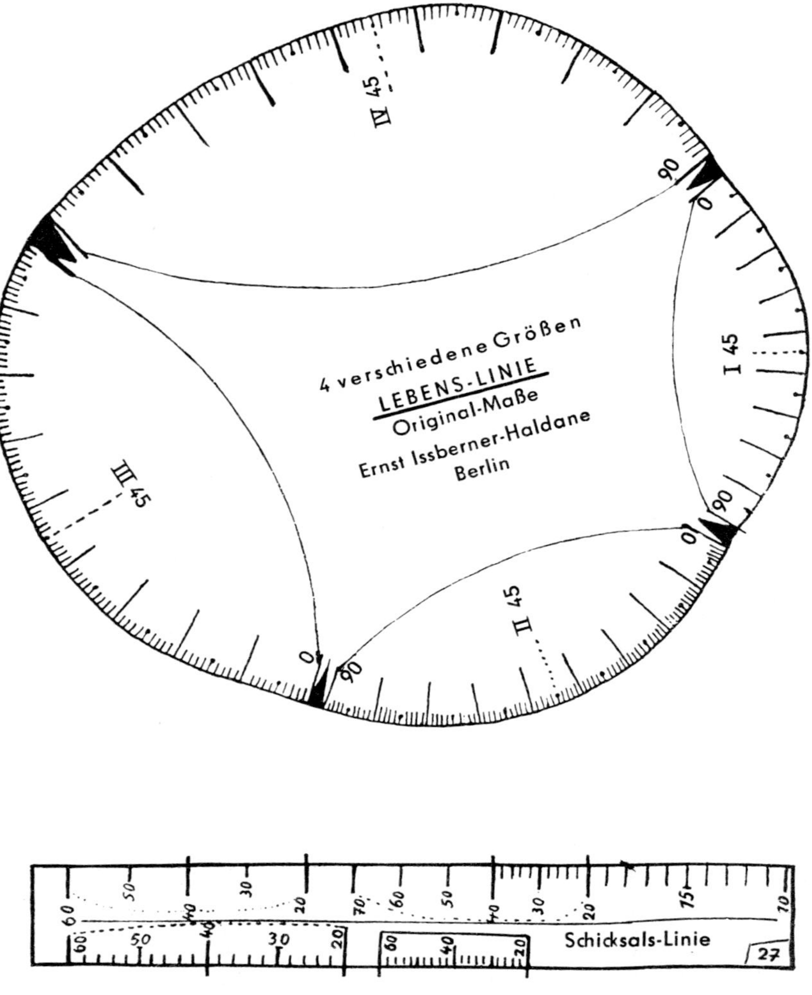

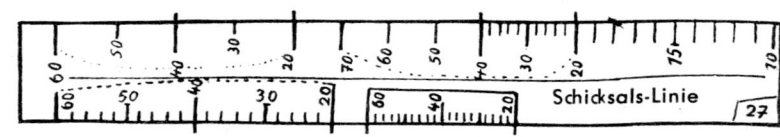

Bild 34a. Meßtafeln für die Handlinien.

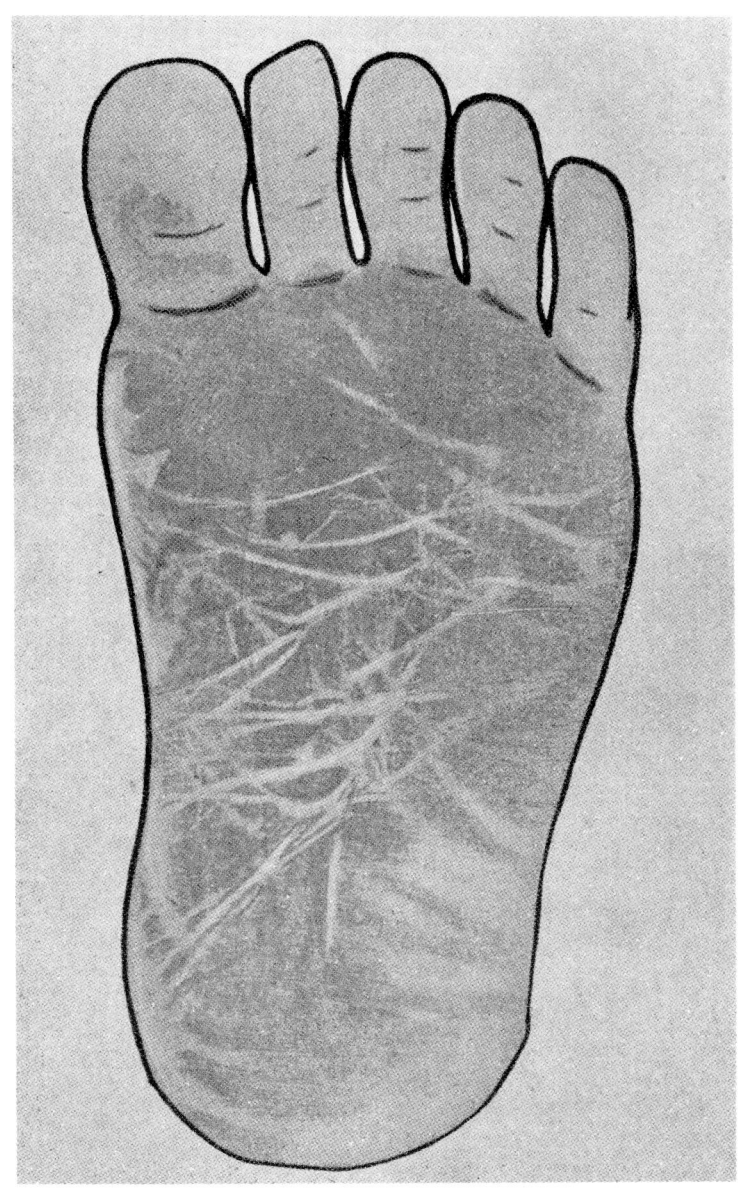

Bild 35. Abdruck der Fußlinien (Herr Unthan, ohne Arme geboren).

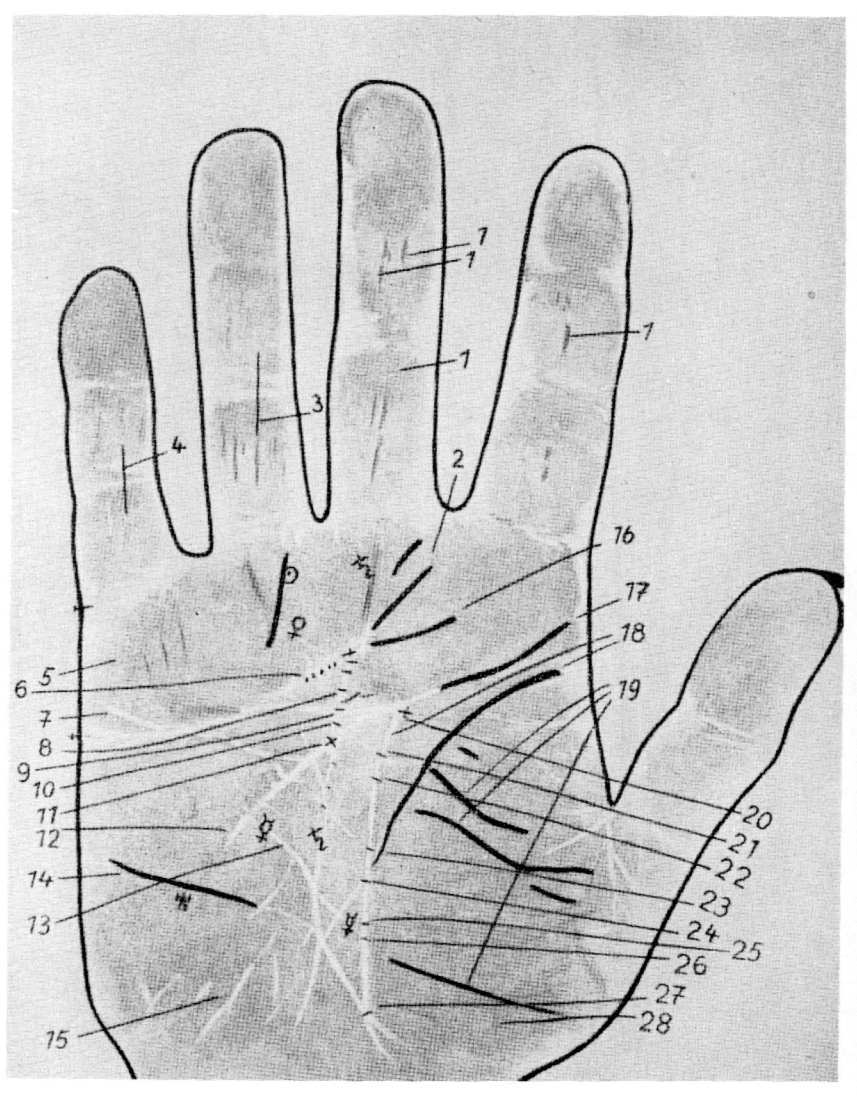

Bild 36. Handabdruck mit wenig Linien, mit Analysenübung.

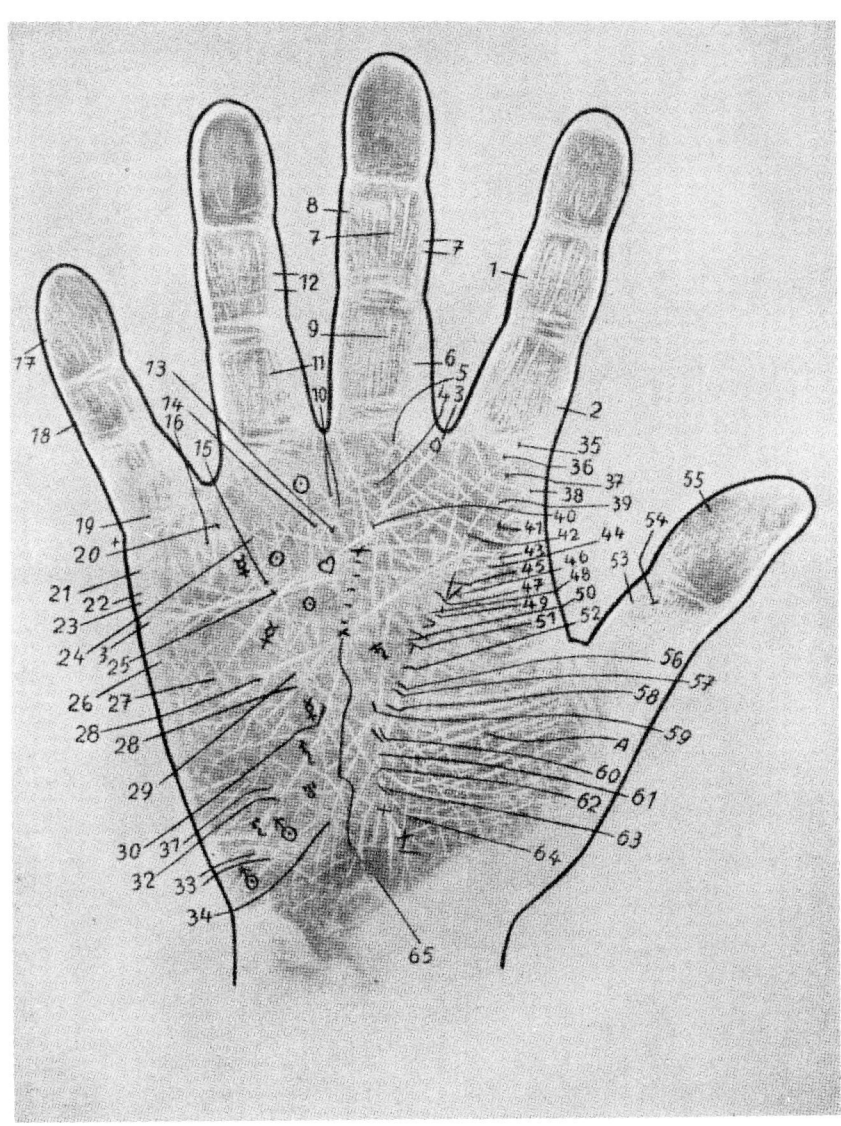

Bild 37. Handabdruck mit vielen Linien, mit Analysenübung.

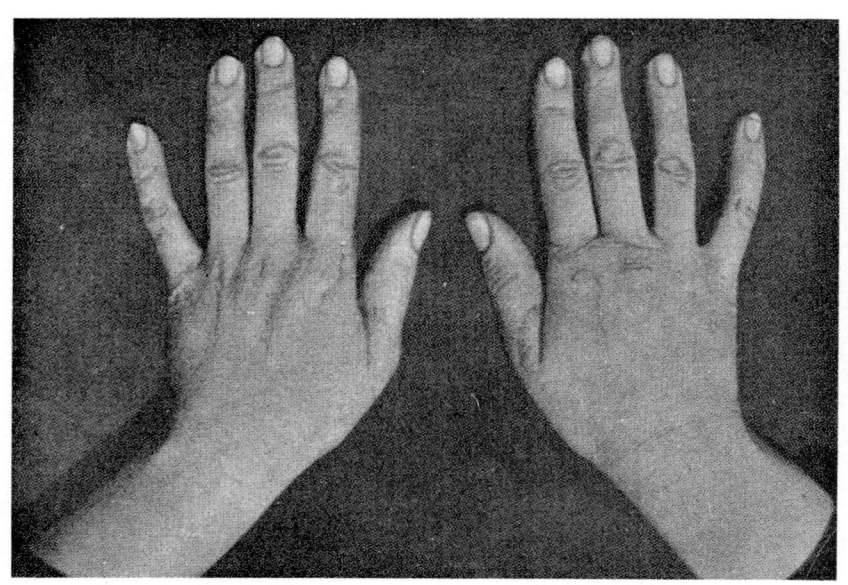

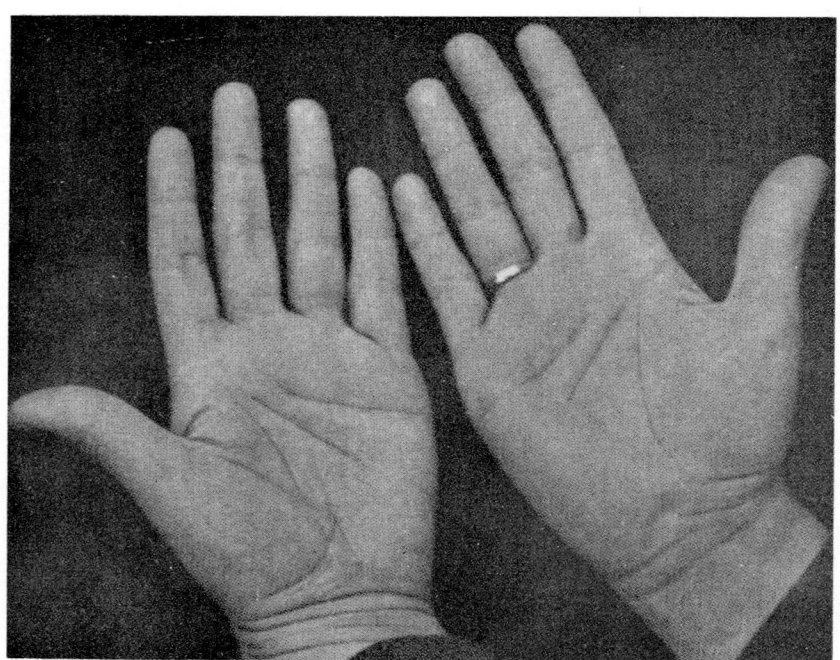

Bild 38. Weiblich: Konische Hand mit eckigem Einschlag.

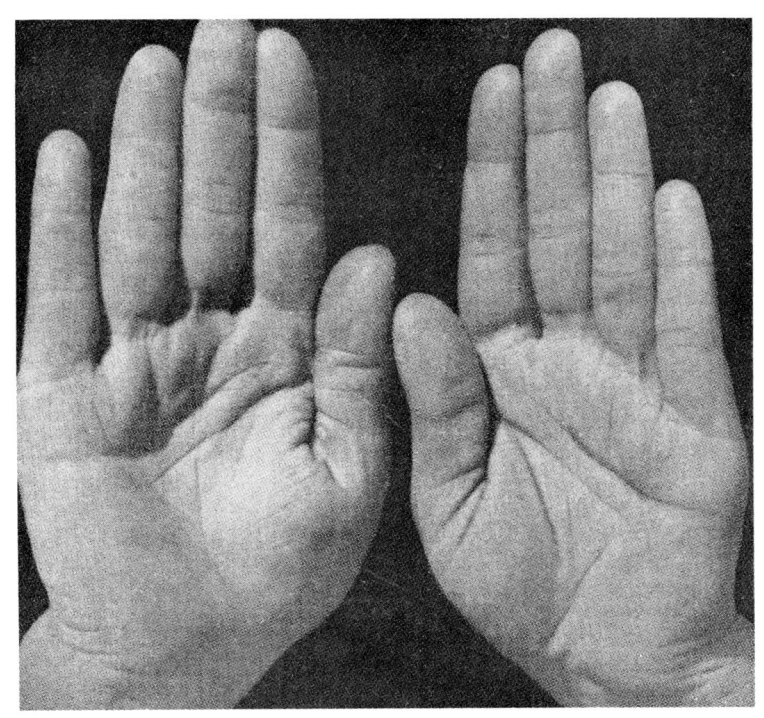

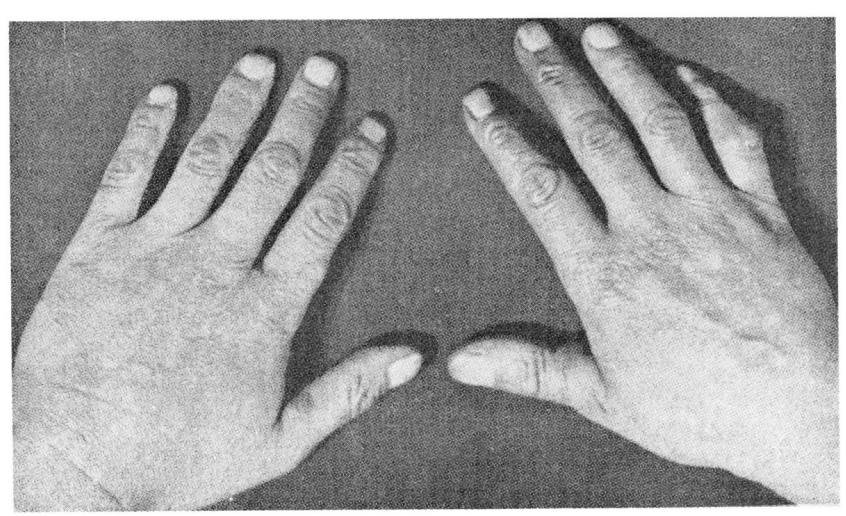

Bild 39. Weiblich: Grundtyp Konisch-Materiell gemischt.

25

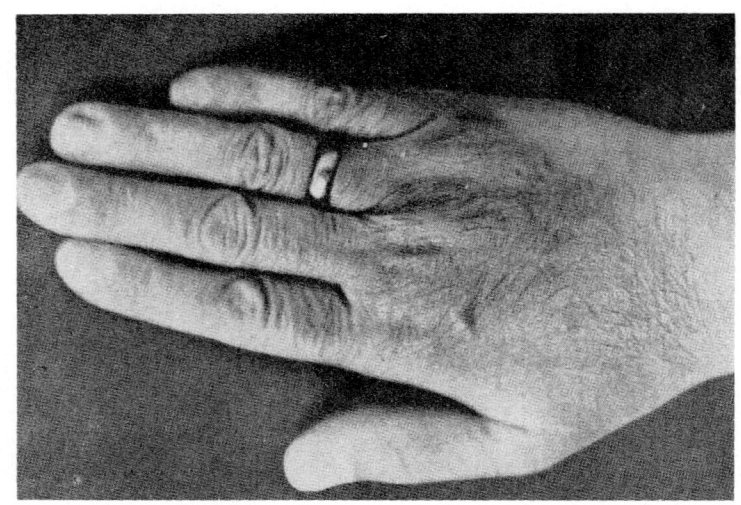

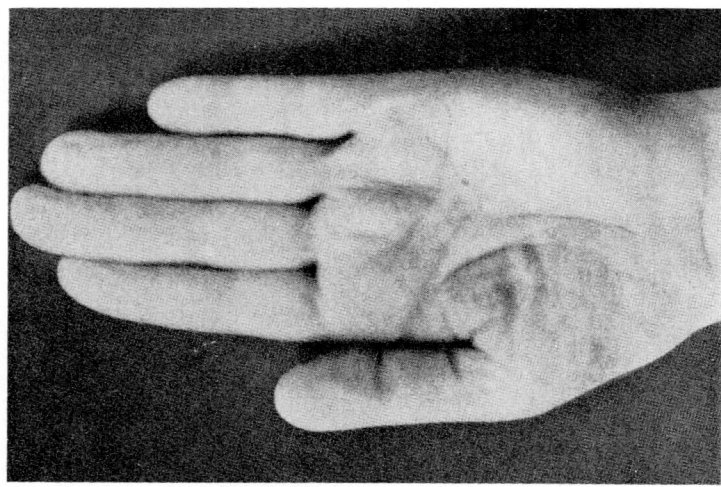

Käthe Kollwitz

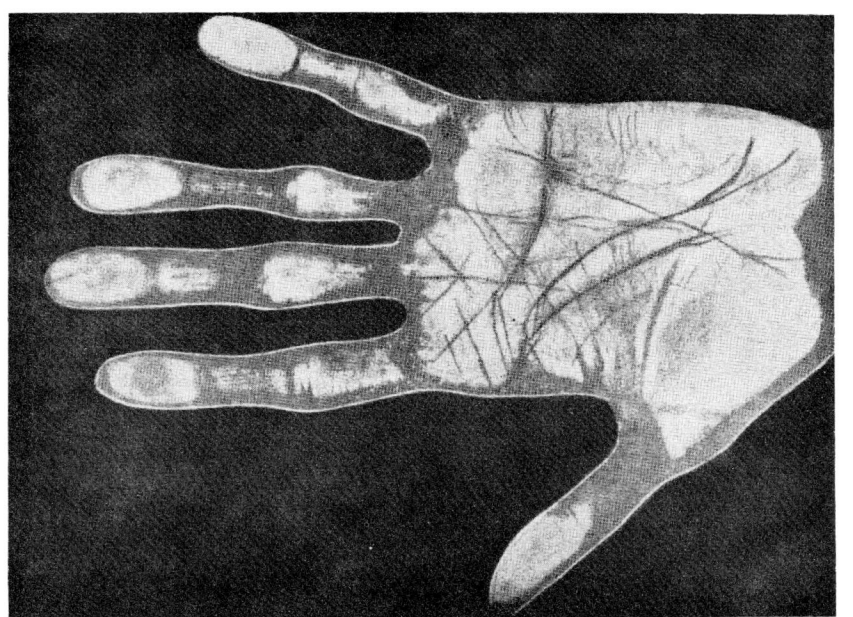

Bild 42. Hand eines Selbstmörders (typische Kopflinienformation).

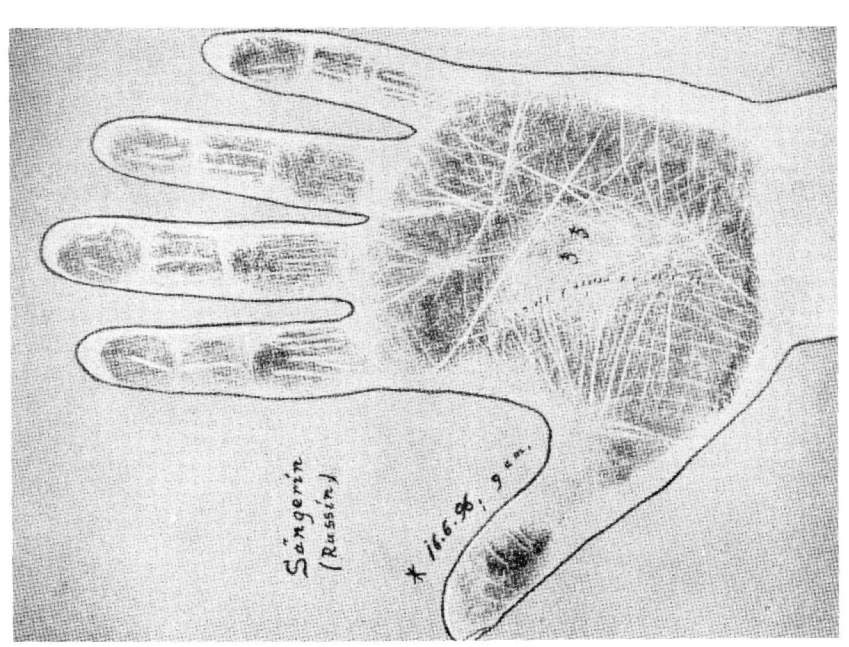

Bild 41. Damenhand mit teilweise sehr guten Linien.

27

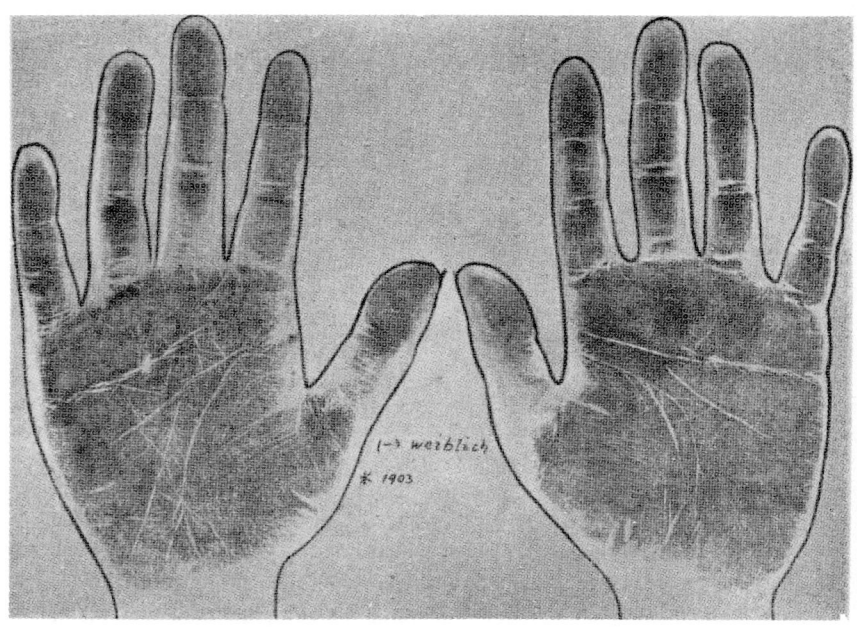

Bild 43. Mädchenhand mit meist schlechten Linienkonstitutionen.

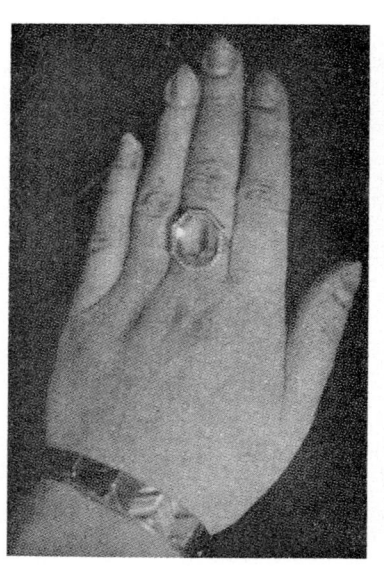
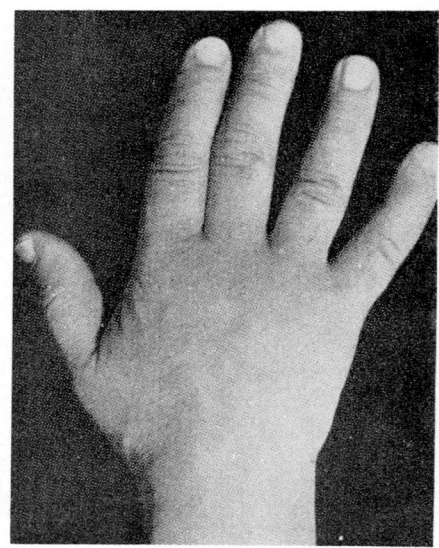

a   Bild 44.   b
a) Sensibel-konisch materielle Hand.
b) Jugend: Praktisch-materielle eckige, gute Handwerkerhand.

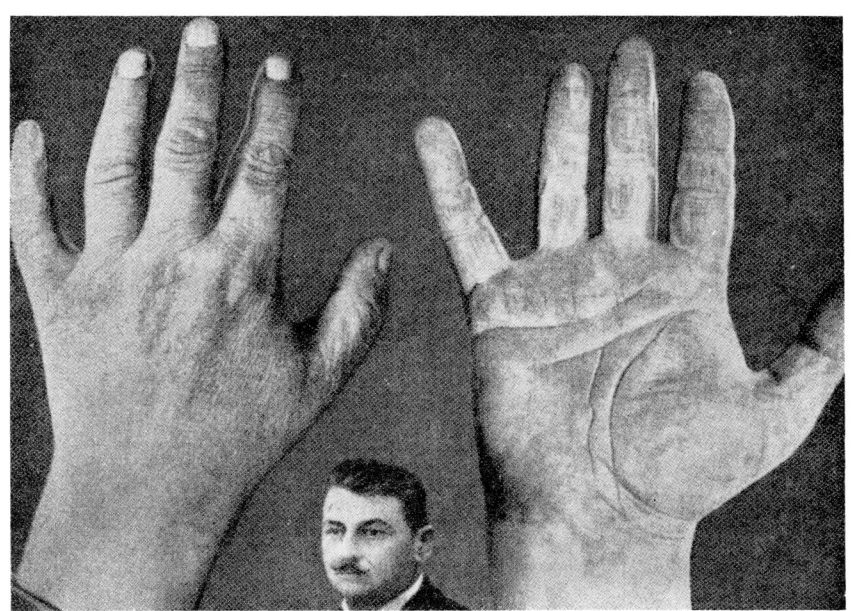

Bild 45. Elementar-konischer Handtyp.

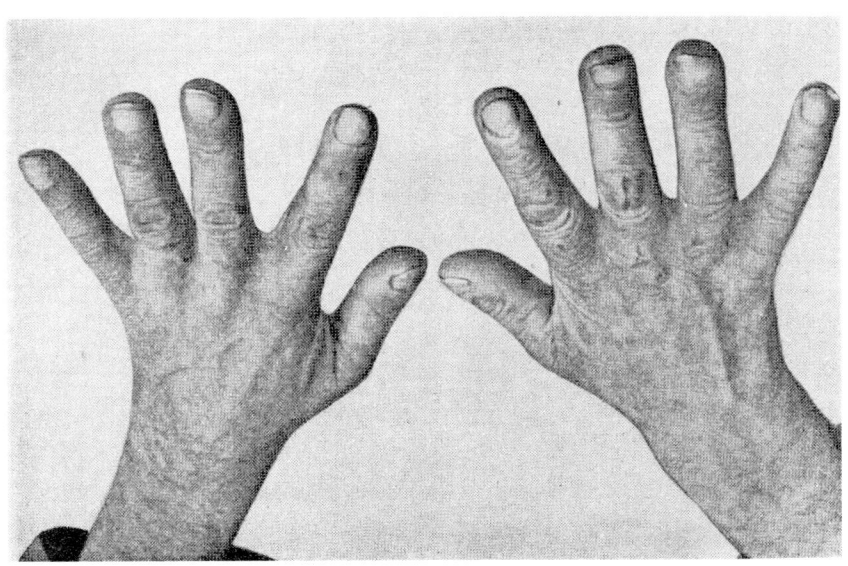

Bild 46. Elementar-eckiger Handtyp, Mörderdaumen.

29

Bild 47. Idealer Frauenhandtyp (mit leicht konischer Beimischung).

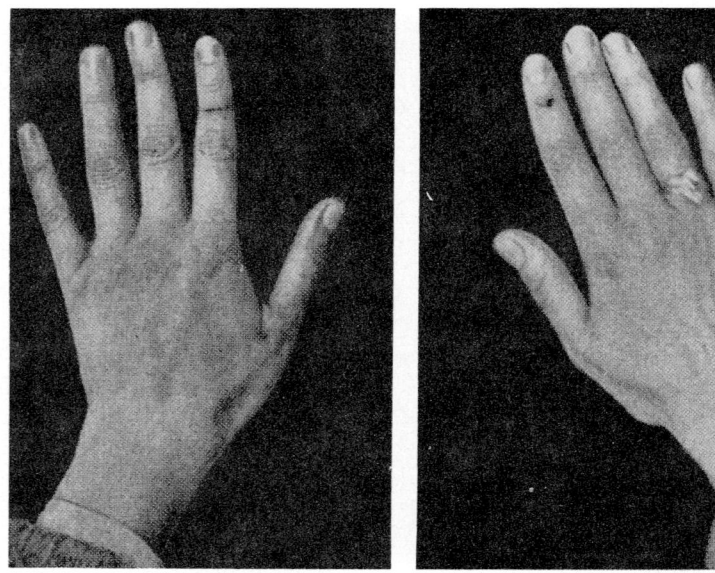

Bild 48. Eckig-konischer Handtyp, idealer Einschlag.

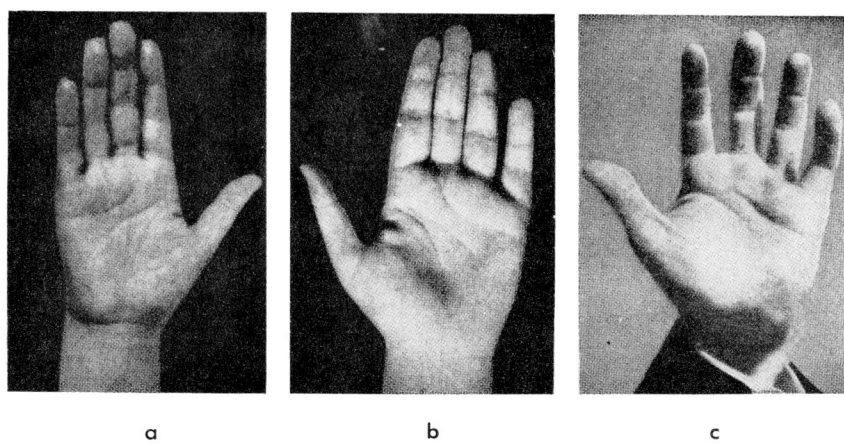

a   b   c

Bild 49. Handtypen der Dreiteilung.
a) Spirituell, b) intellektuell, c) materiell.

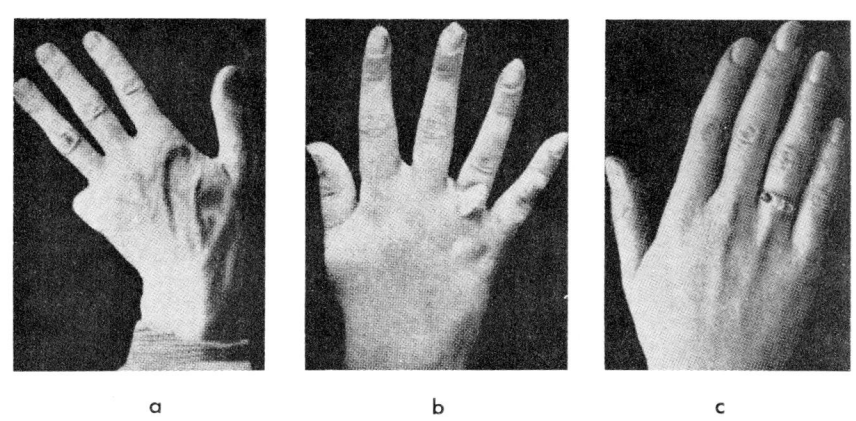

a   b   c

Bild 50. Handtypen.
a) Eckig mit Knoten, b) Konisch weich, c) Konisch-spatel.

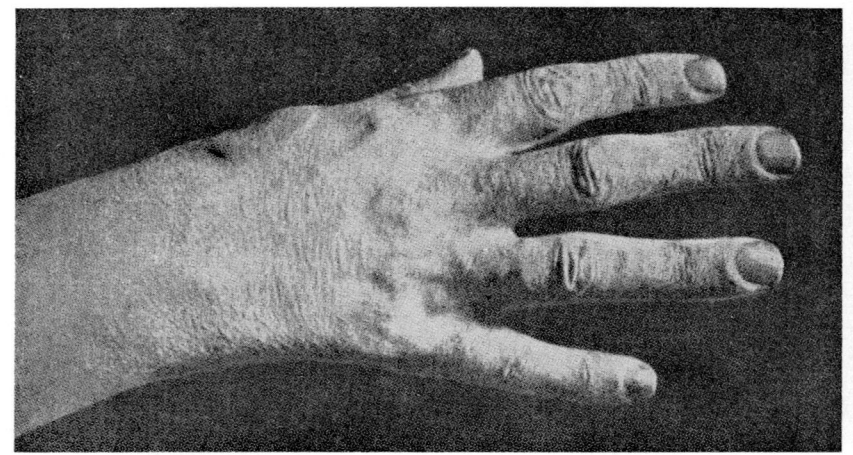

Bild 51. Liszt.

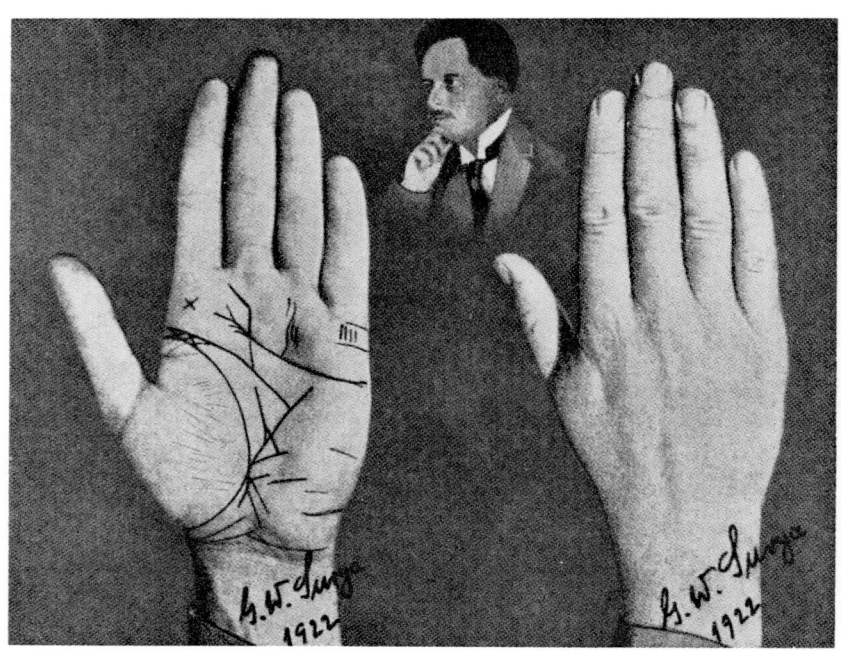

Bild 52. G. W. Surya, einer der bedeutendsten Schriftsteller wissenschaftlich-
okkultistischer Literatur.

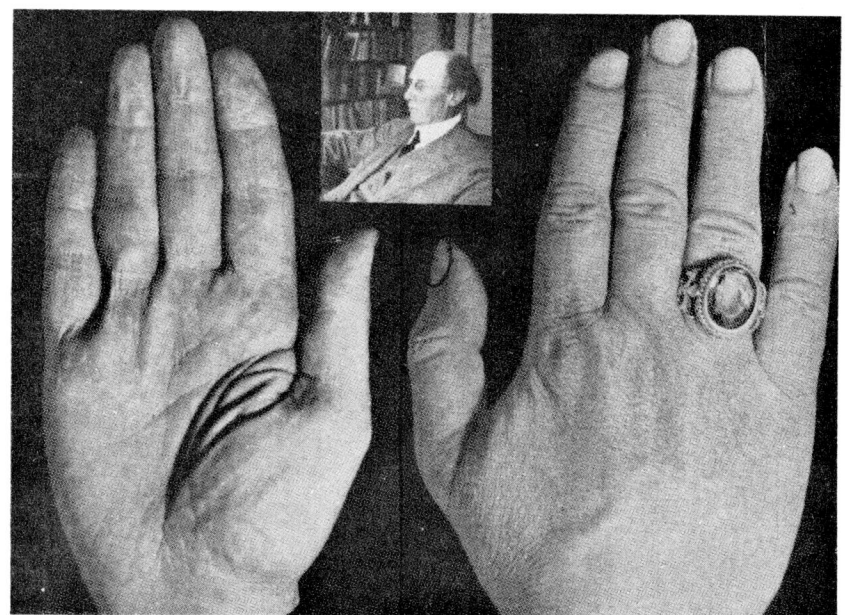

Bild 53. Die Hand des bekannten Anthropologen, Altsprachen- und Religionsforschers, ehemaligen Zisterzienser-Mönches Dr. Baron J. Lanz von Liebenfels.

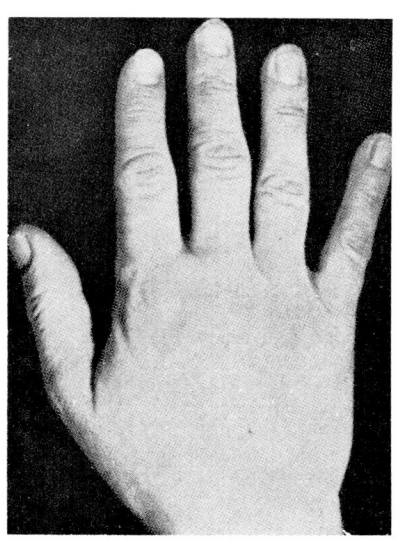 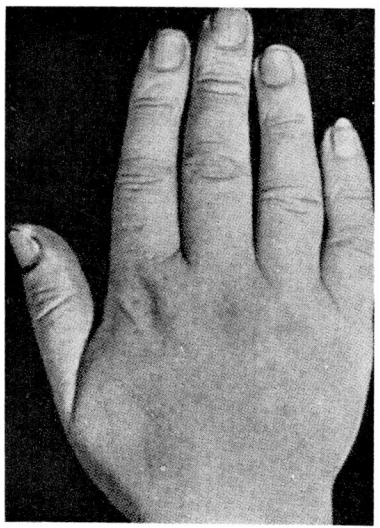

a   Bild 54.   b

a) Die Hand des bedeutenden schwedischen Kunst- und Porträtmalers Ivar Kampke.
b) Die Hand eines weitgereisten Wissenschaftlers.

33

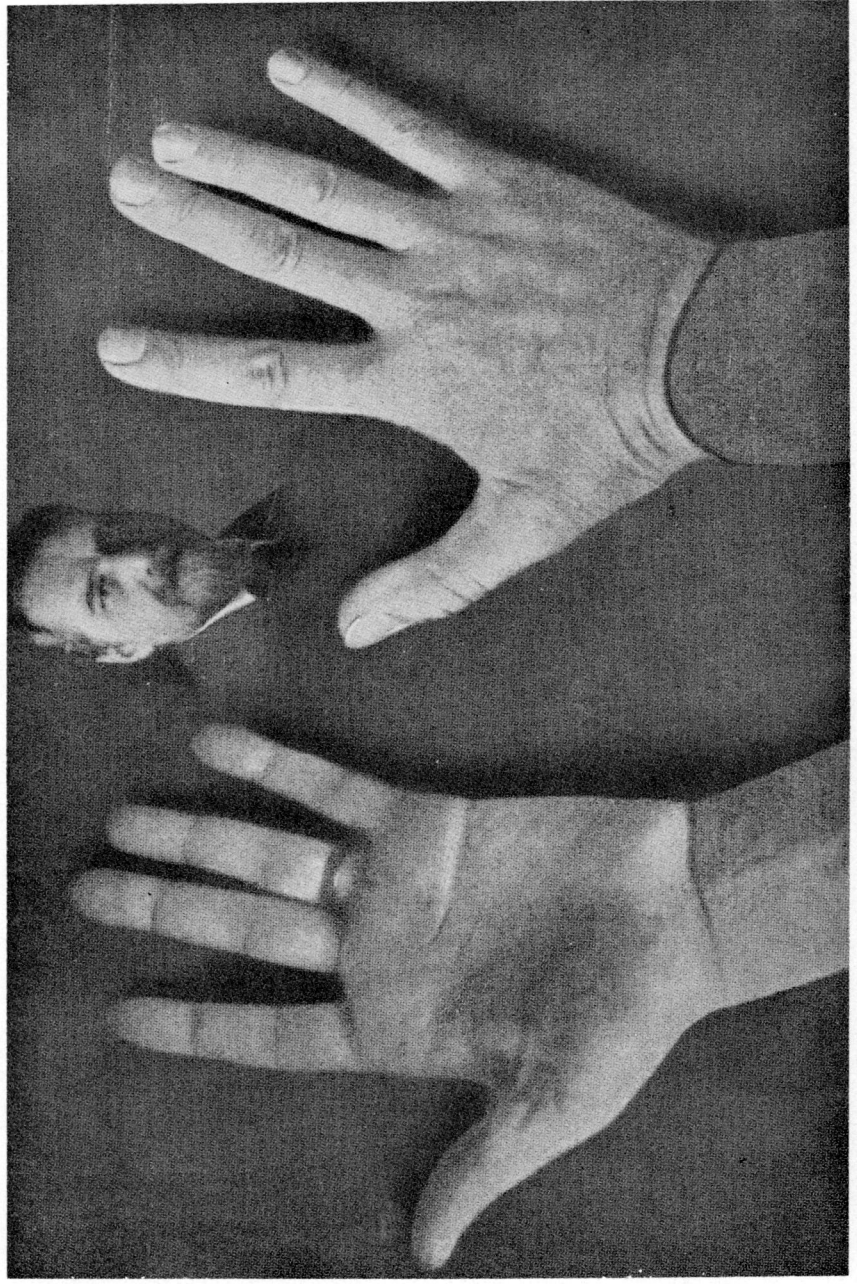

Bild 55. Professor Fahrenkrog, Barmen, hervorragender deutscher Maler.

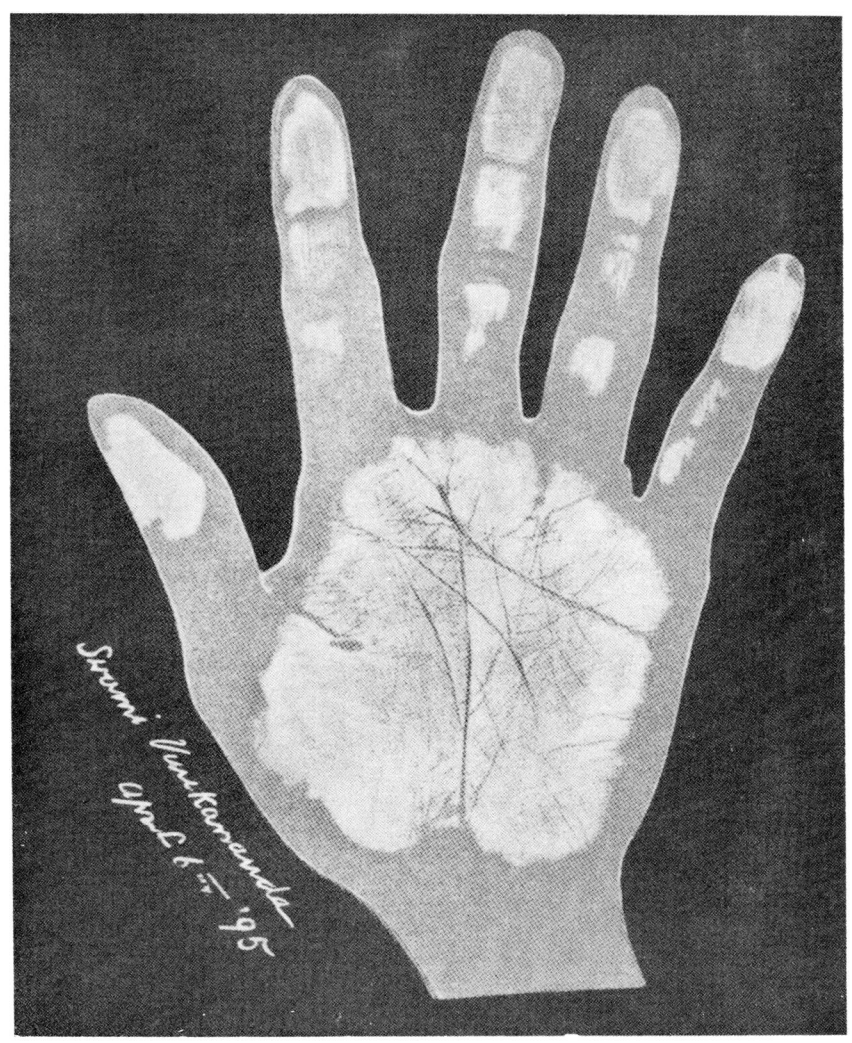

Bild 56. Swami Vivekananda, bekannter indischer Philosoph und Schriftgelehrter.

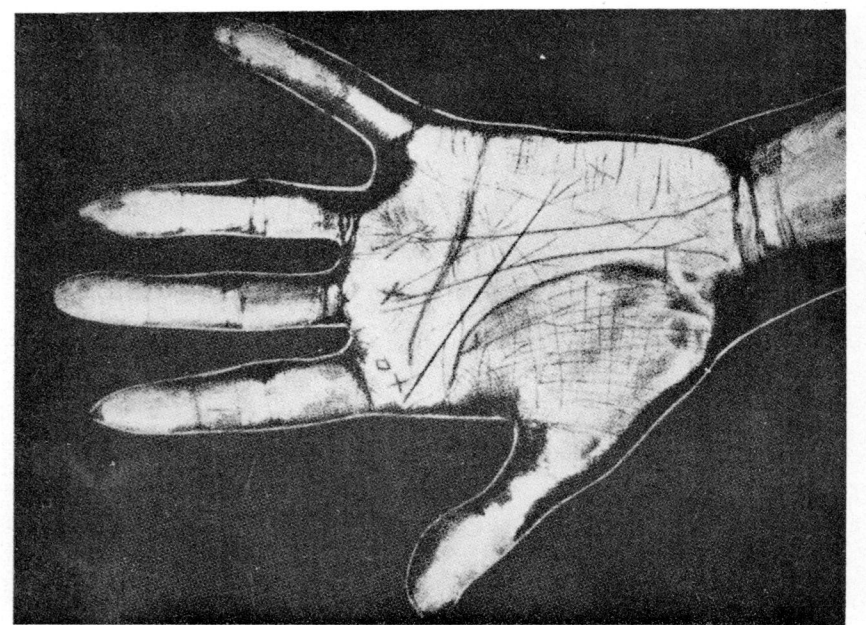

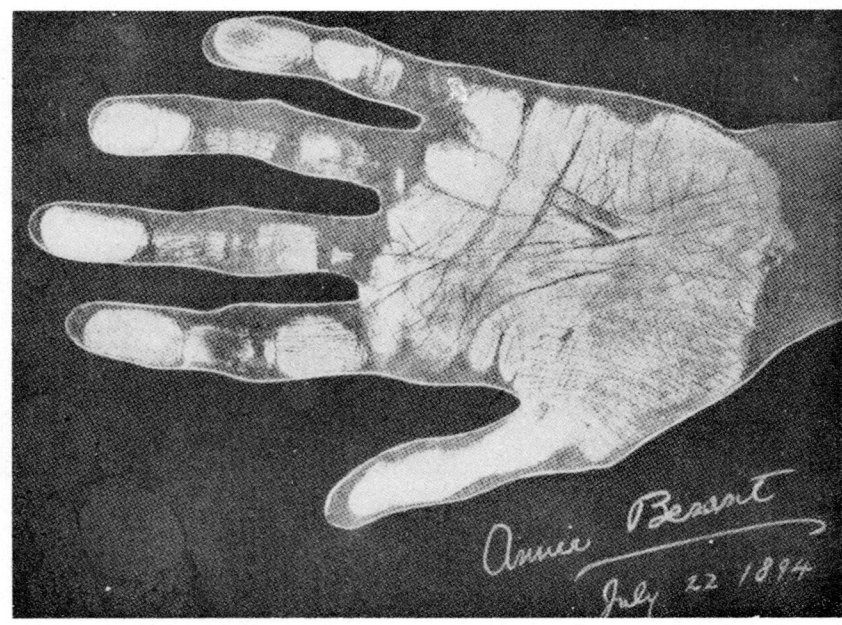

Annie Besant

July 22 1894

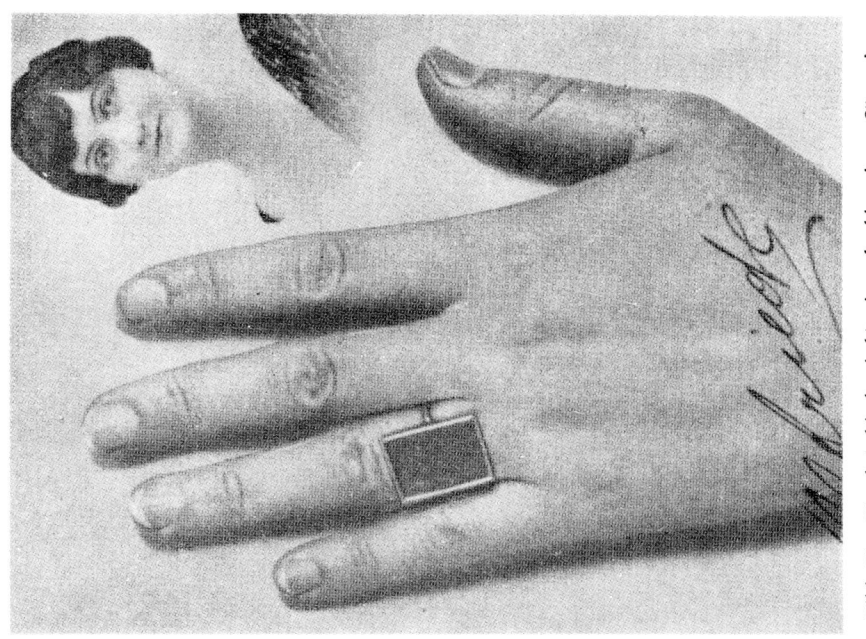

Bild 60. Hand (eckig-konisch) einer hochbegabten Sängerin.

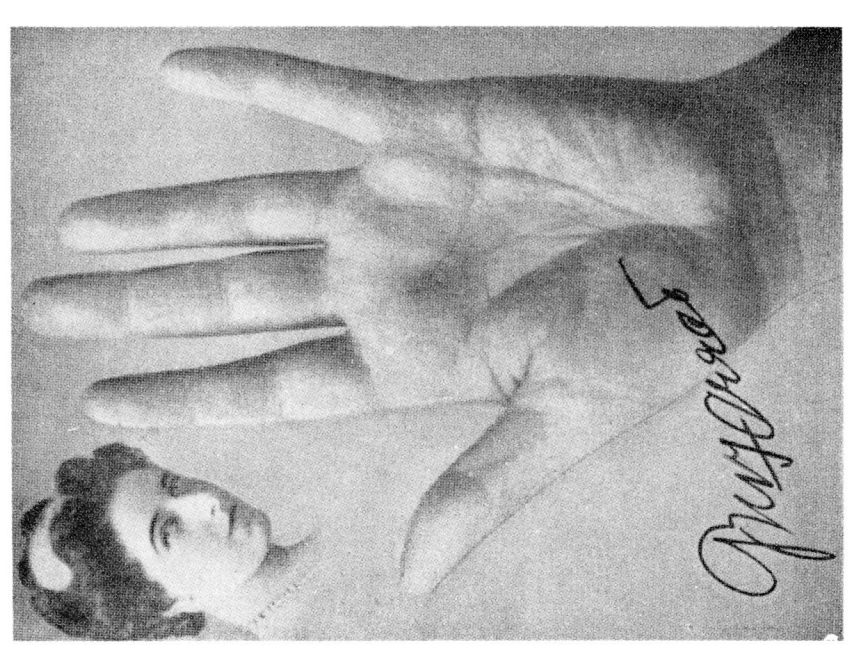

Bild 59. Geraldine Farrar, weltbekannte Operndiva und Kinostern.

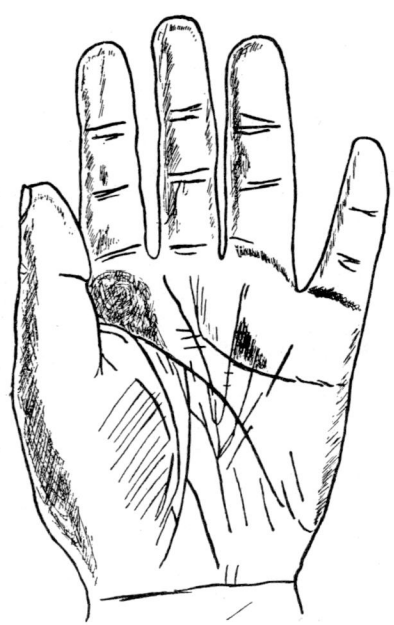

Bild 61. Strindberg (typische Kopflinie für Schwermut).

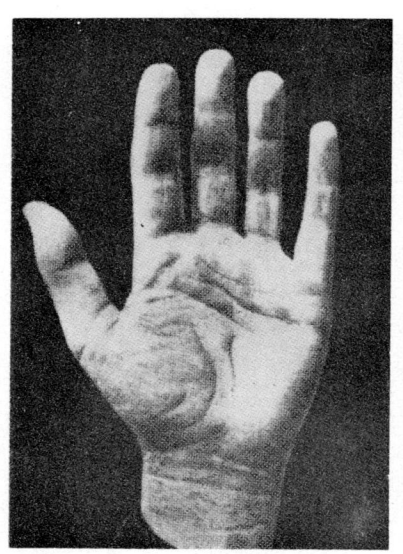
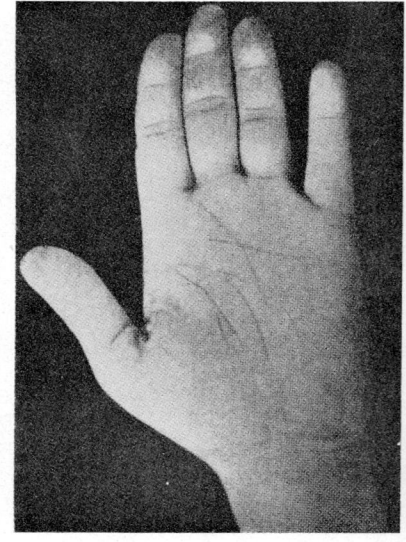

a   Bild 62.   b
a) S. MacManus, Schriftsteller. b) Eugen Carriere, Maler.

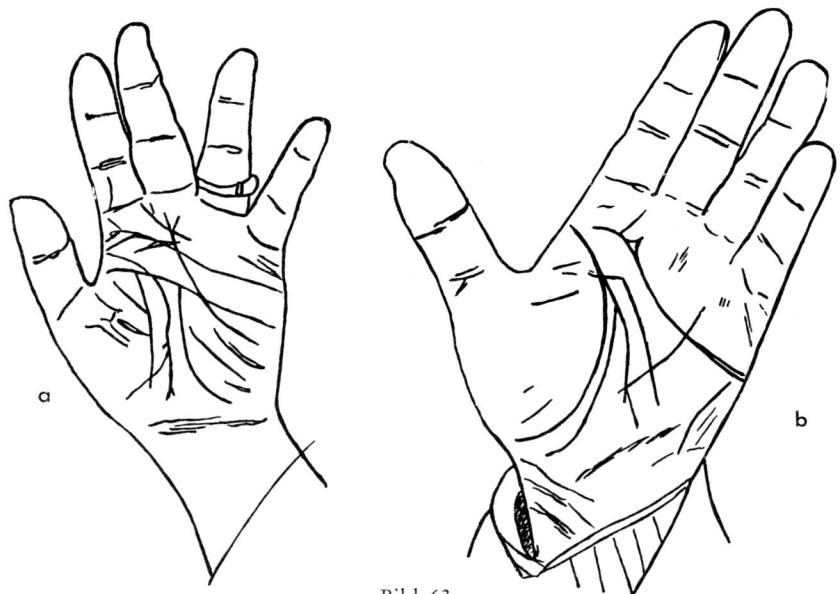

Bild 63.
a) Emile Zola (konische, weiche Genießerhand).
b) Clemenceau (doppelte Kopflinie).

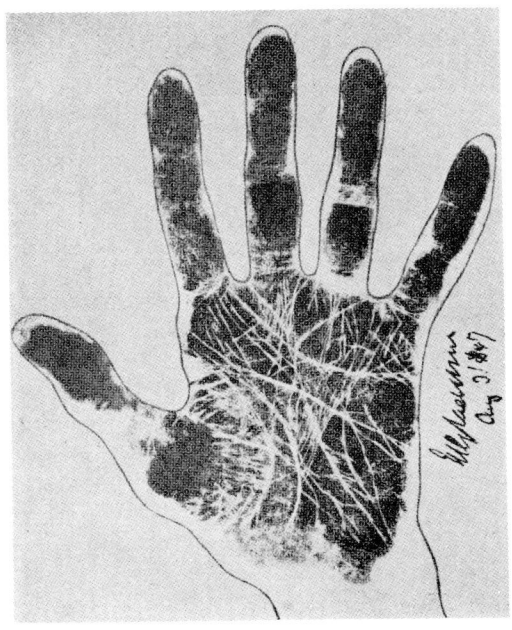

Bild 64. W. E. Gladstone, britischer Staatsmann.

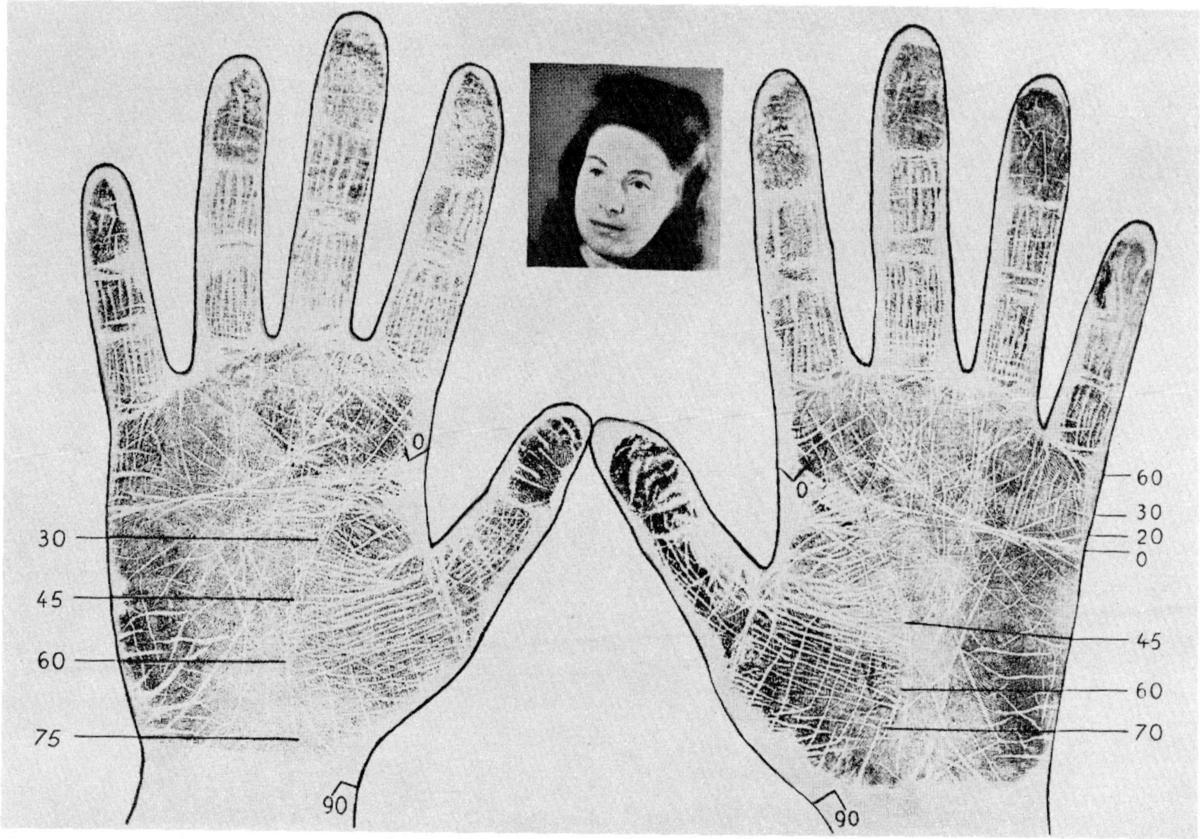

Bild 65. Linienreiche Studienhand einer Stenotypistin.

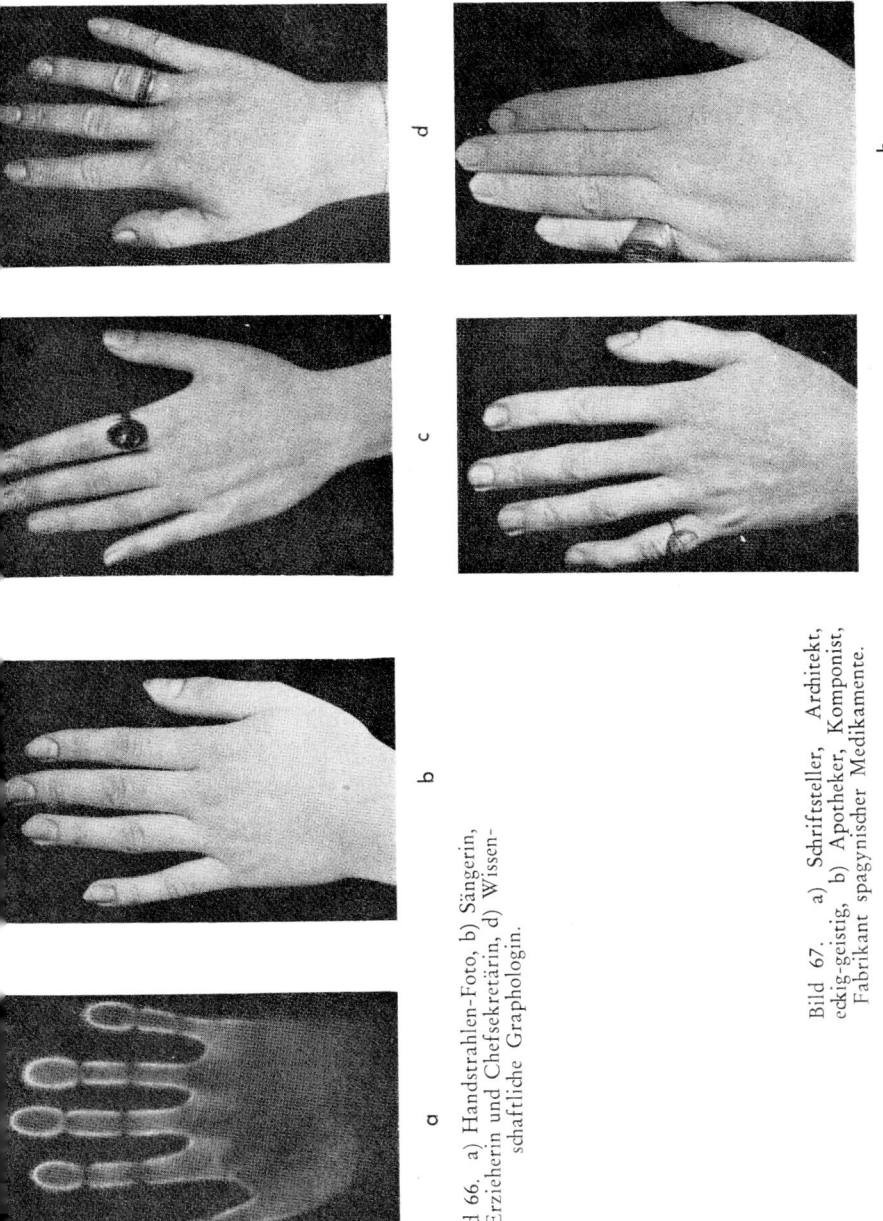

Bild 66. a) Handstrahlen-Foto, b) Sängerin,
c) Erzieherin und Chefsekretärin, d) Wissenschaftliche Graphologin.

Bild 67. a) Schriftsteller, Architekt,
eckig-geistig, b) Apotheker, Komponist,
Fabrikant spagyrischer Medikamente.

41

Oben: Bild 68. a) Theologin, b) Theologe, c) Dipl.-Ingenieur elekt., d) Studentin rer. pol.
Unten: Bild 69. a) Kunstgewerblerin, b) Medizinerin, c) Un[...], d) Kün[...]

42

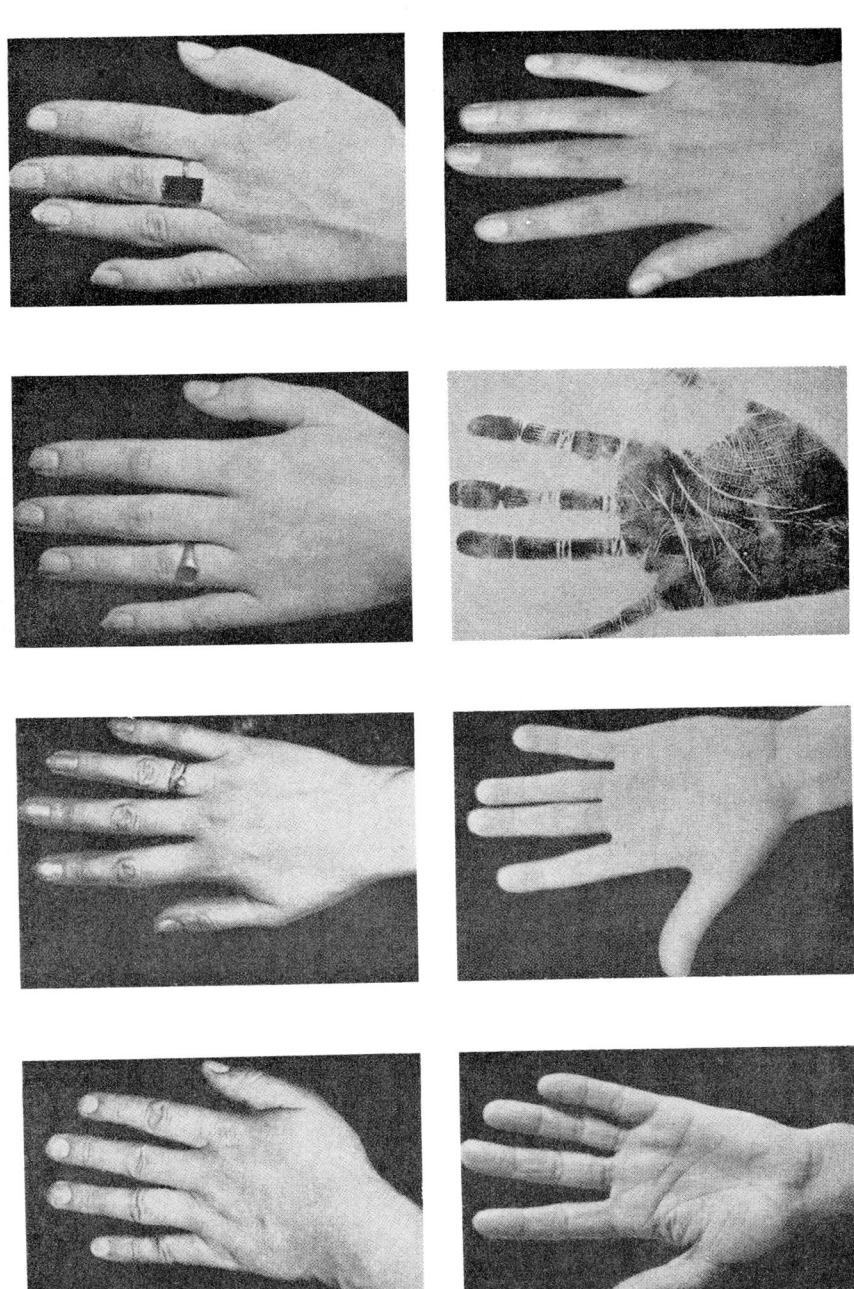

Oben: Bild 70. a) Dr. med. R. Steintel, b) Ärztin, c) Kinderhortnerin, d) Schullehrerin.
Unten: Bild 71. a) Malerin, b) Bildhauerin, c) und d) Innen- und Außenhand eines Mädchens.

43

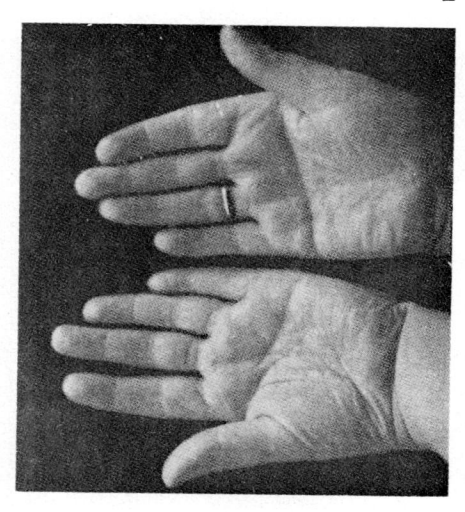
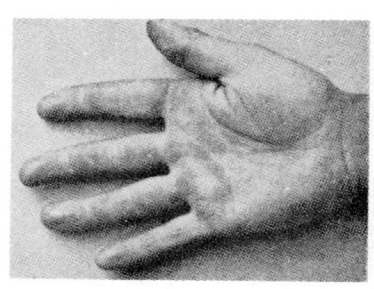
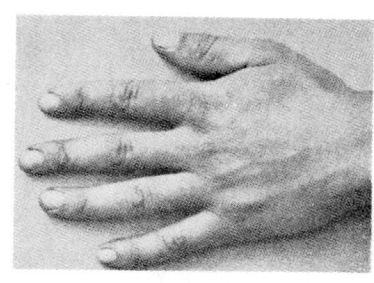
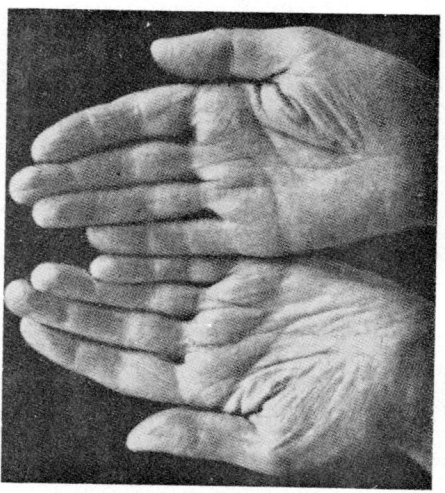
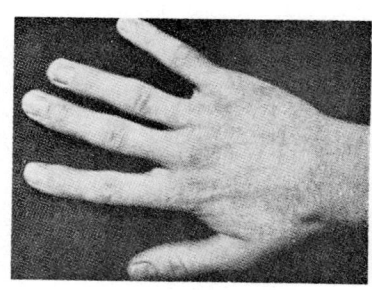
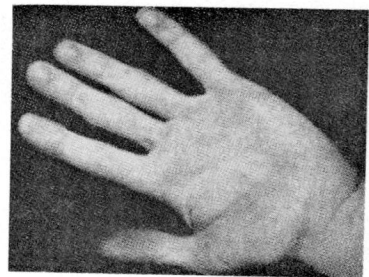

Oben: Bild 72. a) Damenschneiderin, b) Gutsbesitzerin

Unten: Bild 73. a) Studentin der Phil.

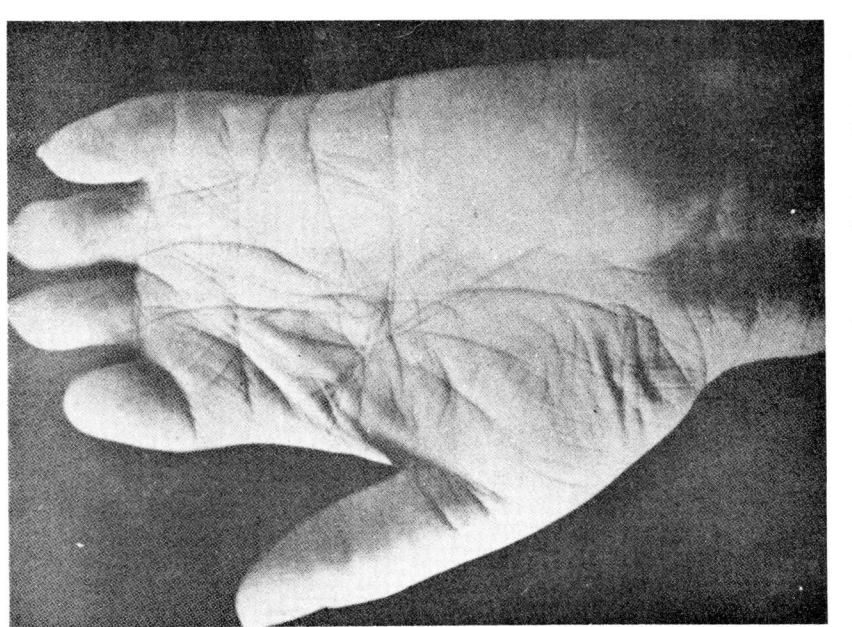

Bild 75. Angeborene Verwachsung (Dekadenzerscheinung).

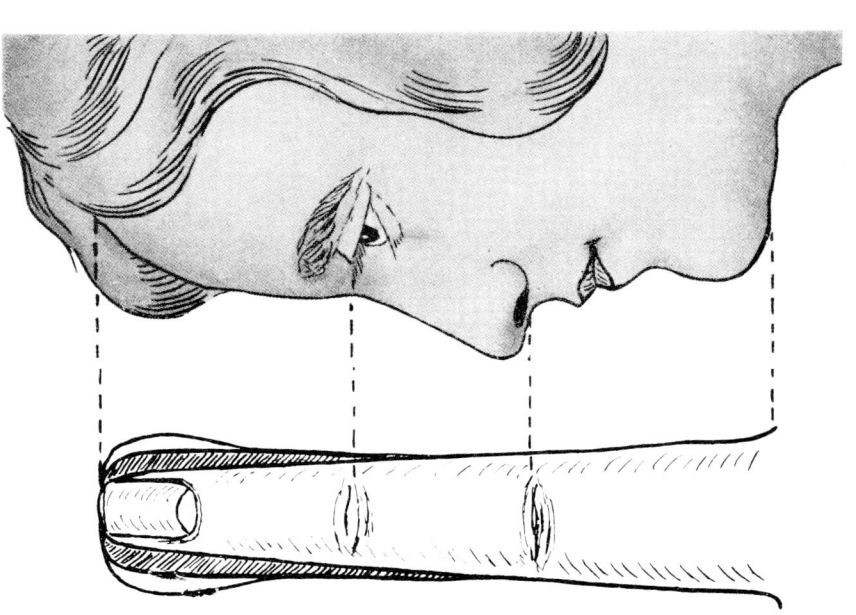

Bild 74. Die drei Zonen an Kopf, Gesicht, Finger.
Drei Fingertypen übereinander zeigt Unterschiede deutlich.

ASTRO-CHIROMANTIE
nach Th. W. Wulff, Hamburg 24

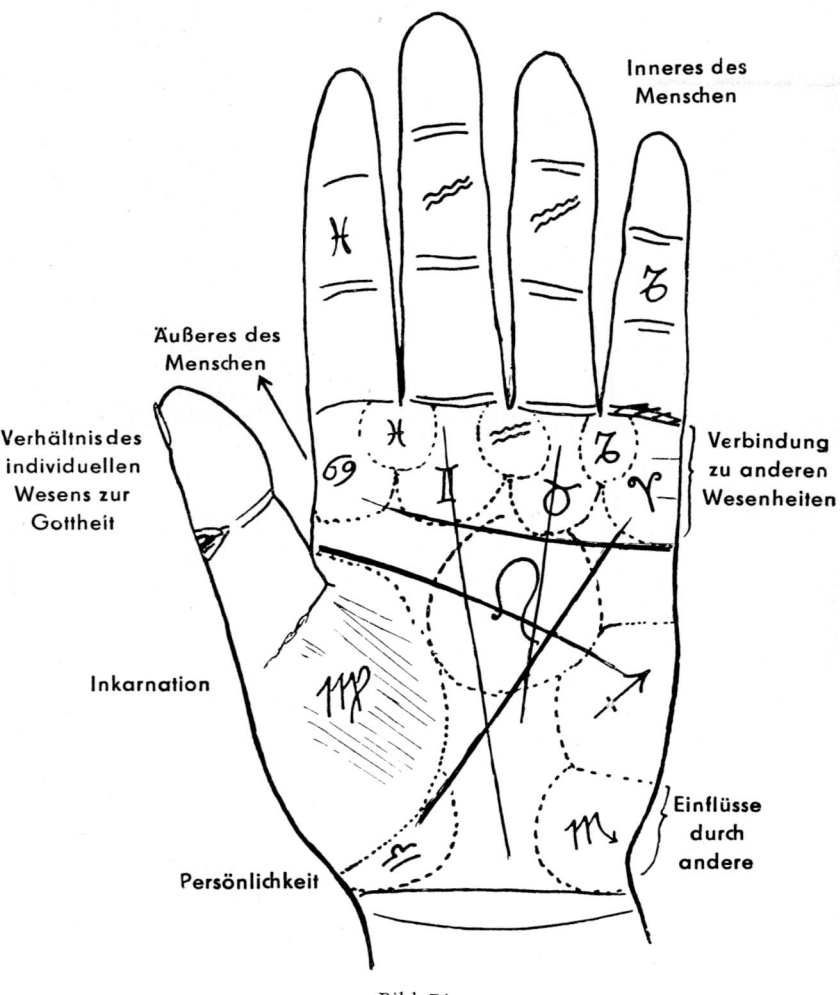

Inneres des Menschen

Äußeres des Menschen

Verhältnis des individuellen Wesens zur Gottheit

Verbindung zu anderen Wesenheiten

Inkarnation

Einflüsse durch andere

Persönlichkeit

Bild 76.

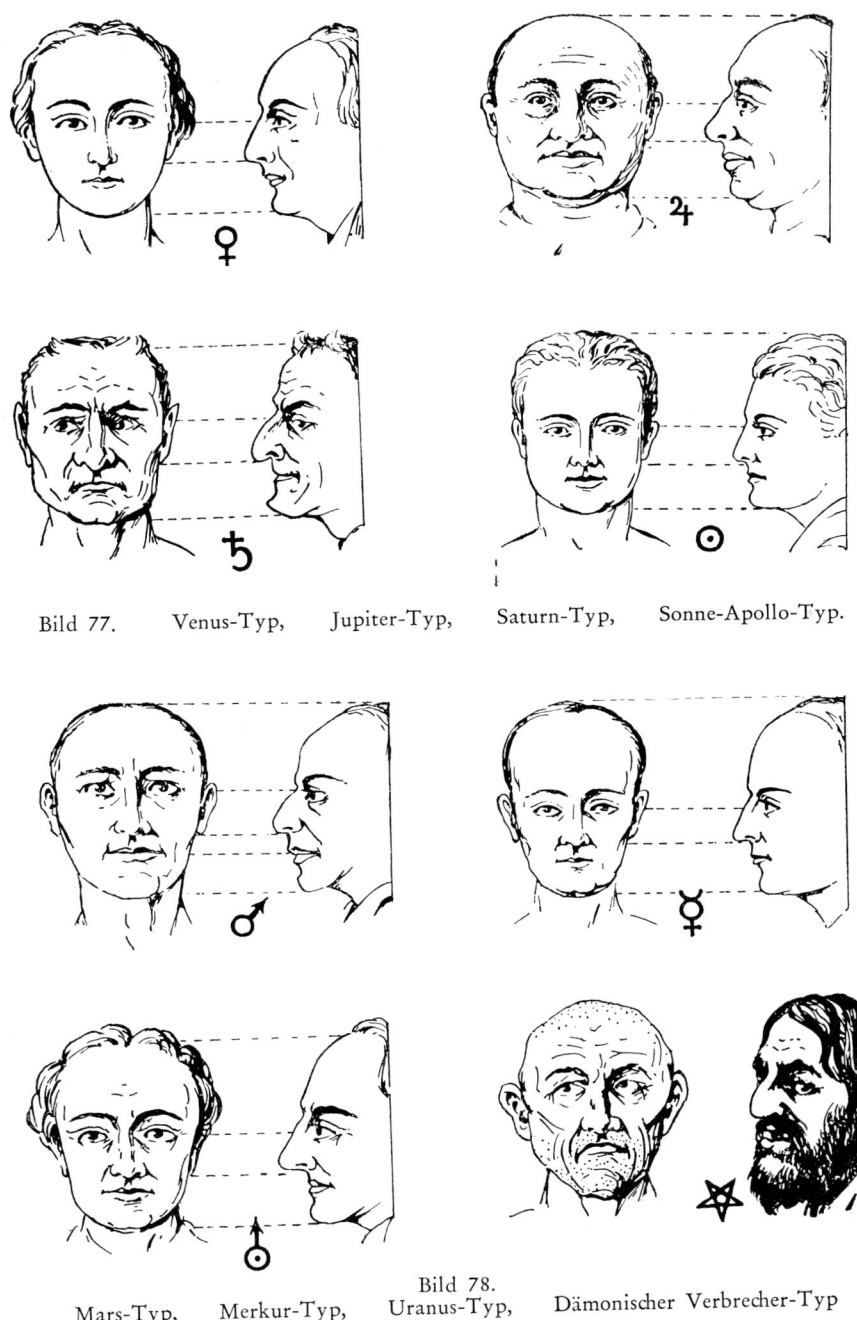

Bild 77.   Venus-Typ,   Jupiter-Typ,   Saturn-Typ,   Sonne-Apollo-Typ.

Mars-Typ,   Merkur-Typ,   Bild 78.
Uranus-Typ,   Dämonischer Verbrecher-Typ

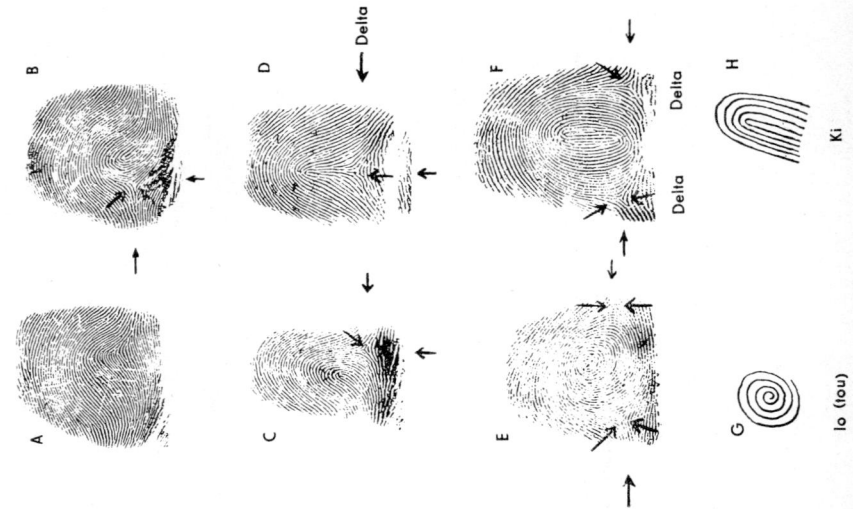

Bild 79. Fingerabdruckmuster.

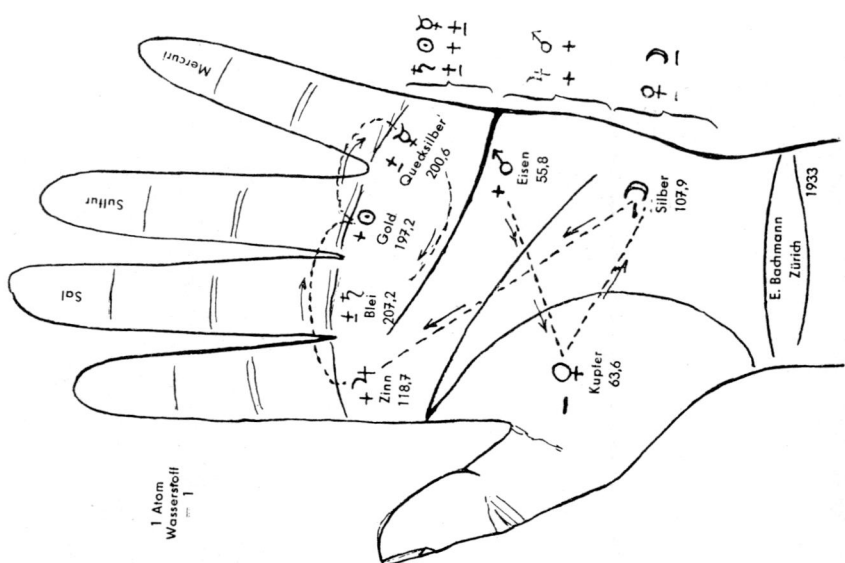

Bild 80. Die Ausdehnungen der einzelnen Handflächen (Berge) verhalten sich im umgekehrten Verhältnis zu ihren zugeeigneten Atom-Gewichten. D. h. die Handfläche mit dem kleinsten Atomgewicht Mars (Eisen) beansprucht den größten Teil, im Gegensatz zu Saturn (Blei) mit dem größten Atomgewicht und der kleinsten Flächenausdehnung.